P9-EKS-691

RENEWALS 458-4574
DATE DUE

WITHDRAWN
UTSA Libraries

A companion to her earlier study of memory in medieval culture, *The Craft of Thought* is Mary Carruthers's examination of the techniques of medieval monastic meditation as a disciplined craft for making thoughts. Called "the memory of God," this craft recognized the essential roles of emotion, imagination, and cognition in the activity of recollection, a term actually closer in meaning to the modern "cognition," the creative process of thinking. Deriving examples from a variety of late antique, Carolingian, and twelfth-century sources (with excursions into modern architectural memorials and late medieval manuscript marginalia), this study emphasizes meditation as a procedure of literary composition, a craft of rhetorical invention. The techniques of this craft particularly involved making mental images or "pictures" for thinking and composing, a use derived from practices taught in both Jewish spirituality and late Roman rhetoric. The book explores the influence of these imaging techniques on, and their realization in, medieval literature, architecture, and art.

CAMBRIDGE STUDIES IN MEDIEVAL LITERATURE 34

The Craft of Thought

CAMBRIDGE STUDIES IN MEDIEVAL LITERATURE

General Editor
Alastair Minnis *University of York*

Editorial Board
Patrick Boyde, *University of Cambridge*
John Burrow, *University of Bristol*
Rita Copeland, *University of Minnesota*
Alan Deyermond, *University of London*
Peter Dronke, *University of Cambridge*
Nigel Palmer, *University of Oxford*
Winthrop Wetherbee, *Cornell University*

This series of critical books seeks to cover the whole area of literature written in the major medieval languages – the main European vernaculars, and medieval Latin and Greek – during the period c. 1100–1500. Its chief aim is to publish and stimulate fresh scholarship and criticism on medieval literature, special emphasis being placed on understanding major works of poetry, prose, and drama in relation to the contemporary culture and learning which fostered them.

A complete list of title in the series can be found at the back of the book

The Craft of Thought

Meditation, rhetoric, and the making of images,
400–1200

MARY CARRUTHERS

New York University

CAMBRIDGE
UNIVERSITY PRESS

Library.
University of Texas

PUBLISHED BY THE PRESS SYNDICATE OF THE UNIVERSITY OF CAMBRIDGE
The Pitt Building, Trumpington Street, Cambridge CB2 1RP, United Kingdom

CAMBRIDGE UNIVERSITY PRESS
The Edinburgh Building, Cambridge CB2 2RU, United Kingdom
40 West 20th Street, New York, NY 10011–4211, USA
10 Stamford Road, Oakleigh, Melbourne 3166, Australia

© Cambridge University Press, 1998

This book is in copyright. Subject to statutory exception and to the provisions of
relevant collective licensing agreements, no reproduction of any part may take place
without the written permission of Cambridge University Press.

First published 1998

Printed in the United Kingdom at the University Press, Cambridge

Typeset in Garamond 11/13pt [CE]

A catalogue record for this book is available from the British Library

ISBN 0 521 582326 hardback

Library
University of Texas
at San Antonio

This book is for Erika

Contents

Illustrations

xi

List of illustrations

ILLUSTRATIONS IN THE TEXT

Abbreviations

BAC	Biblioteca de autores cristianos
CCCM	Corpus christianorum, continuatio mediaevalis
CCSL	Corpus christianorum, series latina
CLCLT	*CETEDOC* Library of Christian Latin Texts
CSEL	Corpus scriptorum ecclesiasticorum latinorum
DMA	*Dictionary of the Middle Ages*
DNB	*Dictionary of National Biography*
DS	*Dictionnaire de spiritualité*
Etymol.	Etymologiae
FC	The Fathers of the Church (series)
Hom. in Hiezech.	*Homiliae in Hiezechihelem prophetam*
Inst. orat.	*De institutione oratoria*
Latham	R. Latham, *A Revised Medieval Latin Word List*
LCL	Loeb Classical Library
Lewis & Short	C. T. Lewis and C. Short, *A Latin Dictionary*
Liddell & Scott	H. Liddell & R. Scott, *A Greek–English Lexicon*
MED	*Middle English Dictionary*
MGH	Monumenta Germaniae Historiae
OED	*The Oxford English Dictionary*
OLD	*The Oxford Latin Dictionary*
PL	*Patrologia latina*, ed. J. P. Migne
SBO	*Sancti Bernardi Opera*
SC	Sources Chrétiennes
TLL	*Thesaurus linguae latinae*

All Biblical references are to the chapter and verse numbering of the Latin Vulgate Bible. In the Book of Psalms, this numbering differs from that of most English translations in that all psalms after Psalm 9 carry a number one greater than that in the Vulgate; the verse numbers can also differ.

Acknowledgments

I wish to acknowledge those institutions and people who helped me most directly. I was gifted with uninterrupted time for research and writing, first by means of a Senior Research Fellowship from the National Endowment for the Humanities, and then as a guest of the J. Paul Getty Research Institute for the History of Art and the Humanities. New York University has been most generous with a variety of small grants for research assistance, including a grant in aid of publication from the Abraham and Rebecca Stein Faculty Publication Fund of the Department of English.

The unexpected gift of nine months at "the Getty" was particularly welcome, because it afforded me the complete freedom I needed to rethink and recast this book in the company of knowledgeable and supportive colleagues on the staffs of the library, the museum, and the research institute and allied Getty organizations, as well as the remarkable community of scholars, artists, and their families, non-medievalists all, visiting from Europe and America that year. Their conversation was stimulating and refreshing always, and Erika and I are much enriched by the friendships we formed during that year. Particularly revealing for my project was the task instigated by Anne and Patrick Poirier of putting my ideas into images for our "Curiositas" cabinet. And two old friends were especially welcome visitors: Professor Lina Bolzoni of the Scuola Normale Superiore in Pisa and Dr. Jean-Philippe Antoine of the University of Lyon. The generosity of the Getty in making sure that three students of the arts of memory, ordinarily working so far distant from one another, had the leisure to talk and study together was characteristic of what I experienced there.

I have read preliminary studies for parts of this book as talks at a number of institutions, including the Universities of California at Los Angeles, Santa Barbara, Berkeley, and Riverside, The J. Paul Getty

Acknowledgments

Center, the Claremont Graduate Center, Brown University, Barnard College, Columbia University, the University of Minnesota Twin-Cities, the University of Notre Dame, Rice University, Wellesley College, The Medieval Academy of America, The Newberry Library, the University of Toronto, The Warburg Institute, the colloquium "Ars memorativa II" held at the University of Vienna, and the colloquium "Lieux ou espace de la mémoire?" held at the Villa Gillet in the city of Lyon.

I have always been blessed with a variety of interesting, learned, and generous colleagues, in North America and Europe, who have enriched my own thought-craft with their conversation; the conversations I sought in connection with this book were no exception. I cannot begin to name them all, and hope that most will recognize my thanks in my use of their work. As usual, I have profited greatly from the work of specialists in other fields: for this study, I read works on the philosophy of mind and on cognitive biology. These do not often appear in the notes, so I would like to mention here in particular the work of Ned Block, Stephen Kosslyn, Mark Johnson, Patricia Churchland, John Searle, Hanna and Antonio Damasio, Joseph LeDoux, and Howard Margolis.

I would like to thank my research assistants in various stages of this project: Beverly Freeland at the Getty, and Simonetta Cochis, Fred Roden, and Heide Estes, at New York University. I also thank those who read the manuscript at varying stages of completeness: Paul Gehl, Alastair Minnis, Rita Copeland, and Linda Seidel. They saved me from many stupidities and infelicities, and are certainly not to blame for those that remain, or those that I have introduced since they last saw this project. Various of my friends and relations have put up with a lot while this book was in preparation: special thanks for cheerful support to Bruce and Wendy, Elspeth, Martha and Robin, Sonya, and Lisa.

I also thank my editors and the production staff at Cambridge University Press, in particular Dr. Katharina Brett, who encouraged me throughout the actual writing of this book, and Dr. Hilary Gaskin and Karl Howe, who oversaw it through the production phase. My copy-editor, Dr. Rosemary Morris, gave the book the careful, critical attention every manuscript needs and should have, and I especially thank her for her expert corrections, queries, and comments. Valerie Elliston has given the book a far better index than I possibly could have. And my special thanks to my friend Josie Dixon, who func-

Acknowledgments

tioned (not for the first time) as *dea ex machina* at a critical point in the editorial process.

I regret that my mother did not live to see the work of mine which she would most have enjoyed and best understood. My greatest thanks are to and for the person to whom this book is dedicated.

Introduction

Orthopraxis is a category developed for the comparative study of religions, specifically Christianity and Buddhism.[1] Orthodox believers seek, in the words of Paul Gehl,

> to reproduce the experience of learning from the teacher, whose teaching lives on in authentic texts, verbal traditions or creeds. An orthopractical adept, by contrast, seeks to achieve an immanent experience of the divine equivalent to that of the founder, usually by following a devotional practice presumed to be similar.

Orthodoxy explicates canonical texts, whereas orthopraxis emphasizes a set of experiences and techniques, conceived as a "way" to be followed, leading one to relive the founder's path to enlightenment. Because it seeks an experience, an orthopraxis can never be completely articulate; instead of normative dogma, it relies upon patterns of oral formulae and ritualized behavior to prepare for an experience of God, should one be granted. Like chance, grace also favors a prepared mind.

Orthopraxis and orthodoxy often co-exist in the same religion. Christianity, though a religion primarily of orthodoxy, has always had groups within it who have created for themselves an orthopraxis. Monasticism is one such practice.[2] It began as a movement of pious laypeople, not clergy (monks were not ordinarily priests until late in the Middle Ages, and nuns never) and as a particular way of living to be adopted only as an adult, often after one's dynastic obligations to marry and have children were fulfilled.

Yet orthopraxis is a concept not unique to religion. Any craft develops an orthopraxis, a craft "knowledge" which is learned, and indeed can only be learned, by the painstaking practical imitation and complete familiarization of exemplary masters' techniques and experiences. Most of this knowledge cannot even be set down in words; it

1

must be learned by practicing, over and over again. Monastic education is best understood, I think, on this apprenticeship model, more like masonry or carpentry than anything in the modern academy. It is an apprenticeship to a craft which is also a way of life.[3] It is "practice" both in the sense of being "preparation" for a perfect craft mastery which can never fully be achieved, and in the sense of "working in a particular way."

The craft of making prayer continuously, which is the craft of monasticism, came to be called *sacra pagina* in Latin, the constant meditation based on reading and recollecting sacred texts. The early desert monks called this set of practices *mneme theou*, "the memory of God." This kind of "memory" is not restricted to what we now call memory, but is a much more expansive concept, for it recognizes the essential roles of emotion, imagination, and cogitation within the activity of recollection. Closer to its meaning is our term "cognition," the construction of thinking. Monastic meditation is the craft of making thoughts about God.[4]

I have chosen to deal with meditation primarily as a rhetorical process and product. This choice of analytic method is somewhat unusual. Monastic spirituality, in this century, has most often been examined in the context of psychology, an analytical focus set by William James and Sigmund Freud. It has been very fruitful; I do not wish to deny this. But I hope to demonstrate in my study of spiritual texts that to bring rhetoric to bear upon them redresses an imbalance which psychological analysis has tended to impart: over-concentration on the individual and personal. In medieval monasticism, the individual always had his or her being within a larger community, within which a single life was "perfected," "made complete," by acquiring a civic being and identity. That civic being, I will suggest, was brought into consciousness through learned practices that were both literary and rhetorical in their nature. This aspect of monasticism, the civic, can be best seen, I believe, through the lens of rhetoric, not psychology.

The monks never themselves produced any textbooks of rhetoric by which we might now recognize, as we can for antiquity, an orthodoxy of written principles and rules. They did, however, produce an orthopractice for the invention of meditation and the composition of prayers. Such "creative thinking" was learned by a method of apprenticeship based upon imitating examples, and mastery came only to a few and only after long discipline and continual practice. This craft is what I mean in this study by "monastic rhetoric."

Monastic rhetoric emphasized "invention," the cognitive procedures of traditional rhetoric. Rhetoric was thus practiced as primarily a craft of composition rather than as one primarily of persuading others. The typical product of monasticism, the meditation – even though, as an example for others to follow, it was obviously addressed to an audience – presented itself as a product of disciplined cognitive activity, or "silence," *silentium*, the term for it in monastic rhetoric.[5] This was also called *competens silentium*, suggesting the "compentency" of those adept in a craft, a "spirit" or attitude of mind towards what one was doing, the "fitness" of craftsman, craft, and work.

The monastic practice of meditation notably involved making mental images or cognitive "pictures" for thinking and composing. The use of such pictures, I will argue, derives both from Jewish spirituality and from the compositional practices of Roman rhetoric. The emphasis upon the need for human beings to "see" their thoughts in their minds as organized schemata of images, or "pictures," and then to use these for further thinking, is a striking and continuous feature of medieval monastic rhetoric, with significant interest even for our own contemporary understanding of the role of images in thinking. And the monks' "mixed" use of verbal and visual media, their often synaesthetic literature and architecture, is a quality of medieval aesthetic practice that was also given a major impetus by the tools of monastic memory work.[6]

These tools, as in all rhetoric, were made of language and image, primarily the tropes and figures and schemes discovered in the Bible, the liturgy, and the arts produced by their means, understood and handled as rhetoric. Monastic art is, as monastic authors themselves talked about it, an art for *mneme*, "memory," rather than one for mimesis. This is not to say that the aesthetics of "representation" were unknown to it, only that in it mimesis was less of an issue, less in the forefront of their conscious practice, than *mneme*.

The questions raised about a work by *mneme* are different from those raised by mimesis. They stress cognitive uses and the instrumentality of art over questions of its "realism." *Mneme* produces an art for "thinking about" and for "meditating upon" and for "gathering" – a favored monastic metaphor for the activity of *mneme theou*, deriving from the pun in the Latin verb *legere*, "to read" and also "to gather by picking." An art of tropes and figures is an art of patterns and pattern-making, and thus an art of *mneme* or *memoria*, of cogitation, thinking. To observe the obvious, tropes cannot exist unless they are recognized. That is a function of memory and shared experience, including shared education. Thus tropes are also social phenomena, and in monastic culture they were considered, as they had been in late ancient culture, to have ethical, communal instrumentality.

Tropes and figures are the memory-resident tools, the devices and machines of monastic reading craft. I have occasionally been asked if I believe that different mnemonic techniques in themselves produce different material expressions (various book layouts, different literary structures or architectures). The question seems to me to show misunderstanding of the nature of mnemotechnic. Like other rhetorical tools, it is not a single systematic entity with a rigorous intrinsic grammar, according to which, for example, "$2x - 3y$" must always produce a result different from "$2x + 3y$." The tools of mnemotechnic (that is, the specific schemes an individual may use) are more like a chisel or a pen.[7]

So I must ask of my readers a considerable effort of imagination throughout this study, to conceive of memory not only as "rote," the ability to reproduce something (whether a text, a formula, a list of items, an incident) but as the matrix of a reminiscing cogitation, shuffling and collating "things" stored in a random-access memory scheme, or set of schemes – a memory *architecture* and a library built up during one's lifetime with the express intention that it be used inventively. Medieval *memoria* was a universal thinking machine, *machina memorialis* – both the mill that ground the grain of one's experiences (including all that one read) into a mental flour with which one could make wholesome new bread, and also the hoist or windlass that every wise master-mason learned to make and to use in constructing new matters.

Meditation is a *craft* of thinking. People use it to make things, such as interpretations and ideas, as well as buildings and prayers. Since I focus on the craft and its tools, I am not particularly concerned in this study with hermeneutics, the validity or legitimacy of an interpretation, but rather with how an interpretation, whatever its content, was thought to be constructed in the first place. I do not think that hermeneutical validity is an unimportant or simple issue: far from it. But the main emphasis in literary studies for the past twenty-five years has been on this matter, while the basic craft involved in making thoughts, including thoughts about the significance of texts, has been treated as though it were in itself unproblematical, even straightforward. It is neither. In the idiom of monasticism, people do not "have" ideas, they "make" them. The work (and I include both process and product in my use of this word) is no better than the skillful hand, or in this case the mind, of its user. The complexity of this cognitive craft renders even more problematic, I think, the question of "validity" in interpretation, and though I will not argue this matter directly in this book, I hope that my readers will come to the same conclusion.

A final point about craft education is important also in the craft of meditative thought. People most often now buy tools ready made. But in many crafts even now, and in all crafts during the Middle Ages, an apprentice learned not only how to use his or her tools but how to make them. Scribes prepared their parchments, made their pens, and mixed their inks; masons made their adzes, mallets, and files. And monks composing made their cognitive pictures and schemes. Tool-making is an essential part of the orthopraxis of the craft.

I must caution my readers that I am not trying to write a comprehensive history of anything. This book is a companion study to my *The Book of Memory*, but it was not conceived of as a simple extension of my previous work into an earlier time. This book has a different, if related, subject. It ends with the twelfth century, not because I think some wholly new cognitive practices came into being then but because European demography changed significantly, and with it, the occasions to which the monastic rhetoric I discuss was asked to respond. Specifically, the twelfth century in Europe marks the development of a much larger, much more disparate, more urban audience, with a large contingent of vernacular-speaking, uncloistered, married laypeople. Such a citizenry makes for very different rhetorical dynamics than does the relatively small, relatively homogeneous citizenry of a monastery. Especially in the twelfth century, certain orders, such as the Augustinian canons of St. Victor, addressed their spirituality to such a heterogeneous audience. Others, such as the monks of Cîteaux, continued to address a small, homogeneous elite. I see the resulting differences in style and emphasis (to cite only the most obvious matters) as explicable through rhetorical analysis, rather than looking simply to changes in technology or ideology or the selection of one medium over another.

I have chosen materials produced by a variety of monastic orders at a wide variety of times. And though I refer for the sake of convenience to "monastic rhetoric," by no means all my examples are produced by people who had taken monastic orders, let alone were members of the same order. Moreover, even when they were, the difference in outlook and experience between a Carolingian Benedictine and a twelfth-century Benedictine was enormous (to say the least).

My Carolingian and twelfth-century authors had all read the basic works that set forth, both in principles and through examples, the practices I am examining: works by John Cassian, Augustine of Hippo, John Chrysostom, Boethius, Prudentius, and Gregory the Great. I have chosen texts from the fourth through sixth centuries, from Carolingian authors, and from the twelfth century. They are not grouped chronologically – rather, my selection is meant to illustrate certain recurring tropes and themes, aspects of the cognitive orthopraxis I am describing. I have focussed on works that either helped to establish basic practices, or offer particularly valuable or interesting examples of the cognitive craft I want to examine.

Collective memory and *memoria rerum*

Ut sapiens architectus fundamentum posui: alius
autem superaedificat.

St. Paul

AN ARCHITECTURE FOR THINKING

I. *MACHINA MEMORIALIS*

This study could be thought of as an extended meditation on the myth that Mnemosyne, "memory," is the mother of all the Muses. That story places memory at the beginning, as the matrix of invention for all human arts, of all human making, including the making of ideas; it memorably encapsulates an assumption that memory and invention, or what we now call "creativity," if not exactly one, are the closest thing to it. In order to create, in order to think at all, human beings require some mental tool or machine, and that "machine" lives in the intricate networks of their own memory.

In terms of the five-fold "parts" of rhetoric formulated memorably in antiquity for teaching the subject, *The Book of Memory* centered on *memoria*; this one centers on *inventio*. The order will seem backwards, since "everybody knows" that the ancients taught Invention, Disposition, Style, Memory, Delivery, in that order. Medieval scholars took Cicero's early treatise "On Invention" (*De inventione*) as the First Rhetoric, calling the *Rhetorica ad Herennium*, then attributed to Cicero, the Second or New Rhetoric. This latter is the textbook that describes an art of memory based upon the building plan of a familiar house, in whose rooms and recesses an orator should "place" images that recall to him the material he intends to talk about. So in medieval textbook tradition too, Invention precedes Memory.

Mnemonics, "artificial memories," and "memory tricks" (as they were called in the nineteenth century) have been viewed with skepticism; they were so even in antiquity, and certainly are now. One early seventeenth-century Chinese student, to whom the Jesuit missionary Matteo Ricci taught the art of memory as a help in studying for the onerous examination for the imperial civil service, finally complained to a confidant that the system was itself so cumbersome to learn that it was easier and took less memory just to memorize the original material. And surely, his assumption must have been, the good of an art of memory is to remember things in order to regurgitate them by rote later on.[1]

In this matter, as so often, the presentation of a subject in textbooks is misleading about daily practice: it seems to have been at least as much so to Ricci as to the exasperated student. For the orator's "art of memory" was not in practice designed to let him reiterate exactly in every detail a composition he had previously fabricated. For one thing, to sound as though he were reciting from memory like a parrot was one of the worst faults a Roman orator could commit. It was also foolish, for if he were to forget his lines or if (very likely in the debates of the Republican Senate) he were flustered by some unexpected event or attack, he would have nothing to say. The goal of Roman oratory was to speak eloquently *ex tempore*; this was the sign of a master.[2]

Thus the orator's "art of memory" was not an art of recitation and reiteration but an art of invention, an art that made it possible for a person to act competently within the "arena" of debate (a favorite commonplace), to respond to interruptions and questions, or to dilate upon the ideas that momentarily occurred to him, without becoming hopelessly distracted, or losing his place in the scheme of his basic speech. That was the elementary good of having an "artificial memory."

The example given in the *Rhetorica ad Herennium*, of imagining the scene of a sick man in his bedroom, to whom a physician, carrying a ram's testicles on his fourth finger, offers a cup, is intended to recall the chief issues of a case at law, not to enable a word-by-word recitation of a previously made up and memorized speech. Remembering these themes as a readily reconstructable quasi- narrative scene of related figures, each of which cues a particular subject in the case, will help an orator readily to compose his speeches *ex tempore*, in response to the actual flow of the court proceedings.

All scholars who study the subject of rhetorical memory remain much indebted to Frances Yates. But for all its pioneering strengths, her work unfortunately does reinforce some common misconceptions about the possible cognitive uses of "the art of memory," and thus the nature of its influence on the making of images and "places" for this purpose. Yates herself believed that the goal of the art of memory was solely to repeat previously stored material: she characterized the medieval versions of the ancient art as "static," without movement, imprisoning thought.[3] She could not have been more wrong.

She also found what she called "the Ciceronian art," for all its fascination, preposterous and unworkable.[4] Agreeing, if reluctantly, with people like Matteo Ricci's Chinese student, she presented mnemotechnic as becoming first a pious and then an arcane study after antiquity, valued by Renaissance practitioners precisely because, even while they made extravagant claims for its practical utility, it was secret and difficult. Yates presented the medieval authors (such as the Dominican friars Albertus Magnus and Thomas Aquinas) who linked mnemonic craft to piety as mistaken and misdirected. Preferring the arcane to the mainstream, she ignored the basic pedagogy of memory in the Middle Ages, finding only a few medieval sources for the sixteenth- and seventeenth-century authors with whom she was primarily concerned.[5]

I repeat: the goal of rhetorical mnemotechnical craft was not to give students a prodigious memory for all the information they might be asked to repeat in an examination, but to give an orator the means and wherewithal to invent his material, both beforehand and – crucially – on the spot. *Memoria* is most usefully thought of as a compositional art.[6] The arts of memory are among the arts of thinking, especially involved with fostering the qualities we now revere as "imagination" and "creativity."

This is not a development that one can trace by analysing the textbook tradition of rhetoric. As a "part" of rhetoric, *memoria* was added to the textbook tradition by the Stoics, and its place in the order was not set for quite some time.[7] When it is discussed, authors pay scant attention to it, repeating a few general precepts. The only elaborated examples of mnemotechnical schemes are in the *Rhetorica ad Herennium*. And yet Cicero also says that the master orator's memory is fundamental to his craft. This opinion is repeated often, and classical pedagogy strove to furnish each student's mind with a solid foundation of memorized material. The technique, though not the content, was similar in the Jewish schools that produced the earliest Christian teachers.[8]

The meditational practice of monasticism is not particularly indebted to the pagan rhetorical practice described in the *Rhetorica ad Herennium*. I will make this point at length and often in this study; I emphasize it now because many scholars have assumed, as Yates did, that there was ever only one art of memory, "the" art of memory. It is clear, however, that the monks also developed what they called an "art" or "discipline" of memory. This is different in many respects from the "Ciceronian" one, but because those who developed it had the same general rhetorical education, the methods used share certain essentials. There are enough similarities that when the art described in the *Rhetorica ad Herennium* was revived in the thirteenth century, it could be made to seem familiar to late medieval culture. But the medieval revival of this specific art, transmitted and adapted primarily by the orders of canons and friars, took place fully within the context of monastic memory craft. That is why it seems to historians now that the ancient art of the *Rhetorica ad Herennium* suffered a peculiar sea-change, and why its cultural translation seems filled with "mistakes" when they read descriptions of it from the later Middle Ages.

Monastic *memoria*, like the Roman art, is a locational memory; it also cultivates the making of mental images for the mind to work with as a fundamental procedure of human thinking. Because crafting memories also involved crafting the images in which those memories were carried and conducted, the artifice of memory was also, necessarily, an art of making various sorts of pictures: pictures in the mind, to be sure, but with close, symbiotic relationships to actual images and actual words that someone had seen or read or heard – or smelled or tasted or touched, for all the senses, as we will observe, were cultivated in the monastic craft of remembering.

2. INVENTION AND "LOCATIONAL MEMORY"

The relationship of memory to invention and cognition may sound straightforward; it is not. For the notions of what constitutes "invention" have changed significantly from the small-group societies of the pre-modern West to the rationalist individualism of the nineteenth century. Most importantly, in antiquity and through the Middle Ages, invention or "creative thinking" received the most detailed attention in the domain of rhetoric, rather than of psychology or what we would now call the philosophy of mind. We should not forget this critical difference from our own intellectual habits.

We tend now to think of rhetoric primarily as persuasion of others, distinguishing "rhetoric" from "self-expression" (a distinction now often built into the syllabi of American college composition courses). But in western monasticism, the craft of rhetoric became primarily focussed not on tasks of public persuasion but on tasks of what is essentially literary invention. It is not true to say (or imply), as histories of the subject have done, that the monks killed off rhetoric. They redirected it to forming citizens of the City of God, a characterization made long ago by Christopher Dawson:

> alike in the East and the West, [the Church Fathers] were essentially *Christian rhetoricians* who shared the culture and traditions of their pagan rivals ... Throughout the Church, rhetoric had recovered [its] vital relation to social life: in place of the old *ecclesia* of the Greek city it had found the new ecclesia of the Christian people.[9]

The writings of those Church Fathers, each with an excellent rhetorical education – Augustine, Jerome, Basil, Cassian, Cassiodorus, and Gregory – formed an essential part of the basic curriculum of monasticism.

The Latin word *inventio* gave rise to two separate words in modern English. One is our word "invention," meaning the "creation of something new" (or at least different). These creations can be either ideas or material objects, including of course works of art, music, and literature. We also speak of people having "inventive minds," by which we mean that they have many "creative" ideas, and they are generally good at "making," to use the Middle English synonym of "composition."

The other modern English word derived from Latin *inventio* is "inventory." This word refers to the storage of many diverse materials, but not to random storage: clothes thrown into the bottom of a closet cannot be said to be "inventoried." Inventories must have an order. Inventoried materials are counted and placed in locations within an overall structure which allows any item to be retrieved easily and at once. This last requirement also excludes collections that are too cumbersome or too unparticular to be useful; think about why it is so daunting to locate one's car in a vast parking lot.

Inventio has the meanings of both these English words, and this observation points to a fundamental assumption about the nature of

11

"creativity" in classical culture. Having "inventory" is a requirement for "invention." Not only does this statement assume that one cannot create ("invent") without a memory store ("inventory") to invent from and with, but it also assumes that one's memory-store is effectively "inventoried," that its matters are in readily-recovered "locations." Some type of locational structure is a prerequisite for any inventive thinking at all.[10]

These structures need not bear a direct relationship to the "art of memory" described in the Republican Roman *Rhetorica ad Herennium*. To limit the study of "locational memory" to this one variety has obscured both the generic concept and the medieval and even Renaissance developments of *memoria*. More important than (at least through the mid-thirteenth century), and in addition to, the precepts of the *Rhetorica ad Herennium*, there developed very early on in Christianity a *disciplina* or *via* of inventive meditation based on memorized locational-inventory structures (deriving from Biblical sources, but more of that later), which was called by the monks "memoria spiritalis" or "sancta memoria." This traditional practice of meditation also was deeply implicated in the pedagogy of ancient rhetoric as well as the textual pedagogy of Judaism, making many of the same assumptions about "invention" and how it is to be done that we find more generally in non-Christian sources. As a consequence, it did not develop in total isolation from the ancient rhetorical practices of invention and composition. The monastic art also employed a "locational memory" as its foundational schema.

The model of memory as inherently locational, and having a particular cognitive role to play, is quite distinct from another philosophical model, equally influential in the West and equally ancient. This is the idea, known to the Middle Ages primarily through the works of Aristotle (and hence not influential in the monastic practice of *sancta memoria*) that defines memories temporally, as being "of the past."[11] Augustine too had emphasized the temporal nature of memories in his meditations, in the *Confessions* and elsewhere, on how we perceive "time" in our minds. The two traditions are frequently confused, even now, and to help sort out their differences, it might be useful to pause over the analysis of prudential *memoria* by Albertus Magnus, the first medieval philosopher to try seriously to distinguish and reconcile them. Albertus is an early scholastic figure, and wrote some fifty years after 1200, but his analysis clearly shows the continuing influence of monastic *memoria*.

Albertus retained a conviction that a locational model of memory was essential for purposes of cognition. In his treatise "On the Good" (ca. 1246), when discussing the nature of prudence, he raises the apparent conflict between describing memory as essentially temporal and describing it as essentially locational. The *Rhetorica ad Herennium* states that "artificial memory consists of backgrounds and images."[12] How can memory *consist of* "places" when Aristotle says that its essence is temporal?

Albertus responds that "place" is required for the mental task of recollection. While it is true that memory can only be "of" matters that are past, presented to us in "images," the *task* of remembering requires that the images so stored be in places. Two very different questions are being inappropriately confused by the erroneous observation of a "conflict" between Aristotle and Cicero concerning the nature of memory, Albertus implies. The one question, "What is memory?" (answer: "Memory is stored-up images of past experiences") is an ontological one, "What is the content of memories?"[13] But the other question, "What is memory?" (answer "Memory consists of backgrounds and images") is a psychological one having to do with cognitive use, "What is the structure of memories?"

"Place," Albertus says, is "something the soul itself makes for storing images." He cites Boethius' commentary on Porphyry's *Isagoge*, one of the basic logic texts of the medieval school, to the effect that "Everything which is born or made exists in space and time." The images which memory stores are such creations. But their temporal quality, that they are of the "past," does not serve to distinguish them, for "pastness" is a quality which they all share. So, in order to remember particular matters, one focusses on what distinguishes one memory from another, namely the qualities that constitute "place."[14]

Our minds "know" most readily those things that are both orderly and distinct from one another, for "such things are more strongly imprinted in it and more strongly affect it." The two qualities which Albertus emphasizes are *solemnis* and *rarus* – "orderly" and "spaced apart" from one another. These are not their actual properties, but are imagined to be so. Albertus understood that mnemonic places are entirely pragmatic; they are cognitive schemata rather than objects. They may entail *likenesses* of existing things (a church, a palace, a garden) but they are not themselves real. They should be thought of as fictive devices that *the mind itself makes* for remembering.

The mental "places" are associatively related to some content, "through analogy and transference and metaphor, as for example, for 'joy' the most similar 'place' is a cloister garth [pratum], and for 'feebleness' an infirmary [infirmaria] or hospice [hospitale] and for 'justice' a courtroom [consistorium]." Thus, what we would call an allegorical connection, and seek to attach to some real content (though that reality is conceptual rather than material), is understood here by Albertus as primarily a convenience, made necessary by the epistemological condition that no human being can have direct knowledge of any "thing." All knowledge depends on memory, and so it is all retained in images, fictions gathered into several places and regrouped into new "places" as the thinking mind draws them together.

3. HAVING A PLACE TO PUT THINGS

Before I discuss further how creativity was related to locational memory, however, I need to make some more elementary definitions. These are not peculiar to any one mnemonic technique, but are shared by many because they appear to build upon the natural, biological requirements of human learning and thinking. First of all, human memory operates in "signs"; these take the form of images that, acting as cues, call up matters with which they have been associated in one's mind. So, in addition to being signs, all memories are also mental images (*phantasiai*).[15]

In rhetoric, the term *phantasiai* is generally reserved for emotionally laden fictions that act powerfully in memory and on the mind.[16] Some traditions in ancient philosophy also recognized an emotional component in all memory. Memory images are composed of two elements: a "likeness" (*similitudo*) that serves as a cognitive cue or token to the "matter" or *res* being remembered, and *intentio* or the "inclination" or "attitude" we have to the remembered experience, which helps both to classify and to retrieve it. Thus, memories are all images, and they are all and always emotionally "colored."

Pre-modern psychologies recognized the emotional basis of remembering, and considered memories to be bodily "affects"; the term *affectus* included all kinds of emotional reactions.[17] This link of strong memory to emotion is, interestingly enough, also emphasized by at least some contemporary observation. A news article on developments in neuropsychology reported that "emotional mem-

14

ories involving fear [other emotions seem not to have been part of the test] are permanently ingrained on the brain; they can be suppressed but never erased."[18]

But more is involved than simply an emotional *state* associated with a memory. Latin *intentio*, derived from the verb *intendo*, refers to the attitudes, aims, and inclinations of the person remembering, as well as to the state of physical and mental concentration required. It involves a kind of judgment, but one not that is simply rational. Memories are not tossed into storage at random, they "are put in" their "places" there, "colored" in ways that are partly personal, partly emotional, partly rational, and mostly cultural. Without this coloration or "attitude," *intentio*, which we give to the matters we know, we would have no inventory and therefore no place to put the matters we have experienced.

Cicero sometimes used the word *intentio* almost as English uses the word "tuning," as a musician tightens (the root meaning of *intendo*) the strings of his instrument. In his *Tusculan Disputations* (a work revered by Augustine, as he tells us), while reviewing various Greek theories of the soul's nature, Cicero mentions with favor Aristoxenus of Tarentum, "musician as well as philosopher, who held the soul to be a special tuning-up [intentionem quandam] of the natural body analogous to that which is called harmony in vocal and instrumental music; answering to the nature and confirmation of the whole body, vibrations of different kinds are produced just as sounds are in vocal music."[19] The Stoic concept which Cicero is rendering is *tonos*, "tone" (as of muscles and of strings), a word also used generally for the "modes" of music.[20] The concept is recognizable in monastic *intentio*, but it was applied spiritually and emotionally.

The monks thought of *intentio* as concentration, "intensity" of memory, intellect, but also as an emotional attitude, what we now might call a "creative tension," willingly adopted, that enabled productive memory work to be carried on (or that thwarted it, if one's *intentio* were bad or one's will ineffectual). Reading of the sacred text, both communal and in "silence," needed to be undertaken with a particular *intentio*, that of "charity."

This "intention" is not a matter of doctrinal or philosophical content, of definitions and classifications. Rather, it bears an analogy to the rhetorical notion of *benevolentia*, the attitude of good will and trust which an orator hoped to evoke in his audience by first approaching them in that spirit. As Augustine famously stated: "I call charity *a movement of the mind toward* [the goal of] *fruitfully enjoying* God for His own sake, and [my]self and my neighbor for God's sake."[21] A "movement of the mind toward" something involves not only *affectus*, or emotion, but also *intentio*.

This conception of *intentio* is certainly related to the one I just discussed; if *intentio* is a part of every memory image, if it is the coloration or attitude we have towards an experience, on the basis of which we have determined where to "hook" it into the linked chains of our "places," then rekindling that sort of *intentio* will enable us to start finding those memories again. Notice also that in this cognitive model, emotions are not discrete mental "entities," but are intricately woven into exactly the same memory networks as are the facts and objects of our experience, what we now call "data."[22] And, though our memories are "intended" in this sense from the start, we constantly restructure and recompose them by means of the different other *intentiones* we bring to our various occasions of remembering.

In such a psychology, there can be no such thing as either a truly objective or a truly unconscious memory, because each remembered thing requires to be intentionally "marked" and "hooked in" to our own places. But like the cogs and wheels of a machine, the mnemonic "places" enable the whole structure to move and work. Mnemonic images are called "agent images" in rhetoric, for they both are "in action" and "act on" other things.

The power of this elementary technique is that it provides immediate access to whatever piece of stored material one may want, and it also provides the means to construct any number of cross-referencing, associational links among the elements in such schemes. In short, it provides a random-access memory, and also sets of patterns or foundations upon which to construct any number of additional collations and concordances of material. This latter goal, the making of mental "locations" for "gathering up" (*collocare*) and "drawing in" (*tractare*), is where *memoria* and invention come together in a single cognitive process.

4. "LIKE A WISE MASTER-BUILDER"

In ancient mnemotechnic, architecture was considered to provide the best source of familiar memory locations. Architecture also plays an essential role in the art of memory which is basic to my present study, but the monastic version of architectural mnemonic carries non-

Roman resonances that make something rich and strange from the forensic orator's set of memory "rooms." These resonances, as one might have predicted, are Biblical.

The monastic architectural mnemonic is founded, like a vast super-structure, on a key text from St. Paul, who, in 1 Corinthians 3:10–17, compares himself to "a wise master-builder":

> According to the grace of God which is given unto me, as a wise master-builder, I have laid the foundation, and another buildeth thereon. But let every man take heed how he buildeth thereupon. For other foundation can no man lay than that is laid, which is Jesus Christ. Now if any man build upon this foundation gold, silver, precious stones, wood, hay, stubble, Every man's work shall be made manifest: for the day of the Lord shall declare it, because it shall be revealed by fire; and fire shall try every man's work of what sort it is. If any man's work abide which he hath built thereupon, he shall receive a reward. If any man's work shall be burned, he shall suffer loss: but he himself shall be saved; yet so as by fire. Know ye not that ye are the temple of God, and that the Spirit of God dwelleth in you? If any man defile the temple of God, him shall God destroy; for the temple of God is holy, which temple ye are.[23]

This passage gave license to a virtual industry of exegetical archi-tectural metaphors. Both as activity and artifact, the trope of building has, as Henri de Lubac noted, "une place privilégiée dans la littérature religieuse, doctrinale ou spirituelle."[24] The trope was used by Philo, the second-century Jewish exegete, and there are also intriguing connections between early Christian use and the mystical "work" of Jewish *merkabah* meditation, which uses several of the same basic structures as early Christian exegesis.[25] In medieval Christianity, this Pauline text soon became the authority for a fully developed mne-monic technique, using the *planus* (and sometimes also the *elevatio*) of a building laid out in one's mind as the structure for allegorical and moral meditation, the "superstructures" (*superaedificationes*) of *sacra pagina*.

Paul uses his architectural metaphor as a trope for invention, not for storage. Likening himself to a builder, he says he has laid a foundation – a foundation which can only be Christ – upon which others are invited to build in their own way.[26] From the beginning of Christianity, the architecture trope is associated with invention in the sense of "discovery," as well as in the sense of "inventory." The foundation which Paul has laid acts as a device that enables the inventions of others. This may seem a minor point in this text, but it acquired major significance later on as exegetical scholars elaborated this "foundation" for meditational compositions of their own, invited to do so by St. Paul himself.

The structures to be built upon were, initially, limited to those measured out and described in the Old Testament. This is an early tradition, probably with Jewish roots. De Lubac quotes Quodvult-deus (an associate of Augustine of Hippo): "If you have a taste for building, you have the construction of the world [Genesis 1], the measurements of the Ark [Genesis 6], the enclosure of the Tabernacle [Exodus 25–27], the erecting of the temple of Solomon [1 Kings 6], all aspects in earthly terms of the Church itself, which they all figure forth."[27]

The earliest uses of this trope indicate that the compositional devices which utilized Biblical buildings were never treated solely as having a single content, like a diagram, or one specific task, in the manner of a mathematical theorem, but rather as dispositive heuristics, devices for "finding" out meanings.[28] The distinction between these two cognitive attitudes resides in whether a book or a church is thought of as an object to be observed and studied for what it is in itself – for example, assuming that it just *is*, all by itself, an encyclopedia in symbol-language, which we thus can describe as it "really" is – or whether one thinks of a book or a church as a machine, a tool that people use for social purposes such as symbol-making. It's the difference between considering the work you are contemplating as an end or as a means – or, in familiar Augustinian terms, between enjoying something for its own sake and using it for social, that is ethical, purposes (remembering that Christians strive to be "citizens" of the City of God).

Gregory the Great articulated the "four senses" of Biblical exegesis in the form of a powerful mnemonic, a composition tool which works on the model of the inventive *circumstantiae* (for example, who, what, where, when, how) of ancient forensic rhetoric:[29]

> First we put in place the foundations of literal meaning [historia]; then through typological interpretation we build up the fabric of our mind in the walled city of faith; and at the end, through the grace of our moral understanding, as though with added color, we clothe the building.[30]

This maxim, much quoted later in the Middle Ages, is a recollection *ad res* of Paul; Gregory could expect his audience to recognize it as such. And he also casts the act of Biblical interpretation as an invention process, an act of composing and fabrication.

The literal text is treated as though it presented a set of memorial cues for the reader, a "foundation" which must then be realized by erecting on it a mental fabric that uses everything which the "citadel of faith" tosses up, and then coloring over the whole surface. In the context of Scriptural hermeneutics, the "walled city" (*arx, arcis*) puns both aurally on *arca* ("strongbox" and "Ark") and visually on the Temple citadel of Ezekiel, the "city on a hill" in Matthew, and the Johannine "Heavenly Jerusalem."[31] It is a useful coincidence too that Gregory uses the word *historia* where later writers speak of *sensus litteralis*: for the Biblical histories, especially of the Old Testament, are treated as though each were a story-outline, one of *One Hundred Great Plots*, whose chief purpose is to be retold.

In the minds of monastic writers, every verse of the Bible thus became a gathering place for other texts, into which even the most remote (in our judgments) and unlikely matters were collected, as the associational memory of a particular author drew them in. Associations depending upon assonance and dissimilarity are just as likely to end up being collated as those of consonance and likeness. A memorative web can be constructed using either principle, and often (as in rememberings of the Last Judgment) using both together.

And the proof of a teller is in the quality and character of his fabrication and coloring – the reconstruction, not the repetition of the "facts" of foundational plots. There seems to be very little interest in "the facts" *per se*. Instead, retelling a story is cast as a question of judgment and character. Paul says that "the fire shall try every man's work." He emphasizes that this is not a determinant of salvation – a poor workman will be saved even if his work burns up (1 Corinthians 3:15). But the assaying fire will manifest the quality of individual work – whether your walls are built of gold or of stubble. The concern in Paul, as in later writers using this theme, is with ethics, not with reproduction, or – to put the matter in terms of memory – with recollection not with rote. *You* are God's temple, the commonplace went, and the inventive work of building its superstructures is entrusted to your memory. This Pauline theme is realized over and over, in literary works, in monastic architecture, and in the decoration of both.

The inventional nature of the master-builder trope is still clear in its twelfth-century use. That master-teacher, Hugh of St. Victor, says that since sacred scripture is like a building, those studying it should be like masons, *architecti.*

> Take a look at what the mason does. When the foundation has been laid, he stretches out his string in a straight line, he drops his perpendicular, and then, one by one, he lays the diligently polished stones in a row. Then he asks for other stones, and still others … See now, you have come to your [reading], you are about to construct the spiritual building. Already the foundations of the story have been laid in you: it remains now that you found the bases of the superstructure. You stretch out your cord, you line it up precisely, you place the square stones into the course, and, moving around the course, you lay the track, so to say, of the future walls.[32]

Notice how this passage recalls the Pauline text, without ever directly mentioning it (a very common device for intertextual *memoria*).[33] A student is to use the mental building he has laid out on the foundation of his "historical" knowledge of the Bible – that is, of its "story" – as a structure in which to gather all the bits of his subsequent learning. Such mnemotechnically constructed "super-structures" (a Pauline word) are useful not as devices for reproduction alone (rote), but as collecting and re-collecting mechanisms with which to compose the designs of one's own learning, and "be able to build [i]nto [t]his structure whatever [one] afterwards finds" in the "great sea of books and … the manifold intricacies of opinions" that one will encounter throughout one's own life.[34] It is as important to get this foundation right as it is for any builder to make his foundations "true."

But the foundation is not to be confused with the completed structure. It is the *ground*, but not the key: it "authorizes," in the medieval sense, by initiating and originating further construction. The "key" – the "character" and "finish" of the master-mason's craft – will lie in the relatively beneficial use which one makes of this common grounding. This is, as St. Paul stressed, a matter not just of salvation but of beauty and benefit, of *ornamentum* conceived of in the classical sense in which "usefulness" is merged with "delight." Medieval reading habits are based upon a model of craft mastery, the "courses" of stone or brick or other materials which a master mason may make in building a wall, with concomitant emphasis upon preparation (the ground), routines of exercise (discipline), and stages in a *way* towards making a finished artifact, a mastery that affords pleasure.[35]

When the foundation plan has been laid out with one's internal builder's measuring line, one's *lineus* or *linea*, and picked out with stones, then the walls may be raised:

> and if [the mason] by chance finds some [stones] that do not fit with the fixed course he has laid, he takes his file, smoothes off the protruding parts, files down the rough spots and the places that do not fit, reduces to form, and so at last joins them to the rest of the stones set into the row ... The foundation is in the earth, and it does not always have smoothly fitted stones. The superstructure rises above the earth, and it demands a smoothly proportioned construction. The divine page is just the same ... The foundation which is under the earth we have said stands for history, and the superstructure which is built upon it we have said suggests allegory.[36]

The shape or foundation of a composition must be thought of as a place-where-one-invents. Everything is fitted onto it. And as the composer, acting like a master builder or *architectus*, fits his tropes onto the foundation stones of a text, he must smooth, scrape, chip off, and in other ways adapt and "translate" the *dicta et facta memorabilia* he is using as his materials.[37] So the edifice of one's life (so to speak), although created from stories available to all citizens, is also a fully personal creation, an expression (and creation) of one's character.[38] This is plain in St. Paul's injunction to be like a wise master-builder: the fire will try the quality of your work.

Thus, because it builds entirely through the associations made in some individual's mind, memory work has an irreducibly personal and private or "secret" dimension to it. That is also why it is a moral activity, an activity of character and what was called "temperament."[39]

At the same time, because most of its building materials are common to all – are in fact common places – memory work is also fully social and political, a truly civic activity. The constant balance of individual and communal, *ethos* and *pathos*, is adjusted and engineered with the tools of rhetoric: images and figures, topics and schemes. Essential among these tools are the memorial *res*, the building blocks of new composition.

5. THE WISE MASTER-BUILDER'S MACHINE

However, a memory, no matter how beautifully put together, is not itself invention. It is, as my heading should emphasize, a machine for performing the tasks of invention. This constructional view of human memory is very difficult for modern students to grasp intuitively: we are deeply attached to the belief that memory should be for reiterating and repeating things like a parrot, that memory is only good for passing examinations; we profess to be appalled (while knowing it all along to be true) that our memories can be "wrong."

Another kind of difficulty for some of us may arise from modern ideas of machines. As we use the word, "machine" is often contrasted to "human," betraying our deep assumption that what is mechanical (like what is artificial) is antithetical to human life and particularly to human "values." We can think of machines as suspiciously non-human and indeed as rivals of human endeavor, as we can think of technologies as self-sufficient "systems," perhaps even with lives of their own. But pre-modern, pre-industrial, cultures did not share this assumption. Their machines were fully human.

A *machina*, according to Isidore of Seville, is a device that architects or *masiones* ("masons") use in order to construct the fabric of buildings.[40] In classical Latin *machina* was any sort of a hoist – hence its association with building. Isidore derives the word *masiones* from *machina*, because masons, also called *architecti* or "master-builders," build upon foundations and so require *machinae* in order to work on the high walls and the roof.[41] So the concept of an *architectus* seems for Isidore to be someone who particularly fashions walls and roof: he may also lay the foundation, as St. Paul says of himself, but the proof of his excellence will lie in his superstructures, Paul's "super-aedificationes." A mason or *architectus* is also an inventor and maker, as was the inventor of architecture, Daedalus. And Isidore ends this discussion by observing that St. Paul called himself an *architectus* because, like a wise master-builder, he built up and added onto a foundation.

Machines move. They are engines which move other things about, and they themselves have moving parts. An early Christian specification of the trope is as the *machina universalis*, the cosmic machine constructed and raised by God, as first artificer and master builder. "He indeed, the artificer of this world, fabricated a machine, and like a wise master-builder he hung the heaven on high, formed the earth

22

into a great mole or dam, bound together the seas in links."[42] A machine is the essential tool of the Pauline "wise master-builder."

Any structure that lifts things up or helps to construct things is a *machina.* Isidore says that the wheel driven by water in a water mill is a kind of *machina.* Tertullian called the Cross "the machine of the pierced body," and in a much later monastic trope, the human body was sometimes called *machina rerum*, a microcosmic analogy to the *machina aetherea* of the cosmos.[43] Machines could also be destructive engines: the word is used for siege engines in many chronicles. It can refer to the trellises which lift and support the vines (in Jerome) or – in a riddle of Aldhelm's – to the hoist that was used to build on top of a cliff a beacon for seafarers.[44] All these structures lift, raise, and move. They are also all constructions of a variety of materials, made for a variety of purposes, good and ill. They are all *tools* for lifting and making.

Mental constructions can also be called machines, and it is this use of the metaphor that most interests me here. In one of his letters, Augustine recalls 1 Corinthians 8:1, "scientia inflat, charitas aedificat," "knowledge puffs up, but charity builds." This verse is yet another Pauline turn on the trope that thinking is like constructing a building (that is, "edification"). Augustine then comments that "knowledge should be used as though it were a kind of machine, by means of which the structure of charity rises up, which lasts forever, even as knowledge shall be destroyed."[45] Gregory the Great, invoking the same figure, says that "the machine of the mind is the energy of love" by which in this existence we are lifted on high.[46] This "machine" is contemplation, which can lift up the human soul. Implicit in this characterization, of course, is that "contemplation" is also an inventive act, a "construction."

Medieval *memoria* thus includes, in our terms, "creative thought," but not thoughts created "out of nothing." It built upon remembered structures "located" in one's mind as patterns, edifices, grids, and – most basically – association-fabricated networks of "bits" in one's memory that must be "gathered" into an idea. Memory work is also process, like a journey; it must therefore have a starting-point. And this assumption leads again to the need for "place," because remembering is a task of "finding" and of "getting from one place to another" in your thinking mind.

Hugh of St. Victor, master-constructionist that he was, exploited the building trope at many points (several of which we have already examined) in his treatise on education, which he called *Didascalicon*. In characterizing geometry, of all the seven liberal arts the one essential for a wise master-builder, he calls it "well-spring of perceptions and source of sayings."[47] This is an odd characterization, we might suppose, for such a non-verbal, abstract art. Hugh was quoting Cassiodorus; but Cassiodorus was characterizing the *topica* of argument, the "seats of argument, the well-spring of perceptions, the origin [as initiator] of speaking."[48] In other words, Hugh understood geometry, the science of "forms," to apply not just to the physical world but also to the cognitive one, to the fabricating of the schemes and patterns for thinking, for constructing the buildings of the mind from and within the *sedes* or locations of remembered "things": *sensus* (perceptions, feelings, attitudes, judgments), *dictiones* (sayings and speakings), and *facta* ("events" as stories).

MEMORIA RERUM, REMEMBERING THINGS

6. INVENTORY FABLES: TEACHING THE LORE OF ONE'S CRAFT

The literary criticism directed in this century at mythic and visionary stories has considered them mostly in terms of their mimesis, their "representation of reality" in Erich Auerbach's phrase – whether that "reality" be natural, social, or psychological. I have a somewhat different set of questions to ask about them, having to do with their cognitive functioning. I can best illustrate this difference by considering a category of common mnemotechnical myths.

Astronomers are accustomed to divide up the visible stars into "constellations" named for various things – animals, mythic beings, implements. For sky charts, artists draw a more or less naturalistic figure of a hunter (for example) around the stars that make up Orion – his belt, his dagger, his feet, his arms – and the two dogs which follow him, Canis major and Canis minor.

Such charts are very old. Plate 5, from a manuscript made about the year 1000 by a famous scribe, Abbot Odbert of the monastery of Saint-Bertin in north-western France, shows a chart of the northern sky made for a common textbook, Aratus' *Phainomena*, a Greek poem about the constellations that was translated into Latin in antiquity and used as an elementary astronomy text in monastic pedagogy.[49] It was common in monastery libraries, and contained both descriptions of individual constellations (with drawings in some manuscripts), and charts of the whole sky with the circles of the Celestial Equator, the Ecliptic (with all the Zodiac constellations painted in it), and the Milky Way (labeled *lacteus circulus*). In Plate 5, Orion and his dogs are visible in the lower right quadrant, between the Ship (Puppis) and the Whale (Cetus), and just below Gemini. At the center of this chart are Ursa minor, the Little Bear, with Polaris, the North Star, in its tail, and Draco, the dragon, snaking around to point at Ursa major, the Great Bear.

In explanation of the origins of these figures, we are earnestly told by some modern encyclopedia articles that vaguely defined "primitive peoples," viewing the night sky, thought the star groups "looked like" such creatures, and they then named them accordingly and made up myths to explain how they got there. All the star myths are assumed to be of a genre known as etiological fable, a story to explain the origin of something. The book of Genesis is filled with such stories; Kipling's *Just-So Stories* are an example as well (as indeed, is the encyclopedia explanation I just cited).

When I look up at the grouping of stars called "Orion" I confess that I see nothing "like" a human hunter – and in fact I'm never sure which stars (beyond the basic pattern, which I can see readily) "belong" to Orion and which do not. Orion's dogs seem to me even less imitative of the shapes of dogs I have known. So, either "primitive people" (the Hellenistic Greeks!!) were a lot more easily satisfied with what constituted the likeness of a hunter and his dogs than I am, or something else was going on in their minds than recognizing earthly shapes in the skies.

Indeed, the makers of Aratus manuscripts, and other medieval encyclopedias of the constellations, seem to have felt it necessary to describe the individual constellations as star *patterns* first of all: patterns which were then keyed to a constellation's name by drawing a rough figure around them. Plate 6 shows several such groupings from a ninth-century manuscript of a work by Isidore of Seville (itself liberally incorporating material from Aratus), also made in northern France. These books, though made for students whose minds were as primitive as the minds of beginning students always are, do not counsel a student "now look up in the sky and find the dog." Instead they counsel "look in the sky for thus-and-so pattern of stars in thus-and-such position," the same way we do now. In other words, the teachers who made these books assumed that *the pattern* is what one would recognize, not a "dog" or a "bull": they recognized, just as we now do, that such names are conventional.

But if the constellation figures are not imitative of some *thing*, even if it is only fantastical, then what are they for? What people needed from star charts was a way of quickly and unerringly picking out certain stars, for their position was essential in the conduct of daily life – to calculate the calendar, to navigate, to plant, to know when to do a host of things. And a great many random items, such as the individual stars, are not retrievable, and so cannot be learned unless they are organized into patterns that allow people readily to find them.

The constellations form a stellar inventory, one that is easily reconstructable, both in part and as a whole, and also one whose plan is completely distinctive. A sky map has the qualities of being both *solemnis* and *rarus*, to use Albertus Magnus' terms. The purpose of organizing stars into constellation patterns is not "representation," but to aid human beings, needing to find various stars, to locate them by means of a recognizable pattern retrieved immediately and securely from their own memories. Constellations are mnemotechnical *tools*.

The constellation patterns were also embedded in stories (though few people now know them): narratives that attach the patterns together, or embed important characteristics about the particular constellations, such as where and at what season they appear in the night sky. "Locating" things to be remembered in a story is an elementary human mnemonic principle; known in practice to every society, the mnemonic power and flexibility of narrative was confirmed in the experiments of F. C. Bartlett earlier in this century.[50]

In the case of Orion, several stories are told. Nearly all of them refer to the constellation's position in the sky. He is associated with Artemis (another hunter, though she especially used a bow) in some; or he was stung to death by a great scorpion (on Artemis' order); or he was chasing the Pleiades when they were all turned into stars. Orion is a constellation of the late fall – hunting season, the season marked by the Zodiac constellations of Scorpio (the scorpion) and Sagittarius (like Artemis, an archer, and one who, embodied in Chiron the centaur, was instructed by her). The position of Orion is such that as the stars move, Orion could be said to "chase" the Pleiades. A myth of the birth of Orion has him "born from urine," making a pun on his name, Orion, and the Greek word for urine, *ouron*.[51]

These many stories all incorporate a few basic mnemonic principles. The stories about the archer and the scorpion associated the star pattern "Orion" with the Zodiac constellations of its season; the Pleiades story links it to a neighboring constellation. The "etymology" that derives Orion from *ouron* is not our sort of etymology at all, but an application of a basic mnemonic technique that associates items via a pun: indeed, the widespread pre-modern interest in such "etymology" is an expression of a very common mnemonic technique.[52]

Many of the star myths are late-comers among Greek stories, dating from Alexandrian times. They are not true etiological fables but what I call "inventory fables," stories devised to help make an inventory of elementary learning. Such a story supplies a form for some basic materials, relating (note the double meaning) several bits of information in a readily stored and retrievable web – the purpose of memorial inventory. These star myths share some features of other pedagogical stories, such as those of "Physiologus" (the Bestiary) and the fables of "Aesop." These form a genre of mnemonic story-telling that also serves basic training in *memoria* and was cultivated in Hellenistic schools.

Another example of an inventory fable concerns the "origin" of *memoria* itself, the story that the pre-Socratic Greek poet Simonides of Ceos invented the art of memory when he was able to identify the bodies recovered from a banquet-hall that had collapsed on his niggardly patron, by reconstructing the order of the seats which each guest had occupied during the fatal feast (he had fortunately been called away from it, perhaps by the gods Castor and Pollux, just before the disaster).[53] The story provides a way of remembering the principles of a mnemonic technique of constructing an order of "seats" into which items to be recalled are "placed" so that one can readily reconstruct and thus find what one needs.

The story has also the requisite mnemonic feature of being attached to a "beginning" or principal – namely Simonides, a famous poet some of whose lines a boy would already have memorized in the course of his grammar training, and whose name, as a mental heading, was therefore available as a convenient and reasonably familiar "place" for this tale.[54] And finally, it is bloody and violent, features always recognized to be especially memorable.

In this book, the questions I ask about the story of Simonides do not concern its truth-content. I am not interested in considering such questions as "Did Simonides actually invent the art of memory that is memorialized in this story?" or "What can we infer about Greek social customs from the fact that all the participants in the story are men, and/or that the poet was denied his fee at the banquet by his patron?" or "What does it say about human (or ancient Greek) psychology that a story about the origins of memory is about violent deaths?" or "What does it signify that the gods, Castor and Pollux, called Simonides out of the hall in the nick of time?" These are all interesting questions in their own right, but not for my present concerns. The questions which I will ask in this study are about the usefulness of such a story in thinking and learning: in this case its proven utility (nobody who knew it seems ever to have forgotten it) as a mnemonic for several elementary aspects of memory craft.[55]

The Simonides story, like the star myths, like the fables of Aesop and Avianus, like the tales of the Bestiary as well, is heuristic and inventional (for the two words are synonyms, one Greek the other Latin), rather than mimetic. It is not about origins or about poets or about feasts, but about learning some principles of a craft.

As representations of real life star fables are absurd, and one might well ask why the kindred of Euclid would have perpetuated such stuff, even for their children (by contrast, our contemporary prejudice is to make sure that children get "just the facts" about their stars). But that quality of absurdity is *exactly* what makes them memorable, and therefore valuable to cultures in which people relied on their memory to keep all that they knew, cultures which also recognized the essential role of memory in human cognition. Another invention fable from this same culture is the one that makes the Muses daughters of Mnemosyne, and "generates" the seven liberal arts in a similar way.

Mnemonic narratives of this sort are a common feature of many practical, technical arts before the rationalist reorientations of the eighteenth century. Alchemists embedded their craft lore in weird narratives which encoded the procedures and ingredients of various chemical processes.[56] The strangeness of these stories has been attributed solely to desires to keep knowledge among an elite guild. But the impulse to clothe difficult technical knowledge in such tales is also accounted for by the need to remember processes exactly: the alchemists' tales are a variety of techno-babble, but a jargon consciously made more memorable than our own. It is a principle of mnemotechnics that we remember particularly vividly and precisely things that are odd and emotionally striking, rather than those that are commonplace. Sex and violence, strangeness and exaggeration, are especially powerful for mnemonic purposes. Given that craft knowledge, like that of the alchemists, consisted until very recently of a large amount of orally transmitted and memorially retained lore, the mnemotechnical role of such story-telling becomes less alien and more intelligent as human behavior.

Medieval craft "mysteries" turn out to be less mysterious (in our sense) than they are mnemonic. Geometry had a whole iconology of mythic animal names for complex geometrical figures, many associated with the craft of builders. Roland Bechmann has recently studied a number of drawings in the notebook of Villard de Honnecourt (thirteenth century), the only surviving text of its kind from the craft of medieval master-builders. These drawings of natural and human forms, some with geometric figures contained in them, have been analyzed by Bechmann to show the complex relationships of arcs and angles which they contain. Bechmann has also found structures in surviving buildings from the period that show how these forms were practically applied. They bear names like "the sheep," "the eagle," "the bearded man," and "the two lions." Some particularly complex geometrical figures acquire names like "the peacock's tail" (for the figure in Euclid's *Elements* III.8) or "the bridge of donkeys" (*Elements* I.5).[57]

7. TEXTS AS *RES*

So long as *memoria* remained the "machine" of thinking, the limitations it placed on human knowledge were a constant theme and preoccupation. "Inside me," says St. Augustine, "in the vast cloisters of my memory ... are the sky, the earth, and the sea, ready at my summons, together with everything that I have ever perceived in them by my senses, *except the things which I have forgotten* [my emphasis]."[58] In the ready, even cheerful, acceptance of that last phrase lies an essential difference between the medieval and modern worlds. To have forgotten things is seen by us as a failure of knowledge and a reason for distrusting memory altogether; to have forgotten some things was seen in Augustine's culture as a necessary condition for remembering others.

The key to understanding the link between memory and invention lies in the mnemotechnical use of the word *res* or "(subject-)matter," especially in the common phrases *memoria ad res, memoria rerum,*

29

and remembering *sententialiter* and *summatim*.[59] These are distinguished from *memoria verborum* or remembering *verbaliter* or *verbatim*, the ability to repeat exactly. Throughout the pre-modern world, students were advised of the virtue of remembering by *res* rather than solely by rote. This is not to suggest that accuracy of recollection was unimportant: it clearly was valued for many tasks. But such accuracy was best performed by essentially stupid tools, like rolls and codices, and the professional "living books" of the ancient Mediterranean world, such as the Jewish *tannaim* and the Homeric rhapsodists, who were trained to recite the canonical texts exactly. Xenophon says of these latter that "they were very particular about the exact words of Homer, but very foolish themselves."[60]

One also needs to keep in mind that throughout the Middle Ages, it was the usual practice to study the elementary canonical books, such as the Psalms, twice. First one learned the texts *verbaliter*, in order to fix the syllables in memory (for people were taught to read Latin by syllables). Then the student went through it again, this time attaching mentally the gloss and commentary to the units of text which were already laid out like "seats" within his or her memory. This technique is described in detail by Hugh of St. Victor in the early twelfth century.[61]

To treat text in this way, as a habitually retained "foundation" for other material, is to use it like a set of mnemonic places, or backgrounds. A text can only serve in this way when its customary context is "forgotten," at least for this occasion, by a deliberate act of the author's will. As Lina Bolzoni has noted, one basic principle of successful mnemotechnic is that the normal semantic links of words and images are suspended, wholly or in part.[62] Only this kind of "forgetting" enables someone to hear a word solely as sounds, see an image solely as shapes, or isolate a phrase or image from a conventional context, and thus free herself to make her own intended associations with them.[63] For medieval scholars, there was much merit in liberating the mind from the rules and commentaries learned in successive layers during their schooling.[64] It is this willed forgetting that actually enables creative mental "play," the recombinatory engineering of meditative *memoria*.

The essential generative process in composition was recollection of "things." *Memoria verborum* was a task best accomplished without thinking, a first task for children or for slaves. But *memoria rerum* was the task that produced wisdom and built character, and could help to perfect one's soul ("perfect" in the sense of "fill in," inscribe things in all those empty tablets of memory). It built upon matters stored *verbaliter* by habit, but built up from the various cues they supplied as links in associational chains. The goal of an education was not to become a "living book" (by rote reiteration, the power of an idiot) but to become a "living concordance," the power of prudence and wisdom.

8. THE "THINGS" OF MEMORY

But just exactly what is being remembered when one claimed and was taught to "remember things"? A crucial text for understanding this ancient idiom is Augustine's rumination on the contents of his memory in *Confessions*, Book X:

> Great is the force of memory, O Lord, I know not what, to be amazed at, profound, and of infinite multiplicity. And yet it is my mind: it is myself. What, then, am I, my God? What is my nature? Ever-changing, with many different forms, is life, and exuberantly limitless. Observe! in the wide plains of my memory and in its innumerable caverns and hollows filled beyond reckoning with varieties of countless things [innumerabilium rerum generibus]; either through images [per imagines], as of all material things [omnium corporum]; or directly [per praesentiam], as are basic skills and know-how [artium]; or by means of I know not what notions or notations [per nescio quas notiones uel notationes], as are emotions [affectionum animi]; for the memory retains them even while the mind does not experience them, although whatever is in the memory must also be in the mind. Through all these I range, and freely move from this to that, digging into them as far as I can, and never finishing. Such is the energy of memory, such the life-energy in human beings living mortally![65]

Augustine uses the word "thing," *res*, in this passage to refer to many varieties of mental phenomena: to "images" of things he has experienced, to the cognitive skill and "know-how" which is present in his mind, and to emotional experiences which take the form of "I know not what notions or notations" in his memory. All of these – note well – are subsumed in the word "things" in this sentence. And Augustine can "freely move from one to the other" of any of these matters, along the associational *catenae* of his recollections.

Intellectual historians have sorted out the mental "objects" to which Augustine refers in this passage, and have noted that he says, here and elsewhere, that memory contains images derived through the power of his imagination from sensory experiences (emotions and corporeal objects), and also "ideas" and concepts. That he seems to admit the real existence in the mind of abstract non-sensory-derived concepts (even more so in his treatise *De trinitate* than here) has led many modern historians to define him as a Neoplatonist.[66]

Yet we should also consider what Augustine says here in the context of some rhetorical uses of *res*, especially in regard to *memoria*. Augustine was always a rhetorician even more than a philosopher; perhaps that is why he so often contradicted himself, and why his definitional vagueness, as in the phrase "nescio quas notiones uel notationes" in the passage just quoted, is so characteristic. I am not implying that rhetoricians can't think, only observing that they are in their composing more tolerant of the polyvalence of words, the energetic leaps of cogitation. Augustine is not averse to showing the unsteady movements of his thinking. He links up the words "notiones" and "notationes" by their homophony, employing a basic habit of an orator's *memoria*. This link does not clarify or define the "real nature" of what he is talking about, for it blurs a crucial distinction in philosophy between "idea" and "image"! Perhaps in Augustine's mind the conceptual fuzziness produced by the homophony served to correct, but without canceling, a distinction that is often more apparent in abstract argument than in cognitive practice. He does freely say (and this is also characteristic of him) that he doesn't quite know what he's describing.

9. THE "DEVICES" OF THINKING

Not only does Augustine's memory contain multiple varieties of *res*, it also contains *rationes*. Like *res*, the meaning of *ratio* acquires an enriched content if one views it in the practical context of rhetorical *memoria*, not restricting ourselves only to the question of the truth-content of what is in our memories. Augustine says that in addition to *res*:

> Memory also contains schematic devices of numbers and measurements, and innumerable principles [numerorum dimensionumque rationes et leges innumerabiles], which no physical sense has impressed onto it, for they are not colored nor do they sound nor smell nor are they tasted or touched ... I have seen measuring-lines

used by artisans even as fine as a spider's filament [uidi lineas fabrorum vel etiam tenuissimas, sicut filum araneae]; but these are of another sort, not images of those things which my bodily eye has reported to me: whoever learns to use them knows them intuitively without any reference to a physical body.[67]

This is a vexed passage among historians of ideas, usually taken as evidence for Augustine's Neoplatonism. While the matter is important in assessing the sources of Augustine's philosophy, and while I agree that he is surely suggesting in this passage that some mental structures and measuring abilities are somehow innately found in his memory, I would like to consider Augustine's characterization here of his memory's *rationes* in the context of rhetorical *memoria*.

Memory's "rationes" are not reasons of the sort that engage a philosopher but "schemes" or "ordering devices," something like what structures and activates my computer's memory in particular ways. They put matters in relationships and proportions, and make thinking possible. Latin *ratio* means "computation" or "calculation," not "reason" in exactly our sense of the word. Bede wrote a treatise on chronology called *De ratione temporum*, meaning a "design" or "structure" for calculating calendars. Bede's understanding of the term is similar to Augustine's. Augustine's memorial *rationes* are "of numbers and dimensions" – locational measurements, notice – because numbering and measuring, calculating, is the essential mnemonic means by which we make the mental webs and fabricate the patterns with which we are then able to think.[68] Consider closely what Augustine says in this passage, taken as describing "mathematical memory." He has just discussed how he remembers ideas and concepts: these, he says, are not stored as single entities in his mind, but result from the action of cogitation, from gathering together "those same things which the memory did before contain more scatteringly and confusedly."[69] Abstracting thought is here seen (as it is generally in memorial tradition) as a process of meditative composition or collocative reminiscence – "gathering," *colligere*.

But "gathering" requires structured "dispositions" of "places" in the mind – mental maps, in short – from which and into which collecting proceeds. In addition to translating *rationes* as "schemes," I would understand *leges* to mean the "principles" of a craft, the kinds of "laws" by means of which one makes or composes or – in this case – calculates and measures. Craft "rules," unlike Divine Law, are variable, and must be adapted to different situations.

Thus, the *rationes* Augustine recognizes within his memory are not like rigid scaffoldings for "data banks" (the way we tend to think of "diagrams" now), nor the rigidly hierarchical "flow charts" that model categories of information, nor are they descriptive models of real objects. Memorial *rationes* are tools of the mind, as "ratios" function in arithmetic. They move "things" into relationships with one another, they find out and gather in and build patterns out of memory's *res*. The simile Augustine uses, comparing such cognitive devices to the "measuring lines" of artisans, makes the point clearly: mental *rationes* are constructing instruments, only as good as the craft of their user.

One further point needs to be made here. Although in his meditation on the powers of his memory Augustine often mentions its chambers and recesses, he is ambiguous as to how literally one should understand the notion of such "places" in memory; in this regard he echoes general rhetorical teaching on the subject of mnemotechnical *loci*. Placement and location, the "mapping" of material, are necessary to remembering and thinking, however like or unlike our mental "places" may be to material ones. In the same way, the ability to calculate, Augustine says, is innate to the mind, not abstracted or "gathered" from images of material objects.

Augustine did not have a "faculty" model of human psychology. Faculty psychology tends to try to locate mental procedures in specific places in the brain. Augustine modeled the activity of human thinking on the Trinity, the activity which embodies the way in which human beings were made "in the image of God," as Genesis says. A trinitarian model of psychology is emphatically not "regionalized" in the way a faculty model is – the Trinity, after all, is everywhere and nowhere, a constant energy that is always also quiet and changes not. Although Augustine and others use a vocabulary that is also found in faculty psychologies, and Augustine distinguishes *memoria* and *intellectus* and *voluntas*, he understands these terms as complementary actions and processes in which the mind as a whole is always engaged.[70]

Human beings by nature make patterns in order to know. This medieval idea seems akin to the modern view that all knowledge requires "grammar," but it is not bound to language as its sole model. Medieval cognitive pattern-making "locates" knowledge, but *within* and *in relation to* other "things." The locational networks – finer even than the filaments of a spider's web – are rich devices of thinking, constructing patterns or "scenes" within which "things" are caught and into which they are "gathered" and re-gathered, in innumerable ways, by individual human minds.

Thus comes about a curious but fundamental quality of the medieval analysis of *res memorabiles,* one very difficult for many moderns to understand. What is "truthful" about them is not their content, that is *what* they remember, but rather their form and especially their ability to find out things, that is *how* they cue memories. It is some essential event and/or characters in a story, the general shapes and "faces" of a building, the shapes and relationships of images within a picture, and most often the *place* each "thing" occupies within a civic topography, that seems to matter most to its long-term success as an ingredient in people's memories. *Res* retain their role as *memorabilia* – literally, something "that is able to be remembered" – because of their ability to fit into and to "locate" social and mental inventories that do not resemble data bases so much as they do maps for thinking and responding.[71]

The "things" in such a map act as the common grounds (common places), important not so much for what they are as for what they do or rather, what we do to and with them. *They* are not memory, but cues and clues for remembering. A florilegium by Valerius Maximus (a sort of archival collection of such common places), which was much read and copied through the Middle Ages, was called *dicta et facta memorabilia,* "sayings and events for remembering." That title captures exactly the nature of *res* in the phrase *memoria rerum.* The very phrase requires that *res memorabiles* be set, like stones in a mosaic (a common metaphor), into a *pattern* that renders them memorable and invent-able.

10. THE VIETNAM WAR MEMORIAL AS AN EXAMPLE OF *MEMORIA RERUM*

To analyze the phenomenon of *memoria rerum* in terms that contemporary readers will recognize, I would like now to digress in what medieval monastic writers might call a "tropological meditation," and to consider a couple of famous modern American memorials as examples of *memoria rerum.* In the course of this discussion, I hope it will become clear exactly how the concept of *memoria rerum* differs from that of our contemporary "collective" or "cultural memory," and provides, to my mind, a more satisfactory and complex account of the social phenomenon of civic story-telling.

One of the more successful additions to contemporary American public memory is the Vietnam Veterans Memorial in Washington, DC. Visiting this structure has proven to be a remarkable experience for a greatly diverse public, from those who fought the war with unchanged belief in its rightness to those who opposed it as utterly corrupt. It is worth pausing over, because I think it can teach us a bit about how memorials are memorable. This is a matter of what we can think of as the "rhetoric" of this structure.[72]

The Vietnam Veterans Memorial includes and abets the memories of "the public." Not authoritarian, it "authors" memories in the sense of a medieval *auctor*, the originator of stories each of which augments (from *augeo*, another root of *auctor*) the bare names carved into the stones.[73] The Vietnam memorial remembers the war *ad res* – its gist – not *ad verba*.

Yet it does so by presenting what seems at first to be a crowd of individual names – of *verba*. It has far more "information" on it than does the nearby Iwo Jima memorial; in fact, the Vietnam memorial is more than anything else a chronological list of names. Edward Tufte, a noted teacher of graphic design, has analyzed its success as a matter of what he calls "editing":

> the names on stone triple-function: to memorialize each person who died, to make a mark adding up the total, and to indicate sequence and approximate date of death ... The spirit of the *individual* created by the wall – both of each death and of each viewer personally editing – decisively affects how we see other visitors. The busloads of tourists appear not so much as crowds but rather as many separate individual faces, not as interruptions at an architectural performance but rather as our colleagues.[74]

Tufte emphasizes that the crowd is engaged in an activity that is both *common* and *individual*, indeed achieves its essential individualness within the context of being part of an on-going common activity. "Common" does not mean "the same thing" – what totalitarian propaganda seeks to ensure – but rather a community activity that focusses on a "common place," literally presented by the site. The Wall (no one needs to call it anything more particular) presents a ground upon which a nearly infinite number of memories can meet and be generated, overlapping in the "gist" (*res*) of what is recalled but sharply particularized and individual in respect to time and place.

The Wall functions rhetorically as a repository of public memory. The specific data it provides are meaningless as given (indeed, for those wanting to find a name, a separate directory is provided). The Wall is a collective common place in the most literal sense: it has "located," as a collection, the *res* (the materials) for making memories about a particular set of events. And in so doing, it provides each individual who looks at it with an occasion and with material clues for remembering, as "the word begins to glow" and reverberate in that person's associational networks.[75]

This remembering is of a particular sort not often encouraged in our days. The Wall is not itself a story-teller, but it invites – even requires – story-telling from all who see it. And it is, of course, those stories that make it memorable to each viewer in ways that are both personal and shared. In the time of the emperor Justinian (d. 565 AD), the Roman public archive was called *scrinia memorialis*, "the memorial treasury." The Vietnam memorial is also worthy of that description.

It is not the content of those private or public stories that creates the communal sense – the sense of what Tufte calls "colleagues" – among the crowds at the Wall. It is rather the shared activity of recollecting stories about that time and that place in this time and this place, stories that are individually different from one another and yet share the authoring *res* of the *locus* itself: the black granite mirror cut sharply into the ground, the need to walk down into it and then up again, and the seemingly endless crowd of names from that war.

Of course, the *res* of the Vietnam memorial are not neutral. The conventions it uses have great social resonance in western society: polished black granite, the individual naming of the dead, the deep wedge into the ground cut by the stone panels. And its site next to the Lincoln Memorial locates it in regard to other *res* that resonate (as each visitor may choose to remember) richly in American memories. All these "attitudes" and "orientations" are, so to speak, the *intentiones* of the memorial's structural *res*. But it is best to think of a work's "intentions" not in terms of conceptualized meaning or even of specific emotions (grief or anger, such as a human being has) but simply in terms of their locating function. They *place* what we think.

The common "story" of the Vietnam war presented on the Wall not only invites but *requires* that visitors take elements from it and make them part of their own stories. Their particular stories have now also formed sets of commentaries on the text of the Wall. People bring pictures, flowers, medals, and other memorial tokens to place near the names of those whom they knew. This activity began spontaneously even before the monument was completed. And people also take away photographs or rubbings of particular names on the wall (rubbing also began spontaneously). The *res* of the memorial afford people the materials for a shared activity of remembering. This, and not some particular "meaning" or even "value," is what makes it truly and successfully a common place.

In other words, the Vietnam memorial is a communally, ethically useful tool for fashioning certain kinds of memories. This is true of many other memorials in other cities, nearly all of which can at least be used as location guides (any memorial's fundamental social utility), a place whereby people, remembering and recognizing, can find out where they are. But some memorials can be used more fruitfully than others, and I suspect that their particular popularity (if such a thing could be measured) would directly correlate with their utility and resonance in the present to a community, rather than with the particular content they were initially intended "forever" to enshrine.

This observation is apparent in another monument, beside which the Vietnam memorial is directly situated, the Lincoln Memorial. It too has become socially and ethically useful, though in ways the original designers did not foresee or intend. Following another set of architectural conventions than those of the Vietnam Wall, the Lincoln Memorial is modeled on the Parthenon: it is built entirely of white marble, with the enthroned, gigantic portrait-statue of Lincoln surrounded by memorably brief maxims derived from his speeches (the *dicta memorabilia*). The building invites one to contemplate the dead Lincoln in the conventions of ancient divinity: Lincoln "enshrined," as the motto over the statue has it. The gnomic maxims, presented *breviter*, invite one to read and gloss them in meditative repose. One need only to stand in this place for a few minutes to recognize that an impulse to gloss the maxims is irresistible to most visitors – and to learn that "private meditation" requires neither being alone nor being quiet.

Lincoln has thus "collected," as it were, an on-going gloss on his words that has translated them – *ad res* – into a kind of publicly accepted commonplace commentary tradition. This commentary importantly includes – again, *ad res* – such re-memberings of the gist of Lincoln (as it were) as Martin Luther King's "I Have a Dream" speech, the Marches on Washington for women's rights and other civil rights, the Vietnam Veterans Against the War rallies, and – since they share contiguous "places" within the overall "map" of the Mall site – the Vietnam memorial too. Various films, from *Mr. Smith Goes to Washington* (1939) to *Nixon* (1995), have also remembered the *res* of the Lincoln Memorial. And there have been competing rhetorical "dilations" of its gist, as groups with opposing political goals have "located" themselves exactly in the same place.

What is significant about this various copiousness, however, is that the gist of the memorial plays a virtually identical role in the "map" of each story. Lasting cultural *res* have (or acquire) rhetorical brevity: this ensures their copious flexibility. Socially successful gists (*res*) are virtually ineffable, matters of lasting *place* not content.[76] This quality is especially evident to us in very old cultural places like the Pantheon and St. Denis, about both of which I will have more to say shortly.

Successive rememberings over time by those who have used it in their various stories have "intended" the gist of the Lincoln Memorial in quite different ways. These range from the divinely wise Athena-figure supposed in the design's initial conventions to the tragic hero of a just war for human freedom to (now) an ironically perceived, compassion-filled, but ultimately betrayed and failed focus of civic aspirations.[77]

A particularly clear instance of the distinction between *res* and *intentio* can be seen in the following incident involving the burning of a high school in Alabama in 1994. The day after the destructive fire, white residents gathered at the site to lay wreaths and mourn the devastation of "all our glory days"; as one said, there were "so many memories, so much personal history revolving around one building." Black residents stayed away; one commented, "it may be a symbol of glory for them, but for me it's the place where they used to . . . throw rocks at me as I walked past it on the way to the black high school."[78] In this instance (as so often), a social "gist" or *res* attached to the high school building, the place itself, as both speakers made plain – but the *intentio*, how the citizens remembering that *res* were "attuned" to it, could not have been more opposite.

On the analogy of literary text, the Vietnam Wall and the Lincoln Memorial both provide "common memory," the *res* or "thing" which we experience and remember. What individual visitors (who are literally readers) do with it is "editing" of a kind, I suppose. But it is more accurate to use a medieval concept to describe this process. Individuals "draw from" the material presented by the memorial various "things" (matters) which are then "gathered into" their own stories. This isn't editing so much as adapting or "translating,"

39

literally understood as carrying from one "place" to another, from a place on the Wall (for example) to a "place" of one's memory. It is not editing so much as making something new, something that is one's own. Douglas Kelly, a historian of medieval literature, has written that "[t]ranslatio is a diversified and fundamental character-istic of medieval composition ... Topical invention is [its] means in the Middle Ages."[79] In the Vietnam memorial, we can study a contemporary instance of how such memorial/compositional "places" still work, not in the abstract, but with the specific sensory, experiential quality that "topical invention" should have.

The inventional use of places (topics) was far better understood by medieval artists than it is now. As I've suggested in the case of the Lincoln Memorial, "successful" public monuments acquire this cul-tural inventiveness (in the sense I've been developing here) *whether or not* their designers and patrons intended them to have such rhetorical power. In fact, given modern culture's dedication to enduring *meaning* and its worship of the author's intentions, both (we assume) fully expressed in "enduring" language, it is very unlikely that the designers of the Lincoln or Vietnam memorials thought in terms of rhetoric at all; probably they would be offended at the very idea.

These memorials *are* rhetorical, however, powerfully so. This fact may keep them "successful" in the future, not because they are somehow uniquely transcendent of time and place, but precisely because they are commonplace, and may thus remain common places. In a century or two, the Vietnam Wall will excite the kind of memories that modern visitors now feel for the village or college plaques honoring the dead of earlier wars. But the "stories" of those later viewers will not be "misunderstandings" or "illegitimate" readings of the monument. A memory, by its very nature, requires a remembering mind: it cannot be abstracted from times and places and people.

II. JERUSALEM PILGRIMAGE AS A MAP FOR REMEMBERING

It is a common mistake to confuse the activity of remembering with the "things" humans may use to locate and cue their memories. One often hears concern these days over who owns and shapes "the collective memory" or "the cultural memory" or even "the book of memory."[80] But memory does not inhere directly in objects.[80] I would now like to examine a few cases from the early Christian period, when a number of cultures were competing over the same *res memorabilia,* for they can help us learn more about the nature of what we now incoherently call "the collective memory."

Some objects (for now I'm using the English term as co-extensive with Latin *res*) are more memorable than others for many people – ancient and medieval mnemonic techniques tried to articulate and capitalize on some observations about the characteristics that make them so. But creating an object for remembering – even using means that every *memoria* handbook says should be forcefully and vigorously memorable – doesn't guarantee that it will play a particular role in people's memories.

An example of this is the Basilica of St. John Lateran in Rome. Designed by the emperor Constantine as part of his project to create a monumental Christian Rome to overlay (by surrounding) the old monumental pagan center, the Lateran basilica was to be in actuality the principal Christian monument. It was to be the "starting-point" of a Christian route through the city.[81] But it was built all the way next to the eastern wall of the city, a location that ran counter to the demographic movement of the population, which was moving to the west of the old center and across the Tiber. Demographics – that is, people with memories – centered the Christian map primarily instead on the tomb of St. Peter, which was located more nearly in the city's center.

But this was not the only reason for the dominance of St. Peter's. At least in part it was also because Constantine had failed to take sufficient account of a commonplace Christian convention which attached particular moral significance to gathering at martyrs' tombs. The Lateran basilica was not located at such a tomb and St. Peter's was.[82] The emperor's command could not make the Lateran basilica function as the memory site he intended it to be. He failed because he did not observe the cultural *intentiones* that "placed" St. Peter's in a particular "location" within the Romans' memorial map of their city. He failed in his rhetoric to take account of what Aristotle called the *pathos* of his audience, their "feelings and notions" – or rather, their *intentiones,* which in this case included the actual direction of the city's demographic movement.

The reverse public policy, destroying an object in order to eradicate memory, can also be unsuccessful. This policy has been tried many times, from the Roman general Titus' razing of the ancient Temple compound of Jerusalem to the German post-war destruction of Nazi-identified buildings to the (unsuccessful) urgings of some clerics after the 1979 Iranian revolution that the site of the Shah's coronation in the ancient ruins of Persepolis be destroyed. There are countless other examples.

Buildings can powerfully cue memories, but they are not themselves Memory. Even when a building is gone, the site itself often continues to play the same role in people's memories, as a "common place" in their mental maps and a cue for their remembered images. The lack of success speaks to the futility of the destruction policy. For example, what was left of the city of Jerusalem was obliterated by order of the emperor Hadrian in 132 AD, who ordered it rebuilt as a pagan city. Yet when the first Christian Jerusalem pilgrim whose account has survived, the pilgrim from Bordeaux, visited the still-ruined city in 333, s/he was shown sites, including at least one on the rubble-filled Temple platform, connected with various tales of the Bible.[83] There is no reason to suppose that there had been any cessation or discontinuity in the connection of the stories to these same places and objects, despite the Roman effort to consign the very topography of the city to oblivion.[84]

On the Temple mount, the Bordeaux pilgrim was shown the altar before which the priest Zachariah was murdered (Matthew 23:35): "you can see today where the blood flowed on the marble before the altar; so too the traces of the transport wagons of the soldiers who killed him appear in the entire area as though they had been imprinted in wax," s/he observes.[85] S/he was prepared to see as well the sycamore tree from which Zaccheus watched Jesus, the palm whose branches were strewn before Jesus, and a stone in the ruined Temple as the very one which the builders rejected (Psalm 118.22).[86]

It is crucial to understand, in all this, that what is important to these early pilgrims is not the site as an authentic, validated historical object. Many pilgrims – in a reaction that seems quite peculiar to us now – were well aware of and yet undisturbed by the improbability that the actual objects, such as the palm and sycamore trees, had survived for so many centuries. What is authentic and *real* about the sites is the *memory-work*, the thinking to which they gave clues.

For the places themselves were experienced by these early pilgrims as locations for recollecting memory images, which they had made on the basis of their prior reading of the Bible. Jerome wrote to the Roman matron Marcella concerning the Jerusalem pilgrimage that *"whenever we enter* the Holy Sepulchre [in Jerusalem] *we see* the Lord lying in his winding sheet, and dwelling [in thought] a little longer, *again we see* the angel at his feet, the cloth wrapped at the head." The images that "we see" are derived from memorized and recollected texts and stories, in this case John 20:5–12. Jerome clearly understands the experience as one of lingering, meditative review – in memory, using mental images constructed from one's reading.[87]

The pilgrims thus came not to see something new, but to recollect things well known to them already, their "dicta et facta memorabilia." As E. D. Hunt remarks of the Bordeaux pilgrim, "the past [s/he] went in search of was the narrative of the Bible." Because it was the narrative which determined the sites (and not, as can sometimes be the case, the other way around), the pilgrimage routes became a path in physical actuality for "making one's way through" the Bible readings. Best known among the early pilgrims is Egeria, who wrote an account for her fellow-nuns, some fifty years after that of the Bordeaux pilgrim. She described enough about the places she saw (she wrote) "so that when your affection [affectio uestra] may read the holy books of Moses, it may more feelingly [diligentius] picture thoroughly all that happened in these places."[88] By the standards of modern realism, Egeria's descriptions are notably brief and unde-tailed: she evidently thinks of them not as substitutes or correctives for her sisters' mental visualizations of their reading, but rather as useful cues for that process – they may see "diligentius." Note also her idiomatic use of *affectio*, "emotion," as the prime cognitive agent of reading.

The holy sites were embedded within liturgical processions, in which the pilgrims moved from site (and sight) to site across a correlated map grid made up from both topographical and calendrical features. There is some indication of this phenomenon already in the Bordeaux pilgrim's account. Egeria's descriptions of the sites she visited are fully embedded within a liturgical journey which she enacted among them, with appropriate readings, hymns, and proces-sions timed to visit the sites at the optimal moments.[89] The pilgrimage had developed into a route fully "colored" in the rhetorical sense, one in which the key events of the Old and New Testaments were recalled by the contiguous sites, topographical and chronological, at which they were said to have occurred. The place where Jesus was baptized and the place where Elijah the prophet was taken to Heaven were next to each other; the altar which Abraham set up to sacrifice Isaac and the place where the Cross had stood were also next to each other.[90] The narrative of the Bible as a whole was conceived as a "way" among "places" – in short, as a map.

In his excellent study of the earliest development of Christian stational liturgies in the cities of Jerusalem, Rome, and Constantinople, John Baldovan calls them expressions of the "public nature of the *ecclesia* and its means of incorporating its members."[91] The "commonality" is created through a narrative mnemonic procedure. "Remembering" is constructed in such processions by means of a communal walk-about among a set of "places" made literally "common." The processions are the routes and networks among the memories placed (as cues) within the various textually derived sites. The physical activity exactly mirrors the mental activity in which the participants were engaged.

12. MAKING A COMMON PLACE

In his study of the rhetorician's role in the eastern Roman empire, Peter Brown recounts a story told in one of Libanius' orations. Libanius, whom we will shortly meet again, was the Orator of the City of Antioch in the middle of the fourth century, and a member of its ruling class – indeed, by his estimate, the chief member. "Confronting the legal advisers of a newly arrived governor ... Libanius posed the crucial question: 'How did Odysseus rule when king of Ithaca?' 'Gently as a father,' was the instant reply." Brown comments, "[t]hrough a shared *paideia*, [men of the urban ruling class] could set up a system of instant communication with men who were, often, total strangers to them," but in this way showed themselves to be members of the same social group.[92] These men referred to themselves as "servants of the Muses": they shared a common education and consequently a common store of *res memorabiles*. This education did surely provide a shared means of communication, but above all else it constructed the web of a community or commonality.

Another example of this phenomenon is the "neck verse" of late medieval England, which enabled someone to escape hanging provided he could recite or read a verse of the Bible, thus proving himself to be a member of the clerical class.[93] The content of the verse was almost immaterial; what counted was the articulation of someone's "common ground" with an educated class, who were immune from hanging because of legal custom. Christian *paideia* could do no less than its pagan counterpart. It too was the means for re-creating in every generation the *civitas Dei* of the monastery, "the servants of Christ," as it were.[94]

The fifth-century bishop of Ravenna Peter Chrysologus (the "golden-worded"), a confidant of the empress Galla Placidia who is thought to have influenced the program of mosaics she commissioned at Ravenna, describes the process of reading the Gospel parables as follows:

> A potential spark is cold in the flint, and lies hidden in the steel, but it is brought into flame when the steel and flint are struck together. In similar manner, when an obscure word is brought together with meaning, it begins to glow. Surely, if there were no mystical meanings, no distinction would remain between the infidel and the faithful.[95]

As is the case with Libanius' allusion to the story of Odysseus, the "mystical" meanings are those hidden in the memory nets of educated Christians, part of their shared *paideia*. What is important is that for a member of the community, a word will "glow" with associated meanings.

Notice that the "obscure" word is not spoken of as having content itself: in itself, it is dark. It only starts to glow when "meaning" is brought to it by someone's mental networks. It is the ability to make it glow, not any specific content, that Peter Chrysologus thinks is crucial. This is a question of *intentio*, that "gut feeling" about and "snap judgment" of a thing that reveals both whether and at which points one is "clued in" to a particular community. *Intentio*, more readily and more reliably than content, will reveal to what community someone belongs.

An example is the logo first used for the 1984 film *Batman*, which featured a yellow circle with a large jagged-edged black form, basically oval in shape, on it. Where (if one were properly "clued in") one was supposed to see this shape as a bat, some people (myself included) saw a set of Rolling-Stones-style teeth surrounding an open mouth, and only with conscious effort were we able to see what we were supposed to. The point I am making is not that I was wrong about the object which this image was "representing": the point is that what the form "represented" had exclusively to do with which network of remembered associations I was plugging it into.

In medieval terms, while the *Batman* image's *similitudo* was identical each time, the *intentio* I gave to it changed completely, as I linked it into two different patterns or networks of my associations. The problem was not with the logo painter's representational abilities but with my personally and culturally induced "inclination" or "aim" towards the thing I was experiencing.

The social "tuning-in" of an individual can be thought of as a function of what we now call conventions. I spoke earlier of the "attitudes" and "intentions" that are a part of the memorial *res*, which serve to initiate and orient a person's responses to a particular common place, such as the Vietnam memorial. Just as individual memory images were analyzed as "colored" with an *intentio* which served to place and locate them in a particular mind, so public memory clues can also be said to have *intentio*, or emotional color. It is an aspect of their "conventional" and commonplace nature as rhetorical sites, and again the sorts of clues the *res* give are matters more of direction and location than of "meaning" *per se*.

When, inevitably, the *dicta et facta memorabilia* of a particular society are challenged – when an attempt is made or the need arrives to "forget" them – the most successful challenges have concentrated not on the "things for remembering" themselves, but on the networks into which they are placed.[96] Obliterating the "thing" will not guarantee that its memory will also disappear, as we have seen; but changing the "colors" in terms of which it is remembered and retold is an effective means for a kind of "forgetting." We can see this principle at work in the fourth-century incident I next want to examine, which is particularly instructive as an example of such social "remembering" and "forgetting."

13. THE WAR AT DAPHNE BETWEEN THE BLESSED BABYLAS AND APOLLO

One of the memorable moments during the fourth-century struggle of Christianity to assert itself publicly was cast as a story of "turf battles" between the Christian martyr Babylas and the god Apollo, over the site of a spring at Daphne. Most of the story we know comes from a panegyric homily about the events by John Chrysostom, who personally witnessed them but composed his version of them nearly twenty years afterwards, when the outcome had been clear for some time.

The immediate cause of this battle was the retrograde effort of the emperor Julian to re-establish the old civic religion in Antioch during the year 362. Julian's main ally was Libanius, the "servant of the Muses" and Orator of the City whom we met earlier in this chapter, "one of the most articulate and zealous champions of the old religion."[97]

The "turf war" in Daphne was not just over a physical place, and only apparently about two contending religions. Certainly, it was a battle between an interloping emperor and a citizenry that on balance preferred its own ways. But it also involved a literary war between two distinguished orators, Chrysostom (the "golden-mouthed") and his old teacher, Libanius.[98] Having two eminent literary men involved has given a self-consciously crafted aspect to these events, which demonstrates very well the issues involved in successfully crafting public memory which I have discussed earlier.

Daphne had traditionally been the site of an oracle of Apollo. There had been a grove and a spring, temples and villas had been built about them, and though the spring had ceased flowing nearly two centuries earlier, in the middle of the fourth century Daphne was still a famous place, indeed a well-established location of the cultural map of late antiquity, known for rich living and fleshly indulgence (and so occupying a place similar to that of "Beverly Hills" on our own similar "map"). The temple of Apollo still had its resident priests; the god's rituals were still conducted.

By the fourth century the city of Antioch had been a major Christian center for a long time. The city had its chief patron in the person of a former bishop who had become a local saint, Babylas. The blessed Babylas had died a martyr some one hundred years earlier, during a persecution of Christians by the pagan emperor Decius, and was buried in a martyrium in the Christian cemetery within the city.

Sometime around 353, the emperor Gallus (then residing in Antioch, and by all accounts something of a zealot) decided to translate the remains of Babylas to Daphne. Gallus had the bones reburied in a mausoleum which he built there, and the site became a focus of Christian processional worship. All this while, remember, the rituals of Apollo were still being maintained in Daphne.

Gallus' step-brother was the even more zealous emperor Julian (360–363), who attempted to revive pagan religion in the old empire. Julian's program was particularly pleasing to men like Libanius. In July, 362, two years after his proclamation as emperor, Julian visited Antioch, which he regarded (wrongly as it turned out) as a major bulwark of the old religion. He restored Apollo's temple in Daphne, setting up in it a huge statue of the god made of gilded wood; he tried to "purify" the major festival of the god, which had acquired a bad reputation as an occasion for bacchanalian excess; and he tried to cleanse the old spring, which had ceased flowing in the time of the emperor Hadrian.

Apollo's spring failed to resume flowing, despite Julian's efforts; and, being advised that the site had become irredeemably polluted by the presence of Babylas' corpse (pagan Romans scorned the Christians as bone-worshippers who lived amongst their own dead, a custom abhorrent to the Romans), Julian had him removed from Daphne.[99] The body of the martyr was taken back to the city accompanied by a large, fervent procession (the Christians having decided to make the best of the emperor's decree), and reburied in the city's martyrium, whence Gallus had orginally removed it.

The instant Babylas re-entered the city, according to Chrysostom, the roof of Apollo's temple in Daphne and the statue of the god were destroyed by fire. The Christians took this to be divine retribution upon Julian and all his works. Libanius composed an oration lamenting the loss of the temple. Julian ordered an investigation of the fire, and regarded the temple's priest as a possible conspirator in what he took to be a Christian arson; apparently even the pagans of Daphne were annoyed by Julian, because his version of the old religion was puritanical, involving the "cleansing" of the lubricious festivals. The citizens of Antioch turned on Julian, who retaliated by ordering a persecution of the Antiochine church (winter 362/363), though it seems not to have been carried out. The emperor left Antioch; he was killed on the Persian frontier in June, 363. His successor, the emperor Jovian, restored the Christian religion, and the brief pagan revival (such as it was) came to an end.

Chrysostom was a young witness of these events (he was born in Antioch c. 347). His homily on the travails and triumph of Babylas seems to have been composed just before a new church was built (in about 380) to rehouse the martyr's relics. There are a great many fascinating threads in this story – which, I emphasize, is self-consciously a story. Neither Chrysostom nor his audience would ever have been so naive as to suppose that "the facts speak for themselves" – except in a rhetorician's commonplace.

As an incident of social memory-making and (crucially) of social forgetting, the narrative has much to teach us. For the contest between Babylas and Apollo, as between Christ and Julian and Chrysostom and Libanius, is cast as a contest over *remembering*. As such, it is also a contest of stories.

The war at Daphne between Babylas and Apollo

We should think of Daphne not just as a literal place but as a memory site, reverberating with conventional associations. It is one of the *res* of the old culture, reclaimed for the new by the emperor Gallus through an act of "emplacement" – the body of the Christian martyr "placed" into Apollo's Daphne.

Notice that Gallus did not destroy the pagan shrine. Instead he changed the map, the habitational pattern, of the old Daphne by locating the Christian martyr next to the god, thereby, as his intention was understood, introducing a note of sobriety to temper (in the best tradition of classical ethics) the debauched excess with which Daphne had come to be associated. This tempering was carried out in the hymn-singing processions to the martyr's tomb which counter-weighed the rituals performed in Daphne for the pagan gods (besides Apollo, there was a temple of Zeus and possibly also one of Aphrodite). Thus within Daphne, the various sites acted as locations on a route; the movement among them was crucially as important to their "meaning" as the buildings themselves. Indeed, the route(s) made an ethical map of Daphne, virtue and vice and the shift between them enacted in the streets of the town. This aspect of the processions was completely understood by all the participants, as we will soon see.

Chrysostom is absolutely clear that the issue at stake in these events is memory. The saints' tombs carry this power:

> the power that they have to excite a similar zeal in the souls of those who behold them. If anyone approaches such a tomb, he immediately receives a distinct impression of this energy. *For the sight of the coffin, entering the soul, acts upon it and affects it in such a way that it feels as if it sees the one who lies there joining in prayer and drawing nigh.* Afterwards, one who has had this experience returns from there filled with great zeal and [is] a changed person ... *[T]he vision of the dead enters the souls of the living* ... as if they saw instead of the tomb those who lie in the tomb standing up ... *And why speak of the location of a grave? Many times, in fact, the sight of* a garment alone and *the recollection of* a word of the dead move the soul and *restore the failing memory.* For this reason God has left us the relics of the saints. (My emphases)[100]

Notice the emphasis on seeing and on memory. What Chrysostom describes here is very like the characterization given of Jerusalem pilgrims: "[w]ith the sight of the holy places [pilgrims] renew the picture in their thinking, and behold in their minds."[101] I will say more in a later chapter about the nature of such mental imaging as this; here it is important to note that the crucial "power" of the saint lies in the ability of his site/sight to enter the soul (through the eye), *affect* it (a question of *intentio*) and so cause one to *feel as if* one sees the saint himself – both in "the mind's eye" and "heartfully." The mental image has both *similitudo* and *intentio* – but crucially it has the latter. This power is not limited to the confines of a place, Chrysostom says: it is a power in the perceiving soul, that comes not from the "site" in itself but from the recollective affects which the "sight" has *on the perceiving mind*.

The martyr's tomb at Daphne, he says, acted like a *pedagogus* with a young student: "exhorting him *by look* to drink, eat, speak, and laugh with proper decorum" and measure. When one ascends to Daphne from the city and sees the martyr's shrine and then hastens to the coffin, one's soul is ordered "decorously in all respects" (par. 70). Through such recalling looks the presence of Babylas had an ameliorating effect on Daphne, Chrysostom claims, the dissolute and licentious persons becoming temperate, as under the gaze of their *pedagogus*.

In Chrysostom's culture this metaphor is important, for the *pedagogus* was the parent-like household slave who first taught a boy to read, taught him by rote the elementary *dicta et facta memorabilia* of the culture, including the canonical poems, and also accompanied him about the city, making sure he didn't get into trouble. The *pedagogus* was the cultural foundation-builder. Babylas acts like a Christian *pedagogus*, a provider of "places to put" in decorous order all the "things" in Daphne. It is not the site alone of Babylas that is crucial but the "sight."

Chrysostom places the local contest within the schema of the Old Testament struggles of God against such deities as Dagon and Baal (par. 116). Chrysostom does not reveal the full parallel until the end, by which time even the dullest of his readers should have gotten the point; but the stories continually reverberate, one within the other. He introduces the events with an Edenic description of Daphne, which "God made ... fair and lovely by the abundance of its waters" (par. 68). But it became polluted and perverted by "the enemy of our salvation," who installed in it the demon Apollo. "Remembering" Babylas is thus cast in terms of the Old Testament requirement of "remembering" Jahweh; at issue is not similitude ("accuracy" of "representation") but intention, will. The battle for Daphne was conducted by procession and festival; the citizens performing at the site like *imagines agentes* in a mnemonic "place" or *scaena*. The processions to the sites provided both remembering minds and memorable images. Both Julian and the Christians understood this.

Julian began his attack on Babylas with a procession of "male and female prostitutes [says Chrysostom] he made rise from the brothels ... and form a cortège which he himself led around the streets of the entire city" (par. 77). This was perhaps a procession to honor Aphrodite: in any event, it was followed by a series of imperial processions up to Daphne with "quantities of offerings and sacrificial victims" (par. 80). These events are understood by Chrysostom as deliberately theatrical: "the madcap emperor, as if acting on a stage and playing a part in a drama" (par. 81), resolved to move upon the tomb of Babylas.[102]

Staged scene succeeded staged scene: the coffin of Babylas, ordered from Daphne, "was dragged all along the road, and the martyr returned, like an athlete, carrying a second crown into his own city where he had received the first ... Like some champion he joined great and wonderful triumphs to greater and more wonderful triumphs" (par. 89). This procession, involving all the inhabitants of the city, is used in Chrysostom's account like an overlay image that "crowds out" and blocks the processions staged by the emperor. What is at stake is not objects *per se*, not *res*, but rather the picture, the pattern, the *scaena* in which those same "things" are embedded. The processions are not staged to impress some passive audience of townsfolk, but to establish for the participants (and those who cared to join them) the cognitive "way" through the sites, and thus "through" the memories they would evoke. It is not the event but the memory networks, their directions or "intentions," that are crucially contested.

It is also for this reason that Chrysostom liberally quotes from Libanius' lament over the destruction by fire of Apollo's temple. Fire is often a key element in scenes of forgetting. There are discussions of "how to forget" as well as of how to remember: several of these from the Renaissance counsel making an image of what one wishes to forget and "burning" it up. Interestingly, however, in practice such a technique turns out not to be necessarily successful. One subject of a now-famous case study of a "memory artist" in the twentieth century, when asked how, after his performances were over, he was able to forget the many items he had committed to memory, said that he had at first tried in his mind seeing them written out on a piece of paper and then imagining the paper burning up. But this did not make him forget. What it did was to make him remember the materials *as burned up*.[103] They were still there, but seen differently and so differently "directed," differently turned. The role of the fire in Chrysostom's story serves a similar mnemonic function. He shows us Apollo *burning up*, and he uses the pagan "matters" offered by Libanius' monody, a well-known poem by a then-major literary figure, as one of his main tools for doing this.

Chrysostom quotes at some length Libanius' description of the fire in Apollo's temple:

> Beams collapsed, carrying the fire which destroyed whatever it approached: Apollo [the statue], instantaneously, since he was close to the roof, and then the other beautiful objects: images of the founding muses, gleaming stones [?mosaics], lovely pillars ... Great was the wail raised by the nymphs, leaping from their fountains; and by Zeus situated nearby, at the destruction of his son's honors; and by a throng of countless demons residing in the grove. No less a lament was raised by Calliope from the middle of the city, when the gladdener of the muses [Apollo] was injured by fire" (par. 112).

By the end of this description, the devastation of the fire is clearly pictured in the mind of any reader. But the deserted ruin of charred beams and destroyed columns mourned by Libanius is "turned," like the trope it is, in a different "direction" by Chrysostom. The key to "forgetting" Apollo in this incident is not to destroy his temple but to re-position it and remember it, in a different, though closely related, "story."

14. WHY WAS APOLLO'S TEMPLE BURNED?

Chrysostom raises several times a critical matter: why didn't the emperor, so abhorring Christian ways, destroy the corpse of Babylas completely? And (more importantly) why didn't God destroy the emperor outright or at least burn down the whole temple? Because of the requirements of memory, he replies. If God had struck the emperor with a thunderbolt, the memory of such a calamity would have awed the onlookers, "but after two or three years the memory of the event would perish and there would be many who would not accept the prodigy; if, however, the temple receives the flame, it will proclaim the anger of God more clearly than any herald not only to contemporaries but also to all posterity" (par. 114). And why is this more effective? Chrysostom responds:

> Just as if someone from above breaking into the cavernous lair of a robber chief should lead out the inhabitant in chains and, having taken all his things, should leave the place as a refuge for wild beasts and jackdaws; then every visitor to the lair, as soon as he sees the place, pictures in his imagination the raids, the thefts, the features of the earlier inhabitant [though obviously not his actual features, since "every visitor" had not seen the robber] – so it happens here. For, seeing the columns from a distance, then coming and crossing the threshold, he pictures to himself the malignity, deceit, and intrigues of the demon and departs in amazement at the strength of God's anger ... See: it is twenty years after the event and none of the edifice left behind by the fire has perished ... Only one of the columns around the back vestibule was broken in two at the time, and it did not even fall down ... The part from the foundation to the break leans sideways towards the wall, while the part from the break to the capital is on its back, supported by the lower part. Although violent winds assailed the place many times and the earth was shaken, the remains of the fire were not even shaken but stand firmly, *all but shouting that they have been preserved for the chastisement of future generations.* (pars. 115–117; my emphasis)

Notice the lingering detail with which Chrysostom "paints" the picture of the single broken column in Apollo's temple. It is not obliterated at all, quite the oposite. But it is dis-placed into a different associational map. Burnt and broken, it serves as a memory cue "for the chastisement" of future generations, who can remember both the pagan "thing" associated with the column and that this "thing" is now broken and has been re-placed.[104] "Forgetting" is accomplished not by erasure but by placement within a scene – a basic mnemonic technique. Forgetting is a variety of remembering.

What crucially counts is not the "things" taken objectively – the hill, the spring, the grove, the columned temple, the martyr's tomb – but their relationship, the *picture* that they make, and which *as a picture* is taken in and immediately "placed" into our other experience. Chrysostom, using the rhetorical figure called *enargeia* (of which I will have much more to say later), carefully paints the picture of the burned temple, as he earlier did (par. 70) that of the tomb of Babylas at Daphne. Thus the attentive reader must paint each image *in a scene* in his imagination and memory: approaching from far off, the reader-viewer comes closer, he sees the details of the site, the ruined building, and finally, as though in closeup, the column snapped in two, its lower half leaning against the wall, its top half reversed, with its capital resting on the ground.

The two locations in Daphne – Babylas' tomb, Apollo's broken column – bracket the homily. They are deliberately paralleled, the one overlying the other. Like a palimpsest, the scene of the wholesome, sweet-aired martyr's tomb "bleeds through" to the scene of the abandoned temple with its broken column. One cannot remember the one without the other. Thus is the memory of the pagan Apollo appropriated cognitively (*a-propria*, 'from its place') from one network into a network of other "places" fashioned by the schema of this sermon, as also by the actions of Gallus, of Julian, of Libanius.

The relics of Babylas were never physically returned to Daphne, as we might expect them to be now. Deliberately, Bishop Meletius of Antioch built the martyrium for his relics in the city cemetery where he had first been buried, and to which he was returned for his "second crown" by the procession accompanying his coffin from Daphne. On the "map" of its citizens, Antioch's triumph over Daphne was complete.

15. THE CONSTRUCTION OF PUBLIC "FORGETTING": OVERLAY AND REMAPPING

Mnemotechnically speaking, as I observed earlier, mere erasure is not a successful means of forgetting. We will look more closely at the phenomenon of individual forgetting in the next chapter, but "communal forgetting" was also mastered by the Christians – not through some variety of amnesia, but by applying carefully the mnemotechnical principles of blocking one pattern of memories by another, through "crowding" or overlay, and by intentional mnemonic replacement. Keep in mind that when we speak of "place" in memory, we refer not to a literal spot or space, but to *location within a network*, "memory" *distributed* through a web of associations, some of which may involve physical space (as Babylas' tomb was actually placed into the route of shrines at Daphne), many of which are socially constructed and maintained conventions (the polished black marble of the Vietnam memorial, listing the names of the dead), and all of which only become active in the minds of people making such webs of association.

The battle of processions that is such a feature of Chrysostom's story is a case in point. "Crowding" was a well-recognized principle of "forgetting." Too many images overlapping one another in a given location, images that are too much alike, will confuse and even cancel one another out. Students were consistently given advice always to memorize from the same codex and page, lest too many competing images of the words formed from different books blur and block their memory of the text.

One can apply this principle to the events at Daphne. Julian's processions up to Daphne were designed to overlie and thus "crowd" or even "block" the earlier Christian processions to the martyr's shrine; they also were supposed to "purge" the debauched, debased processions that Apollo's rites had become. In retaliation, the Christian citizens' procession accompanying Babylas back to Antioch overlay the memory of all those Julian processions and thus "forgot" them.

It has been said of the eastern Mediterranean in the fourth century that it featured a war of processions. That is true: and no culture has better understood the social purpose of procession (the only contemporary culture that comes close in my experience is Hindu culture).[105] Patterned movement, as in procession, is a basic memory foundation; it "places" us individually within a community as an *imago agens* within a memory location. The principles governing these processions are mnemonically sound: they consist of images moving within locations, locations spaced distinctly apart and in a clear relationship to one another (*solemnis* and *rarus*), having the qualities that make them both strike and fix in the mind. Participant and audience together *make up* these processions, and remember them viscerally, the way we remember how to ride a bicycle, or how to dance. Such knowledge cannot really be obliterated: it can, however, be re-located.[106]

John Baldovan comments that in Rome the liturgies that developed about the stational churches are "the classic example of the relation between urban life and Christian worship. Every part of the city was employed to manifest the unity-in-diversity of the Roman church as it moved toward the pinnacle of the Christian Year, the paschal feast."[107] This public memory network (for that is how it functioned) developed over time as "a grand, well-conceived tour of the Christian city." During Easter, for example, each major basilica (the Lateran, Santa Maria Maggiore, St. Peter's, San Paolo, San Lorenzo, Sancti Apostoli, Santa Maria ad Martyres) was visited in the order of the importance of the saints in the city's life. The journey thus provided a walk-through, in processional order, of the city as memorized network, for clergy, laity, and neophytes alike. Each basilica was a node of this network, a site for memory-making: and at other seasons, other churches were incorporated into the stational schemata.

The origins of the Roman stational liturgy are the pagan urban processions, both those that (continuing into Christian times) accompanied the emperor, and also popular processions, like the processions in Daphne. Exactly when and how the Christian liturgies came into being is a vexed matter, the story hampered by lack of evidence. However, it seems that only gradually did the Christians in Rome begin to develop their public processions. But by the seventh century the first pagan temple to be "converted," the Pantheon, was dedicated as Santa Maria ad Martyres, and incorporated into the stational liturgy of Easter. And around the same time, the Christian procession of the Great Liturgy on April 25 replaced the old civic procession of Robigalia, appropriating not only the date but also the route and the goal (civic supplication and penitence) of its pagan original.[108]

These appropriations were carried out with a profound understanding of how human memories work. Exactly the same mechanisms are at work in the re-placement of the Pantheon and the Robigalia as in Chrysostom's story of Babylas and Apollo at Daphne. The Pantheon was inserted into a different social network by being attached to a closely related web of memories which overlay the first, blocking and reforming them. And what remained recognizably the same in the two webs is as important to understanding why the appropriation worked effectively as is the difference between them. It is the principle that allowed and even encouraged the use of *spolia*, Roman columns and other decorative materials re-placed in Christian buildings.[109]

In his study of the art of late antiquity, *The Clash of Gods*, Thomas Mathews gives a number of examples of this technique for "forgetting" the images of pagan gods in making the iconography of Christianity.[110] One example is the "appropriation" (and now we understand exactly what that means cognitively) of the philosopher icon for Christ; another the positioning of a colossal image of Christ in the "bill-board space" afforded by the apse of the early Christian basilica. This colossal figure centers the sightlines within the church, as the colossal statue of the god had occupied them in the old god's temple (for example, the statue of Apollo that burned at Daphne).

Mathews's book is filled with such examples both of mnemotechnical crowding and of relocation (though these are not terms he uses), as the Christians successfully developed their art out of the materials of their pagan past. They were extraordinarily adept at communal forgetting/remembering, utilizing the cognitive power of *memoria rerum*.

Things that are completely different and separate do not block each other: they act instead as two distinct memory sites. Where two or more competing patterns exist in one site, however, only one will be seen: the others, though they may remain potentially visible, will be blocked or absorbed by the overlay. What will block out every pattern but one is our *intentio*, the mental "tone" we select, whose vibrations, like those of the taut strings of an instrument, create the patterns which connect a particular experience into everything else we know and enable us to see a bat instead of teeth, or the Great Liturgy instead of Robigalia. If the people of a city come conventionally (which is only another way of saying habitually) "to see" the Great Liturgy, it matters not at all that some in the crowd may for a time persist in "seeing" the Robigalia procession, or some particular story of their own devising. Eventually ... well, when I now see the yellow circle with the jagged black center, I instantly see a black bat, and must willfully struggle to see golden teeth again (and I have begun to wonder how I ever thought the circle enclosed a picture of teeth at all). Nobody "brainwashed" me. I have, however, changed the "direction" from which I habitually "see" that particular logo, and it is literally colored differently in my eyes. I see the black part now as the primary shape and color, the yellow part as filler, instead of the other way around as I first did, before I was "tuned in."

16. EARLY CHRISTIANS RECOLLECT VIRGIL

A similar effort at "forgetting" also occurred in Christian Latin literature, especially centered on the foundational author of the Roman curriculum, Virgil, and in particular his *Aeneid*, the poem everybody had by heart. The ability to recite it backwards and forwards, though notable, was not uncommon. The late fourth and early fifth centuries saw a phenomenon that has troubled and puzzled modern literary historians: the re-writing of Virgil, especially in the form called *cento*. The contributions of two Christian poets, Ausonius and Proba, are best known; Macklin Smith has pointed out, however, that Prudentius' *Psychomachia*, too, is virtually a *cento* in many passages.[111]

A *cento* is a playful poem that is made up of a pastiche of half-lines and phrases from a canonical poet; it cannot succeed except for an audience who know the original poet as intimately as does the composer of the *cento*. It is a kind of puzzle poem; in a preface, Ausonius likens the *cento* to a Greek bone puzzle called *ostomachia*. The player struggles to fit the disparate shapes of the bones together, and with skill, a delightful picture can be made, perhaps of an elephant or a flying goose, a tower or a tankard – a variety limited only by the ingenuity of the players. "And while the harmonious arrangement of the skillful is marvellous, the jumble made by the unskilled is grotesque."[112]

I have already made brief reference to the pedagogical custom of learning canonical texts twice, the first time by rote, syllable by syllable and phrase by phrase. One result of this education was that the text was perceived as a foundation "divided" into mnemonically sized chunks or bits, which could then be fitted together to build a whole structure. As clauses were "made up" of phrases, and phrases of words (this was particularly evident in metrical material, such as poetry), so words were constructed of syllables. This attitude seems never to have been outgrown in Roman literary taste. As a result readers of these works have to acquire a taste for word-play and puzzle-solving of a sort that modern readers of English are rarely taught to discover or enjoy.[113]

Indeed one major study of *Vergil in the Middle Ages* characterizes a love of *centi* as possible "only among people who had learnt Vergil mechanically and did not know of any better use to which to put all these verses with which they had loaded their brains."[114] The composers and audiences of *centi* had considerably more sophistication concerning the uses of memory than does this modern writer, however. They took Virgil apart not in order to obliterate him nor (I think) to ridicule him but to save him. And the only way to save him was to re-member him, re-locate and re-pattern him, into a Christian.[115]

In the next chapter I will discuss more specifically the dynamic of "forgetting" that the *centi* and such poems as Prudentius' *Psychomachia* employed. But it is akin to the dynamic that remembered the Pantheon as Santa Maria ad Martyres. Such cultural *res* as these are so habitually embedded as memorial *loci* that obliterating them is a

58

pointless, socially disruptive exercise. But the cognitive effect of *memoria rerum* allows them to be remembered faithfully and changed radically at the same time. The Pantheon building looked pretty much as it had always done, and (most importantly) remained *where* it had always been, at the center of the "map" of the city: what changed were the "routes" to it, the webs into which it was re-located, not literally but by forming some additional and different associations in the life of the city. It was given a new label (carved into its portal), and then simply taken over into the new context, its gist as the central landmark of the city reassuringly unchanged. Was this an act of forgetting or remembering? How one answers that question depends entirely on one's own "angle," or *intentio*, the "pattern," including emotional "tones," in terms of which one sees the event.

Ausonius understood that composing *centi* was exclusively an act of memory, "a task for the memory only, which has to gather up scattered tags and fit these [cut-up] scraps together."[116] The Christian poet Faltonia Proba composed a *cento* of Virgilian half-lines, which retells the stories of Scripture; the poem divides into two symmetrical sections of stories from the Old Testament and the New. Proba clearly states her motive: "I will speak a Virgil who has sung of Christ's sacred gifts."[117] Of course, to save Virgil in this way will surely seem to many moderns akin to the American program for saving Vietnam.

But it did finally save Virgil. His work was not destroyed; as a poet who sang of the journey of a man's whole life (the "intention" of Virgil, as articulated by medieval school exegesis), his lines were fitted (with a good bit of chipping and scraping) onto the "foundations" and into the essential curriculum of medieval authors.[118] I don't mean to suggest that *cento* treatment alone accomplished this. But it helped to form a cultural expectation that placed Virgil among the *dicta et facta memorabilia* of Christian culture, as he assuredly had been of pagan. We should not think of parody solely as a destructive, diminishing kind of literature. One cannot read Proba's pious *cento* without first knowing Virgil as intimately as she did; one cannot read Prudentius' *Psychomachia* without being familiar with the *Aeneid*. The *res* remains centrally located, faithfully remembered. I am punning, obviously, as the *cento* form itself does, on its use of half-lines, exactly repeated, members of an earlier work re-membered, like old bricks in a new wall.

2

"Remember Heaven": the aesthetics of *mneme*

Sede in cella quasi in paradiso. St. Romuald of Camaldoli

I. *VIRTUS MEMORIAE*

I suggested in my first chapter how properties of memorability figure importantly in the construction of public memorials and cultural "forgetting." But of course the public, cultural success of these activities depends entirely, as we have just seen, on how well such performances respect the recollective needs of individual human memories. One of the chief contributions of monasticism to rhetoric was to develop the craft of meditation upon one's reading as a self-conscious, practical art of invention, grounded in familiar rhetorical and mnemotechnical principles.

Monastic rhetoric developed an art for composing meditative prayer (its typical product) that conceives of composition in terms of making a "way" among "places" or "seats," or (in a common variation on this trope) as climbing the "steps" of a ladder.[1] These "places" most commonly took the form of short texts from the Bible, or of stories also taken from that source. The trope of "steps" or "stages" was commonly applied to the affective, emotional "route" that a meditator was to take in the course of such composition, from "fear" to "joy" – perhaps even that inarticulate, sensory joy that Augustine characterized as the earthly memory of the vision of God.[2] These "routes," emotional and rational, are always characterized as routes through the things in one's memory.[3]

Along with this trope, and acting always in sympathetic conjunction with it, there also developed the trope of thinking and learning as building, "machines" of the mind "raising" one towards God as masons use hoists to raise the fabric of buildings – and also as millers use mill-wheels (another meaning of *machina*) to grind grains for bread.

The routes of the liturgy and the routes of a mind meditating its way through the sites (and "sights") of Scripture became for the fourth-century Fathers their essential conception of Invention, the mind thinking. In rhetoric, this development is both new, and distinctively fourth century. Teachers of rhetoric in late antiquity developed a concept to describe it, *ductus*, which they related in turn to the old rhetorical concept of *colores*. I will say more about this later in this chapter. It is significant in the practices of monastic rhetoric, as expressed in both meditative and liturgical prayer.

The distinctive practices of meditation also drew upon some core concepts of traditional rhetoric. I will begin with these because they are fundamental to the idea of *ductus* as well. They include the qualities known as *brevitas* and *copia*, which in ancient rhetoric were usually analyzed under style, but in monastic rhetoric develop self-consciously into tropes of invention. When rhetoric was taught again as a school subject after the late eleventh century, they turned up (in Geoffrey of Vinsauf's *Poetria nova*, for example) as the related tropes of "abbreviation" and "amplification," judged to be essential for composing literary work.

Much of this chapter will focus on some of John Cassian's *Conferences* as an essential foundation of monastic rhetoric. These dialogues on the method of prayer and reading, held with various masters living in the Egyptian desert, strongly influenced both Benedict of Nursia and Gregory the Great.[4] Though monastic historians have no need to be reminded of this, it may be useful for other readers if I review very briefly the basis of Cassian's pre-eminence. The Benedictine Rule specified Cassian's *Conferences* as the reading after Vespers on fast days, and named the *Conferences* and *Institutes*, Basil's *Long Rule*, and the Lives of the Fathers (Benedict referred to the desert Fathers, but Gregory's *Dialogues* or lives of the Italian saints, including Benedict, were soon added) as among the suitable readings after supper every day (*Regula Benedicti*, ch. 42; see also ch. 73).[5] This was the last reading before the liturgical office of Compline, after which general silence was observed until the Night Office. It is as though Benedict sent his monks off to their lucubrations with the most suitable of counsel possible. The *Conferences* are about the practice of meditation, and night-time was, in classical pedagogy, the best time for memory work, *meditatio*.[6]

2. THE ENGINE OF MEMORY

The sole work in all of Migne's *Patrologia latina* to bear the title *Tractatus de memoria* appears to be nothing of the sort, but instead is a meditation on such subjects as the Trinity, the Church, and sin. It is the work of Hugo of Rouen, from the middle of the twelfth century. He was a Benedictine monk, of the same generation as the great contemplative Peter Damian, and also a revered elder master for Abbot Suger, the inventive rebuilder of St. Denis. Why and how a sophisticated contemplative would call a meditation on God a work on memory, "in laudem memoriae" even (according to the introductory colophon), is a continuing theme of this chapter.

In a prefatory letter, written to "his dear brother Philip," Hugo observes that while Philip has devoted himself wholly to the study of Scripture, he will not discover what he seeks all at once.[7] For its copiousness is contained in it *breviter* and must be teased out of it by a mind on tenterhooks, irritated, working at fever-pitch, as Hugo describes his own state of mind in composing this meditation for Philip. He is in a state of anxiety, distressed by summer's heat ("aestate praesenti caloribus admodum ... anxiatus") as he sends his meditation off to Philip. However hot the summer may actually have been, this restless, anxious mood described by Hugo was regarded in monastic practice as a common, even necessary, preliminary to invention as we will see later.

But the matters which Hugo sends to Philip are themselves cold and brief and written in a pinched, contracted style. Philip, with "solicitude" (a word that figures prominently in monastic memory craft), is invited to expand them.[8] These various emotional stances and cognitive activities are all presented as the work of *memoria*: "These are matters of faith, holy, divine, set before you after being revealed by the Holy Spirit: they are [subjects] for memory-work, because [Psalm 110:4] 'the merciful and compassionate God hath made His wonderful works to be remembered.'[9] We propose to speak about memory, which God makes vigorous in us."[10]

This view of the work of memory both as producing a concentrated, "brief" matter for storage, and in recollection as exfoliating it through the "routes" of its associations, is fundamental to the earliest monastic art of memory, as it was also in ancient mnemotechnic. In a passage we looked at earlier, Peter Chrysologus speaks of how, in meditation, one looks inwardly at a word from Scripture, recalled from memory and seen with the mind's eye, until it starts to glow and radiate, resonating with the charged spiritual energy of a mind beginning its memory work.[11] But how this activity comes to be thought of specifically as *memoria* – instead of cogitation or meditation or reasoning, words we would be more likely to use now – has to do, I think, with the memory-centered pedagogy, including practice in mnemonic technique, that surrounded the teaching and learning of reading and writing too, of course, which was thought to be part of the memory work of reading.[12]

Many of the basic notions of monastic meditational praxis are illuminated by equally fundamental principles or "rules" of mnemotechnical praxis. Among these principles is the pairing of *brevitas* with *copia*, both as a practical cognitive matter and as an equally practical matter of judgment on the part both of the original author of the meditation and of the audience (should there be one other than God), who can in turn receive the "arcta et brevia" products of *memoria* in order to author and initiate meditations of their own.

The idea that memory requires *brevitas* is also one manifestation of another basic distinction in memory technique, that between someone *meminens verbatim* and *meminens summatim*, remembering by words and remember by "things," *in verbis vel rebus*.[13] This first task of reading is to divide a text up into "brief," memory-sized chunks. This procedure is made very clear in the following advice. Though I am quoting from a collection of maxims by Hugh of St. Victor "on the method of learning and meditating," similar advice is found in fourth-century texts, such as the rhetoric textbooks of Consultus Fortunatianus and Julius Victor, two of the main sources for rhetoric in the earlier Middle Ages.[14]

Human *ingenium* or "ingenuity," one's native thinking ability, and *memoria*, Hugh says, must always work together. But human memory is limited in how much it can store and recall at one time: therefore, in order to remember something long and complicated one is required to divide it for the purpose of memory storage into pieces that respect the length of human "short-term memory" (as we now call it), or (as medieval writers said) what the mind's eye can take in at a single glance (*conspectus*). Each mnemonic background or scene is constituted by the sweep of one such mental gaze, and the individual mnemonic clues within each scene cannot be more in number or complexity than what one can distinguish clearly in one look of the memory.

When we read anything, we are obliged by nature to "divide" it up for this purpose. Then, having stored these pieces in memory, we must re-collect them (*colligere*) for any creative thinking procedures, whether ordinary cogitation or profound meditation (meditation, Hugh says in these maxims, is a variety of cogitation):

> [Mnemotechnically speaking] "to collect" is to reduce those things which are written or spoken about at greater length to a brief and commodious summary; of the sort which is called by ancient authorities an epilogue, a brief recapitulation of the matters spoken about earlier. For indeed human memory delights in brevity, and if something is divided into many pieces it will seem shorter [taken] one piece at a time than it would as a single whole. We should therefore from every study or lesson gather up things brief and secure, which we hide away in the little chest of our memory, from which later they may be drawn when any subject has need.[15]

Such "briefing" is the proper method of learning.

But we must not simply confuse "brief" with "short." Medieval summaries are also, as Hugh says here, "commodious": they resonate and glow just as Biblical words do for Peter Chrysologus. In fact, the Bible texts are made *breviter*. In another sermon, Peter Chrysologus analyzes the mustardseed parable (Luke 13: 18–19) in terms that are derived from the linkage in rhetoric of *brevitas* with *copia*. The mustardseed is tiny, but

> if we would only sow this grain of mustardseed in our memories in such a way that it will grow into a great tree of knowledge, and to the full extent of our consciousness be raised toward the sky; that it will spread out into all the branches of the sciences; that it will burn our tingling mouths with the pungent taste of its seed! Thus it will burn for us with all the fire of its seed, and break into flame in our heart.[16]

The work of memory ("in our heart" and "in our memory") is to take the "brief" mustardseed and make it grow and spread copiously into a "great tree of knowledge."[17]

Augustine, writing for those who would teach beginners in Scriptural study, describes the powers of recollecting *summatim* as follows:

> but, even if we have memorized the words [ad uerbum], [when we teach] we should not either just recite by rote the whole Pentateuch, and the entire books of Judges, Kings, and Esdras, and the whole of the Gospels and Acts, or, by retelling in our own words, disclose and explicate everything contained in these volumes, for neither does time allow it nor does any necessity require it; but having

grasped them all as a whole in summary [summatim] and essential terms, we can select certain things as [being] more worthy to be examined closely, which may be listened to and set forth more agreeably just as they were written; and likewise, it is not right to show such a thing [still] in its wrappings and then immediately remove it from view, but dwelling on it a piece at a time as though to loosen it up and expand it, [one should] offer it for inspection and wonder [miranda] by the minds of the audience: the other matters in these books can be connected up by a cursory run-through.[18]

This is a fine statement of *memoria rerum*, remembering Scripture for homiletic purposes as a set of summarized plots, within which are embedded a number of gems to be held up individually and admired. The word *miranda* has a distinctive resonance in classical culture as the initial act of philosophical speculation, derived from *mirari*, "to look with wonder."[19]

These gems are the dark, difficult parts in the text which one can isolate, holding one or two up at a time to the audience for admiration, and proceeding to loosen up its knots and expand its meaning, as one explicates and expounds, composing a homiletic meditation.[20] Notice that it is the historical books – not the Psalms or the prophets or the epistles of Paul – which Augustine suggests should be treated in this way. And notice also – for this is crucial – that the purpose of such memorial summary is to make new compositions of gloss and interpretation. Thus *memoria rerum* is essential for literary invention; its purpose is to compose new discourse, not really convenience of storage. The most interesting assumption Augustine makes in these remarks is that even if you have the whole Bible word for word by heart, you still need to recall it *summatim* when you come to teach others.

In reading, *memoria rerum* manifests itself also as the principle of *brevitas*. Hugo of Rouen continues,

All that intellect discovers, that study [studium] pays heed to, that pious love desires, a wise memory gathers together at once as a whole, prudently attends to, providently stores away. ... Memoria is, they say, the key of knowledge about the world [clavis scientiae], it raised the ladder of Jacob from earth to heaven.[21]

And, among all the powers of each human mind,

the energy of memory [virtus memoriae] thrives more fertilely: it

65

alone makes the past present, binds together things, recalls divine wisdom [sapientia], gazes upon the future.[22]

The various moral, intellectual, and spiritual virtues or *habitus*, in the language of scholastic moral philosophy, are equipped for their jobs, confirmed, and powered by memory. *Memoria* is like an engine (in our sense of that word) of the mind.[23]

Hugo calls the type of memory work that is his subject "sacra memoria" (1314) and "pia memoria" (1307). It is an art of memory, though no pagan teacher of rhetoric would have recognized it as such. Yet *sacra memoria* was taught as a craft, a conscious discipline with principles and "rules" and stages of mastery. It incorporated a number of techniques and principles similar to those of Republican mnemotechnic, but it is not derived closely from it. In so far as I can find sources for it, it seems to owe a good deal both to Hellenistic (including Jewish) elementary pedagogy and to late-antique Jewish meditational practices.[24]

In trying to clarify the sources and paths of dissemination of craft lore such as the various mnemotechnics, one should not make too much of similarities in their basic principles (such as the need for clear order, for "locations" in which to "place" things, or the mnemonic preference for vivid, shocking, emotion-laden "images-in-action"). There is overlap among the variety of practices and techniques applied in different cultures: to be successful – obviously – all these techniques need to incorporate at the very least the observed actualities of how humans remember. The Roman *auctor ad Herennium* says, after all, that "this memory art" he is about to describe (the demonstrative is emphasized in the Latin) accords with human nature.[25] It will strengthen and improve memories that are capable and talented, but cannot help a person whose memory is poor or injured to begin with. No silk purses from sows' ears are promised though one supposes, from some disparaging remarks made by Quintilian, that there were masters in antiquity quite happy to give improving-your-memory lessons to members of the adult public who would pay for them.

3. REMEMBERING THE FUTURE

God, said the Psalmist, made his works for remembering: *"memoranda sunt ista."* This is a statement obvious in memory cultures, such as those of the Psalmist and of Hugo of Rouen and his contemporaries: as obvious as a statement that "God made his works to be measured" would be to us now. Yet many scholars now seem to me to have overlooked the implications of believing such a thing about fictions, human and divine. All crafted things are made in the first instance for human remembering – both directly, to attract attention and thus to be remembered (what we ordinarily mean when we now say that a thing is "memorable"); and then *through the work of memory* for knowing, for cognition. At the very least this conception of artistic product requires that all art, at some basic level, must engage the procedures of human memory, for one cannot know or even think about what one does not "have in mind," that is, has remembered.

The injunction to "remember," "be mindful of," is characteristic of the Hebrew Bible, memorably throughout the one book that every monk in the Middle Ages learned by heart: the Psalms. The understanding of memory that underlies and nourishes the monastic art of memory, *sacra memoria*, is that typified in Psalm 136: "Super flumina Babylonis illic sedimus et flevimus cum recordaremur Sion"; "By the waters of Babylon there we sat down, yea, we wept when we remembered Zion." Early Christian commentary traditions, while recognizing the historical setting of this psalm in the experience of the Captivity, had attached it allegorically (in Augustine's characterization, "loosened it up and expanded it") to the Heavenly City of the New Jerusalem, which Christians, exiled in this world beside the rivers of the devil's city, Babylon, remembered as they wept and hoped for their heavenly "return."[26] The trope lies as a foundation of Augustine's *The City of God*; it is a fundamental model of the monk's life.

This "remembering," affective (this psalm begins with weeping and ends with calls for angry revenge) and goal-oriented, bears only partial resemblance to the familiar model of memory as the mind's storehouse of things we have experienced in the past. "Remember Jerusalem," like the American equivalent, "Remember the Alamo," is a call not to preserve but to act – in the present, for the future. The matters memory presents are used to persuade and motivate, to create emotion and stir the will. And the "accuracy" or "authenticity" of these memories – their simulation of an actual past – is of far less importance (indeed it is hardly an issue at all) than their use to motivate the present and to affect the future. Though it is certainly a form of knowing, recollecting is also a matter of will, of being *moved*, pre-eminently a moral activity rather than what we think of as intellectual or rational.

This notion of memory has not been very well identified or described in Greek-derived philosophical traditions, which have more typically developed a faculty model for thinking, splitting the process among particular mental "centers" in the brain, and giving to memory the particular function of storing what is past.

The Biblical notion of remembering has tended to be dismissed, until quite recently, as "re-created memory," scarcely different from outright lying, and of no interest in the philosophy of mind at all. Instead, a "storehouse" model of memory, and the idea that memory is "of the past," have been emphasized to such a degree that memory has been accorded only a reiterative, reduplicative role – all else is "unreal" and thus "untruthful." Western ideas of memory have been concerned at least since the Enlightenment with what the philosopher Mary Warnock calls "the crucial distinction, with which we are all familiar in real life, between memory and the imagination (close though these may often be to one another). ... [w]hat distinguishes memory from imagination is not some particular feature of the [mental] image but the fact that memory is, while imagination is not, concerned with the *real*."[27]

One could displace these categories, in order to save the general formulation for medieval conditions by arguing that Heaven, for medieval monks, was real – but this merely obscures a critical difference in early medieval understandings of memory. Heaven was real, but it was certainly not "of the past": if it were, one would have to admit some version of a real transmigration of souls.[28] Christianity does not. So, as we will see, this modern "crucial difference" between memory and imagination (however familiar it may be in our modern "real lives", and though something like it was recognized during the Middle Ages in certain contexts) is not in fact crucial to the meditational arts of monastic culture.[29] In fact, the medieval boundary between "memory" and "imagination" is, from the point of view of our modern notions about them, shifting and very permeable – a feature which is to my mind one of the most interesting things about pre-scholastic medieval *memoria*.

In common monastic idiom, one "remembers" the Last Things, death, Heaven, and Hell: that is, one *makes* a mental vision or "seeing" of invisible things from the matters in his memory. A twelfth-century monk wrote that "[t]he frequent recollection of the city of Jerusalem and of its King is to us a sweet consolation, a pleasing occasion for meditation."[30] A rhetoric professor at Bologna in 1235, Boncompagno da Signa, included in his discussion of rhetorical *memoria* sections "De memoria paradisi" and "De memoria inferni," and comments that "we must assiduously remember the invisible joys of Paradise and the eternal torments of Hell."[31]

Boncompagno gives us a clue for understanding how we may "remember the future." He says that *memoria*, the means by which humans comprehend time, enables us to recall past things, embrace present things, and contemplate future things *through their likeness to past things* ("et futura per preterita similitudinarie contemplamur").[32]

The sources for such remembering are both literary and sensory: texts, commentaries, other literary works, sounds, smells, foods, paintings of all sorts, buildings and their parts, sculptures. Sometimes they might also include more idiosyncratic things one had experienced: Boncompagno says that when he remembers Hell, he particularly remembers an eruption of Mt. Etna, when he saw the mountain throwing out many sulphurous, burning globs as he sailed near it. The mother of Guibert de Nogent in her dreams recalled the Virgin Mary in the likeness of the Virgin in the cathedral at Chartres.[33] And Thomas Bradwardine suggests that if one needs a mnemonically valuable image for an abstract quality, like the Trinity, one should make use of "an image as it is usually painted in churches."[34] These are recognizably uses of memory, but for thinking, for inventing, for making a composition in the present that is directed towards our future.

4. THE WAY OF INVENTION: JOHN CASSIAN'S STORY OF SARAPION, MONK OF EGYPT

If asked now to describe how we compose something, we would probably say that we compose by using our "imagination." And so when we read in a medieval description of religious meditation or in a medieval poem that composition begins in "recollection," we tend to assume one of two things: either that medieval people had no concept at all of "creativity" in our sense and were devoted to a more or less slavish reiteration of other people's creations; or that what they call "recollection" is something completely other than anything we would recognize as "memory" – and that they have made a category error by using the wrong term. So, in her 1911 study of *Mysticism*, Evelyn Underhill felt compelled to apologize for "[t]he unfortunate word *Recollection*, which the hasty reader is apt to connect with remembrance."[35]

This statement, and others like it, assumes that our understanding of the process of composition is the natural one, and that the mental "faculties" we now say it uses, "observation" and "imagination," are the "correct" ones – but not memory. It assumes as well that all descriptions of mental activities are mimetic ontological efforts: to describe what "is" memory, what "is" imagination, what "are" the emotions. It allows little room for the possibility that what these terms describe is not psychic "objects" but arbitrary divisions of a single procedure taking place unceasingly in a human mind. Of course, when pressed, every philosopher and psychologist will tell you that he is perfectly aware that the "faculties" can't be separated out from the seamless process of thinking – but the vocabulary and form of scholastic analysis militate against this and in favor of faculty distinctions.[36]

But if we can get away for a moment from "faculties" analysis, and think instead of human cognition in terms of paths or "ways" (like the *via* of the ancient liberal arts), and then focus on the cognitive way called "composition," we can see that this process can be presented and analyzed as "recollective" because it was assumed to involve acts of remembering, mnemonic activities which pull in or "draw" (*tractare*, a medieval Latin word for composing) other memories. The result was what we now call "using our imagination," even to the point of visionary experience. But medieval people called it "recollection," and they were neither wrong nor foolish nor naive to do so.

In the second of his two conferences with the monk Isaac on the nature of prayer, John Cassian recounts the story of an elderly monk named Sarapion who lived as a hermit in Egypt, in the desert of Scetis. Sarapion, together with his peers, became greatly disturbed when a new doctrine was promulgated by Theophilus, the patriarch of Alexandria. Theophilus had become distressed by what he took to be an overly literal interpretation among some of the monks of Genesis 1: 26, that man is made in the image of God.[37] The Coptic monks' response to the bishop's new-fangled interpretation was hostility, until (in Cassian's smoothed-over account of this complex affair) an orthodox deacon, Photinus, explained to them in council that the image and likeness of God, *imago et similitudo Dei* in the language of Genesis 1:26, should be understood "not in an earthly, literal sense but spiritually."[38]

With compelling arguments, in Cassian's story, Photinus was able to persuade the monks of the error of their understanding. The Coptic group included Sarapion, a most holy though "simple" old man. Photinus and his cohorts arose to thank the Lord that their brothers had been drawn back to the true faith:

> And then amid these prayers the old man became confused, for he sensed that the particular human image of God [illam anthropomorphon imaginem deitatis] which he used to draw [proponere] before him as he prayed was now gone from his heart. Suddenly he gave way to the bitterest, most abundant tears and sobs. He threw himself on the ground and with the mightiest howl he cried out: "Ah the misfortune! They've taken my God away from me, and now I don't have one I might hold on to, and I don't know whom to adore or whom to call out to."[39]

The group of younger men is distressed by Sarapion's evident anguish, but they do not know how to respond to it. They return to the monk Isaac for guidance. Isaac explains that Sarapion is still subject to pagan ways in his anthropomorphic image of divinity, for "such people believe they are holding on to nothing at all if they do not have some image [imaginem quamdam] in front of them, to which they may address themselves in prayer, and may carry about in their mind and bear always fixed before their eyes."[40] Those who pray most purely will not only "reject all representations of the divine and all that is of human shape" but will banish from their minds even the memory of words or actions, whatever mental form they may take.[41] But these young monks are beginners, not yet among the *purissimi*. And so Isaac gives them a way to pray suited to their experience. They are always to hold before their minds the beginning words of Psalm 69: "Deus in adiutorium meum intende," "Come to my help, O God."

There are several interesting features to this story, but for my purposes the least interesting is the one that has received most attention: its doctrinal iconoclasm and Origenist sympathies. Historians of religion have rightly, given their concerns, focussed on this aspect of the story as evidence of John Cassian's own Origenist sympathy, and as a test-case of the quarrel between the Coptic, anti-Origenist ascetics of Egypt and the new-fangled Greek Origenists, who were also iconoclasts, believing that "true knowledge of God" could not be found in images.[42] Elizabeth Clark has cogently summarized the dilemma for the fourth-century iconoclasts: "Were images of *any* sort conducive to spiritual progress, or was the Christian's goal a kind of 'mental iconoclasm' [the position, Clark argues, of the extreme iconoclast Evagrius Ponticus]? Yet if the mind is conceived as a picture-making machine, how could worship and contemplation proceed *without* images?"[43]

As Cassian's dialogue develops, it seems that at issue in this conference are two quite distinct understandings of the words *imago* and *similitudo*. Sarapion's fault is in his doctrine, not in his practice. Understanding the word "likeness" to mean "truthful representation of an object" – that is, as a matter of mimesis – has led him and his colleagues to imagine divinity as a human being, based upon the verse in Genesis that man was created "in the image of God." This is idolatry of a sort that the triumphant iconoclasm of the late fourth century could not tolerate, and had Sarapion's distress been caused by this alone he would have received little notice from Cassian.

But that is not Sarapion's chief problem, and clearly not the motivation for Cassian's choice to tell this incident sympathetically. Sarapion grieves because without the image he was accustomed to use in order to pray, he can no longer *find* God: "[t]hey've taken my God away from me, and now I don't have one I might hold on to [tulerunt a me deum meum, et quem nunc teneam non habeo] ... I don't know whom ... to call out to." This is a complaint about cognition, about the invention of prayer and its "habitation" in a method. Pichery's translation of the Latin clause "quem nunc teneam non habeo" captures the issue of location better than my English: "Je n'ai plus où me prendre."

The crucial issue from this point on in Cassian's dialogue is not the "truth content" of images but their cognitive utility, their necessity as sites upon which and by means of which the human mind can build its compositions, whether these be thoughts or prayers. Having lost his customary way via the image of God he has been using, Sarapion now cannot find where to grab hold of God or to rouse Him up. His is a problem of cognitive invention.

5. THINKING IN IMAGES

Unlike the younger brothers, Abba Isaac understands the inventional problem immediately. No, one cannot imagine God as a human being. But "[w]hile we still hang around in this body we must reproduce some image [similitudinem quamdam] of that blessedness promised for the future to the saints."[44] This image is first of all a location, the *place* of withdrawal: "if we wish to pray to God ... we must withdraw from all the worry and confusion of crowds."[45] In such a place, the soul with its inner gaze may see "the glorified Jesus coming in the splendor of his majesty,"[46] a probable reference to the picture known as the "majestas Domini." In other words, though he rejects Sarapion's anthropomorphic image of God, Abba Isaac nonetheless argues that human beings, in order to know, must *see*, and what they see is an image. If they live in cities and towns and the villages, they see Jesus in earthly forms, *humilis* and *carneus*.[47] If they are spiritually adept and go to "solitude," they may see the glorified Jesus in the splendor of His majesty. But in any case, they *look upon* a kind of image.

The word "image" is being used in two quite distinct ways in these passages, one doctrinal and the other cognitive. One – the doctrinal referent – is concerned with the verisimilitude of an image: does God look like a human being? The answer is unequivocally no. But Abba Isaac also understands what truly upset Sarapion. Having lost his images (on doctrinal grounds) the old monk no longer has a way to think about God at all: all he can do is howl in grief. The understanding of "images" as "cognitive representations" (as contemporary cognitive scientists sometimes call them) underlies the rest of what Isaac says in this conference about the way – the invention and disposition – of prayer. As the "places" of the "way," images are understood as the localizations or nodes of thought, what keeps thinking from being merely "noise" and structures it inventively. The issue regarding images from this point on in the Conference is not "truth" so much as "usefulness."[48]

Composition begins with clearly and deliberately locating oneself in a place, which may be an actual location but is most importantly conceived as a mental position, both a habitation for the mind and a direction. Peter of Celle, articulating a commonplace (he acknowledges Augustine as his source) wrote that in contrast to the direct vision of God *there* ("ibi"), *here* "spiritual seeing is constructed by means of our recollection of images of corporeal things."[49]

This starting place, the essential *here* of human thinking, determines the kind of "things" one will see in the way of one's meditation on God, as the beginning of a journey sets the length and direction of one's subsequent route. Thus, Isaac says that while Jesus is seen by those who live in cities (that is, the "city" of active monastic life), he is not seen "with clarity." For that, solitude is needed, a withdrawal from noise and crowding.

Meditation is a way of advanced *memoria*, as the monks understood it. It is no accident that several mnemotechnical requirements are invoked in Isaac's instructions: solitude, lack of crowding, clarity of light for the inner eye. To those whose inner looking is pure, Christ's face ("vultus") and the "image of His brightness [claritatis . . . imaginem]" is revealed.[50] It is important to note as well that this text does not distinguish, as a philosophical discourse might, between *imago* and *similitudo*. Both words are used as synonyms throughout Cassian's text, as they are in Genesis 1:26.

The younger novices confess that though they understand that the goal of the monk is "to possess in this life an image of future happiness [imaginem futurae beatitudinis],"[51] they are "discouraged when we see how little we know of the route [disciplinam] which would lead us to such heights."[52] Although the word *disciplina* is not attached by ancient grammarians to words meaning "route" or "path," it was thought to be derived from the verb *discere*, "to learn."[53] And since ancient education was fundamentally modeled as "ways" and "routes," the *trivium* and *quadrivium* of the arts, disciples are those who journey along the paths marked by the practical experiences of their masters and ancestors. The disciple, Germanus, says to Abba Isaac that just as children learn to read in incremental steps, beginning first with the shapes of letters, then syllables, then whole words, and finally sentences, so he and his fellow novices need a way, "the method for finding and holding God in our thoughts":

> we desire to have shown to us some material form [materiam] for the memory, by means of which God may be taken hold of [teneatur] by our mind or be grasped continuously so that, as we keep it before our eyes, we may have something to return to immediately whenever we find that we have somehow slipped away from it.[54]

The novices stress the point to Isaac: they are confused because "we had nothing particular, no formula which we could hold constantly before our eyes, one to which the wandering mind could return after many wanderings and various travels, one that the mind could enter as into a haven of peace after long shipwreck."[55]

Isaac praises the understanding revealed by their questions and teaches them his device ("instrumentum"), one he says is "handed on to us by some of the oldest of the Fathers."[56] "You were quite right," Isaac says,

> to make the comparison between training in continuous prayer and the teaching of children who at first do not know the alphabet ... Models are put before them, carefully drawn in wax. By continually studying them, by practicing every day to reproduce them, they at last learn to write ... You need a model and you keep it constantly before your eyes. You learn either to turn it over and over in your spirit or else, as you use it and meditate upon it, you lift yourself upward to the most sublime sights.[57]

This "model," "device," "prayer formula," to be held constantly before the praying monk's inner eye, is the Psalm text "Deus in adiutorium meum intende; Domine ad adiuvandum me festina," "Come to my help, O God; Lord, hurry to my rescue" (Psalm 69:1). And in an extended meditation, Isaac proceeds to show how this text can ensure that in any daily activity or temptation, the monk will be in a state of constant prayer. A short excerpt will help give the flavor of the whole:

> I am assailed by a desire for good eating. I seek out food of which a hermit should know nothing. Into my filthy solitude come the fragrances of royal dishes and I feel myself dragged unwillingly along by my longing for them. And so I must say "Come to my help, O God; Lord, hurry to my rescue." ... The due hour has come to bid me eat, but bread disgusts me and I am held back from my natural necessity. And so I must howl aloud "Come to my help, O God; Lord, hurry to my rescue." ... In my soul are countless and varied distractions. I am in a fever as my heart moves this way and that. I have no strength to hold in check the scatterings of my thoughts. I cannot utter my prayer without interruption, without being visited by empty images and by the memory of words and doings. I feel myself bound in by such sterility that I cannot bring to birth any spiritual feelings within me. And so if I am to deserve liberation from this squalor of spirit, whence I have not been able to save myself by my many groans and cries, I must cry out, "Come to my help, O God; Lord, hurry to my rescue."[58]

The language of elementary schooling permeates this entire Conference. The words that are translated into English as "formula" and "method" include, most frequently, *materia* and *formula*. Neither of these words means in Latin what modern English speakers might assume, especially in the context of the schoolroom, which is Cassian's context. Latin *formula* is not an abstract mathematical rule but a little *forma*, a word which continued to be used in schoolrooms throughout the Middle Ages to refer to the various schemata that were used to present material in a memorable way to students. In the teaching of grammar, the first school subject for beginning-readers, *formulae* are the schematic renderings of declensions and conjugations which were memorized by being chanted, like a little song, in Roman classrooms (and were still so learned when I studied elementary Latin in the 1950s).

Much later, and in the context of rhetoric, Geoffrey of Vinsauf speaks of the mnemotechnical utility of medieval *formae*, to be preferred to the "subtle" Ciceronian rules for *imagines verborum* described in the *Rhetorica ad Herennium*. The word *materia* is used by Cassian as a synonym of *formula*. The elementary exemplary declensions and conjugations memorized schematically for pedagogical purposes were also sometimes called *materia*, as they are by Germanus in this dialogue.[59]

It might be thought significant, especially by scholars wedded to modern distinctions and hierarchies among "the visual" and "the verbal," that the anthropomorphic picture or *imago* of God used by Sarapion is rejected definitively in favor of a Psalm *text*, of words.[60] I do not believe there is any particular significance to this change, either for Cassian or for his many audiences through the Middle Ages – other than the obvious one, that God does not look like a human being. Isaac's point is that for human cognition to be usefully enabled, God must be given some "likeness" – whether it be pictorial or verbal. But there is no final truth in this "likeness": it is a concession to human cognitive ways.[61]

Whatever *materia* or *formula*, *imago* or *similitudo beatitudinis* a monk uses, it is something one gazes upon, that is grasped ("teneatur") with one's mental "senses." Beginners see a corporeal Jesus, adepts will see a Jesus of glorified countenance – but they both "see." John Cassian's text does not suggest any substantive distinction between images and words. It is crucial for modern scholars to grasp this fact. To be sure, some images – Christ coming in glory – are more "advanced" than others (for example, of the earthly mission of Jesus), more particularly products of the trained inner eye. But all, including the Psalm verse *materia*, are *similitudines* that are presented "prae oculis," both by and for memory, as *cognitive* representations. They are images "qua Deus mente concipiatur," "by which God may be taken hold of in the human mind." To keep their minds disciplined, the novices require "speciale aliquid," "something to look at," just as children learn their letters by observing and copying out exemplars onto their waxed tablets.

Isaac is quite clear about this. When the novices first introduce the metaphor of classroom procedure, together with its language of *materiae* and *formae*, the old monk congratulates them on their "precision and subtlety." They have asked, in the words of an old colophon to Chapter 8 of the Latin text, "super eruditione perfectionis per quam possimus ad perpetuam Dei memoriam pervenire," "about the Way of perfection by means of which we may come to the constant remembrance of God." It is a craft or discipline of perfection, that is also conceived to be in essence an art or method of *memoria*. Like all arts, it requires *instrumenta*, another word that Isaac uses to characterize such tools as the words of Psalm 69:1. And these "instruments" are mentally constructed, memorially held *imagines* and *formae*.

The prayer devices keep the mind "on track": this is clear from the various applications which Isaac envisions in his advice. Most particularly they can return a distracted or bored or preoccupied "wandering" mind (engaged in *evagationes*) to the routes of its cogitation. Though the main influence of this essentially monastic model of invention lies in meditative practice itself, it found expression also in the teaching of rhetoric in the late fourth century, in the newly defined (or refined) concept of compositional *ductus*, the "route" in which one moves through a composition, a path marked by the "modes" or "colors" of its varying parts.

6. THE CONCEPT OF RHETORICAL *DUCTUS*

As a technical term, *ductus* was defined first in the rhetoric textbook of Chirius Consultus Fortunatianus, probably a contemporary of Augustine, whose work reflects the pedagogy of rhetoric that Augustine also knew and taught.[62] The *ductus* is what we sometimes now call the "flow" of a composition. *Ductus* is an aspect of rhetorical "disposition," but it is the movement within and through a work's various parts. Indeed, *ductus* insists upon movement, the con*duct* of a thinking mind on its *way* through a composition.[63]

Although the word was not defined as a separate textbook term before Fortunatianus, the concept was certainly known to Quintilian. Analyzing a sentence from Cicero's second Philippic oration, he praises the masterly use of word-order by which the orator humiliates Antony without saying anything actionable. He describes how Mark Antony "in conspectu populi Romani vomere postridie," "in the sight of the people vomited on the next day." The particularly contemptible weakness Antony showed by vomiting publicly on *the day after* a binge is the point Cicero makes: Quintilian admires how "totius ductus hic est quasi mucro," "the *ductus* of the whole [sentence] is here like a knife-point [in the final word *postridie*]."[64]

So *ductus* is the way that a composition guides a person to its various goals. This meaning is apparent in another use Quintilian makes of the concept, this time using a verbal form of the root *duc-*. In the preface to his third book, he speaks of other writers on the subject of rhetoric, all of whom shared the same goal (of making the subject clear) but each of whom constructed different routes to that goal, and drew his disciples along those various ways: "diversas ... vias muniverunt atque ... induxit sequentes," "they constructed their various ways [through the subject] and ... [each] drew along his pupils [in his own route]."[65]

Even when he speaks of how a subject-matter must be analyzed into parts and distributed into its places within a dispositive scheme, Quintilian uses a verb compounded from the same root, *di-duc-ere*: "not only must the whole matter be analyzed [diducenda est] into its questions and topics, but these parts themselves require to be arranged in their own order too."[66] Sometimes translated as "treatment" (as in "the treatment of a subject"), *ductus* conveys a greater sense of motion than the English word "treatment" does. As Martianus Capella says (he borrowed extensively from Fortunatianus), *ductus* is the "tenor agendi" or basic direction of a work, which flows along, like water in an acqueduct, through whatever kinds of construction it encounters on its way.[67]

The movement among a composition's parts is not uniform: it can and should vary. Fortunatianus pays most attention to this feature, though the qualities and degrees of variation are evident also in Quintilian's use of the word and its compounds. According to Fortunatianus, there are five kinds of *ductus*: simple, subtle, figurative, oblique, and mixed.[68] These are distinguished by how direct and easy a path you make for your audience – whether you let them just step along with no obstacles, or whether you want them to work a bit, to look beneath or through your words to another agenda you may have. *Ductus* is born of deliberation and choice, says Fortunatianus, echoed by Martianus Capella.[69]

What marks out the variation in route(s) of the overall *ductus* is the figures, modes, and colors of the way. Fortunatianus reserves the term *modus* for the movement of particular parts of the composition, *ductus* for that of the whole. Martianus Capella uses the word *color* where Fortunatianus uses *modus*: evidently in this context they were synonyms. Since *colores* is a term most commonly used (including by Martianus Capella) for the ornaments of rhetoric, the figures and tropes of style, its adoption by Martianus Capella in connection with way-finding is significant, for it suggests that to Martianus the ornaments played a key marking function for finding one's "way," *ductus*, through a literary composition, such as the works of Scripture. But that is the matter of my next chapter.

Fortunatianus introduces a third term, *skopos*, into the discussion. This term is also important in meditation: John Cassian uses it as a basic concept, as we will soon see, in his First Conference on monastic meditation. *Skopos*, a Greek word, is literally the target of a bowman, the mark towards which he gazes as he aims. (Notice the emphasis on *gaze* in this metaphor.) For Fortunatianus, as for Cassian, *skopos* means goal, that to which the *ductus* and *via* lead. Fortunatianus emphasizes that these terms define aspects of the movement of a composition: *ductus*, *modus*, and *skopos*. They differ, he says, "in that *modus* is the *ductus* in each part of the composition, and *skopos* is that which the whole *ductus* produces."[70] Such a rhetorical conception of *ductus* is invoked, I think, by Boethius in this speech of Lady Philosophy's that came to be much quoted:

> I will fasten wings to your mind by which it may raise itself on high so that, having pushed aside your wavering, you may turn again safe and sound by my course [meo ductu], by my path [mea semita], and by my conveyances.[71]

Indeed, the term *skopos* was important not only in rhetoric, but also in the discourse of philosophical meditation. And the "aerial view" produced by the ancient philosophical trope of the heavenly journey was sometimes called *kataskopos*; it was a chart for a "way" of meditation – playing a role perhaps rather like that of the "cartographic" plan of the Tabernacle-Temple in Jewish and early Christian tradition.[72]

But it is in Augustine's writings that rhetorical *ductus* and the meditational "way" most closely connect. When Augustine thinks about the process of meditation, he, like John Cassian, models it as a "way." Such a model is central to his notion of "conversion" as a procedure of changing orientation and way-finding, as though within a topography of locations among which there is a variety of routes. One notable passage where the word *ductus* is used by Augustine in this rhetorical sense is in his commentary on Psalm 41, a passage I will discuss at length in a later chapter. In it, he describes the experience of meditative prayer as walking through "the place of the Tabernacle." A notion of *ductus* also informs how Augustine writes about meditation in his work *De doctrina christiana* ("On Teaching Christianity"), modeling it as a "turning" (of direction) in fear, and then climbing through emotional stages on a mental ladder from fear to joy to tranquility:

> Above all the work [of reading Scripture] requires that we be turned by fear of God toward knowing His will ... this fear may both inspire in us thought about our mortality and our inevitable future death, and, as our flesh begins to crawl [*lit.* our flesh looking as though it had broken out in prickles], may affix all the wrigglings of our pride to the wood of the cross. ... [The second step is piety, the third knowledge, the fourth strength, the fifth mercy, and then] he ascends to the sixth step, where he cleanses that eye by which God may be seen, as much as He can be by those who die to the world insofar as they can. ... And now however much more certain and not only more tolerable but more joyful the sight of a [divine] light may begin to appear, nonetheless still *darkly* and *in a mirror* it is said to be seen, for it is approached more *by faith* than *by sight* when in this world *we make our pilgrimage*, although we have our *conversation in heaven*."(My emphases)[73]

The seventh step of this ladder is wisdom, and "from fear to wisdom the way extends through these steps."[74]

Spatial and directional metaphors are essential to the conception of the "way" of monastic meditation, as is well known. And the rhetorical concept of *ductus* emphasizes way-finding by organizing the structure of any composition as a journey through a linked series of stages, each of which has its own characteristic flow (its "mode" or "color"), but which also moves the whole composition along. And the "colors" or "modes" are like the individual segments of an aqueduct, carrying the water, yes, but changing its direction, slowing it down, speeding it up, bifurcating, as the water moves along its "route" or "way." For a person following the *ductus*, the "colors" act as stages of the way or ways through to the *skopos* or destination. Every composition, visual or aural, needs to be experienced as a journey, in and through whose paths one must constantly *move*.

7. THE MONASTIC ART OF MEMORY

In all its situations, from individual reading and meditation in cloister or cell to the stational and processional ways of liturgy, the monastic life of prayer incorporated fundamentally an art of memory, of "spiritalis memoria" (the phrase is Cassian's) or "sancta memoria."[75] Though this monastic art shares (as, I have observed, all locational memory schemes do) some general similarities with the art described in the *Rhetorica ad Herennium*, the monastic art of "holy recollection" is quite different in its goal and the details of its practices.

One major difference is exactly the degree to which the monastic art models memory as a construction machine for invention. The ancient art in the *Rhetorica ad Herennium* lays much of its emphasis upon having secure, simple backgrounds of familiar places. A student is counseled to use existing buildings as his backgrounds, buildings he can revisit and so constantly refresh his memory. This emphasis tends to reinforce the storehouse model of memory, memory as an attic or perhaps an apothecary's chest. But the monks, as we will see later, tended to construct their mnemotechnical buildings in their minds, as a prelude to prayer. They built their own locations for memory work – and for that they needed, in Gregory the Great's phrase, "machinae mentis," machines of the mind. Gregory ascribes great energy to these machines:

> indeed the vigor of love is a machine of the mind which, while [the mind] draws away from the world, lifts it on high;
>
> But a human mind, having been raised by the machine (so to speak) of its contemplation, the more it looks above itself at higher things, the more fearfully it trembles in its very self;
>
> Allegory indeed, for a soul placed far from God, creates a kind of machine, that by its means [the soul] may be lifted to God.[76]

Such powerful engines need careful tending and direction.

The meditational "way" provides the necessary cognitive *dispositio*, both "ordering" the whole and "localizing" it and its parts. One meaning of the Latin verb *meditare*, the one which is closest to the meaning of the Greek verb *meletein* (which *meditare* translates in many early ascetic texts), is *exercendo preparare*, "to do preliminary exercises, to learn an art or science by practicing": over and over like a wheel ("rote") one's *res, dicta*, and *facta memorabilia*.[77] But one does not practice these randomly. The metaphors buried within the English word *rote* ("wheel" and "route") imply the orderly disposition of these "bits" of memory. The "things" of any art, including that of memory, are learned in repeated sequences – that is what the "little forms" are for. They provide the structured/structuring "backgrounds" or "places," the "habits" (as in "habitation") of one's own thinking mind. Notice the crucial locational emphasis that underlies these common concepts. They are not significant as ideas themselves, but are the forms upon which, out of other memories, ideas are constructed. They give us what poor Sarapion feared he had lost – a "where," a place to start off from.

8. CURIOSITAS, OR MENTAL FORNICATION

The great vice of *memoria* is not forgetting but disorder. This came to be called by some monastic writers *curiositas*. Clearly "curiosity" did not mean to them what it means to us now; I want in this section to explore its medieval contexts in relation to memory work. In terms of mnemotechnic, curiosity constitutes both image "crowding" – a mnemotechnical vice, because crowding images together blurs them, blocks them, and thus dissipates their effectiveness for orienting and cueing – and randomness, or making backgrounds that have no pattern to them.

Curiositas is well described by John Cassian, though his word for it is "wantonness," *fornicatio*, which is an aimless, fruitless, shifting expenditure of energy.[78] Abba Moses speaks of the need for *skopos* or "aim," in terms of direction. And "a mind which lacks an abiding sense of direction veers hither and yon by the hour, and by the minute is a prey to outside influences and is endlessly the prisoner of what strikes it first."[79] Notice how the root meaning of *skopos* is invoked as the mind, like a unbalanced arrow, veers off its course uselessly, aimlessly.

The mind can never be empty of thought. But it is inclined to laziness and to a kind of wandering about, which Cassian also categorizes as a form of mental fornication. He describes what he means by this:

> Our minds think of some passage of a psalm. But it is taken away from us without our noticing it, and, stupidly, unknowingly, the spirit slips on to some other text of Scripture. It begins to think about it, but before it has been fully considered, another text slides into the memory and drives out the previous one. Meanwhile another one arrives and our mind turns to another meditation. So the spirit rolls along from psalm to psalm, leaps from the gospel to St. Paul, from Paul to the prophets, from there it is carried off to holy stories. Ever on the move, forever wandering, it is tossed along through all the body of Scripture, unable to settle on anything, unable to reject anything or hold on to anything, powerless to arrive at any full and judicious study, a dilettante and a nibbler on spiritual interpretation rather than being its creator and possessor ... If I am praying, my mind thinks about some psalm or another reading. If I am singing, it is preoccupied with something other than what is in the psalm I am chanting. ... Three things keep a wandering mind in place [vagam mentem stabilem faciunt]: vigils, meditation, and prayer. Constant attention to them and a firm concentration upon them will give stability to the soul.[80]

Also essential to keeping a wandering mind in its place is "to keep a firm hold of that little verse which you have given us as a cognitive form, so that the comings and goings of our thoughts should not flow in and out in their own eddying way but should hold together as our own composition."[81]

The basic metaphors in these passages are entirely locational: *wandering* against *having a way* or *a route*. Or being *mobilis* and *vaga* as contrasted to having *status*, a place to stand, and so to be *stabilis*.[82] Cognition, in cultures that value *memoria*, is presupposed to require various sorts of mental maps and organizing structures, the *rationes* which Augustine described as being in his memory. But we do not just "have" these, by virtue of brain physiology or Nature: we must be able *to make* such patterns of places in which to "stand" mentally by way of our "little forms." Cassian indeed implies in this passage that the mind by nature has *no* maps or structures innately but, like the primordial void, requires an artificer (in this case not God but the monk) to make them for cognitive "remembering." Of these structures, too, one could say, with Hugo of Rouen, "memoranda sunt ista." Not every one of Cassian's contemporaries would have agreed in detail with this claim (Augustine seems to imply that at least some of the mind's *rationes* are innate), but all would agree that the bulk of these schemes must be consciously constructed as a fundamental feature of memory work. Mnemotechnical *curiositas* results from sloth, laziness, a mind that neglects to pay attention to thinking as a process of *building*. We cannot build without patterns – foundations and *formae* – which, like good craftsmen, we have made (or adapted) to suit our own level of mastery and our own tasks.

9. BERNARD OF CLAIRVAUX: CURIOSITY AND ICONOCLASM

It is in the context of rhetorical mnemotechnic, I think, that one might with profit consider the cautions against curiosity of a much later ascetic master than John Cassian, Bernard of Clairvaux (d. 1153). In Bernard's famous apology (1125) written to Abbot William of St. Thierry, he excoriates lazy monks who rely on other people's images (those of painters and sculptors) and thus get distracted from the interior prayer which they should be continually constructing. Lay people and clerics who are not part of a contemplative order, comparative *illiterati* in the craft of memory, may need such props and aides, but not Cistercian monks.

Bernard excoriates distraction as an inhibition and depression of *aspectus* and *affectus*. These are both words that resonate in memory training as the concentrated inner "seeing," and the richly sensory, emotional, and fully experiential recreation of "things," that profound memory work requires. The sculpted figures of beasts and monsters on capitals which the Cluniac monks, among others, had placed in their cloisters, were bad because they "divert the inward-seeing [aspectus] of those praying, and also hinder their emotional concentration [affectus]."[83]

Meditation is the interior reading of the book of one's memory, in the richly "gathering" way of medieval reading. For that task, the function of stylistic ornament is a mnemonic one. Ornaments mark out the *colores* or *modi* (as "rhythms" and "moods") of a composition's *ductus*. The banishing of wall paintings, historiated capitals, and other figural ornament in Cistercian monasteries is not motivated by a simple Evagrianism, the dismissal of any sort of image as "impure." Were that true, one could not account for Bernard's sermons, lavish in their extended development of figurative ornament, except as a kind of literary hypocrisy; nor could one account for the continued presence of the Bestiary in most Cistercian libraries, nor the continued painting of Cistercian books.

Rather, I think, Bernard's "iconoclasm" signals an effort to encourage (even to force) his contemplative elite, his master-craftsmen of memory work, to perfect their own mental machines, to make their own images to fill the "places" provided by the unadorned, un-"colored" cloister and oratory, both of them buildings which are made up of regular patterns of "places" for "drawing" thoughts together in liturgical and individual prayer. The "little rooms" indicated within these structures, so typical of Romanesque monastic architectural style in general, can be seen in the modular bays of the nave and apse of Pontigny and in the "sections" formed by the patterns of capitals and vaulting in the cloister at Fontenay: see Plates 25, 26, and 31. I will have more to say later about the trope of using little rooms, *cubiculi* or *cellae*, for memory work.

One readily sees Bernard's attitude towards making images in his *Sermons on the Song of Songs*, addressed to his own followers, the most spiritually sophisticated, most ascetically elite among monks: "The instructions that I address to you, my brothers, will differ from those I should deliver to people in the world [including other clergy]; at least the manner will be different."[84] The Song of Songs, he says, is not fare even for novices:

> it is not a noise of the mouth but the music of the heart, not a trilling of the lips but the movement of joy, harmony not of voices but of wills. It is not a melody heard on the outside, it does not sound off among crowds; only he who sings hears it and the one to whom he sings, bride and groom ... It is not for the novices, the immature, or those recently converted from worldly life to sing or hear this song, but only a mind disciplined by persevering study.[85]

Yet his *Sermons on the Song of Songs* are filled with figurative language that deliberately evokes mental pictures, painting elaborately in the mind. What seems for Bernard to separate the novice from the master in the discipline of spiritual reading is the ability to create meditational compositions *entirely* within the mind, relying on a repertoire of images already in place, and not needing other people's programs to stimulate (or, worst of all, substitute for) his own fiction.

Even a Cistercian monk never left off making his pictures. The acme of the craft for Bernard is not to free oneself altogether from the need for images and become cognitively an-iconographic, the state of perfection envisioned by Evagrius Pontinus.[86] It is rather, as Bernard says here, to vibrate harmoniously in and through a text, to make the true "music of the heart" through the associational symphony of all the matters in one's inventoried and inventive memory, one's "intuned" and "affected" heart.

The goal of meditation, Bernard also writes, is to build oneself into a "templum spiritualis." And the temple into which one constructs oneself is richly decorated, completely unlike the white-washed, undecorated austerity of the stone oratory in which the Cistercians prayed. This fact, it seems to me, demonstrates as clearly as any how Bernard's "iconoclasm" needs to be understood. Decoration is vital to moral life, but it is interior. It is created lavishly in the mind, out of all that is precious and rich in the images invoked through recollective technique alone:

> Study then how to cover these girders [of the temple that one is] and bind them with woods that are also precious and beautiful, of whatever may be at hand to form ceiling panels [opus laquearium] for the embellishment of the house, for example words of wisdom or knowledge, prophecy, the gift of healing, the interpretation of words, and the rest of such things, which we know are more sensibly thought of as ornamentation than as essential for salvation. ... Other timbers may be prepared for the paneling, which, though they may appear less splendid, are no less worthy [these include peace, goodness, cheerfulness, compassion] ... Or would you not consider that same house, as regards the ceiling-work you have inspected, to be sufficiently and abundantly enough decorated with planks made from these woods [of the ordinary virtues]? "Lord, I have loved the beauty of your house" [Psalm 25:8]. Always give me wood like this, I ask, so that I may show you the ever-adorned bedroom of my conscience ... With this I shall be content. ... But you also, most beloved, even though you may not possess such [rare] woods, have confidence, nonetheless, if you have this much; ... let us think nothing of building ourselves up as living stones on the foundation of the apostles and prophets, as indeed houses in which to offer spiritual sacrifices acceptable to God.[87]

Commenting on the contrast between the unadorned Cistercian oratory and the lavish rhetorical ornament of Bernard's literary style, Georges Duby found it "strange" that Bernard felt no need to ornament the house of God as he did his language.[88] I see no contradiction. What Bernard counsels is lavish decoration of one's own making within the "temple" of one's soul, fiction-making which is "supported" by the plain surfaces and clear articulation of the unadorned church and cloister.

Yet notice also that Bernard, in the spirit of St. Paul, says such ornament is not necessary for salvation, and that each brother will build his own kind of *superaedificationes* upon the foundation according to his own gifts. It is in the context of 1 Corinthians 3, the text underlying this sermon, that one must understand Bernard's so-called iconoclasm. According to Bernard, other people's images, presented in programs of sculpture and murals and book illuminations, not only may promote spiritual laziness and *curiositas* among those too adept to require them any longer, but also promote the vice of pride. They may make someone building in "gold" feel morally superior to one building in "wood," just as someone with the gift of tongues may feel superior to one who has the gift of healing.

Bernard's is not the iconoclasm of a John Cassian or an Origen, worried about the perpetuation of old mental habits attached to sets of pagan images, but is more like the concern that leads parents to forbid their children to watch television or play video games lest their imagination and attention span remain undeveloped, ineffectual, and "torpid." And, like those of many such parents, his strictures seem at times both prudish and bullying; indeed (as scholars have often pointed out) the Cistercian order re-embraced images, in moderation, soon after Bernard's death.

Yet the observations about imagination and memory which motivated his judgments were sound enough, and based on the ordinary practice of meditation. As masters – not novices or journeymen – of *sancta memoria*, Cistercian monks, Bernard thought, required mnemotechnical "solitude" in their surroundings – and needed them to be as *raris* and *solemnes* as the cloister at Fontenay (Plate 31) – so that they could make their own images by reading, and seeing internally what they were reading without constant visual "noise" and "crowding."

As Conrad Rudolph has properly emphasized, Bernard saves his particular horror for the programs of images that in some monasteries (Moissac and Cluny, for instance) had invaded the cloister itself, where the monks customarily read and, even more importantly, where novices were instructed and formed their reading habits: "what is this ridiculous monstrosity doing in the cloister, in the presence of the brothers *while they are reading*?" (my emphasis).[89] Reading, the essential work of *memoria*, needs particularly to be shielded from *curiositas*.[90]

10. CURIOSITY AND CARE: JOHN CASSIAN ON HOW TO
FORGET PAGAN SUBJECT-MATTERS

Patterns, of simple words and stories (text) and of decoration (including punctuation of all sorts), become incised permanently in the brain, like the ruts that kept cartwheels on medieval roadways. Distraction leads to "error," wandering from "the ways" of one's thinking. Such errors are of three general kinds. One can lose one's mnemonic associations, the matters that the mental cues one has adopted are supposed to call up (perhaps the most common fault of novices in *memoria*); or one can lose the map itself (the "locations" in their order); or one can slip from one "map" (perhaps a psalm) to another unbidden one (perhaps a scene in the *Aeneid*) via a common cue or key word.

The remembering mind, said Geoffrey of Vinsauf, is a "cellula deliciarum," a little chamber of pleasures.[91] That is both its power and its liability, and like the rest of the physical body it needs disciplined exercise, but it also needs to have its limits respected: not to be over-worked, and to be given a suitable regimen, both of mental "matters" and of physical diet and rest.

In his fourteenth Conference, on the study of Scripture, John Cassian discusses a problem of *curiositas*. It is often taken by historians as a problem of how to forget, but Cassian is really talking about a problem of mnemonic praxis rather than one of the complete obliterating of one's memory. It is a problem that comes up with some frequency in the confessional literature of early Christians who had grown up with a traditional Roman education: the continuing emotional hold on their memories of the pagan literature they had learned by rote as children.[92]

This particular conversation is held with the Egyptian monk Abba Nesteros, to whom Cassian and some companions have come for training. The problem with which Nesteros has been presented by Cassian is the young man's inability to forget his classical education.

> The insistence of my *paedogogus* and my own urge to read continu- ously have so soaked into me that at this point my mind is infected by poetry, those silly stories of fable-tellers [like Ovid], and the tales of war in which I was steeped from the beginning of my basic studies when I was very young. ... When I am singing the psalms or else begging pardon for my sins the shameful memory of poems slips in or the image of warring heroes turns up before my eyes.[93]

This is a case of mnemotechnical distraction, when the pathways "leak," as it were, from one associational network to another.

The case is to be rectified by consciously applying mnemonic technique: one must develop new structuring habits ("backgrounds") and "little forms." Abba Nesteros counsels Cassian to "re-place" his memory network, blocking one set of locations by another: "All you need is to transfer to the reading and meditation of spiritual writings the same care and the same concentration which, you said, you had for worldly studies."[94]

This solution embodies a fundamental assumption about how human beings think. First, thinking is not a disembodied "skill"; there is no thought without matters to think with. Secondly, people can think only with the contents of their memories, their experiences. And human memories are stored as images in patterns of places (or "locations" or "topics"). Nesteros' solution to "forgetting" is one by one to replace the "topics" in his novice's memory with a new set of "places," this time drawn from the Bible. Notice that the condition of *remembering* is considered to be the cognitive norm – the novice suffers from an excess of remembering. So "forgetting" will require particular acts of concentrated attention, during which one "drives out" one set of memory "topics" and replaces them with another. And this in turn is analyzed as a problem of orienting the will, of care and attentiveness.

The difficulty spoken of by Cassian results from a particular elementary procedure in a classical education, a set of methods that built solidly upon processes of memory. The idea was to lay so fixed a foundation that it would never fail. This foundation was laid in earliest education by rote. Children were taught the foundational texts twice, once to learn by heart the sounds of the words, syllable by syllable, and then a second time, using this rote foundation, to attach to those words their meaning and commentary.

In this method, the phrases of the foundation text were first "divided" into syllables, roots, and phrases of short-term memory length, not unlike modern sound-bytes. Then *in that form* they were fully "digested" and made virtually a part of the child's physiological make-up by rote exercises. These brief segments of language then served as the orderly sets of backgrounds to which further matters, such as commentary and exegesis, could be attached, in the manner of basic mnemonic technique. The role of "rote learning" then – as now in Koranic, Talmudic, Vedic, and Buddhist scriptural schools – was to lay a firm foundation for all further education, not simply as information ("content" in the modern sense) but as a series of mnemonically secure inventory "bins" into which additional matter could be stored and thence recovered. This is the problem that the novice John Cassian has encountered: his old backgrounds are getting in the way of his new learning.

The "poems of his childhood" have "steeped" and "infected" and saturated him. Notice how physiological these words are, as though the basic, rote-learned texts were a part of his very body. That in fact was the desired effect. The rote material was thought to provide the scientific and ethical templates, the predispositions and even the moods, for virtually all subsequent ethical, religious, cultural, and intellectual activity. John Cassian writes of it literally as the mind's "fodder," its "guts":

> Of necessity, your mind will be taken up by those poems [which you learned by rote in childhood] for as long as it fails ... to give birth to matters spiritual and divine in place of those unfruitful and earthly things. If it manages to conceive these deeply and profoundly, if it feeds upon them, either previous "topics" will be pushed out one at a time or they will be erased altogether. The human mind is unable to be empty of all thought. If it is not engaged with spiritual matters it will necessarily be wrapped up in what it previously learned. As long as it has nowhere else to go while in its tireless motion, its irresistible inclination is toward matters with which it was imbued since infancy, and it mulls over incessantly those materials which long commerce and attentive meditation have given it to think with. Spiritual knowledge must therefore achieve a similarly long-lasting, secure strength in you. ... It is something to be hidden away within you, perceived as though it were palpable, and felt in your guts. ... If thus these matters were lovingly gathered up, put away in a compartment of your memory, and marked with an identifying sign impressed during a period of silent reading, they will be to you ever afterward like wine of sweet aroma bringing joy to the heart of man ... they will pour forth like a great fragrance from the vessel of your breast ... And so it will happen that not only your memory's concentrated meditations but all its wanderings and strayings will turn into a holy, unceasing rumination of the Law of the Lord.[95]

Notice the assumptions that John Cassian makes here. The mind never stops thinking – it cannot be emptied of thought. Not only is a "good" memory supplied with rote material, but this has been made

90

into its "places," the laid-out compartments or bins of memory. The matter in each location is appropriately marked out and indicated mnemonically ("in recessu mentis condita atque *indicta* fuerint ...*signata*"; my emphases). Whatever new is taken in and learned must then be linked into this memory construction by meditation, the "rumination" of mnemotechnical murmur ("silent" reading).[96] If one has constructed such a memory, holy thoughts will "flow out from the channels of experience" (that is, the networks of a linked-up memory) and "bound forth ... unceasing, from the bottomless ocean of your heart."[97] Even at rest, even when day-dreaming (and night-dreaming too), one's mind, wheeling through the routes of its "in-habited" images, cannot think about anything else than the Law of the Lord, because – ideally – it has nothing else to think with.

The infantile habits, the inviscerated texts ("inviscerata" is the word Cassian uses) of childhood, can, with effort, be dis-placed ("expel-lenda sunt"), presumably into an unfrequented corridor of memory. The figure of human digestion, including excretion, that lies behind this whole discussion is evident, and deliberate. It is fundamental to this commonplace that reading is food, thought is its digestion, cogitation is both rumination and a kind of cooking ("concoction").[98]

In his first conference, Cassian likens the mind thinking to a great mill-wheel grinding flour for bread:

> This exercise of the heart [that is, meditation] is not inappropriately compared ... to that of a mill which is activated by the circular motion of water. The mill cannot cease its operations at all so long as it is driven round by the pressure of the water, and it then becomes quite feasible for the person in charge to decide whether he prefers wheat or barley or darnel to be ground. And one thing is clear. Only that will be ground which is fed in by the one who is in charge. ... if we turn to the constant meditation on Scripture, if we lift up our memory to the things of the spirit ... then the thoughts deriving from all this will of necessity be spiritual ... However, if we are overcome by sloth or by carelessness, if we give ourselves over to dangerous and empty gossiping ... there will follow in effect from this a harvest of tares to serve as a ministry of death to our hearts.[99]

Notice that Cassian places the entire ethical burden upon the miller, the person who feeds raw material into the mill to be ground by the whirling millstone. This is a statement like our own "garbage in, garbage out," and it recognizes the same fact about ethical agency: no machine is better than the craftsman who works with it.

II. *MACHINA MENTIS*: THE MILL CAPITAL AT VÉZELAY

Latin *machina*, in addition to "hoist," can also mean "mill-wheel" and "millstone," though it is not the word which John Cassian used in the passage I just discussed. Nonetheless, I want to suggest that the passage in Cassian may have helped (together with some Biblical passages) to create a trope of somewhat mysterious sources that one finds in Romanesque decoration. Plate 7 shows a representation of this trope of "the Mystical Mill." In addition to this capital from the twelfth-century nave of the pilgrimage church of the Madeleine at Vézelay, a similar scene figures prominently in a stained-glass roundel in Abbot Suger's apse at St.-Denis, built at about the same time, during the 1130s and 1140s.

At St.-Denis, Suger placed the mill scene in one of the double-windowed chapels in the ambulatory, directly behind the main altar. The scene has been linked to segments of two Scriptural verses, one from Isaiah and one from Matthew. Suger identified the miller specifically as St. Paul, grinding the Old Law to make the salvific bread of the New. But the miller figure at Vézelay is not so identified, and it is not necessary to make such a specific "allegory" in order to understand why a flour mill would be a suitable subject within churches frequented by many pilgrims, such as both St.-Denis and the Madeleine.[100]

The Isaiah text attracted a patristic gloss which interpreted the prophet's command to "Take the millstones and grind meal" (Isaiah 47:2) as referring to the meditational labor of Biblical interpretation: John Cassian certainly knew of and commented within this tradition. The scene on the capital at Vézelay shows the mill-wheel virtually at the center: the bent figure of the miller who pours a pannier of grain into the hopper and the figure of the man who receives the flour ground for his bread to form a circle about it. The passage from Cassian may be an additional source of the miller/mill figure, one appropriate to be placed carefully in buildings designed to be "read," and a text which the communities of Vézelay and St.-Denis would have known well.

The church of the Madeleine at Vézelay was affiliated to the great Burgundian abbey of Cluny. Rebuilt in the second quarter of the twelfth century, it housed relics of Mary Magdalene, and so was the object of a major pilgrimage. It also became a starting-point for the pilgrimage route across France to Compostella.[101]

Machina mentis: *the mill capital at Vézelay*

The capital showing the mill was placed prominently in the nave, on the fourth pier (of nine in the nave) forming the south aisle, on the side facing west, towards the entrance. As one walks along this aisle towards the choir, one readily sees on each pier a set of two or three figured capitals: those on the pier itself which face west and south, and one facing north, which is placed on a pilaster opposite each pier, on the outer wall of the aisle. There is a Way marked out among these capitals, which follows the emotional stages of meditative orthopraxis. And though I am well aware that generations of art historians have developed a complex iconology for the scenes depicted, I will describe them as simply as I can in order to convey their basic *ductus*, which is first of all a matter of "moods" and "colors" – and only then of knowledge.[102]

Approaching the mill capital, which is halfway up the aisle, one will journey from fear to conversion. The west-facing capital of the third pier shows a conversion story, the legend of St. Eustace. On the first two piers, in this same west-facing position, capitals show scenes of combat, monsters and armed men fighting; the capitals facing south show wild-haired, grimacing demons, an eagle carrying off a child in its beak (identified as the Ganymede story), and a naked woman (identified as *luxuria*, though perhaps John Cassian's *spiritus fornicationis* is just as appropriate) with a snake consuming her genitals.

On the south aisle wall, a capital on the pilaster facing north into the aisle opposite the third pier (St. Eustace) is a scene of education, Achilles being instructed by Chiron the centaur. In the same position opposite the fourth pier (the mill) is a scene of people taking counsel together; four are seated, one prominently on a chair, and great clusters of grapes form a frame for the scene (grapes commonly recall judgment in Christianity, of course). The pilaster capital opposite the fifth pier shows a scene of masters and students, with an open book prominently displayed.

The other capitals of the fourth and fifth piers continue the meditative experience. The west-facing capital of the fifth pier, the one that comes just after "the mill," shows figures identified as the four winds, who carry a bellows and cone-shaped baskets. The winds might bring several things to mind, perhaps including the Pauline warning that "knowledge inflates, but charity builds" – appropriate in a general context having to do with meditation and reading, and in so wondrous an edifice.

On the fourth pier (on which the mill capital occupies the west face) facing south into the aisle is a scene of the contrasting deaths of Dives and Lazarus, the one carried off by a demon, the other saved in Abraham's bosom. The capital in this same position on the fifth pier shows a scene of triumph, a man (David) vanquishing a lion.

So as one enters from the porch and starts up the south aisle toward the relics of the Magdalene, one passes from scenes of combat with vice (embodied in devils and monsters), to conversion, to scenes having to do with reading and learning, accompanied by scenes of salvation (or damnation) and triumph. The invitation of this *ductus* of capitals to "struggle" against vice and "convert" to one's good the spiritual "breads" presented within the building is plain – to those whose recollective mechanisms are "clued in." The mill image reminds a viewer/reader that whether the mill-stone (*machina*) grinds wheat or tares is a matter of the miller's choice, of *intentio* and will, and to beware of pride and distraction – "curiosity."

12. FORGETTING AND "CONVERSION"

There is another dimension of *curiositas* relevant to meditation besides the one of the "crowding" and *confusio* of the images and *formae mentis*. This meaning of *curiositas* has to do with the mental stance of the thinker. Recall how important "where you stand" is to the way of meditative prayer. Being *curiosus* is the opposite of the state of being *attentus*, "attentive" and "concentrated." It is what happens when you lose track of what your images are cues *for*. This meaning will become clear in the final example I want to discuss of an effort to "forget" that resolves itself not as a need to obliterate but as an ethical need to resist *curiositas* and to find one's "stance" or "ground" against the wandering and wantonness of "mental fornication" (an image that had, after Cassian, a very long life in the monasteries).

In 1140 Bernard of Clairvaux composed a sermon for men who sought to enter the Cistercian order. He was addressing an audience who were already clerics and seeking to become part of an elite: masters of a particularly difficult art of memory work.[103] *Curiositas*, as we have seen, is a failure to pay attention, a vice of dilettantism, when we become so charmed by the play of our mental images that we lose our "place" and cannot remember what path they were supposed to mark. The solution is not to do away with these images but either to focus them and order (discipline) them, or to will them into different, less frequented "places" altogether.

Bernard gives counsel to the young clerics about how to forget their memories of past, pre-claustral experiences before their conversion. The root metaphor of "turning" in the verb "convert" is very much a part of Bernard's play in this sermon: turning memories, turning associations – questions of use and goal that resolve themselves into questions of will. Bernard begins, memorably, with a turn on the trope of "the stomach of memory" (a variety of the memory-as-digestion trope). Quoting Jeremiah 4:19 (a conventional text), "Ventrem meum doleo," literally "I have pains in my gut," Bernard asks rhetorically, "How can I not have pain in the gut of my memory when it is filled with putrid stuff?"[104] The problem is posed as one of memory. And the answer lies in *conversio*, a matter of will and also a matter of location.

It has been suggested that what Bernard wants (and what this whole monastic trope of cleansing memory, which one also finds in Cassian, intends) is the replacement of the empirical facts of one's past life by ideas: "Bernard's monk seems to have trained himself to an habitual loss of self, distinguished by a purged memory and a capacity for remembering only the universal experiences of the sensual delights of Scripture."[105] But is oblivion of self what Bernard in fact counsels? Is amnesia what he means by a laundered memory ("memoria munda," as he calls it)?[106] In other words, is forgetting, as Bernard understands it in this sermon, equivalent to obliteration?

As we have seen in Abba Nesteros' counsel to John Cassian about displacing his childhood texts, the simple obliteration of deeply rooted memories, while held out as a theoretical possibility for a master of the art, was recognized to be extremely difficult. Abba Nesteros spoke of "expelling" such memories by dis-locating them, deliberately pushing them off to a different place. The advice persists to the late Middle Ages in the common counsel to "expel worldly cares" or preoccupations, in preparation for meditative thought. As we saw in the case of public remembering, this is often most successfully achieved not by literal displacement but by placing something into a different network of associations, by changing its "direction" or "intention" within a cognitive "map." The same principle works also on an individual level.

"Expelling worldly cares" does not at all mean, however, that one should not think of one's past life or future death in the most excruciating detail. Augustine described the steps of meditative prayer as beginning in fear, self-created by the most hair-raising, goose-flesh-inducing recollection and imagining of one's own death. Well before Bernard's time, this initial step came to be called *compunctio cordis*, the emotion which is the beginning of prayer. A monk who had completely forgotten himself by obliterating his own past would not be able to pray. Bernard says in this sermon that *only our own sins* can move us to shame and contrition: we may think about those of other people but they will not touch us, not *affect* us.[107]

Bernard addresses the problems of obliteration through another figure later on in this sermon "De conversione." Having begun with Jeremiah's cry about pains in his belly, he changes his governing figure from that of excretion (*expellare*, in Cassian's term) to that of "coloring," dyeing a fabric or writing on a parchment:

> In what way will my life be displaced from my memory? A thin, fragile parchment deeply soaks up the ink; by what craft may it be erased? For it does not take the dye just at the surface, but the skin has been colored straight through. In vain should I try to scrape it away; the parchment rips before the messy letters are erased. Amnesia could completely erase my memory, as, deranged in my mind, I should not remember the things I had done. Short of that, what scraper could bring it about that my memory would remain whole and yet its stains be dissolved? Only that living, powerful word, more cutting than any two-edged sword: "Your sins are forgiven you." ... [God's] forgiveness blots out sin, not in causing it to be lost from my memory but in causing something which before used to be both in my mind and dyed into it by my moral habits to still be in my memory but no longer to stain it in any way. ... Cast out guilt, cast out fear, cast out confusion, for this is what full pardon of sins brings about, in such a way that not only are they no obstacle to our salvation but cooperate in our good.[108]

The issue for Bernard is specifically not "oblivion" in the sense of total obliteration. That would be amnesia, which he sees as a form not of health but of derangement.

The master metaphor in this passage is that of writing on parchment. This figure derives from the fundamental model of memory as a waxed tablet, of the sort most familiar to every ancient and medieval person from elementary school work, upon which one wrote one's earliest letters and phrases, and, in order to erase it (which needed to be done often), smoothed them out with the blunt end of one's stylus.

But unlike wax, parchment is very difficult to erase completely: most scholars who have worked with manuscripts are familiar with the phenomenon of being able still to read the original letters despite an erasure. Bernard compounds this familiar attribute of parchment by making the folio in his example especially poor in quality and therefore one which takes the ink porously, leaving letters which are ragged and blotched. The only way to erase such a parchment is to destroy it altogether: the knife or scraper (or pumice stone) which medieval scribes used to efface their mistakes will only tear such fragile material.

The point of Bernard's metaphor, therefore, is that one *cannot* and should not try simply to obliterate one's own memories. Whatever one does to erase what is written there (short of killing off the parchment, as it were) will be ineffective: one will still be able to read the letters in the manuscript of one's memory. So the only way to "forget" one's sins is to ask God's forgiveness and then change one's attitude, one's "intention," towards them.

This idea derives from a basic fact of memory images: that they are composed of both a "likeness" and an "intention," or emotional coloration, as we saw in Chapter One. What forgiveness changes is that *intentio*, the emotional direction (the root metaphor in *converto*) towards the memory images that still exist in one's mind, including all those personal memories that make up "my life." The key, as usual, is the moral use one makes of them: no longer producers of guilt or fear or *confusio*, they can "cooperate in our good," if we "take care" to use them well.[109]

This may be very odd idea to us, for it assumes a degree of conscious control over one's own emotions that is foreign to our own popular psychologies, predicated as many of them are on notions of a powerful unconscious mind that, by definition, is not subject to our mental control. The idea that memories have *intentio* also couches this conscious control in terms of attitude, how one is "turned" or "tuned" *in regard to* them (notice the sensory implications of this language). One's *stance* towards one's memory images is critical to their moral utility – and this fact brings us around again to the importance of *status* and *stabilis*, of *where* we place ourselves when we are thinking. Notice again the fundamentally locational and visual nature of the metaphor buried in this mnemotechnical advice.

Forgetting is thus analyzed in this tradition as a matter largely of *willed* "re-placement" and displacement. A modern parallel, though inexact, is instructive. In my previous chapter I referred to the experience of "S," the Soviet memory-master who complained of his inability to forget anything. He tried many methods, including writing down some of his schemes and imagining them burning up in a fire, but only when he realized that all he needed to do was *choose to forget* them did they securely disappear. This is an instance of mnemotechnical "curiosity" and its cure: careful, willed attention.[110]

I would like in conclusion to trace the *ductus* of Bernard's sermon, which is marked out through a set of puns. A "clean memory," in this sermon, is the equivalent of being "pure of heart," the phrase consciously played upon in Bernard's structure. The essential two links in his organizational catena or chain of syllables in this sermon are two Beatitudes: "Beati misericordes" ("Blessed are the merciful") and "Beati mundo corde" ("Blessed are the pure in heart"). In addition to sharing an identical sentence structure, beginning with "beati," the two are linked by a pun, sharing the root syllable *cor(d)*-, "heart" (which is of course a synonym of *memoria*).

Such coincidences are among the most common of invention tools, deliberately cultivated to set the mind "in play" through its associative routes. You remember that the "pure in heart" are blessed because they "shall see God," shall have the divine *theoria* or "seeing." Those "mundo corde" who see God are possessed of "munda memoria." And the path to being "mundo corde" from "munda memoria" is – Bernard's structure reveals this – through becoming "miseri*cor*des." This structure of puns provides the "way" in this sermon through human memory to the vision of God.

The *misericordes* are *miseri*. Bernard sets this pun in play with his initial image of the parchment of memory stained with *miseris litteris*. The root *miser-* gave rise to words meaning both "miserable" and "merciful"; the root *cord-* can mean "heart" and also "memory." By a sort of conversion through pun, "wretched in memory" (*misericord-*) turns into "merciful of heart." Again, the structural, "rational" link is made in the first instance by the play of coincident syllables and latent meanings – pieces of words, which make visual and aural patterns and invite the mind to play, to wake up from its torpor. The puns mark out the path of the argument, as the various syllables in the word *misericordes* move through this work. And homophony affords Bernard a coincident visual pun from his memorial concordance (for to be miserable is to weep), by which he moves from memory to misery to weeping to washing clean: "Lava per singulas noctes lectum tuum, lacrimis tuis stratum tuum rigare memento," "Wash your bed each night, remember to wet your couch with your tears" (recalling

Psalm 6:7, the first of the Penitential Psalms).[111] And remembering your sins in order to weep is the first task of monastic *memoria*.

13. SOLLICITUDO, OR HOLY CURIOSITY

In the *Summa theologiae* Thomas Aquinas, while discussing the virtue of prudence, announces that the memory rules given in the *Rhetorica ad Herennium* are the best art of memory. He then gives a digest of them, in the course of which he makes what appears to be a mistake. Where the *Ad Herennium* author, cautioning against the mnemotechnical vice of crowding, had said that "solitude" conserves the clarity of memory images, Thomas writes that "solicitude" does so. He quotes the *Ad Herennium* exactly, except for this one word: he writes, "sollicitudo conservat integras simulacrorum figuras."[112] This shift reflects a medieval diagnosis of mnemotechnical crowding as a form of *curiositas*, and thus also an indication of its cure.

Like other vices, *curiositas*, properly directed, can be a virtue. Peter of Celle begins his treatise "On Conscience" by observing that "[t]he religious mind inquires with religious curiosity [religiosa curiositate] about religious consciousness."[113] And Hugh of St. Victor characterizes meditation as "the ability of a keen and curious [curiosa] mind to explore obscurities and unfold perplexities" in Scripture.[114] Notice how by Hugh of St. Victor's time meditation has become identified with "opening up" the Bible (his verb is *evolvere*), and especially with illuminating its "dark" passages.

Curiositas, together with the adjective *curiosus* and the adverb *curiose*, is derived from *cura*, "care," and its classical meaning, and meaning still occasionally in the Latin of Jerome's Bible, is "carefulness."[115] So there is both bad *curiositas* or distraction, a sort of extreme remembering (both overly much and overly little), and good *curiositas* or "carefulness" and "attentive mindfulness." The good sort is more often known by its synonym, the word for it one finds most often in medieval mnemonic technique: *sollicitudo*.

Memoria was thought to be strongly physiological (using the adverb in its philosophical sense). I have elsewhere described the procedure by which memory images were thought to be physically formed, according to Aristotle and his medieval commentators:[116] however ignorant or uncaring non-philosophers may have been about Aristotle's work, the notion that memories are produced and recalled affectively, that memory itself is an "affection" of the body, was basic. Desire and will therefore underlie remembering, and just as the mind is always in motion, like the great mill-wheel of Cassian's description, so too it always has "intent," or emotional content, the "coloring" so critical in classical rhetoric.

But these emotions are not entirely personal and private; they are also called up and directed within the work, as the word "intention" implies. Recall that movements through a work, *ductus*, are carried by its varying *colores*, to use the late classical rhetorical categories.[117] As one might speak of the "intention" of a work of art not as an intellectual content but as direction and coloring conveyed rhetorically in choices of site, materials, shape, story subjects, and so on, so a work of literature also has "intent," which the reader can "loosen up" and "expand" through *careful*, "solicitous" meditation.[118] But the "care" at issue here is not so much intellectual or scholarly carefulness (our notion of virtue) as emotional "caring."

The idea of "neutral" or "objective" remembering was foreign to monastic culture. As much as it is involved with cognition, memory was recognized to be involved also with will and desire. Without arousing emotions and so moving the will, there will be no remembering and thus no creating of thoughts. The classic statement of this idea is in Augustine's *De trinitate*; I have no wish to analyze further what has often, and eloquently, been analyzed before.[119] But I wish now to focus on an important result of this belief: the need for a reader/thinker to feel, even deliberately create, emotion as a part of reading.

To get at this idea in terms that respect its genesis in rhetoric, I want to focus first on a trope that brings together, as a rhetorical "common place," the physiology of *memoria* and its requirement of strong emotion. This trope clusters on Latin *pung-o, punc-tus*, literally meaning "to pierce, puncture," and thus "wound" some surface. This word quickly came as well to mean emotional vexation, anxiety, grief, and so on, and its close relative, *compunctus*, had much the same range of meanings, both the sense of piercing a surface and the emotional sense, of goading and vexing the feelings. In medieval Latin, *punctus* came to be used also as the word for the dot or point pricked into the parchment surface, which helped to mark up and "divide" a written text for comprehension in reading, and so to "punctuate" it, in our modern sense. The earliest citations given in the *OED*, from the sixteenth and seventeenth centuries, use "punctuation" particularly in the context of religious meditation and liturgical song texts, such as the Psalms: it is the method of marking up units of text into mnemonically useful length by means of "pointing" them.[120]

So we have here a chain (*catena*), mnemonically associated through the key syllable *punct-*, which attaches physical puncture-wounds, with (page) punctuation, with affective compunc-tion of heart – and so from heart to memory, via a dual meaning of Latin *cor(d)-*.

14. MNEMOTECHNICAL ANXIETY: THE SECOND MEDITATION OF ANSELM OF BEC

The "wounding" of page in punctuation and the wounding of memory in *compunctio cordis* are symbiotic processes, each a require-ment for human cognition to occur at all. Several scholars working on *memoria* in medieval culture, among them Eugene Vance, Louise Fradenburg, and Jody Enders, have noted how violence seems to be a recurring preoccupation, almost a mnemotechnical principle.[121] Cer-tainly memory writers who knew the precepts of the memory art described in the Roman Republican textbook *Rhetorica ad Here-nnium*, all emphasize that making "excessive" images for secure remembering (on the observation that we recall what is unusual more readily and precisely than what is common) includes making very bloody, gory, violent *imagines agentes*.

I am well aware that current psychoanalytical theory has empha-sized the role of trauma in memory making. I do not wish to be thought to believe that analysis based on these psychoanalytic con-structs has no role to play in our perception of medieval cultures. But medieval people did not construe themselves in this way, and I have noticed that scholars who use psychoanalytic language to talk about the importance of "trauma" in the undoubtedly violent lives of medieval people can neglect the more social, rhetorical roles such violence played, at least in their art and their pedagogy. So instead of talking about psychic trauma, I will concentrate on the rhetorical figure of puncture-wounds.

I also want to talk about cognition and learning, not neurosis. The *trope* of violence in memory work plays a specifically mnemotech-nical role. One sees its mnemonic use not only in the cultivation of anxiety-provoking images but in the actual, pervasive brutality of ancient and medieval elementary pedagogy, precisely the time in a child's life at which the most important foundational memory work was being done. One can speak of this violence as a neurosis of medieval pedagogy, but to do so seems to me unhelpfully anachronistic. Medieval people clearly saw it as necessary to impress memories upon the brain, those all-important, rote-retained "habitations" and "pathways" of their culture.[122]

In his sermon on conversion Bernard uses, as we saw, one of the master tropes of *memoria*: that memory is like a waxed tablet, or in manuscript cultures, like the page of a parchment, upon which we each individually write with the "stylus" or "pen" of our memory. I have described this model and some of its implications at length in *The Book of Memory*: one finds it as early as Homer, certainly in Plato, the Book of Proverbs, Cicero, Quintilian, Augustine, Jerome, and then down through the ages. This model of memory is essentially a locational one: matters are written into a "place" in memory as characters are impressed into a tablet or incised onto parchment. The physical book's surfaces provide "support" for the laid-out page, including its decoration and punctuation, and these features in turn support the memory of a reader by providing forms for the "matters" (*res*) of a work, visual markers in the form of written letters, dots and curlicues, painted scenes, and so on, which make the matter readily memorable and thus make it into a subject for meditation.

I think most modern scholars contemplating this image of memory as a written tablet are inclined to imagine it much too statically and even indolently, for writing to us involves little physical exertion. But we should keep in mind the vigorous, if not violent, activity involved in making a mark upon such a physical surface as an animal's skin. One must break it, rough it up, "wound" it in some way with a sharply pointed instrument. Erasure involved roughing up the physical surface even more: medieval scribes, trying to erase parchment, had to use pumice stones and other scrapers. In other words, writing was always hard physical labor, very hard as well on the surface on which it was being done; this vigorous physical aspect, I believe, was always part of that master-model of memory as a written surface.

For example, there is a well-known manifestation of this trope, popular in later medieval piety, that likens the body of Christ to a written parchment page. One especially gory version of it is an English poem, the so-called "Long Charter" of Christ from the fifteenth century. The author of this poem calls his image a "memoria" and also a "pictura," both designed for meditation. Christ is imagined to speak from the Cross. He likens himself to a piece of vellum, stretched out "as parchment ought to be." The blood which runs from his wounds is the ink (both red and black) which we see on the page, and the scourges and thorns of His torture are the pens which incised those inked letters onto the surface.[123] For medieval cultures, implied in the very word *recordari* is an act of remembering not in Wordsworthian tranquility, but by means of very strong emotions that both punctuated and wounded memory.

As the praxis of meditation developed, *compunctio cordis* became elaborated in a variety of "ways" to induce strong emotions of grief and/or fear, including an emotion-filled imagining as one recites or chants the Psalms, the Passion, and other suitable texts; strongly emotional reflection upon one's sins and sinful state; and the specific tasks of remembering Hell and remembering death in vigorous sensual detail.

Emotion is initiated and called up by detailed imaging, a recollective cue that most often takes the form of what we would now call a picture.[124] Remember how Augustine describes frightening himself with thoughts of his death until the hairs of his skin stood up like little nails. Astonishing examples of detailed imagining in just this mode can be found in many later medieval texts. Some of the best, and best known even now, are in several prayers and meditations composed by Anselm of Bec between 1070 and 1080 as examples for the devotions of others, including both monks and seculars, especially aristocratic women. They were "to stir up the mind of the reader," and to be "taken a little at a time" and pondered slowly; Anselm even reminds his reader that s/he need not begin at the beginning each time, but wherever s/he chooses. For ease of meditation, Anselm took care to divide the individual prayers into memory-sized pieces: "the sections are divided into paragraphs, so that the reader can begin and leave off wherever he or she chooses, lest too great a length, or having to go over the same place again and again, produce boredom."[125] Such advice is mnemotechnically sound: the memory is easily overwhelmed and fatigued, therefore reading must be divided into bits that short-term memory can manage to recollect. Tedious reiteration is deadly to the mind; hence Anselm's additional comment that dividing a very long text into short pieces can make it easier to remember because of the variety of the individual units, as compared with the dullness provoked by having endlessly to repeat the same length of wordy prose. The presentation Anselm makes of this work is carefully laid out for maximum memorability, the needs of a reader/meditator being clearly understood. The work was also provided with a set of historiated initials, quite possibly made at the direction of Anselm himself when he sent the collection, "which I edited at the request of several brothers," to Countess Matilda of Tuscany in 1104.[126]

The second meditation, "A Lament for Virginity Unhappily Lost," was perhaps written first for lay nobles and novices.[127] It seems to be part of another meditation "to stir up fear," the first step in the way of meditation, as we know. The language of Anselm's prayers and meditations is sufficiently different from previous works in this genre that Anselm is credited with having invented a new form of piety: certainly his style is very personal. Here is a sample:

> My heart considers and reconsiders what it has done and what it deserves. Let my mind descend into 'the land of darkness and the shadows of death', and consider what there awaits my sinful soul. Let me look inwards and contemplate, see and be disturbed; O God, what is this that I perceive, the land of 'misery and darkness'? Horror! horror! What is this I gaze upon ... a confusion of noises, a tumult of gnashing teeth, a babble of groans. Ah, ah, too much, ah, too much woe! Sulphurous flames, flames of hell, eddying dark-nesses, [I see you] swirling with terrible sounds. [Living worms] in the fire ... Devils that burn with us, raging with fire and gnashing your teeth in madness, why are you so cruel to those who roll about among you? ... Is this the end, great God, prepared for fornicators and despisers of your law, of whom I am one? Even I myself am one of them! My soul, be exceedingly afraid; tremble, my mind; be torn, my heart .... Good Lord, do not recall your just claims against your sinner, but remember mercy towards your creature.[128]

This section of Anselm's second meditation is a "loosened up" and copious version of two verses from Job: "Before I go, and return no more, to a land that is dark and covered with the mist of death; A land of misery and darkness, where the shadow of death, and no order, but everlasting horror dwelleth."[129] In fact this entire composition is woven from remembered texts and common images, from Job, the Psalms, Apocalypse, and the Gospels, together with their accrued commentary, including (especially by the time Anselm was writing in the eleventh century) programs of meditational pictures that were part of the interior "viewing" of death and Hell during prayer.

But the texts are vivified and given a cognitive energy through Anselm's own emotions. "Rumination," a word often used for this activity in studies of spirituality (and in discussions of memory work), is perhaps too peaceful and too introspective in its modern connotations to quite suit the anguish of Anselm's reading. He is literally getting himself all worked up. The "careful" internal viewing of these remembered texts, their syllables allowed to "gather in" other *dicta et facta memorabilia* as Anselm's associations collect them up, is done with as much "care," in the emotional sense, as possible. He scares himself, he grieves himself, he shames himself: this is literally *com-punc-tio cordis*, wounding oneself with the *puncti* of text and picture. It is cued to the texts as "punctuated" in the book, both the actual book and that in Anselm's memory, those clauses of text each of which is in length one unit of the mind's *conspectus* or mental gaze, and inscribed and inviscerated in our bodies as small puncture wounds inscribe a tattoo on skin ("tattoo" being another ancient meaning of *compunctio*).

15. MOLDING CHARACTER THROUGH EXERCISE: THE SOLDIER-MONK

I have discussed at length elsewhere exactly how reading was thought to model character through memory:[130] it is the method of ethical and civic modeling of character summed up in the Greek word *paideia*. Speaking of Libanius, the pagan orator of Antioch whom we met earlier, Peter Brown has well summarized just what the scheme of education called *paideia* was supposed to produce: "[t]he rhetorical education provided by a teacher such as Libanius amounted to nothing more than the patient re-creation, in every generation, of the 'collective memory' of the urban upper class."[131] In this education method and practice are just as important as the content itself.

This re-creation involved much more than the study of theoretical subjects. It was based on a careful gradation (a "ladder of perfection") of exercises, founded upon the verbal *via* of grammar, rhetoric, and dialectic. Much has been written about the compositional exercises of the *paideia*,[132] but there were also memorizing exercises, notably the recitation, which "primarily consists in saying over and over to oneself, either quietly or more loudly, certain sentences which the student wishes to engrave on his memory."[133] Thus was moral character molded by means of responses and reflexes inculcated by the ruminative reflection upon "domesticated" texts and stories, the *res memorabiles*. This educational goal, with obvious alterations in its content, also took hold in cenobitic life, as the monastic teachers too sought patiently to recreate in each generation the *res memorabiles* of the monastery.

The many memory exercises were designed on the model of physical exercises: in the Greek physician Galen's phrase, they are a "gymnastic of the soul." "The process was gradual, painstaking – and painful. Like the athlete trained in the old gymnasium, the student of literature slowly acquired his knowledge and skills by replacing unrefined habits with good habits," exactly the displacement process counseled to the novice John Cassian.[134] I have already noted that the Latin verb *meditare* was used to translate the Greek verb *meletein* in many early ascetic texts (fourth to fifth century). *Meletein* referred both to physical exercises, such as those soldiers do, and also to the memory exercises associated with learning to read and write.[135] Such exercises were thought to shape the brain as athletics shape the body – or as a gardener prunes trees or a sculptor cuts away stone or a scribe incises parchment (all of these are commonplace tropes for the process). And the agency of this shaping is memory.

Thus training in the trivium, the arts of language, was thought of as a kind of athletic, even military training. This conflation helped to support another common model of monastic life, one which often seems to us incompatible with the solitude and rumination of prayer. The idea that a monk was always in battle against the enemies of Christ has many sources, of course. But it fitted readily as well into the ancient model of the orator as soldier. There was always a military aspect both to rhetorical education and to the office of an orator in civic life: one need search no further than Cicero's Philippic orations (taught as part of the standard rhetoric curriculum during the whole imperial period) for splendid examples of this.[136]

Cicero's orator is a warrior, doing battle against the (false) persuasions of Rome's enemies. The *res memorabiles* are defensive weapons in this battle, and the art of rhetoric itself is thought of as a kind of military art. To find such a model of reading in the rhetoric of monasticism, one need look no further than the preface to Benedict's Rule:

> So indeed, brothers, we have asked the Lord, who will dwell in his tabernacle [Psalm 14:1], we have heard His requirements for those living there, but we must fulfill the duties of those citizens. There-fore [ergo] our hearts and our bodies are prepared to do battle in holy obedience to his commands. ... And therefore [ergo; notice the causal connection] we are going to establish a study-center for the service of the Lord."[137]

Cenobitic monasticism from the beginning thought of itself as a City

– a city protected and sustained by its own kind of civic oratory, derived, in this case, from Scripture. It was a city in the desert, serving like the Tabernacle for the Jews of the Exodus, but a kingdom nonetheless, whose inhabitants were therefore citizens, not simply lone individuals.[138]

16. PETER OF CELLE, "ON AFFLICTION AND READING"

There is a particularly interesting treatise for novices that encapsulates these issues, especially the close relationship between *sollicitudo* and persuasion. This work is "On Affliction and Reading," by the twelfth-century Benedictine Peter of Celle. He was a writer much admired also by the Cistercians, and a friend of both Richard and John of Salisbury; having been abbot first of the monastery of Montier-la-Celle in northern France, and then of St. Rémi in Rheims, he succeeded John of Salisbury as bishop of Chartres, where he died in 1183. The title of Peter's text has long proven intriguing, being something of an oxymoron for many modern readers; it will serve to focus the topic of how bodily affliction – vexation, anxiety – is one of our primary memory tools, even for activities we tend to consider entirely "mental" or spiritual.

Peter sees the connection of affliction and reading primarily in military terms, the training exercises and tests which soldiers must always engage in because that is who they are – as monks practice their exercises and disciplines of prayer. Here again is the trope anciently found in the Greek word *meletein*:

> newly enlisted soldiers of Christ, who fight under the banner of the cross, are subjected to a strenuous, three-fold test: bodily affliction by which the body's wantonness is curbed; reading of the Old and New Testaments, by which the soul is fed; prayer of compunction for sins ... which raises the spirit to God.[139]

Peter's asceticism is based on ideas of temperance and balance that accord with medieval biological theory. "The proper measure for affliction is to mount a campaign against one's wantonness, rather than against one's nature."[140] Bodily asceticism is couched in terms of persuasion: sinning is a process of persuasion, by oneself but also by "the Persuader," the Adversary, who offers arguments that "solicit" consent from a mind that has wandered (*errare*), become curious, and fallen into the state of mental fornication and curiosity that Cassian described. This model of sin is thoroughly rhetorical in its terms; to look at it only psychologically is to miss the *social*, even civic, setting of monastic ethics.

As ascetic discipline is modeled in part on rhetoric, so reading, the primary preparation of the orator, is a kind of battle, providing textual weapons to defend the citadel against the Enemy. This is the most extraordinary aspect of Peter's treatise, and the best measure of how affective he considered reading to be. The activity of reading, for Peter, is the battleground of virtue and vice:

> [One who does not devote himself to holy reading] disarms his ramparts of a thousand shields which might hang down from them. How quickly and easily is the little citadel of your cell captured if you do not now defend yourself with God's help and the shield of the sacred page? ... Take projectiles from your armory/bookcases [armaria] so that when you are struck you may strike back at the one who struck you.[141]

Much of Peter's advice is couched in the commonplace tropes of meditative reading, which include, importantly, the language of educated *memoria*. These images of the "the little citadel of your cell," of the "bookcases" (with a play on a possible meaning of Latin *armarium* as "armory") in which are stored the weapons with which to defend yourself have much resonance in mnemonic technique. Even language which we may not recognize as metaphorical is: the Benedictine and Cistercian monks of Peter's audience did not actually have bookcases in their cells, for the monastery book-chests were usually in (or just off) the cloister, and these monks did not have private cells. So the "bookcase" in "your cell" should be understood figuratively, as the monk's memory-cell, in which the texts he has armed himself with are kept ready to hand (or rather, ready for secure recollective invention). And of course, Peter, as abbot of Celle, had an additional, personal reason to play on the word *cella*.[142]

Reading is food, "a steaming oven full of breads made of the best wheat flour"[143] (Peter also wrote a treatise "On the Breads" of the Temple), and

> as you amble through the field of Scripture, you will not stub your toe against a rock [Psalm 90:12; Matthew 4:6]. Rather, like a bee harvesting flowers, you may compose from it a honeycomb [Luke 24:42; also Seneca, *Moral Epistles* 84], which will bring sweetness to your taste [cf. Psalm 118:103], light to your eyes, and wonderful scents with which you can sprinkle the walls of your room.[144]

This description is composed of a pastiche of (mixed) metaphors and tropes of memory: no master of the focussed style, Peter is remarkable for the sheer volume of lumber in his memory, and his eagerness to let it all gather together in one place without apparent editing. Notice again the basic structural method of collating short pieces of text, drawn together not only by theme but also by coincident word. But also notice how the same elementary techniques of memory and recollection have been used by two strong personalities, Anselm and Peter, to fashion two entirely different personal literary styles.

Reading, Peter says, is a kind of walking through the contents of Scripture. Its components vary in the speed with which they can be traversed:

> In this book [of Genesis] journey through the greater part of your reading, coming to paradise ... Walk with God, like Enoch ... Enter the Ark at the time of the Flood ... So go with a deliberate but light step through the contents of this book ... interpreting what is obscure, retaining and memorizing what is straightforward. Whenever you enter a pleasant meadow of prophetic blessings, loosen the folds of your garment, stretch your belly, open your mouth and extend your hand ... Then come to Exodus [grieving for] the entry into Egypt ... Then admire the foreshadowing of our redemption in the blood of the sacrificial lamb. Observe how the law was given on Mt. Sinai and how it is open to spiritual understanding. By progressions of virtues run through the forty-two stopping places [in the Sinai] with what they signify. With an angelic mind construct within yourself the Tabernacle and its ceremonies.[145]

Peter clearly thinks of the matters in Genesis in terms of a map; reading it is for him a series of journeys, a sight-seeing pilgrimage. In each site he commands us to observe the stories and events as mental scenes. This is exactly the manner of the early pilgrims who made the actual journey through the Holy Land; the sites mark the *ductus* of a reader making his "way" through the Biblical narratives.

As a means of finding the way, Peter particularly values the variations of tempo and mood, the *colores* of the journey determined in each site: Genesis is taken with a "deliberate but light step"; prophetic passages are places to rest and feast; Exodus is to be traversed with grief and awe. His language is filled not only with commands to the reader to "walk," "enter," "travel," but also with commands to look and to touch, taste, and hear. Notice how he has constructed the Biblical text *summatim*, as a map of "places":

paradise, the Ark, Mt. Sinai. And notice also his command to "build in yourself," from the written text, the holy Tabernacle and its ceremonies. Such building is done by mentally seeing the description as one reads it, by the same careful and keen meditation that Peter counsels at each site on the Biblical map.

In the journey, Peter pays some attention to those parts of Exodus that construct sets of places, like mnemonic places. A chief one of these is the place of the Tabernacle, which we are to construct in our minds. This is undoubtedly a recollection of the metaphor of the monastery as the Exodus Tabernacle, which plays a large part in the familiar prologue to the Benedictine Rule. But there are other such sites which are less obvious. For instance, Peter advises that one should "[b]y progressions of virtues run through the forty-two stopping places [in the Sinai] with what they signify."[146] This particular prescription makes little sense except in terms of mnemonic technique. But in memory work, the forty-two places, *mansiones*, of Sinai serve well as another compositional mapping structure. Like the word *sedes*, *mansiones* is used to refer to the individual areas within a diagrammatic structure. These *mansiones* are related, Peter writes, "profectibus virtutum." *Profectio* means "point of departure," and while the phrase is obscure, if Peter is thinking of a mnemotechnical diagram of the sort often seen in twelfth-century books, one can make some sense of it. Each area or *mansio* would be labeled – conveniently, by the name of a virtue, arranged perhaps in sets, maybe six sets of seven virtues each. Then into each *mansio* of the mental map all manner of "signification" can be collected. In this way, the forty-two places of the exodus through Sinai can be made to serve as a florilegial collection topically arranged (by virtues), very convenient for all kinds of later scholarly use.

Thus one "sees" one's reading, and one "walks" through it, not just to store it away conveniently and safely, in order to be able to reconstruct it as it was, but also in order to meditate on it, digest it, interpret it, and make it fully useful, ethically and compositionally. A reader is constantly in motion, all senses continually in play, slowing down and speeding up, like a craftsman using his various instruments. In eleventh and twelfth-century counsel about reading, as here, the emphasis tends to be on the building process rather than the built object; thus on the interpreting mind rather than on the interpretation, or even the text, except as it "intends" and energizes the mind. This is also the emphasis of Cassian and Gregory. Monastic reading is reading undertaken with "intention" and *sollicitudo* – directed, engaged feeling that is regarded as the foundation of all the good of meditation.

As one would expect, one vice of *sollicitudo* is torpor, bored disengagement (the disengagement produced by misdirected *curiositas* is the other). Peter explains how to counter scholarly sloth:

> The nourishment of holy books is indeed so fruitful and abundant that in them our every boredom will be countered by as many varieties of readings as there are moments in our lives ... According to the inclinations [appetita] of our various feelings one should read now things new, now old, now obscure, now plain, now complicated, now simple, now examples, now commands, now serious, now funny. If the soul is compassed about with such a harmonious variety, it will avoid tedium and acquire its remedy.[147]

The relation of emotion to reading is conceived of by Peter in terms of rhetorical decorum. Our "feelings" require – for support, for remedy – readings that are "appropriate" to them. I don't think what Peter seeks is psychological mood music (as we might now) so much as to balance a mood with its opposite to produce what he calls a "harmonious variety," *varietas concorda*. So just as there is good *curiositas* and bad *curiositas*, so there is also good *sollicitudo* and bad. Getting the right balance is a matter of decorum and equity, as though one had a social relationship with one's reading of the sort that an orator and audience have with one another.

As Jean Leclercq has written, a medieval monk was above all "une âme de désir."[148] Leclercq was describing Peter of Celle's spiritual writings, and cited this clause of the Rule: "Vitam aeternam omni concupiscentia spirituali desiderare," "to desire eternal life with all the passion of our spirit" (*Regula Benedicti*, cap. 4.46). *Concupiscentia* refers most commonly to sexual desire, and its intensity was not supposed to be diminished by monastic life, but directed, like a gaze. This is another reason why Cassian could with justice describe as a type of *sexual* sin the kind of inattentive reading we have all experienced, when our minds are far from our eyes, mental and/or physical. But in the context of reading – a context in which we often encounter the notion of "fornication" in monasticism – we are not dealing exclusively, or perhaps even primarily, with individual psyche but with the community, and that must bring us again to the context of rhetoric. Monastic reading, in all its cognitive complexity, has its sources and results in *social* activity. For "desiring heaven," as Leclercq also noted, "gives the soul an appetite in expectation of

Heaven" and a craving, a bodily need or anxiety, to have more and more of it – to the end, however, of making "the monk *a citizen* of the heavenly Jerusalem" (my emphasis).[149] Citizenry is a construct of rhetoric and *paideia*.

17. FISHING FOR THOUGHT: ROMUALD OF CAMALDOLI

I'd like to close this chapter by examining a well-known bit of advice about meditational method. It was written down by Bruno of Querfort, a disciple of the famous eleventh-century mystic St. Romuald of Camaldoli, who seems not to have written anything down himself. In it, as in virtually all such advice, we should notice the primary importance given to physical location and then to the devices used to engage the audience in forms of mental play, especially through using "puns" of coincident shape as well as verbal puns:

> Be seated within your cell as though in paradise; cast to the rear of your memory everything distracting, becoming alert and focussed on your thoughts as a good fisherman is on the fish. One pathway [to this state] is through reciting the Psalms; do not neglect this. If you cannot manage to get through them all [at one sitting] as you used to do with the fervor of a novice, take pains to chant the psalms in your spirit, now [starting] from this place, now from that, and to interpret them in your mind [intelligere mente], and when you begin to wander in your reading, don't stop what you are doing, but make haste to correct [emendare] by interpreting; place yourself [pone te] above all in the presence of God with fear and trembling, like one who stands in the gaze of the emperor; pull yourself in completely and crouch down like a baby chick, content with God's gift, for, unless its mother provides, it neither knows nor gets what it should eat.[150]

While Romuald, it is true, founded a reformed order of monasticism (the Camaldolese) that involved both cenobitic and eremetical stages, and emphasized a goal for the perfect of living in solitude, "cell" is not to be taken only literally here: indeed the passage contains several word-plays, a number of which resonate within memory technique.[151] *Sede in cella* plays on the standard metaphor of memory as a room or *cella*, as well as a "cellar" where nourishment is stored (inventoried) in an orderly fashion. A cell is also a cube made up of four-sided figures or central squares: a favorite shape, in monastic orthopraxis, with which to initiate meditation.

The command "sede" also plays on a common metaphor for the locations of memory as the "seats" or *sedes* in which materials, such as the memorized psalms, are stored in their order. So the command "sede in cella" is a directional one: locate yourself in a "seat" of memory "as though in paradise" – for the memory work of Heaven. A good way is by means of a journey through the Psalms. Notice the admonition to begin "now from this place, now from that." The individual psalms are imagined as "seats" or "places" in a journey (*via*), whose map is in your memory. Hugh of St. Victor, some hundred years later, uses virtually the same image for the "sedes" of the Psalms in his mnemotechnical preface to his Chronicle.[152] Evidently the Psalms, for Romuald as for Benedict of Nursia before him and Hugh of St. Victor after him, are the foundation of *memoria*; as a novice, one learned them all and could recite them straight through (or however one chose to do so). Even a tired, fading, old memory can begin reading – that is, mentally – starting "now from this place, now from that." The word used is "locus," and it is clear that this description assumes that his own trained, stocked, locational memory inventory is at the monk's individual disposal at all times.

You should be in a state of focussed alertness, *sollicitudo*, like a fisherman watching out for fish. This is another common trope for memory work; it has ancient antecedents, and we still "fish" for a memory.[153] When your mind (and memory) wanders, you must call it back to its path. You do this by giving yourself an emphatic emotional jolt. In fear and trembling, you "place yourself" in imagination, in the presence and gaze of God. In other words, anxiety is a requirement of *mnemonic* art, and so also of invention. The emotion "locates" you and stabilizes you in your reading place, which is also your "starting-off" place for meditation. The difference between simple *legere* (to read) and *intellegere* (to understand) is art, the recollective art that enables you to *locate* and to find what you are reading within the "ways" that lead to God.

But you do not stop with the simple emotion of fear. Notice how Romuald (speaking through Bruno) next starts up his inventing mind by means of an amusing and multivalent little picture: the scene of a baby chick ("pullus"), cowering fearfully under the gaze of an emperor. Bruno-Romuald gets to this picture via a chain of memorial associations, starting off from the technical requirement to manufacture in oneself a state, a place, of "fear and trembling" (*sollicitudo*, anxiety, *compunctio*). Imagine yourself in a frightening situation: for

113

example, as something totally helpless in the presence of a mortal enemy. Choose to be a tiny chick, which is a creature sufficiently different from yourself to "catch your fancy" and to require your imagination and thought to be roused. Since the imperial bird is an eagle, you are to imagine the imperial gaze as that of an eagle contemplating its next meal – you, the chick. Visualize this to yourself.

A chick is food for an eagle – unless it can hide itself away, and unless God saves it. God protects and feeds us, acting as our mother hen who feeds her chick (and saves it from the hungry eagle-emperor). Not all these connections are explicitly made; to do so would defeat the purpose of the device. Enough are made, and the image is amusing enough, to catch our attention and to put our bored, wandering minds "in play," as a "way in" to our own further creative meditation, which is the point. Such associational play is the very stuff of *memoria*.

But the play is set in motion and controlled *consciously*, through the rhetorical "coloring" and clothing of the composition. The emperor–eagle–chick–hen complex is a stylistic ornament (employing the rhetorical figures of *metaphora* and *metonymy* and perhaps *allegoria* as well), a bit of decoration, willfully chosen and applied in accord with well-known rhetorical conventions by a well-educated and stocked mind, stocked like a monastery fish-pond. The associations are not primarily caused by a *spontaneous* overflow of powerful feelings. Nor do they express a rapture of the *unconscious* mind, in the course of which (perhaps) an eleventh-century missionary-monk reveals (without knowing it) both his rural upbringing and his nascent imperialism.

I concede that modern interpreters could look into this text and find such interesting connections (the final connection Bruno makes, from God to mother, is noteworthy to me). But to Romuald and Bruno and the audience whose memories they expected to put in play, the obvious connections would have been to the Bible, for instance, to Matthew 23:37, where Jesus, in an apocalyptic address to the city of Jerusalem, laments that he would often have wished to gather up her children "as the hen doth gather her chickens under her wings" – and so, the hen with her chick becomes yet another way of "remembering Jerusalem," the task with which this chapter began.

But in any event, we need to be clear that both Romuald (if this textual picture originates with him) and Bruno were knowingly

applying a careful technique of cognitive invention located in habituated texts, a technique which they assumed could be learned and
mastered by most people, and whose *virtus* or energy was carried in
the seriously playful chain-making made possible by two things: a
well-furnished memory, and sets of conventions, themselves in
memory, that all together made up the social "habitations" and
"common places" within which these contemplatives lived and wrote.
These conventions, these common places, are, traditionally, the matter
of rhetoric, and their masterly *use* in making new things is what
rhetorical training primarily afforded.[154]

By now it should be clear that virtually *any* meditative work is
susceptible to the kind of mnemotechnical analysis I have applied in
this chapter to Anselm, to Romuald, to Bernard, and to Peter of
Celle. As John Cassian made clear, the art of meditation is fundamentally an art of thinking with a well-furnished memory. Though the
goal of spiritual life is the unmediated vision of God, divine *theoria*,
one can only get there by traveling through one's memory. A person's
entire memory is a composition among whose places, routes, and
pathways one must move whenever one thinks about anything. This
is why the most powerful, the most fruitful engine of the mind in
meditation was considered to be that *pia memoria* of which Hugo of
Rouen spoke. In this chapter we examined the cognitive "maps"
made to reach that goal. In the next, I will focus more specifically on
cognitive markers and sites, that is, the ornaments and figures by
which we make our way.

3

Cognitive images, meditation, and ornament

Cellula quae meminit est cellula deliciarum.   Geoffrey of Vinsauf

The way of meditation was initiated, oriented, and marked out by the schemes and tropes of Scripture. Like sites plotted on a map, these functioned as the stations of the way, to be stopped at and stayed in before continuing; or they could serve as route indicators, "this way" or "slow down" or "skim this quickly" or "note well." I have already talked about how medieval public memory, in pilgrimage and in liturgy, was conducted processionally, as a way among sites, such as those in Jerusalem or Rome or Daphne. In a meditative composition, the "stations" are marked by stylistic ornaments, the colors and modes of the figures of rhetoric. All figurative language can function for a reader in this way, but for monastic composition the "difficult tropes" and schemes of the Bible were particularly important, what Augustine called *obscuritas utilis et salubris*, "productive and health-giving difficulty."[1]

If we adopt for a moment the central figure in the concept of rhetorical *ductus* – that of flow and movement, as through an aqueduct – we can think of the ornaments in a composition as causing varieties of movement: steady, slow, fast, turn, back up. They not only signal how something is to be "taken" (like a pathway) – whether straight on (literally) or obliquely (metaphorically or ironically) – but can also give an indication of temporal movement, like time signatures in written musical composition. Compositional *ductus*, moving in colors and modes, varies both in direction and in pace, after it takes off from its particular beginning (the all-important point "where" one starts) towards its target (*skopos*). If a thinking human mind can be said to require "machines" made out of memory by imagination, then the ornament and decoration, the "clothing," of a piece will indicate ways in which these mental instruments are to be played. A stylistic figure, an "image," signals not just a subject-matter (*res*) but a "mood" (*modus, color*), an "attitude" (*intentio*), and a reading "tempo." Movement within and through a literary or visual piece is performed, as it is in music. Choice is involved for the author in placing ornaments in a work, and choice for an audience in how to "walk" among them. And as in all performances, variation from one occasion to another is a given.

An essential first step of invention is thus recollective cogitation. For the process of meaning-making to begin at all, one's memory must be "hooked up" and "hooked in" to the associational play of the mind at work. That is the essential function of any ornament, and it explains why many of the basic features of the ornaments are also elementary principles of mnemonics: surprise and strangeness (for example, *metaphora*, metonymy, *allegoria*, oxymoron, and, in art, grotesquery), exaggeration (hyperbole and litotes), orderliness and pattern (chiasmus, tropes of repetition, various rhythmic and rhyming patterns), brevity (ellipsis, epitome, synecdoche, and other tropes of abbreviation) and copiousness (all tropes of amplification), similarity (similitude), opposition (paradox and antithesis) and contrast (tropes of irony). All of these characteristics are essential for making mnemonically powerful associations.

And they are all also deliberately playful and surprising, for mnemonic and recollective techniques have all relied heavily on emotion as the quickest and surest way to catch the mind's attention. Recall John Cassian's description of the human mind as a never-ceasing mill-wheel, Romuald's concern to wake the thinking mind from torpor with a sharp emotional surprise. "Cellula quae meminit est cellula deliciarum," "the little cell which remembers is a little chamber of pleasures," wrote Geoffrey of Vinsauf, towards the end of this long meditative tradition.[2] This is a mnemotechnical commonplace: the cogitating mind tires easily, is easily bored, easily distracted. So the craft of *memoria* requires energizing devices to put it in gear and to keep it interested and on track, by arousing emotions of fear or delight, anger, wonder and awe.[3]

In this chapter I will deal with two distinct though related matters. First, I wish to consider carefully the nature and function of mental images, according to the essentially rhetorical analysis given by Augustine and, deriving entirely from his account, by the Carolingian scholar Alcuin. In the rest of the chapter, I will consider the cognitive "way-finding" function in rhetorical *ductus* of three important stylistic ornaments: *enargeia* ("bringing-before-the-eyes"), *paronomasia* ("punning"), and *allegoria* ("difficulty"). These three in turn give rise to many specialized varieties of themselves, such as *ekphrasis* and *etymologia*. My goal is not to classify ornaments but to analyze how they were designed to catch hold of our constantly moving minds and set them in a particular motion, or give them a particular task. I will include examples from manuscript paintings as well as literature, though such things are not usually discussed as examples of rhetorical figures.

I. THINKING WITH IMAGES: AUGUSTINE AND ALCUIN

Thanks to the labors of many excellent scholars, it is now a truism that in the Middle Ages the created universe was thought to be one great symbolic mirror of divinity. At first glance the statements "human beings think in images" and "human thought is symbolic" may seem identical. In some respects they are. But not in all, and to treat them as simply identical is to obscure something quite remarkable about how medieval people were taught to engage and order their cognitive procedures, how they learned how to think. One can make the statement, "the human mind requires a sort of image with which to think," about human epistemology generally. Classical and medieval philosophers were inclined to make just such a statement, thereby articulating a major limitation (as Christians saw it) of human thought.[4]

But I am concerned here with a more particular variety of mental image, one made up especially for effective thinking. A cognitive image is designedly functional (though its author may have some epistemological aspirations for it as well). In monastic rhetoric such an image can have effects that are both pedagogical and ethical, but those effects occur within the alert mind and coloring emotion of a viewer/listener. The image is used by its fashioner and, if it finds artistic form, by its audience as a cognitive tool. The first question one should ask of such an image is not "What does it mean?" but "What is it good for?"

The great Northumbrian Carolingian scholar Alcuin (d. 804), head of Charlemagne's palace school at Aachen, wrote a little treatise "De animae ratione" for Eulalia – his name for a nun named Gundrada. It is a digest of Augustine's teaching on the "trinitarian" soul. Augustine had said that the human soul's trinitarian nature is the interconnected

118

working of intellect, will, and memory. In speaking of how humans learn, Alcuin says this:

> Now let us consider the remarkable speed of the mind in shaping material which it takes in through bodily senses, from which, *as though acting through a kind of messenger-service* [nuntios], whatever it takes in of sensible things known or unknown at once with indescribable speed it forms within itself figures of them, and hides these "in-form-ations" in the treasury of its memory. (My emphasis)[5]

The idea is that some sort of mental "messengers" translate, both physiologically and mentally, the raw sense data into a different form as memory images, which are then, in this translated form, hidden away in memory. Alcuin emphasizes the incredible speed with which the mind performs these translations. It is important to recall that Latin *translatio*, a rhetorical concept, fundamentally means "to carry from one place to another": it is a very active kind of word. Alcuin's bustling metaphor of the mind as a messenger-service is compatible with John Cassian's emphasis on the unceasing activity of the mind, as an ever-turning mill-wheel. Alcuin's image, however, suggests not only activity but *conscious* activity: *nuntii* are not unwilled or "unconscious" servants (nor, of course, is the miller who feeds grain to the mill-wheel in Cassian's image). This is an important difference in emphasis and underlying assumption between modern psychologies and medieval ones.

Alcuin continues:

> Thus one who sees Rome also fashions [an image of] Rome in his soul, and forms it as it actually is. When he may hear or remember "Rome," immediately its essence [for *animus*, with the sense of "gist," i. e. a memory *summatim* of Rome, not *verbatim* and thus in undigested detail] recurs to his memory, where he has stored its image, and he recalls it from that place [*ibi*] where he had put it away. And it is more remarkable, that with respect to unknown things, if they come to our ears from reading or hearing something, the mind immediately fashions a figure of the unknown thing. So perhaps one of us might have formed in his mind an image of a putative Jerusalem: however greatly different the actuality may be, as his mind has fashioned [its image] for itself so [Jerusalem] will seem to him. ... He does not imagine the actual walls and houses and squares of Jerusalem, but whatever he has seen in other cities known to him, these he fashions as being possibly like those in

Jerusalem; from known shapes he fashions a thing unknown ...
Thus the human mind makes up images concerning each matter;
from what it knows it fashions things unknown, having all these
particulars in itself. ... By means of this swift activity of the mind,
by which it thus fashions in itself all that it has heard or seen or
touched or tasted or smelled, and again recalls its fashionings, by the
marvellous power of God and the efficacy of its nature, from any
circumstances it may acquire knowledge.[6]

The products of fantasy and memory are the matrix and materials of
all human thought. That is what Alcuin says here, following his
master. And these thought-devices, these fictions by which we can
grasp God (or any concept) in our mind, are constructions that
someone can hear, smell, taste, touch, and above all *see* mentally.

Images for thinking are not primarily useful because of their
objective truth content or their mimetic ability: they have none, or
have it at best incidentally. Nor are they useful because they "trace"
some past experience in unaltered detail, for instance a previous visit
to Rome. What one recalls, Alcuin says, is not the exact, verbatim
copy of the raw experience, but its essence, its *animus* – an example of
memoria rerum. For Alcuin to say that "human beings think in
images" is a statement about cognitive process – people use these
images to think with (and remember with). It makes no difference to
its cognitive value whether my mental image of "Jerusalem" is like
yours or not. And it certainly doesn't matter whether or not either of
our mental images resembles the actual city.

As an example of how idiosyncratic variations in a generalized
image seem to have been untroubling to painter and audience, notice
how the architectural detail of the city of "New Jerusalem" varies
even among images copying the same original picture: the Saint-Sever
Heavenly City, made in southern France, has the rounded arches of
its time and place, while the Facundus Beatus from Spain shows the
"key-hole" arches of Mozarabic architecture (Plates 2 and 3). And a
painting of the Heavenly City in the thirteenth-century "Trinity
Apocalypse," an English copy of this same Beatus image, shows
pointed Gothic arches.[7] Because such images were used as cognitive
fictions rather than thought to be depictions of an actual object, such
detail can be altered quite freely, so long as the gist is remembered.[8]

Alcuin is indebted to the eighth book of Augustine's *De trinitate*
for his idea that human beings must know things in terms of the
images of what they have experienced. For example, Augustine says

that "when we give credence to any earthly thing which we have heard or read about but have not seen, our mind must represent it to itself as something with bodily features and forms, just as it occurs to our thoughts."[9] Whether this image that we fashion is true to life or not, he says, does not matter: what is important is that "it is useful for some other purpose," namely, knowledge. "For," he continues,

> who, upon reading or listening to what Paul the Apostle wrote or what has been written about him, does not fashion in his mind both the appearance of the Apostle and also of all those whose names are there remembered? And since among the large number of men by whom these words are so noted, one person represents his features and figure in one way, and another in a different way, it is assuredly uncertain whose thoughts are closer to and more like the reality. . . . Even the earthly face of the Lord Himself is represented differently by all the different people having thoughts about Him, even though in actuality His face was only one, whatever it was really like. *But for our faith in the Lord Jesus Christ, it is not the image which the mind forms for itself* [to use for thinking] *(which may perhaps be far different from what he actually looked like) that leads us to salvation,* but, according to our mental representation, what [sorts of thoughts we have] about his humankind. (My emphasis)[10]

Augustine goes on to say, of course, that these mental images are significant only as cues to the "matter" being known; they function in the way mnemonic images do, "pointing to" something else (the matter). In a somewhat similar way, Aristotle argued that humans can only think about the concept of "triangleness" by forming a cognitive representation of a triangle in their minds.[11] Even things one has never encountered oneself are "seen" and thought about using an image, however inadequate it may be to the real object.

What interests me most in Augustine's account, however, is the casual way that he observes how anyone "hearing or reading" the writings of St. Paul "draws a picture in his mind" of the saint's face. The implication is that any reader, while hearing or seeing a literary text, will be painting pictures in his mind and that this task is essential in cognition. It is how we retain and therefore are able to know Paul's texts. Augustine suggests that he is thinking of such images as mnemotechnical markers as well: "who does not fashion in his mind both the face of that apostle [Paul] and also of all those whose names are there remembered [*ibi*, 'in that place']?" The image serves as a location marker for a cluster of readings remembered by means of the name tagged together with the image of the face, as though by a coded file name.[12]

It is also apparent in this comment that Augustine does not associate such mental "painting" with only one type of reading. His coupling of "reading or listening to" is an allusion to the dual practice of reading a book "out loud" or "in silence," the former being the common practice of the school (and other occasions of social reading) and the latter that of the meditative, ruminative reading, often in a murmur, that is identified with prayer and other mental composition. During both sorts of reading, Augustine says, one may be painting mental pictures fashioned from materials familiar in one's memory.

2. ORNAMENT: PUTTING THE MIND IN PLAY

In *The Book of Memory* I developed at length the observation that medieval and ancient writers do not distinguish between what we call "verbal" and "visual" memory; that the letters used for writing were considered to be as visual as what we call "images" today; and that as a result the page as a whole, the complete parchment with its lettering and all its decoration, was considered a cognitively valuable "picture." I would now like to explore the related phenomenon of literary "pictures," organizations of images that are designed to strike the eye of the mind forcefully, and to initiate or punctuate a reader's "progress" through a text, in the way that particular images (or parts of images) structure the "way" of one's eye through a picture.[13] Indeed, the manufacture of mnemonic imagery could be analyzed as a process of mental "ornamentation."

Given the cognitive role assigned to memory in pre-modern psychologies, such ornamentation is no frill, but plays the essential role of catching the attention of a reader and orienting his/her cogitative procedures. All of the figures and tropes, but especially the "difficult" ones like allegory or oxymoron, were understood to offer to a hearer or viewer a site for his or her further invention, acting as a marker on the text's "surface" of matters that might especially require attention, concentration. In teaching mnemotechnic, students were counseled similarly to use *notae*, figures and signs, to mark important matters for secure memory retrieval.[14]

To some extent, the monastic focus on ornament was inherited from Roman rhetoric. In his description of how a Roman citizen-orator should be educated, Quintilian paid a good deal of attention to the ornamentation of a composed work. He was conventional among the Roman authors of rhetorical textbooks in doing this. It is this emphasis in Roman rhetoric – its attention to the surface rather than to the "ideas" and rationale of a work – that perhaps has most convinced many philosophers and historians of rhetoric since the Renaissance of the special triviality of Roman, late Greek, and medieval rhetoric. In an influential textbook, George Kennedy has said of Augustine's rhetoric text, *De doctrina christiana*: "[its] weakness ... is that it encouraged the identification of rhetoric with style and gave still greater authority to the categorization of styles and figures which was already an obsession of classical rhetoric."[15]

The emphasis on ornament, however, corresponded well with the attention paid in early Christian exegesis and spirituality to recollection *summatim* of the Bible – for which its "gems" served crucial heuristic and inventive purposes – and to its "obscurities" as a convenient focus for textual dilation and meditative prayer. In addition to Roman rhetoric, an important source of monastic rhetoric's emphasis upon the value of difficult ornament lies in the exegetical traditions of early rabbinical Judaism, with its particular attention to the "difficult" passages of the Torah.[16] The rabbinical traditions within which early Christianity came into being and was nourished offered an augmentive, dilative method of textual study, organized as the explication and moral elaboration especially of "difficult" passages. Roman rhetoric's attention to stylistic tropes provided a classification system within which the oblique language of Scripture could be explained and examined as "schemes and tropes" of inventive mnemonic importance.

The major treatises on rhetoric in the monastic Middle Ages include a work in dialogue form by Alcuin, part of a series on the liberal arts that the Northumbrian scholar produced for Charlemagne ("On Rhetoric and the Virtues" – note the connection),[17] and Bede's brief treatise on the schemes and tropes of the Bible. Bede's work in particular has been dismissed in some modern histories of rhetoric as a bit of idle (or "peculiarly English") monkishness, its precepts being merely quoted from Donatus (a grammarian, not a rhetorician) but with the examples drawn from Scripture. The whole treatise, some modern historians have said, is designed to show that the Bible not only has all the elegance of the Latin writers, but had it first.[18] It is also accused, as is Augustine's rhetoric, of emphasizing style over invention, thereby betraying its author's lack of understanding of what rhetoric "really" is about.

But we should take the work more seriously than this. We might begin by asking why a monk like Bede should give such paramount importance to identifying and classifying what he calls the "embellishment" of the Bible. Obviously Bede did not think of textual "adornment and clothing" as superficial and trivial. And why? Evidently he thought that his treatise would chart out the most richly texturized nodes of Scripture, those places (topics, loci) that will "catch" a student, invite him or her to engage them recollectively, to ruminate on the text in meditative prayer – those figures that are crucial because they are *fruitful*. Or, to invoke another trope, effective reading requires that a monk should "eat the book," and these tropes are particularly the breads of Scripture. The more they need "chewing," the more difficult they are, the richer their nourishment for a mind engaged in memory work.[19]

3. INVENTION AND DIFFICULTY: AUGUSTINE AND HRABANUS MAURUS

Scripture's figures and tropes are, for Bede as for Augustine and Gregory, the places that particularly generate new compositions in meditative reading and prayer. Indeed, by the time of Hugh of St. Victor, obscure figures have become the particular object of meditation: "meditation is an assiduous and keen attentiveness of thought, gleaming brightly to illuminate something dark [obscurum] or looking closely to see something hidden [occultum]."[20]

In insisting that a text like Bede's is truly a rhetoric and not just a grammar, I am parting company with some scholars, who have discussed Bede's interest in the tropes of Scripture as a matter solely of grammatical explication, and therefore as an important stage in the "literature-izing" (my translation of the Italian jaw-breaker, *letteraturizzazione*) of written material at the expense of a more inventive, performative, oral rhetoric.[21] Scholars who believe this also insist that starting in later antiquity, the trope of *allegoria* became, as it were, "grammarized," its interpretive readings codified in much the way that ordinary paradigms of grammatical correctness were.[22] But to argue this is to ignore the paramount spiritual role given in monasticism to meditation, and the continuing – even increasing – emphasis in monastic reading upon what was obscure, hidden, and dark.[23] In his text on reading (as I have noted earlier), Hugh of St. Victor carefully distinguishes meditation from *lectio*, the annotative, explanatory work of textual exposition. Grammar is necessary as the foundation of useful meditation, but meditation "is bound by none of [its] rules." In meditation the mind is free to roam its inventory, to cast its gleam on the obscure, to scrutinize the dark and secret. Foundations are made only to be built upon; meditation is the real good of reading.[24]

An additional distinction should be kept in mind by modern scholars between the verbal ornament which the rhetoricians called *allegoria* (the "gems" spoken of by Peter Chrysologus, the "obscurities" praised by Augustine, which are "set" in varieties of other, non-allegorical language) and the specifically late-classical exegetical method, deriving from Origen and others, of understanding an entire narrative fiction "allegorically" (whether the events it incorporates be imaginary or actual – Virgil's *Aeneid*, for example, or the Books of Kings). These categories were recognized in the common pedagogical distinction made between an allegory of words and that of (narrated) events – and strictly speaking, only God could create true allegories in history. But the two types of *allegoria* share an essential feature. A major aim of the verbal figure is to encourage someone to make familiar and "domestic" what seems at first obscure and strange. Applied as a tool of narrative exegesis, allegory has the same effect: to de-emphasize the strange otherness of texts, including their historical particularity (an effect Origen's many critics immediately realized). Allegory's *skopos* is ethical and contemplative, and since it operates entirely within the associative orthopractice of meditative *memoria*, allegory will inevitably focus on the present, and look to future *theoria*. In characterizing meditation as cognitive refreshment and spiritual delight, *but not as ordinary reading*, Hugh of St. Victor shows a more acute and practical knowledge of the functioning of allegory than many later literary critics have done.

The two Biblical texts used to justify the continued Christian study and use of pagan art and literature, Exodus 12:35 and Deuteronomy 21: 11–13, are well known to medieval historians, and much has been written about them as justifications for such appropriation. I would like to consider their use by two important medieval authors from the standpoint of these texts' emphasis upon ornament, for this reveals quite clearly, I think, the paramount role of *decus*, "fitting adornment," in monastic concepts of rhetorical invention and meditation.

"[A]nd they demanded of the Egyptians vessels of silver and gold, and also much raiment."[25] This text received its most influential treatment from Augustine, who wrote in the second book of his *De doctrina christiana* that pagan philosophers, "especially the Platonists," have said true things in their books, and so:

> Just as the Egyptians had not only idols and heavy burdens which the people of Israel condemned and avoided, so also they had vessels and ornaments of gold and silver and clothing, which the Israelites fleeing Egypt in secret claimed for themselves, as if to put them to better use – not on their own authority but at God's commandment, the Egyptians having unwittingly fitted them out with the things which they themselves did not use well – so too all the teachings of the pagans [gentilium] contain ... liberal studies ... suited to the uses of truth, and some very useful precepts concerning morals ... which are, as it were, their gold and silver, which they did not find on their own but dug up, as it were, from some quarries of divine Providence ... a Christian should take this treasure from them for the just use of teaching the gospel. And their clothing ... may be taken and kept for turning [conuertenda] to Christian use.[26]

Modern commentary upon this passage in Augustine has emphasized the mined-treasure aspect of this metaphor: the gold and silver truth hidden away in pagan books but useful to Christians. And since the treasure Augustine begins with is nuggets of philosophy, commentators have cast the whole passage as counsel to dig out and use the *ideas* of philosophers (especially Platonists). Augustine does indeed say this, but his main emphasis here is on moral utility, on how materials can be socially and rhetorically "converted" to Christian use. He is thinking not like a Platonist in this passage but like a rhetorician. Mining the *auctores* for treasure is a metaphor not found in Exodus, but it is very common in accounts of rhetorical invention. And Augustine treats the "gold and silver" of the pagans in the way that rhetoric treats its tropes and common places, which are useful precisely because they are not absolutely invariable in their form, but can (and must) be "turned" (the basic metaphor in "convert" as it is also in "trope") in the speaker's own ethos.[27] Augustine says, after all, that pagan literary "treasure" (the memorial treasure of an orator's inventory) is "for the just use of teaching the gospel" – the pre-eminent early Christian rhetorical activity.

And then Augustine also counsels appropriating the "clothing" of the pagans. The *vestis* which the Israelites took is mentioned only once in the two Exodus verses which recount how they spoiled the Egyptians (Exodus 11:2 and 12:35), so Augustine is giving it particular emphasis in his comments. Just as much as the trope of "treasure," the metaphor of "clothing" has specific resonance, for that is how ornament – style – was denominated in the pedagogy of rhetoric, in reference not only to literature but also to architecture. *Venustas*, "clothing," is what happens to a composition after it has been first invented and ordered. So to "convert" the *vestis* of the "Egyptians" means to mine not only (rhetorically) their treasury of moral common places but also their style.

The other textual commonplace for this sort of cultural "conversion" is a passage in Deuteronomy 21, the law instructing Jews who capture gentile women whom they wish to marry to de-clothe and otherwise de-culture them before reclothing them as Jews and thus as proper bed-fellows:

> And [if thou] seest among the captives a beautiful woman, and hast a desire unto her, that thou wouldst have her to thy wife; Then thou shalt bring her home to thine house; and she shall shave her head, and pare her nails; And she shall put the raiment of her captivity from off her, and shall remain in thine house and bewail her father and her mother a full month: and after that thou shalt go in unto her, and be her husband, and she shall be thy wife.[28]

The gentile-captive trope is invoked by Hrabanus Maurus in the ninth century, when he gives his program "of education for clerics" (*De clericorum institutione*). What is particularly interesting is that Hrabanus attaches it to how Christian students may ethically use the "flowers of eloquence," the tropes and figures of pagan rhetoric. In a brief discussion of grammar, defined as "the knowledge of understanding the poets and story-tellers" – a discipline that devoted itself, among other things, to pointing out and grammatically analyzing the "difficult" figures and schemes of Scripture (and indeed much of Hrabanus' teaching is a brief digest of Bede's treatise on the schemes and tropes of Scripture) Hrabanus says that:

> If we wish to read the poems and books of the gentiles [= the pagans] on account of the flower of their eloquence, we should hold fast to the [story] outline of the captured woman described in Deuteronomy: for it recounts that the Lord commanded that if an Israelite wished to have her as a wife, he should make her bald, cut her nails, remove her hairs, and when she was completely clean and naked, then he might embrace her as a wife. If we understand this

literally, isn't it ridiculous? And thus we do ... when we read the gentile poets ... whatever in them we find useful, we convert to our teaching; however whatever superfluous matter we find about idols, or sex, or worldly preoccupations, this thing we should scrape away; these, having been shaved, we should draw a line through; this we should cut out with a very sharp knife.[29]

This is a very odd commentary, because it comes to exactly the opposite meaning from that which the words have in Deuteronomy (that is why Hrabanus calls the Deuteronomy verses "literally ... ridiculous"). The foreign clothes which distinguish the gentile captive (and of which she must be cleansed) would seem logically to attach as a metaphor to the "flowers of eloquence," the "clothing," of pagan poetry. But these ornaments are exactly what Hrabanus wants to save.

So he invokes the device of the mind as a parchment upon which one is writing, in this case copying out the texts of the "gentile" poets. As we read them, we should correct them as a scribe corrects his mistakes, by scraping, excising, and striking out. Via a set of punning associations – on erasure as scraping a parchment "bald," on hair-plucking (parchments have hair- and skin-sides), on the idiom of punctuating *ad unguem* (literally, "to the toenail"), meaning to mark up a text with precision for reading and memory work – Hrabanus "gathers in" the situation of reading a pagan book to the otherwise "ridiculous" parallel with how to deracinate and make Jewish a Canaanite captive one fancies for her beautiful appearance. Only because the *flores eloquentiae* can be coverted, exfoliated independently and translated from pagan contexts to Christian good can the gentile captive be cleansed, erased, scraped, and, pared of her wrongful ideas, fashioned into a suitable wife.

So, although he is evidently concerned with the moral perils of reading Virgil and Ovid and Horace, Hrabanus assumes that they must be studied not for their content but for their "flos eloquentiae," their style or clothing, the *vestis* of the Egyptians which Augustine had shown how to convert. The "nakedness" of the properly expurgated texts (the pagan *mulieres* made *mundae* or "clean") reduces them, it would seem, not to their content, but to their style alone, their "raiment," the flowers of their eloquence without the ideas that made them dangerous.

Thus, the ethical value of these pagan books lies almost entirely *in their ornamentation alone*. And the ornaments can only be "converted" by a procedure of rhetoric, working a set of tropes that serve as the sites for *Christian* invention, just as the schemes and tropes of the Bible do – only the ornaments derived from pagan poetry are completely freed and dilated from their original contexts and shape. This kind of reading is, of course, what is also now called "allegorization," but I stress that it is fundamentally a procedure of rhetorical invention. The tropes gain their value solely from being able to be "copiously" converted. Before it became an exegetical method, *allegoria* after all was classified as a stylistic ornament of "obscurity" and indirection.

The point I wish to make is not that a scholar like Hrabanus was a religiously fanatical mis-reader of classical texts (and of the Bible, for that matter). It is rather that this comment of his shows clearly the extraordinary moral and inventive power that he awarded to ornamentation, even in otherwise dangerously immoral works. Hrabanus could simply have counseled outright that such works should not be studied. That he did not, and that generations of monastic readers before and after him did not either, indicates that they invested stylistic ornamentation with great ethical power during the act of meditative reading, power that came in the first instance not from some putative "meaning" in these texts – remember that their *ornament* is what makes them worthwhile – but from the games of ingenious meditation they encouraged, indeed required, of Christians. Reading the pagan poets was clearly regarded as especially stimulating ethical and cognitive exercise; the pitfalls were fearful but the rewards exhilarating.

The virtue of the "obscure" rhetorical ornaments is a fundamental aesthetic principle for Augustine. He speaks in *The City of God* of how the world order (*ordo saeculorum*) itself incorporates the trope of *antithesis*: "a rhetoric not of words, but of events," as though God intended it should be adorned and laid out with the most elegant of rhetorical figures, "like a most beautiful poem."[30]

And in his discussion of how to teach Christianity (*De doctrina christiana*), Augustine pauses memorably over the difficult simile in the Song of Songs 4:2: "thy teeth are as flocks of sheep." Augustine praises this Scriptural *allegoria* on the grounds of aesthetic *pleasure*: "I contemplate the saints more delightfully when I see them as the church's teeth ... I recognize them most amusingly as shorn sheep."[31] Part of the pleasure surely lies in the initial surprise one may feel at such an absurdity (saints as grazing sheep). Notice, even more basically, that the vehicles for this aesthetic pleasure are mentally picturing the reading ("I see") and memory ("I recognize"). Delight leads on to contemplation, but that initial amusing absurdity, engaging mental sight and recollection, puts his mind in play. Recall how Romuald of Camaldoli, seeking to shock a bored and wayward mind back "on track," also used an absurdity, imagining oneself as a terrified, cowering chick.

4. *ENARGEIA*: PAINTING IN THE MIND

A major symptom of "decadent" late-classical style, in the judgment of some historians, is its abundant use of *enargeia*, or vivid, sensuous word-painting. This ornament can either be found as a textual set-piece and "site" for mental painting, such as a description of a work of art or architecture, imagined or actual (*ekphrasis*), or it can be a quality of the language used to describe vivid action, to give vividness to fictive speeches (*prosopopeia*), or for the word-portrait of a person, actual or imaginary (*ethopoeia*).[32] Though it is not the only ornament to do so, *enargeia* contributes greatly to the "picture-making" of literature, and it was taught in the composition exercises in Roman and Byzantine rhetorical pedagogy called the *progymnasmata*, which every student practiced assiduously.[33]

Many seeming faults of style, Quintilian says, can be made into ornaments when deliberately used for an effect like laughter or understatement, emphasis or irony. But one fault is always unredeemable, and that is monotony, "a style which has no variety to relieve its tedium, and which presents a uniform color; this is one of the surest signs of lack of art, and produces a uniquely unpleasing effect ... on account of its sameness of thought, the uniformity of its figures, and the monotony of its structure."[34] In a composition without ornament, the mind is without landmarks.

For Quintilian *enargeia* seems the basic ornament, the ornament that subsumes most of the others. "[W]e must place among ornaments that *enargeia* which I mentioned [in Book IV.ii.63] ... [f]or oratory fails of its full effect ... if its appeal is merely to the hearing and ... not displayed to the eyes of the mind" (VIII.iii.61–2). And he counsels, as he did earlier (in IV.ii.63), that an orator should learn to construct "rerum imago quodammodo verbis depingitur," "an image of the matters which is, in a way, painted by the words."[35]

He then praises Cicero (the master) for his ability in this department, and quotes from the orations *Against Verres*: "There on the shore in his sandals stood the praetor of the Roman people, in his fancy purple cloak, his underwear down around his ankles, hanging onto his bimbo of a girlfriend."[36]

> Is there anybody [Quintilian remarks] so incapable of forming a mental picture of a scene that ... he does not seem not merely to see the actors ... the place itself and their very dress, but even to imagine to himself other details that the orator does not describe? ... For my own part, I seem to see before my eyes his face, his eyes, the unseemly blandishments of himself and his paramour, the silent loathing and frightened shame of those who viewed the scene.[37]

And for *my* own part, I seem to see Congressman Wilbur Mills of Arkansas, Chairman of the House Ways and Means Committee, emerging from the Reflecting Pool in Washington with Fanny Fox, the Argentine Firecracker. You, depending on your age and background, will doubtless see some other couple altogether. What matters is not whom we raise up before our minds' eyes, but the gist (contempt, in this case) which our images convey.

Quintilian expected that readers normally tried to "see" what they read, that seeing or listening to language could – and should – involve some procedures of mental imaging. And indeed many moderns, when they can participate in that now-rare activity, reading aloud, will make some sorts of mental images as they listen to the reading. Quintilian, addressing a society where reading aloud was commonplace, says that it behoves an orator to tap into this normal human response by providing pictures painted (as it were) with his words, in order to "thrust [his work] upon our notice" and make us raise up a picture in our minds.[38] A primary use of ornament even in Roman rhetoric, in short, is to slow us down, make us concentrate, set up moments of meditation – and so help us to think and remember.

Quintilian says approvingly that "the more remote a simile is from the subject to which it is applied, the greater will be the impression of novelty and the unexpected which it produces."[39] The cognitive value of surprise and novelty applies particularly to memory, for we remember best what is unusual and so catches our attention. So the "arresting" simile serves as an inventory marker, a heuristic for our recollection. The reader is slowed down, the auditor is required to notice – and then encouraged to make a "picture" in his mind.

Like Augustine after him, Quintilian also supposed that a mental picture would vary in its specifics from one individual to another (indeed how could it be otherwise?). *"Ego certe mihi cernere videor* [for my own part, I seem to see]," he writes: the emphasis on the individual nature of the "seeing" couldn't be clearer. Notice moreover that he assumes each person's mental "picture" will likely contain details that are not even in the author's words: an audience member seems to see "not merely the actors in the scene ... but even to imagine to himself other details that the orator does not describe."[40] The emphasis is not on faithfully "illustrating" the words, as we might demand, but on making some "picture" in order to feel, to remember, and thus to know. Reading, one must conclude, must have been, ideally, as deliberative and inventive a process in Roman culture as it became in monastic, and the making of mental pictures, far from being thought childish or an unnecessary frill, was clearly thought to be essential to cognition, to our ability to take in and indeed to work with any conceptual material. And here again we can detect a fundamental assumption that language-produced and sense-produced memory is cognitively the same thing, made in the same way.

Enargeia addresses not just the eyes, but all the senses. It is easy to forget this when we read rhetoric texts, because the emphasis is so much on the visual sense. But the visual leads on to and is accompanied by an engagement of all the other senses in a meticulously crafted fiction. The emotionally affective meditational recollection that we encounter in Anselm and in Peter of Celle – the close connection of "affliction" to "reading" – has some of its antecedents in Roman rhetoric. The procedure is recognizably similar to one which Quintilian (and Cicero before him) recommended to an orator preparing for court:

> the first essential is that those feelings should prevail with us that we wish to prevail with the judge, and that we should be moved ourselves before we attempt to move others. But how are we to generate these emotions in ourselves? ... There are phenomena which the Greeks call "phantasias" and we Romans judiciously call "visiones," by means of which the images of absent things [imagines rerum absentium] are shown to our mind with such vividness that they seem to be before our very eyes. ... it is a power that all may readily acquire if they will. When the mind is unoccupied or is absorbed by fantastic hopes or daydreams, we are haunted by these visions of which I am speaking to such an extent that we imagine we are travelling abroad, crossing the sea, fighting, addressing people ... and seem to ourselves to be not dreaming but acting. Surely it is

132

possible to turn this mental power to some use. Suppose I am presenting the case that a person has been murdered. Shall I not bring before my eyes all the circumstances which it is reasonable to imagine must have occurred on this occasion? Do I not see the murderer suddenly spring out? his victim tremble, cry for mercy or help, or try to flee? Do I not see the fatal blow, and the stricken body fall? Will not her blood, her pallor, her final groan, and her death-rattle be impressed indelibly in my mind? In such a way arises that *enargeia*, which Cicero translated as "illustratio" and "evidentia," and which makes us seem not so much to talk about what we have seen as actually to show it, while our emotions are as actively engaged as if we were present at the events themselves [rebus ipsis].[41]

What Quintilian describes is a rhetorical use of images to persuade. But before persuading the judges of the court, one must first persuade oneself by means of these *visiones*, consciously crafted images designed to generate specific emotions *in oneself*. Notice how Quintilian uses *visiones* as a Latin equivalent for Greek *phantasias*, the images which our imagination (or fantasy) consciously crafts to generate both the "way" and the emotions necessary for effective recollective and cognitive work, to rouse up and channel them, giving them both movement and direction (fearful, vexed, saddened, amused) – the elements of *ductus* within a work.

5. "PAINT IN YOUR HEART": THE HEAVENLY CITY AS EKPHRASIS

In fourth-century Christian Scriptural exegesis, *enargeia* was recognized (though not specifically called this). For example, in his commentary on Ezekiel, Jerome spoke of painting in our hearts the images that the text caused us to see. Clearly this idiom, *(de)pingere in corde nostro*, derived from the common rhetorical trope of *enargeia* and its emphasis upon experiencing, "seeing" what one is reading. Painting *in corde*, of course, is the emotionally engaged work of making memory images.[42]

As Jerome comments on Ezekiel, he treats the various temple descriptions (both that in chapter 8 and those of the glorified City in chapters 40–43) as a sort of *ekphrasis*. The various details are moralized and spiritualized on the basis of an internal picture which the words paint in our mind. We have an internal temple and tabernacle, says Jerome, and because all the things in Ezekiel are shown to us and to the prophet in a sort of image and picture, we can paint them in our own hearts and minds.[43] For example, commenting on the verse describing the Egyptian gods painted on the exterior walls of the temple (Ezekiel 8:10), Jerome counsels that "we also may display idols painted on the walls in our [interior] temple, when we submit to all vices and we paint in our hearts the consciousness and various imaginings of sins. ... For indeed there is no human being who does not have some image, whether of sanctity or of sin."[44] To be sure, this is a caution against mental painting for immoral purposes, but the vividness of mental picturing is, you will notice, taken for granted by Jerome's remark. More important, so is the assumption that reading will raise pictures in the mind's eye. The examples Jerome gives of human qualities, good and bad, that are so "imaged" include such figurative speech as "generation of vipers" and "don't be like a horse or a mule, lacking intelligence" – all examples of *enargeia*, words that paint our thoughts.

In several of the fourth-century texts, "painting in the heart" is associated with making "a temple of the heart." In sermons, Augustine associates the two. Preaching on Jesus' command to "make friends of the mammon of inquity" (Luke 16:9), Augustine rejects a particularly facile, Robin Hood-style justification of robbery which had been offered for this paradoxical text, and says to his congregation, "Do not paint [pingere] God to yourself in such a way, do not gather such an idol into the temple of your heart."[45] And commenting on a verbal image used in Psalm 74:8, "in the hand of the Lord there is a cup," Augustine says, speaking to those in the congregation who are learned, that "you should not paint for yourselves in your heart God circumscribed in human form, in case you raise up likenesses in your heart of an enclosed temple."[46] In this sermon (though not everywhere in his writings, as we have seen) Augustine treated mental painting somewhat gingerly, as something only experienced Christians should do.

It is important to consider Augustine's audience in weighing these remarks. He was concerned, as many fourth-century Christians were, about memories of the anthropomorphized pagan gods, the world of statues, paintings, and mosaics in which Romans lived at that time, and his strictures reflect this. But he was concerned about a particularly literal-minded, worldly, and vivid kind of mental painting. His comments in *De trinitate* on the human need for cognitive images make clear that while he may have regretted the fact, he did not deny that humans need to see and feel in order to think. The vivid quality of his own language, its *enargeia*, is demonstration of that.

One final example of the idiom I have been discussing puts mental painting in a fully positive light (though, you remember, Jerome spoke of painting images both of sanctity and of sin in one's heart). In the middle of the fifth century, the monk Arnobius, commenting in an apocalyptic vein on Psalm 98, prays for the Lord to come. As he invites his audience to contemplate the Lord's coming, he asks them to paint before their eyes the lineaments of the heavenly Jerusalem:

> Paint, paint before your eyes the various fabricated things, whenever you chant of these [while reciting the verses of the psalm]. Of what sort? Those which were seen with wonder by the apostles [chiefly John]; paint the temples, paint the baths, paint the forums and the ramparts rising on the high summit. And while you consider these, remember some little hut woven out of an enclosure of boughs. This will not be more contemptible to you than you will be confounded at these marvels.[47]

Like Jerome, Arnobius considers John's description of the Heavenly City as an instance of ekphrasis, greatly expanded (and conflated with Ezekiel's mountain citadel) in the contemplative "painting" of his mind and memory. He invites his audience to *fabricate* it in their minds as they chant the textual description, including items (like bath-houses) which are in neither John nor Ezekiel. And using the trope of antithesis, he contrasts these heavenly urban splendors to those of the earthly imperial city, alluding "briefly" to a well-known Virgilian moment of remembered Edenic pastoral, when, in the First Eclogue, the shepherd Meliboeus fears he will never again "see" his woven hut, and asks Tityrus, his comrade, to recount the occasion of his "seeing" the great city, Rome. Such an allusion can only work for an audience accustomed to paying attention to *enargeia*, the invitations in a text which ask a reader to "see" what he reads.

6. AN EXCURSUS ON LEARNING TO VISUALIZE: PRUDENTIUS' *DITTOCHEON* AND OTHER PICTURE VERSES

Because my study focusses on the meditative, inventive remembering of texts and images, I have not stressed the pedagogical functions of many of these same images and texts. Yet one cannot really talk about

135

the one without the other. Meditation was an essential part of learning and of teaching; the purpose of meditation is both to memorize and to "loosen up and expand" what one has memorized. The two meanings of the word "invent" are nowhere more closely related than in this one mental act. All education teaches students how to think, the "ways" of thinking and the "mental habits" that were called, well into the seventeenth century, the *formae mentis*, designs and devices of the mind, first cousins to *machinae mentis*.

The importance given in basic ancient and medieval education to memorizing texts has long been recognized by historians. As Henri Marrou once wrote, "[a] classical culture defines itself by a collection of master-works, the recognized foundation of its structure of values."[48] "Recognized" is a key adjective in this characterization. These works form the "common places" of thought and of moral judgment in later life, and the assumption that a child should memorize at least long passages from them carefully, a verse or two at a time, and lay them away diligently and securely in his memory with the aid of various mnemonic *rationes* or dispositive schemes, can be found from the earliest descriptions we have of ancient education. The practice did not alter in the Middle Ages. For whatever the changes in curriculum, in learning to read Latin the elementary procedure was to build up from the shortest units (letters and syllables) to longer and yet longer ones: words, and phrases, and then sentences.

This pedagogy had at least two consequences that are strange to modern concepts of language learning. First, the tendency throughout the Middle Ages is to see words in the first instance as single letters variously combined in syllables, rather than to "comprehend" them at once as semantic units (the way I think most moderns are taught to). Words are thus understood to be *constructions made up* out of syllables, not simplexes of meaning. The manner in which ancient texts were written out, without word divisions, reinforces this mental habit, for a reader had to analyze the syllables first before they could be "glued" together in semantic units. There is a well-known poem by the fifth-century Christian poet Optatianus Porfirius (much admired by some Carolingian writers), which plays upon this ability, for if its syllables are analyzed in one way it makes a poem in Latin, but if analyzed differently it makes a poem in Greek![49]

The letters are visual shapes that cue sounds. Every word is thus analyzed in the first instance as a sensory pattern of simpler units, visual and aural, that do not in themselves have conceptual meaning. Meaningful signs result from a "play" of non-semantic units, in a way akin to graphic design or musical design made up of tone and pitch and length. The elementary pedagogy of Latin pre-disposed anyone who underwent it to first recognize letters in patterns of syllables, made out of one of the five vowels and one, two, or three consonant sounds. The tolerance, at times even vogue, in these cultures for "shaped verse," like that of Optatianus, is instructive again. As William Levitan writes of Optatianus' verses (in the literary genre also called *technopaegnia*), "in none of the lines does the wit depend on the reference of its words. . . . writing no longer functions primarily as the record of speech but as the medium of a[n] . . . artifact."[50] Not everyone who learned Latin (including Optatianus) was thereby rendered incapable of assigning references to words, of course: that is not my point. It is rather that discerning and then building up meaningful patterns from sub-semantic elements of language, which were considered to have at the same time equally visual and oral resonance, was an elementary habit of mind that could always be invoked among those who had experienced this education.

A second consequence of this basic pedagogy is the tendency to view knowledge less as a "language" in our sense of that word, whose rational units are semantically whole and only referential or "conceptual" in function, and more as involving recombinant sets of design elements, whose units are sub-semantic "signs" of all sorts that *make* meanings (rather than necessarily "having" them) in constantly varying combinations with other "signs." It encourages that ability to manipulate and calculate with letters which makes a few people even now extremely good at acrostics and anagrams. A good many of the first words which schoolchildren had to memorize for drills were not "real" words in our sense at all: they were either wholly made-up or extremely rare (this was done in order to include rarely used letters like *x*). And these letters and syllables were practiced in variations that ran the gamut of possibilities, whether or not one was apt to encounter them in "real life" (that is, in our terms, whether or not they had the status of "facts").

The result must have been to give earliest education the aspect of a calculational game, in which pattern recognition was a key to success. Such calculative facility depends on a well-stocked memory "disposed" in patterns that allow one readily to "see where to put" new material, associating it with matters already "in place."[51]

Memorizing gave children an education in the elements of graphic design of an internal, mental sort. These amounted to locational techniques of division and recombination for "disposing" material in memory for cognitive purposes. The visual forms of letters were a sort of graphic devising scheme, elements for "picturing" reading; they were not just transparent signs pointing to sounds. This is clear from Quintilian's advice (given also, over a thousand years later, by Hugh of St. Victor) that students should always memorize texts from the same papyrus or codex, lest the overlapping images of the same written texts in different books muddle and confuse their memory.[52]

Cassiodorus seems to have drawn diagrams and other pedagogical pictures for some of his books.[53] This practice was a recognized accompaniment to reading, especially to devising otherwise structure-less "information." But such visual aids are not the most commonly "seen" features of what became monastic pedagogy. The importance given to learning to visualize as one read (silently or aloud) is emphasized by the fact that several standard medieval elementary readers are also books of pictures: the Bestiary, the *Aratus* or book of constellations, and number of narrative "picturing books," including Prudentius's quatrain-length plot summaries of stories from the Bible, collectively called *Dittocheon*.

Like the Bestiary, *Dittocheon* had an extremely long life as an early reading book, and an equally long life as an iconographical source of key narrative episodes of the Old and New Testaments in figural relationship to one another. Readers are asked to "look" and to "see" as each episode is epitomized in a simple, often single, image. Here is an example:

> Covered with tombs, the field Aceldama, sold for the price of an unspeakable crime, receives bodies for burial. Here is the price of Christ's blood. In the distance [eminus], Judas, despairing for his great sin, squeezes his neck tightly in a noose.[54]

This location is treated by Prudentius like a memory place, whether or not his verses initially described some actual painting. First we see the field, covered with tombs above ground, in the Roman manner. Its Hebrew name means "field of blood" (Matthew 27:5; Acts 1:19); this etymology (which a student has to supply from his own textual knowledge, or a teacher give him in commentary) recalls Judas' blood money for betraying Jesus. Then, following the poet's invitation in these lines to look over the scene, one views in the distance (that of "a spear's throw" rather than that of hand-to-hand combat) the figure of Judas hanging.[55] Finally, in order to see the detail of his neck compressed in the noose, the language brings the image to our eyes from a distance to close-up. Such telescoping of one's viewpoint can easily be done mentally, but it is difficult to accomplish physically (especially if, as is usually assumed, these quatrains described scenes painted "afar," on a church wall).

The point I wish to stress is that even if these stanzas were first written as a description of material images, Prudentius treats them (as, obviously, did the generations after him) as prescriptions for mental visualization, using the device of rhetorical *enargeia*. He makes them mnemotechnically effective rememberings *summatim* of the chief events of the Bible. So effective were they, in fact, that these forty-nine scenes offered standard iconographical tropes for church decoration throughout the Middle Ages.[56]

But *Dittocheon* was also (a fact less well known) a common elementary reader, in use throughout the Middle Ages.[57] The question arises why this should be so, especially since no images accompanied the reading. There were other texts ("Cato"'s distychs, for instance) whose Latin was equally simple and edifying. What *Dittocheon* does is to present the Bible stories in language that is highly visualizable as a series of epitomized tableaux. It not only summarizes content, it trains a habit of mind. A reader moves from one carefully visualized scene in its "place" to the next, as though from picture to picture, through the separate quatrains that make up the whole poem. Each scene has at least one image given the stylistic quality known as *enargeia*, vivid visual and indeed synaesthetic description that paints it before the *mind's* senses. The name *Dittocheon* means "double nourishment," providing a feast for meditation by the remembering, sensory mind, of the sort we have been analyzing.

Medieval pedagogical literature of this type also sometimes explicitly gave locational and descriptive directions for mental painting – "place," "paint," "make," and the like. A good example is the Bestiary, which in its medieval lifetime was not a natural-history book so much as a reading-and-memory book, providing some of the "common places," the foundational blocks, of inventional mnemonics.[58] The description of the creature is called *pictura*, and as one "paints" its picture mentally from the description in the words, maxims are attached to the features of the image.[59] Thus each complete *pictura* in the Bestiary provides the organization of the moral themes – their *forma* or *ratio*, to use two other technical words that are synonymous in the practical context of memory work.[60] So the Bestiary, in addition to being a compendium of moralized content, also teaches a particular cognitive, inventive technique, which (as medievalists will recognize) is one of the commonest ways in the Middle Ages of making a composition.

Other elementary verse "pictures," common in later manuscripts and associated particularly with schoolbooks, have been well described by Michael Curschmann.[61] These are the so-called *versus rapportati*, whose existence in manuscripts dates from the late eleventh century: there was a well-known example in the *Hortus deliciarum*. This figure is of particular interest because, while clearly designed for elementary pedagogy, it was also used as a trope of invention by learned adults, a heuristic design useful for meditation and sermon-making. This type of school figure, which is made up of both words and drawings, is not unlike the complex brain (and imagination) teasers of the antique poets and the Carolingian *carmina figurata*.

The *versus rapportati*, unlike the genres of complex word play at work in more sophisticated shaped verse, are specifically exercises: they provide elementary practice in cognitive pattern formation of the sort that these more sophisticated genres exploit. The drawings are of monsters, fashioned out of animal shapes. But the shapes, in turn, figure the constituent parts of the verses. Neither drawing nor verse can be isolated from the other: the shapes arise from the words, and vice versa.

Figure A shows two pictures, functioning rather like stanzas in poetry (that is, compositions of verses) made from these *versus rapportati*. The Latin text associated with the bird-like figure is

> Bos lepus ales equus homo serpens pavo leo grus
> pes caput os pectus manus ilia cauda juba crus.

Associated with the horned creature is the stanza

> Latrans vir cervus equus ales scorpio cattus
> Dente manu cornu pede pectore retro vel ungue
> Mordeo cedo peto trudo neco scindo.[62]

To read either of these "poems" and make any meaning from it, one must read each phrase vertically (*Bos–pes, lepus–caput, ales–os,* or *latrans dente mordeo* and *cervus cornu peto*). Notice that these

Fig. A Two monstrous figures composed of *versus rapportati*, from f. 255v of the twelfth-century *Hortus deliciarum*. After R. Green, *Hortus deliciarum*.

phrases are grammatically unrelated – they have no syntax – since all the subject-nouns are only given in the nominative singular, and yet the verbs, where they occur, are in the first person singular. The verses are meaningful only when one relates the phrases to the drawing. Since much has been written on them, I will not discuss them at length here. I will only point out that the way these verse figures require "division" of the whole into smaller parts, which must be combined or "composed" to make any sense-patterns from either the words or the images, exactly encapsulates the twin tasks of reading and memory work: *divisio* in order to absorb, and *compositio* in order to use what one has absorbed for further thinking. The verses demonstrate the technique of *divisio*, and the line drawings "made up" from them that of *compositio*.

As Curschmann says of them, the figures and poem are drawn as separate manuscript items, occupying page space unassociated with any particular context. They are "stored very much like a *tabula*, a school figure designed to initiate or structure discussion in various ... contexts; not to promulgate any particular lesson on its own."[63] The entire complex of words and drawing is called, by Gerhoch of Reichersberg (middle of the twelfth century), a *pictura*. He uses these figures as the structural form for an exegetical treatise on some of the Psalm texts.[64] For example, when Gerhoch explicates Psalm 37:4, particularly the phrase "the face of my sins [facies peccatorum]," he says that to be a sinner is to be like the beasts. Thus, the "face of sins" can be seen as a composite of animal shapes. Gerhoch will show this to his readers "in pictura," for "those things which we toil to express in words, will appear more clearly through looking at the following picture [subiecta pictura]."[65] Opposite this text in the manuscript are drawn the *versus rapportati* figures. However, as Curschmann demonstrates, these conventional figures are greatly expanded and rhetorically dilated in the course of the exegetical composition. So it would appear that the *subiecta pictura* to which Gerhoch refers is not just the line drawing of this manuscript but the whole composition which he makes, using that as a base.

I would modify the common understanding of the various diagrams and drawings and even, in some cases, the full illustrations that we find in monastic manuscripts. They are not just "aids" to understanding, as we would say, implying their subservient role to language and that they are in some basic way unnecessary to knowing. They are exercises and examples to be studied and remembered as much as are the words. Words and images *together* are two "ways" of the same mental activity – invention. In addition to acquiring a repertory of words – *dicta et facta memorabilia* – children also gathered into their memories a repertory of images.[66]

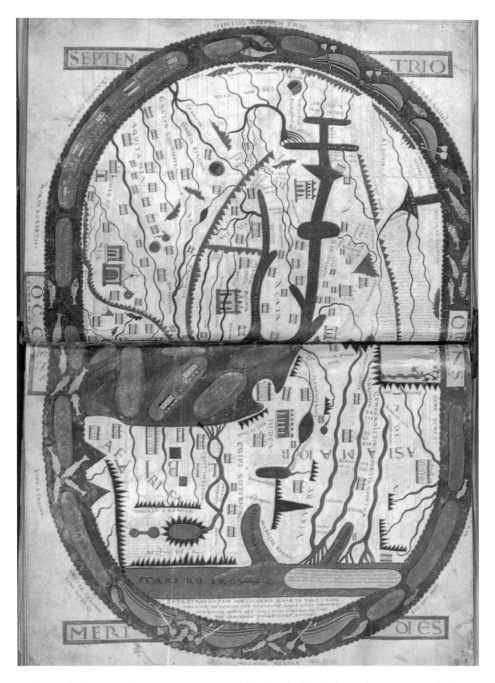

Plate 1: "Mappamundi," a schematic picture showing the hemisphere of Terra surrounded by Oceanus; from the Beatus of Saint-Sever. Made at the abbey of St.-Sever (Gascogne), third quarter of the eleventh century. Paris, Bibliothèque Nationale, MS lat. 8878, ff. 45v-46.

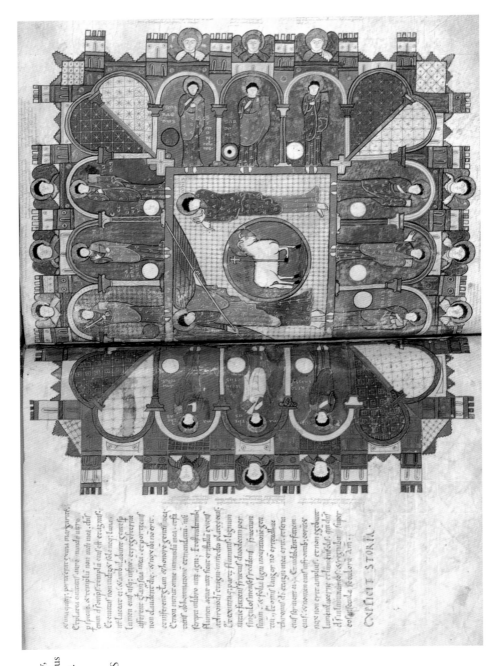

Plate 2: The Heavenly City, from the Beatus of Saint-Sever. Paris, Bibliothèque Nationale, MS lat. 8878, ff. 207v-208.

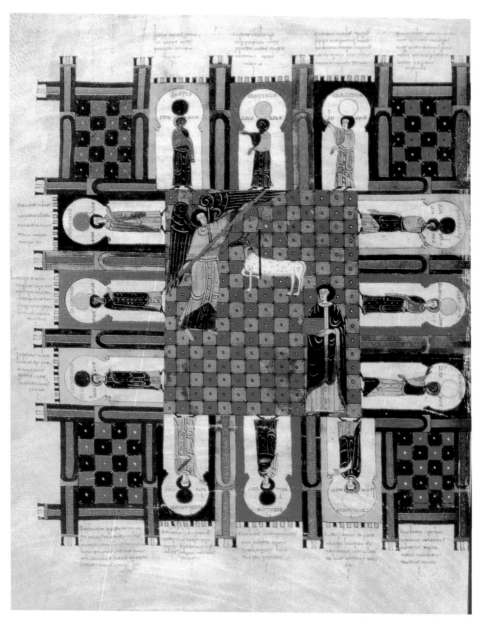

Plate 3: The Heavenly City, from the Facundus Beatus. Made in León (Spain), 1047.   Madrid, Biblioteca Nacional MS Vitrina 14-2, f. 253v.

Plate 4: The opening of the sixth seal of the Book of the Lamb, which caused a great earthquake and the stars to fall from heaven (Rev. 6:12-17). The Beatus of Saint-Sever; this page was painted by Stephanus Garsia, the master-illuminator of this manuscript.

Paris, Bibliothèque Nationale MS lat. 8878, f. 116.

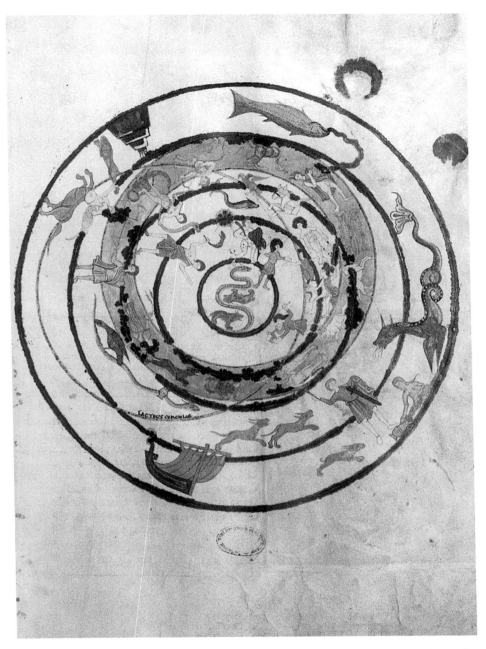

Plate 5: Aratus, *Phaenomena*: the heavenly circles and the constellations of the northern sky. At the centre are the two Bears and Draco. Made c.1000 by Abbot Odbert at Saint-Bertin (Pas de Calais). Boulogne-sur-Mer, Bibliothèque municipale, MS 188, f. 20.

Plate 6: Isidore of Seville, *De natura rerum*: constellations. Each constellation is drawn as a pattern of stars, with descriptive accompanying text. On these two pages appear Gemini, Cancer, Leo, "Agitator" (Auriga, the Charioteer), Taurus,

Ceppheur habet incapite ftellar fplendi
dar duar & indextera manu fplendidam
unam inutroq; humero una inzona trer
indextis latere extransuerfo super illi
um septem infiniftro genu duar infum
mitate pedum quattuor funt omner XXI hicautem infepten
trionir incissione conftituit inter medium septentrionalir cir
culi & eftiuali folftitio

Carropia habet incapite ftellam
fplendidam una Inutroq; humero
fplendidam una Indextra parte
pectorir fplendidam una Indextis
cubito una inutrifq; manibur fum
mitatem fplendidam una inumbilico
fplendidam & magnam unam infinif
tro femore duar ingenu fplendidam una & per fingulor angu
lor infummitatem ftellae una funt omner tridecim

Andromedae habet ftellam fplen
didam incapite una inutroq;
humero una Incubito dextro una
infiniftro una Insummitate manur
fplendidam unam inpedalium fum
mitate fplendidar duar in Zona
trer super zona quattuor Inuno
quoq; genu fplendidam unam indextro pede duar infinif
tro una funt omner uiginti & una

Equur quia & bellorum
fonr dicitur habet ftel
lar inroftro duar obfcu
rar incapite fplendidam una
inmaxillam unam inutrifq; auribur fplendidam unam in
ceruice quattuor inumero unae inpectore unae infpino unae
inumbilico una nitidam inutroque genu una per fingularan
gular anteriorer una funt omner decim & octo

Plate 7: "The Mill": capital in the south aisle of the basilica of Sainte Madeleine, Vézelay (Yonne); second quarter of the twelfth century.

Plate 8: A picture of "Prudentius," drawn just before the closing prayer of *Psychomachia*, the text of which begins on the next page. The text written on this page is lines 880-887: the legend in the margin reads "Prudentius gratias Deo agit," "Prudentius gives thanks to God." Cambridge, Corpus Christi College MS 23, f. 40; first half of the eleventh century, from Malmesbury Abbey.

Plate 9: The sixth angel pours out his bowl upon the river Euphrates (Rev. 16:12), from the
Morgan Beatus. Made by Maius, c. 940-945, in Spain, perhaps in Tábara.
New York, Pierpont Morgan Library MS M. 644, f. 190v.

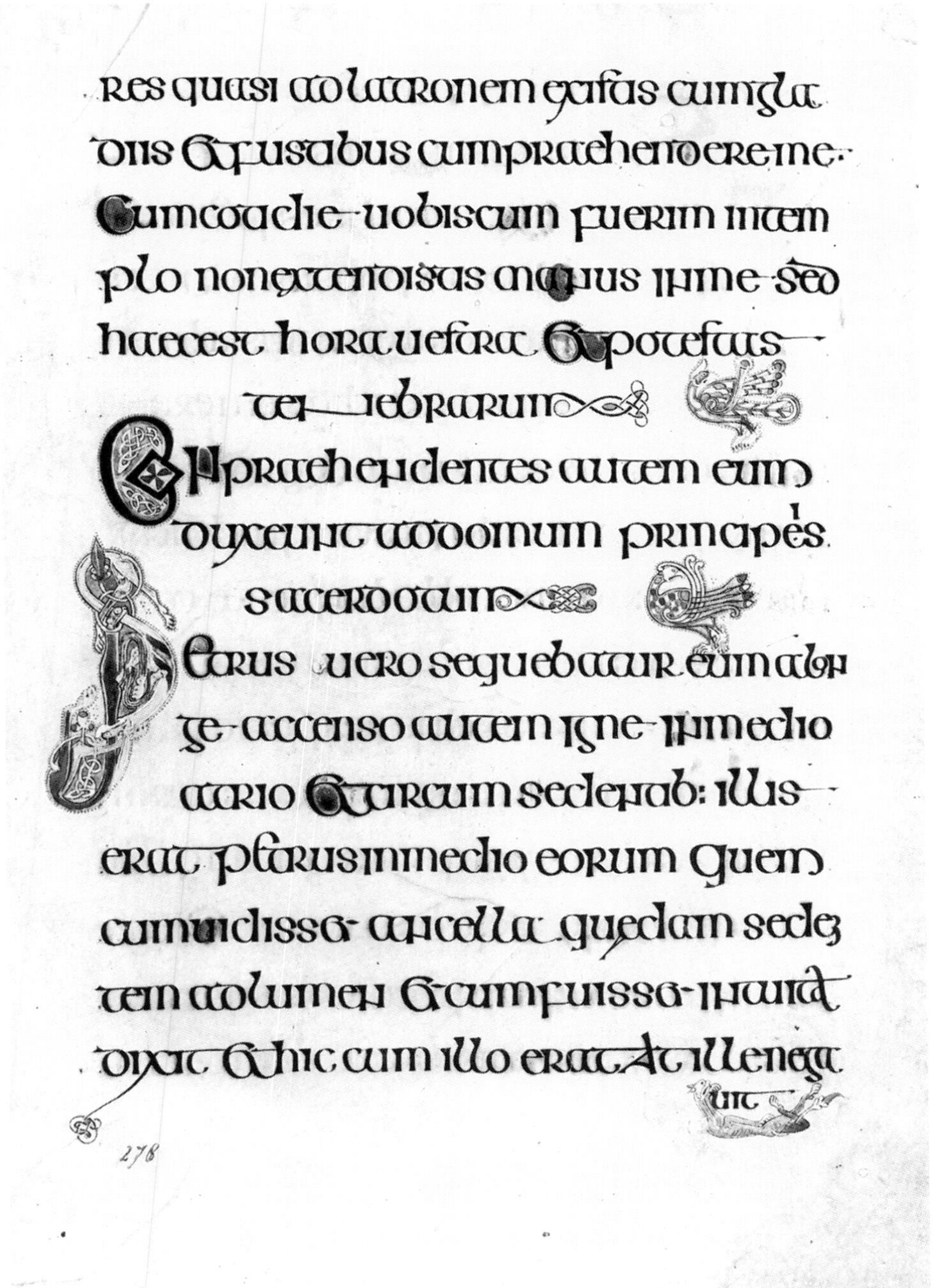

res quasi ad latronem exastis cumgla
diis & fustibus cumpraehendere me·
Cumcotidie uobiscum fuerim intem
plo nonextendistis manus inme· sed
haecest hora uestra. & potestas
uel iebrarum

Apraehendentes autem eum
duxerunt addomum principes.
sacerdotum

Petrus uero seguebatur eum alon
ge· accenso autem igne inmedio
atrio & circum sedentab: illis
erat petrus inmedio eorum quem
cumuidisset ancella quedam sede
tem adlumen & cumfuisset intuita
dixit & hic cum illo erat At illenega
uit

Plate 10: A punctuated page from the Book of Kells, an Insular Gospel book made in the ninth
century, probably in Northumberland. Dublin, Trinity College MS 58, f. 278.

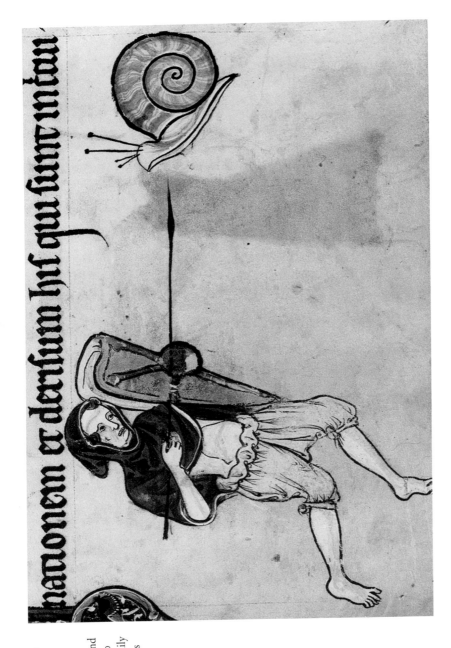

Plate 11: A limasson (snail) bording (sparring) with a knight in a lower border of the Rutland Psalter, made c.1260 for the de Lacy family in England, perhaps London.
London, British Library MS Add. 62925, f. 48.

Plate 12: A monster chews on severed limbs in a border of the Rutland Psalter. London, British Library MS Add. 62925, f. 83v.

Plate 13: A hunting dog (lymer) tracks a hidden rabbit in a border of the Rutland Psalter. London, British Library MS Add. 62925, f. 57v.

Plate 14: A chain of pretzel and biscuit breads surrounds the margin of a prayer; from the Hours of Catherine of Cleves, made in Burgundy in the 1430s. New York, Pierpont Morgan Library MS M. 917, p. 228.

Plate 15: Cubiculum M, in the Villa of Fannius Synestor, Boscoreale; Roman, 40-30 BC. The complete installation is modern, and neither the floor mosaic nor the couch and stool came from the same villa. New York, the Metropolitan Museum of Art, Rogers Fund, 1903 (03.14.13).

Plate 16: A cross-carpet page initiating the Gospel of Luke, from the Lindisfarne Gospels, made in the abbey of Lindisfarne, early ninth century. London, British Library MS Cotton Nero D.IV, f. 138v.

Plate 17: Wall painting, Panel II, in Cubiculum M from the Villa of Fannius Synestor, Boscoreale. New York, the Metropolitan Museum of Art, Rogers Fund, 1903 (03.14.13).

Plate 18: A picture of Hell, f. 255 of *Hortus deliciarum*, a meditational book made by the abbess, Herrad of Hohenbourg, twelfth century; from a nineteenth-century copy of the original book page, which is now destroyed. After R. Green, *Hortus deliciarum*.

Plate 19: Hell and Hell's Mouth, from the Arroyo Beatus, made in the region of Burgos, first half of the thirteenth century. Paris, Bibliothèque Nationale MS nouv. acq. lat. 2290, f. 160.

Plate 20: Theodulph's church at Germigny-des-Prés (Loire): mosaic of the Ark of the Covenant together with two guardian cherubim. Made in the early ninth century by Italian craftsmen.

Plate 21: Gunzo in his dream (notice his open eyes) sees Saints Peter, Paul, and Stephen with builders' lines measuring the plan of the new church at Cluny. Paris, Bibliothèque Nationale MS lat.17716, f. 43. Detail of a manuscript made c. 1180.

Plate 22: "The mandala of Jnanadakini." Opaque watercolor on cloth, late fifteenth century, Tibet (School of the Ngor Monastery). New York, the Metropolitan Museum of Art. Purchase, Lita Annenberg Hazen Charitable Trust Gift, 1987 (1987.16).

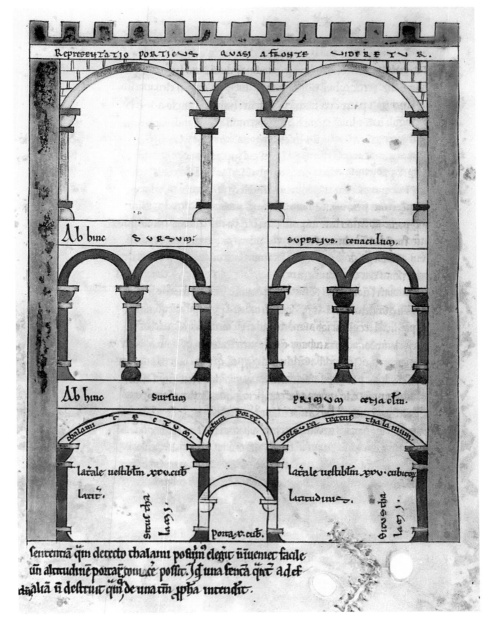

Plate 23: The elevation of the eastern gate to the Temple Citadel of Ezekiel's vision, made for Richard of St. Victor's commentary on Ezekiel. The title of the picture is "Representatio porticus quasi a fronte videretur." English, c. 1160-1175. Oxford, Bodleian Library MS Bodley 494, f. 155v.

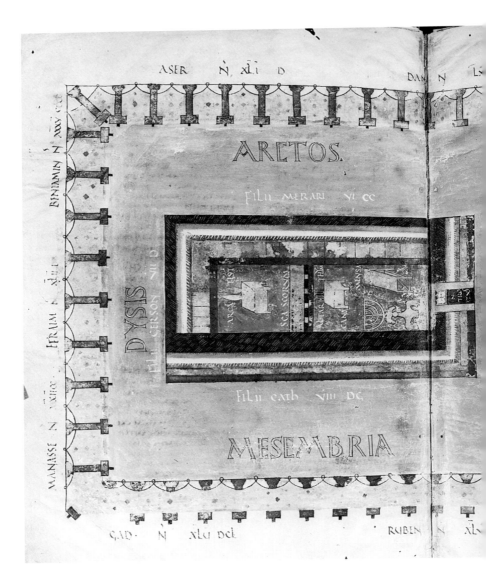

Plate 24: A picture of the Tabernacle, from the Codex Amiatinus, made in England at the monastery of Jarrow, c. 715. Florence, Biblioteca Medicea Laurenziana MS Amiatinus 1, ff. IIv-III.

NEPTHALIM·N ·L̄III·CCC·

ISSACHAR·N·L̄IIII·CCC·

IUDAS·N·LXXIIII·DC

RUBEN·N·L̄VI·CCC

ANATOL

MOSES

ALTARE
HOLOCAVSTI

LABRVM

ZABULON·N·L̄VII·CCC

SIMEON·N·L̄IIII·CC

Plate 25: Part of the ambulatory and two apsidal "rooms" in the church of the Cistercian abbey at Pontigny (Yonne). This section was rebuilt by the monks in the 1180s.

Plate 26: The western portion of the south aisle at Pontigny, constructed in the 1140s.

Plate 27: The ambulatory of Suger's rebuilt apse (c. 1140) at St.-Denis.

Plate 28: The trumeau, Ste.-Marie, Souillac (Lot); middle of the twelfth century.

Plate 29: The western wall of the church porch of the Cluniac abbey of Moissac (Tarn-et-Garonne), showing the story of Dives and Lazarus in the two upper rows of panels, and in the lower, the punishments of Avarice (to the left) and of Luxury (to the right); carved c. 1115-1130.

Plate 30: Noah building the Ark, from the Huntingfield Psalter, a manuscript made in England (perhaps Oxford) c. 1210-1220. New York, Pierpont Morgan Library MS M. 43, f. 8v.

Plate 31: The eastern cloister gallery of the Cistercian monastery of Fontenay (Côte d'Or).

Plate 32: The church of the Cistercian abbey of Pontigny, from the south-east.

Prudentius was one of the first Christian poets, writing at the end of the fourth century; the collection of his poems, with his author's preface, is dated about 405. He was a Roman provincial, like so many early Christian authors, living and working his entire life in Spain.[67] Composed in dactylic hexameters, the traditional meter of epic, *Psychomachia* ("soul-struggle") figures the virtues and vices as warriors, paired in hand-to-hand combat. The virtues are of course victorious, and celebrate their conquest by constructing a great victory Temple, described at length. There is also a verse preamble to the epic, retelling the story in Genesis 14 of Abraham's battle against the heathen kings who imprisoned his nephew, Lot. And there is a concluding prayer which summarizes the work's gist as our soul's constant struggle against its own inner vices, until "building the golden courts of his temple, [Christ], in regard of its moral virtues, crafts ornaments for the soul, delighting in which rich Wisdom may reign forever on her ornate throne."[68] Notice how important ornament and decoration are in this passage, as tokens and products, the "furniture" as it were, of ethical actions.

Psychomachia spawned a huge progeny of moral allegory and picture-making.[69] Remembered *ad res* most frequently, the images of warrior virtues and vices remained a fruitful part of confessional matter throughout the Middle Ages; they crop up in every art form. Having learned at least *summatim* the story of *Psychomachia*, a student had a readily available, heuristically secure scheme that could be used to "re-view" one's own deeds in the structured way necessary for effective penitence, the most vital of all the tasks of remembering.

Prudentius has gotten bad reviews since the nineteenth century. The opinion of H. J. Rose is typical: "Prudentius is often disgusting ... morbid ... puerile and always tedious."[70] Indeed.

Here is a characteristically disgusting, morbid example, quoted from the description of the death of Luxuria at the hands of Sobrietas. Luxuria, "making her drunken way to the war" in a chariot (line 320) is challenged by Sobrietas, who frightens the chariot horses by thrusting a wooden Cross in their faces. They shy in panic, and Luxuria, their driver, is thrown from the chariot and "falls forward under the axle and her mangled body is the brake that slows the chariot down" (lines 415–416). Sobriety hurls a rock at Luxuria:

143

chance drives the stone to smash the breath-passage in the midst of the face and beat the lips into the arched mouth. The teeth within are loosened, the throat cut, and the mangled tongue fills [the mouth] with bloody fragments. Her gorge rises at the strange meal; gulping down the pulped bones she spews up again the lumps she swallowed. "Drink up now your own blood, after your many cups," says the indignant virgin [Sobriety].[71]

Before a work can acquire meaning, before a mind can act on it, it must be made memorable, since memory provides the matter with which human intellect most directly works. As we have seen, this is a fundamental assumption of memorial cultures. If one thinks of the ornaments of a work as mnemonic hooks, as its inventorying heuristics, one will quickly understand that ornaments need minimally to satisfy the requirements of memorability.

In other words, Prudentius' *Psychomachia* is designedly disgusting and morbid because it is those qualities that make it memorable, particularly for the novice, schoolboy minds for which it was written. That, at least, was the assumption in ancient pedagogy. When the novice John Cassian, you recall, had trouble forgetting the epic stories which his *pedagogus* instilled in him as a child, he remembered most powerfully *exactly* the disgusting and bloody parts – the "images of warring heroes" that turned unbidden before his mental eye as he prayed the liturgy or tried to meditate on his psalms.[72]

From the start of its preamble, *Psychomachia* functions as a mnemonic gathering place, a "common place" into which a number of stories are collated. Recollection works through associational chains; the formation of these is a core technique of Prudentius' story-telling. The starting-point, or principle, in the preamble chain is the name Abraham. This name is specially marked by an ornament, etymology, as it also is in Genesis, for it was lengthened by a syllable from the earlier name Abram.[73] This is a meaningless detail to us, but Roman students, who learned to read by syllables, would have paid it full attention.

The name "Abraham" is then treated as a gathering site for a network of stories linked to him, those of Isaac, Lot, Sarah, and the visit of the three angels. But this poem will select the story of Lot, rescued by Abraham from "hard bondage under the barbarians," the kings of Sodom and Gomorrah. In this story, Abraham teaches us "to war against the ungodly tribes ... until the spirit, battling valorously, has overcome with great slaughter the monsters in the enslaved heart."[74]

The remainder of the preamble provides an epitome (which is an ornament of contraction) of Genesis 14:14–18, wherein Abram hears of Lot's capture, arms his servants, rescues Lot and scatters the barbarians, and then returns victorious, to be greeted by Melchisedech, the priest of God, "whose mysterious birth ... has no ostensible author," a detail that ornaments (and so marks specifically) the traditional exegetical association of Melchisedec with Christ. Epitome answers to the mnemonic-cognitive need for *brevitas*; it is the "brief" scheme that allows one to recall a work "plentifully."

Yet Prudentius' epitome of the text is not barren of detail, the way modern summaries tend to be. Lot, "set at liberty by the bursting of his chains, straightens his neck in freedom, where the links had chafed."[75] The detail helps to "paint" Lot in a reader's memory, giving him one of those so-called allegorical attributes that function cognitively to mark this image as worth further mental attention.

Prudentius calls his texturized retelling of the story of Abraham and Lot "haec linea" that he has "praenotata," "sketched out first" (before his main story) "as a model ... which our life should resculpt with due measure."[76] The morally examined life is the work of a careful artist, an artist first of all not in stone or paint or even in words, but in *lineae*, the richly textured lineaments of an educated and well-stocked memory. *Linea* is used here as a synonym of *ratio*, the mental schemes and schedules that Augustine found, along with images and notations of emotions, among the things in his memory. The word resonates richly in medieval mnemotechnic.[77] But notice here how Prudentius uses the word – which later comes to mean "a diagram," and is associated with the mental "sketch" of a composition (by Geoffrey of Vinsauf, among others) – to indicate what we now would probably call the *story*. Prudentius' *linea* is made up of Biblical events recalled *summatim*, like those which Augustine recommended as the basis for teaching.

At the beginning of the series of epic combats, the reader is advised to carefully "see" the pictures which the poem will paint: "The scheme [ratio] for victory is before our eyes if we are able to note at close hand the very faces of the virtues, and their deadly struggle against pestilent men."[78] If we can mentally take close note of the features of the virtues and those struggling against them, then a scheme (*ratio*) will be always present to us (in the memory images we

145

retain from the story) for conquering, with Christ's aid, the rebellious passions and thoughts that arise in us. In other words, we are invited carefully to inspect the text, allow it to paint its synaesthetic pictures in our own minds, and transfer that picture to our memories where it will always be available to us ("praesens") as a sort of ethical device, part of the furnishing of our soul – "furnish" being another meaning of Latin *ornare*, the root of the word "ornament."

These images in the story-line are not iconographic, if by that one means images that signify single specific concepts. Prudentius is concerned to provide a foundation, a "ratio," that will securely stick in our memory: this will enable us at any age to "recognize the features" (as it were) of our own "divided will [fissa voluntas]" (line 760) when sin "attacks." The power of the ornament scheme is precisely its ready memorability as a picture, not as a concept.

The main story of *Psychomachia* is made readily memorable by relying on two elementary procedures. A set of backgrounds is prepared, in this case the episodes of the plot, each the combat of a chief virtue and a chief vice. One ends up with a simple scheme of combats: Faith vs. Worship-of-False-Gods; Chastity vs. Lust; Patience vs. Wrath; Humility vs. Pride; Sobriety vs. Luxuria; Good Works vs. Greed; Concord vs. Discord. In fact the *Psychomachia* is divided into "combats" the way other works are divided into "chapters." One finds similar dividing techniques used very commonly in long narratives later in the Middle Ages: the *Divine Comedy*, in addition to its cantos and its meter (meter being a basic auditory mnemonic) is also divided into a topography of circles, terraces, and spheres; *The Canterbury Tales* into pilgrims; the *Decameron* into a finding system of days indexed to tellers.

Into each background cell of his foundational *ratio*, Prudentius has gathered up related matters. Some are vices and virtues associated with one or both of the central images as helpers (good and bad), such as Hope, who helps Humility to kill Pride; or Luxuria's attendants, Pleasure, Strife, Desire, Jest, Ostentation, and Coquetry, who rush away "in agitated flight" when their master is killed, scattering their toys as they run (lines 445–449). Bible stories are also attached to the combats. So when Lust is slain by Chastity, her victory speech "collates" Judith and Holofernes, the "virgin immaculate" who bore Christ, and the Whore of Babylon shut into Hell. This kind of "chain-making" or *catena* is familiar to all medievalists, from innumerable examples in both Latin and vernacular literatures. I want to emphasize

146

its basis in *memoria*, "gathering" associations into a "place." Nor are the chains confined to what is written down in the text; for example, the killing of Holofernes by Judith is invoked as part of the chain linked to the combat of Chastity and Lechery, but when Hope cuts off the head of Luxuria and holds it up, dripping, the action reverberates (or should) like the rich trope it is, bringing back Judith and Holofernes, and as an antithesis, Salome and John the Baptist.

Psychomachia was one of the earliest non-Biblical works to be illustrated. Sixteen manuscripts still survive, painted between the ninth and thirteenth centuries. But the prototype set of pictures is thought to have been made much earlier, perhaps as early as the fifth century, not long after the poem was composed.[79] The pictures in the program for *Psychomachia* mark the main incidents of its story: indeed, rather as in the case of the eighth-century commentary on the Apocalypse by Beatus of Liébana (which I will examine next), picture and textual episode together make up a series of *storiae*, memorable incidents marked with a picture which serves as a sort of punctuation and "summary." The incident of Luxuria's death was marked by such a picture, as indeed is nearly every incident in the battles in some manuscripts of the tenth and eleventh centuries.

But not only the *imagines agentes* of the story were treated in this way. One eleventh-century manuscript of the poem places a half-page picture of "Prudentius" just before the prayer which concludes and summarizes the gist of his work (Plate 8). Just as Augustine suggested storing in memory things related to Paul under an image of the author which would serve as their mnemonic inventory-marker, so this image may serve as a marker for the authorial *res* of Prudentius' poem.

Intricate chains of stories, woven together in the activities of memory, are a characteristic medieval habit of mind that is not accidental, nor the manifestation of some time-spirit or "mentality." It was *learned in school* from texts like the *Psychomachia*. Like a tuning-fork, the textual trope reverberates in the cultural-made-personal memories of those who read it. So a reader's memory, not confined by worries about "the author's intended meaning," is freed to roam its memorial symphony, "gathering up" harmonies and antitheses in the compositional activity which Hugh of St. Victor described as "meditation," the highest kind of study, that "takes the soul away from the noise of earthly business" (such as grammatical commentary) and "renders his life pleasant indeed" who makes a practice of it.[80] Interpretation can then become a form of prayer, a journey through memory like that Augustine took with his mother Monica, by means of which, at moments, the soul seems to recollect beyond its self, to find out God's own sweetness.[81]

Prudentius' images are painted for the mind's eye. Effort is made not to overwhelm the student with detail: the narrative details are few but they are particularly vivid and specific. This accords with a basic technique for making such images: one must be careful not to overwhelm the mental eye with an excess of images. And those one has must be extreme, "eye-catching" of course, but also fully *synaesthetic*, a fully realized sensory experience that includes recreated sound (the screams and cries and battle trumpets) and taste (chiefly of blood and crushed bone) and odor (vomit and blood but also crushed violets) and touch (chiefly pain).

The battles are described in extreme ways: the lurid description of Luxuria's death which I quoted earlier is repeated with minor variations for all the vices. Each one is made dead, dead, dead – with blood dripping and bones smashed, strangled until the eyeballs pop from their sockets, beheaded, the corpses torn to pieces and thrown into the air. Luxuria, a decadent hothouse flower, "throws violets and fights with rose-leaves" before she is crushed under the wheels of her chariot.[82] Discord, smiling cheerfully, insinuates herself into the ranks of the victorious virtues. But she has a dagger hidden under her cloak, with which she stabs Concord. Then, revealed by the blood staining her robe, she renames herself Heresy, and is torn to pieces by countless hands, the bits of her corpse scattered to the wind and thrown to dogs and crows, and then, after they've been trampled in stinking sewers, fed to the fishes.[83]

These pictures stick in the mind, not as "concepts" or "objects" but *as an inventory* of synaesthetic, syncretic memory cues, to be drawn upon, drawn out from, and *used* for constructing new work. Many later artists, when considering the subject-matter of the virtues and vices, write or paint or carve "in Prudentius" the way that Augustine wrote his Latin in the vocabulary and cadences of the Psalms.[84] Even in their sophisticated, mature age, medieval churchmen would still pull forth the heuristic *schema* of a combat of vices and virtues. Gregory the Great, writing as Pope, provides a penitential scheme of eight sins, with Pride as the mnemonically crucial "beginning of all sin," followed by its seven Princes, each captain of a military troop of associated sins.[85] It is an effective scheme, a useful heuristic – the "beginning" of a meditation, which is then expanded (*Moralia in Job* xxvi.28).

The narrative of *Psychomachia* seems to have become translated entirely into a series of pictures. In the copy-book which he made at the end of the tenth century at the abbey of St. Martial in Limoges, the monk Adémar de Chabannes first drew all the (by then) conventional sketches of *Psychomachia*'s scenes in their narrative order, and then wrote out the text of the poem following these pictures.[86] Another example, somewhat later, is the set of *Psychomachia* drawings in Herrad of Hohenbourg's *Hortus deliciarum*, which was placed in the book without any supporting text from the poem, presented just as a set of picture *topoi* with labels on some of the individual images.[87] And when *Psychomachia* had become to many audiences little more than a gathering of famous tropes, each of which amounted to a sort of picture epitomized for memory by a phrase or name, Chaucer could paint in his description of Mars' temple in *The Knight's Tale* the image of the smiler with the knife under the cloak, while Dante – invoking the same memory icon, but heading down a different associational pathway – shows the discord-sowers of the eighth circle with bodies rent and horribly torn.[88]

Psychomachia ends with the victorious virtues entering the New Temple (recalling both Ezekiel and the Apocalypse) that has been laid out by Faith and Concord. This is constructed out of a variety of Biblical motifs (the Tabernacle, the Temple, the New Jerusalem, and Wisdom's house in Proverbs 9). The composition is described as the laying out of a Temple plan (foundation – we are surely expected to recall 1 Corinthians 3:10) and then the raising of the walls of various precious stones (a detail remembered from Revelation), using a building-crane or "machina."[89] Faith begins by *remembering* that Solomon laid out a temple to celebrate the end of the strife that tore his father David's reign, for "it is when blood is cleansed that a temple is built and an altar set up":[90]

> Then it was that Jerusalem was made glorious with her temple and, herself now divine, received her God to rest there, now that the homeless Ark was established in its place on the marble altar. In our camp too let a sacred temple arise, that the Almighty may visit its holy of holies.[91]

Ark (of Noah), Ark (of the Covenant) in its Tabernacle carried in the camps of the Israelites, and Temple of Solomon in the citadel of

Jerusalem are all brought together, a "common place" of Christian memory by this time. To these structures are added the visionary citadels (*arces*) of Ezekiel and of John. Faith and Concord set to work "to lay out the new temple and set its foundation" (line 825).

First, Faith measures out a central square with her golden measuring rod, and the square-shaped city walls are laid out, with three gates in each side. Measuring the building with a golden rod is an action taken from Ezekiel, both directly and via its appearance in John's vision, and the city which the virtues lay out from that square is the Heavenly Jerusalem of Apocalypse 21, the visionary citadel of Ezekiel 40, and the "city on a hill" of Matthew 25, the three "gathered up" into a pattern by their shared word, *civitas*. It is also called a *templum* both in Ezekiel and here, another word that brings together the New and Old Testament sets of buildings.

This is literary troping built up by means of a basic mnemonic *catena*. The objects collated begin with the same syllable, *arc-*: *arc-a*, "ark" or "chest," both of Noah and of the Covenant, where God's *arc-ana*, "secrets," are hidden away; *arc-es*, "citadels," the walled cities of Ezekiel's and John's visions; and also *arc-us*, "arches," the shape of each of the triple triumphal doorways in the walls. Above the gateways gleam the names of the "apostolic senate" written in gold.[92] Here *enargeia* becomes ekphrasis, the sensuous description of *making* a building. And the ekphrasis is, in some sense, constructed out of puns or *paronomasia*, another basic rhetorical ornament of great inventive power.[93]

Concordances of sound (at the level of syllable) and shape (arch, gateway, chest, and walled city) are fundamental to meditative troping, making a mnemonic machine that can serve to inventory and "find out" a multitude of "things" hidden away (as *arcana*) in memory. The story-telling proceeds by "picture-making," each episode being a "frame" or "form" on which (or into which) one learns to hook up a multitude of diverse material. Each also can serve as the "form" for a number of different meditations, on a variety of occasions.

8. THE BEATUS "HEAVENLY JERUSALEM": A PICTURE WITH
WHICH TO INVENT

An ekphrasis, such as the temple description we have just examined in *Psychomachia*, need not be confined only to literature. As the literary ornament acts as an invention site, a sight for meditation, so I would suggest do certain ekphrastic pictures. I realize that I seem to be stretching the term here (and I am), but cognitively speaking there is no reason why a word picture and a painting cannot both "paint pictures in the mind," and more to the point, function in similar ways as meditative "gathering" sites.

I want now to consider a famous picture of the Heavenly Jerusalem as just such a rhetorical ornament, an ekphrasis in paint. This example is a picture which is part of a set of images in an apocalypse commentary first put together (out of older materials) in the eighth century by a Spanish monk, Beatus of Liébana. I have included several of its pictures from a number of different manuscripts of the work (Plates 1–4, 9, and 19), but to begin with I want to focus on the "Heavenly City" image alone (Plates 2 and 3).

Plate 2 reproduces one version of it from an eleventh-century manuscript of Beatus' book, made in Gascony between 1028 and 1061 at the monastery of Saint-Sever. Plate 3 reproduces the same picture, this one from a manuscript made in the middle of the eleventh century in León.[94] The very ornateness of the picture made it a remarkably flexible meditational tool. It is the sort of thing one wants to look at and look at again; the ways and routes within and among its remarkably various patterns conduct one's sight, mental and physical, in endless yet coherent directions. The apostle images, each in its arch (each arch positioned as one of the three gates in each of the City's four walls), are each also identified with one of the twelve stone foundations that make up the Heavenly City in John's vision (Revelation 21:14). Each type of stone is also marked by an angel poised over the gate (cf. Revelation 21:12): a scribe has written out *summatim* what the commentary says of their properties.[95]

The picture is in one way a simple visual summary of the literal text of Revelation 21:10–22, and yet the design elements of this picture encourage someone looking at it to form for him- or herself shifting patterns of shapes (arches and columns), of graphic elements (dots and cross-hatching), of individual images in the multiple "places" of the pages, and of its strong, distinct colors. As O. K. Werckmeister has written about the Saint-Sever set of these pictures, their "conceptual clarity ... suited the exact literal comprehension of the text [at the level of the story] required for its elaborate exegesis."[96] The same can be said of the Heavenly City picture in the Facundus Beatus. It is a picture of surfaces: everything is bright and distinct. Nothing about it suggests obscurity or darkness, nothing requires elucidating. And it is exactly this quality that makes it an exceptional inventive gathering site.[97]

Each design element can serve, if one chooses, as a relatively simplified, "empty" location in which to "gather" other material, verbal and visual (and for all we know, depending on the interpreter, olfactory, tangible, and gustatory too). The simpler and "emptier" (I am using this word in its mnemotechnical sense, as the opposite of "crowded"), the more variously useful the location can be made to be. These places in this picture, each carefully marked by color and ornament, serve as a schema of compositional backgrounds, as powerful as the textual order itself. They are in fact an alternative text – not an "illustration" of the words. The ornaments of this picture can be dilated, "loosened up and expanded" in just the way verbal texts treated as *memoria summaria* can be, by procedures of shuffling, collating, gathering in – devising and composing meditation.

Greatly influential in the development of the Beatus picture book was the Spanish scribe who made the manuscript now in the Pierpont Morgan Library in New York, sometime about 945.[98] Though not the first to illustrate the commentary, this scribe comments on the role of the pictures in his book and his reasons for making them, in language that clearly indicates their meditative purpose. Maius' colophon reads: "As part of its ornamental order [decus] are the picture-making words of its stories [uerba mirifica storiarum] which I have painted [depinxi] in their order, so that they may inspire fear among those who are learned [scientibus] of the coming future judgment at the world's future end."[99] Recall that meditation begins most effectively with the emotion of fear – the chilling terror that raises prickles on our flesh, which make us stick tight when we throw ourselves upon the redeeming Cross. Maius says that his paintings were made to raise up such terrors in the learned, the *scientes*, "those who have knowledge." Evidently, as all historians who have studied the Beatus tradition have recognized, this picture book was not for beginning students or for illiterate laity. It is a book designed for monks remembering Hell and the Last Things.

And, in accord with meditative practice, the book provides an orderly ("per seriem") way, constructed of images to gaze on and scrutinize and "turn over" with the eye. Moreover, as Maius writes, he has painted completely (the force of *depingere*) those pictures which are in the words of the *storiae* – as Beatus called the sections, each a few verses long, into which he divided the narrative of St. John's vision. "Mirifica verba" are words which make images to be looked at: they are "marvellous," *mirifica*, but what makes them so are the wonderful sights, the images (*mir-*, "gaze with wonder") which they fashion (*fac-*, the root of *fica*). These are what Maius says he has depicted. The verb *depingere*, an intensive form, serves a dual purpose in this sentence, for it refers to both the letters of the *verba* which Maius wrote (in medieval Latin, *pingere* is commonly used for the scribal task of lettering)[100] and also to the *mirifica* pictures which these words raise up in his mind and, through his brush, are translated as paintings to the book. There they, together with the words, may paint pictures in the minds of other monks as they engage in meditative reading.

This union of words and pictures is apparent in the layout of the Beatus commentary. Plate 9 shows a typical page, the section of the text which describes the sixth angel pouring out his bowl. This example is from Maius' book. Notice that the complete book chapter starts with the *storia*, a short segment of Revelation (16:12, in this case), written immediately under the "incipit" in the left-hand column. As one reads the chapter from beginning to end, one then must immediately continue on to the picture of the sixth angel, pouring his vial into the river Euphrates so that it dries up. This picture is framed, a device that seems to be Maius' contribution to the Beatus tradition.[101] And it has a verbal "title" which identifies the scene, written in the right-hand part of the L-shaped frame.

The commentary on the Apocalypse text is then written below the picture. Notice that it begins in the right-hand column, under the picture, following directly upon it. And notice particularly that it is introduced as "the explanation of the above-written *storia*." A reader must proceed through both the written verse and the picture in order to get to their gloss, or "explanatio." Williams characterizes these pictures as "a surrogate" for the text, mediating "between the text and the reader's imagination." Werckmeister has called them a translation of the literal text into "a dense sequence" of equally literal "tableaus."[102] I would go further than either of these statements to suggest that word and picture together make up, equally, the *res memorabiles* for meditative reading. Neither surrogate nor translation, word and picture both constitute "the above-written *storia*." Together they make up the "verba mirifica storiarum" which Maius has fully painted. Like the text, the picture is also a memory site, a place for inventive "gathering" or *collatio*. This concept of the picture is emphasized by the frame Maius painted around it: like the column of text, it provides a definite "place" on the page, both of the vellum and of *memoria*.

In the Saint-Sever book, the pictures were not only adapted as they were copied, but some were also expanded, translated in the inventive way I have described. The scenes are treated as images-for-memory-work, rather than as objects in need of exact reduplication. Werckmeister has pointed out that elements in some of this manuscript's pictures actually depart both from the traditional pictures in Beatus manuscripts and from the literal text in Revelation, the master-painter (a monk, of course) clearly using the picture as an inventive site, just as we have seen monks doing elsewhere with material that is entirely verbal. Made some hundred years after Maius' book, this manuscript, written for the Cluniac abbot of Saint-Sever, Gregory of Montaner, adapted the traditional matter of the *storiae* specifically to themes in the liturgy of the dead, a concern of the abbey's noble sponsors and the occasion of the intercessory prayers which the monks of Saint-Sever promised to them.[103]

In one case, the picture of "the Lamb and the One on the Throne," part of the narrative (*storia*) of the opening of the sixth seal depicted in Revelation 6:12–17 (Plate 4), the Saint-Sever painter has added an inscription to the traditional one found in other such scenes, crowding the lettering into the space in order to bring together two quotes that are unrelated and out of textual sequence; the two quotes make one statement, however, to explain a feature of his picture that is, in fact, not found explicitly in the Bible. On each side of the enthroned deity, the sky is rolling up like a book-scroll. This feature is made from a phrase in Revelation 6:14, which depicts the sky as receding like a scroll that is rolled up. The *tituli* written in the upper part of this picture quote both these words and also a phrase from Revelation 6:16, the words of which are quoted before the words from verse 14, out of sequence. Clearly the painter has departed from the exact sequence of the text in order to pull its pieces together in a new composition – adapted from tradition, to be sure, but "expanded and loosened up."[104]

On the basis of a number of such changes, Werckmeister makes clear how the painters of this manuscript were not just copying verbatim (and "formatim," as it were) from an exemplar, nor just illustrating the words of the Bible. I find this compelling evidence that such pictures were thought of in the same way that textual *ekphrases* were, as sites for further meditational composition. Moreover, the Saint-Sever manuscript version of the picture of the sixth seal (of which the Lamb and One on the Throne is the upper half) appears to be directly the work of Stephanus Garsia, whom François Avril calls "the master of the program," the one who signed the manuscript and was responsible for two other painters working under him; it is also one of the pages that have remained unretouched by later hands, so the alterations to the Biblical text which Werckmeister detected in this image seem to have been part of its original conception.[105]

One question always arises in respect of these "mirificous" books: how were they used? We have very little, if any, direct evidence about this. But the Saint-Sever book was made at the abbot's direction, and one of an abbot's major tasks was to nourish the spiritual life of his brothers, by giving both them and himself food for prayer and meditation. The "stories" in this book are apocalyptic "seeings," *visiones.* They can nurture meditations on the events because they stick in the minds of those who have seen them. The marvellous colors, the extraordinary figures (both noble and monstrous), the clarity of each scene in its background, the frame – these are all effective mnemonic and cognitive agents. The pictures thus serve not as "aids" for memorizing the words, nor even primarily as pictorial "expressions" of an articulated theology, but as the sort of Gregorian *machinae* which could raise the clearing eyes of one's mind towards God.[106]

9. ETYMOLOGY: THE ENERGY OF A WORD UNLEASHED

Another commonly used ornament that many humanistic grammarians have found puerile and disgusting in its own way is etymology (the early twentieth-century philologist Ernst Curtius called most medieval forms of it "insipid trifling," and one late-nineteenth-century editor referred to his author's "most perverse etymologies").[107] To a scientifically trained student of philology like Curtius, this figure is annoyingly playful, for it pays no attention to the actual history of words, but instead whacks up the roots and endings, rearranging them arbitrarily and inconsistently, apparently just to make some whimsical rhymes and far-fetched puns, often in two or more languages at the same time, which may or may not have anything to do with the actual language of the word being "etymologized"! There are plentiful examples of the ornament from antiquity onward, originating both in Hellenic and Judaic traditions.

The connection of etymology to mnemonic technique was clear at least from the time of Cicero, who used the same word, *notatio*, both to translate Greek *etymologia*[108] and for the mnemonically valuable "notes" or "marks" that are the tools of memory work.[109] Whatever its "truth status" – and that question was much argued in antiquity – the *mnemonic* efficacy of etymology was never questioned. Its standing as a valuable pedagogical practice, a sub-set of powerful inventional mnemonics, was to a large extent independent of the philosophical investigations (with differing outcomes) into the truth value of etymologizing.

Isidore of Seville, using definitions traditional in Roman rhetoric, says that etymology

> is [defined as] the origin of words, when the power [vis] of a word or a name is gathered together [colligitur] through interpretation. ... For when you can perceive whence the germ of a name comes, you will more quickly grasp its energy [vim]. The examination of the whole substance [omnis rei] is more plainly known by etymology.[110]

Isidore also observes that not all words are assigned according to the nature of the object to which they refer, but that sometimes the ancients, as we still do (he says), gave out names according to their own whims and desires. Some names reflect their cause, as "reges" ("kings") is from "recte agendo" ("right acting"); some their origin, as "homo" ("man") from "humus" ("earth"); and some refer by means of the principle of opposition, as "lutum" ("mud") is named from "lavando" ("laundering") because mud is not clean.[111] Notice at work here the three basic principles of cognitive association: similarity, analogy (what Aristotle called "neighborliness"), and contrariety.[112]

Notice also that for Isidore, as for Cicero, the purpose of etymology is not primarily to find the true nature of an object (*res*) but to unlock and gather up the energy in a word. It is significant that Isidore stresses that etymology is a way of getting at *vis verbi*: a word's force, power, and – through an echo of *vir* meaning "male person" – fruitfulness (virility). He thinks of *etymologia* at least as much in terms of creativity and invention as he does in terms of "truth" (and not all in terms of historical philology).

Etymology is an ornament of brevity, and like that of all such ornaments, its force consists in the inventive abundance or "copious-ness" which it gathers together in one's mind. This point was made by Cassiodorus, who defined it in his commentary on the first Psalm as *oratio brevis*, "brief utterance, showing through particular conso-nances from what word that word which is sought will come [to mind]."[113] This is a technique of inventive, rhetorical etymology, fully unleashing the energy and copious fruitfulness of a word through recollectively gathering up associations by means of homo-phonies, *assonationes*, puns. It is one of the commonest and most productive of elementary compositional techniques, and while it was grounded in grammar (as invention was always supposed to be), there is no doubt that for composition and for mnemonic effectiveness, ancient and medieval etymologizing rather quickly became a game of consonances, conformations, and other word plays.[114]

One need look no farther than the *Origines*, soon dubbed the "Etymologies," of Isidore of Seville to find an instance of the pedagogical and mnemotechnical power attributed to etymologizing. Isidore's encyclopedia, characterized rightly as supplying "a whole system of education,"[115] begins with an etymology (several, in fact) and proceeds to exfoliate itself on this basis. *Disciplina*, he begins, gets its name from "discendo," "studying"; or it is so called from "discitur plena," "[something that] is learned as a whole."[116] The two etymol-ogies are proferred not as competing explanations whose validity is to be objectively determined (Isidore shows no interest at all in which of these possibilities is correct), but rather as "starting-points" for Isidore's encyclopedic composition. The concern always to have a firm "starting-point" (which is really a "starting-off-point" for a memory chain); the pride of place given to the beginning, the "inventor," recognizes a requirement of human remembering. Isi-dore's pedagogy incorporated the presumption that *all* learning is built up, like a wall or a concordance, upon a memorial base of *notationes* (including etymologies) that serve as recollective inventory markers.

This inventive tool is remarkably persistent, no doubt a symptom of its usefulness to those who had to compose as well as those who had to learn. As invention, *etymologia* is often indistinguishable from punning and other onomastic word play – a characteristic acknowl-edged by Cassiodorus. There are a number of examples in Carolingian poetry, applied both to people and place names. The ninth-century poet Walahfrid Strabo performed florid riffs on the florescent name

157

of his friend, Florus, dean and *magister* of the cathedral in Lyons.[117] A twelfth-century English monk from Pontefract abbey, writing a saint's life, began by etymologizing his name, Thurstan (actually an Anglo-Saxon name) from Latin *thus, thuris* ("incense") or *turris stans* ("standing tower").[118]

One of the most influential and useful aids to preachers for composing their sermons was an anthology of saints' lives called *The Golden Legend*. It was put together about 1260 by an Italian Dominican friar, Jacobus da Voragine, who compiled the materials from many earlier sources. It is Voragine's frequent compositional habit to begin the narrative with a collection of etymologies of the saint's name.[119] These are taken from Latin, Greek, and Hebrew words – though Voragine himself and most of his sources knew little Greek and no Hebrew. So, for example, Stephen is from Greek *stephanos*, "crown," but the word in Hebrew (!) means "example." Or the name is from Latin *strenue fans*, "speaking with zeal," or *strenue stans*, "standing up strongly," or *fans an[ib]us*, "speaking to old women, widows." So, summarizes Jacobus, "Stephen is a crown because he is first in martyrdom, a norm by his example in suffering and his way of life, a zealous speaker in his praiseworthy teaching of the widows."[120]

Here is another example, starting off the life of St. Cecilia:

> "Cecilia" is as though [quasi] "lily of heaven" [celi lilia] or "way of the blind" [cecis via] or from "heaven" [celo] and "Leah" [lya]. Or "Cecilia" is as though "free of blindness" [cecitate carens]. Or she is named from "heaven" [celo] and "leos," that is "people." For she was a "lily of heaven" because of her virgin chastity. Or she is called "lily" because she had the white of purity, the green of conscience, the odor of good fame. She was "way of the blind" because of her teaching by example, "heaven" for her devoted contemplation, "Leah" for her constant busyness. ... She also was "free of blindness" because of the brilliant light of her wisdom. She was also "heaven of people" [celum + leos] because in her, as in a heaven, people wanting a role model might in a spiritual way gaze upon her sun, moon, and stars, that is the far-sightedness of her wisdom, the greatness of her faith, and the variety of her virtues.[121]

Voragine's etymologies resolve themselves into a series of homophonies, puns on the syllables of the saint's name, and images derived from those puns that serve as mnemonics for some of her virtues. Peter Chrysologus spoke of how a word begins to glow in the mind of a believer; for Voragine a word begins to ring changes. "Ce-ci-li-a" *sounds like* "caeca" and "lilia," or like "caeci" and "via," and so on. Lilies – at least for audiences used to seeing them painted in images of the Virgin and described in sermons – are white, with green stems and a sweet scent. Semantics is banished in favor of sounds, a play of coincident likenesses and oppositions: ce-ci-li-a is "like" [quasi] "lilia" and "via" and "Lya," like "caelum" and "caecus," because the syllables of her name *sound like* those words – "sort of [quasi]." Such associative play is the method of the game of charades. It is also the fundamental stuff of remembering.

These elaborately punning riffs of memory do to a word what jazz does to a written musical phrase. The etymologies are indeed *oratio brevis*, as Cassiodorus characterized them, for each one can serve as the germ for an expanded composition. Voragine has given preaching friars, the orators of his time, a very useful digest, *breviter* and *summatim*, of ethical subject-matter in memorable, inventive form: first in puns and rebuses, and then in summary narratives. The stories collected in *The Golden Legend* are organized according to the liturgical year. What better mental fodder for a busy preacher, or a meditating lay person or cleric?[122]

The moral common places summarized in the etymologies that accompany Cecilia's story should be used (if used at all) as the *beginning* of our reading of her story, not as definitive statements of its meaning. The whole point is to invent as many variations on the basic syllables of the name as one's recollective ingenuity, working within its memory store, can manage. These "associations" with the name "Cecilia" invent a composition, very much in the manner that a performer/composer of music uses a phrase (or "trope") as the foundation for "inventions."

The purpose of reading about Cecilia is, as Voragine says, "ad imitandum," "as a role model." The literal story of the saint must be turned ethically into one's life. And a major vehicle for this is etymological troping, "turning" via homophonies. Inventionally re-membered, the syllables of Cecilia are treated as locations into which material of various sorts has been "gathered" by a chain of puns.[123] Why should one wish to remember Cecilia? Not in order to know the facts about her, but to "re-member" her story, by re-telling it in our own selves, in literary, ethical meditation. Reading, says Gregory the Great, in the preface to *Moralia in Job*, "presents a kind of mirror to the eyes of the mind, that our inner face may be seen in it. There indeed we learn *our own* ugliness, there *our own* beauty," for "we should transform what we read into our very selves."[124] It is in that activity, the troping of a literary work that goes on in a memory, that the "meaning" of reading resides.

10. VISUAL ETYMOLOGY: THE BOOK OF KELLS

Etymologia can be a visual as well as a verbal ornament. The ubiquitous leaves and branches used as decorative patterns in manuscripts can express the commonplace etymology of Latin *liber* ("book") from *liber* ("tree bark"). In medieval Germanic vernaculars, this pun is translated exactly in the etymological link of *boc* ("book") to *boc, bec* ("[beech] tree"). The Biblical linkage of one who meditates the law of the Lord with a tree (in Psalm 1) strengthens this particular cultural chain, for a book is for meditating.

As we have just seen, rhetorical etymology is a form of punning. One type of visual pun depends on the position of the punning elements in the graphic design of the page. Used in this way, such puns function almost like a variety of punctuation: they become wayfinders and signals to a reader going through a book. An early example is found in the eighth-century Book of Kells, where some of the line-filling ornaments, shaped like elongated birds or chains that turn back on themselves, pun on the Irish scribes' names for these elements, *ceann fa eitil*, "head under the wing," or *cor fa casan*, "turn in the path."[125] Plate 10 reproduces one characteristic page from this manuscript, in this case the text of Luke 22:52–56, the narrative of Jesus' arrest in the garden, followed by Peter's denial. The two "head-under-the-wing" marks on this page signal two breaks between major events in the narrative, the first after Jesus rebukes the soldiers, and the second when he is brought to the high priest's house.

Often in this manuscript (and in other early books), when the last word of text on a line would not fit the remaining space, the scribes would copy its last syllable or two onto the next line, even when the next line was on the next page. The practice reflects the fact that at this time, Latin words were analyzed for writing as syllables rather than as "whole words," as we do now. An example of the scribal custom is in first line of the page shown in Plate 10, for the syllable *-res* which begins that line is the last syllable of the word *seniores*, carried over from the previous page.

The bottom third of the page shown in Plate 10 is the start of a major "event" in the narrative, Peter's denial of Jesus in the courtyard of the high priest's house. Its beginning is marked by a large initial. But this section of the text in Luke was not completed on this page. Contrary to custom, however, the last syllable of the last word, "negavit," was not carried over to the top line of the next page. Instead it was written just under the bottom line on this page, and was "collected up" into the first part of the word by means of a little animal on its back with its legs (*membra*) embracing the orphaned syllable or segment (*membrum*) of the word. In the incident of Peter's denial *negavit* is the crucial word: a reader would need to pay attention to it, and pause over it if reading aloud, even though the page had to be turned. This scribal device accomplishes that end: it both "collects up" the critical word and attracts the reader's notice.

It is thought that this Gospel book was used primarily for reading aloud during services. The decoration, like all good punctuation, marks out the *ductus* of the narrative clearly for someone who was reading an already familiar, mostly memorized text, but who needed cues and markers for the various stages of the route through it. The decoration also makes the pattern of each page distinctive, so one familiar with it could readily find a needed passage. In other words, the book *locates* the various "stories" (to use Beatus of Liébana's word for similar textual divisions) of the Gospel, making them readily discoverable for the occasions of reading within the liturgical year.[126] Such decoration also would have served someone needing to locate and recall matters for compositional purposes, such as making homilies and colloquies on the *dicta et facta memorabilia* of the book.

II. EXCURSUS: MARGINAL PUNNING IN TWO GOTHIC BOOKS, THE RUTLAND PSALTER AND THE HOURS OF CATHERINE OF CLEVES

The greatest variety of visual punning is found in the margins of devotional books made after the middle of the thirteenth century, a custom that began in England and continued especially among owners who had some English connection. They were made for a reading audience of Anglo-Norman clergy and aristocracy who were bi- and even trilingual, in French, Latin, and English.[127]

The margin of the page is, as I have argued elsewhere, especially the area that invites and gives scope to a reader's memory work.[128] Decorating this area is a particularly prominent feature of medieval books after the twelfth century, so the phenomenon falls a bit outside the scope of my present study. Yet the cognitive play it sets up is in principle so like what I have been discussing in this section, though in a way that answers to a more diversified, heterogeneous audience, that I cannot ignore it entirely.[129]

Laura Kendrick has called attention to how the Anglo-French word *bo(u)rdure*, or "border," can help to account for marginal images of play of all kinds, whether of games or musical instruments, via a set of puns on words related to the noun *bo(u)rde*, "play, jest, have fun." The puns also include the verb *bo(u)rden*, meaning "to joust" or "tilt at the quintain," and we see many scenes in English borders of jousting and tilting knights, or creatures dressed as knights. *Bo(u)rde* includes the meaning of sexual intercourse, and it has long been observed that marginal scenes can be bawdy: in addition to the sexual meaning of *bo(u)rde*, a variant fifteenth-century form of "border" is *bordel*, a homophone of the word for "brothel," *bordel*.[130]

Another Anglo-French word for the border is *marges*, English "margin." I would suggest that marginal paintings of daisies ("marguerites") and pearls ("margeries") are verbal–visual puns on their places in the page. They play also on other associations: daisies or marguerites are flowers, and "flowers of reading" are what an attentive reader should be gathering and digesting in her meditative heart while she reads. One often also sees nectar-gathering or fruit-eating insects, such as butterflies or worms, on the flowers. For their part, "pearls," margeries, are not only among the glowing gems of reading, but of course also have specific religious associations, with the parable of the pearl of great price for instance, the heavenly kingdom towards which pious reading is directed.

Creatures who make pearls are also in marginal evidence. Medieval natural lore held that snails made pearls in their heads, which is where a reader should also be creating pearls of great price from the matters of the book. Oysters and mussels also made pearls. One ornamented border in the fifteenth-century Hours of Catherine of Cleves shows a chain (*catena*) of mussels enclosing pearls. The ornament of this manuscript, made in the 1430s, is filled with motifs associated with the readerly activities of devotional *memoria*. The multilingualism of the clerical aristocracy of mid-fifteenth-century Guelders, the milieu of Catherine's household, as also of the Anglo-Norman aristocracy a century and more earlier in England, seems to me important in establishing and maintaining traditions of visual–verbal punning because it is such a resource of homophonic syllables.[131]

A snail, *limax* (Latin) or *limaçon*, "limasson" (French and English), is a creature of the mud or *limus*, according to Varro.[132] A muddy snail is also a liminal creature, via the puns *limus*, "mud"/*limes*, *limitis*, "boundary, limit" and *limen*, "threshold, boundary." Plate 11 shows a marginal snail or limasson "bourding" with a knight in the border of the Rutland Psalter.[133] Furthermore, as a mud creature a snail is like a man, in being "of earth" ("humus"); it also must be cleansed, as a reader must be, before the business of pearl-making can go on.

Yet another set of visual puns appears in the margins of the Rutland Psalter. This is an English and French pun as well, on French *limbes*, meaning both "limbs" and "border," and the English *limes* ("limbs").[134] The Rutland Psalter has in some of its margins (or *limbes*) a number of severed limbs (see Plate 12) – arms, legs, even heads.[135] It is also one of the most grotesque-filled of all manuscripts, somewhat in the playful spirit of the Book of Kells, made five centuries earlier. Though modern taste winces at many of the Rutland Psalter's images, its gory wit is very memorable.

This nest of puns on the syllable *lim-* may also help to account for the popular presence of *lymers* or hunting dogs, as in Plate 13, shown pursuing their goal, a "secreted" rabbit, their and their huntsman's food. Tracking down and hunting and fishing are all common tropes for the work of meditative *memoria*. Creatures which "gather" for their own compositions their "honey" from the flowers of reading (*flori-legium*), or "eat" its fruits, are a generic marginal motif; birds and flying insects of all sorts, classified together as *aves*, are tropes both of souls and of thoughts.

There can also be puns in single languages, of course. The depiction of field pansies in margins refers to the general topic of gathering, *legere*, "the flowers of reading," *florilegium*; but, for the right Anglo-French audience, it will also pun on the French word *pensées*, "pansies/thoughts," what one is supposed to do while reading – meditatively gather and think.

Tropes of fertility – fruits, eggs, plowing, seeding – obviously pun on the need to be "fruitful": to engage in the ethical copiousness of one's mind the *vis verborum*, the germinal, concentrated virtue of the page which one is reading. There are multiple pathways out into various memory networks from such meditational cues as these images provide, and multiple chains of associations to be built from them. A great many of the border ornaments in the Hours of Catherine of Cleves are in the form of chains, the *catenae* a good reader should be making.

All these puns serve as signals and reminders of the *initial* attitudes of reading – how to prepare, how to orient oneself, how to "intend" one's reading, to stay mindful of the goal. The motifs come only indirectly, I think, from tropes of *memoria* in classical rhetoric (at least before the fifteenth century), for their more direct source lies in the orthopraxis of monasticism. Many commonplace monastic tropes are played upon as well in these margins. One of the commonest of these is that reading is basic food, like bread. A number of images in the Hours of Catherine of Cleves refer to this metaphor, but one of the most interesting is the chain of pretzels and biscuit that is reproduced in Plate 14. Rabbits and deer are also food (especially for aristocrats), though the image of a deer can also "collect" in a well-furnished mind the opening, "As the hart panteth after the water-brooks," of Psalm 41, whose gist conventionally was thought to be meditation.

The food of reading must be chewed and digested – and excreted, an activity whose depiction in the margins of prayer books has proved shocking to modern audiences. Yet the advice to "expel worldly cares" as a necessary prelude to prayer may account for these images in the readers' space, the margins, for Latin *expellere* also means "to defecate." To be watchful of mental "fornication" is another trope in meditative orthopraxis, and another word punned on quite explicitly in some margins. The presence of such images also may bring to mind *coniungere*, a verb for sexual union which also describes what cognition does, in its basic sense of "join together."

Curiosity is an ambiguous state in meditation, as we have seen. The grotesques are fearful monsters, and self-generated anxiety and fear are a common beginning to meditation. Yet they are also often amusing, delighting the *cellula deliciarum* of recollection, and startling it from torpor. These grotesques demonstrate too what the brain must do to start thinking: it must gather, put together, conjoin by likeness and by contrast, the bits from its memory inventory, stored there in images. Productive thinking does not involve simple copying, but chain-making and wall-building: the outrageous combinations that make up a medieval grotesque can shock (or humor) a reader into remembering that his own task is also actively fictive, and that passive receptivity will lead to mental wandering and getting "off the track."

None of the verbal–pictorial play I have identified requires specialized knowledge, and it certainly cannot be said to constitute High Iconography in the Erwin Panofsky tradition. Nor is it philologically respectible, most of it. It is witty fun, it gets attention, it gets one started, perhaps off to heavenly things. And that is exactly the point of it. These ornaments delight the *cellula deliciarum* of inventive *memoria*, encouraging us to construct and "gather up" increasingly complex *catenae* of "things" from our own knowledge stores. And it should also be evident that the sorts of walls we build out of them, whether of straw or of gold, may not determine our salvation, but will certainly be a "proof" (both as demonstration and as challenge) of our "character," the memory stamp that all our experience has made in the basic temperament of each one of us.[136] In this way, even the most far-fetched of puns can still be part of the ethical energy, the good, of art.

12. TROPES FOR STARTING OUT: MYSTICAL FIGURES AND IMAGES

Another ornament that frequently requires a reader to recognize a visual–verbal pun has no specific name, though it is common in monastic rhetoric. Of particular inventive importance in this rhetoric are what were called the "difficult tropes" in Scripture, particularly *allegoria*. Here is an example from the prefatory narrative of Lot and Abraham in Prudentius' *Psychomachia*.

Genesis recounts that Abraham took three hundred and eighteen armed servants with him to rescue Lot (Genesis 14:14). Why 318? Because, Prudentius says (following the commentary of Ambrose), in Greek the number is written "TIH" [tau-iota-eta], which is also the Cross (T) and the first two letters of the name Jesus (IH). Notice that this *allegoria* is "unfolded" initially by means of a visual–verbal conformation. IH are letters that are also numbers (as is characteristic of ancient Latin, Greek, and Hebrew); this is an orthographic pun. But the rest of the allegory depends also on a strictly visual similitude, the *shape* of "tau" is like a cross.

The number 318 is treated by Prudentius not as a fact in the story but as a rhetorical ornament. He calls it a "figura mystica" (line 58). This is not to say that the detail wasn't also thought by Prudentius to be "actual" and "literal." But the simple grammatical fact does not interest him. Instead, he immediately treats it as a site for further meditation, a "machine" with which a reader can "lift" his thoughts. The figure has "hidden" meanings, teased out of the encoded number 318.[137]

The associations proceed with mnemonic artistry. The graphs form a rebus, a trope beloved in medieval mnemonic technique because such puns are powerfully memorable. Moreover, the "Jesus" association keys this story of Abraham and Lot into the schema of the Passion, wherein Jesus as a warrior fought the wicked kings and rescued the human soul – a link that also "hooks in" the story of the battle of virtues and vices which follows.

A "figura mystica" for Prudentius "finds out" and gathers material that is hidden away in the recesses of memory. It allows other memory secrets to be found because it is associationally powerful, in this case linking into the most powerful of all Christian memorial common places, the Cross. It operates for Prudentius somewhat as did Libanius' question about Odysseus to the new ambassadors to Antioch: it both establishes and recalls their larger common culture.[138]

This is not, of course, what we would now call a secret. Any "secret" is knowledge whose access is in some way hidden. In our world, this means matter "hidden *from* us" by somebody else because we aren't meant to have it. Frank Kermode invokes this notion of secrecy when he says of Jesus's parables as reported by Mark's gospel: "To divine the true, the latent sense, you need to be of the elect, of the institution. Outsiders must content themselves with the manifest, and pay a supreme penalty [damnation] for doing so."[139] This characterization assumes that a "secret" is always something *unknown*; once you are "in the know" it is no longer a secret. But in the idiom of meditation, a "secret" can also be matter that is hidden *away in* us, "secreted" within a richly textured memorial network whose foundations are laid within our common places, but which needs to be recovered.

This sort of "secret" becomes a test of our community identification because it is a proof of our educated memory. The story of Abraham is "texturized" within memorial networks, and so made into an ethically valuable memorial "secret" by the mnemonically effective ornaments of Prudentius' poem. Allegory in this model becomes a form of learning game, a challenging puzzle with an ethical aspect to it: can you find ways to link this "secret" into a chain? and what are the chains that you find?

In fact, the greatest "secret" in the *Psychomachia* prologue is the immediate starting-point of the whole epic narrative of the poem: "Put on the whole armour of God ... for we wrestle not against flesh and blood, but against principalities ... Stand therefore, having on the breastplate of righteousness ... the shield of faith ... the helmet of salvation, and the sword of the Spirit" (Ephesians 6:11–17). That text is never specifically mentioned in *Psychomachia*, a fact that has surprised some modern commentators. But they are forgetting Prudentius' audience. The text is one that even a Christian *puer* would (or should) know. So for a student to be able to invent it as the initiator of the whole narrative chain – the preamble to the preamble – is both delightful, in the way that solving puzzles always is, and instructive, because that text effectively articulates the story's gist – the psychic struggle of virtue against vice.

Puzzles and secrets make us anxious, but they are also stimulating. Prudentius composed this epic as a school text, a Christian Virgil for students puzzling out the *auctores* as part of their rhetorical education. Thus the specific content of an interpretation (for example, that 318 "means" Jesus) is less the point of finding out its secret than is the richly networked memory of the Bible which the clue finds out in one's mind – if one has done one's homework. The image functions not so much as a cryptogram as a clue. And the interpreting itself becomes a variety of social as well as cognitive activity, of *memoria rerum*. As Paula Fredriksen says, for early Christian "spiritual" exegetes of the Bible (like Tyconius, a fourth-century commentator on the Apocalypse) numerical *mystica* are "elastic, infinitely interpretable," they "resist calculation" for they are not mathematical, but rhetorical figures.[140]

This was also the primary sense of *mystica* for Prudentius: a "figure" which enables a chain of "secrets" to be invented by the craft of recollection, as the Ephesians text is invented in the *Psychomachia* preamble. In this sense, the allegorizing of various "matters" is not a means of mystifying them (in our sense of the word, hiding them from others) but of secreting them away safely and securely in memory recesses. Like other, less complex ornaments, *allegoria* isn't a "category of thought" but a machine for thinking. It is worth recalling here the words of Gregory the Great that allegory operates like a kind of builder's hoist, *machina*, so that by its means we may be lifted up to God.[141]

Inventive interpretation plays off a work's *surfaces*: that is where its ornaments are. We saw this principle at work in Hrabanus Maurus' (distinctly unliteral) interpretation of the verses from Deuteronomy about the captive gentile. For all the emphasis upon the obscurity and hiddenness of Scripture, it is the ornamental husk that first catches us, that orients us, that *reminds* us of the meditative task at hand, and sends us on our way.

Related to the emphasis on ornament, I think, is an equally pronounced emphasis in monastic meditation on beginnings and starting points. And these initiating, orienting devices often take visual form, or are a place for particular verbal *enargeia*. Prudentius' prelude to the main narrative of his epic, as we have seen, is an occasion for a number of *allegoriae*, including the cross "hidden" – though only until one looks carefully – in the number 318.

Beginning with a cross is a very early Christian practice for prayer and meditative reading. Recall how Augustine, describing the stages of the way of meditation, starts off by raising fear and anxieties about one's own death and sinfulness, which then propel one onto the Cross. In this initiating moment, *enargeia* evokes a mentally painted scene; recall how Cassian says that meditation begins with a mental picture, some seeing Christ glorified, some Christ in his earthly form, in order to stir up the emotions for meditation.

Christians have always begun an act of meditation or worship with the sign of the Cross. This was called, in an idiom current in the fourth century and later, "painting" the cross. The shape which the gesture took was the Greek letter *tau*.[142] What is most of interest to me is that memory work, such as prayer and reading, customarily began with a visual marker, the painted Cross. A simple, but telling, example of such a use to orient and start up a meditative prayer was uncovered in an eighth-century oratorium at the ancient monastery of Celles in Egypt (where Cassian spent some time). On the walls were painted the words of the Jesus prayer, the meditational formula developed in the praxis of the eastern Church. Marking its beginning was the outline, painted in red, of a jeweled cross, together with, at its center, the head and shoulders of Jesus, gesturing in benediction.[143]

This visual rhetorical figure serves as an *allegoria*, an ornament that initiates meditative thinking. It is rarely hidden. The jewelled cross that one sees in early Christian mosaics placed prominently in the apse of the church is an example. It is very clear to all what it is, and in this sense it is very much "on the surface" of the church, placed right in the open where all eyes, and minds, will focus during services. Yet it "gathers" everything else in the church into the "common place" it provides. In this way it functions as a rhetorical *allegoria*, "drawing in" matters in the hearts of the worshippers rather as the Tau-initial of the number 318 does for *Psychomachia*.

The painted cross-carpet pages of some Insular gospel books seem to me to function also as rhetorical *allegoriae*. Plate 16 reproduces the cross-carpet page that starts off the gospel of Luke in the Lindisfarne Gospels, made by the abbot Eadfrith about 698.[144] It is thought that the idea came from Coptic and Syrian monastic books, though the designs themselves are mainly Celtic.

The cross-carpet pages in the Lindisfarne Gospels are initiators. They are placed immediately before and opposite to the beginning words of the gospel, so that a reader sees them together with the highly decorated first phrase of text as a single opening. On the back of the page of text is painted a portrait of the gospel writer. The cross design of the carpet page is immediately apparent (far more so in color than in a black and white reproduction). But like all allegories, the more one looks at this page, the more one reads and collates its intricate patterns, the more one will "see into" it. Interlace is the monastic method of Scriptural exegesis, weaving texts together indefinitely. Finding patterns, discovering consonances of form and color: this is the visual equivalent to what verbal *allegoria* also invites. The whole page is a visual *figura mystica*. To read it requires an attitude of "holy curiosity" to discover the multiple routes within its restless forms. And the prickings, scorings, and "woundings" of the parchment which were necessary to draw the designs (and which are still visible on some of the pages) bring to mind – in the inventive way of all good composition – the com*punc*tion with which one should begin prayerfully to read the gospel text. The cross-carpet page offers an act of reading all in itself, and is a fitting ornament of abbreviation to initiate and orient the reading of the gospel.

The notion that acts of composing began with acts of seeing, of vision, is common in monastic praxis. Although I will explore this idea in my next chapter, before I conclude this one I want to look briefly at the beginning of an Anglo-Saxon poem, monastic in its ambiance, which will serve as a summary of this chapter and a path to my next. The dream-vision poem called *The Dream of the Rood*, composed by a monastic author probably in the early eighth century, starts with a "seeing" of a great jeweled cross clad in gold. The poet sees it in a dream, and describes it as a wondrous tree, wound about with light. The cross image itself is that of an early Christian jeweled cross of the sort depicted commonly in churches of Rome and the eastern Mediterranean. This cross is the focus of all eyes in the poem: the angelic host, men upon earth, and all this fair creation. The cross is wondrously decorated. The person beholding it in his vision is "stained" or "decorated" as well, but with sin ("synnum fah") and "for-wounded," he says, with blemishes. And in this mood of compunction, as he gazes at the golden, jeweled cross, he begins to perceive through the gold that it too is bleeding. It too is troubled and wounded; the sight makes the visionary even more anxious. And in this mutually troubled, compunctive state, the cross tells its story to the visionary.

Barbara Raw has written well about the various themes and concerns of this poem: as she says, "it is a true meditation, for prayer looks forward to the next world." Remembering Christ's heroic sacrifice, the vision is also the means of "remembering" Heaven. Scholars have often commented on how the conventions of Germanic heroic poetry have been translated in the poem to the Passion story.[145] But my interest here is in how the decoration of the cross is both mirrored in and transmitted to the visionary, at first apparently ironically (the cross is decorated with gems, the dreamer with sins) but then literally, as the visionary's wounds, his compunction of heart, enables him, as he looks further and more clearly, to see that the cross is also bleeding. Blood and gems waver in the decoration before his eyes, as at times the cross appears bloody, at times golden.

A series of verbal–visual puns accomplishes this transmutation, this *allegoria*. Visionary and vision blend sympathetically, and then the full narrative composition develops, oriented from this beginning, as the dreamer looks ever more deeply upon the cross. And the device that creates this blending, the "machine" for the poem's composition, is the ornamented surface of that initiating picture.

4

Dream vision, picture, and "the mystery of the bed chamber"

Ego dormio, et cor meum vigilat.   The Song of Songs 5:2

I. "VISION" AND "FANTASY"

The mystery of my chapter title is not one that has a solution. I am using the word in an archaic way, to mean "craft" or "technique." The bedroom I will talk about is what both the Romans and the medieval monks called *thalamus* or *cubiculum*. The monks associated it most often with the bridal chamber of the Song of Songs. And while all the sexual associations of fertility and fruitfulness resonate in this bedroom mystery, its goal is cognitive creation, and its matrix is the secret places of one's own mind, the matters secreted away in the inventory of memory, stored and recalled, collated and gathered up, by the "mystery" or craft of mnemotechnical invention.

In addition to prayer and the literary colloquy with the Biblical text known as *sacra pagina*, an important genre of monastic meditation is dream vision. At the end of the last chapter I discussed briefly the Anglo-Saxon poem *The Dream of the Rood* as an example of this genre, and I suggested that it be understood as deriving from the orthopraxis of monastic memory work, which often begins with meditation upon a "picture," either materially or verbally painted in (or for) the mind's eye. In this chapter I want to investigate more closely some aspects of monastic visions which are closely linked with rhetorical procedures of invention. Once again, I will be looking at a well-known monastic genre through the lens of rhetorical composition, rather than that of dogma or psychology. I wish to stress that I do not offer this analysis as an alternative to the other, but rather as a supplement, an enrichment.

The concept that focusses this chapter is "visions," a word that in medieval rhetoric means the mental seeings which most usefully can meet a composer's needs to get started and then sustain the crafting of a particular composition. Recall that Quintilian used the Latin word *visiones* to translate Greek *phantasiai*, and commented that these mental craftings were most powerfully of use to call up the emotional energies of oneself and one's audience.[1] If the mind uses machines and devices for thinking, then these *visiones* are an important source of their energy. Quintilian defines *visiones* at greatest length when he is talking about the rhetorical ornament of *enargeia*, the power in verbal description to call up cognitive "visions" that can be useful for inventive purposes.[2]

This rhetorical concept of *visiones* also influenced Augustine's well-known analysis, in his commentary on the literal text of Genesis, of the three types of human vision. There, very much like Quintilian, Augustine calls the mental images formed by imagination and memory "spiritual" (because they are made in the spirit rather than received by the eye) and fictive. These mental seeings derive and are made from the matters presented to our minds by our senses ("corporeal" vision). But unlike Quintilian, Augustine recognised a third sort of vision, the "intellectual" kind, called in monastic praxis *theoria* or direct vision of God. True *theoria* is very rare, though it is the goal, the *skopos*, of all human "seeings." Ecstatic and prophetic visions recounted in the Bible – even those of Moses, Ezekiel, Isaiah, and John – are still "spiritual" in nature because the visionary sees the likeness of bodies, and immaterial things are made knowable by means of images present to the soul.[3]

In monastic rhetoric more generally, the concept of *visiones* (as in Augustine) was also greatly influenced by the traditions of prophetic vision, especially of the Last Things, Hell and Heaven. Monastic visions, as we will see, take pains to pay their intertextual respects to the master visionary narratives of Ezekiel, Daniel, Isaiah, John, Peter, and Paul, among others. Though prophetic vision has certainly included the foretelling of future events, the role of prophet has also always included that of interpreter, the Christian teacher-orator's role of speaking God's word to people in present societies. Augustine defended this opinion that a prophet is a prophet by virtue of his judgment most fully in the twelfth book of his commentary on the text of Genesis. A true prophet understands truly, as demonstrated by his immediate power of moral discernment and judgment.[4]

2. BOETHIUS' LADY PHILOSOPHY: INVENTIVE VISION

I would like to start off my investigation of "vision" with a famous scene of literary composition, a familiar moment of pure imagination as we now would call it, pure creative vision. It occurs at the very beginning of Boethius' *The Consolation of Philosophy*. The work begins with a poem of complaint (Book I, meter 1). And then the story starts up, as follows:

> While I, in silence, thought to mull over this composition within myself [Haec dum mecum tacitus ipse reputarem] and expected to inscribe with a stylus my tearful protest, a woman was seen by me to be standing up over my head [adstitisse mihi supra verticem visa est mulier]... Who, seeing the Muses of poetry standing over my bed and speaking words to my tears, was momentarily angered and burned with fierce looks: "Who," she said, "has permitted these whores of the theater to have access to this diseased man ...?"[5]

Boethius, we discover, is in his bed when the vision (*imago*) of Lady Philosophy appears to him. After her appearance has been described carefully (an example of *enargeia*), she dramatically reviles the "whores of the theater" – the Muses clustered about Boethius as he lies in bed – whom she chases away "from this diseased man [hunc aegrum]," as he lies prostrate, weeping.

I would like to call attention to some features of this famous narrative that will seem trivial, because they are so commonplace. First, notice that Boethius is engaged in *silent* composition, that is in meditation and memory work. The poem he is working on (meter 1) is at some stage before it gets written down with a stylus, the stages of "invention" and "disposition," whose product was often called *res* to distinguish it from the *dictamen*, the stage at which the *res* was "clothed" with its final words, and also from the *liber scriptus*, when it was (perhaps, if it was worthy) written down in a fair copy, the *exemplar* to be copied by others. From what he tells us (and from the fact that a poem does recognizably exist, however unfinished he implies it to be), Boethius is in the final drafting stages, almost ready to write his composition out with a stylus, but still wanting to mull it over ("reputarem"), still *inventing*.[6]

The reason Boethius is lying down in his bedchamber, as his narrative makes clear, is not in order to sleep but in order to compose poems. He is lying in bed because that physical attitude was among the postures that were commonly thought to induce the mental concentration necessary for "memory work," recollective, memorative composition. It is not the only such posture possible: sitting or standing at a lectern pensively, head in hand or staring into space, eyes open or closed, with or without a book, are also common postures of meditative memory work. In classical as in monastic rhetoric, withdrawal to one's chamber indicates a state of mind, the entry to the "place" of meditative silence which was thought essential for invention.

It is during this activity of mental composing that a woman of grave countenance "was seen by me" ("mihi ... uisa est mulier") standing upright over the composing poet. We are not told whether or not his eyes, at this point, are closed; later manuscript paintings of this scene show him either with eyes closed or eyes open.[7] But his mind is not only conscious, it is fully engaged in recollective composition of his poem, performed, as the rhetoric handbooks all counsel, by means of mental imaging techniques.

Boethius is described by Philosophy as "dis-eased," *aeger* referring often (as it does here) to a state of mental distress. This is primarily understood to refer to Boethius' perilous ethical health, which Lady Philosophy attempts to restore. But mental unease, anxiety, restlessness – Boethius is lachrymose throughout this scene – is also a preliminary state of mind for one composing, and so we can take Lady Philosophy's comment literally as well as "morally." Quintilian speaks (disapprovingly) of one in the first throes of composing as being restless and anxious.[8] More importantly for Boethius and his audience, this mental state came to be understood as an important initiator of the "way" of monastic meditation. Illness, anxiety, and restlessness are common mental states (though not always present) for visionary monks as well, from which the emotional stages of contemplation (which is an act of progressive vision) relieves one, or so one hopes.

The poet carefully regards his vision of the lady, painting her in the eye of his (and our) mind. Then Philosophy spies the Muses "nostro adsistentes toro," "standing over my bed," watching over the composing poet. They leave in confusion. And then Boethius, weeping and astonished ("obstipui"), fixes his countenance upon the ground and *in silence still* (the adjective "tacitus" is repeated) begins to watch for whatever will come next.

The emphasis in this narrative scene on acts of seeing is extraordinary: everybody is watching everybody else. I've already mentioned how Lady Philosophy is seen by the meditating poet. Lady Philosophy calls the Muses "has scenicas meretriculas," these false stage-images, onstage to be looked at.[9] And finally, Boethius says he *watches* Lady Philosophy – the verb used is "exspectare" from the verb *spectare*, "to look."

In order to look upon Philosophy, Boethius *looks at the ground* ("visuque in terram defixo," lines 46–48). That is a very peculiar detail. The manuscript images I have seen of this encounter (mostly painted well after the twelfth century) show Boethius lying on his back (with his eyes open or closed) and looking up at Philosophy.[10] But the text says that after Philosophy banishes the Muses, Boethius turns himself prostrate, face downward, grief-stricken. The only things one can see from such a position are mental.

And indeed, lying prostrate and weeping "in silence" (that is, in meditation) became a standard posture in the Middle Ages for all kinds of invention. In the late eleventh century the monk Eadmer ascribed just such behavior to Anselm during the initial composition of his *Proslogion* and two centuries later, Bernardo Gui said that Thomas Aquinas did the same thing when he composed.[11] *Compunctio cordis*, grief and fear induced to begin the memory work of prayer, is, as we have seen, an early element of inventional practice in monasticism. Many of the Jewish prophets had their visions in fear and illness; some also then fell prostrate as a posture of readiness to see and remember. The prophet Daniel also had some of his visions in his bed (Daniel 7:1).[12] In pagan literature also there are moments of a sort of *compunctio cordis*. For example, Aeneas, in a famous initiating act of memory work, *weeps* before a picture that moves him to remember and then compose for Dido the story of his flight from Troy.

One of the most famous Christian literary scenes in which reading, inventive memory work, and vision "take place" is that of Augustine's conversion in the garden in Milan. As described in *Confessiones* VIII.vii–xii.19–30, Augustine assumes a number of postures. He first is sitting, reading "a book of the apostle" beside his friend, Alypius, in anguish of thought; as he reads he weeps and expresses his mental agony in gestures, such as tearing his hair and locking his hands over his knees. Then in his mind he sees Lady Continence (VIII.27) accompanied by a flock of exemplary figures, a literary *pictura* made up of *imagines agentes* within a background *locus* which help him to recall and resolve his moral dilemmas, his divided will. Still weeping, he stands up and throws himself prostrate under a figtree. In that posture he repeats to himself some texts from the Psalms, and then he hears something like a child's voice chanting "tolle, lege," "take, read." At that point, he stands again, goes back to where Alypius is still sitting and picks up (one meaning of *lege*) the book he had left there, in which he reads (the other meaning of *lege*) his fated passage (Romans 13:13–14). Though not often so treated by historians now, the scene as a whole, from start to finish, is a paradigmatic instance of the inventive orthopraxis of reading described by others among his contemporaries. Its steps include the thinker's initial anguish expressed and maintained by his continual weeping, his cognitive use of mental imaging, his repetition of Psalm *formulae*, his prone posture to resolve the crisis in his thinking.[13]

3. COMPOSING IN BED: SOME ROMAN ANTECEDENTS

In monastic practice, the emotionally wrought inventional posture of lying prostrate is linked, by Bernard of Clairvaux among others, to the verse (5:2) from the Song of Songs: "Ego dormio, et cor meum vigilat," "I sleep but my heart [my *memoria* and my soul] is awake." In his twenty-third sermon on the Song of Songs, Bernard describes the process of what he calls the mystery of the bedchamber (*secretum cubiculi*), divine contemplation.[14] The first stages are characterized by "restlessness," an active mind disposing matters, arranging things. The language is that of inquiry and composition: invention and disposition, the initial stages of creation. Anselm's biographer Eadmer described the first stage of invention as being like an illness (inquietude is dis-ease).[15] Bernard of Clairvaux writes further that this preparatory stage is

> a remote and secret place, but not a place of repose ... the contemplative who perhaps reaches that place is not allowed to rest and be quiet. Wondrously yet pleasurably [the Bridegroom] wears out the one who is scrutinizing and examining, and renders him restless. Further on, the Bride beautifully expresses this ... when she says that though she sleeps her heart is awake.[16]

This languorous, expectant restlessness is what is characterized in the key text, "ego dormio et cor meum vigilat," and in the verses ascribed to the Bride which immediately follow it (Song of Songs 5:3–8).

Roman rhetorical practice also associated composition with going to bed. During Cicero's dialogue "On Oratory," the chief speakers,

Marcus Antonius and Lucius Crassus, pause twice (between the books of the dialogue) in order to collect their thoughts on the subjects put to them by the younger members of the party. Marcus Antonius prefers to compose by walking with Cotta in the portico ("in porticu," a structure that provides the *intercolumnia* often recommended as backgrounds for memory work). But Lucius Crassus retires to an invention chamber:

> Accordingly, Cotta went on to say, after they had separated before noon to take a brief siesta, what he chiefly noticed was that Crassus devoted all this midday interval to the closest and most careful meditation; and that as he [Cotta] was well acquainted with the look [Crassus] wore when he had to make a speech and with the fixed gaze of his eyes when he was meditating, and had often witnessed this in important lawsuits, on the present occasion he was careful to wait till the others were reposing, when he came to the room [exhedra] where Crassus was reclining on a couch [lectulus] placed there for him, and as he perceived that he was deep in meditation, at once retired; and that almost two hours were spent in this manner without a word being spoken.[17]

Notice the "fixed gaze" Cotta comments on: evidently, this memory work takes place with open eyes. The posture of lying on a couch to cogitate also made for some good jokes, that the composer was actually sleeping rather than working. Scholars still complain that their postures for thinking frequently go unrecognized, and are mistaken for boredom or inactivity; would that others were as discreet as Cotta!

The Roman *exedra* was a sort of large bay or recess within a larger space; it could also be a small chamber off a larger area of the house. And at least from the Republican period on, like other rooms in Roman houses it was often painted with images arranged "intercolumnia," in scenes composed between columns, either architectural or painted.[18]

So we may think of Crassus as selecting for his invention process a fully decorated place. Notice that the couch has been specially placed there for him. And since the dialogue takes place at his own villa, we can also presume that this *exedra* is one of Crassus' own particular rooms. It has been set up especially for him on this occasion as a place to invent, and a couch has been put there specifically for this purpose. But he would also have had his habitual study or *cubiculum*, used for his business, for conversation with particular friends, for reading and contemplation. I imagine Crassus' chamber as a room looking rather like the cubiculum from the villa of Fannius Synestor at Boscoreale, shown in Plate 15.[19] That room is just large enough for a single couch. The word Cicero uses, *lectulus*, meant not just a bed for sleeping, but one for conversation and study – perhaps because of its partial homophony with *legere*, *lectus*, "gather by picking" (like flowers) and "read."[20] Its walls are all painted in panels, *intercolumnia*, with fantastic, theatrical architecture, though without any *imagines agentes* within these backgrounds (Plates 15 and 17). It opens off a much larger space, for it is now in the columned Great Hall of the Metropolitan Museum of Art. The original effect was indeed, as many historians have noted, like a stage set – note the theatrical mask in the frame over the mural shown in Plate 17. The murals make a "theater" of locations that, apparently, was assumed to be conducive to inventional meditation – not because it provided subject-matter, but because the familiarity, the route- (and rote)-like quality, of such a patterned series in one's most tranquil space could help provide an order or "way" for compositional cogitation. This villa also had an exedra just next to the cubiculum, whose walls were painted with *faux-marbre* panels with a heavy garland of leaves and fruits draped over them, and fantastical single objects hung from the garland, one per panel: a basket with a snake, a satyr mask, a cymbal.[21]

Such murals can be used to map out one's topics during invention, somewhat as a mandala-picture does in traditions of Buddhist contemplation.[22] They provide "where" to catch hold of the process of thinking something through. It is the very habitual nature of the pictures in one's most familiar place (one's house, indeed one's very bedroom) that makes them inventively fruitful over time for a variety of matters. These matters may or may not have anything to do directly with the subjects of the art. Indeed, an arbitrary association between cueing image and recollected matter can often be mnemotechnically more secure than what is obvious and common. A picture of a Homeric episode (for example) need not cue only literary, formal, and moral associations: one very familiar with it could use it to order his thoughts about anything at all. And by the same token, someone who knew nothing of Homer (or the Bible) could use the same picture to remember whatever he chose. That is the nature of mnemonic association, as was well known. It is personal and often arbitrary, neither universal nor necessary, even within a given culture.[23]

Like Cicero, Quintilian assumes that a person needing to compose might choose to go to bed. He describes someone desperate to invent a composition as "[lying] back with eyes turned up to the ceiling, trying to fire [his] imagination by muttering ... in the hope that something will present itself."[24] Equally, he counsels (as will Martianus Capella, much later) that night-time, when silence reigns and distractions are minimized, is the best time for the meditative stages of composing the *res* and premeditated drafts of the *dictamen*, which require intensive concentration.[25] Writing with a stylus is better done, he says, in daylight. This advice also reverberates within the poetry of the Song of Songs: "In lectulo meo, per noctes, quaesivi quem diligit anima mea," "In my bed, through the night, I have sought him whom my soul loves" (3:1).

This tradition of retiring to a small room or recess for the concentrated memory work involved in composing carries on in both early Christian worship and in monasticism. As we have seen in Romuald's prescriptions and in those of Anselm and Peter of Celle, the meditational trope of withdrawing to a *cubiculum* or *cellula* owes a good deal to these continuing assumptions about the suitable postures, gestures, and places counseled also in ancient rhetoric. "Come now, little man," wrote Anselm at the start of his meditation on the meaning of faith, "enter the little chamber of your soul."[26] Gesture, posture, and space were thought to be significant, because they help to prepare the mental attitude and mood necessary for concentration.[27]

Thus, a small space is associated in particular with meditative memory work. In the fourth century, Paulinus of Nola described "four little rooms within the colonnades inserted in the longitudinal sides of the basilica at Nola, [which] offer suitable places for the isolation of those praying or meditating in the law of the Lord." These also contained memorials of the dead. Each room was also marked by a *titulus*, two lines of verse inscribed over the lintel.[28] These spaces were clearly in the tradition of Roman *exedrae*, as "familiar" spaces – for family graves (for example) are there – set apart as places intended for "silent" meditation, yet open to the public space of the large assembly hall.

4. THE *VISION OF WETTI*: MONASTIC VISIONARY INVENTION

In many examples of monastic visionary literature, the preparatory state of the visionary is recognizably similar to the tropes of composition in antiquity. Monastic *visiones* have their immediate context in Biblical dreams like that of Peter (Acts 10, discussed as a type of *visio* by Augustine in the twelfth chapter of his commentary on Genesis), and the apocryphal otherworld visions of Peter and Paul, but they are not indebted only to these. The Christian models intersect in monastic dream visions with the orthopraxis of rhetorical invention.

These various traditions can be detected, for example, in the *Vision of Wetti*, composed in 824 by the Benedictine abbot Heito of Reichenau. This is a prose version; a verse version was made by Walafrid Strabo, then a young monk at Reichenau, three years later. *Wetti* is of particular interest because it is so thoroughly monastic in its milieu: it was not written for a lay audience, as were some later examples of the genre like the "Vision of Tondal" (1149), but to further a specific clerical cause, the reform movements of the early ninth century associated with Benedict of Aniane and the emperor Louis the Pious.[29] So in the case of the *Vision of Wetti* one cannot argue, it seems to me, that it employs "folk features" as popular concessions to an unlearned audience. Indeed, I do not believe that its compositional features are unlearned at all.[30]

The *Vision of Wetti* is, like all monastic dream poems, a *recollected* vision, a way of "remembering" Heaven and Hell. Brother Wetti becomes ill from drinking a medicinal potion, that the others in his monastery had all received in good health. He vomits repeatedly: think, for instance, of Proverbs 23:8, speaking of a wise man, "The morsel which thou hast eaten thou shalt vomit up, and lose thy sweet words." Given the commonplace link between remembering and digesting, meditation and rumination, books and eating, this illness from food – including the detail of vomiting – "gathers" Wetti's experience, compositionally, into a set of visionary and prudential tropes, all of which are also tropes of recollection. In addition to the motif, found in both Ezekiel and John's Apocalypse, of the visionary "eating the book" as a prelude to a vision of heaven, Ezekiel also became ill with a stroke-like paralysis when he experienced his visions; Daniel fainted. Wetti becomes so ill that he must be carried on a litter to his cell, which (this is emphasized in the story) shares a common wall with the refectory, where his brothers remain at dinner (monastic meals included reading, so that, as the Rule says, monks' souls and bellies alike may be fed).

While Wetti is resting on his bed *not asleep but with his eyes closed*, he sees the devil in the guise of a monk, who puts him in great fear –

he is then comforted by an angel.[31] This preliminary vision serves the function of a brief *summa* for the main vision to come. Wetti "wakes up" ("expergefactus") from his vision (though – notice – he was earlier described particularly as *not asleep*) and then dictates the matter of this first vision to two monks whom he summons to his bed. And, Heito assures us, nothing has been added or subtracted from his account.[32] This account of how Wetti composed is similar to what Eadmer, Anselm's biographer, says of Anselm's composing habits: from the initial composition of his *res* or material by mental "vision," to *dictamen* (in this case literally "dictating" to the two monks), to inscription on parchment, the *liber scriptus*.[33] And the same compositional stages are observed in order to set down the major vision which follows.

Wetti's main vision is preceded by great fear brought on by his first vision, the state of "compunction" that every monastic meditation starts with. "Anxious in the immensity of this fear" he falls face downward, prostrate in the shape of the Cross, arms extended.[34] It is the common posture of inventive recollection, accompanied by an intense emotion, such as fear or grief (Aeneas weeps; Daniel and Ezekiel are afraid and fall prostrate; Boethius weeps, is afraid, and falls face down – the classical and Jewish traditions in this regard do not seem to be readily distinguishable). There is no question but that the prophetic religious tradition insisted that a more profound state followed upon these gestures: the state of *raptus*, visionary ecstasy. This state is also characterized as non-cognitive and thus *beyond* memory except through the "messenger service" of fictive images, made for human eyes and ears. But the way to that ecstatic state is through the gestures and postures associated with inventive memory work.[35]

While Wetti lies prostrate his fellow monks chant the Penitential Psalms and other readings to him, as they occur to their memories ("qui sibi ad memoriam occurrent"). These psalm *formulae* are chanted by his companions ("decantare") to focus and comfort his mind during his distress; recall the practice described by John Cassian, Augustine, and Romuald of Camaldoli, which focusses the mind in meditation in this same manner.

Wetti then gets up and goes to his bed ("resedit in lectulo"). He asks that the beginning of Book Four, the "last book," of Gregory the Great's *Dialogues* be read to him, "to the ninth or tenth page."[36] The specific nature of this request is meant to send us to our Gregory.

181

There we will not be disappointed, for the passage cited deals specifically with the nature of seeing spiritual, incorporeal matters. The *Dialogues* more generally contain as well many accounts of monastic rememberings of Heaven and Hell. We are clearly intended to remember these literary "seeings," as Wetti does, as the basis (or initiating point) for his own visions. Heito makes very clear the literary basis of Wetti's visions: the Psalms, the prayers, the teachings and stories of Gregory. They do not come from some unanticipated divine seizure, but are built in a consciously remembered, highly "literary" manner, from the matter he has just been reading.

Then, while his two companions withdraw to a corner of his cell, Wetti finally falls asleep, and the same angel as in his preliminary dream comes to conduct him through the sights of Hell and Heaven (both seen as citadels set upon mountains). His angel guide particularly commends him "because in his anguish he gave his full attention as much to chanting the Psalms as to his readings." The angel urges him to continue doing this, and even gives him another reading assignment, frequently to repeat Psalm 118.[37]

And then the angel raises him up "and led him along a beautiful path" ("duxit per viam ... praeclaram") to a citadel-like building containing many places in which Wetti views, with angelic commentary on each, images of the evil and the good souls. This map-like configuration of places joined up by paths, among which a guide leads the visionary, with commentary "attached" in each place, is a major organizational commonplace of early medieval otherworld journeys.[38] It is an obvious application of the mnemotechnical principle of a *locus* with *imagines agentes*, and the associated compositional principles of *viae* and *ductus*, which I have already explored.

This organizational trope is not limited to visionary literature. Plate 18 shows a picture of Hell copied in the nineteenth century from the late-twelfth-century meditational book *Hortus deliciarum*, which was made by the abbess Herrad of Hohenbourg for her nuns.[39] Hell's many places are marked off clearly from one another, each containing images of the devils and the damned: one would find a route through these places during a meditative "remembering." Plate 19 shows another picture of Hell divided similarly into background places, with "active images" collected memorably in each one. This picture, with Hell Mouth a prominent addition to the conventional Beatus *pictura* of Revelation 20:1–10, is from the Cistercian-produced Arroyo Beatus, made about a century after Herrad's picture.[40]

When he wakens, Wetti asks his brothers to write his vision down on wax tablets. His reasons for doing this are instructive:

> I fear lest, my tongue being paralyzed, what I have seen and heard will not be revealed, for they were enjoined to me with such a great penalty attaching to my duty to make them public, that I fear if I am accused of remaining silent about this to be condemned without mercy, if by my silence [these sights and sounds] should perish and not become common knowledge through me.[41]

So the monks write his visions down promptly in order on wax from Wetti's dictation. Wetti's fear that his tongue will be paralyzed and prevent him from recounting what he saw seems like an odd detail. But it evokes Ezekiel, the prophet who could not speak of his visions except what and when the Lord told him. Such tropes from Ezekiel very often echo within these monastic visions, as we will see elsewhere.

The human prelude to the vision of the otherworld in the *Vision of Wetti*, both in Heito's and in Strabo's versions, is cast entirely in terms of the praxis of monastic meditation. No effort is made to do otherwise, to make it unique and "personal," for example. Its literary genesis and foundations are made obvious; it self-consciously depends upon the remembering of other literature for its authenticity and its "authority." Far from a unique act, it takes pains to announce itself as being fully a product of the conventional ways of monastic visionary invention. The dream, in homage to its literary ancestry, which includes Ezekiel and John, begins with "eating a book" as a literary activity, as inventive memory work: reading, whether silently or aloud, leads to vision, and vision, the activity of composing, results in writing down a finished new literary work.

5. SEEING THE DRAGON: GREGORY THE GREAT'S *LIFE OF ST BENEDICT*

The otherworld visions in the Bible, though considered true in the ethical sense, were understood at their "surfaces" – that is, in the ornamental detail of their language – to be cognitive fictions. The rhetorically educated exegetes of the patristic period, like Augustine, Origen, and Jerome, instituted what they called a "spiritual" exegesis, but it is also one which insists that some language is completely fictive. Gregory the Great, for instance, commented that Ezekiel's vision of the new Jerusalem was not to be understood literally but figuratively, fictively, and took as evidence of this the fact that the measurements given in the text are not completely coherent. In other words, Ezekiel's vision was not to be thought of as in any way a sort of tourist's guide to the New Jerusalem.

One of the most interesting developments in the exegesis especially of Ezekiel's temple vision during the later Middle Ages is the effort to literalize its text. In the later twelfth century Richard of St. Victor, a major visionary writer himself, commented on Ezekiel specifically to refute the assertion of Bede and Gregory that the plan of the temple citadel was irreducibly incoherent, literal non-sense, and thus only to be read "spiritually" and as metaphor (including synecdoche, ekphrasis, metonymy, and so on). As Beryl Smalley said of this literalizing effort, "a scientific movement is really afoot," a movement to objectify and de-trope the ekphrasis, understanding it less as an instance of rhetorical *allegoria* and more as the linguistically "transparent" description of an object.

Smalley associated this exegesis with a Victorine desire to visualize verbal descriptions of Scripture.[42] But what was at issue, I think, was not whether or not to visualize the words – visualization was always part of the orthopraxis of reading these texts, as we have seen. The issue was rather what sort of "reality" the visionary building should be understood to have, whether it was a wholly "cognitive picture," or was also a picture "of" a factual "object." Monastic seeings, deriving from the orthopraxis of prayerful meditation, occupy an ambiguous ontological ground, at least according to our modern notions of the relative truth status of "real" and "fictional" images. In many of them, their ethical and meditational usefulness is foregrounded to the question of their authority as "objective" truth. Even the having of visions, as the compositional circumstances of the *Vision of Wetti* show, was regarded as a practical cognitive act in Carolingian monastic rhetoric, an effective device for the machinery of thinking, and closely related to the cognitive task of making pictures as "ways" for composing meditation.

The result of this assumption was a weak distinction (from our standpoint) between meditative reading and visionary experience. To demonstrate what I mean by this, I would like to examine some incidents recounted in Gregory the Great's *Life of St. Benedict of Nursia* (composed in 594; Benedict died in 550), one of the most widely read and remembered books in monastic culture. Forming the second book of Gregory's *Dialogues*, the life of Benedict is the central example in Gregory's effort to demonstrate, during a period of great social turmoil in the West, that Italy also had produced saints worthy to be venerated as much as the monastic founders of the eastern desert. The genre which Gregory picked was that of the dialogue, one of the most familiar types of pedagogical literature, having been used for (among many other famous works) John Cassian's Conferences. The speakers are Gregory and his young student, Peter.

There are several incidents of visions in this work, in which the relationships between fictive images and what I suppose we must call "reality," for want of a better word, are perceived in instructive ways. I want to examine three of these now, as presenting instances of *visiones* for cognitive, pedagogical purposes. In each one, as I hope to show, literary materials provide the key to understanding.

> One of [Benedict's] monks had given his mind over to wandering and no longer wished to stay in the monastery. Though the man of God faithfully rebuked him, frequently admonished him, in no way would he consent to stay with the community but with obstinate requests insisted that he should be released, until one day, fed up with his constant whining, the venerable father [Benedict] angrily ordered him to depart. As soon as the monk had gone outside the monastery he discovered [inuenit] to his horror that a dragon with gaping jaws was blocking his way. And when this same dragon that had appeared to him seemed to want to devour him, trembling and shaking he began to call out in a loud voice, "Help me, help me, for this dragon wants to eat me." His brothers, running up, could not see the dragon at all [draconem minime uiderunt], but they led the trembling and shaking monk back to the monastery. He immediately promised never to leave the monastery again, and from that moment he kept his promise, for because of the holy man's prayers he had seen, standing in his path, the dragon that previously he had followed without seeing it.[43]

Notice that nobody except the monk sees the dragon. This is emphasized: neither the other brothers who run to his aid, nor Benedict, see the monster. We now would understand this fact to mean categorically that the dragon does not corporeally exist. And given that circumstance – that there "is" no dragon – the first thing we moderns would most likely do is to convince the visionary to see what we see, or rather don't see: "pas de dragon," as the *Sources chrétiennes* translator puts it. The modern rejoinder, "nobody else sees it," would constitute altogether sufficient proof of the dragon's non-reality, proof of the sort we would expect any other person to accede to, and if he did not, his persistence in taking for real what is clearly a figment of his imagination would demonstrate to us his insanity.

Or we might take a symbolizing approach, and understand the dragon as a psychic phenomenon, a "projection" of the monk's anxiety and ambivalence onto the physical landscape. In this case, the dragon could be said to have a mental "reality." But in both these modern attempts to explain the dragon, we would now agree that the dragon certainly has no actual existence – the proof of this, to us, residing in the acknowledged fact in the story, that no one else sees it.

Gregory, however, casts the whole episode in terms of seeing an actual, corporeal thing. There is no suggestion in his account that the monk's seeing is merely an insubstantial apparition. "As soon as" the monk leaves the place of the monastery he "discovers" the dragon blocking his path with jaws open to consume him whole. This causes him, you will notice, to tremble and shake, a detail that is repeated. The whole time that this monk of wandering mind is located outside the monastery, he is in a state of great fear and anxiety, immediately threatened by this dragon that he has "discovered" in his "path." But "immediately" his location changes, and he is back inside the monastery, he is made ethically whole again, because "he had seen" the dragon. The verb is *viderat*, the pluperfect indicative tense – no subjunctive, a hesitation that Gregory could certainly have made had he chosen to do so.

In an effort to be more "religious" in our interpretation, let us call this dragon a "vision." The change of terminology, however, does little to alleviate our scholarly problem. In our psychology, a vision is close kin to, if not quite the same thing as, a figment of the imagination: it still has no corporeal reality. A vision to us differs from an act of imagination only because we define it either as an unmediated intuition sent directly into our mind by a paranormal agent, or as an unconscious and thus uncontrolled effect of a mind-altering experience (usually chemical in nature). But such notions about visions do not fit the case of this incident either.

The language which Gregory uses for the monk's vision is the language of rhetorical invention. It is granted to him, after all, by Benedict's flash of anger (the "prayers" which are causally invoked at the end of the story must include the saintly anger which immediately precipitates the action). We recognize the emotionally charged state of mind, both of Benedict (in his anger) and of the monk who is its object, to be the first stage of meditation.

There are two locations for this story, separated by a clear boundary, the monastery wall. The monk moves along a "path" (*iter*) from one location to the next (inside to outside to inside again). And he is a monk of erring, mobile, "curious" mind. Strong emotion, the compunction of his fear, concentrates his wandering mind in one single overwhelming picture: the dragon he "discovers" in his path, who opposes any further movement outward from the monastery. The verb used, *invenio*, is mentally charged within this context, especially since the dragon is not "there" as an object.

The monk "invents" the dragon in his path, and he invents it from literary and pictorial sources found in his (or rather, Gregory's) memorial store. For the dragon is remembered from a conflation of texts about the devil, including Revelation 12:9 (where the devil is the great dragon who is thrown to earth from Heaven by Michael during the war in Heaven) and 1 Peter 5:8 (where the devil is a ravening lion who goes about seeking whom he may devour). There also likely existed even at this early date a program of Apocalyptic pictures, made and disseminated within contemplative circles.[44] So the dragon is presented as a figment of the imagination and as vision at the same time. "Figment" means "fiction," something made up from images in the mind stored there by actual experience (including education), something recollected exactly in the manner in which one was taught to remember Heaven – or in this case, Hell.[45]

Moreover, the vision in question is presented as the seeing of a corporeal beast. The monk saw the dragon which had been following him. Both verbs used, "viderat" and "sequebatur," are indicative, the grammatical mood one uses to speak of physical things that one saw or that did something to one. And the dragon is physical – if one assumes, as Gregory and his contemporaries did, that memories are stored physically in the brain as cognitively functioning images, and that this physiology of cognition can be spoken of meaningfully in corporeal terms, just as the physiology of muscle movement can be. Human thinking, we should recall, was considered to be *embodied*, in images and pictures and schemes. In this sense the dragon he invented was indeed corporeally seen by the monk, even though no other person saw it.[46] For Gregory and his audience, the fact that it was "figmented," made up out of fragments of text and pictures the monk had seen before, does not compromise but actually affirms the dragon's existence. It exists neither psychically nor objectively but socially, within the ethos of Gregory's recognizing and recollecting audience.

6. SEEING THE DEVIL AND GOD: THE AESTHETIC OF *MNEME*

The reality of these kinds of vision is fictional and ethical, starting from an aesthetic principle that emphasized *mneme* (as in the idiom *mneme theou*, "the memory of God") over mimesis, and ethical judgment over epistemology. Another story about a wandering monk will help to define further what I mean by saying this. This monk could not concentrate during prayer, but let his mind wander far and wide. His abbot finally sent him to Benedict who rebuked him for laziness, *stultitia*. (Remember that Bernard of Clairvaux prohibited fantastic images in cloisters also for fear of encouraging laziness, for the bad sort of mental *curiositas* is a form of laziness, a failure to pay attention. Gregory's *Life of St. Benedict*, and his analysis of the origins of mental wandering, was certainly well known to Bernard.)

Having set this wayward monk straight, Benedict returned him to his home abbey, but within days the monk was back to his old habits, to his abbot's despair. Then Benedict himself came to visit, to try to diagnose the monk's problem. During the silent prayer following the communal recitation of psalms (*psalmodium*), Benedict

> saw [aspexit] that a kind of little black boy [quidam niger puerulus] was drawing this monk, who was not able to stay at prayer, outside by the hem of his garment. Then Benedict said quietly to the abbot, Pompeianus, and to Maurus, "Do you see who it is that draws this monk out?" "No," they said. "Then let us pray that you also will see [uideatis] whom this monk is following." They prayed for two days, and then Maurus saw but the abbot, Pompeianus, still could not see. The next day, having finished prayers, Benedict, upon leaving the oratory, discovered the monk standing outside, and struck him with a stick on account of the blindness of [the monk's] heart. From that day, the monk did not suffer any more ulterior persuasions from the little black boy, but was able to remain in prayer without moving, and so the ancient enemy did not dare to rule in his thoughts; it was as though [the devil] himself had been struck by the blow.[47]

There are some obvious similarities between this story and the one we just examined. Again, Gregory uses verbs of corporeal seeing (*videre, aspicere*), and again he uses the indicative mood entirely – until the very end, where the sudden introduction of the subjunctive construction "ac si ... percussus fuisset," is immediately forceful by its very difference from the rest of the passage. The difference serves to underscore the real nature of that "sort of little black boy," which Benedict saw, and taught others to see who could not see him at first.

The line, so natural to us now, dividing "imaginary" from "actual" phenomena is instructively permeable in this tale, exactly as it is in the story of the monk who saw the dragon. This vagrant monk, having trouble concentrating on his prayers, is described as suffering from mental wandering: his abbot, Pompeianus, notices that while the others "inclined" in the physical and mental postures of *studium orationis*, the discipline of prayer, this monk goes outside and wanders in his mind over worldly, transitory things. A continuity between the physical postures (being bent over in prayer or standing and walking outside) and what we now think of as separate, the mental "state," is apparent here. The one flows seamlessly into the other, in a dialogue of corporealities of brain and muscles.

Benedict sees the little black boy, but with what we would now insist is "only" his imagination. Again, no one can see the figure but Benedict, at least at first. Both Maurus and then Pompeianus must pray, that is engage in meditative memory work (as Benedict needed to do), in order to "see" the phenomenon that is physically drawing the monk out from the oratory. The event is described as occurring specifically during silent meditation following the *psalmodium*. And in such meditation remembered reading comes into one's mind. Indeed, the "little black boy" has been invented from Benedict's (and Gregory's) memory store. In the *Life of St. Anthony*, Gregory's literary model and an essential monastic text, the devil in the guise of a little black boy, "his appearance matching his mind," tempts Anthony, while he is at prayer, to engage in fornication – that wandering, mental fornication which John Cassian so well described, and which is clearly the moral and cognitive problem of the monk in this story.[48]

Once he has himself learned the real nature of the monk's problem, by connecting it to the remembered story of Anthony, Benedict is able to teach the others. He finds the monk standing as usual outside the place of prayer and hits him with a stick, *virga* – a stick that also should send vibrations through an audience's textured memory stores. In Gregory's culture, the physical gesture made by Benedict was basic to sound education, placing the monk in the position of a lazy schoolboy, with Benedict as his *grammaticus*. Notice that Benedict does not hit "the little black boy," he hits the monk himself. There is no ambiguity about that. The gesture is not hostile but pedagogical. And only after this entirely corporeal action does Gregory use the subjunctive, when the devil, whom we now can recognize because we have searched our own memory inventory to find our image (stored when we first learned the story) of the wholly literary, entirely fictive little black boy, feels as though he himself had been struck when the monk was hit.

The monk is struck on account of the blindness of his heart, his ethical obtuseness resulting from his un-seeing (badly lighted, ill-stocked, and unresonant) memory. As a fable of seeing, the blindness of the monk is contrasted to the clear-sightedness of Benedict – and what Benedict sees with the eye of his mind is a familiar story in his treasury of memorized things (*memoria rerum*), presented here *summatim* to those who, unlike the lazy monk, have the eyes to see and hear it in their own memory stores. Evidently Maurus is a quicker student than is Pompeianus, who must meditate and pray longer in order to find the allusion. But the whole incident is cast in the model of schooling, familiar as a model of monastic life from Cassian and Basil and other early monastic writers; and it is a rhetorical, literary education, one in which the *res*, both *dicta et facta*, which one had learned so painfully and corporeally have all the actuality of the blows from rods and rulers which helped to imprint them in the first place in the matter of one's brain. The devil, of course, having no body, can only feel these blows "as if" – and also cannot learn a lesson.

The dragon and the little black boy are examples of Gregory (and Benedict) recollectively "seeing" their reading via cognitive-memorial images, that are made and stored at the invitation of the rhetorical *enargeia* in the words and "pictures" of other works. In fact, Gregory sees Benedict's life almost wholly in terms of what he has already "seen" in his prior reading – for, as scholars have noted, nearly every incident in the biography has a parallel in the lives of the prophets (Moses and Elisha especially), apostles, and the desert saints like Anthony. The *Life of St. Benedict* is an immensely rich network of texts (I include in the word "texts" as I am using it here the graphic arts programs that Gregory may also have known). And is it not a true observation of our actual human condition that we know much of the world through what we have read and heard? And since we must "see" what we read in order to know it, why wouldn't those images be what we see when we recollect our reading in order to understand a new situation? The dragon and the little black boy, in short, are real, as real as reading and knowing and judging.

The visions in Gregory's *Life of St. Benedict* all have a pedagogical purpose. This is in keeping, of course, with the nature of the dialogue genre itself, designed, as I observed, for learning and reflective conversation, and not as "objective" history. In this process, the focus is on Gregory's pupil, Peter, just as in the accounts of the visions of the two wayward monks the focus is on their pedagogical effectiveness. And as successful pedagogy, educating the citizens of the city of God, they make masterful use of many tools in the craft of rhetoric.

Even the most rapturous of the saint's visions is made a focus for Peter's continuing lessons in the way of meditation, rather than merely cited as a proof of Benedict's sanctity or evidence of his "psychological make-up." Gregory's purpose remains pedagogical and rhetorical: to show Peter the final stage of meditative praxis, when the mind, absorbed in God, is raised up, enlarged and expanded until it can see the whole universe at a glance, and looking down from above, sees how small the world really is. Gregory's description of the vision should not, I think, be taken as simple mimesis. It invokes the ancient literary device of the philosopher's flight or *kataskopos*, pressed into hagiographical service.[49] Nor is this the only literary matter shaping this very carefully crafted account.

Benedict was watching and praying alone before the night office in his room on the uppermost floor of the tower of his monastery, his companion Servandus one floor below and the other monks in their dormitory, when the saint suddenly saw all the world as though gathered up in a single sun's ray, and the soul of one of his fellows carried to heaven in a fiery ball, like Elijah:

> When the time of silence had come, venerable Benedict went up to his chamber on the second storey of the watchtower, his dean Servandus was located in the one below, which was connected to his by stairs. There was a larger building facing this tower, in which the disciples of both rested. The man of God, Benedict, urgently keeping watch [instans uigiliis] while his brothers yet slept, had anticipated the hour of the night office.[50]

Notice how carefully Benedict is positioned in this scene in relation

191

to all the other actors. Servandus has "located" himself in the *locus* just below but connecting with Benedict's chamber, just as Benedict has located himself in the tower. "Down" and "up" are the key spatial orientations in Gregory's shaping of the story. Benedict is in the top of the monastery watchtower, as his disciples sleep, facing him below in their dormitory.

Benedict's watchfulness is underscored. So is the motif of sight. Every detail of this carefully envisioned scene invites rich harmonies with the *dicta et facta memorabilia* which Peter should carry in his mind: the watchmen and watchtowers of the Psalms and Isaiah and the Song of Songs, the shepherds at the nativity, the watchfulness of Jesus over his sleeping disciples, the lives of other saints. Even the seemingly mundane staircase, *ascensus*, connecting the lower to the higher storeys, presages the moment to come – for those who remember the story of Jacob's dream. This is a scene carefully located and colored within the established ways of meditative prayer.

Gregory continues:

> While he was standing at his window and beseeching almighty God, all at once, as he was reflecting in the dead of the night, he saw a light from on high put to flight all the shadows of night, and to shine with such splendor that the light which radiated among the shadows seemed to vanquish the day. And another wonderful thing followed in his sight, for, as he told it himself afterwards, the whole world was drawn up [adductus est] before his eyes as though it were gathered up [collectus] in one ray of the sun.[51]

The *mira res*, the event wondrous to look upon, is sudden, yet neither unconscious nor unprepared. The careful locating of the saint, temporally (in relation to the canonical hours) and spatially (in relation to the rest of his brothers), is a most striking feature of this account. Only by following the path, the monastic way, the implication seems to be, can the goal of *visio Dei* be achieved, however momentarily.[52] Benedict is engaged in meditation, *respiciens*, "looking back" over matters reflectively and recollectively. And the marvelous sight itself incorporates the rhetorical and mnemonic principle of *brevitas*, brevity for the purpose of copious "dilation," the word Gregory uses.[53] This is the lesson which Peter, with Gregory's help, is able to discover in Benedict's wondrous sight. As one's mind enlarges, *dilatatus est*, in holy contemplation, the whole world becomes "gathered up," *collectus*, into a single ray of intense light. "Gathering" is a favored word in later monasticism for recollective, meditative reading, undoubtedly because of the *etymologia* (philologically correct in this case, for *colligere* was actually fashioned from *con* + *legere*) that links it to *legere*, the verb meaning both "gather up" and "read."[54]

7. (RE)BUILDING THE NEW JERUSALEM: CONSTRUCTION BY VISION

The literary, recollective nature of such pedagogy by vision is apparent also in the example I would like to examine next. This incident in the *Life of St Benedict* is a bit different from the ones we have just looked at, for it is not an incident of literary allusion expressed as encountering an image remembered from reading. Rather, it equates a visionary image with bodily presence, and since it is also an early and influential instance of a type of "construction dream" that became conventional in later monasticism, it is worth pausing over. Well-known examples of such dreams include the vision of St. Aubert (eighth century) for the building of Mont- Saint-Michel, and the vision of Gunzo (twelfth century) for the building of a larger monastery at Cluny, a dream I want to examine in detail in my next chapter.

Benedict was asked to found a new monastery on the estate of a nobleman, near Montecassino. He sent a founding group of his monks, promising them that on a particular day he would come to show them where and how to build the various components of the new monastery. Before dawn on the appointed day, both the abbot and prior of the new foundation had a dream in which Benedict appeared and showed them where and how to build each place in the new establishment:

> During that very night, before the promised day dawned ... the man of God appeared to them in their dreams [in somnis], and showed them plainly where they should build each place [of the monastery]. And when each of them had risen from their sleep [a somno], they told each other what they had seen. But not entirely giving full faith and credit to that vision [uisioni], they continued to wait for the man of God, as he had promised to come in person. And when the man of God did not come at all on the appointed day, they went to him very perturbed, saying: "We expected, father, that you would come, as you promised, and show us where we should build what, and you did not come." He replied, "What are

193

you saying? Did I not come as I had promised?" And they said, "When did you come?" And he replied, "Did I not appear to each of you as you were sleeping and mark out each building location? Return, and as you heard [audistis, *though some manuscripts read uidistis*] by means of your dream [per uisionem], so construct each building of your monastery."[55]

This story seems quite clearly to equate an image mentally seen with corporeal presence, a kind of saintly teleconferencing in which Benedict's dream appearance is regarded as having the same cognitive authority as a physical visit. From the monks' failure to recognize the equivalence of the two kinds of manifestation, it is apparent that it was problematical to suppose that dream images and physical visitations were always the same.

Benedict however rebukes the monks' hesitation in this instance. He does not claim – and this needs to be underscored – that he has indeed come physically to them. What he promised was that he would come and show them where and how to build: "et die illo ego uenio, et ostendo uobis in quo loco ... aedificare debeatis." And this is just what he did. What Benedict objects to about his monks is not that they can't tell the difference between a *visio* and a *somnium*.[56] Nor does either he or Gregory explain his visit as an instance of bodily extromission or telekinesis, though both they and their audiences probably held some belief that such things were possible, at least for saints. What Benedict criticizes the monks for is being unable to make the remembered literary connections that authenticate and originate the motif of giving construction plans for divinely sanctioned buildings via a vision – the prime originators being Moses, Ezekiel, and St. John.

After hearing this story, Peter asks Gregory exactly the question that we moderns would be inclined to ask: how was the saint able to travel such a distance in order to give his reply to those sleeping, so that they recognized and heard him in their vision?[57] Gregory does not respond by trying to give a scientific explanation, of the sort we would insist on – he observes only that the spirit is more mobile than the body.

The real explanation of this story comes when the student, Peter, recalls the most apt set of Biblical parallels to the story. Like a good teacher, Gregory gives him a clue: he reminds Peter that the prophet Habakuk was corporeally transported from Judea to Chaldea in order to dine with the prophet Daniel (Daniel 14:32–38): "If Habakkuk could cover such a distance bodily in an instant to take a meal to his fellow-prophet, what sort of miracle would it be if father Benedict were to go in spirit and tell what was necessary to the spirits of his brothers while they were in a quiet state [quiescentium]?"[58] The verb chosen, *quiescere*, suggests the "quiet" mental state of contemplation, most appropriate to *visiones*. But the monks' state is ambiguous, since the word *somnus* ("sleep") is used earlier. As we have seen, such ambiguity persists in later accounts of monastic visions.

One puzzle has been solved only to put forth another. For the reference to a prophet in Chaldea sets another enigma to Peter and even more importantly to us. Neither Peter nor the monks reflect on the building vision itself, which is, after all, the main point of the story. They each get distracted by how and in what manner Benedict could make his appearance. Notice that Gregory does not mention the obvious and closest parallel to the vision: Ezekiel's sight (while he was in exile in Chaldea) of the new Jerusalem, measured out for him with a measuring-rod, building by building, by the man with a brazen countenance, so that by remembering these measurements he could construct the city after the Return (Ezekiel 40). This is a planned "oversight" of the same sort as Prudentius' failure to cite by name the obvious master-text for *Psychomachia*, the verses from Ephesians about putting on the whole armor of God. It is not mentioned so that a reader can invent it on his own, thereby giving his mind both delight and instruction.

Gregory answers the novice Peter's curious question by a curious answer, giving him the farthest-out, the most obscure, link of a chain that should lead him to the far more important, central matter of the story he has just been told. It is an example of what Peter of Celle, so much later, calls "religious curiosity," the sort of literary puzzle-solving that can lead to ethical good as well as serving as a test of one's ingenuity and "character." Habakuk having been set on Peter's recollective fishing-line (as a parent might bait a child's hook), it is then up to Peter – and to us – to reel in the rest of the fishes: Daniel (Habakkuk's host in Chaldea), Ezekiel (via the keyword "Chaldea," and also via Daniel's association with apocalyptic visions), Ezekiel's vision of Jerusalem, John's vision of the Heavenly City – and all of these "things" linked together finally in the "new Jerusalem" trope, that was also implicated (pleated or enfolded) in the buildings and meditative life of every monastery. The obvious but distracting conundrum of telekinesis "conceals" the far more significant "secret" of the story.[59]

I suspect that some readers will consider my having discovered a reference to Ezekiel in this exchange to be "far-fetched" (it is, literally) and thus to be "stretching" the meaning of the text. But this is to strain at gnats while missing the substance – exactly the sort of thing Gregory rebukes in Peter and in the monks of the original incident. The text of Ezekiel is the "inventor," or "starting-off place," with which Benedict's puzzled monks should have associated their visionary experience in order to recognize and judge the authenticity of their own construction dream. Their dullness, like Peter's curiosity about the physics of telekinesis, is rebuked and corrected by Gregory's reminder of the story of Habakkuk's visit to Daniel. Gregory is too aware of his readers' cognitive need to be puzzled and delighted simply to give us all The Answer (and thereby encourage tendencies towards mental laziness). At the end of the episode, Peter assures Gregory that his mental doubt has been wiped clean by his master's reply; we can only wonder still whether he has indeed "gotten it," or whether this is only the temporary triumph of a still befogged mind that, by solving the minor issue, has missed the obvious.

8. THE MNEMOTECHNIC OF "PICTURE"

Aeneas, washed ashore at Carthage after a great storm, comes unseen into the city and into the temple to Juno which Dido has erected "rich in gifts and the presence of the goddess" (*Aeneid* I. 447). Here, to his amazement, he sees a series of pictures on its walls, each showing a scene of the battle for Troy:

> [he scans each object,] while he marvels at the city's fortune, the handicraft of the several artists and the work of their toil, he sees in due order the battles of Ilium, the warfare now known famously throughout the world, the sons of Atreus, and Priam, and Achilles, fierce in his wrath against both. He stopped and *weeping* cried: "What land, Achates, what tract on earth is now not full of our sorrow?" ... So he speaks, and, *groaning often*, grazes his soul upon the insubstantial picture [animum pictura pascit inani].[60] (My emphasis)

Notice that Aeneas weeps. His memory process is pricked by the act of weeping, and this in turn enables him to recollect, and, recollecting, to let his soul graze and then, after inventing and composing here, to tell his story to Dido later at the material feast.

The verb Virgil chose, *pascere*, "to graze," is an allusion as well to the rumination of meditating. But if the act of weeping and groaning – *compunctio cordis*, the emotional trigger – is necessary to invent, so too are the *picturae* he beholds, the orderly series of scenes of Troy, from one to another of which Aeneas walks. The action is presented by Virgil as an actual event, but it mirrors the practice, commonplace to Virgil and his audience, of rhetorical composition located in the pictures of *memoria*.

Memorial cultures are also story-telling cultures, and their typical picture-artifact is also a story-artifact. The artifact makes present – in memory – the occasion for a composition, the "starting-point" of recollection, as these mural paintings do for Aeneas, as his shield recollects the lives of the Greeks to Achilles. The careful technique of the artificer is often stressed when these "pictures" are described, for the craft of memory is being addressed. It is surely no coincidence that the early fifth-century (BC) poet Simonides of Ceos, supposed "inventor" of the ancient mnemonic art of picturing images in backgrounds, was also identified (by Plutarch and others) with the maxim that poetry is verbal painting, painting silent poetry.[61]

A number of works, both Roman and medieval, begin with a picture, and the technique has acquired a name, although the one used by scholars is modern, *Bildeinsatz*.[62] *Bildeinsatz* starts off a work by addressing the memory of both the fictional onlooker and the reader/hearer with a summary of the principal "matters" of the work to follow, seen as a set of painted or sculpted, embroidered or mosaic images. Cicero's *De natura deorum* begins with a cosmic "picture"; so, far more elaborately, does Martianus Capella's treatise on the liberal arts, with its picture narrative of *The Wedding of Mercury and Philology*. Lady Philosophy's robe is another example; so too is the intricate beginning picture of Dame Nature in Alan of Lille's Boethian poem, *The Complaint of Nature*. The technique is common still in the fourteenth century: I described in *The Book of Memory* friar Robert Holcot's *picturae*, which he says he placed mentally on the *initial* of verses in Hosea in order to remember the themes of the commentary, clearly as his invention tool for sermons and lectures involving these texts.[63] And *pictura* is commonly used also as a synonym of *mappa*, "map."

In several texts, a compositional *pictura* takes the form of a vision seen by the author, as it does in *The Consolation of Philosophy*. A good example is the beginning of Prudentius' account of the martyrdom of St. Cassian of Imola (not to be confused with John Cassian), a Christian grammarian whose martyrdom consisted in being stabbed to death in the arena by the pens of pagan school boys. In this poem, the nature of the *pictura* which Prudentius sees is somewhat unclear. The poet depicts himself as a pilgrim visiting the saint's tomb-shrine. He lies prostrate before it, weeping:

> As I tearfully recalled my wounds and all the trials of my life and pin-pricks of suffering, I raised my face to heaven, and opposite me stood [a] portrait [imago] of the martyr, [painted] in brilliant colors [fucis colorum picta], bearing a thousand wounds, his whole body torn, and displaying flesh ripped with tiny puncture marks. Around him, a pitiful sight, countless boys pierced his limbs with strokes from their small styli, with which they were accustomed to engrave their wax tablets and take down in dictation their schoolmaster's lesson.[64]

"The picture recalls the story," "historiam pictura refert" (line 19), as the verger of the shrine says. We recognize in the sequence of Prudentius' meditation the common monastic meditative way, the visionary's *compunctio* (literally echoed in the picture of the martyr's pierced body) leading to weeping and lying prostrate, and then lifting up his face towards Heaven, seeing the saint's painted picture, the action which starts off his composition.

Saint's shrines, like some of the Jerusalem pilgrimage sites, could be outfitted with paintings. Perhaps one of these is what Prudentius saw here. On the other hand, he may well have seen the martyr in the way that visitors to Babylas' tomb saw the very face of that saint. Prudentius is as uninterested in the "scientific" nature of what he saw as Gregory is in that of the monk's dragon or Boethius is in that of the apparition of Lady Philosophy. It is rather the story and ensuing meditation which his seeing recalls that is significant. The picture of St. Cassian does not merely "help" Prudentius to meditate, it *enables* his mind, setting it in the right inventive "tracks."

9. THE PICTURE AS COGNITIVE MACHINE

In her essay on how visual aids were used in ancient education, Eva Keuls has described how the initiating figure of *Bildeinsatz* was used first in the deliberative homilies of Pythagorean and Stoic orators. It is not hard to see the relationship of rhetorical picture-making to the textbook advice to an orator to fashion *imagines agentes* grouped

narratively as scenes within background places, whose relative positions cue the order and subjects of his composition.

Other scholars also have connected the use of mental imaging for
pedagogical purposes with these same two philosophical schools,
which had so great an influence on Hellenistic education.[65] But the
figure is not confined solely to childhood education. It is a trope of
rhetorical invention (though not defined separately in ancient handbooks) that gained great importance in the monastic way of meditation as the initiating picture or vision upon which a meditator
focussed his attentive memory work.

Bildeinsätze have the rhetorical quality called *enargeia*. Often the
figure is also conflated with ekphrasis, the description of a building or
other artifact (such as the Temple of Juno in *Aeneid* I). Ekphrasis, as
we have seen, provides a meditative occasion within a work; it slows
down, even interrupts, the established *ductus* of a work, and often
sends a reader in a new direction. But narrowly defined (which is a
good place to start, though I wish to broaden the definition shortly), a
Bildeinsatz differs from an *ekphrasis* in two ways. It is at the
beginning of a work (or of a major division or change of subject
within a long work), a trope of the introduction whereas ekphrasis
can occur at any point. And because of its location, it acts as the
elementary foundation, the *dispositio* of what follows. Introductory
rhetorical pictures serve as orienting maps and summaries of the
matters which are developed within the work. They provide its
memoria rerum. Every once in a while they are found at the end of a
work, in the position which we now expect; but the beginning is far
more common, probably because a reader can hold the picture in
mind as a way of recognizing the major themes of what follows (one
needs always to keep in mind that reading, particularly before the
fifteenth century, was most often reading aloud, though this is not a
critical point for my purposes here).

Placement is crucial. The images' relative locations within the
picture arrangement ring changes on the three basic modes of
associative recollection: they may be "the same," they may be
"opposite," they may be "neighborly" or "contiguous."[66] In
memory technique, these adjectives refer primarily to an image's
relative position in a common scene, rather than to a conceptual
relationship. And their placements set up the associative paths and
chains onto which one "hooks up" – in various directions – additional
material from these foundational images: hence, as we have seen, the

basic metaphor in the word *error*, a matter of not minding the path and so getting lost.

Secondly, the orienting picture may be, but need not be, a work of art. Whereas ekphrasis always purports to be a meditative description of a painting, sculpture, or the façade of a building, the initiating compositional *pictura* can also describe a schematized landscape in the form of a world map, or a figure like Lady Philosophy, or just about any of several *formae mentis* in common monastic use: a ladder, a tree, *rotae*, a rose-diagram. The rhetorical figures called ekphrasis and *Bildeinsatz*, in other words, are types of the cognitive, dispositive topos called *pictura*, which is the more general term. The most general terms of all for this cognitive instrument would include words like *ratio* and *schema*.

Maps were also commonly called *picturae*. As P. Harvey has written of them, the maps we find in medieval books (see Plate 1) and in large parchment charts "are best understood as an open framework where all kinds of information might be placed in the relevant spatial position."[67] Isidore of Seville defines a picture as "an image expressing the semblance [speciem] of some thing" which, when seen again, will recall to mind some matter that one wants to remember. The "good" of a picture, its underlying aesthetic principle, is thus understood in terms of its role in cognitive function: a picture is for remembering, and its value is dependent on how it serves this function. *Pictura*, Isidore continues, is etymologically related to *fictura*, that is, an image for the purpose of shaping or fixing something in the mind.[68]

Two things in particular stand out in Isidore's account of a picture. It is, he says, distinct to pictures that they have colors, including lights and shadows. These various colors are the fictive order of a work, what fashion it into a "picture." Though it is not a term he uses, rhetorical *ductus* is assumed here, the movement through the order of a picture marked out by means of its colors, as the verbal colors move one through a speech. A picture's colors do not simulate nature, but are conceived of "diagramatically," as indeed they are in medieval *mappaemundi*. For example, the Red Sea was often painted as an oblong red shape, as it is in the Saint-Sever Beatus (Plate 1). This served as an immediately evident orienting device, whose red color on the map is not an attempt to show the actual color of the water, but is a rebus of its name, as well as being (as all agreed) the most memorable of colors.[69]

And also, like words, pictures are cognitive in nature; their degree of mimetic realism is emphatically not a quality of importance to Isidore. Pictures are constructions, fictions, like all ideas and thoughts. And in the same way as words, pictures are made for the work of memory: learning and meditation. *Pictura* is a cognitive instrument, serving invention in the same manner as words do.

The assumption that learning requires the use of picturing was a venerable one in Hellenistic pedagogy: every historian of Roman education has remarked on it. But Eva Keuls has noted that, with all the literary evidence surviving of a "visually evocative technique" for starting off and organizing an oration or a treatise, there is only one clear piece of evidence of the use of a visual aid in ancient oratory. The matter to which scholars have mostly directed their inquiries is whether the common use of verbal pictures also implies the use of material aids to teaching and learning, sometimes realized as wall charts, but more often as the murals, mosaics, sculptured friezes, columns, and elaborately articulated façades that were found everywhere in Roman towns.[70]

For example, the famous marble Iliac frieze in the Capitoline Museum in Rome, dating from the first century, is but the most commonly discussed of Roman reliefs and paintings that recall and retell stories. The organization of this composition follows some familiar mnemonic organizational principles: the center of the composition is occupied by a scene of the destruction of Troy, as it is the "principle," the nodal event of the story web. Around this center are scenes that epitomize the matter of the *Iliad*, book by book, but with emphasis placed upon the *first* book. An epitome of this initial book, in seven scenes, runs in a continuous register along the top, above the central "story" of Troy's destruction and Aeneas' escape. Books 2–12 of the *Iliad* (now missing) ran in descending order along the left side, and 13–24 ascended along the right side. So, one would read this tablet from left to right across the top; look left and down, and then right and up, in a more-or-less counter-clockwise movement.[71]

This pride of place given to the center in mnemotechnical pictures carries through the Middle Ages: for example, a number of people who describe their technique of making a mental "picture" for their composition begin with a central image. In Hugh of St. Victor's *De arca Noe mystica* this is a square in the center of his mental "page," the square (derived from the square shape of the Heavenly City) which forms the building unit for the rest. Much later, Bishop

Bradwardine writes in his instructions for constructing mnemonic "scenes" that one should "look" first to the central image as the "starting-point," and then to the right and to the left, returning each time to the center, in order to recall the order of the cueing images.[72]

There is much debate as to who might have used such an artifact as the Capitoline tablet. Earlier scholars thought it might have been made for schoolboys as an *aide-mémoire*. This suggestion has now been rejected by some scholars, perhaps too quickly. Richard Brilliant suggested instead that it was a "Classics Comics" of its day, made "for a vulgar clientele that cared little for learning."[73] He based this conclusion on the fact that the scenes depicted alter the "pace" and "saliency" of the original text, producing plot "distortions." This would be a handicap, *if* the tablet were designed to "illustrate" in the modern sense, or to "substitute" for the text in the way that a "Classics Comic" sought to do. But if it were designed as a set of reminder-cues, made to order for a patron who knew the text already but wanted the picture summary as a meditational/mnemonic instrument, its "distortions" need not be seen as only vulgar: they may represent mnemonically significant choices for the patron.

The debate among Roman historians over the use of this object, and many others like it, seems to me to incorporate a flawed assumption about the relationship of images and texts – that picture books are for the textually unsophisticated, either children or vulgarians. Richard Brilliant himself contradicts his suggestion that the Capitoline tablet was made for a vulgar audience when he analyzes the central scene of Troy's destruction, which is dominated by multiple appearances of Aeneas (a minor figure in Homer), culminating in his taking ship for Italy. As Brilliant says, the *Iliad* narrative is by this means "charged with a substratum of Roman iconography" that transforms it "into a preface to Roman history" consistent with contemporary Augustan aspirations. The Iliac frieze thus both recalls *summatim* a text already known and invites further reflection, a sort of tropology of pagan history.[74]

An artifact like the Iliac tablet would not have been used to best effect by students memorizing the text for the first time. They did that by other means, including chanting and bodily postures, perhaps like the davening one still sees in rabbinical and Koranic schools. Nor can it reasonably "substitute" for knowing the epic poem, for the whole point was to be able to quote and recognize the words.

But a summarizing picture could have value for teachers and others who already knew the words but might usefully wish to be reminded of where they were in the overall story by means of visual cues, a sort of map. In a long text with many divisions and episodes, like the *Iliad* and *Aeneid* – and also the Pentateuch and other Biblical material – such a finding tool could be quite useful for someone who had occasion to interpret these texts.

It has been claimed that mnemotechnical principles were used in constructing the program of *picturae* of the Utrecht Psalter, made in the ninth century.[75] Scholars have hesitated to accept this explanation fully, however, precisely on the grounds I have discussed here in respect to the Iliac tablet. But if the manuscript were designed for pedagogical and reading use (which seems probable, since it is not lavishly colored), it would have been used most probably in situations where students already knew the syllables of the Psalms by rote. The pictures cue the chief phrases of each psalm for further commentary and exegesis, and would probably be more useful for inventing meditative homilies and prayers than they would to someone just learning the sounds of the words for the first time. In monastic culture, after all, the Psalms were one of the bases of one's life-long memory work.

10. *PICTURA*: A TROPE OF MONASTIC RHETORIC

The initiating convention which had no distinguishing name in ancient rhetoric was sometimes given one by Carolingian writers. It was called, unsurprisingly, *pictura*, a usage perhaps influenced by the Patristic Latin idiom I examined earlier, *(de)pingere in corde*.[76] A *pictura* is a composition of images, either actualized in a visual medium or described in words for the eye of the mind. For instance, this is how, in the eighth century, Bede described some of the treasures brought to England from Italy by Benedict Biscop, to be installed on the walls of St. Peter's church in the monastery at Wearmouth:

> [Benedict Biscop] brought home pictures of holy images [picturas imaginum sanctarum] to equip [ad ornandum] the church of blessed Peter the apostle, which he had built; namely, the image [imaginem] of the blessed mother of God ... and also of the twelve apostles, by means of which he might gird the vault of the said church with a construction of [painted] wood-panels [which] led [ducto ... tabulato] from wall to wall; images of the Gospel story with which he could furnish [decoraret] the south wall of the church; images of the

visions in Revelation, with which he might equip and ornament [ornaret] the north wall also, in order that all entering the church, even those ignorant of [Latin] letters, whichever way they might turn, should either look on the gracious face of Christ and his saints, although in an image; or might recollect in their minds more feelingly the grace of the Lord's incarnation; or, having the perils of the Last Judgment as it were before their eyes, might remember to examine their consciences more exactly.[77]

P. Hunter Blair has pointed out that Bede clearly distinguishes *imagines* from *picturae* in this passage, but "in such a way as to show that by *imagines* he meant the representations of divine or human beings displayed on the *picturae* ... the *imagines* were part of the *picturae* and not distinct objects."[78] *Pictura*, as used by Bede, refers to the arrangement or *dispositio* of a group of images – one could thus make a picture out of images. Notice also that the *picturae* are themselves grouped in an orderly way through the church, as "equipment," markers or stations in the "routes" of meditation upon the various matters which the stories in relationship to one another call to mind. The pictures within the church act like the stations of pilgrimages which I examined in Chapter One; one is led (*ductus*) from one to another. The heuristic role of *picturae* as markers of varying *ductus* within a church was consciously exploited by various abbots, as we will see in the next chapter.[79]

A similar sense of *pictura* as "arrangement of images" seems to me to be at work in the following lines of a poem by the sixth-century poet, Venantius Fortunatus, to his friend, Gregory of Tours, the bishop and historian, written on the occasion of Gregory's rebuilding in 590 of Tours cathedral. Fortunatus describes the new building and its program of images depicting incidents in the life of St. Martin of Tours, who had once held the episcopal see:

> The splendid design of the picture [pompa picturae] arrays the fabric [of the building] more luminously
> and, conducted by it [*referring to* pompa], you might think the picture elements [membra] with their vibrant colors to live.[80]

Pictura is singular. The "picture" is the array of individual painted narrative scenes from the life of St. Martin which the poem goes on to describe; their splendid formal design ("pompa") makes up the *pictura* of which each painting is a "member." The *pompa picturae* is then said to conduct someone through the fabric – the walls and spaces of the cathedral – by means of its artful arrangement of lights and vivid colors. Piers and arches and columns also made fine "conductors" of this sort.

Bede's language also underscores his sense of the images as together forming a whole meditational device. The panel paintings were not hung as single, contextless, items; they made up a construction of wood (*tabulatum*) that led people (*ductus*) from one wall to the other. A *tabulatum* is a single structure, such as a deck, made up from individual pieces of wood fitted together. Thus Bede imagines the panels as parts of one structure, but one with inherent movement – it leads its viewers.[81] The *tabulatum* in this church was similar in function to the meditational, pedagogical construction of pictures that outfitted such earlier Christian churches as those of Paulinus at Nola, or St. Peter's and Santa Maria Maggiore in Rome. In many cases the structure incorporated the scheme of "pictures" set out in Prudentius' *Dittocheon*. Bede uses the verbs *ornare* and *decorare* throughout his description; they are untranslatable in modern English, since we insist on conceptually separating decoration from function. In Latin, these verbs encompassed both. The *picturae* which the various images made both on the wall surfaces and in the beholders' minds are part of the machinery for the large-scale, on-going mental construction project that a monastery invited from those who entered its precincts.

II. PAINTING PICTURES FOR MEDITATION: PETER OF CELLE "ON CONSCIENCE"

Using "pictures" to arrange the matters of a composition is common throughout the Middle Ages. It is found in vernacular as well as Latin traditions, including some quite early vernacular works. For example, in the Anglo-Saxon poem *Beowulf*, King Hrothgar looks upon a sword-hilt which depicts scenes of the Flood. He then fashions a speech, on the basis of the *ductus* he perceives in and among these scenes, praising Beowulf for saving the Danes from the perils of Grendel and his mother, and then reflecting generally upon human life and death (*Beowulf*, lines 1687–1784). It is clear in the poem that looking at the sword enables Hrothgar's meditation, that the decorated artifact acts as not only the "inspiration" (as we would probably now say) but as the inventional, ordering instrument with which he composes. It occurs in a vernacular poem, but it is a moment fully compatible with monastic practice.

A typical use of *pictura* in Latin monastic literature, an example considerably later than the moment in *Beowulf* which I just described, occurs in Peter of Celle's treatise "On Conscience," written around 1170. After a lengthy preface addressed to Alcher, the monk of Clairvaux who asked him for this work, Peter of Celle gets down to his subject, which is the nature of conscience. First he gives its etymology: conscience is *cordis scientia*, "knowledge of the heart" (one needs always to remember the extended meaning of "heart" available in these devotional texts). This instance of the ornament *etymologia* "brings in" to Peter's composition a collation of texts from the Bible, including ones from Exodus, the Psalms, and Job, invented by the mnemotechnical key words *cor, cordis* and *sapiens, sapientis*.[82] This *etymologia* initiates and orders the main themes of Peter's meditation on the nature of conscience.

To introduce the next, and longest, section of his treatise, Peter makes what he calls an *exemplum* for Alcher to use in understanding this concept:

> Concerning conscience's habit [habitudine, having multiple meanings, including "condition," "dwelling-place," and "clothing"] so that I may make an exemplum for you, not by way of idolatrous error but by way of making abstract doctrine evident [to the eye of your mind], form in your mind something that at the same time may prick [compungat] your pious mind to devotion and raise your soul from visible form to invisible contemplation. And so place [in your mind] a table laden with an abundant variety of several dishes. Put there a king crowned with his diadem [cf. Songs of Songs 3:11] and decked out with the grandeur of all his triumphs; he dwells in the first and most principal place [in capite et principaliori loco residere], and the hand of those assisting and serving him with food and drink should be most attendant. Let there be gold and silver vessels [Exodus 11:2] for each service, let there also be cups filled [cf. Song of Songs 8:2] with honey ... Let cithara and lyre and psaltery refresh the hearing of his companions with melodies ... Having put everything into the most well-arranged order possible [dispositissima ordinatione], let nothing be lacking in elegance or be tediously superfluous.[83]

Notice the language of locational memory in this initiating picture. In the way Peter constructs it, one clearly sees the locational verb *pono*, which is the root of "dispose," at work. First, make a place for your mind's eye; mark this location with something that creates a place for the images you will now put into this background – for instance, a table. Then place within the location a central image, in this case a king (derived from a verse in the Song of Songs). Pause over this image, paint it in grand and admirable fashion. Put it in the initial position – at the head of the table. Make the table a banquet table, and furnish the location with images that suggest this function: dishes, servers, courtiers. Make the location not only visual but synaesthetic: hear melody, smell and taste the food, and so on (in approved mnemotechnical fashion, Peter does not describe each detail: as he says, he fashions an example to be imitated, not a recipe). Whatever you do, be sure that the images within your location are as clearly ordered and ordained as is possible (medieval banquets were a good choice for this task, being highly structured). And make sure everything is eye-catching and attention-grabbing, yet never overwhelming with superfluous details or flourishes.

Peter then imagines that the "place" (*locus* again) at table for the queen is empty, for the time being. Then she makes her entrance in theatrical fashion, appearing splendidly as the court, already at table, sigh and gesture their longing for her. Her name is finally announced: "Conscience." Then her appearance, posture, and garments are described in careful order, each rhetorical element or "color" being associated with one of her traits, in the manner of a mnemotechnical catena.

> Reading the overall sequence [tenor] of her beauty abstractly in the habitual way of doing it, I attach closely [subcingo] her moral qualities to the description, and I distinguish each of the limbs of her virtues by means of the variety of [rhetorical] colors ... she has emerald eyes because of the constant vigor of her chastity, her nose is like the tower of Lebanon which faces Damascus [Song of Songs 7:5] because of her discriminating judgment upon the Assailant's attacks.[84]

Tenor, in the usage of fourth-century rhetoric, referred to the overall direction of a composition; here it refers to the orderly, sequential movement of the description of the Bride in Chapter Seven of the Song of Songs, the base text of Peter's picture.

The sequential phrases of this *descriptio* are used as a thematic outline for the rest of this whole section of the meditation. Biblical texts and commentary continue to be attached to the picture elements, in the manner of the brief excerpt I have just quoted. Peter refers to this as a habitual way of reading. The habit was formed in the first instance by books like the bestiaries, which taught exactly this habit of mind, attaching a moral quality to a descriptive element as though belting them together (*subcingo*, from *cingere*, "to cinch," is the verb Peter uses), piece to associated piece. Undoubtedly the contents of such elementary books were "inviscerated" by most children and novices taught in this way, but again, it seems to me that the profound cultural effect was found not just in the curious lore of such books but also, and probably more importantly in the long run, in invisceriating a basic habit of mind.

This is not the only picture in Peter's book. There are several smaller pictures, which serve to structure his materials into paragraph-sized divisions. And when Peter gets to the subject of charity, the next major piece of his composition, he marks it with another initiating textual picture. "Sequitur de pictura dilectionis," he writes, "here follows the picture of charity."[85] In this picture, verbs of painting, *pingere* and *depingere*, are used frequently. The picture of Charity is also called *sculptura*, a sculpture, and *statua*, a statue; evidently as Peter considers what he is making with his mind's eye, it can readily become a three-dimensional object, which he can move around as he uses it to invent his composition.[86] It is thus both a painting and a statue *at the same time*, using the mind's eye.

It is important to remember the features that require one to *move* through a location, both in depth and in sequence, as we try to understand the cognitive utility of medieval mental pictures. Such movement should be limited and moderate, for an image is easily overwhelmed and "crowded" out of focus if one tries to move about too quickly or goes too far away. But such cautions speak to the careful effort of mental manipulation and moving of the image that was an expected aspect of its usefulness. Rhetorical *ductus*, varying its course through the colors of ornament, works at the invention stage as well as the stage of reception, as these colors catch the eye, associate in various patterns, dispose our thoughts in various directions.

And eye-catching these pictures certainly are. After the description of her painted by Peter, Charity picks up a brush to paint too, and proceeds to paint herself more completely, as a statue. She paints ("pingit", the verb repeated throughout this section) the head of the statue with the Trinity, the eyes with Jesus' passion, the ears with the Gospels, and so on. The colors of these images are described: scarlet for the blood, black for the passion and death, green for the resurrection, hyacinth for the ascension, purple for Christ's struggle with evil spirits. "Especially notice the colors," says Peter to his readers – "ecce colores."[87]

Peter of Celle takes on the iconoclasts' objection in this treatise, after he has "painted" his many pictures in the text. God prohibited the making of statues (Deuteronomy 5:8), as the iconoclasts have pointed out. But Peter interprets this stricture ethically, as referring to the cognitive *uses* of painting. We can paint pictures and make statues for ourselves to use in contemplation so long as we are not side-tracked into error by that failure of imagination which is also, as we have seen, a weakness of *memoria*, namely *curiositas* and "fornication." We should use images painted in fantasy for contemplative thinking; but be careful, Peter says, not to paint upon the tablet of the inward imagination those worldly or morally objectionable or vain details which we might have observed in actual statues of stone or wood, out of a misplaced desire to remember on each occasion every detail of what we actually saw.[88]

Peter's implication – a very interesting one – seems to be that, for cognitive purposes, we need to remember all kinds of artifacts. But we should also freely "refashion" these remembered images as our cognitive focus requires. We do not remember a picture in order to reproduce it, as though by simple rote. Too much detail can be distracting and "curious," an aspect of the worldly cares that we must expel before we can focus our minds in prayer. On the other hand, recollected details that help us emotionally to focus and "intend" our thoughts in meditation are not vain or worldly or morally objectionable.

In other words, Peter understands the Deuteronomy prohibition socially and cognitively, not as a moral absolute: as he says, "The prohibition [in Deuteronomy] makes plain the failure of art; charity restores its wisdom and the excellence of its power."[89] He also assumes that a picture or statue is to be approached cognitively in the same way as he has been trained to approach reading, as a "gathering" of recombinative elements. Each occasion of remembering such a picture is also an occasion for rearranging its elements into yet another composition.

12. TWO PICTURE POEMS BY THEODULPH OF ORLEANS

Some features, at least, of western iconoclasm should be reconsidered in terms of the normative praxis of *memoria*. In the context of meditational remembering, as was apparent in Peter of Celle's analysis, the main danger posed by material artifacts is that they may encourage mental laziness and a consequent failure to attend carefully: that is, *accidia, stultitia, curiositas,* and *fornicatio.* But the use of picturing as a machine of thought is both cognitively necessary and morally good. As Augustine said, a picture's value lies not in the image itself but in the cognitive and ethical use someone makes of it, the quality of what we think and think about, using the picture as our instrument.[90]

This implies a rhetorical approach to artifacts rather than a strictly dogmatic one. What I mean by this can be demonstrated from two poems written by the eighth-century Carolingian bishop Theodulph of Orleans. And since Theodulph probably also wrote the *Libri Carolini,* a work that contains some forceful arguments against icons, warning about the dangers of painting, the fact that Theodulph also composed what he called *picturae* is of some interest.[91]

There are two pictures described in his poems, an "arbor mundi" and a "mappamundi." Neither is now accompanied by a drawing: as I will argue, there is no reason to suppose they ever were, though he may very well have been recalling, in the manner of memory craft, details from works that he had actually seen. His descriptions show that he understood the cognitive function of mental imaging in the familiar categories of rhetorical mnemotechnic. Of his map picture, he writes: "A shape for the whole world is briefly here painted, / It will give you to understand a great matter in a small body."[92] The principle of *brevitas* is clearly invoked, embodied in the mental image raised by the words of his poem. A map is a foundational heuristic form for meditation: one major reason, I would suggest, why a *mappamundi* was by tradition included towards the beginning of the Beatus picture books of the Apocalypse (see Plate 1).

Theodulph is also remembered for having built an oratory on his estate near Orleans, now in a village called Germigny-des-Prés. It contains a remarkable mosaic, the earliest still surviving in France, of the Ark of the Tabernacle in the shape of a chest, surmounted (in accord with the Exodus account) by the statues of two cherubim. Bending protectively over it are two immense dark cherubim, their robes outlined in gold (Plate 20). All seem to float upon the gold background of the mosaic, like images in a meditative vision. Indeed, it is a picture both of and for a vision. And, for all the iconoclastic doctrine included in the *Libri Carolini,* some of the most compelling evidence for Theodulph's authorship is a description of this mosaic in those books, to demonstrate the use of pictures as instruments of meditation.[93]

What I have identified as his rhetorical understanding of images is especially clear in the longer of Theodulph's two pictures, a poem of about one hundred lines "On the Seven Liberal Arts Painted in a Certain Picture."[94] Its literary sources have been identified: Ovid, Virgil, Isidore – and Martianus Capella looming behind the whole conception. But the poem differs markedly from something like the wedding narrative that begins Martianus' *De nuptiis*, for it is a description of a set of vivid visual images, arranged in orderly sequence. It thus has the character of what Bede called *pictura*: images *composed* in a manner that is ethically valuable, not by itself so much as because a "picture" is mnemonically effectual, and thus can become a pleasing instrument of prudent judgment.

Yet Theodulph's poem differs from classical (and several later medieval) examples of *picturae* by being self-contained rather than serving as the preamble to a work or section of a work. Then too, it is not (as literary *picturae* often were) specifically described as being "painted" in the author's mind (compare the language of Hugh of St. Victor in *De arca Noe mystica* and of Adam of Dryburgh).[95]

Theodulph begins with a brief setting of his background: "There was a disk formed in the image of the rounded world, / Which a construction [in the form] of a single tree adorned [decorabat]."[96] Notice how the world-disk changes shape suddenly into a tree; such shape-shifting is a convention of visionary literature, as we have seen, and also a fact of mental imaging, but it is hard to do with material pictures. The tree-structure ("opus arboris") "adorns" the world-disk, says Theodulph, invoking a concept of decoration which derives from mnemotechnic. The tree provides the *forma* or supportive frame for images of the poem's chief matters. For example, in its roots sits Grammar with a whip and a knife, holding the one to stir up the lazy and the other to scrape away defects.[97] Each major image is given a few such distinguishing mnemonic markers or *notulae*, as they were commonly called later during the Middle Ages.[98]

The images which make up the picture, all ladies, are arranged in the branches of the tree. The first set of branches holds Rhetoric, on the right, and on the left, Dialectic (Grammar, you recall, sits in the roots). Next to Dialectic, on another branch, Logic and Ethics sit together, and with Ethics sit the four virtues of Prudence, Fortitude,

Justice, and Moderation. Above these on the trunk is "Ars," a section of the tree that contains a great many branches, including Physic; Music and Geometry as twin branches; and finally, as the tree's crown reaches into Heaven, Astronomy. There follows a list of the Zodiac constellations and the seven planets.

The purpose of this *pictura* of the seven liberal arts is stated at the poem's conclusion:

> This tree bore both these things: leaves and pendant fruits,
> And so furnished both loveliness and many mysteries.
> Understand words in the leaves, the sense in the fruits,
> The former repeatedly grow in abundance, the latter nourish when they are well used.
> In this spreading tree our life is trained
> Always to seek greater things from smaller ones
> So that human sense may little by little climb on high,
> And may lastingly disdain to pursue the lower things.[99]

The invitation to *use* the picture is clear: the word-leaves which grow in abundance about the pendant fruit-matters are to act as a training ground and model for one's life, as one "climbs" upwards in knowledge and wisdom and prudent virtue too. Not only does the schematic serve as a mnemonic for the liberal arts and their curricular relationships (the way modern diagrams are used to "accompany" information), but it is intended to be added to and used as a structure for further knowledge and future cogitation. This tree has "plura mystica", rather like the "figura mystica" we examined in Prudentius' *Psychomachia*. Such "mysteries" are, in part, what such a work's ornaments provide. Theodulph considers his tree-picture to be a tool for further thinking, not just an illustration of concepts.

Anybody who has seen manuscript "trees" – of the vices and virtues, of Jesse (the genealogy of Christ), and later of many other sorts of matters – will recognize Theodulph's "picture." But such trees are *cognitive* schematics, pictures whether in words or in paint that are made for the thinking mind. Theodulph's picture is practically the earliest of such "trees" extant, and it is surely significant that it exists as a picture without the actual painting that we moderns require in order to call something a "picture." The ambivalent ontological status of *picturae* means that modern scholars cannot simply assume that the pictures referred to in medieval texts always and only described material images, nor that our ontological distinction of words from pictures was shared by medieval writers. It was not.

13. BAUDRI DE BOURGEUIL'S DREAM IN THE BEDROOM OF COUNTESS ADELA

Another picture-poem, later and longer than Theodulph's works, is a sort of anthology of basic matters to be learned, written in 1367 elegiac verses by the Benedictine monk Baudri, bishop of Bourgeuil (d. 1130).[100] It was written for Adela, countess of Blois (d. 1137), daughter of William the Conqueror, sister of Henry I of England, mother of king Stephen of England and of Henry, bishop of Winchester, who was also a noted patron of the arts in England during the twelfth century. After her husband's death on crusade in 1101, Adela ruled as regent for her son until 1109, when she resigned in favor of her second son (bypassing the eldest as too weak- minded) and entered a convent, where she spent her final years, dying at the age of seventy-five. She was a good friend of Anselm, who stayed with her on several occasions, and she "became his pupil in order to benefit her children by the instruction obtained from him." She was also a friend of Ivo of Chartres, and contributed substantially to the project of rebuilding the cathedral there in stone. She was thus a learned lady and, though a lay person, greatly involved in ecclesiastical affairs as a patron, friend, and diplomat (she intervened usefully in investiture quarrels between Anselm and her brother).[101]

The poem which Baudri wrote for her is now simply called "Adelae Comitissae" ("To the Countess Adela"), a disappointingly vague title for a work that is actually of considerable literary interest, not so much for its style (which is laborious and precious by modern taste), but for the conventions of genre which it evokes and its probable use as some sort of teaching instrument. The poem was composed at Adela's command for the education of her children (lines 55–65, 1360–1368). It was thus a commissioned work, designed specifically for tutoring noble children, likely including the future king Stephen and Henry of Winchester. It describes a decorated bedchamber, supposed (in the poem's fiction) to be Adela's, in the form of a dream vision granted to the author. It is thus a type of picturing poem closely associated with monastic orthopraxis. To use such conventions for teaching laity is typical of twelfth-century clerical literature, but the adaptations are especially clear in this poem.

The poem to Adela aroused great interest earlier in this century because it contains a description of a tapestry or *velum* depicting the conquest of England by Adela's father, and some hapless antiquarians proposed early in this century that it might be a description of the Bayeux tapestry itself. Once this suggestion was firmly refuted, people seem to have lost further interest in the work.[102] It should be noted, however, that material artifacts like those described in Adela's imaginary chamber do exist in scattered locations: a mosaic floor depicting a *mappamundi*, tapestries woven with historical and school-book scenes (such as the wedding of Mercury and Philology), bed-posts of carved ivory, ceilings painted with stars.[103]

The poem describes a vision, recollected in memory, that Baudri says he had of Adela's *thalamus* or bedchamber. Her room is an inventory of images grouped in scenes, which reckon in an orderly fashion the matter of a general education, the "foundations" of what Adela's children will learn. Walls, ceiling, and floor are all covered with images: one must imagine a completely decorated room of moderate size like the *cubiculum* of Boscoreale only, of course, the room in Baudri's poem is completely imaginary.

On the ceiling, vaulted like the sky itself, are all the major constellations of the Ecliptic and the Milky Way. On the floor is a mosaic pavement set out in the form of a conventional T-form *mappamundi*, the three continents all surrounded by Ocean (an example of such a map is shown in Plate 1; Plate 5 shows a cosmological map of the sort Baudri imagines for the ceiling vault). On all four of the walls are tapestries containing the stories of the Old Testament, the Greek myths, and recent history, notably the tapestry showing William's conquest of England. In addition, the chamber contains Adela's ivory bed, on which is carved in relief Philosophy, with seven youths. (Here Baudri's materials are most completely remembered from Martianus Capella.) The youths are grouped about Philosophy as she reclines on her couch: Music and Number to her right, Astronomy and Geometry to her left. At their feet is a three-faceted sculptured bedpost showing Rhetoric, Grammar, and Dialectic. In addition to these seven, there is the image of a grave maiden upholding them all named "Ars medicina" (line 1333).[104]

Baudri presents the chamber as a remembered vision, a mental seeing: "Though I scarcely could see, I nonetheless remember having seen,/ As I now remember dreams I have seen." He likens the visionary images to looking at the new moon, which one cannot really see yet sees: "So often I remember having seen the new moon / or, since I see with difficulty, I think myself to see [it]."[105] In his playfulness, Baudri emphasizes the mental construction of the items in his vision. He "sees things" in the darkness of Adela's chamber, with the clouded eyes of his (uncorrected) myopia. They are things, like the invisible new moon, which one "sees" in the mind's eye, fleeting, blurred glimpses requiring recollection and mental "composing" to fill in the gaps.

Baudri's emphasis upon his own agency in making this vision is striking, and quite unlike the assurance of some previous monastic visionaries (Wetti, for example), who may not have understood what they saw, but saw it clearly. Think for a moment of just how one does see in the dark. The lack of illumination requires the use of peripheral vision, and engages memory to help "envision" what must be there but can't be seen if looked at directly.

This aspect of the physiology of sight resonates in connection with the "dark" figures in certain medieval mosaics, the ones which float against the gold background but are themselves deliberately made hard to see. Many of them are best seen with peripheral sight, rather than by looking at them straight on. An example of such an aesthetic of obscurity is the huge, dark Christ figure floating on a gold background, above the monks' altar at San Miniato, Florence (the mosaic is dated 1297), whose deep purple and black forms are outlined with thin ribbons of gold. A similar aesthetic principle is at work in the ninth-century mosaic which Theodulph had made for his own oratory near Orleans (Plate 20), showing the Ark suspended in a sea of golden light produced by the glass tesserae of the mosaic, all the lighting for this place of vision being originally received from the lantern window which illuminated its moderate interior. The lineaments of the Ark's two cherubim statues and the huge figures of the two large, dark-winged, dark-robed angels protecting it are alike picked out in thin gold lines. A modern "restoration" has destroyed the original effect, but if one mentally blocks out the white plaster surrounding the mosaic, one can imagine to some degree complex diurnal and seasonal plays of shadow and light moving over these forms.[106]

The dimming or even shutting out of ordinary light is connected with the prostrate posture of intense memory work: one shuts out daylight in order to see more clearly inside. The cultivation of peripheral vision is an aspect of monastic aesthetic, though perhaps also connected in a general way to the ancient notion that memory work is best done in darkness, as the latinate word *lucubrations* suggests.[107] In monastic practice both darkness and silence are associated with the creative memory work of meditative reading, as is clear in Chapters 8 and 48 of the *Regula Benedicti*. Obscure and deliberately "strange" ornaments, the visual equivalent of *figurae mysticae*, are particularly what the recollecting mind feeds upon. Recall how John Cassian speaks of contemplative vision as a process of seeing more and more clearly, as the fogs clear from one's eyes while one is "lifted" ever upwards. So too in darkness, the longer and more quietly one sits, the more one's eyes (and mind) can see.

As a quality deriving from the practice of monastic *memoria*, "obscurity" gives a context to what otherwise seems an obtuse error in Albertus Magnus' commentary (written c. 1260) on Aristotle's treatise "On Memory and Reminiscence." Remarking on the ancient mnemotechnical advice to select properly lighted places for one's memory work, neither too bright nor too dim, Albertus changes the whole emphasis of his original by advising that in our own memory technique "we should imagine and seek out dark places having little light."[108] This remark, it seems to me, expresses the same visual aesthetic as the mosaics I mentioned earlier, and the "glimpsing," new-moon quality of light that Baudri describes at the beginning of his vision. Albertus has "corrected" the ancient precept to accord with his own understanding of the matter.

In selecting Adela's bedchamber, Baudri invokes one of the main inventional tropes of monastic meditation: the *lectulus* and *thalamus* of the bride in the Song of Songs. In fact, since this "bride" is a married princess with children, he is able to pun with the notions of "fruitfulness" to a more literal degree than monks commonly did; but the dominant theme is still the ethical and intellectual "fruit" of meditation. Adela's room is called *thalamus*, a word used by the Roman poets, like Ovid, for a woman's chamber specifically – and also for a marriage bed. Baudri intended these classical resonances to be recognized as well as the Biblical ones, for his description culminates in the bed itself, the ivory-framed, carved couch that "pictures" the arts of knowledge. This is the couch of composition as well as of the vision of the bride. Lying upon it, in the prone posture of invention, Adela can meditate as she desires upon the rich matters which the images of her chamber bring into her heart (the Marian echo of Luke 2:19 is also deliberate).[109]

A Diana figure whom Baudri can barely see (he is myopic,

remember) invites the poet into the marvelous bedchamber, where he sees and invites us to see its furnishings: the bulk of the poem is devoted to their abundant description. "Videas," Baudri says to his readers, again and again. Silk tapestries cover the walls, one after another, in which are woven the stories of Genesis (through Noah), and then, splitting into two currents, the history of the Jews from Abraham through Solomon, and, on the opposite wall, the fables of the Greeks. Each tapestry is called a "locus," before each of which the reader is expected to pause and "see" its arranged, story-cueing images. They are arranged "in order": "whichever ones you consider memorable and worthy for relating aloud / You should look at attentively one at a time in the sequence of tapestries."[110] Each tapestry also has a *titulus*, its summary "title."[111] But Baudri does not provide these in the poem: rather, as a student sees the picture which the words are painting in his mind, he is invited to supply them with *tituli* of his own devising.

The arrangement of these stories, Old Testament on one side and Greek on the other, summarizes a common pedagogical scheme of the later Middle Ages: the *Eclogue* of Theodolus (composed in the tenth century) is precisely so arranged, a text that was at this time one of the essential "authors" of medieval education. Adela's *thalamus* is thus set up as an inventory/invention chamber for a standard medieval education.

All of its structural features also accord with elementary mnemonic principles. This is most apparent in the case of the image-groups that are not cues to particular stories, but are the icons for less inherently orderly material, such as the constellations. The constellations are the matter of "Aratus" (which I briefly discussed in Chapter One), conveyed most often in cosmological pictures, such as the one in Plate 5. Their forms are painted ("pinxerat," line 588) in a great wheel or *rota* on the ceiling above the bed. Baudri calls this wheel a "machina" that rotates, however still it may seem to stand, "for so the skill of the artificer had made it."[112]

The images for the constellations are positioned so as to touch one another, a feature introduced to provide the necessary links of the mnemonic. So, from the point of Polaris, the North Star, in Ursa minor, the constellations circle about the pole, beginning with the Bears and Serpens (now called Draco) "in whose fluctuation Ursa minor is set" (line 602). The relative positions of the star patterns are marked out in this poem as a continuous chain. Thus a constellation is not presented separately but in its position relative to its neighbors. As each constellation is named in serial order, it is linked up to the next by its head and its feet (or tail). This is a characteristic mnemotechnical detail, that the images within a "place" be linked together in their order by some physical action that fastens them together, such as hitting, holding hands (or tail), biting. These connecting actions serve the same function as the joining strokes do in cursive scripts.[113] As one sees the wheel and manipulates it mentally, the machine will act as a memorized sky chart, and is readily adaptable, as Baudri explains, to the seasons of the year.[114]

Around Adela's bed itself are curtains made with such skill and beauty that (using another common trope) Baudri says you could hardly believe they were human products. The reason for calling attention to their subtle craft is surely to remind us that these images are human creations, and they must be constructed in our minds as they have been in this imaginary bedchamber. They are valued not as "representational" or "realistic," but as occasions for remembering and retelling. For Baudri, the nature of learning itself is rhetorical, and thus ethical and social, in its character.

Baudri concludes with an effusive compliment to Adela, the usual sort of begging with false modesty conventional in late medieval poetry. But Baudri's compliments have a certain ponderous wit, as he gathers in the various associations of the bed chamber conceit:

> While I exerted myself for you, Adela, while sweating I told tales,
> I painted your beautiful chamber in my songs.
> May you, truly worthy of our song, requite its worth
> and consider at what price the fable was composed,
> for while the work was growing, while the parchment of my song
> was filling,
> the book swelled with elegant wordiness.
> Now take care lest the wakefulness of our study be lost,
> and may you for whom I have plowed not be sterile for me.[115]

Though Baudri is invoking the Horatian trope of begging his patron's favor and hoping his work will fructify (in terms of money and advancement), he also is casting it in the context of *memoria*, in which the ethical "fruit" and "swelling" that results from Baudri's labors will be paid back in the coin of learning. Baudri plays allusively with his poem's literal situation (a man in Adela's bedroom) as he invites her to understand his other meaning: he plows, his book swells up, he hopes she will not prove sterile. "Surely," he continues, festooning his verse with alliterative play, "such a bed is fit for such a countess," "decet talem talis thalamus comitissam" (line 1353). The hint of scandal and the jingle both make his gift memorable, while also (perhaps) testing the countess's good will.

In conclusion, Baudri says, he has sent with his parchment book a person who can "render and recite" ("reddat recitetque") the whole work. He will come himself as well, if the countess orders it.[116] Since the poem was intended as a study-book for Adela's children, these final promises are of much interest. Baudri would not himself have acted as a teacher for Adela's children, but he is sending the poem with one who will be their tutor, and who will use this poem as a basis for instruction. The person will "render" and "recite" it, that is read it aloud and interpret it, employing the standard method of medieval classroom reading.[117]

But the phrase may imply more. The order of the two verbs is backwards, if one thinks strictly in terms of the two ordinary stages to learning Latin verse, first by heart (implied in *recitare*) and then having the meaning of the words "rendered" through explanatory commentary. But *reddere* also means "to give an account of" something. Baudri may be promising a tutor who will give an account of the meaning to Adela's children first, most likely in Norman French, their first language – and who will then recite the verses so they can memorize the Latin words. In a picturing poem such as this one, hearing about the pictures first in one's native language, so they can be readily painted in one's mind, would have the advantage of making the Latin more comprehensible when one got to the actual text. An Anglo-Norman translation was made of another famous school-book of pictures, the Bestiary, for Adela's sister-in-law, Adelaide of Louvain.[118]

The additional, interpretive commentary is not hidden in Baudri's text for his readers to find in the way one is asked to find a limited number of "correct" answers in a puzzle. Rather, Baudri uses a different, and much more flexible, metaphor when he invites Adela and her children to read his work. The text he is sending her is "naked"; Adela must supply it with a covering cloak. "The parchment [on which my poem is written] comes naked, because it is the writing of a naked bard, / Give a mantle to its nakedness, if it please you."[119] Baudri invokes a commonplace idea in rhetoric that the process of poem-making ends with the *venustas*, the "clothing" of the invented material and its arrangement. This is to be Adela's work.

The trope of the "naked text" was also a commonplace of medieval exegesis. In reference to Biblical literature, naked text is distinguished from obscure text, because it is "open," literal teaching.[120] But that evidently is not what Baudri means here. He means that his poem simply has no clothing or cladding yet. It is but a foundation; it has not yet been joined with other matters and so made fruitful in the "bedroom" of Adela's recollecting memory (and those of her children, when they – by dint of hard discipline and long practice – may acquire ones able to bear fruit). Like Theodulph's two "pictures," what Baudri has done is to provide *formae*, the elementary devices and machines with which his students can build the fabric of their further education.

5

"The place of the Tabernacle"

Ingrediar in locum tabernaculi admirabilis, usque ad domum Dei.
Psalm 41

In this chapter, I want to focus on perhaps the most eloquent and certainly the most lasting expressions of monastic rhetoric, the buildings themselves, as a way of bringing together most of the major lines of my study. So far, I have concentrated primarily on the interior way of meditation, its *ductus* from restlessness and compunction through the steps of inventive recollection to divine vision (if one's soul is prepared and God grant) and its dependence on a basic model of thought as a restless, unceasing activity, requiring instruments, machines which can lift the mind and channel its movements, however variously, towards its destination, using as its primary tools its own images mapped out internally in mental pictures.

Following out one particularly rich monastic trope, the "place of the Tabernacle," I wish to explore now some of the ways in which these internal pictures were made external as well. I am no historian of architecture, any more than I am a historian of religions: my comments are made, as they are throughout this book, as a historian of medieval literature and rhetoric. But in medieval cultures particularly, I think that rhetorical considerations have much to offer by way of understanding how these wonderful buildings, like Maius' wonderful pictures, were conceived and functioned as social artifacts.

During the late eleventh and the twelfth centuries, encyclopedic *picturae* became a prominent artistic expression in the west. Hugh of St. Victor's contribution to the literary manifestation of this genre is called, in some manuscripts, "pictura Arche," "a picture of the Ark." His near-contemporary, the Premonstratensian canon Adam of Dryburgh (or Adam Scot), called his literary contribution also a "pictura," and distinguished it (as we will see) from commentary upon the literal meaning of Biblical texts, even those, like Exodus 25–27 and Ezekiel 40–43, that themselves describe detailed plans for buildings.[1]

The making and use of these structures, rooted in the monastic practices of various kinds of memory work for meditation and prayer, found lasting material form during the twelfth century in a great many large-scale works that we can still see and read. Several types, such as the encyclopedic sculpture programs of the west façade (the main entry door) at St.-Denis or Chartres, or of the porch entrance to the sanctuary, as at the Madeleine at Vézelay, preserve the initiating and orienting function of the *pictura* trope, most commonly used for an exordium or introit. A program that also includes historiated capitals in the porch, as at Vézelay or at St.-Benoît-sur-Loire (Fleury), can especially make the whole entry structure of a church into an elaborate rhetorical prefatory *pictura* to the varying *ductus* of the interior.

I. AN ARTIFACT THAT SPEAKS IS ALSO AN ORATOR

I suggested in an earlier chapter that paintings of buildings and other speaking pictures are a variety of rhetorical ekphrasis. Ekphrasis, through its use of verbal *enargeia*, is a trope of vision; it summons in the mind the imagined structures required for inventive meditation.[2] I am about to argue that the actual buildings also are, in monastic rhetoric, instances of what might be called material ekphrasis.

We have already seen that John's description of the Heavenly City was regarded by fourth- and fifth-century rhetorically educated Christians like Arnobius and Prudentius as being most like an ekphrasis. It was understood not as a real thing, but as a cognitively important device to be painted in the mind for purposes of further meditation and prayer. Other visions of buildings in Scripture were also so understood, for example, Ezekiel's Temple vision and the Tabernacle itself, in commentaries both by Jerome and by Gregory the Great. Ekphrases, however, do not always work in the same way, and before proceeding it will be useful to characterize briefly what monastic ekphrasis commonly did.

There is a critical difference between modern and early medieval ekphrases, which goes to the heart (or rather the gist) of medieval aesthetic. One of the best-known examples in English of a modern ekphrasis is John Keats's poem *Ode on Grecian Urn*. Keats's urn, you recall, has almost nothing to say for itself. It displays its mute pictures to the admiring poet, but he is entirely on his own to make sense of them; even his guesses about their narrative are uninformed by any assurance from the urn. What little the urn does say is Delphic in its brevity and enigma. Indeed its speech is so puzzling that there is not even agreement among scholars about which words it speaks. As an orator, the artifact shares nothing with its audience; no common social ground, no story is shared by urn and admirer. It is only an object; he is only a subject.[3] In our century, indeed, the urn's isolated objectivity has been extended to an ideal of poetry that is papable and mute, having nothing to say to any reader.

By contrast, art objects in medieval ekphrases tend to be loquacious, even garrulous. The ubiquitous *tituli* in paintings, mosaics, tapestries, and sculpture give even these material objects speech: they make them orators in conversation with an audience on a particular social occasion. Though the artifacts of medieval ekphrases are marvelous, like the jeweled Heavenly City or the obscure wonders in Countess Adela's bedroom, they are not alien, they are familiar, home. Nor are words the only elements that give "speech" to a medieval artifact. A painting such as the "Heavenly City" of the Beatus cycle is also an ekphrasis, an artifact which engages socially in a meditative dialogue with its viewers through the colors and forms of all its images.

Medieval ekphrases are also pictures of the sort I described in my last chapter. They are organizations of images amongst which one moves, at least mentally, following out the *ductus* of colors and modes which its images set. The ornamentation of such a work forms its routes and pathways, as verbal ornament does that of speech or of chant.

To characterize such works as I have done is to insist that all medieval arts were conceived and perceived essentially as rhetoric, whether they took the form of poems or paintings or buildings or music. Each work is a composition articulated within particular rhetorical situations of particular communities. Regarding a work as rhetoric has the virtue of focussing on it as a social phenomenon first and foremost, on what the rhetoricians called its "occasion," its negotiation of a particular rhetorical economy.[4]

For example, one can consider the difference between the "iconophilia" of Suger of St.-Denis and the "iconophobia" of Bernard of Clairvaux as a matter of rhetorical occasion, considering questions of the contrasting ethos and pathos and ensuing decorum at work in their constructive use of design and figure.[5] Both clerics built monastic churches. As a royal abbey (in fact, Suger hoped, *the* royal abbey), St.-Denis was certainly located in "the world," and Suger's building and liturgical program addressed this social fact with great rhetorical skill; with equal rhetorical skill, Bernard, through the program at Clairvaux, addressed a self-selected community of learned, aristocratic monks who had withdrawn from the world to "the desert."

Both men used theological arguments and justifications for their programs, but they used them rhetorically – to invent and to persuade. In other words, their theological ideas do not constitute a final explanation for what and how they built, but a rhetorically deployed strategy – one of a variety – within a complex work of art, whether that work be the church of St.-Denis, the complex at Clairvaux, Hugh of St. Victor's treatise on Noah's Ark, Bernard's sermons on the Song of Songs, the musical and processional movements of the year's liturgy at Cluny or at Centula-St.-Riquier, or the entry structures of the pilgrimage churches at St.-Benoît-sur-Loire, Vézelay, and Chartres. Each of these material artifacts can be regarded as a rhetorically conceived expression. It was not idle hyperbole that led one Cistercian to revere Bernard as "our Bernard, an Anthony among monks and a Cicero among orators."[6] We now, reading this comment, think only of his sermons. I will argue in this chapter that the monastery buildings of church and cloister were themselves also compelling expressions of monastic rhetoric, made as tools for the ways of monastic meditative recollection that we have been exploring.

2. BUILDING A DREAM VISION: MALACHY OF ARMAGH AND GUNZO OF BAUME

Monasteries are visionary places, a double meaning well understood by the monks themselves. They provide places where "visions" can occur, and they enable one to "see" those visions. They are also built because of a vision – at least this was one of the monks' commonplace stories. This narrative trope began with the tale we looked at in the last chapter, that of Benedict's visit in a vision to show a new establishment of his monks where and how to ordain and dispose the buildings of their new monastery. Echoing through the story of Benedict, of course, are the two great prophetic building visions of St

John and of Ezekiel, and the divine building plan dictated in a direct vision by God to Moses.

One version of this Benedictine master-story occurs in Bernard of Clairvaux's *Life of St. Malachy*, in which the Irish cleric, intent on extending Roman (and continental) institutions over the indigenous Irish Christians, decides to build a Cistercian-style oratory of stone in place of the Irish chapels. He decides on a location for it, finds money to build it, and talks to his brethren about the project, about which many are dubious. But then,

> returning from a journey one day as he approached the place he looked at it from some distance away. And behold a great oratory appeared built of stone and extremely beautiful. He considered it carefully, its position, its shape and its arrangement, and when he undertook the work confidently, he first told his vision to the older brethren, but only to a few. Certainly he had attentively noted everything regarding the place, manner, and quality with such diligent observation that once the work was finished, the completed oratory was so like the one he had seen that anyone would believe that he, with Moses, had heard it said: 'See that you make all things according to the pattern which was shown to you on the mount.' [Hebrews 8:5, citing the Exodus story of God's instructions for fashioning the Tabernacle.] By the same kind of vision the oratory, and in fact the whole monastery built in Saul, had been shown to him before it was erected.[7]

The oratory which Malachy saw in his vision was not just any old building but a Cistercian *oratorium* – specifically Clairvaux, which he had visited in 1140. On that visit he was so impressed with Bernard's way of life that he sought to be relieved of his bishopric and to become a monk at Clairvaux, a request denied to him. Yet the Cistercian ideal had fully caught him; he predicted, we are told, that he would die at Clairvaux and indeed he did. Evidently, the many things that impressed Malachy about Clairvaux were in a particular way summed up in its buildings.

But he did not go back to Ireland and build a duplicate Clairvaux. Having internalized the *oratorium* he had seen, Malachy recollects it in a vision back in Ireland. But notice how the remembered building is fitted and adjusted, made "familiar" and habituated to its location on Strangford Loch, rather in the way that a good orator "copies" into a speech his remembered *copia*, the common places he has selected for a particular occasion.[8] When he has his vision, Malachy is in the location in which he plans to build. The plan and elevation of the building are projected in every detail, laid out with his mental line, in that particular location, and then, when every detail has been drawn in his mind's eye, the actual construction proceeds, rather in the manner that a literary composition is finally *scriptus* by pen on parchment. The actual building (or book) is only a "recollection" of the mental composition, itself composed or "gathered" from the inventory of the artist's memory. The building functions as a reminder, a cue, a machine for thought – but without the human beings who use it, it has neither value nor meaning.

There are a number of such "building visions" associated with actual monastic buildings. For example, Aubert, bishop of Avranches in the early eighth century, had such a vision, indeed three of them, before finally building the monastery that became Mont-Saint-Michel. The narrator of St. Aubert's vision linked this experience to the originary text in Hebrews (8:5) which is also quoted in the *Life of St. Malachy*.[9]

Another building vision is particularly interesting, because in this one the Ezekiel vision appears like a palimpsest through the account. It is a Cluny story (not Cistercian, but notice that both orders found the trope appropriate) of how the abbot of the monastery of Baume, Gunzo, persuaded Abbot Hugh to enlarge and rebuild the church at Cluny. Gunzo, like Ezekiel, was struck down by a grave stroke-like paralysis (Ezekiel was struck dumb, remember), when Saints Peter, Paul, and Stephen all appeared to him in a vision and told him to carry a message to Hugh to rebuild and enlarge the church at Cluny: his miraculous recovery would be proof of the truth of his vision. When Gunzo protested, Saint Peter

> was seen by Gunzo to draw out measuring-ropes [funiculos] and measure off the length and breadth (of the church). He also showed him in what manner the church was to be built, instructing him to commit both its dimensions and design securely to memory.[10]

Having recovered, Gunzo went to Hugh, who ordered the new church built exactly according to the vision which Gunzo recounted to him "in the order in which these things were told or shown to the monk."[11] The monks thus "measure the pattern" as they construct the church, just as Ezekiel was told by the angel to "measure the pattern" so that the new Jerusalem might be built (an act echoed famously in John's vision of the Heavenly City). Plate 21 shows an illustration of Gunzo lying on his back with his eyes open in vision, watching Peter with Paul and Stephen measuring off the design of the church with their builders' lines.

The angel with the brazen countenance who measured out "the dimensions and design" of the newly constituted Temple for Ezekiel, and who instructed him to hold in his memory its exact plans so that he could tell the Israelites how to rebuild when they returned from captivity, is not far to seek behind Gunzo's St. Peter with his measuring rod. And the fact that Gunzo, like Ezekiel, suffered from a grave, paralyzing disease when the vision of the new Temple was accorded him completes the link between these two stories. Gunzo's vision serves as the "machine" that raises him (in the *persona* of every-monk) from inaction and torpor to active contemplation, and it also, quite literally in this account, is the engine which raises up the new church at Cluny.

Discovering the Ezekiel figure in the story of Gunzo and Hugh's rebuilding of the Cluny *templum* is more than a pious curiosity, and I think more than simply another instance of medieval typology. Monastic construction projects followed a well-attested trope, from a vision evoking in some way the divinely sanctioned architectural instructions given to Moses or to Ezekiel and John, to the project's actualization by a particular, Bezalel-imitating monastic builder. The scriptural echo-chamber of these visions, thus of the constructions they gave birth to, extends as well to the Pauline spiritual temple, which each person constructs in his or her own soul, and to the figure of Jesus, the temple's fulfillment. "Measuring the temple," a penitential and salvific act in Ezekiel, is one mode of the *ductus* of salvation itself.

Major monastic building projects were *expected* to be initiated in the form of a "vision." And – more important for my argument here – major monastic buildings were expected to follow the Ezekiel pattern, as mental "pictures" of the sort I discussed in my last chapter, pre-visualized in the manner of rhetorical invention and of meditation, of which the actual stone is the "imitation." The mental picture or scheme *precedes* and informs its actualization. I think this is true of virtually all such monastic inventions, and this habit of mind convincingly indicates that the *picturae* and *formae* which we encounter in twelfth-century literature, such as those in the meditations of Hugh and Richard of St. Victor, should not be presumed to be *de*scriptions of pictures or plans that necessarily existed physically, but to be *pre*scriptions, exemplars and patterns to be "copied" by the means of

227

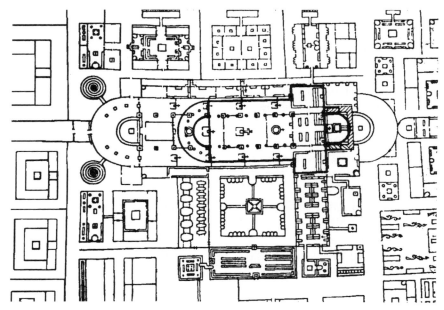

Fig. B A detail of the "Plan of St. Gall." Entrance to the monastery is from the west (left, above) between the two towers flanking the main portal; the square cloister is located to the south of the church. Redrawn from the manuscript, with the scribal glosses (which were added later) omitted, after W. Braunfels, *Monasteries of Western Europe.*

rhetoric: augmentation, abbreviation, and translation. Such ekphrastic pictures have the role in monastic rhetoric of the plan measured out by the angel for Ezekiel to hold in his memory, providing ways and places for the *mental* task of composing prayer.

3. THE "PLAN OF ST. GALL": BUILDING PLAN AS MEDITATION MACHINE

There still exists, drawn on parchment, a monastery plan whose purpose was to serve as a meditational instrument. This is the early ninth-century (c. 820) "Plan of St. Gall," that valuable collection of buildings whose measurements are based on exegetically significant and mnemonically functional numbers like seven, four, and ten: a detail of it, redrawn from the manuscript, is shown in Figure B. Wolfgang Braunfels and Walter Horn both likened the plan to Carolingian literature, to the *carmina figurata* and acrostic picture verses popular at this time – one example of which is the description of sinners in Walahfrid Strabo's *Vision of Wetti*, which we looked at briefly in Chapter Four.

Wetti's vision occurred at the monastery of Reichenau, and the abbot, Heito (governed c. 806–823), who wrote the first account of it, was also the author of the "Plan of St. Gall." This plan, as most scholars now accept, was not intended to show actual buildings (though details of it do reflect actual buildings, and it has, of course, been realized in model form in this century).[12] Its *intentio auctoris* (to use the terminology of medieval literary study) is set out in the dedicatory letter that Heito wrote to abbot Gozbert of St. Gall, who had requested a copy of a plan which Heito had already devised for his own purposes, now the only one extant:

> I have sent you, Gozbert my dearest son, these few designs [exemplata] for the lay-out [de positione] of a monastery, by means of which you might exercise your wits. ... But do not think that I have elaborated this because we considered you to need our instructions, but believe that it was drawn [pinxisse] in God's love for you alone to scrutinize.[13]

As Braunfels comments, "the Plan is to promote meditation upon the meaning and worth of the monastic life."[14]

A French translation of Heito's description of his copy, "exemplata," underscores its cognitive utility; the plan is a summary "vue de la disposition des locaux ... pour te donner lieu de déployer ta propre sagacité."[15] I have translated it as "designs," because *exemplar* is sometimes a synonym for the kinds of mental *picturae* – maps and other such plans – which I discussed in my last chapter. Heito's words also recall clearly the incident in Gregory's *Life of St. Benedict*, when the abbot appears in a vision to his monks to show them the lay-out, *loca singula*, of the unbuilt monastery: an incident which, as I have already shown, is linked to the visionary "measuring of the Temple" in Ezekiel.[16] And like the *formulae* discussed by John Cassian, these *positiones* give one locations, the "where-withal" to practice one's fertile, creative wit. The plan is for Gozbert's mental eyes, his careful cognitive scrutiny.

The "Plan of St. Gall" is the earliest surviving instance of an architectural *pictura*, a device of memory work found commonly, often in very elaborate fashion, in the literature of the later Middle Ages, but whose roots can clearly be perceived in the literature of the early medieval Church. It is the task of this section to sketch out some of that development.

The "Plan of St. Gall" is basically a meditation machine, both in itself and as the plan for a cluster of structures that were *also* meditation machines, especially those parts of the monastery reserved for the monks. Many features that made both architecture and manuscript books suitable cognitive machines were extended and adapted for a much larger clerical and lay audience after the eleventh century but at the time of the "Plan of St. Gall" the anticipated users of such devices would have been monks.

Isidore of Seville says that there are three stages in the making of a building ("aedificiorum partes sunt tres"). These are *dispositio, constructio*, and *venustas*, the planning, the raising, and the "clothing" ("eloquence" or "style") of the building.[17] Within this scheme, architectural *picturae* function as the *dispositiones* for a composition. Echoing this vocabulary in his letter to abbot Gozbert, Heito says he has sent sketches "de *positione*" of the monastery, that are to be used for Gozbert's further invention (*sollertia*). Heito is acting as both a wise *architectus* and a *dispositor*, a word used also sometimes to describe what an architect does.[18] There is an obvious analogy between these three stages and the three stages in rhetoric of constructing a composition: Invention, Disposition, and Ornament.

The monastic practice of using architectural plans as the routes of meditative composition seems to derive most immediately from exegesis of various buildings of the Old Testament. In the case of the St. Gall plan, certain features seem modeled on details of the visionary Temple of Ezekiel, the subject of a set of ten exegetical sermons by Gregory the Great that were a common part of monastic colloquia, the reading in chapter and at meal times. This part of Ezekiel was also, in the twelfth century, endorsed by Hugh of St. Victor as one of the foundational texts for meditation on the *allegoriae* or "difficulties" in Scripture.[19]

A ninth-century commentator labeled the monastery church in the "Plan of St. Gall" the *templum*. This word recalls the temple in Ezekiel, as well as the spiritual and Christological "temples" of Pauline exegesis. Its entry way, which is also the entrance to the whole monastery (see Figure B), is labeled as follows: "This is the way [*via*] to the holy Temple for the multitudes, by means of which they conduct their prayers, and return in joy."[20] As is typical, the entry is given special attention, for the way into the monastery is also the way of the monastic life and the gate-*way* to the Heavenly City of which this plan is an exemplary picture.

Calling the monastery a "way" recalls what John Cassian stressed about monastic prayer, that it is a "route" or "way," a governing metaphor in the ancient notions of *studium* and *disciplina*. Thinking of the Temple compound as a Way is analogous to the use of mandalas in Buddhist meditation. As Grover Zinn has characterized such use of symbols, they have "an initiatory value, for they possessed the potential for ... guiding [a novice] through the levels of experience germane to the life of contemplative asceticism."[21] Not only novices profit from such markers of the way, however: it is worth noting that abbot Heito sent his plan to abbot Gozbert, no novice, for his own meditations.

I am not trying to suggest that there is any direct relationship between oriental mandalas and European devotional *picturae* like the "Plan of St. Gall"; but they have cognitive similarity, a likeness in use. Mandalas too are invention devices, to be imagined and used as "the way" of prayer. Mandala pictures are, in some conventions, architectural complexes built around a central square (an example, a late-fifteenth-century painting on cloth from Tibet, is shown in Plate 22). Indeed, perhaps the closest thing in western monastic practice to the use of mandalas is the church-cloister compound itself.

4. "TO THE PATTERN OF HEAVEN": THE PICTURE OF THE TABERNACLE

There is evidence, tenuous but tantalizing, that versions of Tabernacle and Temple *picturae* may have been made and used as mandala-like meditational schemes in early Christianity and also in Jewish mysticism. The chain of evidence (with many lacunae in it) begins with Ezekiel.[22] The measuring of the Tabernacle in Exodus became in Ezekiel a particularly penitential activity. "Measuring the pattern" of the holy city is the ritual of Israel's penitence and reconciliation with God:

> Thou son of man, show the temple to the house of Israel, that they may be ashamed of their iniquities: and let them measure the pattern, and blush from all they have done. Show them the plan of the house, and of its fabric, its exits and entrances, and its whole description, and all of its precepts, and the rest of its ordering, and all its laws, and write [them] before their sight so

231

that they may store away all its descriptions and its precepts, and fashion them.[23]

In Ezekiel, the measuring of the Temple is an act of contrition and return. The originary text of all such sacred "measuring" is God's measuring of the Tabernacle for the Ark in Exodus. There, the construction measurements are given on the mountain by God to Moses: this is the central act of covenant and reconciliation before the complete reconciliation effected by Christ. Through the work of Bezalel, the master builder, this divinely measured pattern was given material expression in the Tabernacle, later realized again in the temple built by Solomon, described in 1 Kings 6. But similar material realization of the pattern was denied (as far as the prophet's account goes) to the visionary Temple measured for Ezekiel. In its final avatar, as the Heavenly City of John, the pattern is seen in terms that can never have full material expression.

These texts were fundamental commonplaces in medieval monasticism. Their great Christian authority comes ultimately from two meditative catenae made upon them in the Epistles, in 1 Corinthians 3 (the wise master builder building the Temple upon the foundation plan which is Christ) and again in Hebrews 8, a text proclaiming Christ as the true priest of that Tabernacle, whose sketch and pattern is the earthly Tabernacle made by Moses to God's measurements.[24] To these edifices made (actually or in vision) to a divine pattern was soon collated the "measuring" of the Ark of Noah (which resulted in the first of God's covenants) and the original "measuring" involved in the six days of Creation itself.

Notice also that in these texts, as well as in John's vision of the Heavenly Jerusalem, measuring out the plan of the structures is the chief way for the visionaries to receive, remember, and retell their "seeings." The "measurements" are an act of contrition, routed through an architectural mnemonic schema which serves as its *via*. And the goal, the *skopos*, of the way is, of course, "the covenant of salvation," both personal and social. Hrabanus Maurus, commenting on the text in Ezekiel 43, wrote that " 'To measure the fabric' [of the Temple] means to think carefully upon the life of the just. And while we 'measure the fabric,' we must blush in shame over all the things which we do."[25] Thus "measuring the pattern" became in monastic rhetoric a trope of penitential "remembering," and an essential cognitive map, like a mandala, for the routes of memory work, both individual and, in liturgy and procession, civic as well, as the Biblical measurings reconcile an entire community with God.

The Temple plan clearly was a common trope of visionary literature. Ezekiel is one of the earliest examples, but the Jewish apocalyptic book called 1 Enoch (first century BC) uses a vision of the Temple, including a description of its plan and fabric, as a structuring device.[26] It was also used in teaching. Both Henri de Lubac and Beryl Smalley have written the history of this trope in early Christian exegesis: I have already alluded to this. The words addressed by Quodvultdeus to "those who have a taste for building," which I quoted in my first chapter (section four), make it clear that architectural *picturae* like these were in common literary use as inventional schemata at least by the fourth century. John Cassian's Fourteenth Conference recounts an extended meditation by the desert father Abba Nesteros on the Ark and the sacred vessels.[27]

There is also evidence that a map-like image depicting the Tabernacle (or Temple) as a schematic, non-narrative design circulated independently at least in later antiquity.[28] The murals of the synagogue at Dura-Europos (third century AD) feature a picture of the Temple, whose form and placement in the overall scheme of painting seems to derive from its importance in the praxis of prayer. It is placed next to the Torah niche, as though marking a "way" through the narrative scenes which are grouped around the rest of the walls. "[T]he artist here endeavored to suggest ... a city that from his point of view was necessarily of universal significance. In a synagogue this could be only the city of Jerusalem."[29] A similar initiating role, you recall, was given to a *pictura* of Christ in Majesty on the wall of the oratorium at Celles. If the monastic practice had "translated" Jewish orthopraxis, it would make perfect tropological sense to picture Christ in the place accorded to Jerusalem, a translation sanctioned by Paul himself.

A picture schematic of the temple sanctuary with the sacred vessels also could play an initiating and orienting role in manuscript books. Cecil Roth explains that "in the illuminated Jewish Bibles ... it was as it seems conventional to include a double page ... showing the Vessels of the Sanctuary, as the solitary representational illustration ... [T]hey are invariably or almost invariably placed before the entire Biblical text."[30] Illuminated codices of the Hebrew Bible existed in the earliest centuries of the Common Era; many scholars since Roth have demonstrated the complex social interactions of familial communities of

Jews and Christians in the earliest centuries, and how their dialogue, including a dialogue of images, found its way into the early Christian monasticism of Syria and Egypt.

As Roth explains, the sanctuary vessels are shown within a rendering of the sanctuary, either the Temple, or – more frequently – the Tabernacle (the latter form depicts the looped curtains described in Exodus). This basic rendering, of Tabernacle and vessels, is an ancient pictorial tradition: Roth concludes that "both Jews and Samaritans knew of Biblical illuminations of this type, perhaps before or at the very beginning" of the Common Era.[31]

The best known Tabernacle picture of this type is that painted for the early eighth-century (c. 715) Codex Amiatinus (Plate 24). Made at Bede's monastery of Jarrow by Anglo-Saxon scribes, this enormous Bible seems to have been modeled (though how closely is in dispute) upon a no-longer-extant Italian manuscript made at Cassiodorus' monastery in Vivarium, and known as the Codex Grandior.[32]

The stylistic influences and practical associations of the Tabernacle–Temple images provide a fascinating chapter in the cross-currents of Levantine societies in the third-fourth centuries, and (as it becomes a source for the Codex Amiatinus picture) in the diaspora into Merovingian and Anglo-Saxon western Europe of Greek-speaking Christian monks and Jewish scholars, especially from Syria, that resulted from the Arab conquests of the seventh century. But what interests me here is the use of the Tabernacle rendering as a mnemotechnical, meditational *pictura*, of the genre I have been defining.

Roth stressed that a Tabernacle rendering was typically used not as an illustration accompanying Exodus, where modern conventions of illustration would put it; rather it was placed at the beginning of the whole Bible. This is also the position it holds in the Codex Amiatinus, where it now occupies a bifolium, ff. IIv–III. This is certainly not where it was originally. Some scholars think it should be placed at ff. 4v–5, immediately in front of the first textual matters; others that it would have been placed, both in the Codex Grandior and the Codex Amiatinus, where Cassiodorus said it was: "in capite," "at the head" of the book, before everything else.[33] Whichever is correct, the Tabernacle diagram is conceived to be initiatory to the text, holding the traditional position of an inventive, meditational *pictura*. The building plan used in the Codex Amiatinus, moreover, is not an "illustration" of the literal text.[34] However exactly its details may represent the measurements of the Exodus text (some do, some do not), "measuring the pattern" of the Tabernacle–Temple was in itself a visionary, penitential act, "intending" one's emotions and mind to prayerful reading.[35]

Cassiodorus briefly discussed the source for his "pictures" of the Tabernacle and Temple in his Codex Grandior. He refers to it peripherally, because he is really talking about how his source for his commentary on Proverbs was the blind Greek expositor, Didymus. How Didymus had been able to gaze so clearly with his heart ("perspicuo corde conspexit"), though he could not see to read, was something Cassiodorus had found almost incredible, he says, until a Greek "from Asia," named Eusebius, came to Vivarium. This Eusebius had been blind since childhood, and yet:

> he had hidden away in the library of his memory so many authors, so many books, that he could satisfactorily tell others who were reading in what part of a codex they might find what he had previously spoken of. ... He reminded [us] how the Tabernacle and Temple of the Lord was fashioned according to Heaven's pattern [ad instar caeli fuisse formatum]; which, painted skillfully in its proper configuration [depicta subtiliter lineamentis propriis], I have adapted suitably in the larger Latin pandect of the Codex Grandior."[36]

After the dispersal of the library at Vivarium shortly after Cassiodorus' death (around 580), this pandect (a pandect contains all the books of the Bible in one volume) was brought to England by Benedict Biscop during the next century and was used by Bede at Jarrow. In the early eighth century, Bede commented both on the Tabernacle description in Exodus and on Solomon's Temple, described in 1 Kings 6, and in each of these commentaries he mentions having seen the "pictura" drawn by Cassiodorus.[37] Bede's commentaries on these objects in turn, along with those of Jerome and Gregory the Great, were standard until they were gradually replaced during the twelfth and later centuries.

The Tabernacle *pictura* was in the initializing and orienting position in the Codex Grandior, as it is now in the Amiatinus. The context of Cassiodorus' remarks suggests that he assumed its usefulness for memory work. Notice how the *pictura* comes up in a discussion of remarkable memories, those of two blind expositors who each possessed such clear-sightedness "of heart" as to be able to read easily and find instantly whatever they wanted in the much-admired "library of texts" stored up in their memories. It is clear from what

Cassiodorus says here that he associated Eusebius' great memory with his knowledge of the "pattern" or plans of the Tabernacle and Temple, and that he included them in his Codex Grandior as an important device for its readers.

Notice also that the Tabernacle picture was drawn "in its proper configuration" to the plan or pattern (*ad instar*) not of an earthly building, but "of heaven." In other words, it "remembers Jerusalem" in the way that the visionary measuring of the city in Ezekiel does. Ezekiel in turn is the precursor of John's vision of the Heavenly Jerusalem; remember that John also saw an angel with a golden rod, with which he measured the City. This feature is prominent in the Beatus Heavenly City pictures. And "memory of heaven" or "memory of Jerusalem" are, as we have seen, perhaps the most common monastic metaphors for meditative memory work. Cassiodorus' picture made to Heaven's pattern, I would suggest, served like a mandala, providing the "way" or *dispositio* of meditative composition, the basic "way" of reading the Bible. The Amiatinus Tabernacle picture would have this function as well, the same rhetorical function as the more common cross-carpet pages. For Christians, beginning meditation with the picture of the Tabernacle is another form of beginning by painting the Cross, for (via Hebrews 8) Christ is the "true" tabernacle, the exemplary pattern shown to Moses upon the mountain ("tabernaculum verum ... exemplar quod tibi ostensum est in monte").

The Codex Amiatinus picture is not exclusively derived from the Exodus text, as several of its details indicate. For instance, written on the diagram are the Greek names for the four compass points, Arctos, Dysis, Anatol, Mesembria: according to an exegetical tradition, the initials of these names spell the name Adam. The names and census populations of the Hebrew tribes, cited from the Book of Numbers, are also written on the diagram. Such details function in the inventive way ornament was supposed to, inviting further meditation. They suggest (also an exegetical commonplace) that the Tabernacle "embraces the four corners of the world and with it the entire progeny of Adam."[38] And one may link this remembered trope with the ancient (especially Hellenistic) convention of cosmic geographies, seen, for example, in the divine topography of Cosmas Indicopleustes, who drew the world in the shape of the Jerusalem Temple, and in the "cartographic" drawing of the Temple–Tabernacle in Greek Octateuch manuscripts.[39]

The Amiatinus tabernacle picture is thus a kind of map, a map for reading. The advantages for memory work of providing such a cognitive chart also suggest why a *mappamundi* was furnished in monastic meditational works that would seem to have nothing to do with terrestrial geography, such as the Beatus Apocalypses. Yet in these manuscripts, a map (as in Plate 1) is found among the front pages of the book, whereas the Heavenly Jerusalem is placed as part of the story-picture of Revelation 21.

There is another peculiarity of the Amiatinus picture. Half of the columns about the perimeter of the sanctuary are shown in front of the curtains and half are behind them. Elisabeth Revel-Neher has linked this curious double perspective to a pictorial tradition found also in both Jewish and early Octateuch manuscripts, in which the Tabernacle is seen both from the interior (where the columns are in front of the curtain) and the exterior (where the curtain covers the columns). These two perspectives divide the rectangle diagonally. Yet a third perspective, truly "bird's eye," is used for the Sacred Vessels and the *sancta sanctorum*. The varying perspectives cause the "mind's eye" to move about, not as an observer looking or even pacing from a fixed distance, but in the manner of one walking about the building in his or her mind, thus looking from different angles as s/he moves through the "places" of a mental schema. The Codex Amiatinus *pictura* is not a static plan: it requires one (if one is paying attention) to imagine oneself moving about inside the picture. In short, it provides rhetorical *ductus* within its simple, rigorous plan.

5. ARCHITECTURAL MNEMONIC IN MONASTIC RHETORIC: TWO TWELFTH-CENTURY EXAMPLES

The mnemotechnical use of buildings by an orator to lay out and recall the structure of his composition is most familiar to modern scholars in the form it assumed in ancient rhetoric. This was described at some length in the *Rhetorica ad Herennium*, and there are allusions to some similar schemes in other ancient rhetorics, notably in Quintilian's discussion of rhetorical *memoria* and in remarks of two teachers from the late empire, Julius Victor and Martianus Capella.

But this scheme is not the most influential form of architectural mnemonic known in the Middle Ages, especially before the late thirteenth century. The meditational structures of monastic rhetoric also commonly included buildings, and so this mnemotechnic bears a superficial resemblance to the classical scheme. But the sources of monastic practice are quite different, as we have seen. As "locational memories," however, the two techniques are enough alike in practice to have made the architectural mnemonic described in the *Rhetorica ad Herennium* seem familiar when Albertus Magnus revived it as the best art of memory. He married classical advice to monastic practice when, as the paradigm of an architectural mnemonic, he substituted the monastery for the Roman house.[40]

In the ancient method, a student of rhetoric was advised to first use an actual building, such as his own house, which he would revisit frequently, thus establishing it so firmly in his memory that its layout provided him with the fully habituated routes and "backgrounds" of his recollecting mind. One can also make up imaginary plans to use as backgrounds. But these are supplementary, says the *ad Herennium* author, to be fashioned by one's imagination if one is not content with one's ready-made supply.[41]

In monastic teaching, by contrast, the ordinary practice was to construct a wholly fictional building, rather than to use an actual one. When invoking a building plan as the device for a compositional structure, monastic writers did not customarily use the monastery buildings that they lived in daily, but rather laid out a typical, exemplary construction – not unlike those idealized monastery buildings in the "Plan of St. Gall."

For example, Peter of Celle (whose penchant for making compositional pictures I described in the last chapter) used a whole monastery as one of the structuring *picturae* in his *Liber de panibus*, a meditation upon the *panes propositionis* or breads of the Presence, which are placed on the table among the Sacred Vessels within the Tabernacle (Exodus 25:30). The "book of breads" is thus another of his meditations on the structure of the "Tabernacle of Moses."[42] Peter writes:

> The chest of Jesus is there, the refectory; the breast of Jesus is there, the dormitory; the face of Jesus is there, the oratory; the width, breadth, height and depth of Jesus is there, the cloister; the company of Jesus and all the saints is there, the chapter-house; the stories of Jesus about the unity of Father, Son, and Holy Ghost, and the first mystery of his incarnation is there, the auditorium.[43]

Peter could have been looking at an internalized "Plan of St. Gall" – indeed, I think he was using a similar, though wholly mental, picture, and inviting his audience, to whom a monastic plan was utterly familiar, to use it as well. With his repetitive "ibi est" he is clearly marking off the locations of the monastery, for both himself and his audience. Notice also how the corporeal measurements of Jesus ("width, breadth, height, and depth") and the measured plan of the tabernacle (as the monastery) are fully conflated by Peter's image, amplifying the originary conflation in Paul's Epistles. What is created is a useful and powerful mnemonic for all manner of doctrinal and exegetical matter, "placed" upon the locations of an exemplary monastery.

When actually drawn, monastic plans for imaginary buildings will often use details that are derived from structures the artist may have seen (this is apparent, for example, in the varying style of the arches and crenelations in "Heavenly City" plans); but at the same time, these pictures are obviously not intended as reproductions of any actual buildings. Richard of St. Victor's treatise on the literal sense of Ezekiel incorporates many detailed plans of the buildings, and is accompanied by drawings that incorporate features of contemporary monastic architectural style (Plate 23).[44] In monastic fictions, one can always use one's own experiences to help one "remember Jerusalem," being conscious as well that, as both Augustine and Alcuin wrote, one person's fictive image of Jerusalem will differ from another's, for such pictures are products fashioned from *memoriae*.

At the same time such buildings are not "wholly imaginary," in our sense of that phrase. They exist as words in a text (the Bible) that can be "revisited" often, and in this way made fully familiar and habitual, through the power of *phantasia* responding to the *enargeia* of the original texts. The ideal monk's memory contained several sets of biblically derived structures that presented themselves as a series of plans and elevations, available for cognitive use.

A simple example of the basic technique occurs in one of Bernard of Clairvaux's sermons on the Song of Songs. Bernard expands the text of Chapter One, verse three: "Introduxit me rex in cellaria sua," "the king has brought me into his store-rooms." The subsequent meditation is constructed as a set of rooms, imagined as numbered "places":

> *To begin with,* let us imagine them to be *perfume-laden places* within the Bridegroom's quarters, where varied spices breathe their scents, where delights are manifold. *In this same manner, the products of garden and field are put away surely for safe-keeping. . . .* The bride runs, so do the maidens; . . . The door is promptly opened

to her ... But what of the maidens? They follow at a distance. (My emphases)[45]

Notice how Bernard gives us a clear beginning, and encourages us to make a synaesthetic imagining of our "places." They are storerooms for the products of garden or field, two commonplaces for *memoria*'s products, for Bernard refers to the flowers and fruits of Scripture stored up in the "rooms" of a trained memory. Lest there be any doubt, Bernard at once begins to "collect" a selection of such "flowers." He quotes allusively from Romans, from the Gospel of John, and from Matthew, as he "places" into this first "room" – literally by opening its door – the running Bride, filled with the Spirit, and her maidens following at a distance.

Next Bernard describes the plan of his entire sermon in terms of a simple organization of rooms:

> Further on [in the Song of Songs] there is mention of a garden (5:1) and a bedroom (3:4), both of which *I join to* these rooms and make part of this present discussion. When examined together the meaning of each becomes clearer. By your leave then, we shall search the Sacred Scriptures for these three things, the garden, the storeroom, the bedroom. ... *Let the garden, then, be the plain, unadorned narrative sense of Scripture, the storeroom its moral sense, and the bedroom the mystery of divine contemplation.* (My emphases)[46]

Notice how Bernard "joins to" his first "place" the two locations of a garden and a bedroom. Notice also that the finished sequence of places – garden, storeroom, bedroom – is not at all reflective of the order of their appearance in the Bible text, but rather responds to an "artificial" order which Bernard has contrived for this sermon. It is a rhetorical strategy, responsive to the requirement of Bernard's mnemonic-inventive craft and that also of his audience. These places, in their simple scheme, then serve as the "draw-ers in" (*formae tractandi*) of more subject-matter (carried in texts remembered both *ad verba* and *ad res*).[47]

One textual storeroom expands to three, "three apartments as it were in the one storeroom." One "apartment" Bernard identifies with the "wine-room" to which the Bride is admitted in Song of Songs 2:4 – he then decides on his own, he says, to "give names to the other two: the room of the ointments and the room of the spices."[48] And into these three apartments further texts are gathered in their turn. After he has completed his circuit of the storerooms, Bernard

240

proceeds to the bedroom (*cubiculum*),[49] and so, with a meditation on the nature of silence, that which is "collected" in the bedroom, the sermon ends. But before he stops, Bernard sums up his *res* for his audience:

> And now, so that your memories can hold a summary [memoria vestra compendium teneat] of my lengthy discussion of the store-room, the garden, the bedroom, remember the three divisions of time, three kinds of merit and three rewards. Connect the times with the garden, the merits with the storeroom, the reward with the threefold contemplation of one who seeks the bedroom. I am satisfied that I have said enough about the storeroom. With regard to the garden and bedroom, if there is something to add or anything already said that needs to be modified, we shall not skip over it [and be unable to find it] in its own place.[50]

This summary is a *pictura* of his previous meditation (though in the final instead of initial position), a summary diagram of its major themes. Yet, if one looks back at Bernard's actual text, one will see readily that he himself has not used in his present composition all the "places" in the triple locational scheme he describes in this summary. For example, he spends almost no time on the "three divisions of time" that he has associated with the garden (indeed he hardly mentions the garden at all). Rather than a diagram limited to his own actual sermon, therefore, what Bernard gives his audience – *for their memory's sake* – is a set of places which they can hold on to and use to fill with more matter, when he decides to return in further sermons to these same places. Notice particularly how Bernard insists that his audience – "you" – must "remember" the places he suggests, and keep them in mind to fill with relevant additions and modifications as they listen to the rest of his course of sermons.

6. A "SORT-OF" BUILDING: GREGORY THE GREAT ON THE TEMPLE COMPOUND IN EZEKIEL

One must keep in mind that such rhetorical uses among monks of an architectural memory scheme were not new in the twelfth century. A hint of one can be found in John Cassian. In the Tenth Conference, Abba Isaac does not just commend the use of a psalm verse (the first verse of Psalm 69) as a meditational tool, he also employs a scheme of architectural *loci* derived from the Exodus material. Speaking of the stages of a monk's education in the discipline of prayer he tells the novice, Germanus, and his companions that since they have now advanced somewhat beyond "the doorway of true prayer," they can, with Isaac's guidance, be brought in "from the porch ... into the inner sanctum."[51] He also tells Germanus to write the verse *in adiutorium meum intende* "upon the threshold and gateway of your mouth, ... on the walls of your house and in the inner sanctuary of your heart."[52]

Besides the Exodus Tabernacle, the most exegetically familiar avatar of the Tabernacle–Temple for twelfth-century monks was the visionary citadel complex described in Ezekiel. As is the case with the Tabernacle, the Temple citadel is described at length with detailed, elaborate building plans, whose "measuring" was interpreted by both Jerome and Gregory the Great.[53] Jerome's exegesis proceeds verse by verse through the Biblical text, and though he at various points encourages mental "painting" in response to the rhetorical *enargeia* of the descriptions, his organizational structure is that of the Biblical verses.

Gregory the Great, however, composed a set of ten sermons on the first forty-seven verses of Ezekiel 40, now collected as the second book of his *Homilies on the Prophet Ezekiel*. These can be read as separate meditations, and though each takes a specific piece of the text as its immediate focus, they also range widely across the whole text. They emphasize the penitential, contritional nature of the activity of measuring the Temple plan. Gregory comments that Ezekiel is called "son of man" by the angel in order to emphasize the distance between the divine vision and his humanity. What can these words plainly mean, he says of Ezekiel 40:4, except "look upon divine realities spiritually and yet remember your human limitations."[54] The idea that the measuring of the Temple is an act of penitential *remembering* is fundamental in understanding how the trope continued to be used.

Gregory also emphasizes that the Temple is called "quasi aedificium." Thus, he says, it is not a physical building, but a spiritual one; therefore it cannot be understood literally but only as a variety of ekphrastic ordering scheme, a *dispositio* for other matters. The measurements given in Ezekiel are incompatible with one another – it is a "sort-of" building, thus a mental image.[55] This is Gregory's justification for considering all its architectural features as mnemonics. The seven levels up to the sanctuary (these are also in the "Plan of St. Gall") are a mnemonic for the seven stages of Wisdom: "In our mind the first level of the staircase is the fear of God, the second piety, the third knowledge, the fourth perserverance, the fifth counsel, the sixth understanding, the seventh wisdom."[56] This commonplace is then elaborated in the rest of this section, from one stair to the next, and a summary statement is also provided. In other words, the structure he has adopted shows how acutely aware he is of the mnemonic requirements of his audiences, and the way that mental picturing importantly "disposes" the words being heard.

Thus, though Gregory does not use the term, these sermons on Ezekiel use the building described in the text as a *pictura* for his set of meditations on the requirements of good citizenship in the heavenly Jerusalem. Gregory does not even pretend to be commenting here on the *littera* of the vision in Ezekiel: he says this cannot be done, because the building in the text has no "literal" being. In other words, he seems to have understood the vision in Ezekiel itself as a *pictura* of "Jerusalem," shown to the prophet for recollective, inventive use by human minds, to compose the mental "places" of penitent prayer.

7. HUGH OF ST. VICTOR'S PICTURE OF NOAH'S ARK

Thus, the tradition of architectural mnemonic in ancient rhetoric gives way to a monastic tradition of composing with inventional, mnemonic *picturae*, often also of buildings. There are two twelfth-century building plans of encyclopedic scale, each called a "picture," that I would like to examine next. They are both fictive *picturae*, though (like the "Plan of St. Gall") one of them has recently been materially realized, at least in part.[57] Both are the work of canons, clergy whose vocations put them into a rhetorical situation in which they were required to address a more varied audience than a familiar elite. The two works are Hugh of St. Victor's *De pictura Arche* (or *De arca Noe mystica*),[58] and Adam of Dryburgh's *De tripartita arche* (the Ark in this case being the ark in the tabernacle).

Hugh of St. Victor's work is encyclopedic not just in its content, but in the way it brings together a number of different, smaller-scale structures common in earlier meditational literature. Invoking the measurements of the Ark given in Genesis 6, Hugh begins with a square "cubit," the unit of measurement for his mental image. First of all, as the base of his picture, he "paints" this cube, which is also the form of the Heavenly City, and the form first laid out by Prudentius' victorious virtues when they build their victory temple. It was also, by Hugh's time, the common shape of the church crossing, just in front of the altar, and of the cloister. He divides the square into four, and then colors the resulting cross with gold. Each quadrant is painted a different color, and as the composition is elaborated, these colors repeat to become a mnemonic color code for various kinds of information.

In the very center of this central cross he paints a Lamb, the ruler of the (square) Heavenly City. The rest of the plan is measured out in this unit, and when Hugh turns to drawing the building's cross-section, this cubit, the basic unit of measure, also becomes the top of the Ark's central column and forms a lantern window. The central cubit, which is the Lamb of God, provides number and light for the whole structure. The picture is, as it were, measured out in units of "Christs," via the commonplace rhetorical catena which translated the ark of the Tabernacle–Temple (and Noah's ark) to the visionary square temple citadel of Ezekiel and the square Heavenly City of the Lamb. The Lamb (Christ) is also the Tabernacle, and we, in prayerful meditation, must raise the temple in ourselves.[59] A "square schematic" is also at work in the "Plan of St. Gall" church – even though, tellingly enough, it was not used in actual buildings at the time.[60]

In Hugh's description of this mental project, he is careful to show exactly how each piece is articulated in the scheme of the entire structure and how the storeys and rooms are divided, and then to "place" information in the form of images within these divisions, used as mnemonic *loci*. It is apparent, as one reads the complex description, that Hugh *saw* this building in his mind as he was composing: he "walked" through it, and – especially given how often he returns to the Ark trope in his own compositions – he used it himself as he advised others to, as a universal cognitive machine.

The basic structure of Hugh's Ark *pictura* is a three-tiered set of rectangular boxes: the *arca* as a "chest," a pun which associates the Genesis Ark with the Ark of the Covenant, described in Exodus, for which God also gave measurements and in which were stored the texts of the Law (on which the righteous man meditates day and night, according to Psalm 1). The mental painting is driven by sound-associations, homophones and polysemous words as much as it is by coloring and shape. Puns transform the treasure chest of memory into the salvational ark of Noah, into a treasure chest (the ark of Moses) that contains the matter of salvation (God's law) which, stored in the chest of memory and thus available for meditation, will redeem and save, as the citadel (*arc-*) of "Jerusalem" will save God's people – provided they remember to "measure the pattern." And the triple-tiering of the Ark, as Hugh paints its mental image, fashions – literally – this triple pun on *arca* (Noah's ark, Moses' ark, Jerusalem ark) from the material in the "ark" of his memory. Hugh's *pictura Archae* is a picture constructed by puns.

Besides the three-storeyed rectangular Ark, Hugh uses in his encyclopedic picture several smaller-scale *formulae*. There is a genea-logical *linea* (like the builders' *lineae*, with which a building's founda-tion was measured). Into this form, images of some of the prophets and apostles are placed in two "theater" structures, each set in a semi-circle about the central column, thus making the form of a complete amphitheater. There is a tree diagram (conflated with the wooden centerpost of the Ark) that structures a variety of virtues and vices. There are a great many ladders, filled with various labeled human forms as well as the books of the Bible. Superimposed on all of this is a *mappamundi*; the place-names of the map graph in a generalized way the people named in the genealogy, the "line" ordering the historical narrative; various virtues are indexed as well on the compass grid of the map. About and "above" the whole rectangular form is a Creation diagram, which is a (concentric) circle figure, containing an image of Divine Majesty, and both the celestial and angelic circles.

As we have seen, most of these genres of schematic *picturae* are found fairly commonly, even in Carolingian manuscripts, though more often described in words (as here) than painted. In the manner of rhetorical ekphrasis, Hugh was surely recalling several of these that he had seen. Unusual is the combination of such a variety of forms, the complexity of their disposition, and the manifold ways that they are "scanned" and moved about to accord with the varying view-points of Hugh's mental eye as he describes himself "painting" them. But Hugh was a master of *memoria*.

Some scholars believe that the text describes an actual painting, perhaps made on a number of parchment folios fastened together in the manner of the "Plan of St. Gall," or of the (much larger) parchment made up of several ox-hides onto which some meditational pictures were painted by Opicinus de Canistris, a scribe working in the 1330s for the papacy at Avignon.[61] Though some actual drawings and diagrams have been constructed recently from Hugh of St. Victor's directions, I think that he was engaged in "painting" rhetorical *picturae*, and not describing an object physically before him. The reason for this is simply that if the treatise were importantly linked to a painted schematic, one would expect some version of it, however garbled and simplified, to have survived – as renderings have survived of various versions of *genealogiae, mappaemundi,* and so on.[62]

But, for reasons I made clear in my last chapter, I do not think the issue of whether or not the "picture" described was actually painted is, finally, essential to understanding how Hugh's treatise was used by its intended audiences. That issue is something of a red herring – akin to worrying about how exactly St. Benedict could have transported his spirit. In the rhetorical circumstances (pedagogical in their goal) which governed the composing of this picture of Noah's Ark, the question whether a *pictura* scheme would be materially painted or not was determined as an issue of rhetorical decorum, whether, from among the available means of persuasion, a material painting would be thought suitable or valuable. Hugh's *pictura* serves its generic function as a summary and orientation, a "way" to the chief themes of the treatise it accompanies, the *De Arca Noe morali.* And given the conventions of rhetorical *picturae,* it seems likely that these two works are really one, as indeed some manuscripts present them.[63] This possibility – that an exegetical treatise can contain a lengthy verbal *pictura* as one of its constituent parts – is confirmed as well by the work I will consider next, called "The Triple Tabernacle" (*De tripartito tabernaculo*).

8. ADAM OF DRYBURGH'S "TRIPLE TABERNACLE, TOGETHER WITH A PICTURE"

Adam of Dryburgh, its author, was a Scot, a regular canon at the Premonstratensian abbey of Dryburgh, one of King David of Scotland's several religious foundations. He worked during the late twelfth century, a younger contemporary of Richard of St. Victor, John of Salisbury, and Peter of Celle. The order of canons to which Adam belonged were followers of St. Norbert, who was a contemporary of Hugh of St. Victor and a student at St. Victor, though he was there before Hugh entered around 1125. The abbey of St. Victor was founded by William of Champeaux in 1110; Norbert founded the canons of Prémontré in 1120. The three parts of Adam's exegesis of the Tabernacle are, first, a commentary on the literal meaning of the Exodus text, the sort of thing which the methods of grammar produce. Most of part two consists of "historical" commentary (using the method of allegorical typology), bringing the history of Christendom down to Adam's own contemporaries, and part three is moralized, "tropological" commentary. The rubric for part two calls it a *pictura*.

Though basing it on the Exodus text, Adam clearly distinguishes his own "picture" of the Tabernacle from the Biblical description. His is a simplified, summary version, one which, he says, his audience can spread before them as they listen, and *use* in such a way that the picture and the words confirm and support one another:

> in [my] visible picture also I have placed such images and colors that by them the mystical content of each spiritual tabernacle, that is of the allegorical and the tropological, may be more aptly indicated. . . . And because the second and third part[s] of this book pertain to the picture, having spread this same picture out before yourselves, you will be able to read competently the first book [i.e. the literal interpretation] under both aspects [i.e. allegory and tropology]: so that perceiving both through your hearing what is being read and through your gaze [aspectu] what is being depicted, you can fit together the book and the picture simultaneously.[64]

In a prefatory letter, which accompanied the transmittal of his work to the canons of Prémontré, Adam says that he had been asked two years earlier by John, abbot of Kelso (and as such, senior among the Scottish clergy), to compose a book "together with a picture [una cum pictura]" of the Tabernacle of Moses.[65] John asked for this exegetical work, he explains, because Bede's commentary no longer fully satisfied; so Adam was asked to prepare a fuller exegesis for teachers that would take the text "syllabicando," "syllable by syllable," the method of ordinary gloss.[66] On the foundation of this complete grammatical commentary, John requested Adam next to build up allegorical and tropological "tabernacles" (that is, meditations in these two modes that take the tabernacle structure as their starting-point), together with a "picture" which will help readers to "enlarge" the literal text (he uses the verb *augeo*) intellectually and morally, thus becoming also inventive "authors" in the work of the commentary.[67]

Adam's reply to the abbot explains how the picture and the book should work together. The work has three parts, explained as follows: "The first part treats the construction and layout of the material and visible tabernacle of Moses. The second pertains to the picture of this same tabernacle, and [treats of] its allegorical meaning. And the third its moral significance."[68] This characterization suggests that the second division of the work is about two different things: first it describes a *pictura* of the tabernacle and next it suggests the tabernacle's allegorical significance.

As he continues to characterize what he has made, Adam distinguishes even more clearly the "picture" from the rest of the work. The second division of the present work is mainly devoted to a *genealogia* or family history that begins with the Old and New Testament lines and continues onward, as many such works did, with a list of the Popes (to Alexander III, 1159–1181), of the emperors since Constantine, the kings of France, and the present kings of England and Scotland, Henry II (d. 1189) and William the Lion (d. 1214). These people, living and dead, are all members of Holy Church, citizens of the second, "allegorical" tabernacle.

The *pictura* portion of part two is distinguished from this "allegorical tabernacle." Its description occupies the first five chapters of the second part. Having finished the first part of his book "about the construction [*factura*] and layout [*dispositio*] of the tabernacle" in accordance with the measurements God gave to Moses, Adam says at the beginning of part two that he will now carry out the instruction from abbot John to paint a picture of the tabernacle "in plano," "as a plan on a flat surface." Adam cautions that such a schematized reduction of the original will involve distortions: he cannot properly show height and depth, nor the red and blue skins that covered the roof. But he will set his hand to this task, insofar as his mental vision can manage.[69]

Adam describes his painting procedure in a manner very like that employed by Hugh of St. Victor. First, he draws a square in the middle of the flat surface.[70] He extends the lines to the south and the west, to make a rectangular figure that is three times as long as it is wide, for the Tabernacle of Moses was thirty cubits long and ten wide. This foundation is then filled in with detail drawn from the Exodus description – the walls, the columns, the atriums, the tablets on the walls, and the roof. The roof cannot actually be seen, he says, because of the limitations of the *planus* genre of diagram: unlike Hugh of St. Victor, Adam does not include an *elevatio* of the structure. The picture is colored with the colors mentioned in Exodus: hyacinth, crimson, scarlet, and byss (linen).

All the verbs Adam uses in this part of his treatise are in the first person singular of the present tense: "I paint," "I draw." We can see Adam's own structure taking shape, in verbs unlike the past-tense verbs he uses during his literal exposition of the Exodus text. The picture takes shape in that present time of narrative and meditation which is "memory time," the story-telling present, in which pictures form in the mind's eye.

So it would seem to be the case that the *pictura* which Adam made to send along with his book is just this schematic exemplar which introduces the second part. It is described in words alone, using the rhetorical tools of *enargeia* and ekphrasis. There is no reason to think that Adam first painted something that we would call a picture, and then described that actual object.[71] The conventions which Adam is using refer to picture-making of the mind, the picture that structures memory, invents thought, and concentrates will by the action of inner seeing.

Adam's picture, in fact, looks rather like the picture-trope of the Tabernacle (which also shows no roof), a version of which is in the Codex Amiatinus. Perhaps he had seen some schematic version of it himself, and was remembering it here; perhaps it had only been described to him by his teachers. Nothing in his text precludes or suggests either method of dissemination. However he learned of it, Adam uses it as his cognitive tool. Into it he proceeds recollectively to "gather" the allegorical and tropological interpretations that occupy him in the rest of part two and all of part three of his work. This is how he understood his picture, as he says. "Now it remains that among those matters, which we have written about the material tabernacle, we should adapt some to the spiritual tabernacle of Christ, which is holy Church, in the picture laid out before us."[72]

At the very end of this part, Adam superimposes another scheme onto the tabernacle, this one derived from the Song of Songs (and thus bearing a likeness to Bernard of Clairvaux's architectural mnemonic). He identifies five distinct areas (*spatia*) of his *pictura*:

> the first was like a field, the second is like a garden, the third a sort of atrium, the fourth a house, and the fifth a bedchamber. In the field were good and bad plants alike, in the garden select plants, in the atrium friends and comrades, in the house [which, in this context, must refer to the "house of God," an oratory] parents and siblings, in the bedchamber the Bridegroom and Bride.[73]

This scheme within the larger scheme is then the basis of his third "tabernacle," which is of the soul in meditation ("in interna cogitatione," according to the colophon of the third part).

So as Adam uses it, his *pictura* is a means to invent the spiritual meditation he wished (and was commanded) to add on to his grammatical gloss of the literal text. It is not a representation in paint of the actual building described in the text of Exodus: he has made very clear that his intention is not to illustrate that object as it might really have looked. This is *his own* mental picture, "quantum sciero et potero," limited both by his own understanding and by his ability to describe it. He does not even think of it as an art object, made up either of words or of paint, but as something preceeding both and thus capable of being realized, though only to a degree, in both physical media, language and paint. But the picture itself "really" exists in his mind, where it serves his orderly invention of his matters, *memoria rerum*. He invites the users of his book to paint it in their minds too, to serve the same purpose.

To this compositional function of a "picture" of the Tabernacle–Temple, one can contrast the work of literal exegesis by Richard of St. Victor on Ezekiel's Temple vision. Several manuscripts of this exist, a number of them (including one from St. Victor itself) containing drawings showing plans and elevations of the Temple complex (Plate 23).[74] There are also several drawings that answer to Richard's calculations of the dimensions of the various service buildings which were part of the Temple.

But though these plans and elevations contain the sort of imaging from which one might derive a *pictura* of the type used by Hugh of St. Victor and by Adam of Dryburgh, Richard's work is *only* concerned with the *litterae*, the words of Ezekiel. It entirely avoids allegorical or tropological reading. Coming from a master of mystical exegesis, one who could certainly derive carefully crafted *picturae* from the Biblical text as he chose to, it is apparent that for his commentary on Ezekiel, Richard was consciously using what he himself thought to be a different type of commentary. Richard's literal exegesis of Ezekiel is the equivalent of part one of Adam of Dryburgh's *De tripartito tabernaculo*, a literal exegesis that *is distinguished from* what is called a "picture."[75] Richard's tropological exegesis of the Tabernacle figure is a separate composition, now known as *The Mystical Ark* (or *Benjamin major*), which, as I noted earlier, is accompanied by a summary verse *pictura* that uses the tripartite Ark trope as its organizing scheme.[76]

250

9. AUGUSTINE IN "THE PLACE OF THE TABERNACLE"

People who were accustomed to cultivating the images painted in the mind by texts read aloud (and ruminated in murmured "silence") were in a better position than we are to appreciate the difference between grammatical commentary and visual cognitive device. Visualizing the information given to you in a technical manual (and in one sense – the literal – the Ezekiel angel's measurements could be seen as that) requires exactness. It may even require a physical surface and a compass and ruler – with which, in fact, some of the diagrams accompanying Richard's literal exegesis seem to have been made. But this illustrative task should not simply be conflated with the task of images fashioned as a foundation for further meditation on various matters, the task John of Kelso identified as "allegorizing." A picture used as an inventive device almost certainly will depart from the literal words on which it is based; it will bear some relationship to those words, as Adam's picture does to the words of Exodus, but exactitude is not its painter's goal. Such a picture will change its lineaments, sometimes quite drastically (Adam's tabernacle "becomes" a church-cloister complex when it suits him), as the mind of one thinking moves about it.

We now are so accustomed to thinking of diagrams as the static and abstracted forms of already-rationalized subject-matter, that it is difficult for us even to think of a "picture" as requiring movement on the part of the viewer.[77] Yet in exegetical traditions the "place of the Tabernacle" (as Augustine called it) was not static. The varying perspectives used to picture it, both in words and in paint, suggest this. Indeed, the invention trope of "the place of the Tabernacle" requires movement through and within its structure, as though within a material building.

In his comments on Psalm 41, preached first as a sermon to a listening congregation, Augustine paints a literary picture of the Tabernacle. This psalm was regarded as being "about" contemplation; that was regarded as its subject or gist, a heading it would commonly have been filed under in any monk's mental florilegium. It begins "As the hart panteth after the water-brooks, so my soul panteth after thee, o God."[78] Verse 5 mentions the tabernacle: "These things I remembered, and poured out my soul in me: for I shall go over into the place of the wonderful tabernacle, even to the house of God: With the voice of joy and praise; the sound of one feasting."[79]

"The place of the Tabernacle"

Augustine comments that "He who has his highest house in a hidden place, also has on earth his tabernacle." This tabernacle is the Church, and in this place is discovered the way by which one can go up to the house of God. He continues:

> When I [remembered and] poured out my soul within me in order to touch my God, how did I do this? "For I will enter [ingrediar] into the place of the Tabernacle." These words suggest that I will first blunder about [errabo] outside the place of the Tabernacle seeking my God. "For I will enter into the place of the wonderful Tabernacle, even to the house of God." . . . And now I look with wonder at many things in the Tabernacle. Behold the things I admire in the Tabernacle. Faithful men are the Tabernacle of God on earth; I admire in them their control over their members, for not in them does sin reign by obedience to their desires, nor do they show off their limbs armed with the sin of inquity, but show them to the living God in good works; I marvel at the disciplined physique of a soul in service to God. I look again upon the same soul obeying God, distributing the fruits of his activities, restraining his desires, banishing his ignorance . . . I gaze also upon those virtues in my soul. But still I walk about in the place of the Tabernacle. And I cross through even that; and however marvellous the Tabernacle may be, I am amazed when I come right up to the house of God. . . . Here indeed is wisdom's water fountain [cf. Psalm 41:1], in the sanctuary of God, in the house of God. . . . Ascending the Tabernacle, [the Psalmist] came to the house of God. Even while he looked upon the parts of the Tabernacle he was led up to the house of God, by following a certain sweetness, I know not what inner and hidden delight, as though some kind of *organum* sounded sweetly all through the house of God; and all the while he might walk about in the Tabernacle, having heard a sort of interior music, led by sweetness, following the instrument making the music, removing himself from all the noise of body and blood, he made his way up to the house of God. For thus he remembers his way and his *ductus*, as though we had said to him: You are gazing upon the tabernacle in this world; how have you come to the hidden place of God's house? "With the voice," he says, "of joy and praise, with the sound of one celebrating a festival." . . . From that eternal and perpetual feast, there sounds I know not what song so sweet to the ears of my heart; as long as the noisy world does not drown it out. To one walking about in that tabernacle and considering the wonders of God for the redemption of the faithful, the sound of that festivity quiets the ear and carries off the hart to the water fountains.[80]

Augustine treats the phrase *locus tabernaculi* as a mnemotechnical place, a "background." To go up to the place of the tabernacle thus becomes, in Augustine's meditation on the phrase, a mnemotechnical walk about the structure, seeing the various "things" that are gathered within it, placed like groups of actors in scenes, or *imagines agentes* in *loci*. Within the Tabernacle, Augustine says, "is found [invenietur] the way [via] by which one may proceed to the home of God." Remember that the annotator of the "Plan of St. Gall" took pains to label the church entry, "this is the way to the holy Temple": the parallel is instructive. Augustine's psalm commentaries were very well known monastic books.

For a living human being here ("in hac terra"), who is seeking God in the context of a pilgrim-church, the "way" lies from outside, wandering in error, through "the place of the Tabernacle," to the ascent up to "the home of God." There are thus three distinct locations in Augustine's structure, three mnemonic loci: outside, Tabernacle, and *domus Dei* (a common phrase in the Psalms, but one that in this context particularly resonates, recollectively, with Ezekiel 43:10).[81]

Entering the place of the Tabernacle, Augustine invites us to look around and walk about with him: the verbs used here repeatedly are various forms of *ambulare* and *admirari* and *specere* and *ire*, walk, gaze upon, look, go. And in the Tabernacle he sees grouped figures of just men, showing their various attributes (here the verb is *ostendere*), the various virtues disposed in *loci* of the building. And then, having made his inspection of the whole place, he walks across ("transibo," "I will walk over") from it to the next place, ascending to the *domus Dei*. At this point, Augustine shifts without explanation from first to third-person, and joins his own vision with the experience of the Psalmist, as they move with one soul through the "place of the Tabernacle."

Augustine is very clear that only by walking about and looking at the parts or *membra* of the Tabernacle can the soul come to ("be led to") God's house. Augustine was certainly familiar with the rhetorical concept of *ductus*. But in this complex text, the handbook notion realizes an extraordinary literary richness. The master trope is of movement channeled by a construction, contrasted to wandering aimlessly and formlessly outside. This need for orderly movement through "places" is caught in Augustine's use of *ductus*, which at its core (though it has a host of derivative uses) denotes an ordered, directed motion – such as practiced movement of human limbs. (Paleographers are familiar with the scribal *ductus*, the precise combination of hand movements that scribes learned for drawing the letters.) As he, now joining his experience to that of the Psalmist, walks about the Tabernacle, following some internalized route of joy-directed movement, the soul's eye modulates into the soul's ear listening to a sort of ("quasi") *organum* or musical instrument, and the walking becomes more like a dance, some choreographed movement (that is how I would understand *ductus* in this context). As he walks-dances through the Tabernacle, *strepitus*, "noise," is replaced with harmony, as wandering was replaced by walking purposefully and then by a kind of dancing.

But the Tabernacle, the mental building constructed by Augustine from the Psalm text by the eye, the ear, and the limbs of his *memoria*, provides the way and *ductus* to God's house, as an ancient *aquaeductus*, a human construction, conducted formless water. And this psalm begins with water, the *aquae fontes* of its first verse.

Thus, when Augustine uses *ductus* in his meditation on the *locus Tabernaculi*, he evidently thinks of it as movement within a composition, and so contained and oriented by its structure. Yet it is movement which the viewer also chooses. So, Augustine chooses his pace, where he will look first and in what order, and the *ductus* of the construction eventually becomes the "way" he follows, like an internal music that leads him on. As Augustine ponders the idea here, compositional *ductus* is only to a limited extent a matter of the author's original choices or "approach"; the work itself has *ductus* which, while it expresses authorial choices (one hopes well), also allows its audiences to choose their *ductus* within its possibilities. And if they do not, they will simply remain in confused wandering, "outside the place of the Tabernacle."

10. BUILDINGS AS MEDITATION MACHINES: TWO MODERN STORIES

In the rest of this chapter, I would like to suggest how the monastery buildings themselves, the oratory (*templum*) and cloister (*pratum*) in particular, were understood to function rhetorically as a support and conduit for the memorial work of both meditation and liturgical prayer. We have seen how, in earliest monasticism, the buildings of Scripture – especially the Tabernacle and Temple – were used as mental devices for the life of prayer (which, we must never forget, encompassed *everything* a monk did). We have also seen how the compositional trope of *pictura*, though the word has a general meaning of "scheme" or *dispositio*, is associated especially with the diagrammatic or cartographical figures that were used for picturing cognitive work throughout the Middle Ages.

The architectural "predisposition" of these schemes – their preferred use of imaginary buildings built mentally out of Biblical descriptions, with particular (though not exclusive) attention paid to the ornamenting of their walls and ceilings, which were considered the special concern of *architecti* – formed a compositional trope that was used also in making actual structures and mural programs.

Around 1246, the Dominican master, Albertus Magnus, composed a treatise (*De bono*) on the virtues. When he discussed Prudence, he commented on the art of memory described in the ancient *Rhetorica ad Herennium*.[82] For his thirteenth-century university audience he translated the list of ancient architectural sites given as examples of suitable mnemotechnical backgrounds (a niche, a house, arches, colonnades) into medieval examples: *templum* (the monastery church), *hospitalis* (the monastery guest-house), *pratum* (the cloister-garth), and *intercolumnia*, a term which he took over from the ancient source, but referred to the commonest of monastic *intercolumnia*, the portico, ambulatory, and aisles of the church and the galleries of the cloister. Note that each of these structures is specifically monastic: Albertus and his audience evidently thought of monasteries as providing particularly familiar and appropriate "places" for memory work.

From the start of his reform, Bernard of Clairvaux emphasized that the daughter-houses of his monastery should be built according to the same plan, as far as was physically possible.[83] Though this desire has sometimes been interpreted as an effort to impose uniformity on the Cistercians or even as the primary expression of a centralizing, authoritarian reform of the western Church at this time, I think another kind of interpretation is also possible. Bernard, like every other monastic founder, was concerned above all with supplying a proper support for the contemplative lives of his brother-monks. I use the word "support" here in a technical sense, as stone, paper, wood, parchment are all called *supports* when they are written or painted upon. The architecture provides a supporting structure within which compositional memory work can take place, for the community in the work of the liturgy, and for the individual in the work of reading, both silent and aloud.

But it does more than this. By providing cognitive *ductus*, it also gives energy and pattern to the mind's ceaseless movements. I can best illustrate what I mean by recounting a contemporary monastic incident. A friend of mine once told me of a conversation he had had many years earlier with an elderly Cistercian monk, who had lived his whole life in the Heiligenkreutz monastery in Austria. Only once in his life had he traveled, sent to a Cistercian monastery in Portugal for study – an experience which, in anticipation, caused him much anxiety lest its strangeness and foreignness would disturb his spiritual peace and his ability to participate fully in the offices of his profession, especially the Night Office, when he could expect to be most disoriented. He was worried about having to worry about finding his way.

But, he said, he was much relieved to find himself instantly oriented by the near-identity of the architecture in the Portuguese house with his familiar home in Austria. The lay-out of buildings was the same, the orientation of the chapel, the location of the cloister, dormitory, library, refectory. But especially helpful was the fact that details were the same, like the number of the chancel steps, of bays in the nave, and (crucially) the location and number of the night stairs. This congruence, he was convinced, enabled him to continue his prayers and meditations without interruption, and to compose his spiritual life as fully in the new place as he was accustomed to doing at home. Because his mnemonic places were undisturbed by his move from Austria to Portugal, the monk was able to continue to know where he was, without interruption or disorientation: he retained that all-important cognitive "where" whose loss so distressed the elderly Coptic desert monk, Sarapion. And notice that the *important* similarities consisted not only in the larger correspondences of the lay-out but even more in the details, like the numbers of stairs and the placement of entries and bays.

There are other contemporary stories of this sort. When Nelson Mandela was released from his prison in South Africa to begin planning a new constitution, he built an exact replica of the prison warden's house in which he had worked during the last months of his imprisonment. When asked why he had done this, he replied that he had grown accustomed to the floor plan of that house and "wanted a place where he could find the bathroom at night without stumbling."[84] The replica was his vacation home, where he went for meditative leisure, his own form of the life of prayer, of the sort he had been forced to construct for himself in prison. The utterly familiar lay-out, as it were "inviscerated" within his brain, enabled his meditation, and it is especially interesting that finding the bathroom at night was a particular anxiety for him, as finding the way for night offices was to the traveling monk.

Buildings become enfolded in people's thinking habits. The remembered familiarity of a building's plan does not just enable one to "purge worldly cares" (such as getting to places in the dark without stumbling) and concentrate on important matters, but it seems actually to channel and "carry" the movements of one's thinking. The mind is entirely freed to make its thoughts when it also has entirely familiar habitations and its familiar routes, a principle well understood in meditative practice.

The new British Library building in St. Pancras occasioned a loud outcry from some scholars whose research habits were completely implicated in the disposition of the old building, and who were disturbed by the interruption to their work that having to learn a new building plan would necessarily involve. This scholarly fear is not just annoyance at having to learn where the new catalogue and study rooms are (scholars are, after all, good at learning things). It is the more fundamental anxiety of not knowing where one is, not being able to recover (perhaps ever) the "places" in one's thinking schemes that the familiar locations of catalogue and study – and the routes between them – had served.[85]

II. MEDITATION REFORM AND BUILDING REFORM: A CISTERCIAN EXAMPLE

It is significant, I think, that both Bernard of Clairvaux and Hugh of St. Victor, using Suger of St.-Denis as his surrogate,[86] should have thought to realize their *meditational* reforms in terms of building reforms. To these two reformers one should add Thierry of Chartres, thought to have had a hand at least in planning the program of the right portal of the west façade at Chartres cathedral; and Peter of Celle, who certainly planned programs of interior metalwork and glass at Saint-Rémi while he was abbot.[87] And of course, there are many earlier instances which indicate how thoroughly meditative orthopraxis depended upon its habitation. The "Plan of St. Gall" is thought to have some relationship, though just what is unclear, to the reform set in motion by Benedict of Aniane. And no less a figure than Benedict of Nursia himself, as we have seen, was at pains to show his monks exactly how their buildings should be disposed.

The twelfth-century reforms, as all know, took varying shapes, according to the situations of various orders. Bernard of Clairvaux pared down the monks' oratory to an unadorned, moderately lighted, moderately sized *locus* variously subdivided into plain backgrounds marked off by the bays, the steps, the lights and shadows within. In the designs of Suger and Hugh, and of Thierry of Chartres, the building included elaborate encyclopedic mnemonic *picturae*, orienting and initiating those entering to the ways of this *locus Tabernaculi*. At Saint-Rémi, Peter of Celle – as we have seen, a master of the rhetorical *pictura* – redesigned the choir (as Suger did at St.-Denis), giving it (as Suger also did) a program of windows that made the space into a jeweled *cella* within which to remember the Heavenly Jerusalem.

Their emphasis on architecture indicates that buildings, especially the church in which the liturgy "took place," were conceived to be meditational mechanisms, structures that not only housed and abetted, but *enabled* the *opus Dei*.[88] Their function is not primarily commemorative or "symbolic": it is to act as engines channeling and focussing the restless power of the ever-turning wheel that is the human mind. Bernard pointedly used the word *oratorium* for the sort of church he wished to build instead of the (by then) more common word *ecclesia* because he conceived of it as a *place* for prayer. This is one of his chief points of contrast between his "praying places" and the excessive scale (as he thought it) of the *ecclesiae* of other monastic orders.[89] His architecture is one of his greatest *rhetorical* achievements. Many of its features are not peculiar to Cistercian buildings at all, but they are clarified, simplified, shrunk in size – in short, they are turned, "troped" – in ways that fashion a distinctively Cistercian praxis.

A Cistercian oratory provides a set of "places" that accord with some general principles of mnemonic backgrounds. These are articulated in the *Rhetorica ad Herennium*, but are evidently also capable of being independently invented: perhaps they are sufficiently basic to human memory processes to be considered matters of "common sense."[90] The building is of moderate extent and enclosed, of a size and shape that can be encompassed (as the cloister also could) by one glance of the mental eye. This quality is enhanced by the mural continuity of the second storey, a continuous wall above the arches. It is lighted moderately, neither dazzling nor obscure, by windows of uncolored glass, made in simple grisaille patterns (Plates 25 and 26). These windows mark out the building's structural units, so that each room-like unit is provided with a moderate illumination. Moderate size is typical also in the cloister galleries, where the capitals (as at Fontenay) are virtually at eye level.

The *templum* and *pratum* also contain elements that readily and obviously mark off the subdivisions of each "place." There is an arcade that provides *intercolumnia*, the "inter-columnar spaces" suggested as backgrounds even in the ancient mnemotechnical lists. The obvious divisions of the building – nave, transepts, apse – are related to one another in modular construction, like a set of *loci* or *sedes* in a mnemonically valuable structure. The square of the crossing provides the basic unit of both plan and elevation, the unit of measure for the bays, one "Christ."

One is thus always secure of one's "place" in the structure; one can *the* indeed mentally "walk" about it. In such a mental walk through the *ruin* nave, for instance, each *locus* between the columns is divided obviously from the next by a form (the column shafts) that acts like an enclosing frame. Thus the bays provide a *linea* of moderately sized seats or places that not only could be used mnemonically, but that also seem artfully to fulfill basic mnemonic requirements.

An example, shown in Plate 26, is the set of rectangular box-like spaces formed by the bays of the aisles at Pontigny, one of the first daughter-foundations of Cîteaux (the nave dates from the 1140's). Each bay of the aisles, clearly marked out by columns, arch, and vault, forms a little room or *cella*, moderately lighted by a single grisaille window. It is the right size for the eye to take in with a single *conspectus* or mental "glance"; it is a plain background of moderate extent clearly defined by a frame; a viewer is set at a moderate distance from the back wall; each background is separated from the next by a moderate interval formed by the piers.[91]

Considered as a single mnemonic place, the interior of a Cistercian oratory seems absolutely plain, a *locus* that has the characteristic, to use Albertus Magnus' terms, of being both *solemnis*, "orderly," and *rarus*, "not-crowded" (indeed so *rarus* that architectural ornament is all but banished). Both of these are also characteristics mentioned in the Ciceronian mnemonic art, yet Albertus would have known them from his own experience, *before* he studied and commented on the ancient text. This is a critical order of events to grasp when one is attempting to understand the history of mnemotechnics. The ancient textbook precepts defined some matters already familiar to Albertus in the buildings where he had prayed; the textbook techniques were comprehensible to him and his audience (as they no longer are to most of us) because they saw them through the lens of their own practices, and those practices reshaped for them the ancient *techne*.

One also needs to consider the *ductus* of these oratories, a rhetorical concept of great value in describing the nature of the meditational support they give. As helping to mark "the way" in and through a building, its light patterns are an important element of this *ductus*. Hugh of St. Victor emphasizes the mnemotechnical usefulness of seasonal and diurnal change in his elementary memory art, the preface to his *Chronicon* – an emphasis not found in the ancient art, and one which puzzled me until I considered monastic architecture.[92] For his emphasis on the need to place oneself diurnally and seasonally, as well as spatially, is best explained as a contribution to mnemonic technique from monastic meditational practice, in which changing intensities of light marked out and accompanied the basic steps of one's way.

The grisaille window, a particular Cistercian feature, allows each "room" to be moderately lighted, while at the same time making a simple pattern of light on the "walls" formed by the columns, which will change with time of day and season. Like the patterns of Cistercian capitals, which will seem at first to be virtually uniform, the light patterns made by grisaille windows require great attentiveness and study – and an attentive memory – to discover. Recalling and supporting such meditational attentiveness, such *intentio* of heart, was an essential part of Bernard's reforms.

This is a different light aesthetic, seemingly more classical in affliation, from the visionary obscure commended in Baudri de Bourgeuil's encyclopedic poem for Countess Adela, the low light which Albertus Magnus, in his comments on the *Rhetorica ad Herennium*, thought was proper to the art of memory (thereby "correcting" what the classical author had advised). Yet I do not think the Cistercian aesthetic was classical at all in its sources; rather, it is a simple device for focussing those "clean," ardent memories which Bernard wanted all his monks to cultivate. The lower-light, "obscure" aesthetic familiar to Albertus was at work in the "Gothic gloom" of other churches of other orders, like St.-Denis and St.-Rémi, whose windows were painted. Such windows also, of course, create complex *ductus* as the colors move with the light through the architectural forms, a *ductus* that seems appropriate to all else we know of the "occasion" of these great works. Different social circumstances are at work in these different buildings, different rhetorical circumstances each requiring its suitable decorum. (And one also needs to keep in mind that "sufficient light" – especially for the mind's eye – is not a standard that can be made normative.)

12. FURNISHING THE ROUTES OF PRAYER

A monastic oratory is a building that experienced practioners in meditational craft can *use*: it can easily be internalized, readily "laid out" in distinct units, each of moderate size, in one's mind, and can be "re-visited" both mentally and physically. It is not a lazy or a jaded person's building, for each individual will need to work at making "his own," *familiaris*, the composition of places which it provides. The *ductus* within church and cloister produces a complex, varying and changeable music, like that of the internalized *organum* which conducts Augustine through the "locus Tabernaculi."[93]

Other orders than the Cistercians, with different audiences and different "common places," had other and additional means of marking the routes of prayer. Light and its varying patterns was a constant means, one that encouraged developing the *intentio* and *affectus* of mind required for rememorative contemplation. So were the corollary patterns marked out by the varying texts and *colores* of the liturgy. But they are not the only means. I have previously discussed how various subjects used for mural decoration, such as the common trope used in both literature and mosaic art of pairing Old and New Testament events, constitute a "machine" for meditation upon scripture, in which decoration and prayer together create continuously various compositions.

Many scholars have noted how the parts of a church are articulated as a kind of journey of conversion, from pre-baptism to baptism to faith. John Onians has suggestively described this motive of using the decorative orders of architecture to mark the *ductus* (a word he does not use) of a construction, such as a façade. By the time of the empire, Romans "expected to scan a building and look for features, especially in the columnar organization, which would articulate it."[94] Roman imperial cities bristled with columns, used in part to mark their owners' status and, in a communal context, to give addresses to the places of the city. These columns, literally and figuratively, "invented" the city as a human community, a network of places by means of which a person could find her way.

This heuristic motive for using ornament intensified with Christian buildings, Onians argues, and was made an essential part of the way that buildings could, as it were, invent prayer, conceived of as the common places and common matter or *res* of liturgy, upon which individual meditative prayer would be a rhetorical dilation. So, for example, Constantine transferred the Composite order, used to mark imperial triumph, to the triumph of the new religion when, instead of using it on his own triumphal arch as previous emperors had, he reserved it for the six spiral-vine columns he had set up about the tomb of St. Peter in his new church. "It is as if Constantine, in gratitude for Christ's aid at Milvian Bridge, decided to surrender the [Composite] order to him. The victory was Christ's, not the emperor's."[95]

Onians continues, "Every step taken in a Christian church, every passage in liturgy, potentially involved psychological transformations and the dramatic realization of some bold metaphor such as rebirth or salvation."[96] But more is at work than simple heuristic, the mapping of a prescribed route for the faithful always to follow. There are, as Augustine reminds us, many ways through the "locus Tabernaculi" to the house of God, but to get there one must journey forth upon them. That journey is not only psychological and interior, but one made with feet and eyes through physical spaces, and colored by bodily sensation and emotion.

In monastic compositions, both personal and communal, the governing metaphor of the Way is critical, as we have seen. Every journey is oriented towards a particular end, its *skopos*. In the vocabulary of late ancient rhetoric, every composition began as a place-from-where (the *stasis* or *status*), a place-towards-which (the *skopos*), and the *ductus* between them, marked out by various *colores* and *modi*. Thus, in a sense, any composition was also a procession of author and audience. For the monks the *skopos* was, of course, the Heavenly City. Moreover, the journey took several moods, from fear (the heart-stopping anxiety, especially in the face of one's death and its consequences, that propelled the self-terrified Augustine on to the Cross), to the emotional restlessness of "ego dormio, et cor meum vigilat," to the musical silence and radiance of the "domus Dei," to the return, in a state of joy, to *strepitus*, the bustle of the mortal world.

Historians have tended to map the *ductus* of a church intellectually and dogmatically, as reflecting *ideas* of rebirth or conversion, or indeed ideological systems (Neoplatonism, for example) far more abstract than these. But in monastic practice, the impelling force, the energy for the journey, is emotional. Anselm of Bec, like Augustine before him, scares himself witless on purpose – to start up and start off his meditations. And as I remarked earlier, this emotional jolt of fear is designed, as John Cassian said, to keep the ever-restless mind on track, in the "Way." The *ductus* of monastic churches, perhaps particularly (in the early twelfth century) those of the monasteries influenced by Cluny, was designed not just to mark out, but to recall and evoke these emotions coloring the "way."

I earlier suggested that the famous capital of the "mystical mill" at Vézelay recalled, both in its subject and in its placement within the church, the essential activity of meditative recollection, milling the grains of one's remembered learning to make the nourishing breads of prayer, an image derived in part at least from Cassian's conferences on monastic life. I also suggested that the placement of this capital, taken with others in its context, could be seen to mark out recollectively some stages in the way from "conversion" (the gist of the great tympanum of the porch and of its trumeau depicting John the Baptist, which "turn" one in towards the nave) to "restlessness," the state of meditative activity, and then through the nave to the astonishing radiance of the choir, as *domus Dei*. I would suggest that in trying to "read" the *ductus* of sculpture in such a church, we should pay careful attention to the *emotions* which the figures direct and "discover," not always, and only, seeking intellectual content. Emotions also make cognitively valuable patterns. Indeed, as we have seen, they, and the images which carry them, were regarded as the primary engines of the way.

So much has been written on the iconography, and increasingly also on the light "symbolism," of Vézelay and other churches that I have no desire to adjust these studies in detail to the cognitive and rhetorical approach I am advocating. But I would argue strongly for more awareness and attention on the part of historians to the social and therefore rhetorical nature of human symbol-making.[97] And I would also urge the value to such analyses of the concept of *ductus*, and of its attendant colors and modes (moods).

A church building itself has, as it were, moving parts. It works as an engine of prayer, not simply as its edifice. In Cistercian churches, this cognitive engine primarily moves in patterns of shadow and light, and in other subtle variations of form which demand intense effort to see. In the churches of other orders, the modes of the way are marked as well by complex programs of sculpture and painted glass. I have referred to the program at St.-Rémi, and to the expressions of Victorine rhetoric in St.-Denis. The double aisle of the ambulatory in this church, which provides the routes for viewing its complex windows, encourages meditative "restlessness" (Plate 27). One needs to be always mindful of possible ways to move about within the manifold little "rooms," the *cellae*, of this complicated space.

Other abbeys produced their distinctive architectural rhetorics of the way. The famous trumeau of the abbey church at Souillac is a case in point (Plate 28). It is set in an unusual location, off-center to the right of the inner portal of the church's west wall. Meyer Schapiro well described the "frantic confusion of struggling, devouring, inter-twining figures," which radiate emotions of "tension, instability, obstruction, and entanglement."[98] They have a frenetic animation that would seem to make mere "restlessness" a relief. And that, I think, is the point. They convey the *mood*, the color, with which a meditation begins. So do the tablets depicting *summatim* the story of the monk Theophilus, who sold his soul to the devil (shown as a ferocious, raptor-headed monster) in order to purchase worldly advancement. Outside the *locus tabernaculi* all is wandering, lacking control, in error, instable, off-kilter. And to be in that state is to experience great fear, even panic.

Similarly, the complex of porch sculptures at Moissac seems designed, at least in part, to evoke fear, particularly the fear of death. This was indeed, as historians have long pointed out, a particular emphasis of Cluniac liturgy at this time: we notice it as well in the adaptations made for the St.-Sever manuscript of Beatus' Apocalypse book.[99]

But I do not think this is the sole, or perhaps even most important, motive for this choice. On the western wall of the porch at Moissac (Plate 29), the grim portrayals of the death of Dives, and the punish-ments of Avarice and Unchastity, are emotionally jarring and ar-resting, establishing a mood much as does the cry which begins Anselm's first meditation, "My life terrifies me," "Terret me vita mea."[100] One need not be a monk, nor have read Augustine, to respond in this way to this fearful picture.

Above, like a distant goal (and one must physically lift up one's head to see it) are the sculptures of the tympanum, the serene, symmetrically "measured" Heavenly City under the crowned Christ. Thus, on the threshold of the church at Moissac, one literally takes one's stand (*stasis* of a kind) in the midst of death, looking ahead to one's target (*skopos*). On the east side of this porch are sculptures presenting, *summatim* as usual, the events of the Incarnation, the way through which (entering the church) that distant goal was opened and can be reached. As one looks at these sculptures, one is struck first, I think, by the way in which they represent movement as a succession of journeys, but the figures move by fits and starts and in different directions. Then, in Schapiro's words, the lintel itself, underneath which one must enter the interior, gives an effect of "intense and sustained movement because of the recurrent radiation [of its patterns]."[101] Rather like the cross-carpet introductory pages of insular Bibles, the entry complex at Moissac puts one not just in mind but in motion, establishing intention and affect for the experiences within.

Yet when one steps into the church's narthex through this portal, one's path is still not simple and direct. Entering from the south of the west tower, where this portal is set, one must turn right to orient oneself towards the altar, an act of literal conversion. And of course the light is much dimmer, the shapes much less clear, inside than out, and consequently the "way" is more difficult. On entering one must allow one's body and eyes to adjust before one can move at all into the nave. (Think of Baudri of Bourgeuil's period of adjustment to the dimness in Adela's visionary bedchamber.) Thus, the main entry complex at Moissac (and other monastic churches were crafted on variations of this same theme) puts one physically in a state of "restlessness," having to cast about to "find a way," the *ductus*, within this particular *locus tabernaculi*.

I have deliberately not presented an erudite "reading" of this material; more learned people can, have done, and will erect much more impressive edifices upon this extraordinary sculptured fiction than I have here. It invites people to do just that. But *almost anybody* can "get" the fundamentals of this composition, because almost everybody will be *affected* and *intended* emotionally by it: the disgust and fear of death lodged in the devils and rotted corpses, the removed but visible serenity of the great Christ in his kingdom looming over all, and the multiple journeys which lead one into the ways of the interior.[102] And on that foundation each can build, as s/he chooses and is able. It may be worth recalling that the local population identified the kingly figure of the Moissac tympanum with Clovis, supposed founder of the abbey.[103] They may not have had the doctrine right, but they certainly got the gist of the image.

The spaces of the porch and narthex have often been analyzed as those mainly of the laity, the unlearned, implying that such imagery is particularly suitable to the naive, who need to be frightened into salvation. But clerics also went on pilgrimages, and not all the medieval laity, especially by the twelfth century, were unlearned: far from it. It is also naive to assume that the resident religious never prayed within the nave of their own church.

We must try to appreciate that in monastic spirituality fear is not an unsophisticated emotion. It is essential in the orthopraxis of monastic prayer that even the most spiritually "advanced" and richly learned of clerics, even Augustine himself, needed a kick of strong emotion – of terror, of grief, of anxiety – to turn himself (*convertere*) and begin upon the Way. Without it, one would likely suffer the fate of Dives, that proud man – and the more learned one was, the more likely.

13. LITURGICAL *DUCTUS*: CENTULA-SAINT-RIQUIER

Cistercians and Cluniacs both were the heirs of previous masters of monastic architectural rhetoric. Carol Heitz has written persuasively about some ways in which processional liturgies determined, in several respects, the articulation of space within Carolingian and pre-Romanesque monastery churches.[104] His work is too rich to be easily summarized here, but one example will perhaps give an idea of his analysis. At the Carolingian monastery of St.-Riquier, built a few decades (in the 790s) before the drawing of the "Plan of St. Gall" (c. 820), there were three churches of varying size, built at the apices of an obtuse triangle, joined by long galleries. Documents have survived from the eleventh century, describing various liturgies that took place within this complex: they involved elaborate, journey-like processions by choirs of the monks through the main church of St.-Riquier, and from one church to another.[105] In these processions the altars in the main church, and the porch, became the markers of this liturgical journey. Figure C shows the route of one of these processions through the church of St.-Riquier; the chronicler's descriptions make clear that such a procession would then have continued into the other, smaller churches.

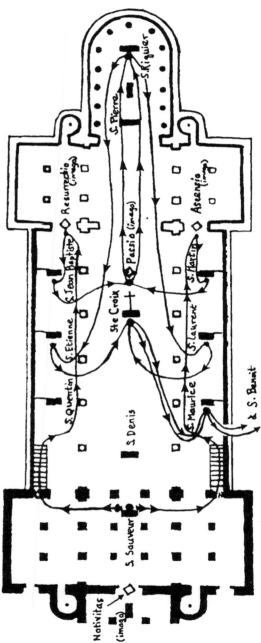

Fig. C The route of one liturgical procession performed in the abbey of Centula-St.-Riquier. After C. Heitz, "Architecture et liturgie processionnelle."

In addition to these altars, four *imagines* (the chronicler's word) also marked out the main *loci* of the "way." Heitz describes them:

> Images, *imagines* – stations for prayer – marked out the liturgical itinerary. ... The first of these, that of the Nativity, was placed in the porch, above the entry door in the crypt of the Savior ... The three other *imagines* were found in the nave and transepts, more or less aligned. In the center, behind the altar of the Holy Cross, was the image of the Passion of Christ. To the north, doubtless at the end of the aisle, the Resurrection; to the south, in the same position, the Ascension.[106]

Various liturgies utilized all these *loci* in a variety of ways. The procession shown in Figure C started in front of the Nativity picture in the porch, then split into two choirs, which moved along each side of the nave to the corresponding *imagines* of the Resurrection and the Ascension, and then across the church to meet in the central *locus* of the altar of the Holy Cross surmounted by the Passion. From there the monks went east, still in two choirs, into the apse, to the altar of St.-Riquier, west again to altars on opposite sides of the nave, met again at the altar of the Holy Cross, and then left the church by the south door, first pausing to chant the office of the dead at the altar of St. Maurice. All this while, of course, they were engaged in communal prayer. Their abbot clearly understood the whole cloister-and-churches complex as, in effect, a single structure whose decoration (both the altars and the mural paintings) afforded a simple map of background "places," within which he could invent an extremely complex set of varying *ductus*.

And the way the *imagines* were used at St.-Riquier also confirms that using images and all forms of ornamentation "for memory" entails more than just meditating on some particular *content* which they represent. The pictures in this church were reminders of particular content of course (the Passion, the Nativity), but they were also way-markers. Whether or not the abbot had Augustine's commentary on Psalm 41:5 in mind (and he may well have, for it was familiar material), he perfectly realized its intent. Heitz stresses that the inventive play of space and liturgy at Centula-St.-Riquier was not unique; it is only the best documented. The processions in St.-Riquier show in a particularly rich way how a locational memory could be woven into the very fabric of monastic buildings.[107]

As I argued in Chapter One, stational liturgies are themselves a powerful means to create a "locational memory," and are consciously crafted for that purpose. Even in Jerusalem, where the places were supposed actually to be those in which the events had occurred, the memorial, recollective motivation for "placing images" derived from reading into "backgrounds" provided by the local topography is clear from the start. It was not the fact of the places themelves, but their rich mindfulness that was important to the visiting pilgrims. Meditational technique developed as mnemonic technique of a kind, with great sensitivity to human memory requirements. Pilgrims went to these sites not just to see the actual place but, using it as a powerful cue, to "see," "refresh," and *locate* the recollective images from their reading, which they already carried in their own memories. This is how they could "visit Jerusalem" in places far distant from the actual city.

14. SHAPE-PUNS: TEMPLE AND GARDEN

Monastic buildings function as meditational engines not only by providing supportive locations, but also by serving as the sites and "collection agencies" for literary–visual punning. Such collations set up different, yet correlative, kinds of rhetorical *ductus* to those in the patterns of stone and light of a particular building.

Both *templum* and *pratum*, church and cloister, are also remembrances *summatim* of the walled Heavenly Citadel. How such a "summary" was thought to work cognitively is an issue which needs to be treated with a keen sense of rhetorical decorum. Many historians have reacted strongly against interpretations which present a medieval church building as the Bible or scholasticism in stone, as though the building's forms were entirely expressive of dogmatic beliefs rather than responsive to pressures of demographics and economics, or to technical considerations. For example, to suggest that carving gutters into gargoyles may allude (in the minds of those prepared for the association) to the essential preparation for prayer of "purging worldly cares," does not in the least compromise their function as down-spouts. Nor does it claim that such a cognitive association is "the meaning of" gargoyles in any authoritative or definitive manner. The relationship of the carving and my humorous use of it is rhetorical, and will convince you (or not) out of your sense of its "fitness," a matter of decorum.[108]

The Heavenly City–Tabernacle–Temple trope, I emphasize, like all cognitive tropes, is a dispositive schema for invention. Such a scheme can, putatively, be used to arrange and link up any kind of content. But obviously, in the context of monastic and devotional buildings that content was spiritual, and if the trope were used publicly for other purposes it would have caused scandal – but scandal rather than heresy. There is nothing inherent in the physical shapes themselves – even in the cross shape – that has meaning wholly independent of the communities which produced and used them. And this is not just a modern observation.

As Augustine wrote, "it is not the image which the mind forms for itself ... that leads to salvation." John Cassian wrote that "Holy Scripture shapes itself to human capacity." And also that "[t]he differences [of prayer] are as great and as numerous as can be encountered within a single soul or rather, within all souls in all their various conditions and states."[109] These are statements of men who thought not only in dogmatic but also in rhetorical terms, such as *decorum* and *imagines rerum, ethos* and *pathos.* And so when a nun or a monk read John Cassian's counsel to "build in your heart the sacred tabernacle of spiritual knowledge," s/he understood that the sacred Tabernacle would take various forms according to the variety of the hearts that built it, and yet still be – *ad res* – the "true" Tabernacle.[110] S/he will know it by recognizing it, not in the manner of a photograph but in the manner of a pun, collating in her own memory a particular avatar of the *templum* with the "sacred Tabernacle" she has built up in the verbal and visual library of her heart.

There are many reasons for the orthopractical traditions giving predominance to the Ezekiel structure as a meditational background image. I have already discussed several. But one basic factor was the happy collation of the *templum* in Ezekiel with the *templum Dei* of 1 Corinthians 3, that *templum* which each of us is. In addition, the Ezekiel *templum* as *lex domus* links up through rhetorical word play with the *lex Domini* upon which a righteous man meditates day and night (Psalm 1). *Lex Domini* is also what is put away in the Ark of the Tabernacle. Moreover, the word for an architectural arch is *arca* or *archa*, a homophony that completes an associational chain to the word for the Ark or the chest in which the precious law (on which one meditates day and night) is enclosed – that is, one's memory chest. So the *intercolumnia* in a church, formed by sets of *arche* or arches, is a perfect unit or scene for memory work. And of course one has only to look at the arches often made to articulate the inter-columnar location of devotional scenes both in late medieval prayer-books and in late medieval churches to see how this trope is worked continually, as a basic memory tool.

Arca is also the Ark of Noah, and standard exegesis, at least from the time of Ambrose, linked Noah's Ark with the Church. Of course. Such a word play is irresistible to a culture so inclined. In late medieval illustrations of Noah building the Ark, the Ark is shaped like a miniature church; thus a "picture" is created of this common-place pun. In the twelfth century, Noah's Ark can be shaped like a triple-storeyed flattened pyramid (the shape Hugh of St. Victor says it had) inside the rounded hull of a medieval boat, as it is in Plate 30.[111]

I have called Hugh of St. Victor's *De pictura Arche* a picture of puns. One could say somewhat the same thing about certain aspects of monastic buildings. For example, having first built a Cistercian-style square apse for their church at Pontigny, the monks, about forty years later, tore it down and built in its place a three-storeyed, soaring, light-filled, semi-circular construction with a number of small meditational cells surrounding the main altar (Plate 25). Looking at this structure from the south-east (Plate 32), over the fields which were always open to that side, it looks like the triple-storeyed, flattened pyramidal shape of the Ark, set within a rounded form like a hull. Or perhaps, especially given its setting within open fields, it may remind one of a barn – the granary of Holy Church that stores the Lord's grain until the Judgment, another exegetical common place.

To point out the possibility of such pun-like "shape-play" is not at all to claim that the new chevet at Pontigny was built in order to look like Noah's Ark. Many far more immediate reasons have been given: a perceived disproportion between the nave and the original square chevet; perhaps a need for more space, or an abbot with ambitions; to say nothing (when construction actually was underway) of technical solutions to problems like wind load and weight.[112] But all these factors play their part without affecting the final structure's rhetorical usefulness as "a reminder," to those who look at it and live within it, that all are part of the earthly Church (as *arca*) seeking the Heavenly Jerusalem (as *arx celestis*). Shapes are also part of cultural *res*, and so are available for *memoria rerum* in the way that stories and sayings are. As happens at Pontigny, not only the forms of a building but the site itself can also invite puns, and such associational punning, various as it is from one person to another, is a part of the way the structure functions as "memory."

15. THE CLOISTER AS MEMORY MACHINE AND ENCYCLOPEDIA

The other richly rememorative structure in monastic architecture is the cloister, a moderately sized quadrangle, well lighted in all seasons, surrounded by *intercolumnia* which, as at the Cistercian abbey of Fontenay, "divide" the space within the gallery walks into a series of visual *cellae* (Plate 31). These are especially evident as, diurnally and seasonally, sunlight of varying intensity moves through the cloister. In many cloisters the capitals, set at eye level, were carved with narrative scenes "told" *summatim*; even Cistercian cloisters had simple but subtly various patterns of capitals. Like the church, the cloister has its *ductus*, its very predictability and simplicity – its "silence" – giving it extraordinary cognitive flexibility.

The source of the cloister's four-sided shape is something of a puzzle, however. As Walter Horn has shown, this orthopractic convention is a Carolingian innovation, built first in the ninth century at Lorsch abbey. Indeed, prior to the "Plan of St. Gall" no quadrangular cloister seems to have been considered in monastic settlements. The word *claustrum*, "enclosure," was used earlier for the wall that surrounded the entire monastery complex.

Horn concluded that the quadrangular-shaped cloister garth, surrounded by a portico (that is, a covered walkway with arches supported by columns at least on the side facing the yard), and flanked by the church and other buildings reserved for the use of the monks, was mainly due to economics, a response to "the association of Benedictine monasticism with a new type of agrarian feudalism" that brought the community necessarily into contact with many non-monks; it was also part of the imperially sponsored desire for uniformity in observance that established Benedictine monasticism over other forms. He also noted that such a galleried court with living units around it is Mediterranean in origin: Lorsch, the first monastery to use it, was converted from the Roman-style villa of a Frankish nobleman.[113]

But in a culture like monasticism, it is difficult to think that some form of *memoria rerum* involving shapes was not also at work in the popularity which this form acquired. The cloister became, by the eleventh century, the pre-eminent place of meditational memory work, where monks read and prayed and also where novices were instructed.[114] Of course the cloister is "paradise," of course it is the garden of the Spouse: but it is also, like the church, a complex machine for memory work, whose shapes provided particularly effective devices for the work of reading.

Even in a Carolingian abbey, St.-Riquier, memory work was already sited within a cloister-like space adjoining the church (or churches, in that instance). The abbot of St.-Riquier built his cloister "in the shape of an obtuse triangle," each of its points marked by a church. This was done, the abbot said, in order that all the faithful (and at St.-Riquier, the laity participated in the great liturgy at Easter) "should confess, venerate, *cultivate in their minds*, and firmly believe in the holy and inseparable Trinity."[115] This abbot clearly expected that his structure should be *used* to meditate upon and "remember" the faith.

The trinitarian form never caught on. But why a Mediterranean-style open atrium surrounded by open arched galleries was adopted and used for so long in northern Europe is a curious matter, and not one, I think, that can wholly be explained on the grounds of (for example) the imperial Roman ambitions of Charlemagne and his bishops, or monastic feudal economics, or other entirely institutional explanations. An open atrium in northern Europe is just not practical. But as a "way" to "Jerusalem" it has considerable mnemotechnical merit.[116]

The visionary city of Ezekiel featured a square "atrium of the priests," which Gregory the Great moralized as the virtuous life.[117] It is associated closely with other elements that came to be rich units of memory in monastic tradition. There are also porticos in the inner courts of Ezekiel's visionary Temple. They are associated with the "treasuries," the *gazophylacia*, which – also according to Gregory the Great – can only signify "hearts full of the knowledge and rich wisdom of the Fathers."[118]

Like the *templum–tabernaculum* and the *archa*, the cloister-garden is an encyclopedic form, as conventional as a multi-volumed encyclopedia with alphabetically arranged topics is for us. In the Middle Ages it was simply one of the major ways that every kind of knowledge could be organized and inventoried. An example from the later Middle Ages helps to clarify this.

The thirteenth-century canon and chancelor of the cathedral at Amiens, Richard de Fournival, described an imaginary library, using as his organizing scheme an *ortulum* or "little garden." The books, classified according to divisions of the liberal arts, are planted in beds or *areolae* on three-stepped terraces (rather like the three-storeyed

Ark). The spines of the books/plants are marked, as they would be in a real library, with a classification letter, although throughout the work they remain described as "plants" in a garden.

Richard called his work *Biblionomia*; Leopold Delisle, the great nineteenth-century bibliographer, thought it one of the most curious relics of the Middle Ages, but was willing to think (after dismissing the absurd metaphor which Richard had used) that it described an actual library. This seems very unlikely; the work is a curriculum rather than a catalogue. But the device of organizing a course of study as a garden of books was less odd in the thirteenth century than it will seem to us, because for Richard, as for Albertus Magnus, "little gardens," cloister-gardens, were excellent structures for organizing memories of "things" read in and plucked from books.[119] We should not be surprised to find that an encyclopedic poem written in a vernacular language might also use a garden as its basic form – the *Roman de la Rose*, to cite an obvious case.

An early twelfth-century text sums up *breviter* many examples of the kind of moralized "remembering" that the structures of the monastery habitually "gathered up." This is the *Gemma animae* of Honorius Augustodunensis, a work often cited as an authoritative encyclopedia of twelfth-century architectural iconography. The interpretive method Honorius uses is the familiar one of building memorial chains of associations upon background locations.

Honorius speaks of the "machina ecclesiae," and as one reads the *Gemma animae* one sees just how rich a meditative machine every aspect could be. The cloister, he says, "is taken from [*est sumpta*] the portico of Solomon, constructed next to the temple in Jerusalem as the cloister is joined to the monks' church," and in which the apostles gathered to preach and commune, as the religious gather in their cloister in community.[120]

Honorius' allegorizing is presented in the familiar conceptual language of monastic rhetoric. The connection between object and concept is made, he says in a recurrent idiom, "ut ... in memoriam revocatur," "so that [whatever thing it may be] may be recalled in memory."[121] He describes his method as "speaking briefly": "We have spoken *breviter* about the Mass, now we should look at a few things [*pauca*] in the church, where it is performed."[122] This brevity should not be mistaken for proscriptive definition. The term is from rhetoric. Honorius composes on the principle of abbreviation, *res* "digested" into units according to the principle of memorial *brevitas*, then to be dilated, expanded, gathered up, and "fructified" in the ways of meditational composition.

Into the *claustrum* of his *machina ecclesiae* Honorius "gathers" a host of Scriptural "things." The cloister makes present again (to the recollecting mind) Edenic Paradise; its font Eden's fountains (and, in other texts, the "sealed up" fountain of the Song of Songs); the trees of the cloister the books of Scripture, via the venerable pun we have encountered before in this study, which recognized a double meaning in Latin *liber* as "book" and "inner bark [of a tree]"; and the allied trope of fruited trees of the garden as the "fruits" of learning. And one who meditates on the law of the Lord "day and night" (Psalm 1) is also like a tree, planted beside the waters: the Tree of Life and the River of Life in John's vision of the Heavenly City. Columns are also the church and cloister's most prolific trees, as their foliated capitals proclaim.

There is a sermon by the ninth-century abbot of Fulda, Hrabanus Maurus, preached "in dedicatione templi," that catches the relationship of architectural ornament and the invention it may cue quite precisely. The trope is repeated in a thousand variations throughout the Middle Ages, but I like this particular version, for in it the decorations of church and mind act together to make a great memory structure:

> you are well met together today, dear brothers, that we may dedicate a house [domum] to God ... But we do this if we ourselves strive to become a temple [templum] of God, and do our best to match ourselves to the ritual that we cultivate in our hearts; so that just as with the decorated walls of this very church, with many lighted candles, with voices variously raised through litanies and prayers, through readings and songs we can more earnestly offer praise to God: so we should always decorate the recesses of our hearts with the essential ornaments of good works, always in us the flame of divine and communal charity should grow side by side, always in the interior of our breast the holy sweetness of heavenly sayings and of gospel praise should resonate in memory. These are the fruits of a good tree, this the treasury of a good heart, these the foundations of a wise master builder, which our reading of the holy Gospel has commended to us today.[123]

Notice how the language of Ezekiel's vision of the "civitas Domini" (*domus, templum*) permeates this sermon. Notice also how the exterior building and liturgy are internalized in each individual as they are made into the structures and ornaments, incense and music, of the *penetralia cordis*, "the secret places of the heart." Notice finally, and most importantly, how each of the brothers is urged to make these congruences *for himself*, and to treat the whole fiction of stone and image and liturgy as a set of gathering places that can resonate in memory with divine sayings and praise. The medieval monastery church is not itself a cryptogram, but rather a tool, a machine for thinking, whose structure and decoration together serve as its functioning parts.

Notes

INTRODUCTION

1 I am indebted to P. Gehl's insightful essay "Competens Silentium," both for the term and the suggestion of how it applies to monastic meditation. He attributes its first developed use to Raimundo Pannikar: see his bibliographical note, p. 157.

2 As I have indicated, "orthopraxis" is a modern term, but early Christian writers used the Greek word *praxis* for the way of prayer which they developed. Two studies of early meditational *praxis* which I have found especially helpful are I. Hausherr, *The Name of Jesus*, and P. Rabbow, *Seelenführung*.

3 On monastic language instruction, see J. Leclercq, *The Love of Learning and the Desire for God*, and P. Gehl, "Mystical Language Models in Monastic Educational Psychology."

4 An interesting effort to discuss various problems of cognitive psychology in terms of an equally rich meditative praxis, Buddhism, is F. J. Varela, E. Thompson, and E. Rosch, *The Embodied Mind*.

5 Whether and how monastic silence can be considered a kind of rhetoric has been the subject of some debate. The term "rhetoric of silence" was proposed by J. Mazzeo, "Augustine's Rhetoric of Silence." Mazzeo was later taken to task for having made too Platonic (and Neoplatonist), too unitary, and too conceptual (as distinct from practical) a presentation of it. M. Colish, writing of Augustine's theory of signification (especially in his rhetorical treatise *De doctrina christiana*), while criticizing Mazzeo's formulations, nonetheless emphasizes that for Augustine silence was also a form of eloquence, indeed eloquence of the highest sort: see "The Stoic Theory of Verbal Signification" and "St. Augustine's Rhetoric of Silence Revisited." The question was thoroughly reviewed by Gehl, ("Competens Silentium") who insightfully emphasized the fact that as a rhetoric "silence was more a practice than a concept" (p. 157). Nearly every writer on monasticism has tried to define silence (see the excellent bibliographies given in the works by Colish and Gehl), but the *silentium* cultivated equally during individual reading and communal liturgical prayer – which is a distinctive aspect of monastic developments in rhetoric – has probably been discussed best by J. Leclercq: see his two studies, *Etudes sur le vocabulaire monastique au moyen âge* and *Otia monastica*; and *The Love of Learning and the Desire for God*, esp. pp. 15–17, 244–270.

6 Cf. the comment of W.J.T. Mitchell that "the purification of the media in

277

modernist aesthetics, the attempt to grasp the unitary, homogeneous essences of painting, photography, sculpture, poetry, etc., is the real aberration ... [for] the heterogeneous character of media was well understood in premodern cultures": *Picture Theory*, p. 107.

7 I advanced this argument also in *The Book of Memory*, in particular against the claims made for true cognitive differences between "orality" and "literacy": see esp. pp. 29–32 and 96–99. A description of the various elementary mnemotechnics used throughout the Middle Ages is in Chapter Three of that book, pp. 80–121. Perhaps the modern misconception arises in part from a confusion of the modern word "technology" (as in the printing press or CD-ROM) with the ancient *techne*, "craft" or "art." "Mnemotechne," anglicized as "mnemotechnic," means "memory craft."

I. "COLLECTIVE MEMORY" AND *MEMORIA RERUM*

1 The anecdote is recounted in J. Spence, *Matteo Ricci*, p. 4; see also the example of applied mnemotechnic which Spence constructs (pp. 6–8) to illustrate how it works; it is addressed to the task of recalling detailed anatomical information for a medical examination.

2 See *The Book of Memory*, pp. 206–208; cf. Quintilian, *Inst. orat.* XI.2.47.

3 F. Yates, *The Art of Memory*, p. 178; see also her comments about Albertus Magnus, pp. 79–80, and Thomas Aquinas, pp. 86–87. Her opinion of medieval mnemotechnic was repeated in "Architecture and the Art of Memory": "The necessity to remember everything in this static way, in the built-up memory, naturally impeded [*sic*!] the free movement of the mind. One of the immensely important things that the advent of printing did, was to liberate the mind and memory from the built-up memory systems" (p. 7).

4 See, for example, *The Art of Memory*, pp. 18–20, 41. It is significant that Yates admits (p. 19) that she never herself tried out the classical precepts. She also assumed that even the classical art was supposed to "enable [an orator] to deliver long speeches from memory *with unfailing accuracy*" (p. 18; my emphasis). "Unfailing accuracy" (in relation to what?) is not a quality which rhetoric ever considered important, let alone commended. We should remember, of course, that truth and accuracy are not synonymous qualities.

5 For expressions of these opinions, see especially the chapters in *The Art of Memory* on "The Art of Memory in the Middle Ages" and "The Memory Theatre of Giulio Camillo." Of Camillo Yates writes that he turned the art of memory into "an occult art, a Hermetic secret" (p. 161). The chief medieval sources she considers for the occult turn she thinks to be characteristic of sixteenth-century mnemonics are Raimond Llull, and before him, Scotus Eriugena and twelfth-century medieval "Platonism." In *The Art of Memory*, she thus manages to divert *memoria* from the main currents of medieval and Renaissance rhetoric altogether. A more recent study of Camillo is L. Bolzoni, *Il teatro della memoria*; see also her edition of Camillo's work, *L'idea del teatro*.

6 A recent effort to redevelop a pedagogy of rhetorical invention as memory-dependent is S. Crowley, *The Methodical Memory*.

7 G. Kennedy, *Classical Rhetoric and its Christian and Secular Tradition*, p. 87.

Aristotle does not discuss Memory separately as a part of rhetoric; it was added in the third century BC, under Stoic influence. In the *Rhetorica ad Herennium* (c. 85 BC), though the author defines the parts of rhetoric as "Invention, Order, Style, Memory, Delivery" in Book I, he actually discusses Memory in Book III and then describes the figures of Style in Book IV. The later textbooks follow the more common order articulated (though with jovial contempt as mere "textbook precepts") in Cicero's *De oratore*, and discuss Memory with Delivery, after Style.

8   See the description of rabbinical pedagogy in B. Gerhardsson, *Memory and Manuscript*, esp. pp. 93–189, and the studies of Mishnah teaching by J. Neusner, perhaps especially *Oral Tradition in Judaism*. On earliest Christian pedagogy, see also L. Alexander, "The Living Voice."

9   C. Dawson, *The Making of Europe*, p. 63 (italics in the original). Gehl argues ("Competens Silentium") that monasticism produced "a genuine rhetoric of silence" (p. 126), impossible as this pairing seems to us now.

10   Though there is a vast number of studies of the term "invention," for my purposes the most instructive are R. Copeland, *Rhetoric, Hermeneutics and Translation*; K. Eden, "The Rhetorical Tradition and Augustinian Hermeneutics" and "Hermeneutics and the Ancient Rhetorical Tradition," and P. Bagni, "L'*Inventio* nell'ars poetica Latino-medievale."

11   Aristotle, *De memoria et reminiscentia* 449b 22–23, and the notes and comments by R. Sorabji, *Aristotle on Memory*. Another fine discussion of this passage in relation to Aristotle's views on *mneme* and *anamnesis* ("recollecting"), in this treatise and elsewhere, is J. Annas, "Aristotle on Memory and the Self." As Annas points out (p. 298), Greek *mneme* is the more general word, from which Aristotle distinguishes two separate mental activities: storage, which he also calls *mneme* ("memory as 'of the past'"), and recollecting – which he usually calls *anamnesis*; but even in this treatise Aristotle uses *mneme* for both. As we will see in the next chapter, the monks' common expression *mneme theou*, "the memory of God," must be added to the already complex background to the medieval versions of this debate on the relationship of memory and "past," both as "the past" and as "my past." An overview of the debate among philosophers concerning memory and "*the* past" is J. Coleman, *Ancient and Medieval Memories*.

12   *Rhetorica ad Herennium* III.xvi.29: "Constat igitur artificiosa memoria ex locis et imaginibus." A translation of Albertus' discussion appears in Appendix B of *The Book of Memory*.

13   A further complication in defining memories as "of the past" is not addressed by Aristotle, though it is a critical one, especially for the philosophy of history. This is the distinction between "the past" and "my past." On this matter see especially Annas, "Aristotle on Memory and the Self."

14   Albertus Magnus, *De bono* tr. iv, "De prudentia" Q. II, art. 2, resp. 7 (ed. Kühle, p. 250.75–82): "cum tempus omnis memorabilis sit praeteritum, tempus non distinguit memorabilia et ita non ducit potius in unum quam in alterum. Locus autem praecipue solemnis distinguit per hoc, quod non omnium memorabilium est locus unus, et movet per hoc, quod est solemnis et rarus. Solemnibus enim et raris fortius inhaeret anima, et ideo fortius ei imprimuntur et fortius movent." Translation quoted from *The Book of Memory*, p. 277. Some relative degree of

"pastness" can be inferred from a memory image, but only as an accidental feature (to use an Aristotelian category) of the cue: for example, in a memory image of a childhood event I may see myself as a child, whereas in an image of what happened to me yesterday I take the form of an adult. But purely among themselves memory images aren't distinguishable as being more and less "past."

15 These ideas were expounded by Augustine: see Coleman, *Ancient and Medieval Memories*. Two earlier essays that contain much good judgment are R. A. Markus, "St. Augustine on Signs" and G. Matthews, "Augustine on Speaking from Memory." The concept of "image" also has a resonance in rhetorical training: Augustine's conception of these terms has as much to do with their rhetorical usage, of which he was master, as with the various philosophical traditions with which he was familiar. On Augustine and Ciceronian rhetoric see the studies of M. Testard, *St. Augustin et Cicéron*, H. Marrou, *St. Augustin et la fin de la culture antique*, and P. Brown, *Augustine of Hippo*.

16 See C. Imbert, "Stoic Logic and Alexandrian Poetics," esp. pp. 182–5.

17 The most careful consideration of the meanings of Latin, Greek, and Arabic terms used to describe these matters remains H. Wolfson, "The Internal Senses"; see also D. Black, "Estimation (*Wahm*) in Avicenna." Crucially important in the consideration of the emotional content of "images" in ancient philosophy are the Stoics: in the Latin tradition, these are represented by the anonymous treatise of "Longinus," *On the Sublime*; see especially Imbert, "Stoic Logic and Alexandrian Poetics." Stoic philosophy has a complicated but fruitful relationship to rhetorical teaching in antiquity, and also to Augustine: on the latter, see especially the second edition of M. Colish, *The Mirror of Language*. Cicero used *intentio* to translate the Stoic concept of *tonos*, the "tension" or harmonic resonance of the mind in apprehending the "things" of its experience (cf. *OLD* s.v. *intentio*, 1b; the citation is of *Tusculan Disputations* I.10. See also the note by J. E. King on Cicero's use of *intentio* in II.23, LCL edition, pp. 208–209). I shall have more to say about this later, in Chapter Two.

18 Quoted from a report by S. Blakeslee on the research chiefly of Joseph LeDoux of New York University and Hanna and Antonio Damasio of the University of Iowa: *The New York Times*, Dec. 6, 1994, section B, pp. 5, 11. See also A. Damasio, *Descartes' Error*, and J. LeDoux, *The Emotional Brain*.

19 Cicero, *Tusculan Disputations* I.10 (LCL, p. 24): "musicus idemque philosophus, ipsius corporis intentionem quandam, velut in cantu et fidibus quae harmonia dicitur, sic ex corporis totius natura et figura varios motus cieri tamquam in cantu sonos"; translated by J. E. King (on *intentio*, see esp. his lexicographical note at pp. 207–208). Cicero also uses the word in II.23, II.65, and IV.3. In *De oratore* III.57 Cicero describes how "the whole frame of a man, and his whole countenance, and the variations of his voice, resonate like strings in a musical instrument, just as they are moved by the affections of the mind [sonant ut a motu animi quoque sunt pulsae] ... the tones of the voice, like musical chords, are so wound up [sunt intensae] as to be responsive to every touch." Cf. *Tusculan Disputations* II.24, in reference to the emotive "voices" of the orator Marcus Antonius, one of the chief speakers in *De oratore*. As will become clear, the monastic concept of *intentio* very much involves a notion of mental resonance and "tone," which, when it is "tuned" properly for meditation, makes of the

mind a kind of inner *organum* or musical instrument; see especially the commentary of Augustine on the *locus tabernaculi*, discussed in Chapter Five below.

20 Aristoxenus of Tarentum was a Pythagorean and Peripatetic; see F. Wehrli, *Die Schule des Aristoteles*, vol. 2, for witnesses and fragments attributed to him. The concept of *tonos* was invoked by the Stoics (according to Calcidius' commentary on Plato's *Timaeus*) in an account of sense perception, particularly vision, which described the soul as "stretched" during the process; see also H. von Arnim, *Stoicorum veterum fragmenta*, vol. 2, par. 10, fragments 439–462. My thanks to Peter Lautner for giving me these references, and for emphasizing to me the Stoic context of Cicero's usage in books I and II. On early Greek accounts of vision, including the Stoic, see also D. Lindberg, *Theories of Vision*, pp. 1–17.

21 Augustine, *De doctrina christiana* III.x.16: "Caritatem uoco motum animi ad fruendum deo propter ipsum et se atque proximo propter deum." Recall Cicero's use of the idiom *motus animi* in the quotation from *De oratore* III.57 (note 19, above), in the context of emotive rhetorical *intentio*.

22 M. Nussbaum has insisted upon this connection also in Aristotle's philosophy of ethical judgment in *The Therapy of Desire*, the portion of which most relevant to rhetoric was reprinted in A. Rorty, *Essays on Aristotle's Rhetoric*, pp. 303–323.

23 1 Cor. 3:10–17: "Secundum gratiam Dei, quae data est mihi, ut sapiens architectus fundamentum posui: alius autem superaedificat. Unusquisque autem videat quomodo superaedificet. Fundamentum enim alius nemo potest ponere praeter id quod positum est, quod est Christus Iesus. Si quis autem superaedificat super fundamentum hoc, aurum, argentum, lapides pretiosos, ligna, foenum, stipulam, uniuscuiusque opus manifestum erit: dies enim Domini declarabit, quia in igne revelabitur: et uniuscuiusque opus quale sit, ignis probabit. Si cuius opus manserit quod superaedificavit, mercedem accipiet. Si cuius opus arserit, detrimentum patietur: ipse autem salvus erit: sic tamen quasi per ignem. Nescitis quia templum Dei estis, et Spiritus Dei habitat in vobis? Si quis autem templum Dei violaverit, disperdet illum Deus. Templum enim Dei sanctum est, quod estis vos." I have quoted the Authorized Version by preference when I can do so, but when the Latin is significantly different, I have either used the Douay or translated it myself.

24 H. de Lubac, *Exégèse médiévale*, vol. 4, p. 44; a compendium of brief quotations from a variety of exegetical writers from the first century (Philo) through the twelfth, demonstrating the pervasiveness of the basic trope, is on pp. 41–60. See also B. Smalley, *The Study of the Bible*, pp. 3–7 (on Philo Judaeus). Origen is credited with crafting the method of "spiritual" or allegorical interpretation of Scripture for the Christians: his indebtedness to Jewish hermeneutical traditions is analyzed in N. De Lange, *Origen and the Jews*.

25 The standard study of *merkabah* mysticism is G. Scholem, *Major Trends in Jewish Mysticism*. But see the cautions expressed by M. Swartz, *Mystical Prayer in Ancient Judaism*, esp. pp. 6–18. A review of the various threads of this tradition with reference particularly to literary cultures is M. Lieb, *The Visionary Mode*.

26 On the possibility that Paul was himself knowledgeable in *merkabah* texts and traditions, see A. Segal, *Paul the Convert*, esp. pp. 40–52. Segal links Paul's reference to the Temple in this passage to antecedent Jewish traditions (p. 168). See also Lieb, *The Visionary Mode*, pp. 173–190, and the bibliography given

there. It should be kept in mind, of course, that an injunction to remember the Temple plan as a meditational act of penance is in the text of Ezekiel (43:10–12). I shall have more to say about this later.

27 Quodvultdeus, *Liber promissionum*, "De gloria regnoque sanctorum capitula," 13.17 (CCSL 60, 221.59–62): "Aedificandi si est affectio, habes fabricam mundi, mensuras arcae, ambitum tabernaculi, fastigium templi Salamonis, ipsiusque per mundum membra Ecclesiae, quam illa omnia figurabant." See also de Lubac, *Exégèse médiévale*, vol. 4, p. 41.

28 A point well made by Lieb with respect to the traditions of interpretive "work" regarding the Throne-Chariot: see esp. *The Visionary Mode*, pp. 83–84. See also Eden, "Hermeneutics and the Ancient Rhetorical Tradition."

29 I made this suggestion in *The Book of Memory*, p. 165. That the rhetorical, inventional function of *circumstantiae*, related closely to mnemonics, continued to exist in the twelfth century is apparent from the title, "De tribus maximis circumstantiae gestorum," of Hugh of St. Victor's preface to his *Chronicon*, a mnemotechnical art (see Appendix A of *The Book of Memory*).

30 Gregory the Great, *Moralia in Job*, Prologue ("Epistola ad Leandrum") 3 (CCSL 143, 4.110–114). "Nam primum quidem fundamenta historiae ponimus; deinde per significationem typicam in arcem fidei fabricam mentis erigimus; ad extremum quoque per moralitatis gratiam quasi superducto aedificium colore vestimus."

31 *Arx* is one of the family of storage-room metaphors for memory (see *The Book of Memory*, chapter 1, for a descriptive catalogue of many of these). The word was linked with *arca*, according to Isidore of Seville, *Etymol.* XV.2: "ab arcendo hostem arces vocantur. Unde et *arcus* et *arca*," "they are called *arces* from the warding-off [*arcendo*] of an enemy. Whence also the words *bow* and *ark* ["storage-chest," with an additional pun in Latin on *arch*]."

32 Hugh of St. Victor, *Didascalicon* vi.4 (ed. Buttimer, pp. 118.10–13, 119.27–120.1): "[R]espice opus caementarii. collocato fundamento, lineam extendit in directum, perpendiculum demittit, ac deinde lapides diligenter politos in ordinem ponit. alios deinde atque alios quaerit ... ecce ad lectionem venisti, spirituale fabricaturus aedificium. iam historiae fundamenta in te locata sunt: restat nunc tibi ipsius fabricae bases fundare. linum tendis, ponis examussim, quadros in ordinem collocas, et circumgyrans quaedam futurorum murorum vestigia figis" (translated by J. Taylor). The masonry "courses" referred to are the parts of the curriculum, likened to the layers of stones laid in building a wall: see Taylor's note 15, p. 223. The trope became realized as a material drawing in the thirteenth century, in the common meditational picture known as the "Torre Sapientiae" or "Tower of Wisdom," one of a great many such secularizings of monastic cognitive commonplaces (chiefly by the orders of friars, as this one was). On the *torre sapientiae* drawing itself see L. Sandler, *The Psalter of Robert de Lisle*, and her bibliographical references. This fourteenth-century English manuscript contains a rich collection of such cognitive-mnemotechnical drawings.

33 See *The Book of Memory*, pp. 98–99. I. Illich, *In the Vineyard of the Text*, has meditated insightfully on Hugh's reading praxis, though I find his analytical terms somewhat more romantic and less rhetorical than I would choose.

34 Hugh of St. Victor, *Didascalicon* vi. 4 (ed. Buttimer, p. 120.6–8): "instructus sit, ut, quaecumque postmodum invenerit, tuto superaedificare possit. vix enim in

tanto librorum pelago et multiplicibus sententiarum anfractibus"; translated by
J. Taylor. P. Sicard, *Hugues de St-Victor*, argues that for Hugh and his students
tropes of "building" acquired a fundamental value. This is certainly true; I am not
convinced, however, that the value placed upon the figure of "building" is so
distinctive as to be considered particularly Victorine.

35 The status of the "letter" in Hugh of St. Victor's exegesis has been, and is still, a
matter of debate among intellectual historians. See esp. de Lubac, *Exégèse
médiévale*, vol. 3, pp. 332–339, and Smalley, *The Study of the Bible*, pp. 97–106.
As Smalley succinctly comments (p. 102): "Hugh's philosophy teaches him to
value the letter. It does not teach him to regard the letter as a good in itself." In
his discussion of the matter, de Lubac emphasizes the construction model, as does
Hugh himself; this seems to me a most valuable emphasis. The tendency to
conceive of the relationships of literal and spiritual "levels" in interpretation as
static hierarchies is modern, I believe, and reflects a failure of historical imagination at the deepest level – a trait not shared by either de Lubac or Smalley. On
Hugh's educational model see J. Châtillon, "Le titre du 'Didascalicon'," and
Sicard, *Hugues de Saint-Victor*, esp. pp. 17–34.

36 Hugh of St. Victor, *Didascalicon* vi. 4 (ed. Buttimer, pp. 118.13–16, 118.20–22,
119.4–6): "et si forte aliquos primae dispositioni non respondentes invenerit,
accipit limam, praeeminentia praecidit, aspera planat, et informia ad formam
reducit, sicque demum reliquis in ordinem dispositis adiungit ... fundamentum in
terra est, nec semper politos habet lapides. fabrica desuper terram, et aequalem
quaerit structuram. sic divina pagina ... quod sub terra est fundamentum figurare
diximus historiam, fabricam quae superaedificatur allegoriam insinuare." It
should be noted that the word *pagina* (as in "divina pagina") refers both to the
columnar layout of manuscript pages and to the compressed and compositionally
incomplete nature of what was conventionally written in this format: see *The
Book of Memory*, pp. 92–93.

37 On the rhetorical theory of medieval translation, and its roots in classical poetic,
see especially Copeland, *Rhetoric, Hermeneutics, and Translation*, and D. Kelly,
"*Translatio Studii*." The construction trope is a particularly rich image of the
translation process, for the building stones are literally borne across from one
place to another.

38 The relationship between "character" and the contents of one's memory images is
discussed in *The Book of Memory*, esp. pp. 178–183. The word *character* literally
meant "stamp," as in wax: it was thus related to the master trope that memory
was "stamped" or "impressed" by one's experiences. One's "character" was thus,
quite literally, an important result of one's memories: but "temperament," like the
varying qualities of the wax, is a crucial factor that ensures that memories of
"things" will never be entirely identical from one person to another. A particularly cogent medieval statement of this principle of "character" is in Canto 2 (esp.
lines 121–148) of Dante's *Paradiso*, in which Beatrice explains the nature of the
spots on the moon.

39 I have detailed elsewhere how and why meditative reading as memory work was
analyzed as a moral activity, and how *memoria* came to be thought of as basic to
prudentia, the virtue of ethical judgment, esp. in Chapter Five of *The Book of
Memory*.

40 Isidore of Seville, *Etymol.* XIX.8.1–2: "In fabricis parietum atque tectorum Graeci inventorem Daedalum adserunt; iste enim primus didicisse fabricam a Minerva dicitur. Fabros autem sive artifices Graeci *tektonas* vocant, id est instructores. Architecti autem caementarii sunt, qui disponunt in fundamentis. Vnde et Apostolus de semetipso 'Quasi sapiens,' inquit, 'architectus fundamentum posui.' Maciones dicti a machinis in quibus insistunt propter altitudinem parietum."

41 See N. Pevsner, "The Term 'Architect'," for a description of which actual task(s) an *architectus* performed at a medieval building site. The word seems to have often implied (and always did in antiquity) the one who planned, "disposed," the building, and who or may not also have overseen the construction. Evidently for St. Paul (who matters most for the cultures I am discussing) an *architectus* was such a figure. Isidore of Seville, in the influential etymology I just discussed, associates the architect with a mason, and thus with building walls: as Pevsner notes, another etymology made him a fashioner of roofs (as an *archi-tectus* or "roof-fashioner," *tectum* being Latin for "roof").

42 Quoted from Sermon 13a of Maximus, the fifth-century bishop of Turin (CCSL 23, p. 45.47–50): "Ipse enim artifex huius mundi machinam fabricatus est, tanquam sapiens architectus caelum sublimitate suspendit terram mole fundavit maria calculis alligauit." Cf. his older contemporary, Augustine, addressing God in the eleventh book of his *Confessiones*: "Quomodo autem fecisti caelum et terram et quae machina tam grandis operationis tuae?" "But how didst thou make heaven and earth? And what engine hadst thou to work all this vast fabric of thine?" (*Confessiones* XI.v.7.1–2; CCSL 27, p. 197). The translation (from 1631) is that of William Watts.

43 Isidore of Seville, *Etymol.* XX.15.1. Tertullian speaks of the Cross as *configendi corporis machina*, "the machine of the body of the pierced one": *Ad nationes* I.xviii.10 (CCSL 1, p. 38.13). "Machina rerum" as a metaphor for the body is found in a poem by Petrus Pictor, a twelfth-century Flemish canon, called "Liber de sacramentis" (Prol. 32; CCCM 25, p. 12), and also in the *Speculum virginum* (XI.352–3; CCCM 5, p. 324). The phrase *machina aetherea* is used by Augustine, *De Genesi ad litteram*, liber imperfectus (CSEL 28, p. 486.13–14).

44 See the citations in both *OLD* and *TLL* s.v. *machina*. A search in CLCLT, s. v. *machina* and related forms, produced most of the patristic citations. Citations are from Jerome, *Commentarii in Hiezekielem* IV.15 (CCSL 75, p. 157.719); Aldhelm, *Aenigmata* 92 (CCSL 133, pp. 512–13). On the design and technical uses of water-wheels and windlasses, see J. Gimpel, *The Medieval Machine*, and A. Matthies, "Medieval Treadwheels."

45 Augustine, *Epistulae* LV.xxi.39.1–6 (CSEL 34, p. 213): "sic itaque adhibeatur scientia tamquam machina quaedam, per quam structura caritatis adsurgat, quae manet in aeternam, etiam cum scientia destruetur."

46 The phrase is used in Gregory's *Moralia in Job* 6.37.58: "*Machina* quippe mentis est uis amoris quae hanc dum a mundo extrahit in alta sustollit" (CCSL 143, p. 328.118–119). In the previous book of the *Moralia*, Gregory speaks of contemplation as a "machina" (5.31.55; CCSL 143, p. 258.81), and in his *Expositio in Canticum canticorum* he writes of allegory as a kind of machine that lifts the soul which is far from God (par. 2; CCSL 144, p. 3.14–15).

47 Hugh of St. Victor, *Didascalicon* II.15 (ed. Buttimer, p. 34.23): "fons sensuum et origo dictionum." See the note on this passage in J. Taylor's translation of the text. "The Geometry of the Mind" is the title of a fine essay on medieval diagrams by M. Evans, who cites this phrase of Hugh's.

48 Cassiodorus, *Institutiones* II.iii.14, a discussion of Dialectic; quoted in Isidore, *Etymol.* II.xxix.16: "Nunc ad Topica veniamus, quae sunt argumentorum sedes, fontes sensuum et origines dictionum." An important study of how the structuring "geometry" or *rationes* of music were thought essential to the invention of lyric poetry in the Middle Ages is R. Edwards, *Ratio and Invention*.

49 Aratus was a Greek poet of the third century BC, attached to the Macedonian court. His work is not considered important to the history of the science of astronomy, but was a focal point throughout antiquity of what one might call the grammatical-rhetorical-literary uses of astronomy. It was translated, at least in part, into Latin by Cicero, Varro, and the emperor Germanicus. The Middle Ages knew it primarily through a fourth-century Latin prose paraphrase. A major disseminator to the Middle Ages was the poem on the seven liberal arts by Martianus Capella, as well as Isidore of Seville's *Etymologiae* and *De rerum natura* (Martianus, unlike Aratus, gives prominence among the celestial circles to the Milky Way; see W. Stahl and R. Johnson, *Martianus Capella*, vol. 1, pp. 178–179). On Isidore's sources, and his contribution to "literary astronomy" see J. Fontaine, *Isidore de Seville et la culture classique*, vol. 2, pp. 457–467, 503–539. Aratus' role in the ancient liberal arts curriculum is discussed by H. Marrou, *History of Education in Antiquity*.

50 F. C. Bartlett, *Remembering*. It is interesting that some New Testament scholars now believe that the earliest segment of the "Jesus tradition" was in the form of "sayings," which were then woven into narrative forms. The sequence would seem to follow the basic mnemotechnical use of story-telling which Bartlett sketched out in his experiments.

51 Succinct summaries of many star myths are in P. Harvey, *The Oxford Companion to Classical Literature*; examples s.v. *Orion, Pleiades, Callisto*. Isidore of Seville repeats the Orion–ouron pun, as well as a number of other such stellar "etymologies" (*Etymol.* III.71ff). As we will see in Chapter Three, punning is an essential learning and invention technique.

52 Such association via pun is described in the earliest mnemonic advice known, in a text of c. 400 BC called *Dissoi logoi*: see *The Book of Memory*, p. 28, and Yates, *The Art of Memory*, pp. 44–45.

53 This story makes its earliest surviving appearance in the first-century BC Latin text known as the *Rhetorica ad Herennium*, but it is Greek in provenance; it is also told at length by Cicero in *De oratore* II.86. It was known in the Middle Ages through a very brief account in Martianus Capella, *De nuptiis Philologiae et Mercurii* (*The Marriage of Mercury and Philology*) V.538.

54 Plutarch, for example (early second century), frequently quotes bits of Simonides (the same few bits, most famously that poetry is articulate painting, and painting is silent poetry), but never recounts this story. It is a common ancient and medieval phenomenon that tales like this get "attached" to famous names. I do not think this is primarily because of a desire to pass off inferior, apocryphal stuff

on a gullible public, but more importantly because a few famous names are those which people readily remember from one school generation to another.

55 Matteo Ricci told his Chinese students the story of Simonides and the banquet when he taught them the art of memory described in the *Rhetorica ad Herennium*. Jonathan Spence describes his astonishment when he recognized a set of Chinese characters in Ricci's writings as the ideographic equivalent of "Simonides" (*Matteo Ricci*, pp. 2–3).

56 Though he lived much later than the medieval alchemists, the writings of the English alchemist-chemist Robert Boyle on chemical processes have been analyzed in these terms: see especially the studies of L. Principe, "The Gold Process" and "Robert Boyle's Alchemical Secrecy."

57 R. Bechmann, *Villard de Honnecourt* and "La mnémotechnique des constructeurs gothiques." On the names given to figures in Euclid, see G. Beaujouan and P. Cattin, *Philippe Eléphant*; Beaujouan and Cattin describe several medieval geometric figures.

58 Augustine, *Confessiones* X.8.14.43–45 (CCSL 27, p. 162): "Intus haec ago, in aula ingenti memoriae meae. Ibi enim mihi caelum et terra et mare praesto sunt cum omnibus, quae in eis sentire potui, praeter illa, quae oblitus sum." See also X. 9.16. My translation, after consulting those both of William Watts (from 1631, printed in the LCL), and Henry Chadwick (Oxford World's Classics, 1991); all my quotations of *The Confessions* were subjected to the same process.

59 On the concept in medieval rhetoric more generally, see M. Woods, "'In a Nutshell'."

60 Gerhardsson, *Memory and Manuscript*, pp. 93–112; Gerhardsson cites Xenophon, *Memorabilia* 4.2.10.

61 See Hugh of St. Victor's preface to his chronicle of universal history, translated in *The Book of Memory*, Appendix A. This "twice-over" teaching method was in use for a very long time. Gerhardsson describes how it is related to the *mishnah* teaching in rabbinical schools of the time of Jesus (*Memory and Manuscript*, pp. 122–130 and the citations there of studies of other Hellenistic cultures that used this same method); also see J. Neusner, *The Memorized Torah*. At the end of the Middle Ages, Tuscan masters advertised different price schedules for teaching texts according to whether one were taught only the words or the words plus their meaning: P. Gehl, *A Moral Art*, pp. 82–106, and "Latin Readers in Fourteenth-Century Florence."

62 L. Bolzoni, *La stanza della memoria*, esp. pp. 87–102.

63 An acquaintance of mine who is a practiced mnemotechnician uses as his preferred "backgrounds" a list of his students, in their seated arrangement, dating from some twenty years ago. It is well to remember that the backgrounds don't have to be architectural or natural places; the phrases of the Bible acted in this way for scholars of both the Jewish and Christian exegetical traditions. See Gerhardsson, *Memory and Manuscript*, pp. 148–156, on some of the mnemonics used at the time of Christ and somewhat later, for the study of the Torah in Hellenistic Palestine.

64 This is exactly how Hugh of St. Victor distinguishes the difference between "lecture" (*praelectio*) and "meditation": one must learn all the glosses and commentaries first, but then in meditation, the mind is "bound by none of

reading's rules or precepts": *Didascalicon* III.6. See *The Book of Memory*, pp. 162–170.

65 *Confessiones* X.17.26.1–13 (CCSL 27, p. 168): "Magna uis est memoriae, nescio quid horrendum, deus meus, profunda et infinita multiplicitas; et hoc animus est, et hoc ego ipse sum. Quid ergo sum, deus meus? Quae natura sum? Varia, multimoda uita et immensa uehementer. Ecce in memoriae meae campis et antris et cauernis innumerabilibus atque innumerabiliter plenis innumerabilium rerum generibus siue per imagines, sicut omnium corporum, siue per praesentiam, sicut artium, siue per nescio quas notiones uel notationes, sicut affectionum animi – quas et cum animus non patitur, memoria tenet, cum in animo sit quidquid est in memoria – per haec omnia discurro et uolito hac illac, penetro etiam, quantum possum, et finis nusquam: tanta uis est memoriae, tanta uitae uis est in homine uiuente mortaliter!"

66 See the discussions by Colish, *The Mirror of Language*, and Coleman, *Ancient and Medieval Memories*.

67 Augustine, *Confessiones* X.12.19.1–11 (CCSL 27, pp. 164–165): "Item continet memoria numerorum dimensionumque rationes et leges innumerabiles, quarum nullam corporis sensus impressit, quia nec ipsae coloratae sunt aut sonant aut olent aut gustatae aut contrectatae sunt ... Vidi lineas fabrorum uel etiam tenuissimas, sicut filum araneae; sed illae aliae sunt, non sunt imagines earum, quas mihi nuntiauit carnis oculus: nouit eas quisquis sine ulla cogitatione qualiscumque corporis intus agnouit eas."

68 See *The Book of Memory*, esp. Chapter Three.

69 Augustine, *Confessiones* X.11.18.3–4 (CCSL 27, p. 164): "nisi ea, quae passim atque indisposite memoria continebat, cogitando quasi conligere." He continues in the same vein: matters so "collected" and diligently attended to, are "placed ready to hand in that same memory, where earlier they had remained hidden, scattered and neglected, but now, having been made our own, readily presenting themselves by our intention," "atque animaduertendo curare, ut tanquam ad manum posita in ipsa memoria, ubi sparsa prius et neglecta latitabant, iam familiari intentioni facile occurrant" (p. 164.4–7). This process refers not just to the craft of memorizing, but more importantly to the whole cognitive procedure involved in thoughtful reading. I analyzed this at some length in *The Book of Memory*, esp. Chapters Two and Five.

70 The essential passages describing the "trinitarian" psyche are in Augustine's *De trinitate*, perhaps especially Books IX-X, XIV-XV. This "trinitarian" model remains essential in Christian spiritual writing, though the more familiar Aristotelian "faculty" model dominated the later medieval universities. Though there are many accounts of how the Augustinian psychic model works, one of the best in English for my purposes remains that of C. Butler, *Western Mysticism*, pp. 19–62.

71 Something of the same cognitive phenomenon may be at work in the success of some medieval document forgeries. In *Phantoms of Remembrance*, P. Geary describes how the documents forged for St.-Denis in the eleventh century imitated the forms of archaic, seventh-century scripts (as best as could be done with the wrong kind of pen), and reused old papyri glued to parchment as a writing surface. To these were then attached the bulls of Merovingian popes,

287

taken from authentic documents. As Geary says, "it was this visual impression more than the precision of the content that was paramount in this set of forgeries" (p. 113). They looked like old documents: that allowed them to serve as the familiar "markers" and "way-finders" for a whole new story of St. Denis.

72 The words *ethos* and *ethic* share the same root; on rhetorical *memoria* and ethical judgment, see *The Book of Memory*, esp. pp. 179–188.

73 M.-D. Chenu, "*Auctor, actor, autor*"; see also A. Minnis, *Medieval Theory of Authorship*, esp. pp. 10–12, 118–159.

74 E. Tufte, *Envisioning Information*, p. 44. Tufte's book is a fascinating discussion of how one can make "information" (data) into knowledge by shaping it with those particular qualities which medieval writers would have recognized as ones enabling someone to retain and recollect, especially those governing the mnemonically successful use of "backgrounds," including the rhetorical principle of *brevitas* (which invites and enables *copia*), and the need for images to have the qualities of *solemnitas* and *raritas* in the graphic design of knowledge.

75 The quoted phrase is from the fifth-century preacher Peter Chrysologus, and is discussed at length in my next chapter. A good rhetorical analysis of this monument is C. Blair and E. Pucci, "Public Memorializing in Postmodernity."

76 An example is Justice William Brennan's comment that "the gist of the First Amendment [protecting freedom of speech] is controversy." This is a statement of its "spirit" or "subject-matter," though the word itself never is used in the language of the amendment. "Controversy," in Brennan's formulation, also refers to this amendment's social *function* – its "*place* in our culture" – rather than to any ideological content.

77 An interesting attempt to show the changing significance of the Lincoln Memorial as the modern civil-rights movement made use of it is S. Sandage, "A Marble House Divided."

78 Reported in *The New York Times*, August 8, 1994.

79 Kelly, "*Translatio Studii*," p. 291. This same idea, carried out in much greater detail, informs Copeland, *Rhetoric, Hermeneutics, and Translation*.

80 A recent study of Holocaust memorials, for example, confuses this issue by saying that while monuments are "of little value" in themselves, they gain value from being "invested with national soul and memory" (J. Young, *The Texture of Memory*, pp. 2–3). This sentence fails to distinguish exactly the point I am discussing here, for "the national memory," like "the collective memory," does not exist as an independent entity. Many discussions of public memory now seem to me to show an essentially reified, even commodified concept of memory (note Young's use of the verb "invest"), so the key questions become variations upon "who owns the national memory?" (note the definite article). A rhetorical understanding of "public" memory-making is more complex than this.

81 On the role (and lack thereof) of the Lateran basilica in the processional "map" of the city see J. Baldovan, *The Urban Character of Christian Worship*, pp. 108–115.

82 The best history of the role of the martyrs' tombs in early Christian architecture is still A. Grabar, *Martyrium*; see also R. Krautheimer, "Mensa-Coemeterium-Martyrium," reprinted in his *Studies in Early Christian ... Art*. On the demographic topography of St. Peter's and St. John Lateran, see J. Baldovan, *The Urban Character of Christian Worship*, pp. 110–113. On the crucial role of the

heroic martyr figure in early Christian epic see the study of Prudentius' *Peristephanon* by M. Roberts: *Poetry and the Cult of the Martyrs.*

83 The Bordeaux pilgrim may have been a woman. The first effort by M. Halbwachs to analyze the social nature of collective memory focussed on the fourth-century development of the holy places in terms of Constantine's Christian remaking of the memory "places" of Jerusalem; see his *La topographie légendaire*. The material is summarized in his *On Collective Memory*. In "Loca Sancta" S. MacCormack takes a more mystical and sacral view of the essence of Holy Places than I do, arguing that some terrestrial spots were "inherently" sacred by nature as "focal points of sacred power" (p. 19). MacCormack's approach is less sociologically and rhetorically conceived than that of Halbwachs. Yet she concludes as well that the Christian make-over of the sacred places was rhetorical, social, and memorial. See also the thoughtful studies of how sacred places are developed in J. Smith, *To Take Place* and P. Connerton, *How Societies Remember.* J. Fentress and C. Wickham, *Social Memory* contains (among much else) a fascinating study of the socially charged topography of the Camisard rebellions in the south of France: see esp. pp. 87–114. A thoughtful analysis of sites and ritual movements as themselves a complex rhetoric is in D. Ochs's study of ancient panegyric, *Consolatory Rhetoric.* See also R. Ousterhout, "Loca Sancta and the Architectural Response to Pilgrimage."

84 F. Peters, *Jerusalem and Mecca*, p. 83. There are many excellent studies of the earliest Jerusalem pilgrimages, among which I have found helpful Halbwachs, *La topographie légendaire* and E. D. Hunt, *Holy Land Pilgrimages*. Particularly useful for my purposes has been Baldovan, *The Urban Character of Christian Worship.* Modern editions of the earliest Latin accounts are collected in *Itineraria et alia geographica*, CCSL 175. Among translations, a useful collection of short selections is in J. Wilkinson, *Jerusalem Pilgrims Before the Crusades*; see also his translation of the *Itinerarium Egeriae*, *Egeria's Travels to the Holy Land*, which also contains an extract from the account of the Bordeaux pilgrim.

85 *Itinerarium burdigalense* 591.1–3 (CCSL 175, pp. 15–16): "in marmore ante aram sanguinem Zachariae ibi dicas hodie fusum; etiam parent uestigia clauorum militum, qui eum occiderunt, per totum aream, ut putes in cera fixum esse." MacCormack has discussed how "the interpretation of Scripture, initially by Jews and then also by Christians, favored the formation of a sacred topography of the Holy Land" ("Loca Sancta," p. 20).

86 *Itinerarium burdigalense* 596.5–6, 595.1, and 590.3 (CCSL 175, pp. 18, 17, 15); a good account of these landmarks is in Hunt, *Holy Land Pilgrimage*, pp. 84–85.

87 Jerome, *Epistula* 46:5 (PL 22.486): "quod [sepulchrum Domini] quotiescumque ingredimur, toties jacere in sindone cernimus Salvatorem: et paululum ibidem commorantes, rursum videmus Angelum sedere ad pedes ejus, et ad caput sudarium convolutum." Such mental seeing was a commonplace experience of pilgrims: many accounts are summarized in Hunt, *Holy Land Pilgrimage*, pp. 83–106. In one site, at Mamre, a fourth-century account reports that the pilgrims' imaginings were aided by a picture of Abraham greeting the three strangers (Genesis 18:1–2). MacCormack rightly comments of the Christian holy places that their "sanctity of place arose primarily from sacred history and sacred texts and not, as the pagans believed, from nature" ("Loca Sancta," p. 21). In

other words, in Christian belief itself the sanctity of geographical places is not an inherent characteristic but is historically (that is, socially) acquired, from their locations in a recollected story.

88 *Itinerarium Egeriae* V.8 (CCSL 175, p. 44.42–44): "sed cum leget affectio uestra libros sanctos Moysi, omnia diligentius peruidet, quae ibi facta sunt."

89 Hunt gives a synopsis of Egeria's liturgical journey in *Holy Land Pilgrimage*, esp. pp. 110–117. Baldovan notes that from the initial phases of the Christian re-making of the Roman town of "Aelia Capitolina" (the name given to the settlement which was built after the old city was razed) as a new Jerusalem, "the buildings around Golgotha were constructed with a view to a liturgy that called for much movement" (*The Urban Character of Christian Worship*, p. 48).

90 MacCormack, "Loca Sancta," pp. 25–26.

91 Baldovan, *The Urban Character of Christian Worship*, p. 87.

92 P. Brown, *Power and Persuasion*, p. 40, citing Libanius, *Oratio* 46.3; Libanius alludes to *Odyssey* II.333.

93 On the custom of the neck verse see M. T. Clanchy, *From Memory to Written Record*, p. 234, and note 42 on that page. It is alluded to also in the fourteenth-century English poem *Piers Plowman*, B-Text, XII.189–191 (C-Text, XIV.128–30).

94 On the essential idea of the monastery as "city," there has been rich commentary, but see esp. R. A. Markus, *The End of Ancient Christianity*, pp. 139–197.

95 Peter Chrysologus, Sermo 96, lines 6–10 (CCSL 24A.592): "In lapide friget ignis, latet ignis in ferro, ipse tamen ignis ferri ac lapidis conlisione flammatur; sic obscurum uerbum uerbi ac sensus conlatione resplendet. Certe si mystica non essent, inter infidelem fidelemque … discretio non maneret"; translated by G. Ganss, FC 17, p. 152.

96 A different, though evidently related, phenomenon of societal "remembering" involves adding to and extending an already existing "story." A great deal of sometimes quite radical change can be accommodated in traditional societies by this means. It is a dual sort of forgetting–remembering, as a text or image is continually reshaped for present audiences by its accrued glosses and interpretations. I discussed the phenomenon in literature, focussing on the medieval glossed book as an especially graphic depiction of such additive "remembering," in *The Book of Memory*, pp. 189–220.

97 S. Lieu, *The Emperor Julian*, p. 43.

98 The relevant materials are translated, and the authenticity of their accounts assessed, together with a generous introduction to the historical context of the events, in Lieu, *The Emperor Julian*; the whole homily is translated by M. Schatkin in *St. John Chrysostom Apologist*, in the FC. Libanius' oration, giving the pagan side of the events, is now known only from extensive quotations in Chrysostom's homily. The likely role of Libanius in Chrysostom's education, and the complex interplay of Christian and pagan values in rhetorical education in Antioch at this time, is assessed in A. Festugière, *Antioche païenne et chrétienne*. On Libanius and the role of the civic rhetorician in the eastern Mediterranean in late antiquity see Brown, *Power and Persuasion*, and on the pedagogy of rhetoric at this time see G. Kennedy, *Greek Rhetoric under Christian Emperors*. It should be noted that the war of orators I speak of was one-sided: Chrysostom took on

Libanius only after the orator's death, as he himself was starting his career as a priest in Antioch, a role that took over the social "place" of the pagan orator of the city.

99 Of the many accounts of the pagan–Christian cultural clashes over burial and funeral customs, one of the best is P. Brown, *The Cult of the Saints*, which has an excellent bibliography. On the development of the architecture associated with this struggle the authoritative account is Grabar, *Martyrium*.

100 John Chrysostom, "Discourse on Blessed Babylas," par. 66; translated by M. Schatkin, pp. 112–113. All my quotations of "Blessed Babylas" are from this translation; further references are given in parentheses in the text.

101 Asterius of Amasea, a fourth-century Cappadocian bishop, quoted by Hunt, *Holy Land Pilgrimage*, p. 103.

102 The relationship of mnemotechnic to theater is ancient, the "theater of memory" being a common variation upon the idea that memory requires an architecture. Among recent studies of this trope see especially J. Enders, "The Theatre of Scholastic Erudition" and *Rhetoric and the Origins of Medieval Drama*.

103 A. Luria, *The Mind of a Mnemonist*, pp. 66–73.

104 It is clear in this homily that Chrysostom had in mind the razing (by Hadrian) of Jerusalem and its reconstruction by Constantine; one of Julian's "demonic" designs was to rebuild the Temple in Jerusalem and reinstall Jewish ritual there (as usual, Julian showed little knowledge of the people whose cultures he wished to "revive"): see paras. 118–119. The Jerusalem pilgrimage which Egeria described included services at the column where Jesus was scourged (*Itinerarium Egeriae*, 37.1; cf. Baldovan, *The Urban Character of Christian Worship*, p. 62). Given the reminder of Jerusalem, specifically of the Temple, Chrysostom's focus on the Daphne column may also invite a "reminiscence" of the Scourging, to be "gathered up," as an ironic, admonitory echo, with the column in Apollo's temple. In this manner, a powerful story of resurrection is overlaid on that of the defeated god.

105 Interesting studies of the importance of ritual and procession in late antique Mediterranean culture include S. Price, *Rituals and Power*, and S. MacCormack, *Art and Ceremony*.

106 A remarkable journal of how such muscular, as well as interior, seeing habits can be cognitively relocated is D. Sudnow, *Ways of the Hand*. The author is a classically trained pianist who learned to play improvisational jazz, a process that he describes largely in terms of "re-routing," "pathways," "shaping of distances" (on the keyboard) and digital "courses through terrain," until he had acquired true "jazz hands." It is valuable to have such a self-aware description of a craftsman learning "hands" for his craft; what Sudnow says about piano playing is applicable to virtually all manual crafts.

107 Baldovan, *The Urban Character of Christian Worship*, p. 155.

108 Ibid., pp. 116, 130, 159.

109 The scholarship on *spolia* is vast; interesting studies of how they act as devices of complex remembering include S. Settis, "Des ruines au musée," and (in specific medieval contexts) D. Kinney, "Spolia from the Baths of Caracalla in Sta. Maria in Trastevere" and "Making the Mute Stones Speak."

110 T. Mathews, *The Clash of Gods*, passim, but esp. pp. 33–39, 95–109. A much

later parallel is found in the self-conscious Christian "translation" to native cultures in the Americas. The work of S. MacCormack has been particularly illuminating of this matter; see especially her early essay, "From the Sun of the Incas to the Virgin of Copacabana."

111 M. Smith, *Prudentius' Psychomachia*, esp. pp. 282–300, which analyze in detail the Virgilian half-lines in several passages of *Psychomachia*; see also the remarks on the *cento* by M. Malamud, *A Poetics of Transformation*, esp. pp. 30–45.

112 Ausonius, *Cento nuptialis* (LCL, vol. 1, pp. 374–375): "sed peritorum concinnatio miraculum est, imperitorum iunctura ridiculum"; translated by H. White. H. Marrou, *A History of Education in Antiquity*, discusses the pedagogical use of the game of knuckle-bones, pp. 119, 143.

113 Several good recent studies of Latin word play include J. Snyder, *Puns and Poetry* (on Lucretius); F. Ahl, *Metaformations* (mostly on Ovid, and the most theoretically ambitious); and W. Levitan, "Dancing at the End of the Rope," on the late Latin puzzle acrostic poems of the Christian poet Optation (which were much imitated by Carolingian poets). On these last, see esp. U. Ernst, *Carmen figuratum*.

114 D. Comparetti, *Vergil in the Middle Ages*, p. 53.

115 It has been plausibly suggested that the Virgilian *cento* by Proba was written in response to the emperor Julian's decree (in 362) forbidding Christians to explicate or teach the pagan classics; this was done on the grounds of "mental health," Julian believing that a healthy person could not teach one thing and believe another. Christian parents were generally concerned that pagan literature was corrupting, but, for the reasons we have been examining, they also could conceive of no other way to teach sound Latin and Greek. As a Christian mother responsible for her children's education, Proba's motives for providing a "Christian Virgil" make some practical sense. See E. Clark and D. Hatch, *The Golden Bough, the Oaken Cross*, pp. 98–100. An edition and translation of Proba's *cento*, together with an extensive commentary including identification of all the Virgilian references, is published in this work.

116 Ausonius, *Cento nuptialis*, preface (LCL, vol. 1, p. 370): "solae memoriae negotium sparsa colligere et integrare lacerata"; translated by H. White. Ausonius was a teacher of Paulinus, the bishop of Nola: a good introduction to his life and work is N. Chadwick, *Poetry and Letters*, pp. 47–62. Ausonius' nuptial poem is comic eroticism, designed to be amusing, but other *centi* are serious. The technique of quoting familiar bits out of context, either for serious or comic effect, was employed long before Ausonius wrote: see M. Smith's discussion, *Prudentius' Psychomachia*, pp. 259–264.

117 Proba, "Virgilian Cento," line 23: "Uergilium cecinisse loquar pia munera Christi." This particular line, of course, is not Virgilian in origin, but most of the poem is.

118 Samples of the standard eleventh-century (and later) statement of the *intentio auctoris* of Virgil can be readily found in A. Minnis, A. Scott, and D. Wallace, *Medieval Literary Theory and Criticism*, esp. pp. 62–64 (Conrad of Hirsau) and pp. 150–153 (Bernardus Silvestris).

2. "REMEMBER HEAVEN": THE AESTHETICS OF *MNEME*

1 This common trope found visual expression relatively early in the meditational text with pictures called *The Ladder of Paradise*, written in the early seventh century by the abbot of Mt. Sinai monastery, John Klimakos (Greek *klimax* means "ladder"): see esp. J. R. Martin, *The Illustration of The Heavenly Ladder*. Perhaps the best known use of it in western monasticism is in the ladder of humility in the Rule of Saint Benedict (Benedict of Nursia, *Regula Benedicti* vii) which invokes Jacob's ladder, the commonplace textual "author" of the trope. In fact Benedict quoted this chapter from the somewhat earlier "Rule of the Master." The fact that the ladder has Biblical authority is important to its cultural eminence, of course; but the further question I ask myself is why so many people found a ladder figure so useful for so many different pedagogical applications. What I suggest is that the "ladder" as a mental picture was considered (correctly) to be especially useful cognitively, because it provides a clear, rigid (and thus, paradoxically, heuristically more flexible) disposition of places. See *The Book of Memory*, pp. 33–45, 107–121.

2 Augustine, *Confessiones* X.xl.65.18–23 (CCSL 27, p. 191): "Neque in his omnibus, quae percurro consulens te, inuenio tutum locum animae meae nisi in te, quo conligantur sparsa mea nec a te quidquam recedat ex me. Et aliquando intromittis me in affectum multum inusitatum introrsus ad nescio quam dulcedinem, quae si perficiatur in me, nescio quid erit, quod uita ista non erit," "But in all these places [in my memory] which I run through, seeking your guidance, only in you do I find a secure place for my mind, into which my scattered pieces may be collected, where nothing of me may be held back from you. And sometimes you inwardly admit me into an emotion I am not used to, I know not what delight, which if it were perfected in me, I know not what it would be, though it would not be in this life." More famous still is Augustine's synaesthetic characterization of God in *Confessiones* X.xxvii.38.5–8 (CCSL 27, p. 175): "Vocasti et clamasti et rupisti surdidatem meam, coruscasti, splenduisti et fugasti caecitatem meam, flagrasti, et duxi spiritum et anhelo tibi, gustaui et esurio et sitio, tetigisti me, et exarsi in pacem tuam," "Thou calledst and criedst unto me, yea thou breakedst open my deafness: thou discoveredst thy beams and shinedst unto me, and didst chase away my blindness: thou didst most fragrantly blow upon me, and I drew in my breath and I pant after thee: I tasted thee, and now do hunger and thirst after thee: thou didst touch me, and I even burn again to enjoy thy peace." This translation by William Watt (1631) captures in English the sensuality of Augustine's Latin as no modern one seems able to.

3 The *locus classicus* of this experience is Augustine's conversation at Ostia with his mother, Monica: *Confessiones* IX.x.24.21 (CCSL 27, p. 147): "uenimus in mentes nostras et transcendimus eas." Notice the journey metaphor implied in the verbs *venire* and *transcendere*, from the root *scand-*, "to climb." I discussed this passage briefly in *The Book of Memory*, pp. 170–171.

4 A good account of this influence is in the introduction by O. Chadwick to C. Luibheid's English translation of John Cassian's Conferences; see also C. Lawrence, *Medieval Monasticism*, esp. pp. 116, 144.

5 These monastic *auctores* were read and revered, sometimes in florilegial form,

throughout the Middle Ages and long after. As C. Lawrence writes, these books are "the ascetic's quintessential library" (*Medieval Monasticism*, p. 36). It has been too bad, in American literary criticism at least, that so much exclusive emphasis has been placed on Augustine that many of these other writers go unread and unquoted.

6 As the fifth-century rhetorician Martianus Capella says, "memory is stimulated more readily at night than during the day, when the silence all about is also an aid, and concentration is not interrupted by sensations from outside" (*De nuptiis* V. 539). See *The Book of Memory*, pp. 170–174 (my error in transcribing the Latin text resulted in my mistranslating it on p. 173; this has now been corrected there and by this note).

7 The text of this "Tractatus de memoria complectens tres libros in laudem memoriae" is in *PL* 192.1299–1324. Further references will be to column numbers only. A bibliography and brief account of Hugo's works by G. Oury is in *DS* s.v. *Hugues de Rouen*. Born and educated in France, at Amiens and Laon, he was brought to England by Henry I, and installed first at Lewes and then, as its first abbot, at Reading, in 1125. In 1130 he was elected Archbishop of Rouen; he died there in 1164. He is probably best known for being mentioned by Abbot Suger of St.-Denis as the bishop who presided at the dedication of the chapel of St. Romanus (Suger, *De administratione*, 26; all references are to the edition of E. Panofsky, *Abbot Suger on the Abbey Church of Saint-Denis*). It is worth noting, given Hugo's comments here about the memorable nature of art, that Suger speaks of his own efforts rebuilding St.-Denis as "institutionum memorandam," "the establishment of something for remembering" (ibid. 24).

8 Hugo of Rouen, *Tractatus de memoria* (*PL* 192.1299–1300): "Ego quidem aestate praesenti caloribus admodum teneor anxiatus, senio fessus, pede collisus, morbo gravatus, sollicitudinem tuam nolo offendere, quam proposui semper honorare. Arcta quidem sunt et brevia quae tibi mandamus, et stilo contracta porrigimus; ... haec itaque studiosus attendas, gratanter relegas, prae memoria teneas," "Indeed, summer being here, I am held in a state of complete anxiety by the heat, weak from old age, bruised in my foot, oppressed by affliction I do not wish to offend your sollicitude, which I have undertaken ever to honor. These things which we send you are contracted and brief, and we offer [them] in an abbreviated style; ... and so may you being studious pay attention to these matters, may you joyfully read [them] over, keep [them] before your memory."

9 There is a change in the Latin wording, though it is insignificant to the meaning, between the "Gallican" version of the Psalms (which is the Vulgate text) and the so-called "Hebrew" version, an English translation of which I have quoted here. The "Hebrew" version of this verse reads: "memoranda fecit mirabilia sua," "He made His wondrous works for remembering." The Vulgate, which Hugo quotes, uses the direct object, *memoriam*, to express the result of the verb, *fecit*. In both cases God creates His wonders so that humans will make memory of them.

10 Hugo of Rouen, *Tractatus de memoria* (*PL* 192.1300): "Fidelia sunt ista, sancta, divina, Spiritu sancto revelante tibi proposita; memoranda sunt ista, quia *memoriam fecit mirabilium suorum misericors et miserator Dominus* [Psalm 110:4]: super memoria loqui proponimus, quam in nobis sanam efficiat Deus."

11 Peter Chrysologus, *Sermo* 96, quoted in Chapter One, section 12, above.

12 I discussed this purpose, evident in elementary ancient pedagogy, in *The Book of Memory*: see *passim*, but perhaps esp. pp. 107–114.

13 This commonplace distinction may be the source of the word *rebus*, now meaning a far-fetched punning visualization of a name or phrase, the visual equivalent of a charade; see *OED* s.v. *rebus*. The earliest occurrence in English listed is 1605, a time when the ancient distinction in memory craft was still understood. It articulates one of the most common of memory techniques, one that is not at all unique to any particular version of the arts of memory.

14 The mnemotechnical need to "divide" reading is discussed at length in *The Book of Memory*.

15 Hugh of St. Victor, "De modo dicendi et meditandi," *PL* 176.878 (cf. Hugh of St. Victor, *Didascalicon* 3.11, and *The Book of Memory*, pp. 83–85): "Colligere est ea de quibus prolixius vel scriptum vel disputatum est ad brevem quamdam et compendiosam summam redigere; quae a majoribus epilogus, id est brevis recapitulatio supradictorum, appellata est. Memoria enim hominis brevitate gaudet, et si in multa dividitur fit minor in singulis. Debemus ergo in omni studio vel doctrina breve aliquid et certum colligere, quod in arcula memoriae recondatur, unde postmodum cum res exigit aliqua deriventur." We must also, he continues, often recall this matter from the stomach of our memory to our palate, lest a long interval obscure it: this is a reference to the common practice of recollective murmuring.

16 Peter Chrysologus, *Sermo* 98, lines 28:33 (CCSL 24A.603): "si modo hoc granum sinapis nos sic nostris seminemus in pectore, ut intelligentiae magnam nobis in arborem crescat, et sensus altitudine tota leuetur ad caelum, ac totum scientiarum diffundatur in ramos, atque ita ora nostra feruentia uiuido fructus sui sapore succendat, et ita igne seminis sui toto nobis ardeat, flammetur in pectore." Compare Theodolph of Orleans's poem describing a "picture" tree of the seven liberal arts, discussed in Chapter Four, section 11, below.

17 The phrase *sacra pagina* refers to this process specifically, Latin *pagina* meaning something written in contracted, brief form, like a note or memorandum, and needing to be expanded by a reader or speaker. See *The Book of Memory*, pp. 92–93.

18 Augustine, *De catechizandis rudibus* III.5(2).3–15 (CCSL 46, pp. 124–125): "Non tamen propterea debemus totum pentateuchum, totosque iudicum et regnorum [sic] et Esdrae libros, totumque euangelium at actus apostolorum, uel, si ad uerbum edidicimus, memoriter reddere, uel nostris uerbis omnia quae his uoluminibus continentur narrando euoluere et explicare; quod nec tempus capit, nec ulla necessitas postulat: sed cuncta summatim generatimque complecti, ita ut eligantur quaedam mirabiliora, quae suauius audiuntur atque in ipsis articulis constituta sunt, et ea tamquam in inuolucris ostendere statimque a conspectu abripere non oportet, sed aliquantum immorando quasi resoluere atque expandere, et inspicienda atque miranda offerre animis auditorum: cetera uero celeri percursione inserendo contexere."

19 See *OLD* s.v. *admiror* and *miror*; a famous statement of the idea is Aristotle, *Metaphysics* I.2. There is no reason to think that Augustine knew the passage in Aristotle, but the idea was a commonplace.

20 Amplification of a single, simple phrase is one of the most common techniques of

composition from the earliest Middle Ages. M. Roberts discusses an excellent example from the sixth century in "St. Martin and the Leper."

21 Hugo of Rouen, *Tractatus de memoria* (*PL* 192.1300): "Omne quod intellectus invenit, quod studium attingit, quod pius amor appetit, totum simul sapiens memoria colligit, prudenter attendit, provide custodit ... Est, inquit, clavis scientiae memoria, haec scalam Jacob a terris ad coelum elevat."

22 Ibid., 1301: "Inter omnis rationis humanae valetudines, memoriae virtus viget uberius: sola haec praeterita reddit praesentia, instantia ligat, sapientia reportat, futura prospectat; haec prudentiam ornat, justitiam firmat, fortitudinem roborat, temperantiam illustrat; haec fidem astruit, spem erigit, charitatem producit."

23 Scholars have tended to attribute opinions like these entirely to the strong influence of Augustine, and the philosophy of Neoplatonism more generally. I think this places an emphasis far too exclusively on intellectual sources alone – on memory only as an idea – and does not sufficiently take account of the *practice* of memory craft, which was developed in monasticism primarily as the activity of *sacra pagina*, the genesis of prayer in meditation upon the Biblical texts, treated as expandable nuggets of matter remembered *summatim*. An equally important part of such reading-craft lay in the community prayer of the liturgies, not only their texts but their chant and physical movement. See Chapter Five below.

24 A useful overview of the praxis tied into the phrase (of admirable mnemonic *brevitas*) "the memory of God" (*mneme theou*) is Hausherr, *The Name of Jesus*, esp. pp. 158–165. See esp. the uses cited there from St. Basil's Longer Rule, a key document in western monasticism. As Hausherr shows, however, the idea of prayer as *mneme theou* does not begin with Basil: as I've said, it is a major theme of the Hebrew Bible.

25 *Rhetorica ad Herennium* III.xvi.29.

26 For example in the influential commentary of Cassiodorus on this psalm (*PL* 70.974–979). According to Cassiodorus, the "daughters of Babylon" whose infants will be dashed against a stone are wicked thoughts and desires which must be dashed against the rock, Christ. The whole psalm, via this tropology, is made into a meditation on penitence, the pre-eminent act of remembering.

27 Mary Warnock, *Memory*, pp. 16, 34 (emphasis in the text). The chapter which these two quotations frame gives a valuable, succinct account of "philosophical accounts of memory," roughly from Hobbes to Sartre: pp. 15–36.

28 Summary discussions of the Platonist conceptualizing that continued to haunt patristic discussions of the immortality of the soul can be found in J. Pelikan, *The Emergence of the Catholic Tradition*, esp. pp. 45–52, and in E. Gilson, *The Christian Philosophy of St. Augustine*, esp. pp. 46–55.

29 Even as late as Vico, no substantive difference was defined between the phantasia of memory and imagination except that memory images had the quality of "pastness." One could therefore have real memories of past fantasies, a proposition that in part helps to justify the medieval belief in the real nature – as recollection – of fantastical visions. See P. Rossi, "Le arti della memoria: rinascite e trasfigurazioni."

30 An anonymous meditation, from the *Exhortatio ad amorem claustri et desiderium lectionis divinae* (ed. *Analecta monastica* II), translated by Leclercq, *Love of Learning*, p. 62.

31 Boncompagno da Signa, *Rhetorica novissima*, 8.1 (ed. Gaudenzi, p. 278): "invisi-
bilium gaudiorum paradisi et eternarum penarum inferni debemus assidue
memorari." These sections in Boncampagno's rhetoric were described by Yates,
The Art of Memory, pp. 58– 60. I discuss this rhetorical text further in Chapter
Six below, and also in my "Boncompagno at the Cutting Edge of Rhetoric."

32 Boncompagno da Signa, *Rhetorica novissima* 8.1 (ed. Gaudenzi, p. 275).

33 Described by J. Sumption, *Pilgrimage*, p. 52, from Guibert de Nogent, *De vita
sua* I.16. Sumption also cites (p. 52) the experience of a monk of Monte Cassino
who saw a dead brother taken into Heaven by St. Michael; the angel had exactly
the aspect that painters customarily give him ("illa nimirium specie qua depingi a
pictoribus consuevit").

34 *The Book of Memory*, p. 287; earlier Bradwardine speaks of using (manuscript)
paintings as sources of images, p. 284.

35 E. Underhill, *Mysticism*, p. 314. For all its Victorian psychologizing, this study
remains full of keen observation, a mine of source material.

36 Coleman, *Ancient and Medieval Memories*, cautions wisely against the tendency
in writing about mental activities and procedures to divide the "faculties" from
one another: see esp. pp. 231–232.

37 For an account of the context of these events, and the larger controversy over
Origenist teaching in which the Greek Theophilus and the Coptic monks were
embroiled on opposing sides, leading to riots in Alexandria and the expulsion of
Origenism, and probably also of John Cassian, see E. Clark, *The Origenist
Controversy*. The story is also told briefly by O. Chadwick, *John Cassian*,
pp. 24–29.

38 John Cassian, *Conférence* X.3 (SC 54, p. 77): "non secundum humilem litterae
sonum, sed spiritaliter." In making my translations I consulted those of C.
Luibheid, and the French of E. Pichery for the SC. An anthropomorphic
Hekhalot mystical text is known from the late second century, the *Shi'ur Qomah*,
which "includes three lists: a list of the limbs of the divine figure – crown,
forehead, beard, neck, eyes, hands, fingers, etc.; a list of the names of these limbs
... and a list of the measurements of these limbs, given in tens of millions of
parsangs. It is quite evident that ... other Hekhalot texts, when referring to God,
relate to the same enormous figure that is described, named, and measured in this
treatise." (Quoted from J. Dan, "The Religious Experience of the *Merkavah*,"
pp. 294–295.) Dan comments that "such a seemingly crude, anthropomorphic
work" caused "great embarrassment to medieval Jewish thinkers" (p. 294). Is it
possible that the Coptic monks of the Egyptian desert had borrowed this
traditional meditative "way" together with other traditional figures of Jewish
Hekhalot meditation? Medieval Jewish exegetical traditions are as deeply allegorical as the Christian, and are surely related: see E. Wolfson, "Beautiful Maiden
Without Eyes" and F. Talmage, "Apples of Gold," each with full bibliographies.

39 John Cassian, *Conférence* X.3 (SC 54, p. 77): "ita est in oratione senex mente
confusus, eo quod illam anthropmorphon imaginem deitatis, quam proponere sibi
in oratione consueuerat, aboleri de suo corde sentiret, ut in amarississimos fletus
crebrosque singultus repente prorumpens in terramque prostratus cum heiulatu
ualidissimo proclamaret: heu mihi miserum! tulerunt a me deum meum, et quem
nunc teneam non habeo uel quem adorem aut interpellem iam nescio." *Interpello*

suggests a vigorous action, like interrupting or rousing someone: one meaning of its root, *pell-o* is "knock on the door": *OLD* s.v. *interpello*, *pello*, and c.f. s.v. *appello*.

40 The Latin of this quotation is given in the next note. The complaint here may include the very common practice in early Christianity of painting a cross on the eastern wall of a house or oratory, in order to orient (literally) the direction of prayer. The origins of this practice are probably taken from Jewish practices of praying towards Jerusalem. See A. Guillaumont, "Une inscription copte," for a description of these practices, and of an extremely interesting archeological recovery of an eremetical oratory in the monastery of "the Cells" in lower Egypt, dating to about 335 (the oratory is mid-seventh to mid-eighth century, however). On the walls are painted prayer texts, with a jeweled Cross and Christ in majesty painted in a special niche (a traditional mnemotechnical "place") to orient and initiate the prayer. The Torah niche in the fourth-century synagogue at Dura-Europos served the same function. I will have more to say about this in subsequent chapters.

41 John Cassian, *Conférence* X.5 (SC 54, pp. 78–9): "si propositam non habuerint imaginem quandam, quam in supplicatione positi iugiter interpellent eamque circumferant mente ac prae oculis teneant semper adfixam. ... et ita ad illam orationis purissimam perueniet qualitatem, quae non solum nullam diuinitatis effigiem nec liniamenta corporea ... in sua supplicatione miscebit, sed ne ullam quidem in se memoriam dicti cuiusquam uel facti speciem seu formam cuiuslibet characteris admittet."

42 This analysis has been done most cogently by Clark, *The Origenist Controversy*, pp. 43–84, and esp. p. 66.

43 Ibid., p. 4.

44 John Cassian, *Conférence* X.7 (SC 54, p. 81): "ut in hoc corpore conmorantes ad similitudinem quandam illius beatitudinis, quae in futuro repromittitur sanctis."

45 Ibid., X.6 (SC 54, p. 81): "ut si interpellare nos quoque uoluerimus deum ... ab omni inquietudine et confusione turbarum similiter secedamus." This whole passage is an application to the monastic practice of "solitude," after the example of Jesus, who withdrew "to a mountain to pray alone" (Matthew 14:23).

46 Ibid., p. 80: "in maiestatis suae gloria uenientem internis obtutibus animae peruideri."

47 For example, John Cassian writes (ibid.): "Ceterum uidetur Iesus etiam ab his qui in ciuitatibus et castellis ac uiculis commorantur, id est qui in actuali conuersatione sunt atque operibus constituti," "Jesus is also seen by those who dwell in cities and towns and villages, I mean those who are involved in the practical matters and ordinary work [of monastic life]." The adjectives *humilis* and *carneus* are used by Cassian in the first sentence of *Conférence* X.6 to refer to the kind of image of divinity seen by those monks who still have earthly eyes and have not yet climbed up the mountain towards purer vision.

48 The influence of G. Zinn's essay on "Mandala Symbolism" upon my discussion of this Conference is deep. Though written about a work of Hugh of St. Victor, Zinn's comments on the cognitive way that mandala pictures incorporate should be studied by every cognitive scientist.

49 Peter of Celle, *De puritate animae* (ed. Leclercq, p. 181, 17– 18): "spiritalis visio

quae hic fit per recordationem corporalium imaginum aut non erit ibi." Peter is employing the distinction made by Augustine (*De Genesi ad litteram* Book 12) among types of human *visio*; cf. also what Augustine says about cognitive images in *De trinitate* VIII, discussed in Chapter Three below.

50 John Cassian, *Conférence* X.6 (SC 54, p. 80): "illi soli purissimis oculis … qui … ascendentes cum illo secedunt in excelso solitudinis monte, qui … fide purissima ac uirtutum eminentia sublimatus, gloriam uultus eius et claritatis reuelat imaginem his qui merentur eum mundis animae obtutibus intueri," "Only those with the purest eyes, who … ascending with Him withdraw to the high mountain of solitude, which … raised up in purest faith and with greatest [spiritual] vigor, reveals the glory of His countenance and the image of His brightness to those who are worthy to look upon Him with the inward gazings of a cleansed mind." Once again, even describing the highest forms of meditation by the "most pure," Cassian's words are imbued with the activity of seeing, of eyes, of images, of vision. This is one of the chief features that distinguishes him from ultra-iconoclasts like Evagrius.

51 Ibid., X.7 (SC 54, pp. 81–82): "Haec igitur destinatio solitarii … ut imaginem futurae beatitudinis in hoc corpore possidere mereatur."

52 Ibid., X.8 (SC 54, p. 82): "tantum maiore desperatione concidimus, ignorantes quemadmodum disciplinam tantae sublimitatis expetere uel obtinere possimus," "And yet we are very discouraged when we see how little we know of the route which would lead us to such heights."

53 The first sentence of Isidore of Seville's *Etymologiae* derives *disciplina* from *discendo* (I.1). He was echoing a popular ancient derivation. Varro derived *disciplina* from *ducere* "to lead," along with both *docere* ("to teach") and *discere* ("to learn"): *De lingua latina* VI.62. Modern scholars accept neither explanation, but derive *disciplina* from *discipulus* ("student"), derived in turn from *dis* (an intensifier) and *capio*, a verb with several extended meanings, but basically meaning "take hold (of)": see *OLD* s.v. *disciplina* and *discipulus*.

54 John Cassian, *Conférence* X.8 (SC 54, p. 83): "primum [principium] nouerimus qua meditatione teneatur uel cogitetur Deus … Et idcirco quandam memoriae huius materiam, qua deus mente concipiatur uel perpetuo teneatur, nobis cupimus demonstrari, ut eam prae oculis retentantes, cum elapsos nos ab eadem senserimus, habeamus in promptu quo resipiscentes ilico reuertamur." Notice the use of the verb *teneo*, the same use as in the words of Sarapion.

55 Ibid., pp. 83–84: "Quam confusionem idcirco nobis accidere satis certum est, quia speciale aliquid prae oculis propositum uelut formulam quandam stabiliter non tenemus, ad quam possit uagus animus post multos anfractus ac discursus uarios reuocari et post longa naufragia uelut portum quietis intrare."

56 Ibid., X.10 (SC 54, pp. 85–86): "sicut nobis a paucis qui antiquissimorum patrum residui erant tradita est. … Hic namque uersiculus [referring to Psalm 69:1] non inmerito de toto scripturarum exceptus est instrumento."

57 Ibid., p. 85: "Quapropter secundum illam institutionem, quam paruulorum eruditioni prudentissime conparastis (qui alias elementorum traditionem primam percipere non possunt … quam protypiis quibusdam et formulis cerae diligenter inpressis effigies eorum exprimere contemplatione iugi et cotidiana imitatione consuescant), huius quoque spiritalis theoriae tradenda uobis est formula, ac

quam semper tenacissime uestrum intuitum defigentes uel eandem salubriter uoluere indisrupta iugitate discatis „uel sublimiores intuitis scandere ilius usu ac meditatione possitis." On the use of waxed tablets in schools, especially during the Middle Ages, see E. Lalou, "Les tablettes de cire médiévales."

58 John Cassian, *Conférence* X.10 (SC 54, pp. 87–89): "Gastrimargiae passione perstringor, cibos quos heremus ignorat inquiro et in squalida solitudine ingeruntur mihi odores regalium ferculorum atque ad illorum desideria sentio me inuitissimum trahi: dicendum proinde mihi est: *Deus in adiutorium meum intende: domine ad adiuuandum mihi festina.* … Accedens ad refectionem hora legitima suggerente perceptionem panis exhorreo atque ab omni esu naturalis necessitatis excludor: cum heiulatu proclamandum est mihi: *Deus in adiutorium meum intende: domine ad adiuuandum mihi festina.* … Euagationibus animae innumeris ac diuersis et instabilitate cordis exaestuo nec cogitationum disparsiones ualeo cohercere, ipsamque orationem meam fundere absque interpellatione atque phantasmate inanium figurarum sermonumque et actuum retractatione non possum, tantaque me sentio sterilitatis huius ariditate constrictum, ut nullas omnino spiritalium sensuum generationes parturire me sentiam: ut de hoc animi squalore merear liberari, unde me gemitibus multis atque suspiriis expedire non pos[s]um, necessarie proclamabo: *Deus in adiutorium meum intende: domine ad adiuuandum mihi festina.*"

59 See *TLL* s. v. *materia, forma,* and *formula.* Needless to say, both *materia* (which was thought to derive from *mater,* "mother," and can also mean "[subject]-matter") and *forma* are words with a great range of meanings, some precise, some general to the point of vagueness, which is why the overall context, especially if (as in this case) it involves a general metaphor, is extremely important.

60 On the distinction between verbal and visual experience, and the insistence that the two are absolutely incompatible, see W. J. T. Mitchell, *Iconology,* esp. his discussion of George Lessing, who first articulated this theory in the eighteenth century.

61 The complex development of this dilemma in the later Middle Ages, which is beside the focus of my study here, is covered best, to my mind, in Colish, *The Mirror of Language,* and M.-D. Chenu, *La théologie au douzième siècle.*

62 Fortunatianus' exact dates are not known, but he preceded Martianus Capella, who flourished between 420 and 440; Augustine died in 430. His theory of *ductus* is described as "unusual" by Kennedy (*Classical Rhetoric and its Christian and Secular Tradition,* p. 105); *ductus* was certainly first categorized and "theorized" by him and his contemporaries. Fortunatianus' rhetoric was usually copied in the Middle Ages together with a work on rhetoric then attributed to Augustine; thus it shared the aura of the master. In addition, Fortunatianus was named by Cassiodorus as a master of rhetoric, especially on *memoria* and delivery. See J. Miller *et al., Readings in Medieval Rhetoric,* in which appears a portion of Fortunatianus' discussion of *ductus* (somewhat misleadingly translated as "approach").

63 An analysis of the thirteenth-century musical concept *conductus,* with interesting relationships to the more generalized root-word (*ductus*), is in N. Van Deusen, *Theology and Music,* pp. 37–53.

64 Quintilian, *Inst. orat.* IX.iv.30. Cf. IV.ii.53: "it is also possible to make the flow of

the matter [*ductus rei*] credible, as is done in comedy and farce. For some things naturally have such sequence and coherence, that if you have told the first part well, the judge will expect what comes next all by himself." Here *ductus* has to do with narrative credibility. The word shows up again in some thirteenth-century technical discussions: see P. Bagni, "L'*inventio* nell'Ars Poetica latino-medievale."

65 Quintilian, *Inst. orat.* III.i.5.

66 Ibid., VII.x.5: "Non enim causa tantum universa in quaestiones ac locos didu-cenda est, sed haec ipsae partes habent rursus ordinem suum." Notice that Fortunatianus' distinction between *ductus* as the movement of the whole and *modus* as the movement of each particular part is implicit in this advice from Quintilian.

67 Martianus Capella, *De arte rhetorica*, 470 (Halm, p. 463.35– 36): "Ductus autem est agendi per totam causam tenor sub aliqua figura servatus," "*Ductus* is the course of action through the whole cause, held to underneath whatever figure of speech."

68 Fortunatianus, *Artis rhetoricae libri III* I.5–6 (Halm, pp. 84– 86); cf. Martianus Capella, *De rhetorica*, 470 (Halm, pp. 463–464).

69 Fortunatianus, *Artis rhetoricae libri III* I.7 (Halm, p. 86.24): "ductus ex consilio nascitur, consilium autem non omnium semper est unum." The whole discussion (lines 24–33) is of interest.

70 Fortunatianus, *Artis rhetoricae libri III* I.7 (Halm, p. 86.29– 30): "modus est ductus in parte orationis, scopos autem id quod omnis efficit ductus." Cf. Martianus Capella, *De rhetorica* 470 (Halm, p. 464.16–17): "color in una tantum parte, ductus in tota causa servatur."

71 Boethius, *Philosophiae consolatio* IV prosa 1.35–38: "Pennas etiam tuae menti quibus se in altum tollere possit adfigam, ut perturbatione depulsa sospes in patriam meo ductu, mea semita, meis retiam uehiculis reuertaris."

72 In the introduction to his translation of *Orbis terrae descriptio* by the second-century Alexandrian writer Dionysius Periegestes, C. Jacob has analyzed the ancient trope of using a topographical description as a "way" of philosophic meditation: *La description de la Terre habitée de Denys d'Alexandrie*. Jacob elsewhere describes this trope as a "tour du monde littéraire ... en effet le survol d'une carte immatérielle, qui se construit graduellement dans l'imagination du lecteur" ("Lieux de la carte," p. 70). The Hellenistic philosophical genre of *kataskopos* is also found in Latin literature (cf. Cicero's account of the "dream of Scipio"). Of this same genre and Levantine provenance, but composed in the middle of the sixth century, is the Christian topography of Cosmas Indico-pleustes, who (among other things) described the world as being shaped like the Jerusalem temple (which, of course, by then no longer existed, except as ekphrastic descriptions in the Bible). On Cosmas, see W. Wolska-Conus, "La 'Topographie chrétienne' de Cosmas Indicopleustès," and H. Kessler, "Medieval Art as Argument." For more on the cartographic Tabernacle-Temple projections in the early Middle Ages, see Chapter Five, section 5 below.

73 Augustine, *De doctrina christiana* II.vii.9.1–6 and II.vii.11.44–46, 48–52 (CCSL 32, pp. 36, 38): "Ante omnia igitur opus est dei timore conuerti ad cognoscendam eius uoluntatem, quid nobis appetendum fugiendumque praecipiat. Timor autem

iste cogitationem de nostra mortalitate et de futura morte necesse est incutiat et quasi clauatis carnibus omnes superbiae motus ligno crucis affigat. ... ascendit in sextum gradum, ubi iam ipsum oculum purgat, quo uideri deus potest, quantum potest ab eis, qui huic saeculo moriuntur, quantum possunt. ... Et ideo quamuis iam certior et non solum tolerabilior, sed etiam iucundior species lucis illius incipiat apparere, *in aenigmate* adhuc tamen et *per speculum* uideri dicitur, quia magis *per fidem* quam *per speciem* ambulatur, cum in hac uita *peregrinamur*, quamuis *conuersationem* habeamus *in caelis.*" Note how the phrases from 1 Corinthians 13:12 and 2 Corinthians 5: 6–7 are woven into Augustine's sentences, without being set off as a separate quotation, modern style. This is the kind of textual intimacy that only the familiarity of secure memorization can give, and it remains typical of monastic and devotional "intertextuality" until the very end of the Middle Ages. *TLL* cites only this passage from Augustine as a metaphorical use of the already unusual adjective *clauatus.* It was used more frequently for the prickly surfaces of the shells of some molluscs and for a "hooked" pattern sometimes used on the border of the toga; see *TLL* s.v. *clavatus.*

74 Augustine, *De doctrina christiana* II.vii.62–3 (CCSL 32, p. 38): "Ab illo enim usque ad ipsam per hos gradus tenditur et uenitur." *Gradus* is the Latin word for "rungs" of a ladder (or for "stairs").

75 John Cassian, *Conférence* X.8 for "spiritalis memoria"; the phrase "sancta memoria" is used by Hugo of Rouen, quoted previously in this chapter.

76 Gregory the Great, *Moralia in Job* 6.37.58 (CCSL 143, p. 328.118–119): "Machina quippe mentis est uis amoris quae hanc dum a mundo extrahit in alta sustollit"; Ibid., 5.32.56 (CCSL 143, p. 258.80–82): "Sed humanus animus quadam suae comtemplationis machina subleuatus, quo super se altiora conspicit, eo in semetipso terribilius contremiscit"; *Expositio in Canticum Canticorum* 2 (CCSL 144, p. 3.14–15): "Allegoria enim animae longe a Deo positae quasi quandam machinam facit, ut per illam leuetur ad deum."

77 Hausherr, *The Name of Jesus*, pp. 174–175. Cf. *TLL* s.v. *meditari.* The ortho-practice of the Jesus prayer in Coptic monasticism, at least by the eighth century, involved speaking the name of Jesus in a rhythm keyed to breathing, in and out, but centuries earlier Augustine wrote that the desert monks spoke brief prayers in a manner "like jets" ("quomodo jaculatos"). See A. Guillaumont, "The Jesus Prayer among the Monks of Egypt"; this rhythm was part of the method of meditation or *meletê*, which Guillaumont describes as "the assiduous recitation, *sotto voce* and from memory, of Scripture" (p. 68).

78 John Cassian talks about the different kinds of *fornicatio* in Conference XIV.11. Though he agrees that sexual fornication is also a sin, he spends most of the time describing psychological varieties, including "straying of thoughts" ("peruagatio cogitationum"). It seems to be not just "straying" that is an issue, but also the expenditure of energy in fruitless tasks. It is worthwhile, when one comes across the frequent cautions against "fornication" in writing on spirituality, to remember how *fornicatio* was inserted by Cassian into a web of *cognitive* vices. Cassian also discussed *spiritus fornicationis* at length in Book VI of his *Institutiones*, another work carefully studied in a medieval monastic education. That discussion focusses more on fornication as a sin of the body than as a sin of meditation, the extended sense Cassian develops in Conference XIV.

79 John Cassian, *Conférence* I.5 (SC 42, p. 83): "Necesse est enim mentem quo recurrat cuiue principaliter inhaereat non habentem per singulas horas atque momenta pro incursuum uarietate mutari atque ex his quae extrinsecus accedunt in illum statum continuo transformari qui sibi primus occurrerit."

80 Ibid., X. 13–14 (SC 54, pp. 94–95): "Cum enim capitulum cuiuslibet psalmi mens nostra conceperit, insensibiliter eo subtracto ad alterius scripturae textum nesciens stupensque deuoluitur. Cumque illud in semet ipsa coeperit uolutare, necdum illo ad integrum uentilato oborta alterius testimonii memoria meditationem materiae prioris excludit. De hac quoque ad alteram subintrante alia meditatione transfertur, et ita animus semper de psalmo rotatus ad psalmum, de euangelii textu ad apostoli transiliens lectionem, de hac quoque ad prophetica deuolutus eloquia et exinde ad quasdam spiritales delatus historias per omne scripturarum corpus instabilis uagusque iactatur, nihil pro arbitrio suo praeualens uel abicere uel tenere nec pleno quicquam iudicio et examinatione finire, palpator tantummodo spiritalium sensuum ac degustator, non generator nec possessor effectus. ... cum orat, psalmum aut aliquam recolit lectionem. Cum decantat, aliud quid meditatur quam textus ipsius continet psalmi. ... Tria sunt quae uagam mentem stabilem faciunt, vigiliae, meditatio et oratio, quarum adsiduitas et iugio intentio conferunt animae stabilem firmitatem."

81 Ibid., X. 13 (SC 54, p. 94): "certe hunc eundem uersiculum, quem nobis uice formulae tradidisti, inmobiliter custodire, ut omnium sensuum ortus ac fines non in sua uolubilitate fluctuant, sed in nostra dicione consistant."

82 On the importance of *stabilis* in Cassian's thought, see esp. C. Leyser, "*Lectio divina, oratio pura.*" This essay is particularly suggestive on the matter of how rhetoric conditioned Cassian's spiritual teaching.

83 Bernard of Clairvaux, *Apologia* xii.28 (*SBO*, vol. 3, p.104.14): "quae dum in se orantium retorquent aspectum, impediunt et affectum." Recall that memory is always described as a type of *affectus* and inner *aspectus*.

84 Bernard of Clairvaux, *Super Cantica Sermo* 1.1 (*SBO*, vol. 1, p. 3.1–2): "Vobis, fratres, alia quam aliis de saeculo, aut certe aliter dicenda sunt." This, and subsequent translations from Bernard's *Sermons on The Song of Songs*, are those of K. Walsh for the Cistercian Fathers series, unless otherwise noted.

85 Bernard of Clairvaux, *Super Cantica Sermo* 1.6 (*SBO*, vol. 1, pp. 7.25–8.8): "et iure hoc appellaverim 'Canticum canticorum,' quia ceterorum omnium ipsum est fructus. ... Non est strepitus oris, sed iubilus cordis; non sonus labiorum, sed motus gaudiorum; voluntatum, non vocum consonantia. Non auditur foris, nec enim in publico personat: sola quae cantat audit, et cui cantatur, id est sponsus et sponsa. ... Ceterum non est illud cantare seu audire animae puerilis et neophytae adhuc, et recens conversae de saeculo, sed provectae iam et eruditae mentis." The contrast of "strepitus oris" and "iubilus cordis" is also found in the *locus classicus* of memorative meditation, Augustine's conversation with his mother just before her death (*Confessiones* Book IX).

86 On Evagrius' iconoclasm see Clark, *The Origenist Controversy*, esp. pp. 43–84.

87 Bernard of Clairvaux, *Super Cantica Sermo* 46.3 (*SBO*, vol. 2, pp. 60.23–61.21): "Studete deinde his tignis substernere et alligare ligna alia aeque pretiosa et pulchra, cui tamen ad manum fuerint in opus laquearium ad decorem domus, sermonem scilicet sapientiae sive scientiae, prophetiam, gratiam curationum,

interpretationem sermonum, et cetera talia, quae magis noscuntur sane apta ornatui quam necessaria esse saluti. ... magis autem e lignis aliis laquearia praeparari, quae, etsi minus appareant splendida, non minus tamen valida esse probantur ... Annon tu illam domum, quod ad laquearia spectat, satis abundeque ornatam censeas, quam talibus lignis inspexeris sufficienter compositeque tabulatam? 'Domine, dilexi decorem domus tuae' [Psalm 25:8]. Semper da mihi ligna haec, quaeso, quibus tibi semper ornatum exhibeam thalamum conscientiae ... His contentus ero. ... Sed et vos, dilectissimi, tametsi illa ligna non habeatis, nihilominus tamen, si haec habetis, confidate; ... nihilominus super fundamentum Apostolorum et Prophetarum et ipsi tamquam lapides vivi superaedificamini, domos scilicet, offerre spirituales hostias, acceptabiles Deo"; my translation, after consulting that of K. Walsh.

88 G. Duby, *Saint Bernard, l'art cistercien*, p. 94.

89 Bernard of Clairvaux, *Apologia* xii.29 (*SBO*, vol. 3, p. 106,14–15): "Ceterum in claustris, *coram legentibus fratribus*, quid facit illa ridicula monstruositas ...?" (my emphasis). See C. Rudolph's discussions of this theme in both *'The Things of Greater Importance'*, esp. pp. 110–119, and *Artistic Change at St-Denis*, esp. pp. 13–17, 60–63.

90 My understanding of Bernard's iconoclasm accords with Rudolph's interpretation of the famous Statute 80 of the Cistercian Order, "Concerning letters and windows: Letters are to be made of one color, and not depictive. Windows are to be made white, and without crosses and pictures." Rudolph has argued that the aim of this statute was against "distractive and gratuitous miniatures" ("The 'Principal Founders'," p. 24): in other words against providing temptations to *curiositas*. The stricture against window-painting not only comes out of this motive, but also reflects an alternative aesthetic of the light needed for memory work; I shall have more to say about this in Chapter Five, section 9 below.

91 Geoffrey of Vinsauf, *Poetria nova*, line 1972 (ed. Faral): "Cellula quae meminit est cellula deliciarum."

92 The best-known instances include Augustine's regret at how the scene of Dido's death made him weep (*Confessiones* I.13–14) and Jerome's vision of being expelled from Heaven because he was a Ciceronian rather than a Christian (*Epistula* 22).

93 John Cassian, *Conférence* XIV.12 (SC 54, p. 199): "in qua [litteratura] me ita uel instantia paedagogi uel continuae lectionis macerauit intentio, ut nunc mens mea poeticis illis uelut infecta carminibus illas fabularum nugas historiasque bellorum, quibus a paruulo primis studiorum inbuta est rudimentis ... psallentique uel pro peccatorum indulgentia supplicanti aut inpudens poematum memoria suggeratur aut quasi bellantium heroum ante oculos imago uersetur." One such poem was undoubtedly Virgil's *Aeneid*; this problem of Cassian's provides a motive for the composition of Christian *centi*, a type of cultural "forgetting" which we looked at briefly in Chapter One, section 16.

94 Ibid., XIV.13 (SC 54, p. 199): "De hac ipsa re, unde tibi purgationis maxima nascitur desperatio, citum satis atque efficax remedium poterit oboriri, si eandem diligentiam atque instantiam, quam te in illis saecularibus studiis habuisse dixisti, ad spiritalium scripturarum uoleris lectionem meditationemque transferre."

95 Ibid., pp. 199–201: "Necesse est enim mentem tuam tamdiu illis carminibus occupari, quamdiu ... pro illis infructuosis atque terrenis spiritalia ac diuina parturiat. Quae cum profunde alteque conceperit atque in illis fuerit enutrita, uel expelli priores sensim poterunt uel penitus aboleri. Vacare enim cunctis cogitationibus humana mens non potest, et ideo quamdiu spiritalibus studiis non fuerit occupata, necesse est eam illis quae pridem didicit inplicari. Quamdiu enim non habuerit quo recurrat et indefessos exerceat motus, necesse est ut ad illa quibus ad infantia inbuta est conlabatur eaque semper reuoluat quae longo usu ac meditatione concepit. Vt ergo haec in te scientia spiritalis perpetua soliditate roboretur ... ut sensibus tuis inuiscerata quodammodo et perspecta atque palpata condatur ... Si itaque haec diligenter excepta et in recessu mentis condita atque indicta fuerint taciturnitate signata, postea ut uina quaedam suaue olentia et laetificantia cor hominis ... cum magna sui fragrantia de uase tui pectoris proferentur ... Atque ita fiet ut non solum omnis directio ac meditatio cordis tui, uerum etiam cunctae euagationes atque discursus cogitationum tuarum sint tibi diuinae legis sancta et incessabilis ruminatio."

96 I analyzed the crucial role of "murmur" and "silent" reading (*legere tacite*) in mnemonic technique in *The Book of Memory*, esp. pp. 169–74.

97 John Cassian, *Conférence* XIV. 13 (SC 54, p. 201): "de experientiae uenis ... redundabunt fluentaque continua uelut de quadam abysso tui cordis effundent."

98 These assumptions about reading are discussed at length in *The Book of Memory*, esp. pp. 156–170.

99 John Cassian, *Conférence* I.18 (SC 42, p. 99): "Quod exercitium cordis non incongrue molarum similitudini conparatur, quas meatus aquarum impetu rotante prouoluit. Quae nullatenus quidem cessare possunt ab opere suo aquarum inpulsibus circumactae; in eius uero qui praeest situm est potestate, utrumnam triticum malit an hordeum loliumue comminui. Illud quippe est procul dubio conmolendum, quod ingestum ab illo fuerit cui operis illius cura commissa est. ... Si enim ut diximus ad sanctarum scripturarum meditationem iugiter recurramus ac memoriam nostram ad recordationem spiritalium rerum ... necesse est ut ortae cogitationes exinde spiritales ... Sin uero desidia seu neglegentia superati uitiis et otiosis confabulationibus occupemur ... consequenter exinde uelut quaedam zizaniorum species generata operationem quoque nostro cordi noxiam ministrabit."

100 Suger wrote a Latin quatrain explaining his understanding of this trope that is recorded in his *De administratione*, 34. The interpretations put forward for it, and its Biblical sources, are reviewed masterfully in L. Grodecki, "Les vitraux allégoriques," esp. pp. 22–24. Grodecki believes that Suger's linkage of the miller grinding to St. Paul's "processing" the Old Testament is original with Suger. If so, it is another instance of an original meditation made from traditional materials, and of the creative nature of *memoria rerum*.

101 On the history of the abbey see esp. Hugh of Poitiers, *The Vézelay Chronicle*, translated by J. Scott and J. O. Ward. The nave was built between 1120 and 1140, before the narthex. Bernard of Clairvaux preached the Second Crusade to Louis VII of France and his assembled court in the valley just below the hill of Vézelay on March 31, 1146. The relics of Mary Magdalene had a checkered and peripatetic career in the Middle Ages, and those at Vézelay lost their authenticity

in the late thirteenth century, causing a decline in the town's fortunes: see the account by E. Cox in *The Vézelay Chronicle*, pp. 363–375.

102 There are also scenes on some of the capitals facing east, which one would see on one's way out (or if one were to walk around the pier). I am concerned here, however, to describe only a small part of a possible journey through this building, as an example. On the location and iconography of these capitals, see F. Salet (presenting the work of J. Adhémar), *La Madeleine de Vézelay*, though F. Vogade, *Vézelay: histoire, iconographie, symbolisme*, has better reproductions and is more current about the iconography. There is no substitute, however, for moving through the building itself and noticing the capitals in their relationship to one another as one does so. Only in this way can one begin to appreciate the rhetorical *ductus* at work in this building. I return to the subject of decoration and architectural *ductus* in Chapter Five, below.

103 See the introductory remarks by J. Leclercq to his edition of this sermon "ad clericos de conversione." This was the sermon which convinced Geoffrey of Auxerre, already a cleric, to enter monastic life: *SBO*, vol. 4, p. 61. All further references to this sermon are to page and line numbers of this edition.

104 Bernard of Clairvaux, *Ad clericos* III.4 (p. 75.8–9): "Quidni doleam ventrem memoriae, ubi tanta congesta est putredo?"

105 Coleman, *Ancient and Medieval Memories*, pp. 175, 186. While in the main Coleman addresses monastic attitudes towards memory with sympathetic judiciousness, her account, it seems to me, suffers from her disengagement with the praxis of prayer, memory in action.

106 The phrase is found in Bernard of Clairvaux, *Ad clericos* XVI.29 (p. 105.14).

107 Bernard of Clairvaux, *Ad clericos* XV.28 (pp. 103.14–104.3).

108 Bernard of Clairvaux, *Ad clericos* XV.28 (pp. 102.17–104.5): "Quomodo enim a memoria mea excidet vita mea? Membrana vilis et tenuis atramento forte ebibit; qua deinceps arte delebitur? Non enim superficie tenus tinxit; sed prorsus totam intinxit. Frustra conarer eradere: ante scinditur charta quam caracteres miseri deleantur. Ipsam enim forte memoriam delere posset oblivio, ut videlicet, mente captus, eorum non meminerim, quae commisi. Ceterum, ut memoria integra maneat et ipsius maculae diluantur, quae novacula possit efficere? Solus utique sermo vivus et efficax, et penetrabilior omni gladio ancipiti: DIMITTUNTUR TIBI PECCATA TUA ... Huius indulgentia delet peccatum, non quidem ut a memoria excidat, sed ut quod prius inesse pariter et inficere consuevisset, sic de cetero insit memoriae, ut eam nullatenus decoloret. ... Tolle damnationem, tolle timorem, tolle confusionem, quae quidem omnia plena remissio tollit, et non modo non oberunt, sed et cooperantur in bonum."

109 Even sexual and scatological material can be used, so long as one does not get "confused" by it. The fifteenth-century master Peter of Ravenna said that he marked his memory places with images of seductive women, for "these greatly stimulate my memory" – but this is not suitable, he cautions, for those who hate women (i.e. have the wrong stance) or those without control (who are subject to the vice of curiosity): *Foenix*, b.iv.verso. Peter's practice may be seen as a (parodic) turn on an old and well-known ascetic exercise in withstanding temptation – in this case, an exercise against "mental fornication."

110 Luria, *The Mind of a Mnemonist*, pp. 66–73.

111 Bernard of Clairvaux, *Ad clericos* XVI.29 (p. 104.11–12).
112 Discussed in *The Book of Memory*, pp. 173–174. The quotation is from Thomas Aquinas, *Summa theologiae* II-II, Q. 49.
113 Peter of Celle, *De conscientia* prol. 3–5: "religiosa mens religiosa curiositate quaerit de religione conscientiae."
114 Hugh of St. Victor, *De modo dicendi* 8 (*PL* 176.879): "Meditatio itaque est vis quaedam mentis curiosa et sagax obscura investigare et perplexa evolvere." Literally "curiosa et sagax" modify "vis" but in English the adjectives make better sense transposed to "mind."
115 *OLD* s.v. *curiositas, curiosus, curiose*. In the Vulgate, pejorative connotations of being overly inquisitive dominate in these words, but a positive meaning is present in Ecclesiastes 9:1, "Omnia haec tractavi in corde meo, ut curiose intelligerem," "All these things I drew into my heart, that I might think about them more carefully."
116 *The Book of Memory*, pp. 47–71.
117 If this seems to us very like music, it is. *Ductus* in the later Middle Ages is closely related to the musical concept, *conductus*: see Van Deusen, *Theology and Music at the Early University*, pp. 37–53. For Augustine, *ductus* is clearly a concept identified both with music and with architecture: see the passage from his commentary on Psalm 41, discussed in Chapter Five, section 9, below.
118 In *Patterns of Intention*, M. Baxandall has written well about this "intention" of a work, in the making of which the intention of its author plays a greater or lesser, but never completely identical, role: "Intention is the forward-leaning look of things ... '[I]ntention' here is referred to pictures rather more than to painters. In particular cases it will be a construct descriptive of a relationship between a picture and its circumstances" (p. 42).
119 See in particular Colish's discussion of Augustine in *The Mirror of Language*.
120 *OED* s.v. *punctuation*.
121 See in particular E. Vance, "Roland and the Poetics of Memory," L. Fradenburg, "'Voice Memorial'," and J. Enders, "Rhetoric, Coercion, and the Memory of Violence." I discussed the violent, sexual images recommended in Thomas Bradwardine's art of memory in *The Book of Memory*, pp. 130–137.
122 See esp. Marrou, *History of Education in Antiquity*, pp. 158–159 and 272–73. Some recent research in neuropsychology seems to support this widely held ancient belief. As reported in the *New York Times* (December 6, 1994), "emotional memories involving fear are permanently ingrained on the brain; they can be suppressed but never erased ... Researchers have come to realize that emotional brain circuits are just as tangible as circuits for seeing, hearing, and touching. ... Emotions and feelings are not ... ephemeral ... [but] are largely the brain's interpretation of our visceral reaction to the world." See LeDoux, *The Emotional Brain*.
123 I discussed the mnemotechnical aspects of this poem, and its layout in Cambridge University Library MS Ii.3.26, in "'Ut pictura poesis'." This and related texts have been edited by M. C. Spalding, *The Middle English Charters of Christ*.
124 Through the work of L. Martz, *The Poetry of Meditation*, and others, students of English Renaissance literature have long been familiar with such techniques as

the starting-points for poetic composition. I have found, however, that many are content to attribute their origins to Ignatius of Loyola; as will be apparent, Ignatius was working within a very long tradition.

125 Anselm, *Prayers and Meditations*, Prologue (ed. Schmitt, BAC II, p. 290): "Orationes sive meditationes quae subscriptae sunt … ad excitandam legentis mentem ad Dei amorem vel timorem … [N]on sunt legendae … cursim et velociter, sed paulatim cum intenta et morosa meditatione. … Nec necesse habet aliquam semper a principio incipere, sed ubi magis illi placuerit [lector]. Ad hoc enim ipsum paragraphis sunt distinctae per partes, ut ubi elegerit incipiat aut desinat, ne prolixitas, aut frequens eiusdem loci repetitio generet fastidium."

126 The best introduction to Anselm's affective piety is the thorough introduction by B. Ward to her translation of *The Prayers and Meditations*, from which all my subsequent quotations are taken (any changes I have made are indicated by square brackets). Several prayers and meditations were sent to other correspondents during Anselm's lifetime, notably to Princess Adelaide, the youngest daughter of William the Conqueror. Anselm wrote to Matilda that he sent the collection to her "so that if you like them you may be able to compose others after their example" (trans. Ward, p. 90). The work circulated widely later during the Middle Ages among both laity and clergy. On the illustrations see O. Pächt, "The Illustrations of St. Anselm's Prayers and Meditations": a manuscript made for the nuns of Littlemore is now in the Bodleian Library, Oxford (MS Auct. D.2.6). A praying lady is depicted in many of the illustrations, who may represent Matilda (though, given the exemplary nature of the work, she may simply be "the reader").

127 A letter from Durandus, abbot of Casa-Dei in the Auvergne, to Anselm while he was still at Bec speaks of two young men from Bayeaux who have come to visit, bringing praise of Anselm and, presumably, texts of his meditations with them: evidently these were sent as models for the brothers' devotions at Casa-Dei. Durandus asks Anselm to send more (trans. Ward, p. 220).

128 Anselm, *Prayers and Meditations*, meditation 2 "Deploratio virginitatis male amissae" (ed. Schmitt, BAC II, pp. 424, 426): "Cogitet igitur et recogitet cor meum quid fecit, quid meruit. Descendat, inquam, descendat *ad terram tenebrosam et opertam mortis caligine*, mens mea, et consideret quae ibi exspectent scelerosam animam meam. Intendat et contempletur, videat et conturbetur; quid est Deus, quid est quod animadverto in terra *miseriae et tenebrarum*? Horror! horror! Quid est quod intueor, ubi *nullus ordo sed sempiternus horror inhabitat*? Heu confusio ululatuum, tumultus dentibus stridentium, inordinata multitudo gemituum. Vae, vae, quot et quot et quot vae, vae! Ignis sulfhureus, flamma tartarea, caliginosa volumina, quam terrifico rugitu video vos rotari. Vermes in igne viventes … Daemones coardentes, frementes ardore, frendentes furore: cur sic crudeles estis iis quos volutantur inter vos? … Haeccine sunt, magne Deus, quae parata sunt fornicatoribus et contemptoribus tuis, quorum unus ego sum? Ego, ego utique unus horum sum. Anima mea, expavesce; mens mea, defice; cor meum, scindere. … Ne ergo memineris, bone Domine, iustitiae tuae adversus peccatorem tuum, sed memor esto benignitatis tuae erga creaturam tuam." Notice the frequent internal rhymes, providing *catenae* that link the composition together into mnemonically powerful if casual verses: for example, "daemones

308

co-*ard-entes*, frem-*entes ard-ore*, frend-*entes* fur-*ore*." This common feature of medieval Latin seems almost to embarrass even sympathetic scholars (Ward speaks of Anselm's "almost childish play with words, the love of a jingle," p. 57). But exactly this kind of deconstructive word play (syllable play often) and jingle makes pieces of prose text readily memorable. And without memory there is no meditation.

129 Job 10:21–22: "Antequam vadam, et non revertar, ad terram tenebrosam, et opertam mortis caligine: Terram miseriae et tenebrarum, ubi umbra mortis et nullus ordo, Sed sempiternus horror inhabitat."

130 *The Book of Memory*, Chapter Five.

131 Brown, *Power and Persuasion*, p. 40. I would simply modify this statement by underscoring that what Brown calls "the 'collective memory'" (as his quotation marks suggest) is a metaphor for what is more accurately thought of as the *res memorabiles* of a social group.

132 See esp. the essays in J. Murphy, *A Short History of Writing Instruction*, and also Marrou, *History of Education in Antiquity*, pp. 172–175.

133 Hausherr, *The Name of Jesus*, p. 175, citing Rabbow, *Seelenführung*. See also descriptions of early rabbinical pedagogy, such as those in Gerhardsson, *Memory and Manuscript*. See also Marrou, *History of Education in Antiquity*, pp. 150–154.

134 R. Kaster, *Guardians of Language*, pp. 16–17; the citation is to Galen, *Peri Ethon*, 4.

135 Liddell and Scott s.v. *melet-*.

136 Marrou notes, however, that the military aspect in Roman education was "softer" than that of Greek: *History of Education in Antiquity*, pp. 229–241.

137 *Regula Benedicti*, Prol. 39–40, 45 (CSEL 75, pp. 8–9): "Cum ergo interrogassemus dominum, fratres, de habitatore tauernaculi eius, audiuimus habitandi praeceptum: sed si compleamus habitatoris officium. Ergo praeparanda sunt corda et corpora nostra sanctae praeceptorum oboedientiae militanda. ... Constituenda est ergo nobis dominici scola seruitii."

138 One of the most eloquent exponents of this emphasis within monasticism is R. A. Markus: see his two studies, *Saeculum* (on Augustine's idea of the Christian "city") and *The End of Ancient Christianity*.

139 Peter of Celle, *De afflictione et lectione* (ed. Leclercq, p. 231.1–4): "Triplici studio tirones Christi probantur sub uexillo militantes in cella, afflicitione scilicet corporali qua carnis lasciuia infrenatur, lectione Novi et Veteris Testamenti qua anima pascitur, oratione compunctiua pro peccatis qua spiritus ad Deum subleuatur."

140 Ibid., p. 231.12–13: "Modus uero est persequi in afflictione lasciuiam non naturam."

141 Ibid., p. 233, 25–28, 35–36): "Exarmat enim propugnacula sua *mille clypeis pendentibus ex eis* [cf. Song of Songs 4:4] qui non uacat lectionibus diuinis. O quam cito et sine labor capietur ciuitatula cellae, nisi se defenderit auxilio Dei et scuto diuinae paginae! ... Sume nihilominus de armario librorum missilia quibus percussus percussorem tuum repercutias."

142 A number of examples of these common tropes for the memory store are collected in *The Book of Memory*, Chapter One. It was an ideal of monasticism

that one's memory be a library of texts: for example, Didymus, the blind Greek expositor of Scripture whom Cassiodorus admired because he had so stored away all the authors and texts of Scripture in the library of his memory ("in memoriae suae bibliotheca") that he could immediately tell you in which part of the codex any text could be found: see Cassiodorus, *Inst.* I.5. 2. I will have more to say about Cassiodorus' admiration for Didymus in a later chapter.

143 Peter of Celle, *De afflictione et lectione* (ed. Leclercq, p. 234.33): "spirantem clibanum panibus similagineis plenum."

144 Ibid., p. 235.13–16: "ut gradiens et deambulans per campum Scripturae non offendas ad lapidem pedem tuum, sed tanquam apes flores ex eo colligens, fauum mellis componas unde sit dulcedo in faucibus et lumen in oculis et miris odoribus cellae tuae etiam parietas conspergas." In monastic contexts, the trope of the honeycomb gains added force because of the pun in Latin *cella*, which was also the word for the "cells" of a beehive.

145 Ibid., pp. 236.24–237.11: "In hoc quoque libro [Genesi] grandiori passa lectionis ueni ad paradisum … Ambula cum Deo sicut Enoch. … Intra arcam tempore diluuii … Ad hunc modum presso et suspenso pede continentiam huius libri decurre … interpretando obscura, plana retinendo et memoriae commendando. Ubi amoenum pratum prophetalium benedictionum intraueris, laxa sinum, uentrem distende, *dilata os* [Psalm 80:11], manum extende … Ad Exodum dolens pro ingressu Aegypti accede. … Deinde umbram nostrae redemptionis in sanguine immolati agni adora. Legem in monte Sina datam spiritaliter intellectam obserua, quadraginta duas mansiones cum suis significatis profectibus uirtutum peragra tabernaculum, cum suis caeremoniis mente angelica in teipso construens."

146 The forty-two "places" are enumerated in Numbers 33. Some late medieval diagrams used the word *mansiones* as a synonym of *sedes*, the mnemonic "seats" or *loci*, indicating that the word had come by then to have a generalized mnemonic use, perhaps because of the monastic practice of using the Sinai *mansiones* as a structure for a variety of meditations. The original Sinai *mansiones* were part of the Jerusalem pilgrimage route even in the time of Egeria.

147 Ibid., pp. 235.26–7, 236.1–4: "Est autem adeo fertilis et copiosa sanctorum librorum refectio ut in eis tot fastidia nostra habeant lectionum mutatoria quot uiuendi momenta … Secundum appetitum uero diuersarum affectionum nunc noua, nunc uetera, nunc obscura, nunc aperta, nunc subtilia, nunc simplicia, nunc exempla, nunc mandata, nunc seria, nunc iocosa legenda sunt; ut anima circumamicta concordi uarietate uitet taedium et sumat remedium."

148 J. Leclercq, *La spiritualité de Pierre de Celle*, p. 78.

149 Ibid., p. 79.

150 Romuald of Camaldoli (d. 1027), as quoted in Bruno de Querfort, *Vita quinque fratrum* 2 (MGH, *Scriptores* 15.2, p. 738.23–30): "Sede in cella quasi in paradiso; proice post tergum de memoria totum mundum, cautus ad cogitationes, quasi bonus piscator ad pisces. Una via est in psalmis; hanc ne dimittas. Si non potes omnia, qui venisti fervore novicio, nunc in hoc, nunc illo loco psallere in spiritu et intelligere mente stude, et cum ceperis vagari legendo, ne desistas, sed festina intelligendo emendare; pone te ante omnia in presentia Dei cum timore et tremore, quasi qui stat in conspectu imperatoris; destrue te totum et sede quasi

pullus, contentus ad gratiam Dei, quia, nisi mater donet, nec sapit nec habet quod comedat."

151 Romuald was the subject of a biography, written a generation after his death by the great contemplative monk and member of his order Peter Damian, and what we know of Romuald comes mainly from this source, for he left no writings of his own. The account of his meditational method quoted here is by one of his disciples, Bruno of Querfort, who went as a missionary to Russia, where he was martyred in 1009.

152 Translated in Appendix A of *The Book of Memory*, pp. 261–266.

153 Quintilian likens finding the "places" of argument to finding the places where fish, or game, lie hidden: *Inst. orat.* V. x. 20–22. A similar metaphor is found in Greek; see *The Book of Memory*, pp. 62, 247, and Figure 28.

154 An excellent effort to characterize medieval *ars orandi*, together with a bibliography, is that of B. Jaye, in M. Briscoe and B. Jaye, *Artes praedicandi, artes orandi*. No true manual of prayer was produced during the time-span of my study, but John Cassian differentiates some genres of prayer in his first Conference, and Hugh of St. Victor wrote a little treatise *De modo orandi* (*PL* 176.977–988).

3. COGNITIVE IMAGES, MEDITATION, AND ORNAMENT

1 The phrase is used by Augustine in *De doctrina christiana* IV.viii.22.7–8 (CCSL 32, p. 131). An important essay on the inventive power of obscure language is D. Kelly, "Obscurity and Memory," and see also W. Kemp, "Visual Narrative, Memory, and the Medieval Esprit du Système."

2 Geoffrey of Vinsauf, *Poetria nova*, line 1972.

3 There was great difference of opinion on the relative merits of these emotions, of course. Augustine said he was amused by the teeth–sheep–apostles connection that he made, which I will shortly discuss. But most writers put more emphasis on fear (probably rightly) as a reliable emotion to stir up the mind; certainly this is so in the orthopraxis of meditation which Augustine outlines in *De doctrina christiana* II.vii, in Anselm's *Prayers and Meditations*, and in the practice described by Peter of Celle in "On Affliction and Reading."

4 The best introductions to medieval epistemology remain Colish, *The Mirror of Language*, and Chenu, *Nature, Man, and Society in the Twelfth Century* (the English translation of *La théologie au douzième siècle*). And see also G. Ladner, "Medieval and Modern Understanding of Symbolism."

5 Alcuin, *Liber de animae ratione* 7 (*PL* 101.642A): "Nunc autem consideremus miram velocitatem animae in formandis rebus, quae percipit per carnales sensus, a quibus quasi per quosdam nuntios, quidquid rerum sensibilium cognitarum vel incognitarum percipit, mox in seipsa earum ineffabili celeritate format figuras, informatasque in suae thesauro memoriae recondit." The metaphor of a "sort of messenger service" for what, in scholastic Aristotelian psychology, is the *sensus communis* and *vis imaginativa* is taken from Augustine, *De Genesi ad litteram* XII.xxiv.

6 *Liber de animae ratione* 7–8 (*PL* 101.642A–C): "Sicut enim qui Romam vidit, Romam enim [*Forte, etiam*] fingit in animo suo, et format qualis sit. Et dum

nomen audierit vel rememorat Romae, statim recurrit animus illius ad memoriam, ubi conditam habet formam illius, et ibi recognoscit [eam ad memoriam], ubi recondidit illam. Et adhuc mirabilius est, quod incognitarum rerum, si lectae vel auditae erunt in auribus, anima statim format figuram ignotae rei. Sicut forte Jerusalem quisquam nostrum habet in anima sua formatam, qualis sit: quamvis longe aliter sit, quam sibi anima fingit, dum videtur. ... Muros et domos et plateas non fingit in eo, sicut in Jerusalem facit, [sed] quidquid in aliis civitatibus vidit sibi cognitis, hec fingit in Jerusalem esse posse; ex notis enim speciebus fingit ignota ... Sic de omni re facit animus hominis, ex cognitis fingit incognita, habens has omnes species in se. ... Ex qua velocitate animae, quo in se sic omnia fingit audita vel visa, aut sensa, aut odorata, aut gustata, iterumque inventa recognoscit, mira Dei potentia et naturae efficacia, utcunque cognosci poterit." This quotation follows directly after the sentence quoted in the preceding note 5; the material in square brackets, including emendations, appears as printed in Migne.

7 The Trinity Apocalypse is Cambridge, Trinity College, MS R.16.2, made c. 1260. The rounded, "Roman" arch of the Saint-Sever painting may also reflect a tradition dating to late antiquity, which would have been shown in the original image, though the "Romanesque" arch was used when the Saint-Sever image was made in the eleventh century. On the vexed problem of the relationships among styles of the various manuscripts of the Beatus tradition, see the summarizing comments of J. Williams, *The Illustrated Beatus*, vol. 1, esp. pp. 53–78, 143–157; P. Klein, "Les sources non hispaniques et la genèse iconographique du Beatus de Saint-Sever"; and the still-pertinent essay of M. Schapiro, "Two Romanesque Drawings in Auxerre and Some Iconographical Problems" (1954; rpt. *Romanesque Art*, pp. 306–327). My comments do nothing one way or another to clarify matters of influence or genealogy. Art historians seem agreed only that the first Beatus commentary probably incorporated a program of illustrations, but it is impossible to determine what their style might have been: see Williams, *The Illustrated Beatus*, vol. 1, pp. 36–39.

8 This distinction is crucial in understanding the arguments of most religious iconoclasm: see G. Ladner, "The Concept of the Image in the Greek Fathers." An interesting discussion of modern iconoclasm, especially that of Marx, is Mitchell, *Iconology*, esp. pp. 160–208. The role of *memoria* in relation to what he terms "portrait" is briefly discussed by H. Belting, *Likeness and Presence*, pp. 9–14. Belting's definition of "memory" in relation to his own theory of cultic or "holy images," however, is completely at odds with my understanding of how the term was used in the Middle Ages; like many historians, Belting assumes that the concept of "memory" was always limited to repetition and reiteration of the past. See esp. his comments (p. 28) about late Byzantine art, that "[s]tylistic development comes to an end only when the icon has become merely a means of remembrance ... a desire to hold on to a lost tradition." A fruitful analysis of how this view and the rhetorical view of *memoria* have led to "dialogues of the deaf" among modern scholars is F. Wallis, "The Ambiguities of Medieval 'Memoria.'"

9 Augustine, *De trinitate* VIII.iv.7 (CCSL 50, p. 275.26–31): "Necesse est autem cum aliqua corporalia lecta uel audita quae non uidimus credimus, fingat sibi animus aliquid in lineamentis formisque corporum sicut occurrerit cogitanti ... non hoc tamen fide ut teneamus quidquam prodest, sed ad aliud aliquid utile

quod per hoc insinuatur." For my translations of this work I consulted that of S. McKenna for the Fathers of the Church series. Though Augustine uses a plural form to refer to unknown "earthly things" in this passage, I have made it singular in English, for Latin often uses plurals where idiomatic English would use a singular; thus keeping the singular throughout obviates a difficulty English speakers may experience in the switch from "corporalia" to "aliquid."

10 Augustine, *De trinitate* VIII.iv.7 (CCSL 50, p. 275.32–276.47): "Quis enim legentium uel audientium quae scripsit apostolus Paulus uel quae de illo scripta sunt non fingat animo et ipsius apostoli faciem et omnium quorum ibi nomina commemorantur? Et cum in tanta hominum multitudine quibus illae litterae notae sunt alius aliter lineamenta figuramque illorum corporum cogitet, quis propinquius et similius cogitet utique incertum est. ... Nam et ipsius facies dominicae carnis innumerabilium cogitationum diuersitate uariatur et fingitur, quae tamen una erat quaecumque erat. Neque in fide nostra quam de domino Iesu Christo habemus illud salubre est quod sibi animus fingit longe fortasse aliter quam res habet, sed illud quod secundum speciem de homine cogitamus." My translation differs significantly from S. McKenna's in the last phrase. I take the phrase "secundum speciem" as adverbial, modifying "cogitamus," *secundum* meaning "following upon" or "after," and *speciem* meaning an "image" or "representation," the cognitive image that each person makes for himself (such as the image of St. Paul one may conjure up when reading his work), as Augustine has just explained.

11 See Sorabji, *Aristotle on Memory*, pp. 2–17. See also the important comments on Augustine's remarks in *De trinitate* VIII by B. Stock (*Augustine the Reader*, pp. 251–254), who demonstrates how Augustine distinguishes carefully the issues of image verification (an epistemological matter) from those of cognitive use.

12 Robert Holcot, the fourteenth-century Dominican friar, said he "saw" his schematic "pictures" placed in his mind on the initial letters of the major divisions of Hosea; see *The Book of Memory*, p. 231.

13 Mitchell, discussing the early Romantic English poet–painter William Blake, comments that his pictures are "riddled with ideas, making them a visible language," but also that his calligraphy requires us "to pause at the sensuous surface of calligraphic and typographical forms" (*Picture Theory*, p. 147). One observes similarly "sensuous" calligraphy, especially at major divisions in a text, in many Carolingian, Insular, and later medieval manuscripts as well. Blake's is also, of course, an art of meditation. I have found Mitchell's discussion of such issues in Blake most valuable: see esp. pp. 111–150.

14 This practice was mentioned approvingly by Quintilian and it was ubiquitous through the Middle Ages: see my discussion of it in *The Book of Memory*, pp. 107–108, 117–119, 242–245.

15 Kennedy, *Classical Rhetoric*, p. 159.

16 See Gerhardsson, *Memory and Manuscript*, and Neusner, *The Memorized Torah*, on the rabbinical procedures of using brief pieces of Torah text as memory nodes to which to attach considerable amounts of commentary and other kinds of teaching. Some of these pedagogical "breves" even acquired mnemonic nicknames, such as "the thorn-bush" for Exodus 3 (Gerhardsson, *Memory and*

Manuscript, pp. 142–56). On the value of "difficulty" in rabbinical teaching, even in the earliest periods, the remarks of M. Fishbane, "'The Holy One Sits and Roars,'" Wolfson, "Beautiful Maiden Without Eyes," and D. Stern, "The Rabbinic Parable and the Narrative of Interpretation," are illuminating. The concept and practice of "difficult" ornament in various medieval poetries, including Hebrew, is the special theme of *Medievalia* 19 (1996). Several essays in this volume suggest that such obscurity was a conventional feature of early vernacular literatures in both the Celtic and the Germanic traditions: this cultural preference would have reinforced the emphases in patristic exegesis on the merits of "difficulty." On the value of difficulty in Roman rhetoric, see J. Ziolkowski, "Theories of Obscurity in the Latin Tradition." *Translatio* was itself sometimes considered a "difficult" trope: see M. Nims, "Translatio."

17 Alcuin's rhetoric has been edited with commentary and translation by W. S. Howell, who was inclined to think that the treatise on virtues was separate from that on rhetoric. But see the comments on this matter of L. Wallach, *Alcuin and Charlemagne*. The marriage between eloquence and the virtues of government was a goal of rhetorical pedagogy for Quintilian and for the late ancient rhetoricians, like Julius Victor and Martianus Capella, whose work directly influenced Alcuin.

18 J. Murphy is not very interested in it. Noting its reliance on Donatus, he says it shouldn't be considered a rhetoric at all but a grammar: *Rhetoric in the Middle Ages*, pp. 78–80. And the introduction provided to a translation of it in a standard anthology says that its "significance lies" in its being the first treatise on rhetoric written in England and setting "a peculiarly English attitude of the next eight centuries: the equating of rhetoric with style" (Miller, *Readings in Medieval Rhetoric*, pp. 96–97). More recently M. Irvine has treated it as a work solely of grammar; indeed he says that it is "misclassified" as a work about rhetoric (*The Making of Textual Culture*, pp. 293–296).

19 The connections of "eating the book" with meditative reading practices and the associated features of memory work, especially the sub-vocalized murmur of engaged *memoria*, are discussed fully in *The Book of Memory*, esp. pp. 165–173.

20 Hugh of St. Victor, *De modo dicendi et meditandi* 8 (*PL* 176.879): "Meditatio est assidua ac sagax retractatio cogitationis, aliquid obscurum explicare nitens, vel scrutans penetrare occultum."

21 A corrective to the usual identification of "literature-ization" only with *writing* is the use of the term by Enders throughout her *Rhetoric and the Origins of Medieval Drama*; Enders equates *letteraturizzazione* with a late classical trend towards "aestheticizing" legal rhetoric, making it more narrative and pathetic, hence more dramatic. The ethically basic role of such "aestheticized" approaches to Biblical narrative is, of course, emphasized in monastic reading and meditation too, from the fourth-century Fathers onward; this, as well as the dramatic character of processional liturgy, all contributed to the monastic ethos within which medieval drama developed. On the inappropriateness of rigorously identifying grammar with written texts and rhetoric with oral performance in medieval situations, see the comments of M. Woods, "The Teaching of Writing in Medieval Europe," and J. Ward, "From Antiquity to the Renaissance" and *Ciceronian Rhetoric*, pp. 51–73.

22 Though that was not the vocabulary he used, this was essentially the justification of D. W. Robertson for his "historical" exegetical readings even of vernacular and secular medieval literature: see especially his introduction to *A Preface to Chaucer*. Robertson acknowledged his own indebtedness to E. Panofsky.

23 Monastic reform movements typically complained that unreformed monks spent too much time on codified practices that had become simply rote, and did not give sufficient attention to meditation, seen as the key to spiritual growth: probably the best known of these reforms are those of Benedict of Aniane in the ninth century, and the Cluniac–Cistercian "quarrel" in the twelfth.

24 Hugh of St. Victor, *Didascalicon* III.9–10; see also all of Book VI, in which he expounds the "reading as construction" metaphor I discussed in my first chapter. I also discussed the matter in *The Book of Memory*, esp. pp. 156–188.

25 Exodus 12:35b: "et petierunt ab Aegyptiis vasa argentea et aurea, vestemque plurimam."

26 Augustine, *De doctrina christiana* II.xl.60.4–27 (CCSL 32, pp. 73–74): "Sicut enim Aegyptii non tantum idola habebant et onera gravia, quae populus Israhel detestaretur et fugeret, sed etiam uasa atque ornamenta de auro et argento et uestem, quae ille populus exiens de Aegypto sibi potius tanquam ad usum meliorem clanculo uindicauit, non auctoritate propria, sed praecepto dei ipsis Aegyptiis nescienter commodantibus ea, quibus non bene utebantur, sic doctrinae omnes gentilium ... liberales disciplinas usui ueritatis aptiores et quaedam morum praecepta utilissima continent ... quod eorum tamquam aurum et argentum, quod non ipso instituerunt, sed de quibusdam quasi metallis diuinae prouidentiae ... eruerunt ... debet ab eis auferre christianus ad usum iustum praedicandi euangelii. Vestem quoque illorum ... accipere atque habere licuerit in usum conuertenda christianum." In making my several translations from this work, I consulted those of D. W. Robertson.

27 The examples Augustine lists in II.xli.61, of those who are well stuffed ("suffarcinatus," used of Cyprian; CCSL 32, p. 74.29) with the gold and silver and garments of the pagans, are all orators and poets: Cyprian, Lactantius, Victorinus, Optatus, and Hilary.

28 Deuteronomy 21: 11–13: "et videris in numero captivorum mulierem pulchram ... voluerisque habere uxorem, introduces in domum tuam: quae radet caesariem: et circumcidet ungues, et deponet uestem, in qua capta est: sedensque in domo tua, flebit patrem et matrem suam uno mense: et postea intrabis ad eam, dormiesque cum illa, et erit uxor tua."

29 Hrabanus Maurus, *De clericorum institutione* 18 (*PL* 107.396): "poemata autem et libros gentilium si velimus propter florem eloquentiae legere, typus mulieris captivae tenendus est, quam Deuteronomium describit; et Dominum ita praecepisse commemorat, ut si Israelites eam habere vellet uxorem, calvitiem ei faciat, ungues praesecet, pilos auferat, et cum munda fuerit effecta, tunc transeat in uxoris amplexus. Haec si secundum litteram intelligimus, nonne ridicula sunt? Itaque et nos hoc facere solemus ... quando poetas gentiles legimus ... si quid in eis utile reperimus, ad nostrum dogma convertimus; si quid vero superfluum de idolis, de amore, de cura saecularium rerum, haec radamus, his calvitiem inducamus, haec in unguium more ferro acutissimo desecemus."

30 Augustine, *De civitate dei* XI.18.4–21 (CCSL 48, p. 337): "ita ordinem saecu-

lorum tamquam pulcherrimum carmen etiam ex quibusdam quasi antithetis honestaret. Antitheta enim quae appellantur in ornamentis elocutionis sunt decentissima, quae Latine ut appellentur opposita ... ita quadam non uerborum, sed rerum eloquentia contrariorum oppositione saeculi pulchritudo componitur." In the next section of this book (XI.19.1–8), Augustine extolls the virtue of rhetorical obscurity as a moral tool: "when one man thinks this and another that, many interpretations of the truth are conceived and brought forth into the light of knowledge." These are then judged for their relative merit, often "after much debate." There is a strong assumption in this passage that interpretation is often a communal and rhetorical process; this assumption persists in later medieval justifications for rhetorical obscurity, such as those of Hugh of St. Victor. Augustine assumed as well, of course, that such interpretive activities took place over time within a coherent Christian community, which God was directing through human history; his position therefore is protected from both solipsism and cultural relativism.

31 Augustine, *De doctrina christiana*, II.vi.7.22–26 (CCSL 32, p. 36): "Et tamen nescio quomodo suauius intueor sanctos, cum eos quasi dentes ecclesiae uideo ... Oues etiam iucundissime agnosco detonsas." J. Baldwin has translated a brief composition recalled *ad res* from this text by Peter the Chanter (late twelfth century); in a extended gloss on Numbers 3:18, Peter says: "the front teeth are the apostles; the canines those expositors of Scripture who 'bark' against heretics; the molars are modern masters who prepare sacred doctrine to nourish the faithful" ("Masters at Paris," p. 161; text in note 104). Peter of Poitiers, a contemporary, composed a *distinctio* "De dentibus" in his collection of *Distinctiones super psalterium*: in such ways whole sermons were composed from bites of "remembered things."

32 An interesting essay arguing that the "see-ability" of material described in words was a major concern even for the most factually disposed of historians is A. Walker, "*Enargeia* and the Spectator in Greek Historiography." *Enargeia* directly addresses a reader's need for memorability, the crucial cognitive requirement; this may explain why pre-modern "facts" are almost always either tagged in some way (for example, by being set into a story pattern, or into a geography or star-map) or placed into an easily recollected visual pattern (Euclidean geometry, for example).

33 A succinct account of these exercises in medieval schools is in Woods, "The Teaching of Writing in Medieval Europe."

34 Quintilian, *Inst. orat.* VIII.iii.52; the translation is that of H. Butler for the LCL, as are all those of this work, except when otherwise noted: for this reason, I have not thought it necessary to quote the Latin. Of all the faults, only this one, *homoeideia*, literally "all of one shape," cannot be redeemed. The appeal to the mind's eye is implicit in the concept, for *eidos* means visible shape or form.

35 Though he continued to be very influential, Quintilian survived in the Middle Ages mostly through excerpts and digests, his complete work having been "lost." On the medieval reception of Quintilian, see esp. J. Ward, "Quintilian and the Rhetorical Revolution of the Middle Ages."

36 Quintilian, *Inst. orat.* VIII.iii.64, quoting Cicero, *Verrine Orations* V. 33.86: "Stetit soleatus praetor populi Romani cum pallio purpureo tunicaque talari

muliercula nixus in litore" (my translation, consulting that of H. Butler). Part of the effect, not reproduceable in translation, lies in the alliterative jingle. I have tried to convey the contempt in this description by other means.

37 Quintilian, *Inst. orat.*, VIII.iii.64–65.

38 Ibid., 62.

39 Ibid., 75.

40 Ibid., 64.

41 Ibid., VI.xxx–xxxii.

42 The closely related verb *depingere* was also used, perhaps even more commonly, for painting in words or mentally: see the citations in *TLL* s.v. *depingo*, 1.b. Several of these are from the Latin Fathers (Cassiodorus, Jerome, Boethius), as well as from Cicero and Quintilian (see esp. the uses by Quintilian, *Inst. orat.* VIII.iii.63, the passage on *enargeia* from which I just quoted).

43 Jerome, *Commentarii in Hiezechielem* III.viii.7–9.173–174 (CCSL 75, p. 95): "omnia quasi imagine picturaque monstrantur." Jerome emphasizes throughout the commentary that Ezekiel is a vision, that his seeings are images, that they must be seen with eye of the mind and understood meditatively (spiritually) not literally. The images are a divine concession to a basic requirement of human knowing, however, for Ezekiel would know nothing without them.

44 Ibid., 201–207 (CCSL 75, p. 96): "Possumus et in nostro templi parietibus idola monstrare depicta, quando omnibus uitiis subiacemus et pingimus in corde nostro peccatorum conscientiam imaginesque diuersas. ... Quod scilicet nullus hominum sit qui aliquam imaginem non habeat, siue sanctitatis, siue peccati."

45 Augustine, *Sermo* 113 (*PL* 38.649): "Noli tibi talem pingere Deum, noli collocare in templo cordis tui tale idolum."

46 Augustine, *Enarrationes in Psalmis* LXXIV.9.11 (CCSL 39, p. 1032.14–16): "*Calix in manu Domini*, cum dicit, eruditis in ecclesia Christi loquor, non utique ueluti forma humana circumscriptum Deum debitis uobis in corde pingere, ne clausis templis simulacra in cordibus fabricetis." The stricture against painting a likeness of a *clausum templum* is interesting: could Augustine be suggesting that a schematic temple plan is preferable? See my discussion of a "cartographic" Temple image for meditation in Chapter Five, section 4. The strictures in this sermon are against overly "descriptive" mental painting: among other things, such literal-mindedness may have been thought to distract one and to "freeze up" the flexibility of an image whose function is cognitive.

47 Arnobius Iunior, *Commentarii in Psalmos*, 118.81–176 (CCSL 25, p. 199.151–156): "Pinge, pinge ante oculos tuos, qui haec cantas, aliquas fabricas. Quales? Illas quas mirabantur apostoli: pinge templa, pinge thermas, pinge fora et moenia in uertice excelso surgentia. Et dum ista consideras, memento casulae cuiuscumque ex frondium septo contextae. Numquid non tanto illa tibi erit despectior, quanto ista mirabilia stupueris." Some historians believe that a picture cycle of the Apocalypse was circulating as early as the fifth century; though there is no necessary connection, Arnobius' comments here are certainly of interest in this regard. See P. Klein, "The Apocalypse in Medieval Art," in R. Emmerson and B. McGinn, *The Apocalypse in the Middle Ages*, p. 175, and the references cited in note 78, p. 176. The Virgilian allusions are to *Eclogue* I.26, 67–69, occasioned by the poet giving up his farm, and were part of the standard mental

kit of late ancient education. The connection is not made via a common word but via a common image, that of a rural hut woven from boughs (in Virgil, with a turved roof).

48 Marrou, *History of Education in Antiquity*, p. 225.

49 Described by Levitan, "Dancing at the End of the Rope," pp. 255–256. On the scribal institution of word division and its possible effect on reading habits see P. Saenger, "Silent Reading." A comprehensive survey of Carolingian *carmina figurata*, acrostics, and anagrams is in Ernst, *Carmen figuratum*. W. Ong analyzed the syllabic play in a hymn of Thomas Aquinas in "Wit and Mystery," and see also *A Game of Heuene* by M. C. Davlin, a careful study of word-play in the Middle English poem *Piers Plowman*, most of which relies on play at the level of a single syllable.

50 Levitan, "Dancing at the End of the Rope," p. 249.

51 Some contemporary cognitive scientists analyze cognition as fundamentally pattern making and pattern recognition. Of particular interest is the theory of "parallel distributed" processing: see esp. Chapter 17 of D. Rumelhart and J. L. McClelland, *Parallel Distributed Processing*, and M. Johnson, *The Body in the Mind*. H. Margolis, *Patterns, Thinking, and Cognition*, applies the notion of cognitive "pattern" to the making of rational judgments; his discussion of "the Copernican revolution" in these terms is particularly instructive.

52 Quintilian, *Inst. orat.* XI. ii. 32; see *The Book of Memory*, pp. 74–75.

53 Cassiodorus' figures have been discussed several times, and the question of their authenticity is debated, but most scholars now seem to have decided they are original. See the comments of R. Mynors, the editor of the *Institutiones*, pp. xxii–xxiv, and more recently K. Corsano, "The First Quire of the Codex Amiatinus," and F. Troncarelli, "Alpha e acciuga." Some of the varieties and possible uses of school diagrams and pedagogical designs, paticularly of the liberal arts, has been surveyed, from the Carolingian period to the time of Meister Eckhart by K.-A. Wirth, "Von mittelalterlichen Bildern und Lehrfiguren." On the use of diagram-like forms in earliest books see K. Weitzmann, *Late Antique and Early Christian Book Illumination*.

54 Prudentius, *Dittocheon (Tituli historiarum)*, xxxix (LCL 398, p. 364): "Campus Acheldemach sceleris mercede nefandi / venditus exequias recipit tumulosus humandas. / sanguinis hoc pretium est Christi. Iuda eminus artat / infelix collum laqueo pro crimine tanto."

55 *Eminus* is usually translated "from afar," but "far" is a notoriously unreliable measure. All one can say with reasonable sureness is that the word here means "not close up." See the citations especially from Caesar in OLD and in Lewis and Short s.v. *eminus*.

56 *Dittocheon* has no images in any of the extant manuscripts. It has been assumed that the *Dittocheon* quatrains originally served as *tituli* for a set of murals, now lost. They may have – but the "painted" quality of the language alone is not enough to support this assumption. On the role of this poem in establishing a typological iconography of Biblical scenes, see C. Davis-Weyer, "Komposition und Szenenwahl im Dittochaeum des Prudentius."

57 See Gehl, *A Moral Art*, esp. pp. 43–56.

58 On the pedagogical ambiance of the Bestiary tradition see F. McCulloch,

Medieval French and Latin Bestiaries. See also the lengthy introduction to W. Clark, *The Medieval Book of Birds.*

59 An excellent example is the Anglo-Norman translation of the Bestiary by Philippe de Thaon; I discussed this in *The Book of Memory*, pp. 126–127.

60 This has been demonstrated in an important article by B. Rowland, "The Art of Memory and the Bestiary." See also the comments of S. Lewis, "Beyond the Frame," on a related variety of "picture-book."

61 M. Curschmann, "Imagined Exegesis." While I think Curschmann concludes too quickly that visual exegesis was new in the eleventh century, and also that it was a German invention, I completely support his main conclusion, that the relationship between words and images must be discussed in terms of "function: how, irrespective of their own stylistic, iconographic, or intellectual traditions, texts and pictures work together in given instances" (p. 169). Most work done recently on the relationship of text and image has (for obvious reasons) concentrated on materials produced after the eleventh century, but I think it would be wrong to conclude therefore that earlier monastic culture was iconoclastic in a truly practical way. My own research has led me to quite a different conclusion, as should by now be apparent. A preliminary study of the "theory" (if one can call it that) of visual exegesis from Paulinus of Nola and Prudentius to the twelfth century is A. Esmeijer, *Divina quaternitas*, though I find she over-emphasizes Neoplatonic sources for this practice, which therefore is given an esoteric cast that I do not think it had during the Middle Ages. Among many excellent discussions of the *cognitive* use of images in books made around the twelfth century, I have found especially useful the remarks of M. Camille, "Seeing and Reading"; C. Hahn, "Picturing the Text"; and M. Caviness, "Images of Divine Order." H. Bober's early essay, "An Illustrated Medieval School-Book of Bede's 'De Natura Rerum,'" has much relevance to this matter. See also Sicard, *Hugues de Saint-Victor et son école*, esp. pp. 7–45, and *Diagrammes médiévaux*, and J.-C. Schmitt, "Les images classificatrices."

62 "Ox hare bird horse man serpent peacock lion crane / foot head beak chest hand body tail mane leg"; "Barker [dog] man stag horse large bird scorpion cat / With tooth with hand with horn with foot with breast from the back [tail] or with claw / I bite I withdraw I attack I smite I drive I kill I rend." Similar *versus rapportati* are edited by G. Silagi as "Tituli zu Kompositfiguren" in MGH, *Poetae latini medii aevi* vol. 5.3, p. 656 (#11). They remained quite popular, though the "peacock" picture shown here lost a third line that the other examples have.

63 Curschmann, "Imagined Exegesis," p. 161.

64 Gerhoch's use of this device is discussed in Curschmann, "Imagined Exegesis," pp. 162–163.

65 Cited from Curschmann, "Imagined Exegesis," p. 163: "Sed ea quae verbis molimur exprimere, clarius apparebunt per inspectionem subjectae picturae." The original source is Munich, Bayerische Staatsbibliothek MS. Clm. 16012.

66 Several recent studies have addressed both the methods of such early training and the people, chiefly the mother, responsible for it in medieval households. The alphabet, and the basic Psalms and prayers, were the content of this training; pictures formed an essential part of this education. The lay-out and ornamentation of medieval prayer books for the laity should be studied in this educational

context: for example, there is a fifteenth-century Book of Hours made for Marguerite d'Orléans (Paris, BN MS. Lat. 1156B) with a disarranged alphabet (f. 153), of exactly the sort children used to be sure they recognized individual letter forms. See M. T. Clanchy, "Learning to Read in the Middle Ages and the Role of Mothers," and D. Alexandre-Bidon, "La lettre volée." Quintilian emphasizes how a child should learn letter shapes through such tactile means as carved ivory blocks (*Inst. orat.* I.i.25–26). This educational emphasis on shape, it is tempting to speculate, may have contributed to a "graphic design" bias towards written letters that scholars have often remarked on, especially in Insular and Carolingian books. Throughout the Middle Ages, a scribe would write several different forms of certain of the letters (A, for example) for reasons of page design, and there are well-known examples of the use of letters in human and animal shapes.

67 Prudentius was one of the curriculum authors listed in grammar and rhetoric curricula by Conrad of Hirsau (twelfth century). On his curricular role more generally see E. Curtius, *European Literature and the Latin Middle Ages*, pp. 48–54.

68 Prudentius, *Psychomachia*, 912–915: "aurea templi / atria constituens texat spectamine morum / ornamenta animae, quibus oblectata decoro / aeternum solio dives Sapientia regnet." Here and elsewhere, my translations of Prudentius are based on those of H. J. Thomson for the LCL, consulting also the verse translation of M. C. Eagan for the FC.

69 *Psychomachia*'s role in setting the iconographic conventions of later medieval art is detailed in A. Katzenellenbogen, *Allegories of the Virtues and Vices in Medieval Art.*

70 H. Rose, *A Handbook of Latin Literature*, p. 509. There are several fine recent studies which adjust this older judgment. See especially Smith, *Prudentius' Psychomachia*, the first monograph in English on the poem and its sources, both pagan and biblical; Malamud, *A Poetics of Transformation*; and S. Nugent, *Allegory and Poetics.* Some general characteristics of late antique style, especially its "excessive pictorial" quality (to which Rose and others objected), are interestingly discussed by J. Onians, "Abstraction and Imagination in Late Antiquity," and M. Roberts, *The Jewelled Style.* Roberts, *Poetry and the Cult of the Martyrs*, is an excellent analysis of Prudentius' influential poem about the martyrs, *Peristephanon*, another enormously "successful" work both in literature and iconography during the Middle Ages.

71 Prudentius, *Psychomachia*, 421–8: "casus agit saxum, medii spiramen ut oris / frangeret, et recavo misceret labra palato. / dentibus introrsum resolutis lingua resectam / dilaniata gulam frustris cum sanguinis inplet. / insolitis dapibus crudescit guttur, et ossa / conliquefacta vorans revomit quas hauserat offas. / 'ebibe iam proprium post pocula multa cruorem,'/ virgo ait increpitans ..." Commenting on Prudentius' extensive use of Virgil, especially the *Aeneid* (as one might expect), Smith suggests (*Prudentius' Psychomachia*, pp. 290–291) that this scene is modeled on the death of Troilus (*Aeneid* I.474–478), dangling in death from his chariot after being struck by Achilles' spear.

72 John Cassian, Conferences XIV.xii: see Chapter Two, section 9 above.

73 Curtius, *European Literature and the Latin Middle Ages*, gives many examples of etymologies in ancient literature, though he fails to note the many times this trope

occurs in the Bible as well. He treats the ornament as "a category of thought," but complains that much of what is called etymology in antiquity is "more or less insipid trifling" (p. 496), missing the point (as I will argue below) of this ancient ornament.

74 Prudentius, *Psychomachia*, praef. 9–14: "pugnare nosmet eum profanis gentibus / suasit, ... quam strage multa bellicosus spiritus / portenta cordis servientis vicerit."

75 Prudentius, *Psychomachia*, praef. 32–33: "Loth ipse ruptis expeditus nexibus / attrita bacis colla liber erigit." The quotation from the epitome of the Melchisedech story, which immediately follows, is lines 40–43.

76 Prudentius, *Psychomachia*, praef. 50–51: "haec ad figuram praenotata est linea,/ quam nostra recto vita resculpet pede."

77 Hugh of St. Victor used the word for the mental device he describes as a method for recalling the Psalms: see Appendix A of *The Book of Memory*. The word is also used by the early-thirteenth-century professor of rhetoric Geoffrey of Vinsauf, for the preliminary "scheme" of a composition: I discussed this in "The Poet as Master-Builder."

78 Prudentius, *Psychomachia*, 18–20: "vincendi praesens ratio est, si comminus ipsas / Virtutum facies et conluctantia contra / viribus infestis liceat portenta notare."

79 See Katzenellenbogen, *Allegories of the Vices and Virtues*, pp. 3–8. Most of the illustrations were published in R. Stettiner, *Die illustrierten Prudentius-Handschriften*. The figure of Luxuria tumbling from her overturned cart was a staple image in the series. I have elected not to reproduce an example of it, however, because my concern is with readerly mental painting.

80 Hugh of St. Victor, *Didascalicon* III.x (ed. Buttimer, p. 59.20–25): "principium ergo doctrinae est in lectione, consummatio in meditatione. ... ea enim maxime est, quae animam a terrenorum actuum strepitu segregat, et in hac vita etiam aeternae quietis dulcedinem quoddammodo praegustare facit"; "The beginning of learning thus is in *lectio* [grammatical commentary], its consummation in meditation. ... This is the best [stage] which takes the soul away from the noise of earthly business and causes it even in this life to pre-taste the sweetness of eternal stillness."

81 The incident is described in Augustine, *Confessiones* IX.x; see *The Book of Memory*, pp. 171–172.

82 Prudentius, *Psychomachia*, 326–327: "sed violas lascivia iacit foliisque rosarum / dimicat."

83 Ibid., 719–725: "carpitur innumeris feralis bestia dextris; / frustratim sibi quisque rapit quod spargat in auras, / quod canibus donet, corvis quod edacibus ultro / offerat, inmundis caeno exhalante cloacis / quod trudat, monstris quod mandet habere marinis." On the use of epic conventions in this passage see Roberts, *The Jewelled Style*, pp. 28–29.

84 The oldest extant manuscripts containing a program of illustrations for *Psychomachia* are ninth century; the motifs are incorporated into both Romanesque and Gothic sculpture as well. Excellent examples in the Romanesque sculpture of Aquitaine are discussed by L. Seidel, *Songs of Glory*, pp. 48–69. See also Katzenellenbogen, *Allegory of the Vices and Virtues*, pp. 3–13, and the accompanying plates. I discussed Augustine's constant use of phrases and echoes of the

Psalms as a distinct feature of texts completely familiarized in memory in *The Book of Memory*, p. 88.

85 Gregory needn't (and, since he gives a list of eight sins, probably didn't) only have Prudentius in mind. Schemes of the "deadly sins" pre-date *Psychomachia*, as one might suspect: it was Prudentius' particular genius to use the scheme of seven or eight battling vices and virtues in the conventions of the classical heroic epic – thereby "dis-placing," in accord with an elementary principle of mnemotechnical forgetting, the pagan images with Christian ones, though they still appeared in their accustomed cultural packaging, or style. The literary development of the scheme of virtues and vices during the Middle Ages was comprehensively described by M. Bloomfield, *The Seven Deadly Sins*.

86 This copy-book (or "model book") is now Leiden, University Library MS Vossiani lat. O.15; Adémar lived c. 988–c.1035. The drawings occupy ff. 37–43v and the text ff. 45–60v; between the two parts are some unrelated miscellaneous materials. Adémar also drew some images of Biblical scenes and "allegorical figures" at the beginning of his school miscellany. See De Meyier, *Codices Vossiani Latini*, vol. 3, pp. 35–36. K. Weitzmann, *Illustrations in Roll and Codex*, pp. 95–96, thought the drawings were intended as a pattern book for artisans, but it seems to me, given the evident copy-book nature of the other materials in the manuscript, that this is not a very satisfactory explanation.

87 The unique manuscript of the *Hortus deliciarum* was destroyed by a bomb during the Franco-Prussian War. A set of painted copies had been made of its illustrations before the book was lost; these are preserved in the Bibliothèque Nationale in Paris. A reconstruction of the lost book's program of anthology and pictures was edited by R. Green *et al.*

88 See Chaucer, *The Knight's Tale*, line 1999, and Dante, *Inferno*, canto 28.

89 Prudentius, *Psychomachia*, 866–867: "stridebat gravidis funalis machina vinclis / inmensas rapiens alta ad fastigia gemmas," "The hoist groaned in its chains with the weight, seizing to the upper heights the immense gemstones." There is an echo in this description of St. Paul, "seized" (*raptus*) to the third heaven (2 Corinthians 12:2), and perhaps Gregory the Great was "gathering up" these Prudential lines when he used the image of *machina* for contemplation and allegory, in the passages which I have discussed previously.

90 Prudentius, *Psychomachia* 809–810: "sanguine nam terso templum fundatur et ara / ponitur auratis Christi domus ardua tectis."

91 Ibid., 811–815: "tunc Hierusalem templo inlustrata quietum / suscepit iam diva Deum, circumvaga postquam / sedit marmoreis fundata altaribus arca. / surgat et in nostris templum venerabile castris, / omnipotens cuius sanctorum sancta revisat."

92 Ibid., 834–839: "nullum illic structile saxum, / sed cava per solidum multoque forata dolatu / gemma relucenti limen conplectitur arcu, / vestibulumque lapis penetrabile concipit unus. / portarum summis inscripta in postibus auro / nomina apostolici fulgent bis sena senatus," "No building stone is there, but a single gem, a block through which much hewing has pierced a single passage, frames the doorway with a shining arch, and a single stone forms the entrance-court. On top of the gates, written on the posts in gold, gleam the twelve names of the apostolic senate."

93 Like virtually all technical terms for the figures of rhetoric, *paronomasia* was more loosely and generally applied before the fifteenth- and sixteenth-century passion for classification broke the older categories into smaller and increasingly refined definitional units. Medieval *paronomasia* or *adnominatio* was play upon words of similar sound, not only upon those exactly alike. Plays upon words that were exactly alike in sound but different in meaning or function was called *traductio* by Geoffrey of Vinsauf (c. 1200). In some humanist rhetorics *traductio* became known as *paronomasia*, and what Geoffrey called *adnominatio* was called *antanaclasis*. There is no word in rhetoric treatises for visual coincidences. The best word of all for these phenomena, in my opinion, is English "pun," precisely because it is an inclusive and inexact category.

94 On the current state of opinion regarding the making and early provenance of the Saint-Sever Beatus see Klein, "Les sources non hispaniques et la genèse iconographique du Beatus de Saint-Sever" and J. Williams, "Le Beatus de Saint-Sever: état des questions." On the Facundus Beatus (Madrid, Biblioteca Nacional MS Vitrina 14–2), named for its scribe and dated to 1047, see Williams, *The Illustrated Beatus*, vol. 1, esp. pp. 53–55, 61–64. There are two basic shapes for the Heavenly City in medieval art, square and round. The Beatus tradition uses the square shape, which is also the shape of the city described by John, and of that described by Ezekiel. On the variations and possible sources of these two traditions, see the summarizing essay on apocalypse iconology by Klein, "The Apocalypse in Medieval Art," in R. Emmerson and B. McGinn, eds. *The Apocalypse in the Middle Ages*, pp. 159–199 (esp. the bibliography on p. 166, n. 11), and the catalogue of the exhibition *Immagini della Gerusalemme celeste*, edited by M. L. Gatti Perer.

95 Beatus lists his sources as Jerome, Augustine, Ambrose, Fulgentius, Gregory, Tyconius, Iraneus, Apringius, and Isidore in his *praefatio* 1(5) (ed. Sanders, pp. 1–2). On the way in which Prudentius' description of the virtues' temple merges with conventions about the Heavenly Jerusalem, see esp. Y. Christe, "La cité de la Sagesse."

96 O. K. Werckmeister, "The First Romanesque Beatus Manuscripts," p. 169.

97 The suggestion that some of the visual features of the Beatus commentary owed something to mnemotechnic was made by U. Eco, *Beato di Liébana*, pp. 36–37, but he thought the reason was principally to aid initial memorization of the text, not as a meditation tool. This seems to me unlikely; the pictures only would make sense to someone who already knew the literal text well. See also Werckmeister, "The First Romanesque Beatus Manuscripts," pp. 169–170.

98 A handsome facsimile of this book is available: *A Spanish Apocalypse*, with commentary by J. Williams and B. Shailor. On Maius' importance see both the introduction to this volume and Williams's comments in *The Illustrated Beatus*, vol. 1, pp. 75–93.

99 "Inter eius decus uerba mirifica storiarum que depinxi per seriem ut scientibus terreant iudicii futuri adventui peracturi saeculari" is the colophon on the last page (f. 293) of MS Morgan 644. J. Williams's translation of this colophon (for example, "Purpose and Imagery in the Apocalypse Commentary of Beatus of Liébana," p. 226) is somewhat freer with the Latin syntax than the one I have given.

100 See my discussion of this usage in *The Book of Memory*, pp. 224–226. A well-known eleventh-century image of a scribe (reproduced as Figure 8 of *The Book of Memory*), shows the person who was *pictor et illuminator* of the book writing it out under the legend "Hugo pictor." For this scribe, a *pictor* was engaged in writing, an *illuminator* in painting (and, like Maius, he evidently did both tasks).

101 See Williams, *The Illustrated Beatus*, vol. 1, pp. 77–78.

102 Williams, "Purpose and Imagery in the Apocalypse Commentary of Beatus of Liébana," p. 227; Werckmeister, "The First Romanesque Beatus Manuscripts," p. 169.

103 O. K. Werckmeister, "Pain and Death in the Beatus of Saint-Sever."

104 Werckmeister analyzed several other such singular departures in "Pain and Death in the Beatus of Saint-Sever"; the sixth-seal description I cite here is on pp. 595–596.

105 See F. Avril, "Quelques considérations sur l'exécution matérielle des enluminures de l'Apocalypse de Saint-Sever," p. 268.

106 On the profound influence of Gregory the Great's theology of contemplation upon Beatus see the comments of Werckmeister, "The First Romanesque Beatus Manuscripts," and the references there cited.

107 Curtius, *European Literature and the Latin Middle Ages*, p. 496. Curtius' appendix on etymology has a number of examples of *etymologia* from Carolingian and later poetry. My other quotation is taken from W. G. Ryan's translation of Jacobus de Voragine's *The Golden Legend*, vol. 1, p. xvii, citing the editor of Latin text, Th. Graesse.

108 Cicero, *Topica* 35; cf. Quintilian, *Inst. orat.* I.vi.28.

109 Cicero, *De oratore* II.358; cf. *Rhetorica ad Herennium* III.34.

110 Isidore of Seville, *Etymol.* I.29: "Etymologia est origo vocabulorum, cum vis verbi vel nominis per interpretationem colligitur. ... Nam dum videris unde ortum est nomen, citius vim eius intelligis. Omnis enim rei inspectio etymologia cognita planior est."

111 Ibid.: "Sunt autem etymologiae nominum aut ex causa datae, ut 'reges' a [regendo et] recte agendo, aut ex origine, ut 'homo,' quia sit ex humo, aut ex contrariis ut a lavando 'lutum,' dum lutum non sit mundum."

112 These principles are discussed in Aristotle's *De memoria et reminiscentia*: see Sorabji, trans., *Aristotle on Memory*, pp. 42–46, 96–102.

113 Cassiodorus, *Expositio Psalmorum*, Psalm 1:1 (CCSL 97, p. 30): "Etymologia est enim oratio breuis, per certas assonationes ostendens ex quo nomine id, quod quaeritur, uenerit nomen." Cassiodorus' definition in *Institutiones* II.i.2 is a grammatical one (and is taken from Donatus): "etymologia vero est aut verisimilis demonstratio, declarans ex qua origine verba descendant," "etymology is a true or likely demonstration [that] makes known from what origin words are descended." In this latter passage Cassiodorus is defining what one could call "philological etymology," that is the literal sort that grammarians and philologists deal with. This is different from rhetorical etymology, which, like other ornaments, serves inventive compositional purposes ("id quod quaeritur ... nomen") the sort of *etymologia* which Isidore defines, and which was widely practiced as a device for meditation.

114 There is a very long tradition of such word play in classical literature, imitated

with particular enthusiasm by Carolingian poets, though by no means confined to them. A good study of word play in classical Latin, focussing on Ovid, is Ahl, *Metaformations*. Modern readers have to learn to recognize this play; like Curtius, many literary scholars are made nervous by it, and want to confine literary scholarship to "real" (that is, philologically correct) puns. But a consideration of the name plays in Jacobus de Voragine, for example, should quickly dispel any idea that medieval authors and readers felt so constrained.

115 Murphy, *Rhetoric in the Middle Ages*, p. 73.

116 Isidore of Seville, *Etymol.* I.1: "Disciplina a discendo nomen accepit ... Aliter dicta disciplina, quia discitur plena." He also links *disciplina* to *dictum*.

117 Walahfrid Strabo, "Carmina Ad Agobardum Episcopum Lugdunensem," lines 17–32. Florus was probably master of the cathedral school in Lyon: see *DMA* s.v. *Florus of Lyons*. Strabo does not, heavy-handedly, state the obvious etymology, but these lines play (somewhat heavy-handedly) with it.

118 Cited by A. G. Rigg, *Anglo-Latin Literature*, p. 52. Rigg's book has a number of fine examples of etymologizing; see his excellent index for guidance.

119 This was also a compositional tool favored by a somewhat earlier thirteenth-century author, the Anglo-Norman poet Henry of Avranches, whom Rigg calls "the foremost Anglo-Latin poet of the century" (*Anglo-Latin Literature*, p. 179). Henry plays with the names of his patrons and characters: for example, "Roger" from *rosam geris* ("you bear a rose," i.e. the Virgin). See ibid., pp. 180–182. One of the best-known examples of late-twelfth-century *etymologia* is the beginning address of Geoffrey of Vinsauf to his patron, Pope Innocent III (*Poetria nova* 1–9).

120 Jacobus de Voragine, *The Golden Legend*, vol. 1, p. 45; the translation is that of W. G. Ryan, who used the 1850 edition of Graesse.

121 Jacobus de Voragine, *Legenda aurea* (transcribed from Bodleian MS Bodley 336, early 14th c., in W. Bryan and G. Dempster, *Sources and Analogues of Chaucer's Canterbury Tales*, p. 671): "Cecilia quasi celi lilia vel cecis via vel a celo et lya. Uel Cecilia quasi cecitate carens. Uel dicitur a celo et leos, quod est populus. Fuit enim celeste lilium per uirginitatis pudorem. Uel dicitur lilium quia habuit candorem mundicie, uirorem consciencie, odorem bone fame. Fuit enim cecis via per exempli informacionem, celum per iugem contemplacionem, lya per assiduam operacionem ... Fuit enim cecitate carens per sapiencie splendorem. Fuit et celum populi quia in ipsam tanquam in celum spirituale populus ad imitandum intuetur solem, lunam, et stellas, id est sapiencie perspicacitatem, fidei magnanimitatem, et uirtutum uarietatem." Etymologies of the Hebrew names in the Bible were available in Jerome's glossary of them; there *Leah* is interpreted as "worker," "Lia laboriosa" (CCSL 72, p. 68.7).

122 *The Golden Legend* was soon translated into all Western European vernacular languages; it remained greatly popular through the sixteenth century. It survives in over a thousand manuscripts.

123 Counseling the mnemonic value of puns to remember names predates the systematizing of Hellenistic education in the fourth century BC. It is a prominent feature of some general mnemotechnical advice given in the sophist text (c. 400) called *Dissoi logoi*. To remember words, that treatise says, one should connect them via homophonies to mental images; for example, to

remember the word *pyrilampes*, "glow-worm," one might connect it to a flaming torch, via *pyr*, "fire," and *lampein*, "shine."

124 Gregory the Great, *Moralia in Job* II.i and I.xxxiii; see *The Book of Memory*, pp. 164–169 and 179–183 esp.

125 F. Henry, *The Book of Kells*, pp. 157, 174–175; see also J. Alexander, *Insular Manuscripts*, p. 73.

126 Weitzmann, *Illustrations in Roll and Codex*, points out that in the Vienna Genesis, a "mirificous" book of the sixth century, the Genesis texts were excerpted and compressed in order to make room on the page for the pictures (pp. 89–93). This feature also suggests to me a book made for people who were already very familiar with the text, but were either teaching (through homilies and colloquies) or serving as lectors in a liturgical situation, where the need is not to memorize words for the first time, but to be reminded of familiar words from clues provided by the pictures and text summaries.

127 I discussed a number of common marginal motifs in Gothic books as being derived from traditional tropes for memory work in *The Book of Memory*, pp. 246–248.

128 See *The Book of Memory*, esp. pp. 204–205, 214–218, and also M. Camille, *Image on the Edge*. Early monastic books by contrast are dominated by large full-page paintings, set at the beginnings of major divisions in a work and at the beginning of the whole book. I have more to say about this in the next section of this chapter.

129 A number of art historians have written about the puns between written text and marginal decoration in books made between the thirteenth and fifteenth centuries. I have especially profited from the work of Lewis, "Beyond the Frame," C. R. Sherman, *Imaging Aristotle*, and Camille, *Image on the Edge*. A number of essays by L. Randall, most published after her seminal work *Images in the Margins of Gothic Manuscripts*, pioneered in observing such links: see perhaps esp. "Games and the Passion in Pucelle's Hours of Jeanne d'Evreux," "Humour and Fantasy in the Margins of an English Book of Hours," and "An Elephant in the Liturgy," which points out a pun based upon shape as well as on sound, for the bishop-piece in chess was first an elephant (*oliphant*, shortened to *aufin*) and then called a "bishop" in English because of the two horn-like projections in the way it was conventionally carved, which looked like a bishop's mitre.

130 L. Kendrick, "Les 'Bords' des Contes de Cantorbéry." On this cluster of Middle English puns, see MED s.v. *bordure, bordel* (1 and 2), *bourde, bourden* (1 and 2): each of these forms has a similar variety of spellings. These words all are also French: see Godefroy, *Dictionnaire*, s.v. *borde, bordel, behorder* (var. border, bourder, etc.), and *behordeis*, and also *The Anglo-Norman Dictionary*.

131 On the audience for this book, see J. Plummer's introduction to *The Hours of Catherine of Cleves*. L. Seidel, *Jan van Eyck's Arnolfini Portrait*, comments on some of the marginal puns in this book (pp. 85–91), especially one on *nasse*, meaning "(fishing) basket," referring to a common idiom for "entrapment" in marriage (the Book of Hours was for Catherine's marriage). This pun would not exclude, of course, another general pun, on "fishing" as a common metaphor for meditative memory work, as in the usage, for example, of Romuald of Camaldoli (see Chapter Two, section 16, above). These very different associations are part

of what Seidel calls "the play among the images" in this book (p. 85). On the value of homophony in *memoria*, according to John of Garland (ca. 1230), see *The Book of Memory*, p. 125. Davlin, *A Game of Heuene*, demonstrates a number of multilingual puns in English, Latin, and French, in *Piers Plowman*.

132 Varro, *De lingua latina* VII. 64; cf. *MED* s.v. *limax* (plural *limacez*), and the citation there from John of Trevisa (c. 1398). Two essays which make interesting suggestions, far more learned about snail images than mine but not involving this pun, are L. Randall, "The Snail in Gothic Marginal Warfare" and H. Ettlinger, "The Virgin Snail." As Randall notes, the word *limaçon* had a metaphorically extended meaning that referred to a kind of fighting manoeuver: see Godefroy, *Dictionnaire*, s.v. *limaçon* and *OED* s.v. *limaçon*.

133 This book was an English production made about 1260, for the Anglo-Norman de Lacy family, among the earliest of all Gothic manuscripts to have so much marginal ornament. See N. Morgan, *Early Gothic Manuscripts*, no. 112, and L. F. Sandler, "Marginal Illustration in the Rutland Psalter."

134 See *MED* s.v. *lim*, and Godefroy, *Dictionnaire*, s.v. *limbes*. The English word did not acquire its *b* until at least the sixteenth century, probably influenced by the French spelling; cf. *OED* s.v. *limb*.

135 Another pun based in these dismembered limbs suggests itself, having to do specifically with the memory work of reading. It involves the Anglo-Norman and Middle English words *membre*, "member" (a synonym of "limb"), and *(re)membrer*, "to re-member": see *MED* and Godefroy, *Dictionnaire*, both s.v. *membre, membrer*. K. Duys, "Early Literary Literacy in the *Miracles de Nostre Dame* of Gautier de Coincy," has discussed how this pun was elaborately played with in one of Gautier's verse legends, composed between 1215 and 1233, which became immediately popular in England as well as France.

136 I discussed the intricate interplay of remembered texts, familiarized and "domesticated" by one's own memory, for the formation of one's ethical character in *The Book of Memory*, Chapter Five.

137 P. Fredriksen characterizes early Christian exegesis of many Scriptural numbers as instances of the rhetorical figure of synecdoche. The number "1000," for example, was understood to stand for "a great many" and was not to be taken at face value. She has argued that such a rhetorical reading of many of the numbers in Revelation was an important basis of Tyconius' influential "spiritual" exegesis of this book, against literal-minded millenarians and apocalypticists. See "Tyconius and Augustine on the Apocalypse."

138 I discussed this incident in Chapter One, section 12, above.

139 F. Kermode, *The Genesis of Secrecy*, p. 3.

140 Fredriksen, "Tyconius and Augustine on the Apocalypse," p. 26.

141 Gregory the Great, *Expositio in Canticum canticorum* par. 2 (CCSL 143A, p. 3.14): "Allegoria enim animae longe a deo positae quasi quandam machinam facit, ut per illam leuetur ad deum."

142 Jerome, *Commentarii in Hiezechielem* III.9.4–6.525–27 (CCSL 75, p. 106): "extrema 'tau' littera crucis habet similitudinem, quae christianorum frontibus pingitur, et frequenti manus inscriptione signatur," "the last letter, tau, bears a likeness to the cross, which is painted on the foreheads of Christians, and is signed commonly with a gesture of the hand."

143 Guillaumont, "Une inscription copte." It has been suggested that the Torah-niche painted on the wall of the third-century synagogue at Dura-Europos served as an orienting marker for the mural series painted there: see C. Kraeling, *The Synagogue*, p. 54.

144 J. Backhouse, *The Lindisfarne Gospels*. There is dispute among art historians about whether Eadfrith himself wrote and painted the book, though the evidence is that it was the work of one scribe, and early accounts say that he did; see the discussion and bibliography of "The Lindisfarne Gospels" in Alexander, *Insular Manuscripts*. The earliest extant example of a cross-carpet page is in "The Book of Durrow," made somewhat earlier than the Lindisfarne Gospels. On the various sources of the ornamental motifs and the overall pattern, see the works cited in Alexander's bibliography for "The Book of Durrow."

145 See B. Raw, "Biblical literature: the New Testament," p. 240. On the Crucifixion trope in Anglo-Saxon culture more generally, see also B. Raw, *Anglo-Saxon Crucifixion Iconography*. The edition I have used of the poem is that in B. Mitchell and F. Robinson, *A Guide to Old English*, which also contains a summary account of its possible compositional circumstances and sources.

4. DREAM VISION, PICTURE, AND "THE MYSTERY OF THE BED CHAMBER"

1 Latin *visio* refers both to physical and mental seeing: cf. the examples given in *OLD*, s.v. *visio*.

2 See above, Chapter Three, section 4; particularly relevant are Quintilian, *Inst. orat.* VIII.iii and X.vii (in the latter passage, he describes using *phantasiai* for composition). Quintilian uses *enargeia* to mean vivid description that sets something as though before the eyes, where Aristotle used *energeia* to discuss a similar rhetorical objective (*Rhetoric* 3.11; 1411b–1412a). Aristotle does not use the word *enargeia* at all, though it is used by other ancient Greek rhetoricians. The words come from distinct Greek roots, one associated with making visible and seeing, the other with being active, energetic. But at least from Roman rhetoric onward, they were conflated, until Renaissance humanist rhetoricians anachronistically separated them and distinguished them from one another. A good general account of the terms is in R. Lanham, *A Handlist of Rhetorical Terms*, s.v. *enargia* and *energia*; see also the discussion of the two words in K. Eden, *Poetic and Legal Fiction in the Aristotelian Tradition*, pp. 71–75, and R. Moran, "Artifice and Persuasion." In a medieval context, I emphasize, the concepts were fused, and identified (as they were in Quintilian) with the heuristic making of vivid *cognitive* images through description and other means.

3 Augustine, *De Genesi ad litteram* XII.xxvi.53 (CSEL 28, pp. 418–419). The only instance of true *theoria* in Biblical visions which Augustine acknowledges is Paul's *raptus* to the third heaven.

4 Ibid., XII.xiv.29–30. On Augustine's understanding of the nature of prophecy see esp. Markus, *Saeculum*, appendix A: my quotation is from p. 194. As J. Lindblom reminds us, "*pro* in the Greek term *prophetes* does not mean 'before' but 'forth' " (*Prophecy in Ancient Israel*, p. 1, and see his extensive bibliography). This understanding of a prophet's role, based on the textual

examples of Jeremiah, Isaiah, Ezekiel, and others, informs the understanding of some Carolingian visionaries, as P. E. Dutton explains in his discussion of the ninth-century poet Audradus: *The Politics of Dreaming in the Carolingian Empire*, pp. 114– 156, esp. 138–140. Despite this strong tradition in medieval understanding of the prophet's role, however, one must also keep in mind a much narrower but common definition, articulated in Isidore's *Etymologiae* VII.8, which linked *prophetae* with "one who foretells the future truthfully," and distinguished the role of prophet (which by its nature ended with the coming of Christ) from any available in the Church militant.

5 Boethius, *Philosophiae consolatio* I, prosa 1.1–3, 26–30: "Haec dum mecum tacitus ipse reputarem querimoniamque lacrimabilem stili officio signarem, adstitisse mihi supra uerticem uisa est mulier... Quae ubi poeticas Musas uidit nostro adsistentes toro fletibusque meis uerba dictantes, commota paulisper ac toruis inflammata luminibus: 'Quis,' inquit, 'has scenicas meretriculas ad hunc aegrum permisit accedere ...'" The translation is my own, though I have consulted the translations both of "I.T." for the LCL, and of R. Green.

6 I discussed at length the different functions of silent reading and reading aloud in antiquity, and described the vocabulary of the different stages of composing in *The Book of Memory*; see pp. 170–174 and 194–220.

7 Conventions throughout the Middle Ages are ambivalent about whether dreamers should be shown with eyes open or closed. Augustine thinks either condition is possible in "spiritual" visions, which can occur with eyes open or or closed as in deep sleep (cf. *De Genesi ad litteram* XII, xii.25 and xxvi.53). A good motif to consider in this regard is the common "Tree of Jesse" genealogy, often shown as a tree springing from the loins of a visionary Jesse; sometimes his eyes are open, sometimes they are closed. There is so much variation that I am not sure modern scholars can draw any firm conclusions about the state of mind of represented figures from the position of their eyes alone.

8 Quintilian, *Inst. orat.* X.iii.15; see *The Book of Memory*, pp. 196–197.

9 Common ancient and medieval etymology understood the concept of *theater*, like *theory*, to be derived from the act of seeing; cf. Isidore, *Etymol* XV.ii.34–35.

10 The iconography of *The Consolation of Philosophy* has been presented by P. Courcelle, *La Consolation de Philosophie dans la tradition littéraire*; see esp. plates 49, 56–57, 59.

11 These accounts are given in *The Book of Memory*, pp. 199–202.

12 Daniel is a late work, of course, and heavily influenced by Hellenistic traditions. For Ezekiel's visionary postures, which (along with those of Daniel) were particularly imitated in monastic literature, see especially Ezekiel 1:28–2:2; 3:26; and 43: 3–6, 10–11. In addition to Daniel 7:1, see also Daniel 8:17–18, 27; and 10:8–10. There are medieval works on prayer (mostly from the later centuries) that discuss appropriate prayer postures: one of the most interesting is by Peter the Chanter (twelfth century), translated by R. Trextler as *The Christian at Prayer*. On prayer postures more generally, see J.-C. Schmitt, *La raison des gestes*, pp. 289–320. See also the discussion of the gendering rhetoric often associated with these postures in M. Moore, "Assumptions of Gender."

13 On the iconography of this scene in paintings from the late Middle Ages, see the various studies of J. and P. Courcelle, *Iconographie de saint Augustin*. See also

Stock (*Augustine the Reader*, pp. 102–111), who shows some of the literary patterns, the memorative, rhetorical *translatio*, richly and complexly involved in this scene. Even the apparently "supernatural" element of the child's voice echoes literary antecedents.

14 Bernard of Clairvaux, *Super Cantica sermo* 23. IV.10 (*SBO* I, p. 145.19–20), refers to "secretum illud cubiculi, quod suae illi columbae, formosae, perfectae, uni, unicum sponsus servat," "that secret of the bedchamber, which the Bridegroom reserves solely for her who is his dove, beautiful, perfect and unique." Translated by K. Walsh, vol. 2, p. 35.

15 See *The Book of Memory*, pp. 195–200, and the sources noted there.

16 Bernard of Clairvaux, *Super Cantica sermo* 23. IV.11 (*SBO* I, pp. 145–146): "Est locus iste altus et secretus, sed minime quietus … et contemplantem, qui forte eo loci pervenerit, quiescere non permittit; sed mirabiliter, quamvis delectabiliter, rimantem et admirantem fatigat, redditque inquietum. Pulchre utrumque in consequentibus sponsa exprimit … ubi et se dormire, et cor suum vigilare fatetur" (my translation, after consulting that of K. Walsh). Notice the emphasis on place, *locus*.

17 Cicero, *De oratore* III.v.17: "Ut igitur ante meridiem discesserunt paululumque requierunt, in primis hoc a se Cotta animadversum esse dicebat, omne illud tempus meridianum Crassum in acerrima atque attentissima cogitatione posuisse, seseque, qui vultum eius cum ei dicendum esset obtutumque oculorum in cognitando probe nosset atque in maximis causis saepe vidissset, tum dedita opera quiescentibus aliis in eam exhedram venisse in qua Crassus lectulo posito recubisset, cumque eum in cogitatione defixum esse sensisset, statim recessisse, atque in eo silentio duas horas fere esse consumptas." Translated by H. Rackham, LCL.

18 E. Leach has a fascinating study of the literary-mnemotechnic connections of Roman domestic mural painting: *The Rhetoric of Space*, esp. pp. 73–143. In a recent essay, B. Bergmann has discussed a detailed reconstruction of the murals in the "House of the Tragic Poet" at Pompeii in terms of the architectural mnemonic described in the *Rhetorica ad Herennium*: "The Roman House as Memory Theater." Bergmann emphasizes how a viewer would move through the main rooms of such a house, making his own associations with various murals. What she describes is a fine instance of rhetorical *ductus* at work in a meditative and processional visual experience (though Bergmann does not employ this concept).

19 On this villa see M. Anderson, *Pompeian Frescoes in the Metropolitan Museum of Art*.

20 This, as I said previously, is the source of the pun in *florilegium*, which is literally a plucking and gathering of reading-flowers. This figure was a great favorite in monastic discussions of reading. "Gathering," *colligere*, from *con* + *legere*, is Hugh of St. Victor's word of choice for "recollection". An early-thirteenth-century professor and author of a manual of rhetoric and poetic theory, John of Garland, used what he apparently thought was a sort of philological relative, *alligare*, for compositional invention. See *The Book of Memory*, pp. 83–85, 124, 174–178.

21 Anderson, *Pompeian Frescoes in the Metropolitan Museum of Art*, p. 16; the Metropolitan Museum's mural from the exedra is shown in Plate 43 of this book

(most of this exedra's murals are in the Musée Royal et Domaine de Mariemont, Morlanwelz, Belgium).

22 See Zinn, "Mandala Symbolism," for a good general description of how a mandala works, specifically in relation to contemplation. This essay is essential for anyone interested in the cognitive aspects of meditative orthopraxis.

23 It is this characteristic that distinguishes mnemotechnic from semiology. The association of image and cued memory may (and usually does) *acquire* meanings, and these meanings may (and often do) become conventional in a culture: but there is no inherent "content" to a memory image. On this point see the astute comments of Bolzoni, *La stanza della memoria*, pp. 90–102.

24 Quintilian, *Inst. orat.* X.iii.15: "resupini spectantesque tectum et cogitationem murmure agitantes expectaverimus quid obveniat": translated by H. E. Butler, LCL. Quintilian does not approve of such desperation, as he makes clear.

25 Ibid., X.iii.26–27; cf. Martianus Capella, *De nuptiis* V.539, cited in *The Book of Memory*, p. 331, note 67.

26 Anselm, *Proslogion* I (ed. Schmitt, BAC I, p. 360): "Eia nunc, homuncio ... *Intra in cubiculum* mentis tuae"; the immediate reference of the last phrase is to the *cubiculum* of the Song of Songs. Translated by B. Ward.

27 Quintilian, *Inst. orat.* X.iii gives a lengthy description of some of these gestures and postures, also the suitable times of day. In particular, he discusses the need to find a private retreat for creative thought, if not in fact, then by learning how to "retreat" as though to a small room in your mind.

28 Paulinus of Nola, Epistle 32.12 (written to Sulpicius Severus in 403; ed. Goldschmidt, p. 40): "Cubicula intra porticus quaterna longis basilicae lateribus inserta secretis orantium uel in lege domini meditantium, praeterea memoriis religiosorum ac familiarium accommodatos ad pacis aeternae requiem locos praebent. Omne cubiculum binis per liminum frontes uersibus praenotatur." Translated by Goldschmidt. The translated text was reprinted in C. Davis-Weyer, *Early Medieval Art*, pp. 20–23.

29 On the politics of the *Visio Wetti*, see Dutton, *The Politics of Dreaming in the Carolingian Empire*, pp. 63–67. Dutton argues that this famous dream was a calculated part of a clerical campaign to discredit the legitimacy of Charlemagne's heirs after his death, other than the claim of the "right" emperor, Louis the Pious. Walahfrid Strabo's verse redaction of Wetti's dream specifically names the late emperor as a fornicator. During the description of the figure of the emperor in the hell of the lecherous, his genitals being constantly eaten by a fierce animal, the initial letters of the lines spell out (in the fashion of anagram poems) "CAROLUS IMPERATOR" (Walahfrid Strabo, *Visio Wettini*, 446–461). The names of other sinners are similarly indicated, but the series climaxes with the emperor's fate.

30 A. Gurevich, *Medieval Popular Culture*, has argued that features of these visions represent a merging of Latin and non-Latin traditions ("popular" in his definition). I accept this as a general observation, but take exception to one of his instances of a "popular" trope. He suggests that the characteristic topography of the otherworld was a "popular" feature (i.e. non-Latin): "the Other World of visions is a conglomerate of uncoordinated points ... connected only by the path along which the angel leads the travelling soul" (p. 132). This characteristic is consistent, however, with the Latin monastic notion of a composition as a "way"

or route among places. In trying to sift out the "popular" strands of Carolingian literary culture (and the same may be observed of Anglo-Saxon literary culture), it may be well to keep in mind Dutton's sobering comment that none of these works were "the product of the humble or the unknown" (p. 256), whatever conventional tropes of humility and modesty they may employ.

31 Heito, *Visio Wettini* II (ed. Duemmler, p. 268): "Membris ergo in lectulo conpositis, oculis tantummodo clausis et necdum in somnum." Recall that Crassus, in Cicero's account, lay with a "fixed stare," and that Boethius does not tell us whether his eyes were open or shut. As I commented earlier, one cannot determine from the posture alone whether a figure is portrayed as sleeping or as concentrating in mental seeing.

32 See ibid., III.

33 See *The Book of Memory*, pp. 194–196. A similar sequence of stages is described in the author's "declaration" prefacing Hildegard of Bingen's *Scivias* (twelfth century). Hildegard received her visions (she is at pains to claim) while she was not asleep but awake and seeing with a pure mind. She then became sick and took to her bed, a point she also stresses carefully – having refused for a period of time to write down what she had seen. Then, while still ill in bed, she says, she wrote her visions down and completed the composition, with the help of a monk and a nun, over a period of ten years. Hildegard's visions take the form of painted pictures as well as of verbal descriptions; each is followed by her commentary, thus using a lay-out not unlike the Beatus commentary. One needs to be careful in assessing accounts of composition, like this one of Hildegard, for evidence of an author's "illiteracy," because the *dictamen* was a stage intended to be corrected, often extensively, often with the help of other readers, before the final copying out of the work. On Hildegard as author see the comments of A. Derolez, "The Genesis of Hildegard of Bingen's 'Liber divinorum operum.'"

34 Heito, *Visio Wettini* IV (ed. Duemmler, p. 269): "In ipsa ergo inmensitate timoris anxius proruit in terram ... distenso omni corpore in crucis modum postulavit." These details are also in Walahfrid Strabo's poem.

35 Two classic literary accounts of the "way" to *raptus* are Augustine's conversation with his mother, Monica (*Confessiones* IX.10) and the end of Dante's *Paradiso*. In each case, the way is *through* the work of memory to the point where memory fails and pure *raptus* is achieved.

36 Heito, *Visio Wettini* IV (ed. Duemmler, p. 269): "His ergo finitis surrexit et resedit in lectulo, postulans Dialogum beati Gregori sibi legi. Principia ergo ultimi libri euisdem Dialogi audiente eo lecta sunt usque ad consummationem novem aut decem foliorum," "These [chanted psalms] being finished, he rose and sat down again on his bed, asking that the Dialogues of blessed Gregory be read to him. As he listened, the first parts of the last book were read to him up to the end of the ninth or tenth folio."

37 Ibid., V (ed. Duemmler, p. 269): "angelus ... laudavit confugium eius, quod ad deum in angustiis positus tam studio psalmodiae quam lectionis fecerat, hortans eum de cetero sine defectu similiter acturum. Inter ceteros etiam psalmum centesimum octavum decimum, quia moralis in eo virtus describitur, saepe repetendum ammonuit," "the angel ... praised his [means of] refuge [from distress] that in his anguish he gave his full attention as much to chanting the

psalms as to his readings, urging him that he should perform the rest without error in a similar manner. Among the others he especially recommended for frequent repetition Psalm 118, for it describes the power of moral living." The influence of the meditational way described in John Cassian's tenth Conference is evident here.

38 See the comments of H. Patch, *The Other World* (though he makes less of his observation than one might want), and the comments of A. Gurevich, cited in note 30 above.

39 A reconstructed facsimile was prepared by R. Green *et al.*: *Hortus deliciarum*.

40 Williams, *The Illustrated Beatus*, vol. 1, pp. 140–141. Williams considers that there was nothing unusual about Cistercians having illustrated Beatus manuscripts in their libraries: as he says, "[i]t is testimony to the fact that the illustrated Commentary functioned, as was probably always the case, as an integral part of monastic spirituality. It was a tradition which was to expire only with the decline of the institution of monasticism itself" (p. 141).

41 Heito, *Visio Wettini* XXVIII (ed. Duemmler, p. 274): "Timeo enim, ne lingua torpente visa et audita nequeant propalari, quia cum tanto mihi obligationis damno in publicum producenda iniuncta sunt, ut reatu silentii huius sine venia feriri timeam, si meo silentio ita depereant, ut per me publicata non pateant." For my translations from the Latin text, I have consulted E. Gardiner's version in *Visions of Heaven and Hell Before Dante*.

42 Smalley, *The Study of the Bible in the Middle Ages*, pp. 83– 111; the quotation is from p. 97. I discuss these issues more fully, in relation to a distinction between *pictura* and *littera* in the exegesis of Adam of Dryburgh, in Chapter Five, sections 5 and 7.

43 Gregory the Great, *Dialogues* II.25.1–19: "Quidam autem eius monachus mobili-tati mentem dederat et permanere in monasterio nolebat. Cumque eum uir Dei adsidue corriperet, frequenter admoneret, ipse uero nullo modo consentiret in congrrgatione persistere atque inportunis precibus ut relaxaretur inmineret, quadam die isdem uenerabilis pater, nimietatis eius taedio affectus, iratus iussit ut discederet. Qui mox ut monasterium exiit, contra se adsistere aperto ore draconem in itinere inuenit. Cumque eum isdem draco qui apparuerat deuorare uellet, coepit ipse tremens et palpitans magnis uocibus clamare, dicens: 'Currite, currite, quia draco iste me deuorare uult.' Currentes autem fratres draconem minime uiderunt, sed trementem atque palpitantem monachum ad monasterium reduxerunt. Qui statim promisit numquam se esse iam a monasterio recessurum, atque ex hora eadem in sua promissione permansit, quippe qui sancti uiri orationibus contra se adsistere draconem uiderat, quem prius non uidendo sequebatur." The translation is my own, though I consulted those of both P. Antin (in French, for the SC) and O. J. Zimmermann for the FC.

44 Klein, "The Apocalypse in Medieval Art," pp. 175–177.

45 *Figment* is derived from Latin *fingere*, "to make up, fashion, create"; see *OED* s.v. *figment*.

46 This idea may have been facilitated and corroborated by the widely held ancient and early-medieval concept of the "extromission" of sight, that when we see something, a ray from the eye reaches out to the object being perceived and, like hands grasping, pulls in its image, which is then processed by the "common

sense," the "image- forming power," and finally "impressed" in memory, as a seal is stamped into wax. But I would caution that a belief in an impression theory of thinking is not absolutely related to extromission beliefs: a notable example is Aristotle, who did hold that mental images are impressed corporeally, but did not hold an extromission theory of sight. The importance of extromission theories (there are more than one) in various aspects of medieval visual culture, including literary accounts, is explored in several essays in a forthcoming collection of essays edited by Robert S. Nelson, *Seeing as Others Saw*, especially M. Camille, "Before the Gaze: the Internal Senses and Late-Medieval Visuality," and G. Frank, "The Pilgrim's Gaze in the Age before Icons." A useful review of early Western theories of how the eye sees, both extromission and intromission models, is Lindberg, *Theories of Vision*.

47 Gregory the Great, *Dialogues* II.4.14–32: "[E]t constituta hora, expleta psalmodio, sese fratres in orationem dedissent, aspexit quod eundem monachum, qui manere in oratione non poterat, quidam niger puerulus per uestimenti fimbriam foras trahebat. Tunc eidem patri monasterii Pompeiano nomine et Mauro Dei famulo secreto dixit: 'Numquid non aspicitis quis est qui istum monachum foras trahit?' Qui respondentes dixerunt: 'Non.' Quibus ait: 'Oremus, ut uos etiam uideatis quem iste monachus sequitur.' Cumque per biduum esset oratum, Maurus monachus uidit, Pompeianus autem euisdem monasterii pater uidere non potuit. Die igitur alia, expleta oratione, uir Dei, oratorium egressus, stantem foris monachum repperit, quem pro caecitate cordis sui uirga percussit. Qui ex illo die nihil persuasionis ulterius a nigro iam puerulo pertulit, sed ad orationis studium inmobilis permansit, sicque antiquus hostis dominari non ausus est in eius cogitatione, ac si ipse percussus fuisset ex uerbere." Maurus is Benedict's beloved disciple in Gregory's "Life," cast in a John-like role.

48 *The Life of St. Anthony*, 6; this text was so well known that Gregory does not bother even to suggest that the "niger puerulus" has a literary source. This, as we have seen in other cases, is a common rhetorical habit with regard to particularly well-known materials, alluding to without directly "footnoting" an obvious source. I suppose it might be classified as a sort of *enigma*.

49 The two best-known examples were the dream of Er in Plato's *Republic* and Scipio's Dream in Cicero's *De re publica*, best known to the later Middle Ages from the commentary by Macrobius. On the trope see W. Stahl's introduction to his translation of Macrobius' commentary, and Jacob, *La description de la terre habitée de Denys d'Alexandrie*, pp. 23–35. Jacob also discusses this motif in "Lieux de la carte."

50 Gregory the Great, *Dialogues* II.35.10–19: "Cum uero hora iam quietis exigeret, in cuius turris superioribus se uenerabilis Benedictus, in eius quoque inferioribus se Seruandus diaconus conlocauit, quo uidelicet in loco inferiora superioribus peruius continuabat ascensus. Ante eandem uero turrem largius erat habitaculum, in quo utriusque discipuli quiescebant. Cumque uir Domini Benedictus, adhuc quiescentibus fratribus, instans uigiliis, nocturnae orationis tempora praeuenisset . . .' [the rest of this Latin sentence is quoted in the next note].

51 Ibid., 19–26: "ad fenestram stans et omnipotentem Dominum deprecans subito intempesta noctis hora respiciens, uidit fusam lucem desuper cunctas noctis tenebras exfugasse, tantoque splendore clarescere, ut diem uinceret lux illa, quae

inter tenebras radiasset. Mira autem ualde res in hac speculatione secuta est, quia, sicut post ipse narrauit, omnis etiam mundus, uelut sub uno solis radio collectus, ante oculos eius adductus est."

52 This motif returns in final form when two monks have a vision after the saint's death of a richly decorated road leading to Heaven straight from the monastery, and an angel standing upon it tells them that this is the road taken by Benedict (Chapter 37).

53 Gregory the Great, *Dialogues* II.35.7.65–7: "Quod autem collectus mundus ante eius oculos dicitur, non caelum et terra contracta est, sed uidentis animus dilatatus"; [Gregory explains to Peter] "when the world is said to be gathered up before his eyes, it does not mean that heaven and earth are shrunk in size but that the soul of the one seeing is dilated." Peter, as literal-minded as ever, has inquired how the whole world could become so small that one person could see it all.

54 The *visio Dei* as the world gathered up *breviter* in a single concentrated object or light became a major trope in monastic spirituality. And it finds one of its masterful expressions in the divine vision at the end of Dante's *Paradiso*, in which the single light and the world gathered up as one volume (*collectus*) are merged in a *mira res*. On the changing visuality of the divine vision in the Middle Ages see C. Hahn, "*Visio Dei*: Changes in Medieval Visuality."

55 Gregory the Great, *Dialogues* II. 22.14–31: "Nocte uero eadem, qua promissus inluscescebat dies … uir Domini in somnis apparuit, et loca singula, ubi quid aedificari debuisset, subtiliter designauit. Cumque utrique a somno surgerent, sibi inuicem quod uiderant retulerant. Non tamen uisioni illi omnimodo fidem dantes, uirum Dei, sicut se uenire promiserat, expectabant. Cumque uir Dei constituto die minime uenisset, ad eum cum moerore reuersi sunt, dicentes: 'Expectauimus, pater, ut ueniras, sicut promiseras, et nobis ostenderes, ubi quid aedificare deberemus, et non uenisti.' Quibus ipse ait: 'Quare, fratres, quare ista dicitis? Numquid, sicut promisi, non ueni?' Cui cum ipsi dicerent: 'Quando uenisti?,' respondit: 'Numquid utrisque uobis dormientibus non apparui et loca singula designaui? Ite, et sicut per uisionem audistis, omne habitaculum monasterii ita construite.'"

56 These categories as I have just used them are part of a hierarchical set which attempts to define the truth content of dreams (*visio* having the greatest and *somnium* the least); used in this way, they derive from Macrobius' commentary on Cicero's "Dream of Scipio." They acquired authority in the later Middle Ages because of the role played by this commentary in scholastic curriculum. They do not seem to have been paid much attention in these monastic visions, however. On the development of these categories see S. Kruger, *Dreaming in the Middle Ages*.

57 Gregory the Great, *Dialogues* II. 22.34–6: "Doceri uelim, quo fieri ordine potuit, ut longe iret, responsum dormientibus diceret, quod ipsi per uisionem audirent et recognoscerent."

58 Ibid., 43–46: "Si igitur tam longe Abacuc potuit sub momento corporaliter ire et prandium deferre, quid mirum si Benedictus pater obtinuit, quatenus iret per spiritum et fratrum quiescentium spiritibus necessaria narret." The passage in Daniel is not in the Protestant Bible, but it was in the Old Latin and Vulgate Bibles.

59 Gregory's answer has set Peter a puzzle – as he acknowledges when he replies "Manus tuae locutionis tersit a me, fateor, dubietatem mentis," "[t]he hand of your speech has cleansed me, I declare, from the doubt in my mind" (*Dialogues* II. 22.49–50). The odd, though not unprecedented, image of "the hand of your speech" is immediately derived from the action of washing denoted in the verb *tergeo* (past tense "tersit"), the root of modern English *detergent*. I also think, however, that the general pedagogical setting of the dialogue has encouraged Gregory to "break out" (as it were) the image latent in "tersit," associating the "hand" both with the chastising hand of the teacher (for Gregory's speech is a rebuke to Peter) and with mnemotechnical instrumentality, one of the hand's commonest assignments since Peter's task is to recollect. This is a fine instance of a basic inventional procedure, "breaking up" a word via recollective associational chains in order cognitively to dilate it, thus to discover its hidden associations.

60 Virgil, *Aeneid* I.454–460, 464: "dum, quae fortuna sit urbi, / artificumque manus inter se operumque laborem / miratur, videt Iliacas ex ordine pugnas / bellaque iam fama totum vulgata per orbem, / Atridas Priamumque et saevum ambobus Achillem. / constitit et lacrimans, "quis iam locus," inquit, "Acate, / quae regio in terris nostri non plena laboris?" ... sic ait, atque animum pictura pascit inani / multa gemens"; my translation, consulting that of H. Fairclough for LCL. At least one sixteenth-century author, Giovan Battista Della Porta, understood this scene to be Aeneas' memory theatre: see Yates, *The Art of Memory*, p. 203, and esp. Bolzoni, *La stanza della memoria*, pp. 196–197.

61 Plutarch attributes this maxim to Simonides in his oration "On the Fame of the Athenians" (also called "The Glories of Athens"), 346F–347A (LCL, *Plutarch's Moralia*, vol. 4, pp. 500–501; trans. F. C. Babbitt). Though Plutarch quotes a few maxims of Simonides frequently, he does not mention his connection with an art of memory; that story is found for the first time in the *Rhetorica ad Herennium*, though it is retold often enough after that.

62 Discussed by E. Keuls, "Rhetoric and Visual Aids in Greece and Rome." See also Leach, *The Rhetoric of Space*, pp. 86–89, on a "cartographic" picture described by the Stoic speaker to summarize and orient the themes in Cicero's *De natura deorum* II.38–40.

63 *The Book of Memory*, pp. 230–231. These "picturae" were first described and transcribed by B. Smalley, *English Friars and Antiquity*, pp. 165–183; they occur in Bodleian Library (Oxford) MS Bodley 722.

64 Prudentius, *Peristephanon*, IX.7–16: "Dum lacrimans mecum reputo mea uulnera et omnes / uitae labores ac dolorum acumina, / erexi ad caelum faciem, stetit obuia contra / fucis colorum picta imago martyris / plagas mile gerens, totos lacerata per artus, / ruptam minutis praeferens punctis cutem. / Innumeri circum pueri (miserabile uisu) / confossa paruis membra figebant stilis, / unde pugillares soliti percurrere ceras / scholare murmur adnotantes scripserant." Translated by Roberts, *Poetry and the Cult of the Martyrs*, p. 134, slightly altered by me as indicated. Roberts discusses Prudentius' account of St. Cassian, especially this passage, on pp. 132–148; to his analysis I have little to add, except to observe that this description is an early example of the trope, important in later monastic spirituality, of punctured skin as an incised, "punctuated" writing surface. The *murmur* of the scholars writing on their wax tablets is also that of meditational

murmur as one mentally wrote upon the wax of one's memory, an association that I doubt would be lost on Prudentius' audiences. Roberts summarizes the evidence that Prudentius saw a material picture (p. 138), though I remain skeptical, for reasons apparent in my argument so far. Hahn discusses the illustrations to this story in a Prudentius manuscript of c. 900 in "Picturing the Text."

65 Keuls, "Rhetoric and Visual Aids," p. 128. The influence of Stoic philosophy on the visual needs of human thought is examined by J. Onians, *Art and Thought in the Hellenistic Period*, esp. pp. 88–94 and 115–118, and C. Imbert, "Stoic Logic and Alexandrian Poetics." Onians is skeptical about the extent of Stoic influence, crediting Aristotle with more influence than the Stoics on reaffirming "the visual nature of thought" (p. 116). A strong Epicurean (as well as Stoic) influence on Eastern monastic meditational practice is claimed by Rabbow, *Seelenführung*, esp. pp. 127–130. See also M. Colish, "The Stoic Theory of Verbal Significance."

66 These categories are found in Aristotle's *De memoria et reminiscentia*; see Sorabji, *Aristotle on Memory*, and see also *The Book of Memory*, pp. 62–63.

67 P. Harvey, *Medieval Maps*, p. 19. In Latin, the word *mappa* refers to various sorts of cloth coverings like napkins; what we call a map was referred to "using some word meaning either a diagram or a picture" (ibid., p. 7). The Tabernacle plan also functions as a kind of "map": see my discussion in Chapter Five, section 5, and further references there.

68 Isidore of Seville, *Etymol.* XIX.xvi.1–2: "Pictura autem est imago exprimens speciem rei alicuius, quae dum visa fuerit ad recordationem mentem reducit. Pictura autem dicta quasi fictura; est enim imago ficta, non veritas. Hinc et fucata, id est ficto quodam colore inlita, nihil fidei et veritatis habentia," "A picture is an image expressing the semblance of some matter, which when it may be looked upon brings [the matter] back to our mind's recollection. A picture also is [so] called as though for making; it is therefore a fictive image, not realistic. Hence also is it painted, that is suffused with a certain made-up color, having no [qualities] of fidelity or truthfulness [to nature]." This definition certainly supported the commonly held view that pictures were not realistic, and thus should not be taken literally; but by that same token it entirely accepted their utility as fictions for inventive thought.

69 On the particular memorability of red, used also for the orienting rubrics for major divisions of literary works, see *The Book of Memory*, esp. the quote from Andrew of St. Victor, pp. 8–9, and pp. 92–94.

70 Onians comments that second-century Rome "was becoming increasingly like a labyrinth of colonnades" (*Bearers of Meaning*, p. 53). S. Bonner, discussing the use of visual aids in early education, notes that a schoolboy "had only to walk around the city to bring his studies to life" (*Education in Ancient Rome*, p. 130).

71 Bonner summarizes some of the suggestions modern scholars have made: *Education in Ancient Rome*, pp. 129–130, and the bibliography cited in his notes. See also Keuls, "Rhetoric and Visual Aids in Greece and Rome," and R. Brilliant, *Visual Narratives*, pp. 53–58. If medieval experience has any relevance, such an organization of *scaenae* would have been most useful not to children first learning the words of the poem, but to teachers and commenters upon it, for whom the images acted as prompts.

72 Of course one doesn't have to start with a center-based schema: I described several other types in *The Book of Memory*. One highly successful set of mnemotechnical *picturae* is in the Utrecht Psalter; it employs a number of different *ductus* in its image-schemata. R. Brilliant has analysed what he calls "the communication network" of scenes in the Bayeux tapestry (early twelfth century): see "The Bayeux Tapestry." He is talking of its *ductus*, though he doesn't use this word.

73 Brilliant, *Visual Narratives*, p. 57.

74 Ibid., pp. 57–58, but see also his second and third chapters. Brilliant's study generally shows how Roman "visual narratives" of this sort (and some whose organization was far more intricate and puzzle-like) were a cultural commonplace, from the Etruscans through the late empire. As he notes, in late antiquity the continuous scenes of earlier picture narratives, some with several hundred figures, which a viewer would need to "divide" for himself just as ancient readers needed to mark for reading the continuous writing of their papyrus rolls, are replaced by a reductive style to a few images grouped in an epitomizing scene, a "metonymous tableau ... full of rich material for the narrative skills of the observer" (p. 164). This could be explained as a mnemotechnical and rhetorical principle.

75 See the excellent study by Carol Gibson-Wood, "The *Utrecht Psalter* and the Art of Memory." But her analysis falters on exactly this question – how was it used? I also discussed this manuscript's mnemotechnical schemes in *The Book of Memory*, pp. 226–227. I did not then know Gibson-Wood's essay, and am pleased to have found it and to acknowledge it here.

76 Uses of *pictura* referring to writing occur as early as the sixth century, and *pingo*, as I noted earlier, was commonly used as the verb for what a scribe did; cf. Latham s.v. *pictura*. Such a use of *pingo*, however, is unlikely to have greatly influenced *pictura*'s use as the name of a literary trope.

77 Bede, *Vita sanctorum abbatum monasterii in Uyramutha et Gyruum*, 6 (LCL, pp. 404, 406): "[Benedictus] picturas imaginum sanctarum quas ad ornandum ecclesiam beati Petri apostoli quam construxerat detulit; imaginem videlicet beatae Dei genetricis ... simul et duodecim apostolorum, quibus mediam eiusdem ecclesiae testudinem, ducto a pariete ad parietem tabulato praecingeret; imagines evangelicae historiae quibus australem ecclesiae parietem decoraret; imagines visonum apocalypsis beati Iohannis, quibus septentrionalem aeque parietem ornaret, quatenus intrantes ecclesiam omnes etiam literarum ignari, quaquaversum intenderent, vel semper amabilem Christi sanctorumque eius, quamvis in imagine, contemplarentur aspectum; vel Dominicae incarnationis gratiam vigilantiore mente recolerent; vel extremi discrimen examinis, quasi coram oculis habentes, districtius se ipsi examinare meminissent." My translation, consulting that of J. E. King for the LCL. The disposition within the church of the panel paintings which Benedict Biscop brought from Rome is a matter of speculation; see C. R. Dodwell, *Anglo-Saxon Art*, pp. 84–91 for a summary discussion of various possibilities. The monastery at Jarrow was also equipped with panel paintings, these showing the correspondence of the testaments, a theme common in the decoration of early Christian churches: see Bede's *Vita sanctorum* 9 (LCL, pp. 412, 414).

78 P. Hunter Blair, *The World of Bede*, p. 172.
79 Though from much later times, and in a different medium (stone), the sculptural programs ("furnishings" might be a better word) of medieval Christian churches continued to exhibit this fundamental heuristic role in the life of prayer, both communal (liturgical) and personal. An especially rich demonstration of just how complex and site-specific such fiction-making mechanisms could be is L. Seidel's study of the sculptures in the Romanesque church of St.-Lazare, Autun: "Legends in Limestone."
80 Venantius Fortunatus, *Carmina* X.vi.91–2, "Ad ecclesiam Toronicam quae per Gregorium episcopum renovata est" (ed. Leo, p. 237): "lucidius fabricam picturae pompa perornat, / ductaque qua fucis vivere membra putes." This whole portion of his poem is devoted to what he calls the "aula decens" (line 89), the ornamentation in the *aula* or apse area of the cathedral. In lines 89–90, Fortunatus describes how this area is lighted in daylight by large windows, and at night "day is enclosed within it" by artificial lights. This poem and the picture program which it describes are discussed by H. Kessler, "Pictorial Narrative and Church Mission in Sixth-Century Gaul."
81 I base my understanding of this structure on the comments of P. Meyvaert, "Bede and the church paintings at Wearmouth-Jarrow."
82 Peter of Celle, *De conscientia* (ed. Leclercq, pp. 199.29–200. 5). One of these texts is a "gathered-up" recollection of Exodus 35:30–32, recalled by Peter as "dedit Deus sapientiam in corde Beseleel ad facienda omnia opera siue ex auro, siue et argento," "God gave wisdom to the heart of Bezalel for making all the work whether of gold or of silver." The emphasis given to this rather obscure verse in this way, as part of the "matter" of conscience, makes sense when one also recalls that the Tabernacle of Exodus is one of the master "commonplaces of thought" or forms for invention in monasticism. I have more to say about this in my next chapter.
83 Ibid., pp. 200.34–201.12 (since the paragraphs of this treatise are not numbered, I can only give references according to page and line numbers of this edition): "De cuius habitudine ut tibi exemplum faciam, non sub errore idolatriae, sed sub specie euidentioris doctrinae, tale quid in animo finge, quod etiam ad pietatem deuotionis mentem compungat, et de uisibili exemplo ad inuisibilem contemplationem animam accendat. Pone itaque mensam uarietate et plenitudine diuersorum ferculorum refertam. Constitue *regem in diademate suo coronatum* et omni triumphali sublimitate insignitum, in capite et principaliori loco residere, cui manus assistentium et ministrantium tam ad cibum quam ad potum sedulissima sit. Sint *uasa aurea et argentea* in omnem usum, sint et *pocula* melle *condita ...* Cithara et lyra et psalterium auditus conuiuantium suis reficiant modulationibus ... Dispositissima ordinatione ordinata omnia, ita ut nihil desit ad cultum aut supersit ad taedium." Translations of this work are mine, consulting those of H. Feiss. Peter of Celle, as abbot of St.-Rémi in Rheims, was a notable deviser of pictures in other media as well, such as stained glass: his role in the decoration of St.-Rémi is described by M. Caviness, *Sumptuous Arts*, esp. pp. 36–53.
84 Peter of Celle, *De conscientia* (ed. Leclercq, p. 201.27–33): "Cuius pulchritudinis tenorem in habitu ipsius typice legens, rursus tali descriptione mores eius subcingo, et per colorum uarietates uirtutum uniuersa membra distinguo ... habet

oculos smaragdinos propter castitatis perpetuum uirorem; *nasum sicut turris Libani quae respicit contra Damascum* propter incursantium tentationum prudentem discretionem."

85 Ibid., p. 205.29.

86 Anyone picturing a solid object in her mind's eye can see it from all sides, though not all at the same time: try it yourself. To see the back you will have to "move" it or "walk about" it. On these and similar phenomena of mental imaging, see S. Kosslyn *et al.*, "On the Demystification of Mental Imagery," and N. Block, "Mental Pictures and Cognitive Science."

87 Peter of Celle, *De conscientia* (ed. Leclercq, p. 206.23). The entire "pictura caritatis" (p. 206.16) is contained on pp. 205.30–206.23 of Leclercq's edition.

88 These issues are discussed especially in Peter of Celle, *De conscientia*, ed. Leclercq, pp. 207.34–208.15.

89 See ibid., pp. 207.34–208.7. The translated passage is: "Vitia artis lex ostendit, scientiam et consummationem uirtutis caritas reddit" (p. 208.1–2).

90 Stoic signification theory stressed the moral nature of language use. Stoic influence, strong in ancient education, can be seen in Quintilian's famous characterization of the ideal orator as a good citizen speaking eloquently; this essentially moral character informs the teaching especially of the elementary language crafts of grammar and rhetoric throughout later antiquity and the Middle Ages. Certainly, monastic meditation craft was fundamentally conceived, as we have seen, as a procedure for crafting one's soul through eloquence (for "silence" is a type of eloquence) preparatory to salvation. See Colish, "The Stoic Theory of Verbal Signification"; Gehl, "Competens Silentium"; and the illuminating comments on Aldhelm's deliberately difficult literary style in K. Dungey, "Allegorical Theory and Aldhelm's Obscurity."

91 I do not want to examine the matter of Carolingian iconoclasm in detail, for it has been ably done by others. See T. Noble, "Tradition and Learning in Search of Ideology," and R. McKitterick, who concludes ("Text and Image in the Carolingian World,") that "[p]aintings were tolerated, even encouraged, when they were of letters or were visual translations of a text" (p. 301). Pictures are *for* memory work: as Theodulph says in the *Libri Carolini*, "A picture [by this he means a material artifact] is painted in order to convey to the onlookers the true *memory* of historical events and to advance their minds from falseness to the fostering of truth" (translated by McKitterick, p. 298; my emphasis). "Truth" for Theodulph, as for most Carolingians, was a moral value, not simply a matter of "verifiability." Humans remember by means of pictures, and thus pictures are cognitive ethical instruments. We have seen this same idea in Augustine, in Alcuin, and (as I argued in *The Book of Memory*, pp. 221–222) in Gregory the Great. The comments of Mitchell on the phenomenon of William Blake, "that strangest of creatures, a Puritan painter, an iconoclastic maker of icons" (*Iconology*, p. 115) are also suggestive; see also his analysis of Blake's picturing poetry in *Picture Theory*, esp. pp. 109–150.

92 Theodulph of Orleans, "Alia Pictura, in qua erat imago terrae in modum orbis comprehensa" (*Carmen* 47): "Totius orbis adest breviter depicta figura, / Rem magnam in parvo corpore nosse dabit" (ed. Traube, pp. 547–548, lines 49–50).

93 On the authorship of the *Libri Carolini* see A. Freeman, "Theodulf of Orleans

and the *Libri Carolini*" and P. Meyvaert, "The Authorship of the 'Libri Carolini'."

94 Theodulf of Orleans, "De septem liberalibus artibus in quadam pictura depictis," number 46 of "Theodulphi Carmina" (ed. Traube, pp. 544–547; subsequent references are by line number to this edition).

95 Both are authors of the twelfth century: for Hugh of St. Victor, see my discussion in *The Book of Memory*, pp. 232–233; Adam of Dryburgh is discussed below in Chapter Five, section 8.

96 Theodulf of Orleans, *De septem liberalibus artibus*, 1–2: "Discus erat tereti formatus imagine mundi, / Arboris unius quem decorabat opus."

97 Ibid., 3–8: "Huius Grammatica ingens in radice sedebat, / Gignere eam semet seu retinere monens. / Omnis ab hac ideo procedere cernitur arbos, / Ars quia proferri hac sine nulla valet. / Huius laeva tenet flagrum, seu dextra machaeram, / Pigros hoc ut agat, radat ut haec vitia," "In whose root great Grammar sat, / Admonishing it to bear fruit or to hold back. / The whole tree thus seemed to proceed from her, / For art without her does not have the power to be expressed. / Her left hand held a whip and her right a sharp blade, / The one so that she might stir up the lazy, the other that she might scrape away faults."

98 For example, by an early-thirteenth-century professor of rhetoric at Bologna, Boncompagno da Signa; see my essay "Boncompagno at the Cutting-Edge of Rhetoric."

99 Theodulf of Orleans, *De septem liberalibus artibus*, 99–106: "Arbor habebat ea, et folia, et pendentia poma, / Sicque venustatem et mystica plura dabat. /In foliis verba, in pomis intelligue sensus, / Haec crebro accrescunt, illa bene usa cibant. / Hac patula nostra exercetur in arbore vita, / Semper ut a parvis editiora petat, / Sensus et humanus paulatim scandat ad alta, / Huncque diu pigeat inferiora sequi."

100 Baudri was from the village of Meung-sur-Loire, and would have gotten his earliest education at the grammar school there, established by none other than Theodulph of Orleans; for a brief discussion of his life and work, see H. Waddell, *The Wandering Scholars*, pp. 100–104.

101 The main source for Adela's life is Ordericus Vitalis, *Ecclesiastical History*, completed in 1141. See also *DNB*, s.v. *Adela*, from which my information and the direct quotation in this paragraph is taken.

102 These suggestions and refutations were summarized by Phyllis Abrahams in her critical edition of this poem: see her note 61, pp. 243–44, 246–247.

103 See E. Kitzinger, "World Map and Fortune's Wheel," which describes a map mosaic in the floor of the cathedral at Turin, along with similar works, and also Abrahams's notes to her edition of Baudri. Abrahams makes it clear, however, that Baudri's closest and most important source is the wedding description in Martianus Capella's *The Marriage of Mercury and Philology*. On the enduring influence of this work throughout the Middle Ages, see W. H. Stahl and R. Johnson, *Martianus Capella*, vol. 1, pp. 56–79.

104 She is not in Martianus Capella; see Abrahams's note on this figure, p. 253.

105 Baudri de Bourgueil, "Adelae Comitissae," 83–86: "Vix ideo uidi uidisse tamen reminiscor,/ Ut reminiscor ego somnia uisa michi./ Sic me sepe nouam lunam uidisse recordor/ Vel, cum uix uideo, meue uidere puto."

106 On the stylistic affinities of Theodulph's mosaic, see esp. A. Grabar, "Les mosaïques de Germigny-des-Prés"; on the church see A. Khatchatrian, "Notes sur l'architecture de l'église." Not all the original mosaic survives. The original oratory was quite small, built on a quatrefoil plan, and lighted by a lantern window; the mosaic was in the eastern apse (Khatchatrian, pp. 168–169). Some interesting observations on the aesthetics of shadow are in M. Baxandall, *Shadows and Enlightenment*, esp. pp. 28–31, and although this book deals with eighteenth century materials, the observation that shadow is a creation of light seems to me pertinent as well to medieval aesthetic. Of particular interest in Baxandall's study are the meticulous observations of the changing light and shadows in his cell made by Abbé Millot of Lyon (quoted pp. 29–30). Such constant observation of a confined space over many seasons would always have been a feature of monastic life; it is alluded to, I think, in the advice to pay attention during memory work to seasonal and diurnal changes, particularly of light (and thus of shadow).

107 Ancient writers are all agreed that night-time is best for the concentration needed in *memoria*: composing lying down, either face down or with eyes closed, is a way of achieving this effect too.

108 Albertus Magnus, *Commentary on Aristotle's Parva naturalia: De memoria et reminiscentia* (ed. Borgnet, vol. 9, p. 108): "Et hujus causa bene volentes reminisci trahunt se a publico lucido, et vadunt ad obscurum privatum: quia in publico lucido loco sparguntur imagines sensibilium, et confunduntur motus eorum. In obscuro autem adunantur et ordinate moventur. Hinc est quod Tullius, in arte memorandi quam ponit in secunda *Rhetorica*, praecipit ut imaginemur et quaeramus loca obscura parum lucis habentia," "And for this reason, those wishing very much to recollect withdraw from the bright lights and retire to a dark secluded spot: because the images of sensory things are scattered in a public, well-lighted place, and their movements are confused. But in obscure lighting they are joined together and moved about in an orderly way. This is why [Cicero], in the art of memory he described in [*Rhetorica ad Herennium*], advises that we should imagine and seek out dark places having little light."

109 Evidently, a long tradition lies behind Descartes's shutting himself into a chamber in order to "discover" his Method, and behind Proust's preference for compositional recollecting within a bedchamber. A photograph of Mark Twain shows the famous author, cigar in hand, composing in bed.

110 Baudri de Bourgeuil, *Adelae Comitissae*, 159–160: "Que memoranda putes et claro digna relatu, / In ueli serie singula conspiceres."

111 Referred to in lines 145–146 and 233–234.

112 Baudri de Bourgeuil, *Adelae Comitissae*, 585–586: "At, quamvis staret, tamquam tamen ipsa rotabat / Machina: sic studium fecerat artificis." Remember that medieval *machinae* often employed moving wheels and other moving parts: a mill-wheel, a windlass type of hoist, a siege engine.

113 This characteristic advice to connect up the images in a background is found in Thomas Bradwardine's art of memory (composed c. 1335; see *The Book of Memory*, pp. 282–283), and it is interesting that Bradwardine's exemplar for the basic techniques for making mnemotechnical images involves manipulating the conventional figures of the Zodiac constellations. Linking images together in a

background is implied in some ancient mnemotechnic, for example, in the
Rhetorica ad Herennium III.xxiii.37, which advises that the images be active
(*imagines agentes*), and the example of how to make images for *memoria
verborum*, which shows Domitius being lashed by the Marcii Reges (III.xxi.34).
But the specific advice to make links of the sort found in Bradwardine is not in
the ancient texts: it is likely, since Baudri's poem pre-dates the thirteenth-
century revival of the ancient advice, that Bradwardine was articulating a precept
of medieval technique, rather than "misunderstanding" something he discovered
directly from the *Rhetorica ad Herennium*. It is another proof that medieval
mnemotechnic was not particularly beholden to the ancient sources.

114 Baudri de Bourgeuil, *Adelae Comitissae*, 669–674: "His inerant signis superedita
nomina semper, / Stellarum numerus, tempora, circuitus[;] / Littera signabat
superaddita nomina signis, / Signabat cursus, tempus, et officium. / Horologos
etiam possem numerare meatus/ Copia sed fecit me cumulata inopem," "In these
patterns the names [which I have] made known above record always / the
number, seasons, circuits of the stars; / The story-line inscribed the names
attached to the [stellar] patterns, / It marked their course, season, and position. /
Indeed I should be able to enumerate their hourly progressions / Except that the
cumulative abundance [of the task] overwhelmed me." I have stretched the usual
meaning of the word *littera* to suit this context; since in common twelfth-century
medieval usage the *littera* of the Bible refers to its narrative "level," I have
extended that meaning to Baudri's use of *littera* here, referring to the "story"
inscribed in each constellation pattern, linked up into a single "story-line."

115 Ibid., 1343–1350: "Dum tibi desudo, dum sudans, Adela, nugor, / Depinxi
pulchrum carminibus thalamum. / Tu uero nostre fabelle digna repende / Et
pensa, quanti fabula constiterit / Nam dum crescit opus, dum carmine carta
repletur, / Vrbana tumuit garrulitate liber. / Nunc caue, ne studii pereat uigilantia
nostri, / Cuique laboraui, non michi sis sterilis."

116 Ibid., 1367–1368: "Misi, qui nostrum reddat recitetque libellum / Ipseque, si
tandem iusseris, adueniam."

117 F. Raby, *A History of Secular Latin Poetry*, vol. 1, p. 348, commented that
Baudri's poem to Countess Adela "would have been remarkably useful in the
school," but noted (correctly) that there is no direct evidence still extant it was
ever so employed, though "[w]e may imagine it was often put to such a use."

118 See *The Book of Memory*, pp. 126–127.

119 Baudri de Bourgeuil, *Adelae Comitissae*, 1357–1358: "Cartula nuda uenit, quia
nudi cartula uatis;/ Da nude cappam, sique placet, tunicam."

120 See the comments by Copeland on Jerome's justification for translation in
Rhetoric, Hermeneutics, and Translation, pp. 42–55. On the hermeneutic
importance of the literal text in earliest education during the late Middle Ages,
see her "Childhood, Pedagogy, and the Literal Sense of the Text," and see also
the comments of Woods, "'In a Nutshell'."

5. "THE PLACE OF THE TABERNACLE"

1 We need to take note of the fact that both these authors were canons, members
of orders that doctrinally were more involved with "the world" than other

regular orders were at this time. But we must also take care not to over-estimate the significance of their differences from monks. Peter of Celle was a Benedictine: as we have just seen, he used ekphrastic *picturae* extensively in his writings, and so did Bernard of Clairvaux. Caroline Bynum's assessment is properly cautious: the differences between monks and canons, while they exist, are easily exaggerated. See Bynum, *'Docere verbo et exemplo'*.

2 A sixteenth-century professor of rhetoric, Rodolphus Agricola, was the author of a very influential textbook which rationalized rhetorical invention into a scheme of twenty-four logically ordered topics, to be applied in turn when analyzing any proposition. He called his method *ekphrasis*, a choice of term which underscores his understanding of the power of this trope as a tool of mental organization. A good introduction to the themes of Agricola's invention method is M. Cogan, "Rodolphus Agricola and the Semantic Revolution."

3 For this reason, this poem presented the paradigmatic statement for the New Criticism, evidenced in the title of C. Brooks's school-defining book *The Well-Wrought Urn*. Unlike Keats's ode, Archibald McLeish's poem *Ars Poetica* (1926) was a self-conscious statement of the extreme subjectivity of high modern aesthetic. In his chapter on ekphrasis Mitchell, discussing modern ekphrases exclusively, notes that in each case the artifact is viewed as alien and "other," in the manner of Keats's ode: *Picture Theory*, pp. 151–181.

4 On the concept of *economy* in rhetoric see K. Eden, "Economy and the Hermeneutics of Late Antiquity" and *Hermeneutics and the Rhetorical Tradition*.

5 In *Songs of Glory*, a study of the façades of Romanesque churches in Aquitaine, Seidel presents a model analysis of the rhetoric of architecture. These façades are not monastic, but were designed instead within a cultural context that was civic and aristocratic; Seidel demonstrates how each of her subjects makes "a deliberate and original union of specific forms and figures" (p. 13) within communally held traditions – that is, how each addresses its occasion, in the full rhetorical meaning of that word. See also her forthcoming "Legends in Limestone," a study of the complex rhetoric involved in the foundation and sculptural equipment (ornamentation) of the church of St.-Lazare in Autun.

6 "Bernardus noster, monachorum Antonius et Tullius oratorum": see J. Leclercq, "L'art de la composition," p. 153. Another of Bernard's contemporaries called him the "king" of preaching orators: see K. Fredborg, "The Scholastic Teaching of Rhetoric in the Middle Ages," p. 89.

7 Bernard of Clairvaux, *The Life and Death of St. Malachy the Irishman* 63 (*SBO* III, pp. 367–368): "Et die quadam de via regrediens, cum iam loco appropiaret, prospexit eminus: et ecce oratorium apparuit magnum lapideum et pulchrum valde. Et intuens diligenter situm, formam, et compositionem, cum fiducia arripit opus, prius quidem indicata visione senioribus fratribus, paucis tamen. Sane totum quod attente notavit de loco, et modo, et qualitate, tanta diligentia observavit ut, peracto opere, factum viso simillimum appareret, ac si et sibi cum Moyse dictum audierit: 'Vide, ut omnia facias secundum exemplar quod tibi ostensum est in monte.' Eodem visionis genere id quoque, quod in Saballino situm est, antequam fieret, praeostensum est illi, non modo oratorium, sed et monasterium totum" (translated by R. Meyer). Saul monastery, now destroyed, near the town of Downpatrick in County Down, was built where Patrick was

supposed to have been buried. Thus the special significance given to Saul Abbey by the building vision may be related to the fact that building it was a deliberate sort of "forgetting" through site over-lay (or a figural fulfillment, depending on your point of view) of the chief saint of the old Irish church. Malachy was responsible for a number of Cistercian foundations in Ireland, including the first, Mellifont, built by Irish monks whom Malachy took to Clairvaux for training (*Life of St. Malachy*, 39).

8   This is allied to the point made by Richard Krautheimer in his important series of essays on medieval architectural "copying," including "The Carolingian Revival of Early Christian Architecture" and "Sancta Maria Rotonda," reprinted in his *Studies in Early Christian . . . Art*. I would stress that this sort of "copy," from Latin *copia*, is a concept in rhetoric: cf. *OED* s.v. copy and copybook, 2. A sixteenth-century "copybook" was a book of models to imitate in order to help a student acquire rhetorical copiousness; see T. Sloane, "School-books and Rhetoric."

9   See C. Rudolph, "Building-Miracles as Artistic Justification," and C. Carty, "The Role of Gunzo's Dream."

10 "His dictis ipse funiculos tendere visus est, ipse longitudinis atque latitudinis metiri quantitatem. Ostendit ei etiam basilicae qualitatem fabricandae, menti eius et dimensionis et schematis memoriam tenacius habere praecipiens." Text and translation from W. Braunfels, *Monasteries of Western Europe*, pp. 240–241. The source is *Bibliotheca Cluniacensis*, cols. 457ff.

11 "ex ordine quaecumque monacho dicta fuerant, vel ostensa": quoted from Braunfels, *Monasteries of Western Europe*, p. 241.

12 The model was built by Walter Horn and Ernest Born, who describe it in their *The Plan of St. Gall*. They have been criticized for trying to impose an overly rigid square schematic upon the entire drawing: see W. Sanderson, "The Plan of St. Gall Reconsidered." Moreover, the scale of the drawing and the scribes' instructions concerning its measurements do not match up. On the relationship of details in the Plan to some actual buildings of the time, see Heitz, "Architecture et liturgie processionnelle" (the selection and sequence of altars inside the sanctuary are modeled partly on the church of St. Riquier). The fact that "real" details are included is not in any way incompatible with its being an exemplary instrument for meditation; both Augustine and Alcuin said that one will, indeed must, make cognitive images of unknown things from details of things one knows (see Chapter Three, section 1, above).

13 "Haec tibi dulcissime fili cozberte de posicione officianarum paucis exemplata direxi quibus sollertiam exerceas tuam ... Ne suspiceris autem me haec ideo elaborasse, quod vos putemus nostris indigere magestriis, sed potius ob amorem dei tibi soli scrutinanda pinxisse ... crede"; text quoted from W. Braunfels, *Monasteries of Western Europe*, p. 46. On the purpose of the "Plan of St. Gall" see L. Nees, "The Plan of St. Gall."

14 Braunfels, *Monasteries of Western Europe*, p. 46.

15 A. de Vogüé, "Le Plan de Saint-Gall," pp. 301–302. See also Nees, "The Plan of St. Gall" and Sanderson, "The Plan of St. Gall Reconsidered," both of whom argue strenuously against the interpretation of other historians, Horn among them, who understood this work to be a sort of imperial edict for future

monastery-building, and as a key element of an attempt (short-lived, if it ever existed) by Carolingian emperors to impose cultural uniformity. In Hebrews 8:5 Christ is identified as the *exemplar* of the Tabernacle.

16 Gregory the Great, *Dialogues* II.22.2.16–17: "[Benedictus] in somnis apparuit, et loca singula, ubi quid aedificari debuisset, subtiliter designauit." See also the comments of de Vogüé (who edited Gregory's *Dialogues* for the SC) in "Le Plan de Saint-Gall."

17 Isidore, *Etymol.* XIX.9. He says further, in defining *dispositio*, that "est areae vel solii et fundamentorum descriptio," "it is a description of its foundations and of its area or floor," a plan and elevation. One sees exactly these sketched for the visionary temple of Ezekiel in several manuscripts (including one from St. Victor itself, Paris, Bibliothèque Nationale, MS lat. 14516) of Richard of St. Victor's exposition of the literal sense of Ezekiel ("In Visionem Ezechielis"). On these *picturae* see W. Cahn, "Architecture and Exegesis."

18 Pevsner quotes from a life of Benno of Osnabrück, responsible for Speier and Hildesheim, whose author calls him both *architectus* and *dispositor*: "The Term 'Architect'," pp. 554–555.

19 *Didascalicon* vi. 4 (ed. Buttimer, pp. 121–122). The Old Testament readings which Hugh recommends also include the account of Creation (the Six Days, extolled as a memory help also in Hugh's "De tribus circumstantiae": see *The Book of Memory*, Appendix A); the "three last books of Moses"; Isaiah, and the beginning and ending of Ezekiel (these three readings all containing visions that, like the cosmographia in Genesis, were used as basic exegetical *picturae*, namely the six-winged Seraph, the Throne Chariot, and the Plan of the visionary Temple Citadel); also Job, the Psalter, and the Song of Songs.

20 "Omnibus ad Sanctum turbis patet haec via templum qua sua vota ferant unde hilares redeant"; quoted from Braunfels, *Monasteries of Western Europe*, p. 45. The manuscript's *tituli* and rubrics are not Heito's but the work of a somewhat later commentator after the copy came to Saint Gall. Horn published a study of the use of "sacred numbers" in the Plan ("On the Selective Use of Sacred Numbers"); I think it would be interesting to see to what extent these also correlate to specific details in the Ezekiel and Exodus accounts.

21 Zinn, "Mandala Symbolism," pp. 318–319. Zinn's essay is devoted to Hugh of St. Victor, particularly his summary picture of Noah's Ark, but his comments illuminate the meditational way more generally. See also Zinn's comments on this same picture treatise in "Hugh of St. Victor and the Art of Memory."

22 See M. Himmelfarb, "From Prophecy to Apocalypse," and *Tours of Hell*, esp. pp. 56–58, and also C. Rowland, *The Open Heaven*.

23 Ezekiel 43:10–11: "Tu autem, fili hominis, ostende domui Israel templum, et confundantur ab iniquitatibus suis, et metiantur fabricam, et erubescant ex omnibus quae fecerunt. Figuram domus, et fabricae eius, exitus et introitus, et omnem descriptionem eius, et universa praecepta eius, cunctumque ordinem eius, et omnes leges eius ostende eis, et scribes in oculis eorum, ut custodiant omnes descriptiones eius, et praecepta illius, et faciant ea."

24 Hebrews 8:1–5: "Talem habemus pontificem, qui consedit in dextera sedis magnitudinis in caelis, sanctorum minister, et tabernaculi veri, quod fixit Dominus, et non homo ... qui exemplari, et umbrae deserviunt caelestium. Sicut

responsum est Moysi, cum consummaret tabernaculum: Vide (inquit) omnia facito secundam exemplar, quod tibi ostensum est in monte." The high priest of the true Tabernacle is Christ, of whose pattern (*exemplar*) all other priests (and all other buildings) are a shadow. I quoted the relevant text of 1 Corinthians 3 in Chapter One, section 4.

25 Hrabanus Maurus, *Commentarii in Ezechielem prophetam* XVII.xliii (*PL* 110.991): "Metiri vero est fabricam, pensare subtiliter justorum vitam. Sed dum metimur fabricam, necesse est, ut ex cunctis quae fecimus, erubescamus."

26 See Himmelfarb, "From Prophecy to Apocalypse" and *Tours of Hell*, for an analysis of the characteristics and relationships among the ancient texts in this genre. The visionary temple is described in 1 Enoch 90.

27 The Tabernacle trope is also, as I have previously noted, a major presence in the prologue to the *Regula Benedicti*, with specific reference made there to Psalm 14, "Domine, quis habitabit in tabernaculo tuo?".

28 H. Kessler, "Through the Temple Veil": "a cartographic representation of the tabernacle circulated as an independent image already in Late Antiquity" (p. 60). Other essays which discuss these images include C. Roth, "Jewish Andecedents," and E. Revel-Neher, "Du Codex Amiatinus."

29 Kraeling, *The Synagogue*, p. 107. See also K. Weitzmann and H. Kessler, *The Frescoes of the Dura Synagogue*, which discusses how the Temple (or Tabernacle) image may have been disseminated. On the devotional significance of the literary version of the Tabernacle–Temple trope see J. Levenson, "The Jerusalem Temple."

30 Roth, "Jewish Antecedents," p. 25. Though details of Roth's article have been modified by later scholars (see esp. the work of Kessler and Revel-Neher), this essay is an important demonstration, not just of the earliest influences of Jewish traditions on Christian traditions, but of their continuing influence on aspects of Christian art throughout the later Middle Ages.

31 Roth, "Jewish Antecedents," p. 36.

32 Four essays I found most helpful concerning the dating, writing, and sources of this manuscript are (in chronological order) R. Bruce-Mitford, "The Art of the Codex Amiatinus"; Revel-Neher, "Du Codex Amiatinus"; Corsano, "The First Quire of the Codex Amiatinus," and P. Meyvaert, "Bede, Cassiodorus, and the Codex Amiatinus." Though art historians used to consider this manuscript to be an exact copy of classical exemplars, opinion has now shifted to emphasize both its completely Anglo-Saxon making and the Anglo-Saxon elements in its "translation" of classical style. Corsano and Bruce-Mitford are particularly concerned to show the Anglo-Saxon matrix of the manuscript; Revel-Neher, expanding some comments by Roth, is concerned to show that the Codex Amiatinus rendering is not based directly upon Jewish models, but shows evidence of translation through the Octateuch manuscripts (themselves based only partly on Jewish antecedents) made by Byzantine Christians. On this point see also Weitzmann and Kessler, *The Frescoes of the Dura Synagogue*. Meyvaert is particularly concerned with Bede's understanding of Cassiodorus, and in this context examines the Tabernacle image.

33 A picture of the scribe, "Ezra," is now placed between the Tabernacle bifolium and the text; the picture from which it was copied showed Cassiodorus in his

study, a subject mistaken for Ezra by the Anglo-Saxon makers of the Codex Amiatinus. Meyvaert, "Bede, Cassiodorus, and the Codex Amiatinus," argues that the Tabernacle image stood first in the Codex Grandior, followed immediately by an image of the Temple precincts, and that all other matter followed these two bifoliar "pictures"; he contends that the Amiatinus scribes would have followed this order. Bruce-Mitford, "The Art of the Codex Amiatinus," placed the Tabernacle picture in the Amiatinus after some dedicatory verses and the "Ezra" portrait and just before the introductory matter to the text (the divisions of books, table of contents, etc.). See Corsano, "The First Quire of the Codex Amiatinus," on the codicological evidence that these initiatory leaves have been moved.

34 I disagree with Revel-Neher's comment that the Amiatinus diagram is wholly literal, "liée étroitement au texte, le suivant précisément, cherchant à l'illustrer fidèlement," unlike the Sacred Vessels images in Jewish tradition, which serve a symbolic cultural and religious system (p. 16). This is another instance where applying a categorical opposition of "the literal" to "the symbolic" will obscure how an ancient or medieval reading-figure was thought to work.

35 See Ousterhout, "Loca Sancta," for an account of how the transfer of the "measurements," *mensurae*, of holy sites or objects in Jerusalem to European sites was regarded as a type of transfer of relics.

36 Cassiodorus, *Institutiones* I. 5. 2 (ed. Mynors, p. 22–23):"Hic tantos auctores, tantos libros in memoriae suae bibliotheca condiderat, ut legentes probabiliter admoneret, in qua parte codicis quod praedixerat invenirent. ... Commonuit etiam tabernaculum templumque Domini ad instar caeli fuisse formatum; quae depicta subtiliter lineamenti propriis in pandecte Latino corporis grandioris aptavi." Eusebius "from Asia" may have come from Egypt; see Meyvaert, "Bede, Cassiodorus, and the Codex Amiatinus," p. 835, note 45. On Vivarium's general affiliations with the Mediterranean world at this time, the essay by P. Courcelle, "Le site du monastère de Cassiodore," still has much value. Cassiodorus mentions his Codex Grandior pictures also in his commentary on the Psalms, but does not repeat there the story of Didymus. The consensus among scholars is that Bede did not know Cassiodorus' *Institutiones*, but was familiar with the Psalm commentary and had the Codex Grandior with its pictures: see Meyvaert, "Bede, Cassiodorus, and the Codex Amiatinus."

37 Details of the Altar of Sacrifice described by Bede were made, he says, "quo modo in pictura Cassiodori Senatoris ... expressum vidimus," "in the manner we saw clearly defined in the picture of Cassiodorus Senator" (*De Tabernaculo* II, CCSL 119A, 81.1565–1567). And he says he saw the Temple "in pictura Cassiodori" (*De Templo* II, CCSL 119A, 192.28–193.52; my quote is found on p.193.48–49, but the whole passage is relevant). A good general description of the Bible as Bede knew it is Hunter Blair, *The World of Bede*, pp. 211–236, and see also R. Marsden, *The Text of the Old Testament in Anglo-Saxon England*.

38 Corsano, "The First Quire of the Codex Amiatinus," p. 10.

39 Suggested by Revel-Neher, "Du Codex Amiatinus," and see also the comments of Kessler, "Medieval Art as Argument." Meyvaert is convinced not only that the picture derived from Octateuch manuscripts but that it is specifically linked to the topographical picture of the world as the Jerusalem Temple in manuscripts of the

"Topography" of Cosmas Indicopleustes: see the postscript to "Bede, Cassiodorus, and the Codex Amiatinus," p. 883. The case for this influence was argued also by Wolska-Conus, "La 'Topographie chrétienne' de Cosmas Indicopleustès," who gives the most comprehensive description and analysis of Cosmas manuscripts. These all contain a drawing of the world as the Jerusalem Temple. On the genre more generally in pagan literature and pedagogy, see the introduction to Jacob, *La description de la terre habitée de Denys d'Alexandrie*.

40 The revival of the *Rhetorica ad Herennium* mnemonic technique during the last part of the thirteenth century is described in *The Book of Memory*, pp. 122–155.

41 Cf. *Rhetorica ad Herennium* III.xix.32.

42 Peter of Celle wrote two treatises on the Tabernacle of Moses. On the popularity during the twelfth century of using the Mosaic constructions in Exodus as inventional and dispositive devices for composition see de Lubac, *Exégèse médiévale*, vol. 3, pp. 403–418; he notes, as does J. Leclercq, that the texts about the Tabernacle played the same role among Benedictines that the Song of Songs played among the Cistercians, as pre-eminent meditative structures (pp. 406–407, and p. 407, note 1). This would seem to be evidence of fashions at work within meditative praxis, vogues for one structure or another among different orders or/ and in different times and places. In the closed worlds of monasteries, one would expect such a phenomenon. The vogue for using jeweled crosses as initiating pictures, such as the one in *The Dream of the Rood*, may be another example of a meditational fashion; see Raw, *Anglo-Saxon Crucifixion Iconography*, pp. 67–90. Vogues should not, however, be mistaken for capabilities; any of the traditional meditational devices, *formulae*, would have been, at least putatively, available for use by anyone educated in monastic orthopraxis.

43 Peter of Celle, *Liber de panibus* (*PL* 202.965): "Pectus Iesu, ibi est refectorium; sinus Iesu, ibi est dormitorium; vultus Iesu, ibi est oratorium; latitudo, longitudo, sublimitas et profundum Iesu, ibi est claustrum; consortium Iesu et omnium beatorum, ibi est capitulum; narrationes Iesu de Patris et Filii et Spiritus sancti unitate, et de apertione mysterii incarnationis suae, ibi est auditorium."

44 These have been discussed by Cahn, "Architecture and Exegesis."

45 Bernard of Clairvaux, *Sermones super Cantica* 23.1.1 (*SBO* I, p. 138. 14–20): "Cogitemus ea interim loca quaedam redolentia penes sponsum, plena odoramentis, referta deliciis. In istiusmodi nempe officina potiora quaeque ex horto sive ex agro servanda reponuntur. … Currit sponsa, currunt adolescentulae … Sine mora aperitur ei … Adolescentulae autem quid? Sequuntur a longe." In making my own translation, I have consulted that of Kilian Walsh.

46 Ibid., 23.II.3 (*SBO* I, p. 140. 14–20): "In consequentibus mentio fit etiam de horto et de cubiculo, quae ambo nunc adiungo istis cellariis et in praesentem disputationem assumo; nam simul tractata melius ex invicem innotescent. Et quaeramus, si placet, tria ista in Scripturis sanctis, hortum, cellarium, cubiculum. … Sit itaque hortus plana ac simplex historia, sit cellarium moralis sensus, sit cubiculum arcanum theoricae contemplationis."

47 The scholastic distinction of *forma tractandi*, the order which an author chooses for composing, and *forma tractata*, the order which an already-composed work displays, was not employed by Bernard, so far as I know, but the idea of composition being a process of "drawing-in" materials to a formal order was

certainly familiar to him. On the scholastic definitions of these terms see Minnis *et al.*, *Medieval Literary Theory and Criticism*, p. 198.

48 Bernard of Clairvaux, *Sermones super Cantica* 23.II.7 (*SBO* I, p. 142.23–4): "Puto, si bene intellexisti utriusque cellae proprietates, non incongrue me hanc Unguentariam, illam Aromaticam appellasse testaberis."

49 Ibid., 23.IV.9 (*SBO* I, p. 144.19): "Iam ad cubiculum veniamus."

50 Ibid., 23.VI.17 (*SBO* I, p. 150.11–17): "Iam ut horum quae de cellario, horto, cubiculo, longiori sunt disputata sermone, memoria vestra compendium teneat, mementote trium temporum, trium meritorum, trium quasi praemiorum: in horto advertite tempora, merita in cellario, praemia in triplici illa contemplatione cubiculum inquirentis. Et de cellario quidem ista sufficiant. Porro de horto vel cubiculo, si qua addenda, aut alia forte quam dicta sint modo advertenda occurrerint, loco suo non praetereamus."

51 John Cassian, *Conférence* X.9.10 (SC 54, p. 84): "uideo uos ... pro foribus orationis ... ut iam intra aulam quodammodo ipsius oberrantes in adyta quoque ... introducam."

52 Ibid., X.10 (SC 54, p. 90): "Hunc scribes in limine et ianuis oris tui, hunc in parietibus domus tuae ac penetralibus tui pectoris conlocabis." There is an immediate allusion to Deuteronomy 11:8–20, and a more distant one to the Passover narrative (Exodus 12:7), but the building metaphor is used more extensively in this text from Cassian than in either of those Biblical passages.

53 De Lubac summarizes the exegetical traditions of this text in the Middle Ages in *Exégèse médiévale*, vol. 3, pp. 387–403. On pp. 403–404 he takes issue with Smalley's claim in respect of this treatise (*The Study of the Bible*, pp. 108–109) that Victorine exegesis significantly literalized the tradition of Gregory; he is inclined to regard Richard's literal depiction as a special case that cannot be generalized into an exegetical position. As will become clear in my discussion, my understanding of this matter is closer to that of de Lubac; I think we are dealing with at least two different genres of commentary, one an attempt to "measure" out the literal text, and the other responding to the text as an ekphrasis, and creating from it *picturae* of the sort I have been discussing. As de Lubac reminds us, Richard's text caused some adverse comment at the time: Peter the Chanter wondered why so much effort had been wasted (by Richard) on "dispositiones maecanicas in aedificiis et in dispositione templi imaginarii," "mechanical blue-prints for the buildings and for the lineaments of an imaginary temple" (p. 404). Richard's "error," in Peter's judgment, would have been similar to that in the incident in the *Life of St. Benedict*, in which the monks got a monastery plan from the saint, but were distracted by the mechanics of how the saint could "really" be there. The "Plan of St. Gall," as an example of a dispositive, material *pictura* intended for spiritual "seeing," should also be considered by historians debating the nature of "literal" and "spiritual" reading during the Middle Ages: in some modern discussions the distinction between the two may have been drawn too sharply.

54 Gregory the Great, *Hom. in Hiezech.* II. homilia ii. 2 (CCSL 142, p. 226.55–56): "Spiritalia spiritaliter aspice, et tamen carnales infirmitates tuas memorare," referring to Ezekiel 40:4: "Fili hominis, vide oculis tuis, et auribus tuis audi, et pone cor tuum in omnia quae ego ostendam tibi."

55 Gregory the Great, *Hom. in Hiezech.* II. homilia i. 3 (CCSL 142, 208.51–52: "ciuitatis aedificium accipi iuxta litteram nullatenus potest," "it is not possible to take the building of the city literally." See also II. homilia i. 5: "non de corporalis, sed de spiritalis ciuitatis aedificio cuncta discerentur. Qui enim non se aedificium, sed quasi aedificium uidisse perhibet, cor audientium ad spiritalem fabricam mittit," "all these things should be learned with reference to the building not of a physical, but of a spiritual city. And so, the one who admits having seen not the city itself, but a sort-of city, directs the hearts of his hearers to its spiritual construction" (CCSL 142, p. 210.137–140). Jerome and Gregory the Great dominated the exegesis of this important text through the twelfth century: see De Lubac, *Exégèse médiévale*, vol. 3, esp. pp. 388–389, 399.

56 Gregory the Great, *Hom. in Hiezech.* II. homilia vii. 7 (CCSL 142, 321.216–219): "In mente enim nostra primus ascencionis gradus est timor Domini, secundus pietas, tertius scientia, quartus fortitudo, quintus consilium, sextus intellectus, septimus sapientia." I take *ascensio* in its architectural sense as "a flight of stairs" rather than the more abstract "ascent": in general, I opt for a translation of words that allows an English-speaking mind to make pictures from them, for reasons that by now are obvious.

57 See the drawings in D. Lecoq, "La 'Mappemonde' du *De Arca Noe Mystica*," and Sicard's painting of the basic *formae* of this picture in *Hugues de Saint-Victor et son école*, plate 6, and *Diagrammes médiévaux*, plates 7 and 8.

58 See *The Book of Memory*, pp. 231–239. Sicard has retitled this treatise *Libellus de formacione arce*, selecting this title for his edition of it. That is a better title than the *PL* one, *De arca Noe mystica*, but I still prefer the one it was given in a few manuscripts, *De pictura Arche*. Grover Zinn has written cogently about the treatise in his essays on Hugh of St. Victor, especially "Hugh of St. Victor and the Art of Memory" and "Suger, Theology, and the Pseudo-Dionysian Tradition."

59 M. Fassler, *Gothic Song*, pp. 290–320, has demonstrated how the basic "unit" of the Victorine sequence, "Laudes crucis," functioned in constructing the families of later Victorine sequences rather as this "Christ-cubit" does in measuring out the structure of Hugh's imaginary Ark; in Fassler's words, the musical phrase constructs the church as "a huge harp, each of the individual sequences being one of the strings" (p. 319). The turn which the Victorines gave to the "square schematic" as a trope of architecture is also unusually rich, and unusually well recorded. But the trope itself is, as we have seen, much older.

60 On the problem of architectural sources for the square schematic at the time of the Plan, see Sanderson, "The Plan of St. Gall." So far as I know, no one has suggested that the chief source may be textual, not material, but to the extent this is true, it supports the idea that the plan was for meditation, and not designed for material construction.

61 On Opicinus see F. Saxl, "A Spiritual Encyclopedia of the Middle Ages" (where he is discussed briefly) and, more recently, M. Evans, *Medieval Drawings*, esp. Plates 83–85. Some of his drawings are very "cartographic." There is considerable debate over whether or not Hugh of St. Victor described an actual painting: M. Evans, "Fictive Painting in Twelfth-Century Paris" says no, but many other scholars, including Sicard, Zinn, and Rudolph, believe that he did. Based on the philological evidence, I agree with Evans on this point: the use of *pingo* and

pictura in the tropes of ekphrasis and enargeia is so pervasive in monasticism, as we have seen, that in the absence of any other kind of evidence (such as some sort of drawing copied with the text), one cannot conclude from word use alone that a "painted" picture of this sort was ever, or indeed was ever meant to be, materially realized.

62 The several picture-treatises of Hugh of St. Victor's near-contemporary, Hugo de Folieto, are a prime example: see *The Book of Memory*, pp. 239–242. W. Clark, *The Medieval Book of Birds*, reproduces a number of versions of some of Hugh's prefatory *picturae*.

63 I discussed the manuscript evidence in *The Book of Memory*, pp. 231–232, and notes.

64 Adam of Dryburgh, *De tripartito tabernaculo*, proem III.10 (*PL* 198.634): "in pictura quoque visibili tales picturas et colores posui, quibus utriusque spiritualis tabernaculi, allegorici videlicet et tropologici spiritualitas congruentius possit denotari. ... Et quia secunda et tertia hujus libri pars pertinent ad picturam, extensa coram vobis ipsa pictura, utramque praefati libri partem competenter legi facietis: ut percipientes et lecta auditu, et depicta aspectu, librum et picturam simul coaptetis." *Aspectus* often means "inner gaze," though it need not always mean that; cf. *OLD* s.v. *aspectus*. It should be noted that Migne reprinted an edition of 1659 (Antwerp) by Godfrey Gilbert.

65 Ibid., I.3 (*PL* 198.611): "librum, quem de tabernaculo Moysis, una cum pictura, ante hoc biennium, rogatu quorumdam fratrum nostrorum, et maxime viri illustris Joannis cujusdam abbatis, qui in terra nostra est, composuimus, vobis transmitteremus," "we should send you a book, which, at the request of some of our brothers and of a certain abbot John, greatest of the great men in our country, we composed two years ago concerning the tabernacle of Moses, together with a picture." Jean-Philippe Antoine first suggested that I look at this text, and I am grateful to him for doing so. It is briefly discussed by De Lubac, *Exégèse médiévale*, vol. 3, pp. 407–413 (who commented that it is "une œuvre de longue haleine"), and mentioned by Smalley, *The Study of the Bible*, pp. 180–181.

66 The letter of John to Adam; *PL* 198.625. On developments in Biblical exegesis during the twelfth century, including both a move to making more grammatically focussed commentaries on the textual *litterae* and a desire to fill the extensive gaps left by patristic commentaries such as Bede's, see G. R. Evans, *The Language and Logic of the Bible*, esp. pp. 72–100.

67 See the instructions of Abbot John of Kelso to Adam, 6–7 (*PL* 198.626–627): "In textu autem secundae partis, visibile tabernaculum in plano depingens, oculis intuentium ... illius formam aedificii exprime ... Depictis igitur omnibus, in ipsa eadem parte libri, mox ipsam picturam ... per allegoricos sensus expone, ut lectoris studium atque intellectus augeatur," "In the second part of the text, painting in a plan the visible tabernacle for the eyes of those gazing mentally ... portray the form of that edifice. ... And having painted every bit, in that same part of the book, just after the picture, ... comment [on it] in the manner of allegory, that the study and understanding of the reader may increase." On the ancient and medieval *etymologia* which linked *augeo* with *auctor*, see Chenu, "*Auctor, actor, autor*." Whether or not this letter is genuinely by John of Kelso (and in the absence of a critical edition one must exercise some caution), the

statement articulates some contemporary's clear understanding of how Adam's picture was to function in relation to the rest of the work.

68 Adam of Dryburgh, *De tripartito tabernaculo*, proem III.7 (*PL* 198.632): "Prima pars tractat de factura et dispositione materialis et visibilis tabernaculi Moysis. Secunda de pictura agit ejusdem tabernaculi, et de allegorica ejusdem significatione. Tertia vero de significatione ejus morali."

69 Ibid., II.1.77 (*PL* 198. 683): "Finita itaque utcunque libri nostri particula prima, in qua de materiali factura et dispositione tabernaculi quaedam, prout Dominus dedit, tractata sunt[:] juxta vestram, Pater sancte, jussionem, ut saepe dictum tabernaculum in plano quoque, quantum sciero et potero, depingam[,] jam manum appono, quatenus per corporalem etiam aliquatenus cerni possit, visionem," "thus in any event the first portion of our book is finished, in which, just as the Lord gave [them to Moses], various matters concerning the material edifice and disposition of the tabernacle were treated: according to your command, holy father, that I should also describe the tabernacle, [which is] usually [only] spoken about, in a schematic plan as well, insofar as I understood and was able to, I now put my hand to its visualization, insofar as it may be seen in some fashion with bodily sight." Adam is not distinguishing corporeal vision from mental vision, but rather from *theoria*, the direct vision of God, of the sort that Moses experienced when he received the original measurements recorded in Exodus. Just what such "corporeal visualization" of a prophetic text may consist in was clarified by the manner in which the visionary Temple of Ezekiel was commented on by Jerome and (especially) by Gregory the Great; the classification is the familiar Augustinian one. On such mortal "picturing" cf. the excellent essay by Caviness, "Images of Divine Order."

70 This convention, of a flat "page" of memory, is found as early as Martianus Capella – though the oldest convention of all, that of the mnemotechnical *tabula* or waxed tablet, also conceives making memories as being like writing or drawing on a flat surface. John of Garland, writing some thirty years after Adam, speaks of the *area* of memory; Hugh of St. Victor, like Adam, of the *planus*. See *The Book of Memory*, pp. 124–125, 232. Adam likens the basic square to the quadripartite Rule, the "measure" of every monk's life.

71 J.-P. Antoine, "*Ad perpetuam memoriam,*" cites a passage from yet another "letter of Adam" that Migne printed at the end of the *De tripartito tabernaculo* (*PL* 198.791–796). This letter refers clearly to a physical "picture" like a chart, that is used with a pointer ("virga") as the book is read aloud. The letter is a restatement of Adam's letters printed by Migne as Proemia I and III, and is used to introduce both the Tabernacle exegesis (called here "De triplici praefati tabernaculi pictura") and another work, "De triplici genere contemplationis." So far as I know, no surviving manuscripts of "The Triple Tabernacle" have paintings of the structure described: in this respect as in others, Adam's "picture" is much like Hugh of St. Victor's picture of the Ark.

72 Adam of Dryburgh, *De tripartito tabernaculo* II.6.86 (*PL* 198. 690): "Restat nunc, ut aliqua ex his, quae de materiali tabernaculo depinximus, spirituali tabernaculo Christi, quod sancta Ecclesia est, in pictura coram posita adaptemus."

73 Ibid., II.19.137 (*PL* 198.742–743): "Et primus [locus] quasi ager fuit, secundus ut hortus, tertius velut atrium, quartus sicut domus, quintus tanquam thalamus. In

agro bonae simul et malae herbae fuerunt, in horto herbae electae, in atrio familiares et amici, in domo parentes et cognati, in thalamo Sponsus et sponsa." Adam uses *locus* synonymously with *spatium*, his more common choice, in II.17.132 (col. 735).

74 On the sources and style of these drawings see Cahn, "Architecture and Exegesis." Cahn notes that the architectural style employed is Romanesque, answering to Augustine and Alcuin's observation that to make images for unseen or unseeable things (like the visionary Citadel), one makes use of things recalled from one's own remembered experiences. Cahn also observes with some surprise that Richard supplied only a simple ground plan for the complex's most important spiritual building, the sanctuary itself, though its decoration is described in the text. This may well reflect a belief that for truly important memory work one must (as it were) craft one's own tools, and that for "remembering Jerusalem" one should not simply replicate another's ready-made images. On the genre of Temple drawings in the Middle Ages see C. Krinsky, "Representations of the Temple of Jerusalem."

75 Richard says specifically that he intends to fill in the literal exposition of both visions of Ezekiel, of the Throne Chariot and of the Temple, which he felt that Gregory had neglected. He does not comment at all on the narrative introduction to the vision of the Temple (the first four verses of Ezekiel 40), but goes at once to the measurements. His aim, he says, is to provide a firm foundation for meditation by means of an exact comprehension of the grammar: "spiritualis intelligentiae structura firmius statuitur quando in historici sensus solido apte fundatur," "the structure of spiritual understanding is more firmly set in place when it is properly grounded in the solid substance of literal meaning"; Richard of St. Victor, *In visionem Ezechielis*, prol. (*PL* 196.527). At no point in his commentary does Richard give a spiritual interpretation of the details – that is, at no time does he trope "allegorically" upon the literal words. Perhaps a student's mnemonic may help clarify this common distinction in commentary practices: "grammatica componit, rhetorica explicat."

76 The summary picture is included by G. Zinn in his translation of some of Richard of St. Victor's meditational works, including *The Mystical Ark*: see *Richard of St. Victor*, pp. 344–370.

77 In an important article, J.-P. Antoine argues that the changeable perspectives of Trecento painting reflect a mnemotechnical perambulation about the picture-space: "Mémoire, Lieux, et Invention Spatiale." Such *picturae* as these, with changeable perspective (like the Codex Amiatinus Tabernacle), do not fit George Lessing's dictum that paintings differ cognitively from language because they are grasped all at once, without unfolding through time (as words unfold in time for a reader): see Mitchell, *Iconology*, pp. 95–115. In order to grasp the perspectives of these Trecento pictures, however, one must "walk about" in them – and that necessitates a form of temporal progression.

78 "Quemadmodum desiderat cervus ad fontes aquarum, sic desiderat anima mea ad te, Deus." The text I have used in all quotations from this psalm is the Old Latin, the basis of Augustine's comments. Since it differs in several particulars from the Revised Version, I have based my translations on the Douay.

79 "Haec meditatus sum, et effudi super me animam meam, Quoniam ingrediar in

locum tabernaculi admirabilis, usque ad domum Dei, In voce exsultationis et confessionis, soni festiuitatem celebrantis" (Psalm 41: 5).

80 Augustine, *Enarrationes in Psalmis* XLI.8.4–6; 9.1–24, 35–46, 58–62 (CCSL 38, pp. 465–466): "Ergo, ut eum tangerem, *haec meditatus sum, et effudi super me animam meam*. . . . Ille enim qui habet altissimam in secreto domum, habet etiam in terra tabernaculum. . . . Sed hic quaerendus est, quia in tabernaculo inuenitur uia, per quam uenitur ad domum. Etenim cum effunderem super me animam meam ad adtingendum Deum meum, quare hoc feci? *Quoniam ingrediar in locum tabernaculi*. Nam extra locum tabernaculi errabo quaerens Deum meum. *Quoniam ingrediar in locum tabernaculi admirabilis, usque ad domum Dei*. . . . Iam enim multa admiror in tabernaculo. Ecce quanta admiror in tabernaculo! Tabernaculum enim Dei in terra, homines sunt fideles; admiror in eis ipsorum membrorum obsequium; quia non in eis regnat peccatum ad oboediendum desideriis eius, nec exhibent membra sua arma iniquitatis peccato, sed exhibent Deo uiuo in bonis operibus; animae seruienti Deo membra corporalia militare admiror. Respicio et ipsam animam oboedientem Deo, distribuentem opera actus sui, frenantem cupiditates, pellentem ignorantiam . . . Miror et istas uirtutes in anima; sed adhuc in loco tabernaculi ambulo. Transeo et haec; et quamuis admirabile sit tabernaculum, stupeo cum peruenio usque ad domum Dei. . . . Ibi est enim fons intellectus, in sanctuario Dei, in domo Dei. . . . Ascendens tabernaculum, peruenit ad domum Dei. Tamen dum miratur membra tabernaculi, ita perductus est ad domum Dei, quamdam dulcedinem sequendo, interiorem nescio quam et occultam uoluptatem, tamquam de domo Dei sonaret suauiter aliquod organum; et cum ille ambularet in tabernaculo, audito quodam interiore sono, ductus dulcedine, sequens quod sonabat, abstrahens se ab omni strepitu carnis et sanguinis, peruenit usque ad domum Dei. Nam uiam suam et ductum suum sic ipse commemorat, quasi diceremus et: Miraris tabernaculum in hac terra; quomodo peruenisti ad secretum domus Dei? *In uoce*, inquit, *exsultationis et confessionis, soni festiuitatem celebrantis*. . . . De illa aeterna et perpetua festiuitate sonat nescio quid canorum et dulce auribus cordis; sed si non perstrepat mundus. Ambulanti in hoc tabernaculo et miracula Dei in redemtionem fidelium consideranti, mulcet aurem sonus festiuitatis illius, et rapit ceruum ad fontes aquarum."

81 Richard of St. Victor's meditation on the Tabernacle, *The Mystical Ark*, is summarized by its author in terms of a three-fold scheme of "places" very like the one Augustine uses here. My thanks to Grover Zinn for pointing this out to me.

82 Albertus Magnus, *De bono*, discussed more fully in *The Book of Memory*, pp. 137–139 (cf. 279, line 15). My translation there of Albertus' *pratum* should be corrected to "cloister," rather than the generalized meaning of "meadow, garden," since I am now convinced that he specifically had a monastery in mind.

83 See Braunfels, *Monasteries of Western Europe*, esp. pp. 74–89; P. Fergusson, *Architecture of Solitude*, has aptly characterized Cistercian reform as "a way of life in search of an architecture" (Chapter One). See also F. Bucher, "Cistercian Architectural Purism."

84 Reported in *The New York Times*, May 1, 1994.

85 See the 1994 report by the Director of the British Library, Sir Anthony Kenny, "The British Library and the St Pancras Building." Similar scholarly dismay has accompanied the building of the new Bibliothèque Nationale de France in Paris.

86 Following suggestions made by several scholars recently, including Zinn, Rudolph has argued (in *Artistic Change at St-Denis*, esp. pp. 32–47) that Hugh of St. Victor was responsible for the general plan and some of the specifics of the sculptural programs at St.-Denis under Suger. He has also analyzed Bernard of Clairvaux's somewhat arm's-length approval of the plans, presumably because the images at St.-Denis were in the lay portions of the church and not in the monks' own prayer places. See, in addition, Zinn, "Suger, Theology, and the Pseudo-Dionysian Tradition" and P. Kidson, "Panofsky, Suger, and St. Denis." Though not a study of architecture but of music, Fassler's masterful demonstration of how Victorine liturgy constructed "the church" as an expression of Hugh of St. Victor's reformist ideas, is germane to my general point here: see *Gothic Song*, esp. pp. 290–302, 315–320.

87 For Thierry's involvement at Chartres, see A. Katzenellenbogen, *Sculptural Programs*, pp. 27–36; for Peter of Celle's role at St.-Rémi, see Caviness, *Sumptuous Arts*, esp. pp. 44–62.

88 On the role of physical place in ritual and religious observance, see especially J. Z. Smith, *To Take Place*. The work of Heitz on Carolingian processional liturgies and church architecture has been especially illuminating to me of this crucial relationship, and see also C. Waddell, "The Early Cistercian Experience of the Liturgy."

89 Rudolph discusses Bernard's use of the contrast between *oratorium* and *ecclesia* in "*The Things of Greater Importance*," p. 311.

90 The memory-artist, S., described in Luria's *The Mind of a Mnemonist* used principles remarkably like those described in the *Rhetorica ad Herennium*, though he did not know that ancient treatise; neither did Luria. In his notes, Luria mentions a Japanese memory artist who used techniques similar to those of S., but who knew neither Luria nor S. (nor the ancient Greco-Roman mnemotechnical precepts): see *The Book of Memory*, pp. 75–79. A current theory in cognitive neuropsychology describes memories as being stored in "bits" in various parts of the brain, and "recollection" as a process of re-gathering the bits into a whole memory experience: see Damasio, *Descartes' Error*, esp. pp. 90–108.

91 These characteristics of proper mnemonic backgrounds are found in later medieval manuals, for example, Thomas Bradwardine's *De memoria artificiali adquirenda*. They are similar to those in the *Rhetorica ad Herennium*, but are amplified in interesting ways that suggest (to me) the degree to which familiar monastic practice had informed medieval understanding of the ancient principles.

92 Hugh of St. Victor says that a student should pay attention to a variety of factors when seeking to learn something permanently, and these include "the varying nature of the occasions during which we learned something." If we remember the circumstances in which we learned something, these will help to fix our memory of the content, and we can find it again by remembering the whole experience, whether we learned a thing at night or by day, in cloudy weather or in sunshine: *The Book of Memory*, p. 264. See also pp. 77–78 for a description of how S., the memory artist studied by Luria, recalled particular facts by re-placing himself recollectively in the conditions in which he first learned them. Many observers have written about the significance of the play of light in particular medieval churches. I confess that I find some of the conclusions reached too jejune, but I

also concede, as I think one must, that ingenuity employed in studying a building complex over a lifetime will likely produce highly intricate meditations, both individual and collective, upon its various *ductus*. That is, after all, what these buildings as cognitive engines are for.

93 A compelling meditation upon making patterns of subjects, occasioned exactly by finding (actually, by having it thrust upon her) a new *ductus* among the capitals of La Daurade, due to a changed installation by the Toulouse museum, is L. Seidel, "Installation as Inspiration." As she concludes from her re-viewing, as these capitals were installed permanently in the cloister, the monks would have had to make their own narrative way among them, out of the various associations and omissions presented by the forms, reassembling them, shuffling them about, "fict-ing" patterns from them mentally.

94 Onians, *Bearers of Meaning*, p. 58. Though *ductus* is not a concept he uses, it often describes what Onians wants to talk about, while also emphasizing the necessary sense of variation and movement which iconographic studies have too often lacked.

95 Ibid., p. 57. On the use of columns in imperial Rome, see pp. 51–58.

96 Ibid., p. 60.

97 Many scholars have emphasized this same point, many in studies I have already referred to. But a cogent critique of a modernist assumption that language (including the "language of images," iconology) somehow is prior to the actual world is G. Spiegel, "History, Historicism, and the Social Logic." See also the essays in B. Cassidy, ed. *Iconography at the Crossroads*.

98 M. Schapiro, "The Sculptures of Souillac," in his *Romanesque Art*, pp. 114–116. It is impossible now to reconstruct the original appearance of this doorway. Some art historians have wanted to reconstruct the trumeau orthopractically at the center of the door, but Schapiro argued that its position now is probably authentic. See also M. Camille, "Mouths and Meanings," though I disagree with his conclusion that the trumeau was "almost certainly" the creation of illiterate carvers rather than "the literate part of Souillac's 'textual community'." A "scream rent from a human body," Camille's apt characterization of this sculpture (p. 54), was embedded at the start of the monastic way of prayer.

99 Much has been written on the subject of Cluniac spirituality; R. Morghen, "Monastic Reform and Cluniac Spirituality" and K. Hallinger, "The Spiritual Life of Cluny in the Early Days" are places to start.

100 Anselm, *Prayers and Meditations*, Meditation 1; see Chapter Two, section 14, above. Umberto Eco's *The Name of the Rose* captures perfectly the emotional point of such sculptures, when the young monk Adso becomes disoriented and terrified by the Last Judgment sculptures on the tympanum of his church.

101 M. Schapiro, "The Romanesque Sculpture of Moissac II," in his *Romanesque Art*, p. 227; as must be obvious, I am immensely indebted to his two essays on Moissac sculpture, which I first read as an undergraduate, and was delighted to remember again.

102 In ancient rhetoric, the emotions constituted the "common ground" of barbarians, rustics, and the educated: a particularly good statement of this commonplace is in Cicero's *De oratore*, Book III.59, where he makes the point during his general discussion of decorum and delivery.

103 Schapiro, "The Sculptures of Souillac," p. 120. A. Remensnyder has studied what she calls "imaginative memory" at work in the narratives attached to various relics at Conques in "Legendary Treasure at Conques."

104 See C. Heitz, *Recherches sur les rapports entre architecture et liturgie à l'époque carolingienne* and "Architecture et liturgie processionnelle à l'époque préromane."

105 The chronicler who described these processions, Hariulf, represents them as having been decreed by Angilbert, the Carolingian abbot, and therefore to have been performed since the ninth century, but there is controversy over how precisely he is to be understood.

106 Heitz, "Architecture et liturgie processionnelle," p. 35 (my translation).

107 W. Tronzo, "The Prestige of St. Peter's," discusses a somewhat similar "mapping" function of certain motifs in church floor mosaics. Richard Ivo Schneider has argued that Abbot Suger's inscriptions for the various locations within his "new" church at St.-Denis, described in his own *De administratione*, were intended as a sort of "pilgrims' guide" to the church, and conceive of the interior as a set of "places" or stations, at each of which liturgical and/or individual prayer is meant to occur, the pilgrims thus making their "Way" through. Schneider presented some of his research at the Medieval Academy of America meeting in March, 1995.

108 This is related to Baxandall's observation in *Patterns of Intention* that art criticism (and one should add literary criticism) is a matter of decorum between the critic's opinions and observations and the work, the successful "fitness" of which ultimately can only be judged by how well it persuades others.

109 John Cassian, *Conférence* XIV.xi (SC 54, p. 197): "Pro capacitate enim humanorum sensuum [scripturarum] quoque species coaptatur"; the whole passage, which discusses how Scripture's "face" changes as a student proceeds in his studies, is pertinent. The other quote is from *Conférence* IX.viii, in which Isaac talks about the kinds of prayer (SC 54, p. 48): "Vniversas orationum species … conprehendi non posse. Tot enim sunt quot in una anima, immo in cunctis animabus status queunt qualitatesque generari." I discussed the passage from Augustine's *De trinitate* VIII.iv in Chapter Three, section 1. Cassian stresses that the "truth" of a prayer is a matter of a person's character (purity of heart) and of grace, the illumination of the Holy Spirit. The former shares something with Quintilian's *vir bonus*, the orator of good character whose words are true because his character enables him to select them wisely.

110 John Cassian, *Conférence* XIV.ix (SC 54, p. 193): "si scientiae spiritalis sacrum in corde uestro uultis tabernaculum praeparare." In the next section (x) of this Conference, Abba Nesteros develops at some length a meditation on the Ark and some of the Sacred Vessels. Evidently, this was a favored *machina mentis* even at this early date, as we have seen from other evidence.

111 S. Murray, *Notre Dame Cathedral at Amiens*, pp. 38–43, has demonstrated how one of the chief units of measurement, the central square, at Amiens cathedral is based upon the measurements of the Ark of the Covenant, a square which also includes the "golden proportion" of 5:3 (the dimensions of the Ark given in Exodus 27:1 are five cubits by five cubits by three cubits). Murray describes at length the varying *ductus* (though this is not his word) within this great building

as an experience of movements through both space and time. See also his essay "The Architectural Envelope of the Sainte-Chapelle," and M. Davis, "Scenes from a Design."

112 See T. Kinder, "The Original Chevet of Pontigny's Church," for a brief summary of some of the reasons scholars have proposed for the rebuilding. Carlo Ginzburg has an interesting essay relevant to the cognitive power of such shape-punning, pointing out how, in some nineteenth-century circles (such as psychoanalysis), this procedure attained the status of an evidentiary paradigm for establishing the truth: *Clues, Myths*, pp. 96–125.

113 W. Horn, "The Origins of the Medieval Cloister," esp. pp. 37– 48. Seidel, "Legends in Limestone," comments on the effects of light in the patterns of the nave capitals in St.-Lazare, Autun.

114 P. Meyvaert, "The Medieval Monastic *Claustrum*," describes the various activities, including pedagogical, that went on in a cloister. The complex memory work possible in a cloister has been the subject of detailed studies by some historians: see Seidel, "Installation as Inspiration" (on La Daurade); K. Nolan, "Narration in the Capital Frieze at Notre-Dame at Etampes"; and L. Rutchick, "Sculptural Programs in the Moissac Cloister."

115 *Chronicon centulense* II.8: "Quia igitur omnis plebs fidelium sanctissimam atque inseparabilem Trinitatem confiteri, venerari et in mente colere firmiterque credere debet ... tres æcclesias principales ... fundare studuimus." Quoted from Horn, "On the Origins of the Medieval Cloister," p. 43.

116 Cloisters were sometimes glazed: in the later Middle Ages, even the Cistercians did so, especially if the cloister galleries were also used as the *scriptorium*; see J. Hayward, "Glazed Cloisters."

117 Gregory the Great, *Hom. in Hiezech.* II, homilia X.17–18 (CCSL 142, pp. 392–394). For example, Gregory says that the square shape, equally as wide as it is long, signifies how, in a perfect life, all four cardinal virtues (prudence, temperance, justice, and fortitude) are found in equal amounts. The dimensions of the atrium, 100 by 100 cubits, form a perfect number; so life is perfected by long-suffering hope, widespread charity, certain faith, and careful performance of good works. And so on.

118 Ibid., homilia VI.2 (CCSL 142, p. 295.15–19): "Quia sermone Graeco *phylattein* seruare dicitur, et gazae lingua Persica diuitiae vocantur, gazophylacium locus appellari solet quo divitiae seruantur. Quid itaque per gazophylacia designatur, nisi, ut praediximus, corda doctorum sapientiae atque scientiae diuitiis plena?" "Since in the Greek language *phylattein* means 'to save up,' and in the Persian language riches are called *gazae*, the place in which riches are stored is usually called *gazophylacium*. What therefore can be meant by *gazophylacia* except, as we said earlier, hearts full of knowledge and the rich wisdom of the Fathers?" The word *gazophylacium* is unique to Ezekiel, and so when it appears in monastic meditations (for example, in Peter of Celle's meditation on "The School of the Cloister," ch. 13) the allusion is to Ezekiel. Gregory's commentary was repeated by Hrabanus and other commentators on Ezekiel, and so found its way into the ordinary gloss in the late eleventh century.

119 Richard de Fournival, *Biblionomia*, in L. Delisle, *Le Cabinet des Manuscrits*, vol. 2, 520–521. Delisle, dismissing Richard's "metaphor" (and thus his orga-

nizing scheme), sets out instead to give an idea of what Richard's library would have really been like [!], with reading desks and books in cases, larger volumes on the bottom shelves, each volume marked by a letter, and so on (pp. 518–519). I discussed another work of Richard's, the preface to his *Bestiaire d'Amour*, in *The Book of Memory*, esp. pp. 223–229.

120 Honorius Augustodunensis, *Gemma animae* I.148 (*PL* 172.590): "Claustralis constructio juxta monasterium est sumpta a porticu Salamonis constructa juxta templum." The phrase *machina ecclesiae* occurs in I.131 (*PL* 172.586). W. Dynes, "The Medieval Cloister as Portico of Solomon," has shown that the analogy of the cloister and Solomon's portico was common in the twelfth century. Dynes suggests that the specific connection of *claustrum* with Solomon's portico was made by Crusaders, for Crusader maps of Jerusalem labeled the area of the portico of Solomon "Claustrum Templi Salamonis" (p. 63).

121 For instance, in *Gemma animae* I, chs. 132, 141 (*PL* 172.586, 588). A variant is "ut ... jugiter memoretur" (ch. 135; ibid., 587). Various mnemotechnic features characterize Honorius' style, including a marked tendency to rhyme related phrases, such as (in ch. 123; ibid., 584) "templum ... dedicavit, arcam ... locavit[;] Quod quia ... Ecclesiam praefiguravit ... secundum formam ... populus ... ecclesias formavit," and recollectively linking letters to concepts, as in ch. 126 (ibid., 585), in which the seven phonemes in the word *ecclesia* are associated with the seven gifts of the Spirit. Such mnemotechnical devices persisted in the *ars praedicandi* treatises of the later Middle Ages: see *The Book of Memory*, pp. 104–107.

122 Honorius Augustodunensis, *Gemma animae* I, ch. 122, preface (*PL* 172.583): "Haec breviter de missa dixerimus, nunc pauca de ecclesia, in qua agitur, videamus."

123 Hrabanus Maurus, Homilia 39 "In dedicatione templi"; *Homiliae de festis praecipius, etc.* (*PL* 110.73–74): "[B]ene convenistis hodie, fratres charissimi, ut Deo domum dedicaremus ... Sed hoc tunc facimus si ipsi Dei templum fieri contendimus, studemus congruere solemnitati quam colimus; ut sicut ornatis studiosius ejusdem ecclesiae parietibus, pluribus accensis luminaribus, diversis per litanias et preces, per lectiones et cantica, excitatis vocibus, Deo laudem parare satagerimus: ita etiam penetralia cordium nostrorum semper necessariis bonorum operum decoremus ornatibus, semper in nobis flamma divinae pariter et fraternae charitatis augescat, semper in secretario pectoris nostri coelestium memoria praeceptorum et evangelicae laudationis dulcedo sancta resonet. Hi sunt enim fructus bonae arboris, hic boni thesaurus cordis, haec fundamenta sapientis architecti, quae nobis hodierna sancta Evangelii lectio commendat."

Bibliography

GENERAL REFERENCE WORKS

Bell, David N. *An Index of Authors and Works in Cistercian Libraries in Great Britain*. Kalamazoo: Cistercian Publications, 1992.

Blaise, Albert. *Lexicon Latinitatis Medii Aevii*. CCCM 28. Turnhout: Brepols, 1975.

CETEDOC: Library of Christian Latin Texts. CD-ROM version 2. Turnhout: Brepols, 1994.

Dictionary of Medieval Latin from British Sources. Prepared by R. E. Latham. London: Oxford University Press, 1975–.

Dictionary of National Biography. Edited by L. Stephen and S. Lee. London: Smith, Elder, 1908.

Dictionnaire de spiritualité ascétique et mystique. Edited by Marcel Viller. Paris: G. Beauchesne, 1937–.

Godefroy, Frédéric. *Dictionnaire de l'ancienne langue française*. 1881–1902; rpt. Paris: Slatkine, 1982.

Harvey, Paul. *The Oxford Companion to Classical Literature*. Oxford University Press, 1937.

Lanham, Richard A. *A Handlist of Rhetorical Terms*. Second edition. Berkeley: University of California, 1991.

Lewis, C. T. and C. Short, eds. *A Latin Dictionary*. Oxford: Clarendon Press, 1879.

Liddell, H. G. and R. Scott, eds. *A Greek–English Lexicon*. Revised edition. Oxford: Clarendon Press, 1968.

Middle English Dictionary. Edited by H. Kurath, S. M. Kuhn, and R. Lewis. Ann Arbor: University of Michigan Press, 1952–.

Murphy, James J. *Medieval Rhetoric: A Select Bibliography*. Second edition. Toronto: University of Toronto Press, 1989.

The Oxford English Dictionary on Historical Principles. Edited by J. H. A. Murray, et al. Oxford: Clarendon Press, 1933.

The Oxford Latin Dictionary. Edited by P. G. W. Clare. New York: Oxford University Press, 1982.

A Revised Medieval Latin Word List. Prepared by R. E. Latham. London: Oxford University Press, 1965.

Stone, Louise and W. Rothwell. *Anglo-Norman Dictionary*. London: Modern Humanities Research Association, 1977.

Bibliography

Strayer, Joseph *et al. Dictionary of the Middle Ages*. New York: Charles Scribner for the American Council of Learned Societies, 1982–1989.

Thesaurus linguae latinae. Leipzig: Teubner, 1900–.

CATALOGUES AND FACSIMILES

Alexander, Jonathan J. G. *Insular Manuscripts, 6th–9th Centuries. A Survey of Manuscripts Illuminated in the British Isles*, I. London: Harvey Miller, 1978.

Courcelle, Pierre and J. Courcelle. *Iconographie de saint Augustin. Les cycles du XIVe au XVIIIe siècles*. 5 vols. Paris: Etudes augustiniennes, 1965–1991.

De Meyier, K. A. *Codices Vossiani Latini*. 4 vols. Leiden: Bibliotheca Universitatis Leiden, 1973–1984.

De Wald, Edgar. *The Illustrations of the Utrecht Psalter*. Princeton University Press, 1932.

Gatti Perer, M. L. *et al.*, eds. *'La dimora di Dio con gli uomini': Immagini della Gerusalemme celeste dal III al XIV secolo*. Milan: Vita e Pensiero, 1983.

Henry, Françoise. *The Book of Kells*. New York: Knopf, 1974.

Kauffmann, C. M. *Romanesque Manuscripts, 1066–1190. A Survey of Manuscripts Illuminated in the British Isles*, III. London: Harvey Miller, 1975.

James, M. R. *A Descriptive Catalogue of the Manuscripts in the Library of Corpus Christi College, Cambridge*. Cambridge University Press, 1912.

Los Beatos (Europalia 85 España). Edited by Luis Revenga *et al.* Brussels: Chapelle de Nassau, Bibliothèque royale Albert Ier, 1985.

Millar, E. G. *The Rutland Psalter*. Oxford University Press, for the Roxburghe Club, 1937.

Morgan, Nigel. *Early Gothic Manuscripts, 1250–1285*. 2 vols. *A Survey of Manuscripts Illuminated in the British Isles*, IV. London: Harvey Miller, 1988.

Netzer, Nancy and Virginia Reinburg, eds. *Memory and the Middle Ages: Catalogue of an Exhibition at the Boston College Museum of Art*. Boston: Boston College Museum of Art, 1995.

A Spanish Apocalypse: The Morgan Beatus Manuscript (M. 644), Commentary by John Williams and Barbara Shailor. New York: G. Braziller and The Pierpont Morgan Library, 1991.

Stettiner, Richard. *Die illustrierten Prudentius-Handschriften*. 2 vols. Berlin: Grotesche, 1905.

PRIMARY WORKS

Adam of Dryburgh. *De tripartito tabernaculo*. PL 198.609–796.

Alanus de Insulis. *De planctu Naturae*. Edited by N. M. Häring. *Studi medievali*, serie terza 19.2 (1978): 798–879.

Albertus Magnus. *De bono*. In *Opera Omnia*, vol. 28. Edited by H. Kühle, C. Feckes, B. Geyer, W. Kubel. Aschendorff: Monasterii Westfalorum, 1951.

    Commentary on Aristotle's Parva naturalia: De memoria et reminiscentia. In *Opera omnia*, vol. 9. Edited by A. Borgnet. Paris: Ludovicum Vives, 1890.

Alcuin. *De animae ratione liber ad Eulaliam virginem*. PL 101.639–650.

Bibliography

The Rhetoric of Alcuin and Charlemagne. Edited and translated by W. S. Howell. Princeton University Press, 1941.

Aldhelm. *Aenigmata*. Edited by Fr. Glorie. CCSL 133. Turnhout: Brepols, 1968.

Anselm of Bec. *Orationes siue meditationes*. In *Sancti Anselmi Cantuariensis Archiepiscopi opera omnia*. Edited by F. S. Schmitt. 1938; rpt. Madrid: BAC, 1953. Translated by B. Ward as *The Prayers and Meditations of St. Anselm*. London: Penguin, 1973.

Aristotle. *De memoria et reminiscentia*, translated as *Aristotle on Memory*, with commentary and notes, by R. Sorabji. Providence, RI: Brown University Press, 1972.

Arnobius Iunior. *Commentarii in Psalmos*. Edited by K.-D. Daur. CCSL 25. Turnhout: Brepols, 1990.

Athanasius. *The Life of St. Anthony*. Translated by M. Keenan. In R. Deferrari, ed. *Early Christian Biographies*, pp. 127–216. FC 15. Washington: Catholic University of America Press, 1952.

Augustinus Aurelius, Bishop of Hippo (Saint Augustine). *Confessionum libri XIII*. Edited by L. Verheijen. CCSL 27. Turnhout: Brepols, 1981.

De catechizandis rudibus. Edited by I. B. Bauer. CCSL 46, pp. 115–178. Turnhout: Brepols, 1969.

De civitate Dei. Edited by B. Dombart and A. Kalb. CCSL 47–48. Turnhout: Brepols, 1955.

De doctrina christiana. Edited by J. Martin. CCSL 32, pp. 1–167. Turnhout: Brepols, 1962.

De trinitate. Edited by W. J. Mountain. 2 vols. CCSL 50–50A. Turnhout: Brepols, 1968.

Enarrationes in Psalmis. Edited by E. Dekkers and J. Fraipont. CCSL 38–40. Turnhout: Brepols, 1956.

Epistulae. Edited by A. Goldbacher. CSEL 34. Vienna: F. Tempsky, 1898.

De Genesi ad litteram libri duodecim. Edited by J. Zycha. CSEL 28, sect. 3.2. Vienna: F. Tempsky, 1894.

"Sermo CXIII, de verbis evangelii Luce xvi:9." *Sermones ad populum*. PL 38.648–652.

Ausonius. *Cento nuptialis*. Translated by H. G. E. White. LCL 96, pp. 370–396. London: Heinemann, 1919.

Baudri de Bourgeuil. *Baldrici Burguliani Carmina*. Edited by K. Hilbert. Heidelberg: Carl Winter, 1979.

Les œuvres poétiques de Baudri de Bourgueil. Edited by P. Abrahams. Paris: Champion, 1926.

Beatus of Liébana. *Beati in Apocalipsin Libri Duodecim*. Edited by H. A. Sanders. Papers and Monographs of the American Academy in Rome 7. Rome: American Academy in Rome, 1930.

Beda Venerabilis. *De tabernaculo et vasis eius ac vestibus sacerdotum Libri III, De templo Libri II*. In *Opera exegetica*, pars II. Edited by D. Hurst. CCSL 119A. Turnhout: Brepols, 1969.

Vita sanctorum abbatum monasterii in Uyramutha et Gyruum. In *Bede's Historical Works*. 2 vols. Translated by J. E. King. LCL 248. London: Heinemann, 1963.

Benedict of Nursia. *Regula Benedicti*. Revised edition by R. Hanslik. CSEL 75. Vienna: Hoelder, 1977.

Bibliography

Bernard of Clairvaux. *Sancti Bernardi opera*. Edited by C. Talbot, J. Leclercq, and H. Rochais. 6 vols. Roma: Editiones Cistercienses, 1957.

The Life and Death of St. Malachy, the Irishman. Translated by R. T. Meyer. Kalamazoo: Cistercian Publications, 1978.

Sermons on the Song of Songs. Translated by K. Walsh. 4 vols. Kalamazoo: Cistercian Publications, 1971.

Biblia Sacra juxta Vulgatam Clementinam, nova editio. Seventh edition. Madrid: BAC, 1985.

Boethius, Anicius Manlius Severinus. *Philosophiae consolatio*. Edited by L. Bieler. CCSL 94. Turnhout: Brepols, 1984.

Boncompagno da Signa. *Rhetorica novissima*. Edited by A. Gaudenzi. *Scripta anecdota glossatorum*. Bibliotheca Iuridica Medii Aevi, vol. 2. Bononiae [Bologna], 1892.

Bruno de Querfort. *Vita quinque fratrum*. Edited by R. Kade. MGH Scriptores 15.2, pp. 709–738. 1888; rpt. New York: Kraus, 1963.

Bryan, W. F. and G. Dempster, eds. *Sources and Analogues of Chaucer's Canterbury Tales*. 1941; rpt. New York: Humanities Press, 1958.

Cassiodorus, M. Aurelius. *Expositio Psalmorum I-LXX*. Edited by M. Adriaen. CCSL 97–98. Turnhout: Brepols, 1958.

Institutiones. Edited by R. A. B. Mynors. Oxford University Press, 1937.

Cicero, Marcus Tullius. *Topica*, etc. Edited and translated by H. M. Hubbell. LCL 386. Cambridge, MA: Harvard University Press, 1949.

De natura deorum, etc. Edited and translated by H. Rackham. LCL 141. London: Heinemann, 1919.

De oratore, etc. Edited and translated by E. W. Sutton and H. Rackham. 2 vols. LCL 348–349. London: Heinemann, 1942–1948.

Tusculan Disputations. Edited and translated by J. E. King. Second edition. LCL 40. London: Heinemann, 1943.

Clark, Elizabeth A. and D. F. Hatch, eds. and trans. *The Golden Bough, the Oaken Cross: The Virgilian Cento of Faltonia Betitia Proba*. American Academy of Religion, texts and translations 5. Chico, CA: Scholars Press, for the American Academy of Religion, 1981.

Clark, Willene B., ed. and trans. *The Medieval Book of Birds: Hugh of Fouilloy's Aviarium*. Binghamton, NY: MRTS, 1992.

Davis-Weyer, Caecilia. *Early Medieval Art: 300–1150*. Medieval Academy Reprints for Teaching 17. 1971; rpt. Toronto: University of Toronto Press, 1986.

Egeria. *Itinerarium Egeriae*. Edited by A. Franceschini and R. Weber. In *Itineraria et alia geographica* (q.v.). CCSL 175, pp. 27–103. Translated by John Wilkinson as *Egeria's Travels to the Holy Land*. Warminster: Aris and Phillips, 1981.

Fortunatianus, C. *Artis rhetoricae libri III*. In Carolus Halm, ed. *Rhetores latini minores*, pp. 81–134. Leipzig: Teubner, 1863.

Gardiner, Eileen, trans. *Visions of Heaven and Hell Before Dante*. New York: Italica Press, 1988.

Geoffrey of Vinsauf. *Poetria nova*. In E. Faral, ed. *Les arts poétiques des xiie et xiiie siècles*. 1924; rpt. Paris: Champion, 1958.

Goldschmidt, R. C. *Paulinus' Churches at Nola: Texts, Translations and Commentary*. Amsterdam: Noord-Hollandsche Uitgevers Maatschappij, 1940.

Gregory the Great. *Dialogues*. Edited by Adalbert de Vogüé. SC 260. Paris: Editions du Cerf, 1979.

Expositio in Canticum canticorum. Edited by P. Verbraken. CCSL 144. Turnhout: Brepols, 1963.

Homiliae in Hiezechihelem prophetam. Edited by M. Adriaen. CCSL 142. Turnhout: Brepols, 1971.

Moralia in Job. Edited by M. Adriaen. 3 vols. CCSL 143–143B. Turnhout: Brepols, 1979–1985.

Heito of Reichenau. *Visio Wettii*. Edited by E. Duemmler. MGH, Poetae latinae aevi Carolini, vol. 2, pp. 267–275. 1884; rpt. Munich, 1978.

Herrad of Hohenbourg. *Hortus deliciarum*. Edited by Rosalie Green *et al.* London: The Warburg Institute, 1979.

Honorius Augustodunensis. *Gemma animae*. PL 172.541–738.

Hrabanus Maurus. *De clericorum institutione*. PL 107.293–420.

Commentaria in Ezechielem prophetam. PL 110.493–1084.

Homiliae de festis praecipuis, etc. PL 110.1–134.

Hugh of Poitiers. *The Vézelay Chronicle*. Translated by J. Scott and J. O. Ward, with essays by E. Cox. Binghamton, NY: MRTS, 1992.

Hugh of St. Victor. *De arca Noe mystica (De pictura Arche)*. PL 176.681–702.

Didascalicon. Edited by C. H. Buttimer. Catholic University of America Studies in Medieval and Renaissance Latin 10. Washington: Catholic University Press, 1939. Translated by J. Taylor. New York: Columbia University Press, 1961.

Libellus de modo dicendi et meditandi, De modo orandi, De meditando. PL 176.877–880, 977–987, 993–998.

Hugo of Rouen. *Tractatus de memoria*. PL 192.1299–1324.

Isidore of Seville. *Etymologiae*. Edited by W. M. Lindsay. 2 vols. Oxford Classical Texts. Oxford: Clarendon Press, 1911.

Itineraria et alia geographica. Edited by Fr. Glorie. CCSL 175–176.. Turnhout: Brepols, 1965.

Itinerarium burdigalense. Edited by P. Geyer and O. Cuntz. In *Itineraria et alia geographica* (q.v.), CCSL 175, pp. 1–26.

Jacobus de Voragine. *The Golden Legend*. Translated by W. Ryan. 2 vols. Princeton University Press, 1993.

Jerome. *Commentarii in Hiezechielem*. Edited by F. Glorie. CCSL 75. Turnhout: Brepols, 1964.

Epistulae. PL 22.

Liber interpretationis hebraicorum nominum. Edited by P. de Lagarde. CCSL 72. Turnhout: Brepols, 1959.

John Cassian. *Conférences (Collationes)*. Edited and translated by E. Pichery. SC 42, 54, 64. Paris: Editions du Cerf, 1955. Translated by Colm Luibheid. New York: Paulist Press, 1985.

Institutions cénobitiques. Edited by J.-C. Guy. SC 109. Paris: Editions du Cerf, 1965.

John Chrysostom. "Discourse on Blessed Babylas and Against the Greeks." In *St. John Chrysostom, Apologist*. Translated by Margaret A. Schatkin. FC 73. Washington, DC: The Catholic University of America Press, 1985.

Libri Carolini sive Caroli Magni capitulare de imaginibus. Edited by H. Bastgen. MGH, Concilia vol. 2, supplementum. Hanover, 1924.

Lieu, Samuel N. C. *The Emperor Julian: Panegyric and Polemic.* Second edition. Liverpool University Press, 1989.

Macrobius. *Commentary on the Dream of Scipio.* Translated by W. H. Stahl. New York: Columbia University Press, 1952.

Martianus Capella. *De nuptiis philologiae et Mercurii.* Edited by A. Dick. 1925; rpt. Stuttgart: Teubner, 1969. Translated by W. H. Stahl and R. Johnson in *Martianus Capella and the Seven Liberal Arts.* New York: Columbia University Press, 1977.

 Liber de arte rhetorica (Book V of *De nuptiis*). In C. Halm, ed. *Rhetores latini minores*, pp. 451–492. Leipzig: Teubner, 1863.

Maximus Taurinensis. *Sermonum collectio antiqua.* Edited by A. Mutzenbecher. CCSL 23. Turnhout: Brepols, 1962.

Miller, Joseph M., M. H. Prosser, and T. W. Benson. *Readings in Medieval Rhetoric.* Bloomington: Indiana University Press, 1973.

Minnis, A. J., A. B. Scott, and D. Wallace, eds. *Medieval Literary Theory and Criticism, c. 1100– c.1375: The Commentary Tradition.* Oxford: Clarendon Press, 1988.

Mitchell, Bruce and F. C. Robinson. *A Guide to Old English.* Fourth edition. Oxford: Basil Blackwell, 1986.

Panofsky, Erwin and G. Panofsky-Soergel, eds. and trans. *Abbot Suger on the Abbey Church of St.-Denis and its Art Treasures.* Second edition. Princeton University Press, 1979.

Peter Chrysologus. *Sermonum collectio.* Edited by A. Olivar. 3 vols. CCSL 24–24B. Turnhout: Brepols, 1975–1982.

Peter of Celle. *De afflictione et lectione, De conscientia, De puritate animae.* Edited in Jean Leclercq, *La spiritualité de Pierre de Celle.* Paris: J. Vrin, 1946.

 De disciplina claustrali. Edited and translated by G. de Martel. SC 240. Paris: Editions du Cerf, 1977.

 Liber de panibus. PL 202.929–1046.

 Peter of Celle: Selected Works. Translated by H. Feiss. Kalamazoo: Cistercian Publications, 1987.

Peter of Ravenna (Petrus Tommai). *Foenix Domini Petri Ravennatis Memoriae Magistri.* Venice: Bernardinus de Choris de Cremona, 1491 [1492].

Petrus Pictor. *Carmina.* Edited by L. Van Acker. CCCM 25. Turnhout: Brepols, 1972.

Prudentius (Aurelius Prudentius Clemens). *Opera.* Edited and translated by H. J. Thomson. LCL 387, 398. London: Heinemann, 1949–1953.

 Carmina. Edited by M. P. Cunningham. CCSL 126. Turnhout: Brepols, 1966.

Quintilian, M. Fabius. *De institutione oratoria.* Edited by M. Winterbottom. 2 vols. Oxford Classical Texts. Oxford: Clarendon Press, 1970. Translated by H. E. Butler. LCL 124–127. London: Heinemann, 1922.

Quodvultdeus, Bishop of Carthage. *Liber promissionum.* In *Opera.* Edited by R. Braun. CCSL 60. Turnhout: Brepols, 1976.

Rhetorica ad Herennium (Ad C. Herennium Libri IV De Ratione Dicendi). Edited and translated by Harry Caplan. LCL 403. Cambridge, MA: Harvard University Press, 1954.

Richard de Fournival. *Biblionomia.* In L. Deslisle, *Le Cabinet des Manuscrits de la*

Bibliography

Bibliothèque Nationale, vol. 2, pp. 518–535. 1868–1881; rpt. New York: Burt Franklin, 1973.

Richard of St. Victor. *In visionem Ezechielis. PL* 196.527–600.

The Mystical Ark (or Benjamin major). Translated by G. A. Zinn, Jr. *Richard of St. Victor,* pp. 149–370. New York: Paulist Press, 1979.

Spalding, Mary Caroline. *The Middle English Charters of Christ.* Bryn Mawr College Monographs 15. Bryn Mawr, PA: Bryn Mawr College, 1914.

Speculum virginum. Edited by J. Seyfarth. CCCM 5. Turnhout: Brepols, 1990.

Sprague, Rosamond Kent. "Dissoi Logoi or Dialexeis." *Mind* 77 (1968): 155–167.

Strabo, Walahfrid. "Carmina ad Agobardum Episcopum Lugdunensem." Edited by E. Duemmler. MGH, Poetae latini aevi Carolini, vol. 2, pp. 356–357. 1884; rpt. Munich, 1978.

Visio Wetti. Edited by E. Duemmler. MGH, Poetae latini aevi Carolini, vol. 2, pp. 301–333. 1884; rpt. Munich, 1978.

Suger, Abbot. See under Panofsky.

Tertullian, Q. S. Fl. *Ad nationes libri II.* In *Opera omnia.* Edited by J. G. Ph. Borleffs. CCSL 1. Turnhout: Brepols, 1954.

Theodulph of Orleans. *Carmina.* Edited by L. Traube. MGH, Poetae latini aevi Carolini, vol. 1. 1896; rpt. Munich: 1978.

Trexler, Richard, ed. *The Christian at Prayer: An Illustrated Prayer Manual Attributed to Peter the Chanter.* Binghamton, NY: MRTS, 1987.

Varro. *De lingua latina.* Edited and translated by R. G. Kent. LCL 333–334. London: Heinemann, 1938.

Venantius Fortunatus. *Carmina.* Edited by F. Leo. MGH, Auctorum antiquissimorum, vol. 4, pt. 1. 1881; rpt. Berlin: Weidmann, 1961.

Virgil. *Eclogues, Georgics, and Aeneid.* Edited and translated by H. R. Fairclough. LCL 63–64. Cambridge, MA: Harvard University Press, 1978.

von Arnim, H. F. *Stoicorum veterum fragmenta.* Stuttgart: Teubner, 1968.

Wilkinson, John. *Jerusalem Pilgrims Before the Crusades.* Warminster: Aris and Phillips, 1977.

SECONDARY WORKS

Actas del Simposio para el Estudio de los Codices del "Comentario al Apocalipsis" de Beato de Liébana. Grupo de Estudios Beato de Liébana. 3 vols. Madrid: Joyas Bibliográficas, 1978.

Ahl, Frederick. *Metaformations: Soundplay and Wordplay in Ovid and Other Classical Poets.* Ithaca: Cornell University Press, 1985.

Alexander, Loveday. "The Living Voice: Scepticism towards the Written Word in Early Christian and in Graeco-Roman Texts." *The Bible in Three Dimensions,* pp. 221–247. Edited by D. Clines, S. Fowl, and S. Porter. *Journal for the Study of the Old Testament,* supplement series 87. Sheffield: Sheffield Academic Press, 1990.

Alexandre-Bidon, Danièle. "La lettre volée: apprendre à lire à l'enfant au moyen âge." *Annales ESC* 44 (1989): 953–992.

Anderson, Maxwell L. *Pompeian Frescoes in The Metropolitan Museum of Art.* New York: Metropolitan Museum of Art, 1987.

Bibliography

Annas, Julia. "Aristotle on Memory and the Self." In M. C. Nussbaum and A. O. Rorty, eds. *Essays on Aristotle's* De Anima, pp. 297–311. Oxford: Clarendon Press, 1992.

"Memories are made of this and that." *London Review of Books*, 14 May 1992: 21–22.

Antoine, Jean-Philippe. "*Ad perpetuam memoriam*: Les nouvelles fonctions de l'image peinte en Italie, 1250–1400." *Melanges de l'Ecole Français de Rome* 100 (1988): 541–615.

"Mémoire, lieux et invention spatiale dans la peinture italienne des xiiie et xive siècles." *Annales ESC* 48 (1993): 1447–1469.

Avril, François. "Quelques considérations sur l'exécution matérielle des enluminures de l'Apocalypse de Saint-Sever." In *Actas del Simposio para el estudio de los códices del "Comentario al Apocalipsis" de Beato de Liébana* (q.v.), pp. 263–71.

Backhouse, Janet. *The Lindisfarne Gospels.* London: Phaidon, 1981.

Bagni, Paolo. "L'*inventio* nell'ars poetica latino-medievale." In B. Vickers, ed. *Rhetoric Revalued: Papers from the International Society for the History of Rhetoric*, pp. 99–114, Binghamton, NY: MRTS, 1982.

Baldovin, John F. *The Urban Character of Christian Worship: The Origins, Development, and Meaning of Stational Liturgy.* Rome: Pontificale Institutum Studiorum Orientalium, 1987.

Baldwin, John W. *Masters, Princes, and Merchants: The Social Views of Peter the Chanter and His Circle.* Princeton University Press, 1970.

"Masters at Paris from 1179–1215." In R. Benson and G. Constable, eds. *Renaissance and Renewal in the Twelfth Century* (q.v.), pp. 138–172.

Bartlett, Frederic C. *Remembering: A Study in Experimental and Social Psychology.* Cambridge University Press, 1932.

Baxandall, Michael. *Patterns of Intention.* New Haven: Yale University Press, 1985.

Shadows and Enlightenment. New Haven: Yale University Press, 1995.

Beaujouan, Guy and Paul Cattin. *Philippe Elephant (Mathematique, Alchimie, Ethique)*, pp. 285–363. Histoire littéraire de la France. Paris: Académie des Inscriptions et Belles-lettres, 1981.

Bechmann, Roland. "La mnémotechnique des constructeurs gothiques." *Pour la Science* (Paris) 158 (December 1990): 98–104.

Villard de Honnecourt: La pensée technique au XIIIe siècle et sa communication. Paris: Picard, 1991.

Belting, Hans. *Likeness and Presence: A History of the Image Before the Era of Art.* Translated by E. Jephcott from *Bild und Kult* (Munich, 1990). Chicago: University of Chicago Press, 1994.

Benson, Robert L. and Giles Constable, eds. *Renaissance and Renewal in the Twelfth Century.* Cambridge, MA: Harvard University Press, 1982.

Bergmann, Bettina. "The Roman House as Memory Theater: The House of the Tragic Poet in Pompeii." *Art Bulletin* 76 (1994): 225–256.

Black, Deborah L. "Estimation (*Wahm*) in Avicenna: The Logical and Psychological Dimensions." *Dialogue. Canadian Philosophical Review/ Revue canadienne de philosophie* 32 (1993): 219–258.

Blair, Carole Marsha Jeppeson, and Enrico Pucci, Jr. "Public Memorializing in Postmodernity: The Vietnam Veterans Memorial as Prototype." *Quarterly Journal of Speech* 77 (1991): 263–288.

368

Bibliography

Blair, Peter Hunter. *The World of Bede.* London: Secker & Warburg, 1970.

Block, Ned. "Mental Pictures and Cognitive Science." *The Philosophical Review* 92 (1983): 499–541.

ed. *Imagery.* Cambridge, MA: MIT Press, 1981.

Bloomfield, Morton. *The Seven Deadly Sins.* East Lansing, MI: Michigan State College Press, 1952.

Blum, Herwig. *Die antike Mnemotechnik.* Spudasmata 15. Hildesheim: Georg Olms, 1969.

Bober, Harry. "An Illustrated Medieval School-Book of Bede's 'De Natura Rerum'." *The Journal of the Walters Art Gallery* 19–20 (1956–1957): 64– 97.

Bolzoni, Lina. *Il teatro della memoria: studi su Giulio Camillo.* Padua: Liviana, 1984.

L'idea del theatro di Gulio Camillo. Palermo: Sellerio, 1991.

La stanza della memoria: Modelli letterari e iconografici nell'età della stampa. Turin: Einaudi, 1995.

Bolzoni, Lina and Pietro Corsi, eds. *La cultura della memoria.* Bologna: Il Mulino, 1992.

Bonner, Stanley F. *Education in Ancient Rome.* Berkeley and Los Angeles: University of California Press, 1977.

Braunfels, Wolfgang. *Monasteries of Western Europe: The Architecture of the Orders.* Translated by A. Laing. London: Thames & Hudson, 1972.

Brilliant, Richard. *Visual Narratives: Storytelling in Etruscan and Roman Art.* Ithaca: Cornell University Press, 1984.

"The Bayeux Tapestry: A Stripped Narrative for their Eyes and Ears." *Word & Image* 7 (1991): 98–123.

Brown, Peter. *Augustine of Hippo.* Berkeley: University of California Press, 1967.

The Making of Late Antiquity. Cambridge, MA: Harvard University Press, 1978.

The Cult of the Saints. Chicago: University of Chicago Press, 1981.

Power and Persuasion in Late Antiquity: Towards a Christian Empire. Madison, WI: University of Wisconsin Press, 1992.

Bruce-Mitford, R. L. S. "The Art of the Codex Amiatinus." *The Journal of the British Archaeological Society,* third series, vol. 32 (1969): 1–25.

Bucher, François. "Cistercian Architectural Purism." *Comparative Studies in Society and History* 3 (January 1960): 89–107.

Butler, E. Cuthbert. *Western Mysticism.* Second edition. 1926; rpt. New York: Harper & Row, 1966.

Bynum, Caroline Walker. *'Docere verbo et exemplo': An Aspect of Twelfth-Century Spirituality.* Harvard Theological Studies 31. Missoula, MT: University of Montana Press, 1979.

Jesus as Mother: Studies in the Spirituality of the High Middle Ages. Berkeley and Los Angeles: University of California Press, 1982.

Cabanot, Jean, ed. *Saint-Sever: Millénaire de l'Abbaye.* Mont-de-Marson: Comité d'Etudes sur l'Histoire et l'Art de Gascogne, 1986.

Cahn, Walter. "Architecture and Exegesis: Richard of St.-Victor's Ezekiel Commentary and Its Illustrations." *Art Bulletin* 76 (1994): 53–68.

Camille, Michael. "Seeing and Reading: Some Visual Implications of Medieval Literacy and Illiteracy." *Art History* 8 (1985): 26–49.

Bibliography

"Mouths and Meanings: Towards an Anti-Iconography of Medieval Art." In
B. Cassidy, ed. *Iconography at the Crossroads* (q.v.), pp. 43–57.

Image on the Edge: The Margins of Medieval Art. Cambridge, MA: Harvard
University Press, 1992.

"Before the Gaze: The Internal Senses and Late-Medieval Visuality." In R. S.
Nelson, ed. *Seeing as Others Saw*, forthcoming.

Carruthers, Mary. "'Ut pictura poesis': The Rhetoric of Verbal and Visual Images."
Mentalities/Mentalités 7.1 (Fall 1990): 1–6.

The Book of Memory. Cambridge Studies in Medieval Literature 10. Cambridge
University Press, 1990.

"The Poet as Master Builder: Composition and Locational Memory in the Middle
Ages." *New Literary History* 24 (1993): 881–904.

"Boncompagno at the Cutting-Edge of Rhetoric: Rhetorical *Memoria* and the
Craft of Memory." *The Journal of Medieval Latin* 6 (1996): 44–64.

"'Locus tabernaculi': Mémoire et lieu dans la méditation monastique." *Cahiers de
la Villa Gillet, Lyon,* cahier spécial 1996: 7–36.

Carty, Carolyn M. "The Role of Gunzo's Dream in the Building of Cluny III."
Gesta 27 (1988): 113–123.

Cassidy, Brendan, ed. *Iconography at the Crossroads.* Princeton University Press, for
the Index of Christian Art, 1990.

Caviness, Madeline H. "Images of Divine Order and the Third Mode of Seeing."
Gesta 22 (1983): 99–120.

Sumptuous Arts at the Royal Abbeys in Reims and Braine. Princeton University
Press, 1990.

Chadwick, Nora K. *Poetry and Letters in Early Christian Gaul.* London: Bowes and
Bowes, 1955.

Chadwick, Owen. *John Cassian.* Second edition. Cambridge University Press,
1968.

Châtillon, Jean. "Le titre du 'Didascalicon' de Hugues de Saint-Victor et sa signification." In A. Cazenave et J.-F. Lyotard, eds. *L'art des confins: Mélanges offerts à
Maurice de Gandillac,* pp. 535–543. Paris: Presses Universitaires de France,
1985.

Chenu, M.-D. "*Auctor, actor, autor.*" *Bulletin Du Cange* 3 (1927), 81–86.

Nature, Man, and Society in the Twelfth Century. Edited and translated from *La
théologie au douzième siècle,* by L. Little and J. Taylor. Chicago: University of
Chicago Press, 1968.

Christe, Yves. "La cité de la Sagesse." *Cahiers de Civilisation Médiévale* 31 (1988):
29–35.

Clanchy, M. T. "Learning to Read in the Middle Ages and the Role of Mothers." In
G. Brooks and A. K. Pugh, eds. *Studies in the History of Reading,* pp. 33–39.
Reading: University of Reading School of Education, 1984.

From Memory to Written Record. Second edition. Oxford: Blackwell, 1993.

Clark, Elizabeth A. *The Origenist Controversy.* Princeton University Press, 1992.

Clark, Willene B. and M. T. McMunn, eds. *Beasts and Birds of the Middle Ages:
The Bestiary and its Legacy.* Philadelphia: University of Pennsylvania Press,
1989.

Bibliography

Cogan, M. "Rodolphus Agricola and the Semantic Revolution in the History of Invention." *Rhetorica* 2 (1984): 163–194.

Cohen, Adam. "The Uta Codex: Art and Exegesis in the Ottonian Age (Germany)." Ph.D. diss., Johns Hopkins University, 1995.

Coleman, Janet. *Ancient and Medieval Memories: The Reconstruction of the Past.* Cambridge University Press, 1992.

Colish, Marcia. "St. Augustine's Rhetoric of Silence Revisited." *Augustinian Studies* 9 (1978): 15–24.

"The Stoic Theory of Verbal Signification and the Problem of Lies and False Statements from Antiquity to St. Anselm." In L. Brind'Amour et E. Vance, eds. *Archéologie du signe*, pp. 17–43. Toronto: Pontifical Institute of Medieval Studies, 1983.

The Mirror of Language. Second edition. Lincoln: University of Nebraska Press, 1983.

Comparetti, Domenico. *Vergil in the Middle Ages.* 1895; rpt. Hamden, CT: Archon Books, 1966.

Connerton, Paul. *How Societies Remember.* Cambridge University Press, 1989.

Copeland, Rita. *Rhetoric, Hermeneutics and Translation in the Middle Ages,* Cambridge Studies in Medieval Literature 11. Cambridge University Press, 1991.

"Childhood, Pedagogy, and the Literal Sense: From Late Antiquity to the Lollard Heretical Classroom." *New Medieval Literatures* 1 (1997): 125–156.

Corrigan, Kathleen. *Visual Polemics in the Ninth-Century Byzantine Psalters.* Cambridge University Press, 1992.

Corsano, Karen. "The First Quire of the Codex Amiatinus and the *Institutiones* of Cassiodorus." *Scriptorium* 41 (1987): 3–34.

Courcelle, Pierre. "Le Site du Monastère de Cassiodore." (1938). In P. Courcelle, *Opuscula selecta*, pp. 27–75. Paris: Etudes augustiniennes, 1984.

Les Confessions de Saint Augustin dans la tradition littéraire. Paris: Etudes augustiniennes, 1963.

La Consolation de Philosophie dans la tradition littéraire. Paris: Etudes augustiniennes, 1967.

Crosby, Sumner M. *The Royal Abbey of Saint-Denis.* New Haven: Yale University Press, 1987.

Crowley, Sharon. *The Methodical Memory: Invention in Current-Traditional Rhetoric.* Carbondale, IL: Southern Illinois University Press, 1990.

Curschmann, Michael. "Imagined Exegesis: Text and Picture in the Exegetical Works of Rupert of Deutz, Honorius Augustodunensis, and Gerhoch of Reichersberg." *Traditio* 44 (1988): 145–169.

Curtius, Ernst Robert. *European Literature and the Latin Middle Ages.* Translated by W. R. Trask. New York: Harper Torchbooks, 1963.

Damasio, Antonio R. *Descartes' Error: Emotion, Reason, and the Human Brain.* New York: Grosset/Putnam, 1994.

Dan, Joseph. "The Religious Experience of the *Merkavah*." In A. Green, ed. *Jewish Spirituality I* (q.v.), pp. 289–307.

Davis, Michael T. "The Literal, the Symbolic, and Gothic Architecture." *Avista Forum* 10 (1996–1997): 25–30.

"Scenes from a Design: The Plan of Saint-Urbain, Troyes." *Avista Forum* 10 (1996–1997): 15–21.

Davis-Weyer, Caecilia. "Komposition und Szenenwahl im Dittochaeum des Prudentius." In O. Feld and U. Peschlow, eds. *Studien zur spätantiken und byzantinischen Kunst Friedrich Wilhelm Deichmann gewidmet*, Teil 3, pp. 19–29. Bonn: Rudolf Habelt, 1986.

Davlin, Mary Clemente. *A Game of Heuene: Word Play and the Meaning of Piers Plowman B.* Cambridge: D. S. Brewer, 1989.

Dawson, Christopher. *The Making of Europe.* 1932; rpt. New York: Meridian Books, 1958.

De Lange, Nicholas R. M. *Origen and the Jews.* Cambridge University Press, 1976.

De Lubac, Henri. *Exégèse médiévale.* 4 vols. Paris: Aubier, 1959–1964.

Derolez, Albert. "The Genesis of Hildegard of Bingen's 'Liber divinorum operum'." In J. P. Gumbert and M. de Haan, eds. *Texts and Manuscripts: Essays presented to G. I. Lieftinck*, pp. 23–33. Amsterdam: Van Gendt, 1972.

De Vogüé, Adalbert. "Le Plan de Saint-Gall, copie d'un document officiel?" *Revue Bénédictine* 94 (1984): 295–314.

Dodwell, C. R. *Anglo-Saxon Art: A New Perspective.* Ithaca: Cornell University Press, 1982.

Doob, Penelope R. *The Idea of the Labyrinth from Classical Antiquity through the Middle Ages.* Ithaca: Cornell University Press, 1990.

Duby, Georges. *Saint Bernard, l'art cistercien.* Paris: Arts et Métiers Graphiques, 1976.

Duggan, Lawrence. "Was Art Really the 'Book of the Illiterate'?" *Word & Image* 5 (1989): 227–251.

Dungey, Kevin R. "Faith in the Darkness: Allegorical Theory and Aldhelm's Obscurity." In J. S. Russell, ed. *Allegoresis*, pp. 3–26. New York: Garland, 1988.

Dutton, Paul Edward. *The Politics of Dreaming in the Carolingian Empire.* Lincoln: University of Nebraska Press, 1994.

Duys, Kathryn A. "Books Shaped by Song: Early Literary Literacy in the *Miracles de Nostre Dame* of Gautier de Coinci." Ph.D. diss., New York University, 1996.

Dynes, William. "The Medieval Cloister as Portico of Solomon." *Gesta* 12 (1973): 61–69.

Eco, Umberto. *Beato di Liébana: Miniature del Beato de Fernando I y Sancha (Codice B.N. Madrid Vit. 14–2).* Parma: Franco Maria Ricci, 1973.

Eden, Kathy. *Poetic and Legal Fiction in the Aristotelian Tradition.* Princeton University Press, 1986.

"Hermeneutics and the Ancient Rhetorical Tradition." *Rhetorica* 5 (1987): 59–86.

"The Rhetorical Tradition and Augustinian Hermeneutics in *De doctrina christiana*." *Rhetorica* 8 (1990): 45–63.

"Economy in the Hermeneutics of Late Antiquity." *Studies in Literary Imagination* 28 (1995): 13–26.

Hermeneutics and the Rhetorical Tradition. New Haven: Yale University Press, 1997.

Edwards, Robert R. *Ratio and Invention: A Study of Medieval Lyric and Narrative.* Nashville: Vanderbilt University Press, 1989.

Edwards, Warwick. "Phrasing in Medieval Song: Perspectives from Traditional Music." *Plainsong and Medieval Music* 5 (1996): 1–22.

Emmerson, Richard K. and Bernard McGinn, eds. *The Apocalypse in the Middle Ages*. Ithaca: Cornell University Press, 1992.

Enders, Jody. *Rhetoric and the Origins of Medieval Drama*. Ithaca: Cornell University Press, 1992.

"The Theatre of Scholastic Erudition." *Comparative Drama* 27 (1993): 341–363.

"Rhetoric, Coercion, and the Memory of Violence." In R. Copeland, ed. *Criticism and Dissent in the Middle Ages*, pp. 24–55. Cambridge University Press, 1996.

Ernst, Ulrich. *Carmen figuratum*. Cologne: Böhlau, 1991.

Esmeijer, Anna C. *Divina Quaternitas: A Preliminary Study in the Method and Application of Visual Exegesis*. Amsterdam: Van Gorcum, 1978.

Ettlinger, Helen. "The Virgin Snail." *Journal of the Warburg and Courtauld Institutes* 41 (1978): 316.

Evans, G. R. *The Language and Logic of the Bible in the Earlier Middle Ages*. Cambridge University Press, 1984.

The Thought of Gregory the Great. Cambridge University Press, 1986.

Evans, Michael. *Medieval Drawings*. London: Paul Hamlyn, 1969.

"The Geometry of the Mind." *Architectural Association Quarterly* 12 (1980): 32–55.

"Fictive Painting in Twelfth-century Paris." In John Onians, ed. *Sight and Insight: Essays on Art and Culture in Honour of E. H. Gombrich at 85*, pp. 73–87. London: Phaidon, 1994.

Fassler, Margot. *Gothic Song: Victorine Sequence and Augustinian Reform in Twelfth Century Paris*. Cambridge University Press, 1993.

Fentress, James and Chris Wickham. *Social Memory*. Oxford: Blackwell, 1992.

Fergusson, Peter. *Architecture of Solitude: Cistercian Abbeys in Twelfth-Century England*. Princeton University Press, 1984.

Festugière, A. J. *Antioche païenne et chrétienne: Libanius, Chrysostome et les moines de Syrie*. Bibliothèque des Ecoles Françaises d'Athènes et de Rome 194. Paris: Boccard, 1959.

Fishbane, Michael. " 'The Holy One Sits and Roars': Mythopoesis and the Midrashic Imagination." In M. Fishbane, ed. *The Midrashic Imagination* (q.v.), pp. 60–77.

Fishbane, Michael, ed. *The Midrashic Imagination: Jewish Exegesis, Thought, and History*. Albany: State University of New York Press, 1993.

Fontaine, Jacques. *Isidore de Séville et la culture classique dans l'Espagne wisigothique*. 2 vols. Paris: Etudes augustiniennes, 1959.

Fradenburg, Louise O. " 'Voice Memorial': Loss and Reparation in Chaucer's Poetry." *Exemplaria* 2 (1990): 169–202.

Frank, Georgia. "The Pilgrim's Gaze in the Age Before Icons." In R. S. Nelson, ed. *Seeing as Others Saw*, forthcoming.

Fredborg, K. Margareta. "Twelfth-Century Ciceronian Rhetoric: Its Doctrinal Developments and Influences." In B. Vickers, ed. *Rhetoric Revalued*, pp. 87–97. Binghamton, NY: MRTS, 1982.

"The Scholastic Teaching of Rhetoric in the Middle Ages." *Cahiers de l'Institut du Môyen-Age Grec et Latin (Copenhagen)* 55 (1987): 85–105.

373

Fredriksen, Paula. "Tyconius and Augustine on the Apocalypse." In R. Emmerson and B. McGinn, eds. *The Apocalypse in the Middle Ages* (q.v.), pp. 20–37.

Freeman, Ann. "Theodulf of Orleans and the *Libri Carolini*." *Speculum* 32 (1957): 663–705.

Geary, Patrick J. *Phantoms of Remembrance*. Princeton University Press, 1994.

Gehl, Paul F. "Mystical Language Models in Monastic Educational Psychology." *Journal of Medieval and Renaissance Studies* 14 (1984): 219–243.

"Competens Silentium: Varieties of Monastic Silence in the Medieval West." *Viator* 18 (1987): 125–160.

"Latin Readers in Fourteenth-Century Florence." *Scittura e civiltà* 13 (1989), 387–440.

A Moral Art: Grammar, Society, and Culture in Trecento Florence. Ithaca: Cornell University Press, 1993.

Gerhardsson, Birger. *Memory and Manuscript*. Translated by E. J. Sharpe. Acta Seminarii Neotestamentici Upsaliensis 22. Uppsala: Almquist & Wiksells, 1961.

Gibson-Wood, Carol. "The *Utrecht Psalter* and the Art of Memory." *Revue d'Art Canadien/Canadian Art Review (RACCAR)* 14 (1987): 9–15.

Gilson, Etienne. *The Christian Philosophy of St. Augustine*. London: Gollancz, 1961.

Gimpel, Jean. *The Cathedral Builders*. Translated by C. F. Barnes from *Les bâtisseurs de cathédrales* (Paris, 1959). New York: Grove Press, 1961.

The Medieval Machine: The Industrial Revolution of the Middle Ages. New York: Penguin, 1976.

Ginzburg, Carlo. *Clues, Myths, and the Historical Method*. Trans. A. and J. Tedeschi. Baltimore: Johns Hopkins University Press, 1989.

Godden, Malcolm and Michael Lapidge, eds. *The Cambridge Companion to Old English Literature*. Cambridge University Press, 1991.

Grabar, André. *Martyrium: recherches sur le culte des reliques et l'art chrétien antique*. 1946; rpt. London: Variorum Reprints, 1972.

"Les Mosaïques de Germigny-des-Prés." *Cahiers Archéologiques* 7 (1954): 171–183, plates 58–66.

Graham, William A. *Beyond the Written Word: Oral Aspects of Scripture in the History of Religion*. Cambridge University Press, 1987.

Green, Arthur, editor. *Jewish Spirituality I: From the Bible Through the Middle Ages*. World Spirituality 13. New York: Crossroad, 1987.

Grodecki, Louis. "Les vitraux allégoriques de Saint-Denis." *Art de France* 1 (1961): 19–46.

Guillaumont, Antoine. "Une inscription copte sur la 'Prière de Jésus'." *Orientalia Christiana Periodica* (Rome: Pontifical Institute of Oriental Studies) 34 (1968): 310–325.

"The Jesus Prayer among the Monks of Egypt." *Eastern Churches Review* 6 (1974): 66–71.

Gurevich, Aron I. *Medieval Popular Culture: Problems of Belief and Perception*. Translated by J. M. Bak and P. A. Hollingsworth. Cambridge University Press, 1988.

Hahn, Cynthia. "Picturing the Text: Narrative in the *Life* of the Saints." *Art History* 13 (1990): 1–33.

Bibliography

"*Visio Dei*: Changes in Medieval Visuality." In R. S. Nelson, ed. *Seeing as Others Saw*, forthcoming.

Hajdu, Helga. *Das mnemotechnische Schrifttum des Mittelalters*. 1936; rpt. Amsterdam: E. J. Bonset, 1967.

Halbwachs, Maurice. *La topographie légendaire des Evangiles en Terre Sainte*. 1941; rpt. Paris: Presses Universitaires de France, 1971.

On Collective Memory. Edited and translated by Lewis A. Coser. Chicago: University of Chicago Press, 1992.

Hallinger, Kassius. "The Spiritual Life of Cluny in the Early Days." In N. Hunt, ed. *Cluniac Monasticism in the Central Middle Ages* (q .v.), pp. 29–55.

Harvey, P. D. A. *Medieval Maps*. London: British Library, 1991.

Hausherr, Irénée. *The Name of Jesus*. Translated by C. Cummings from *Noms du Christ et voies d'oraison* (Rome, 1960). Kalamazoo: Cistercian Publications, 1978.

Hayward, Jane. "Glazed Cloisters and Their Development in the Houses of the Cistercian Order." *Gesta* 12 (1973): 93–109.

Heitz, Carol. "Architecture et liturgie processionnelle à l'époque préromane." *Revue de l'Art* [Paris, CNRS] 24 (1974): 30–47.

Recherches sur les rapports entre architecture et liturgie à l'époque carolingienne. Paris: SEVPEN, 1963.

Himmelfarb, Martha. *Tours of Hell: An Apocalyptic Form in Jewish and Christian Literature*. Philadelphia: University of Pennsylvania Press, 1983.

"From Prophecy to Apocalypse: the *Book of the Watchers* and Tours of Heaven." In A. Green, ed. *Jewish Spirituality* I (q.v.), pp. 145–165.

Hohler, Christopher. "A Note on *Jacobus*." *Journal of the Warburg and Courtauld Institutes* 35 (1972): 31–80.

Horn, Walter. "The Origins of the Medieval Cloister." *Gesta* 12 (1973): 13–52.

"On the Selective Use of Sacred Numbers and the Creation of a New Aesthetic in Carolingian Architecture." *Viator* 6 (1975): 351–390 + 50 plates.

Horn, Walter and E. Born. *The Plan of St. Gall: A Study of the Architecture and Economy of and Life in a Paradigmatic Carolingian Monastery*. 3 vols. Berkeley: University of California Press, 1979.

Hunt, E. D. *Holy Land Pilgrimages in the Later Roman Empire, AD 312– 460*. Oxford: Clarendon Press, 1984.

Hunt, Noreen. "Cluniac Monasticism." In N. Hunt, ed. *Cluniac Monasticism in the Central Middle Ages* (q.v.), pp. 1–10.

Hunt, Noreen, ed. *Cluniac Monasticism in the Central Middle Ages*. Hamden, CT: Archon Books, 1971.

Illich, Ivan. *In the Vineyard of the Text: A Commentary to Hugh's* Didascalicon. Chicago: University of Chicago Press, 1993.

Imbert, Claude. "Stoic Logic and Alexandrian Poetics." In M. Schofield, M. Burnyeat, and J. Barnes, eds. *Doubt and Dogmatism: Studies in Hellenistic Epistemology*, pp. 182–216. Oxford: Clarendon Press, 1980.

Irvine, Martin. *The Making of Textual Culture*. Cambridge Studies in Medieval Literature 19. Cambridge University Press, 1994.

Jacob, Christian. *La description de la terre habitée de Denys d'Alexandrie, ou, la leçon de géographie*. Paris: Albin Michel, 1990.

L'Empire des cartes: approche théorique de la cartographie à travers l'histoire. Paris: Albin Michel, 1992.

"Lieux de la carte, éspaces du savoir." *Cahiers de la Villa Gillet, Lyon*, cahier spécial 1996: 67–99.

Jaye, Barbara. *"Artes orandi"*. In M. G. Briscoe and B. Jaye, eds. *Artes praedicandi, artes orandi*, pp. 77–118. Typologie des Sources du Moyen Age Occidental 61. Turnhout: Brepols, 1992.

Johnson, Mark. *The Body in the Mind: The Bodily Basis of Meaning, Imagination, and Reason.* Chicago: University of Chicago Press, 1987.

"The Imaginative Basis of Meaning and Cognition." In S. Küchler and W. Melion, eds. *Images of Memory* (q.v.), pp. 74–86.

Kaster, Robert A. *Guardians of Language: The Grammarian and Society in Late Antiquity.* Berkeley: University of California Press, 1988.

Katzenellenbogen, Adolf. *Allegories of the Virtues and Vices in Medieval Art.* 1939; rpt. Toronto: University of Toronto Press, 1989.

"The Central Tympanum at Vézelay: Its Encyclopedic Meaning and its Relation to the First Crusade." *Art Bulletin* 26 (1944): 141–151.

The Sculptural Programs of Chartres Cathedral. Baltimore: Johns Hopkins University Press, 1959.

Kelly, Douglas. "Theory of Composition in Medieval Narrative Poetry and Geoffrey of Vinsauf." *Mediaeval Studies* 31 (1969): 117–148.

"Topical Invention in Medieval French Literature." In J. J. Murphy, ed. *Medieval Eloquence* (q.v.), pp. 231–251.

"*Translatio Studii*: Translation, Adaptation, and Allegory in Medieval French Literature." *Philological Quarterly* 57 (1978): 287– 310.

"Obscurity and Memory: Sources for Invention in Medieval French Literature." In L. Ebin, ed. *Vernacular Poetics in the Middle Ages*, pp. 33–56. Studies in Medieval Culture 16. Kalamazoo: Medieval Institute Publications, 1984.

Kemp, Wolfgang. "Visual Narratives, Memory, and the Medieval Esprit du Système." In S. Küchler and W. Melion, eds. *Images of Memory* (q.v.), pp. 87–108.

Kendrick, Laura. "Les 'Bords' des *Contes de Cantorbéry* et des manuscrits enluminés de l'époque gothique." *Bulletin des Anglicistes Médiévistes* 46 (1994): 926–943.

Kennedy, George A. *Classical Rhetoric and its Christian and Secular Tradition from Ancient to Modern Times.* Chapel Hill: University of North Carolina Press, 1980.

Greek Rhetoric Under Christian Emperors. Princeton University Press, 1983.

Kenny, Anthony. "The British Library and the St Pancras Building" (pamphlet). London: The British Library, 1994.

Kermode, Frank. *The Genesis of Secrecy.* Cambridge, MA: Harvard University Press, 1979.

Kessler, Herbert L. "Pictorial Narrative and Church Mission in Sixth-Century Gaul." In H. L. Kessler and M. S. Simpson, eds. *Pictorial Narrative in Antiquity and the Middle Ages* (q.v.), pp. 75–91.

"Medieval Art as Argument." In B. Cassidy, ed. *Iconography at the Crossroads* (q.v.), pp. 59–73.

Bibliography

"Through the Temple Veil: The Holy Image in Judaism and Christianity." *Kairos: Schrift für Judaistik Religionswissenschaft* 32/33 (1990): 53–77.

Kessler, Herbert L. and M. S. Simpson, eds. *Pictorial Narrative in Antiquity and the Middle Ages*. Studies in the History of Art 16. Washington: National Gallery of Art, 1985.

Keuls, Eva. "Rhetoric and Visual Aids in Greece and Rome." In E. Havelock and J. P. Hershbell, eds. *Communications Arts in the Ancient World*, pp. 121–134. New York: Hastings House, 1978.

Khatchatrian, A. "Notes sur l'architecture de l'église de Germigny-des-Prés." *Cahiers Archéologiques* 7 (1954): 161–169.

Kidson, Peter. "Panofsky, Suger and St. Denis." *Journal of the Warburg and Courtauld Institutes* 50 (1987): 1–17.

Kinder, Terryl L. "The Original Chevet of Pontigny's Church." In M. P. Lillich, ed. *Studies in Cistercian Art and Architecture* 2, pp. 30–38. Kalamazoo: Cistercian Publications, 1984.

Kinney, Dale. "Spolia from the Baths of Caracalla in Sta. Maria in Trastevere." *Art Bulletin* 68 (1986): 379–397.

"Making Mute Stones Speak: Reading Columns in S. Nicola in Carcere and S. Maria in Aracoeli." In C. L. Striker, ed. *Architectural Studies in Memory of Richard Krautheimer*, pp. 83–86, plates 38–40. Mainz: von Zabern, 1996.

Kitzinger, Ernst. "World Map and Fortune's Wheel: A Medieval Mosaic Floor in Turin." *Proceedings of the American Philosophical Society* 117 (1973): 344–373.

Klein, Peter K. "Les sources non hispaniques et la genèse iconographique du Beatus de Saint-Sever." In J. Cabanot, ed. *Saint-Sever: Millénaire de l'Abbaye* (q.v.), pp. 317–333.

"Introduction: The Apocalypse in Medieval Art." In R. Emmerson and B. McGinn, eds. *The Apocalypse in the Middle Ages* (q.v.), pp. 159–199.

Kosslyn, Stephen M. "The Medium and the Message in Mental Imagery: A Theory." In N. Block, ed. *Imagery* (q.v.), pp. 207–244.

Kosslyn, Stephen M. *et al.* "On the Demystification of Mental Imagery." In N. Block, ed. *Imagery* (q.v.), pp. 131–150.

Kraeling, Carl H. *The Synagogue*. Revised edition. *The Excavations at Dura-Europos: Final Report*, 8, pt. 1. New Haven: Yale University Press, 1979.

Krautheimer, Richard. *Studies in Early Christian, Medieval, and Renaissance Art*. New York: New York University Press, 1969.

Krinsky, Carol H. "Representations of the Temple of Jerusalem Before 1500." *Journal of the Warburg and Courtauld Institutes* 33 (1970): 1–19.

Kruger, Steven. *Dreaming in the Middle Ages*. Cambridge University Press, 1992.

Kupfer, Marcia. *Romanesque Wall Painting in Central France*. New Haven: Yale University Press, 1993.

Küchler, Susanne and Walter Melion, eds. *Images of Memory: On Remembering and Representation*. Washington: Smithsonian Institution Press, 1991.

Ladner, Gerhart B. "Medieval and Modern Understanding of Symbolism: A Comparison." *Speculum* 54 (1979): 223–256.

"The Concept of the Image in the Greek Fathers and the Byzantine Iconoclastic Controversy." *Dumbarton Oaks Papers* 7 (1953): 1–34.

Lalou, Elisabeth. "Les tablettes de cire médiévales." *Bibliothèque de l'Ecole des Chartes* 147 (1989): 123–140.

Lawrence, C. H. *Medieval Monasticism: Forms of Religious Life in Western Europe in the Middle Ages.* Second edition. London: Longman, 1989.

Leach, Eleanor Winsor. *The Rhetoric of Space: Literary and Artistic Representations of Landscape in Republican and Augustan Rome.* Princeton University Press, 1988.

Leclercq, Jean. *La spiritualité de Pierre de Celle.* Paris: J. Vrin, 1946.

  The Love of Learning and the Desire for God. Translated by C. Misrahi. New York: Fordham University Press, 1961.

  Etudes sur le vocabulaire monastique au moyen âge. Studia Anselmiana Philosophia Theologica 48. Rome: Herder, 1961.

  Otia monastica. Etudes sur le vocabulaire de la contemplation au moyen âge. Studia Anselmiana Philosophia Theologica 51. Rome: Herder, 1963.

  "L'art de la composition dans les sermons de S. Bernard." *Studi Medievali,* serie terza 7 (1966): 128–153.

Lecoq, Danielle. "La 'Mappemonde' du *De Arca Noe Mystica* de Hugues de Saint-Victor (1128–1129)." In M. Pelletier, ed. *Géographie du Monde au Moyen Age et à la Renaissance.* Memoires de la Section Géographie, pp. 9–31. Paris: CTHS, 1989.

LeDoux, Joseph. *The Emotional Brain: The Mysterious Underpinnings of Emotional Life.* New York: Simon & Schuster, 1996.

Levenson, John D. "The Jerusalem Temple in Devotional and Visionary Experience." In A. Green, ed. *Jewish Spirituality* I (q.v.), pp. 32–61.

Levitan, William. "Dancing at the End of the Rope: Optatian Porfyry and the Field of Roman Verse." *Transactions of the American Philological Association* 115 (1985): 245–269.

Lewis, Suzanne. "Beyond the Frame: Marginal Figures and Historiated Initials in the Getty Apocalypse." *J. Paul Getty Museum Journal* 20 (1992): 53–76.

Leyser, Conrad. "*Lectio divina, oratio pura*: Rhetoric and the Techniques of Asceticism in the 'Conferences' of John Cassian." In M. Caffiero, G. Barone, and F. S. Barcellona, eds. *Modelli di santità e modelli di comportamento: contrasti, intersezioni, complementarità,* pp. 79–105. Turin: Rosenberg & Sellier, 1994.

Lieb, Michael. *The Visionary Mode: Biblical Prophecy, Hermeneutics, and Cultural Change.* Ithaca: Cornell University Press, 1991.

Lindberg, David C. *Theories of Vision from Al-Kindi to Kepler.* Chicago: University of Chicago Press, 1976.

Lindblom, Johannes. *Prophecy in Ancient Israel.* Oxford: Blackwell, 1962.

Luria, A. R. *The Mind of a Mnemonist.* Translated Lynn Solotaroff. New York: Basic Books, 1968.

Lyman, Thomas W. "Theophanic Iconography and the Easter Litany: the Romanesque Painted Program at Saint-Sernin in Toulouse." In L. Grisebach and K. Renger, eds. *Festschrift für Otto von Simson zum 65. Geburtstag,* pp. 72–93. Frankfurt: Propyläen Verlag, 1977.

MacCormack, Sabine. *Art and Ceremony in Late Antiquity.* Berkeley: University of California Press, 1981.

  "From the Sun of the Incas to the Virgin of Copacabana." *Representations* 8 (1984): 30–60.

Bibliography

"Loca Sancta: The Organization of Sacred Topography in Late Antiquity." In R. Ousterhout, ed. *The Blessings of Pilgrimage* (q.v.), pp. 7–40.

McCulloch, Florence. *Medieval Latin and French Bestiaries*. Chapel Hill: University of North Carolina Press, 1960.

McKitterick, Rosamond. *The Carolingians and the Written Word*. Cambridge University Press, 1989.

"Text and Image in the Carolingian World." In R. McKitterick, ed. *The Uses of Literacy in Early Medieval Europe*, pp. 297–318. Cambridge University Press, 1990.

Malamud, Martha A. *A Poetics of Transformation: Prudentius and Classical Mythology*. Ithaca: Cornell University Press, 1989.

Margolis, Howard. *Patterns, Thinking, and Cognition: A Theory of Judgment*. Chicago: University of Chicago Press, 1987.

Markus, R. A. "St. Augustine on Signs" (1957). Rpt. in R. A. Markus, ed. *Augustine: A Collection of Essays* (q.v.), pp. 61–91.

Saeculum: History and Society in the Theology of Saint Augustine. Cambridge University Press, 1970 (revised edition 1988).

The End of Ancient Christianity. Cambridge University Press, 1990.

ed. *Augustine: A Collection of Essays*. New York: Anchor Doubleday, 1972.

Marrou, Henri I. *A History of Education in Antiquity*. Translated by G. Lamb from *L'Histoire de l'education dans l'antiquité* (Paris, 1948). 1956; rpt. Madison: University of Wisconsin Press, 1982.

Saint Augustin et la fin de la culture antique. Paris: Boccard, 1938.

Marsden, Richard. *The Text of the Old Testament in Anglo-Saxon England*. Cambridge Studies in Anglo-Saxon England 15. Cambridge University Press, 1995.

Martin, John R. *The Illustration of The Heavenly Ladder of John Climacus*. Princeton University Press, 1954.

Martz, Louis L. *The Poetry of Meditation*. New Haven: Yale University Press, 1954.

Mathews, Thomas F. *The Clash of Gods: A Reinterpretation of Early Christian Art*. Princeton University Press, 1993.

Matter, E. Ann. *The Voice of My Beloved: The Song of Songs in Western Medieval Christianity*. Philadelphia: University of Pennsylvania Press, 1990.

Matthews, Gareth B. "Augustine On Speaking from Memory" (1965). Rpt. in R. A. Markus, ed. *Augustine: A Collection of Essays* (q.v.), pp. 168–175.

Matthies, Andrea L. "Medieval Treadwheels: Artists' Views of Building Construction." *Technology and Culture* 33 (1992): 510–547.

Mazzeo, Joseph A. "St. Augustine's Rhetoric of Silence." *Journal of the History of Ideas* 23 (1962): 175–196.

Meyvaert, Paul. "The Medieval Monastic Claustrum." *Gesta* 12 (1973): 53–59.

"The Authorship of the 'Libri Carolini'." *Revue Bénédictine* 89 (1979): 29–57.

"Bede and the church paintings at Wearmouth-Jarrow." *Anglo-Saxon England* 8 (1979): 63–77.

"Bede, Cassiodorus, and the Codex Amiatinus." *Speculum* 71 (1996): 827–883.

Minnis, A. J. *Medieval Theory of Authorship*. Second edition. Philadelphia: University of Pennsylvania Press, 1988.

Mitchell, W. J. T. *Iconology: Image, Text, Ideology*. Chicago: University of Chicago Press, 1986.

Bibliography

Picture Theory. Chicago: University of Chicago Press, 1994.

Moore, Marilyn. "Assumptions of Gender: Rhetoric, Devotion, and Character in Chaucer's *Troilus and Criseyde*." Ph.D. diss., University of Illinois at Chicago, 1997.

Moran, Richard. "Artifice and Persuasion: The Work of Metaphor in the *Rhetoric*." In A. O. Rorty, ed. *Essays on Aristotle's* Rhetoric, pp. 385–398. Berkeley: University of California Press, 1996.

Morghen, Raffaello. "Monastic Reform and Cluniac Spirituality." In N. Hunt, ed. *Cluniac Monasticism in the Central Middle Ages* (q.v.), pp. 11–28.

Murphy, James J. *Rhetoric in the Middle Ages*. Berkeley: University of California Press, 1974.

Murphy, James J., ed. *Medieval Eloquence: Studies in the Theory and Practice of Medieval Rhetoric*. Berkeley and Los Angeles: University of California Press, 1978.

A Short History of Writing Instruction from Ancient Greece to Twentieth Century America. Davis, CA: Hermagoras Press, 1990.

Murray, Stephen. *Notre-Dame Cathedral of Amiens: The Power of Change in Gothic*. Cambridge University Press, 1996.

"The Architectural Envelope of the Sainte-Chapelle." *Avista Forum* 10 (1996–97): 21–25.

Nees, Lawrence. "The Plan of St. Gall and the Theory of the Program of Carolingian Art." *Gesta* 25 (1986): 1–8.

Neusner, Jacob. *The Memorized Torah: The Mnemonic System of the Mishnah*. Chico, CA: Scholars Press, for the American Academy of Religion, 1985.

Oral Tradition in Judaism: The Case of the Mishnah. New York: Garland Press, 1987.

Nims, Margaret F. "Translatio: 'Difficult Statement' in Medieval Poetic Theory." *University of Toronto Quarterly* 43 (1974): 215–230.

Noble, Thomas F. X. "Tradition and Learning in Search of Ideology: The *Libri Carolini*." In R. E. Sullivan, ed. *"The Gentle Voices of Teachers": Aspects of Learning in the Carolingian Age*, pp. 227–260. Columbus: Ohio State University Press, 1995.

Nolan, Kathleen. "Narration in the Capital Frieze at Notre-Dame at Etampes." *Art Bulletin* 71 (1989): 166–184.

Nugent, S. Georgia. *Allegory and Poetics: The Structure and Imagery of Prudentius' 'Psychomachia'*. Studien zur klassischen Philologie 14. Frankfurt: P. Lang, 1985.

Nussbaum, Martha C. *The Therapy of Desire: Theory and Practice in Hellenistic Ethics*. Princeton University Press, 1994.

Ochs, Donovan J. *Consolatory Rhetoric*. Columbia, SC: University of South Carolina Press, 1993.

O'Keeffe, Katherine O'Brien. *Visible Song: Transitional Literacy in Old English Verse*. Cambridge University Press, 1990.

Ong, Walter S. "Wit and Mystery: A Revaluation in Medieval Latin Hymnody." *Speculum* 22 (1947): 310–341.

The Presence of the Word: Some Prolegomena for Cultural and Religious History. New Haven: Yale University Press, 1967.

Bibliography

Onians, John. *Art and Thought in the Hellenistic Age*. London: Thames & Hudson, 1979.

"Abstraction and Imagination in Late Antiquity." *Art History* 3 (1980): 1–24.

Bearers of Meaning: The Classical Orders in Antiquity, the Middle Ages, and the Renaissance. Princeton University Press, 1988.

Ousterhout, Robert. "Loca Sancta and the Architectural Response to Pilgrimage." In R. Ousterhout, *The Blessings of Pilgrimage* (q.v.), pp. 108–124.

Ousterhout, R., ed. *The Blessings of Pilgrimage*. Chicago: University of Illinois Press, 1990.

Pächt, Otto. "The Illustrations of St. Anselm's Prayers and Meditations." *Journal of the Warburg and Courtauld Institutes* 19 (1956): 68–83.

Patch, Howard R. *The Other World According to Descriptions in Medieval Literature*. Cambridge, MA: Harvard University Press, 1950.

Pelikan, Jaroslav. *The Emergence of the Catholic Tradition (100–600)*. Chicago: University of Chicago Press, 1971.

Peters, F. E. *Jerusalem and Mecca: The Typology of the Holy City in the Near East*. New York: New York University Press, 1986.

Pevsner, Nicholas. "The Term 'Architect' in the Middle Ages." *Speculum* 17 (1942): 549–562.

Plummer, John. *The Hours of Catherine of Cleves*. New York: Braziller [1966].

Price, S. R. F. *Rituals and Power: The Roman Imperial Cult in Asia Minor*. Cambridge University Press, 1984.

Principe, Lawrence M. "The Gold Process: Directions in the Study of Robert Boyle's Alchemy." In Z. R. W. M. von Martels, ed. *Alchemy Revisited*, pp. 200–206. Leiden: Brill, 1990.

"Robert Boyle's Alchemical Secrecy: Codes, Ciphers, and Concealments." *Ambix: Journal of the Society for the History of Alchemy and Chemistry* 39 (1992): 63–74.

Rabbow, Paul. *Seelenführung: Methodik der Exerzitien in der Antike*. Munich: Kösel Verlag, 1954.

Raby, F. J. E. *A History of Secular Latin Poetry in the Middle Ages*. 2 vols. Oxford: Clarendon Press, 1957.

Radding, Charles M. and William W. Clark. *Medieval Architecture, Medieval Learning: Builders and Masters in the Age of Romanesque and Gothic*. New Haven: Yale University Press, 1992.

Randall, Lilian M. C. *Images in the Margins of Gothic Manuscripts*. Berkeley and Los Angeles: University of California Press, 1996.

"The Snail in Gothic Marginal Warfare." *Speculum* 37 (1962): 358–367.

"Humour and Fantasy in the Margins of an English Book of Hours." *Apollo* 84 (1966): 482–488.

"Games and the Passion in Pucelle's Hours of Jeanne d'Evreux." *Speculum* 47 (1972): 246–257.

"An Elephant in the Litany: Further Thoughts on an English Book of Hours in the Walters Art Gallery (W. 102)." In W. Clark and M. McMunn, eds. *Beasts and Birds of the Middle Ages* (q.v.), pp. 106–133.

Raw, Barbara C. *Anglo-Saxon Crucifixion Iconography and the Art of the Monastic*

Revival. Cambridge Studies in Anglo-Saxon England 1. Cambridge University Press, 1990.

"Biblical Literature: the New Testament." In H. Godden and M. Lapidge, eds., *The Cambridge Companion to Old English Literature* (q.v.), pp. 227–242.

Remensnyder, Amy G. "Legendary Treasure at Conques: Reliquaries and Imaginative Memory." *Speculum* 71 (1996): 884–906.

Revel-Neher, Elisabeth. "Du Codex Amiatinus et ses rapports avec les plans du Tabernacle dans l'art juif et dans l'art byzantin." *The Journal of Jewish Art* 9 (1982): 6–17.

Rigg, A. G. *A History of Anglo-Latin Literature 1066–1422.* Cambridge University Press, 1992.

Roberts, Michael. *The Jeweled Style: Poetry and Poetics in Late Antiquity.* Ithaca: Cornell University Press, 1989.

Poetry and the Cult of the Martyrs: The Liber Peristephanon *of Prudentius.* Ann Arbor: University of Michigan Press, 1993.

"St. Martin and the Leper: Narrative Variation in the Martin Poems of Venantius Fortunatus." *The Journal of Medieval Latin* 4 (1994): 82–100.

Robertson, D. W. *A Preface to Chaucer.* Princeton University Press, 1962.

Rorty, Amélie O., ed. *Essays on Aristotle's Rhetoric.* Berkeley: University of California Press, 1996.

Rose, H. J. *A Handbook of Latin Literature.* 1936; rpt. New York: E. P. Dutton, 1960.

Rossi, Paolo. "Le arti della memoria: rinascite e trasfigurazioni." In L. Bolzoni and P. Corsi, eds. *La cultura della memoria* (q.v.), pp. 13–34.

Roth, Cecil. "Jewish Antecedents of Christian Art." *Journal of the Warburg and Courtauld Institutes* 16 (1953): 24–44.

Rouveret, Agnes. "Peinture et 'Art de la mémoire': le paysage et l'allégorie dans les tableaux grecs et romains." *Comptes-rendus des séances (Oct. 1982) de l'Académie des Inscriptions et Belles-Lettres* (1982): 571–588.

Rowland, Beryl. "The Art of Memory and the Bestiary." In W. Clark and M. McMunn, eds. *Beasts and Birds of the Middle Ages* (q.v.), pp. 12–25.

Rowland, Christopher. *The Open Heaven: A Study of Apocalyptic in Judaism and Early Christianity.* London: SPCK, 1982.

Rudolph, Conrad. "The 'Principal Founders' and the Early Artistic Legislation of Cîteaux"." In M. P. Lillich, ed. *Studies in Cistercian Art and Architecture 3*, pp. 1–45. Kalamazoo: Cistercian Publicatons, 1987.

Artistic Change at St-Denis. Princeton University Press, 1990.

"The Things of Greater Importance": Bernard of Clairvaux's Apologia and the Medieval Attitude Toward Art. Philadelphia: University of Pennsylvania Press, 1990.

"Building-Miracles as Artistic Justification in the Early and Mid-Twelfth Century." In W. Kersten, ed. *Radical Art History: Internationale Anthologie*, pp. 288–291, 399–410. Zürich: ZIP, 1997.

Rumelhart, David E., and J. L. McClelland. *Parallel Distributed Processing.* 2 vols. Cambridge, MA: MIT Press, 1986.

Rutchick, Leah. "Sculpture Programs in the Moissac Cloister: Benedictine Culture, Memory Systems, and Liturgical Performance." Ph.D. diss., University of Chicago, 1991.

Saenger, Paul. "Silent Reading: Its Impact on Late Medieval Script and Society." *Viator* 13 (1982): 367–414.

Salet, Francis and J. Adhémar. *La Madeleine de Vézelay: étude iconographique par Jean Adhémar.* Melun: Librarie d'Argences, 1948.

Sandage, Scott A. "A Marble House Divided: The Lincoln Memorial, the Civil Rights Movement, and the Politics of Memory, 1939–1963." *The Journal of American History* 80 (1993): 135–167.

Sanderson, Warren. "The Plan of St. Gall Reconsidered." *Speculum* 60 (1985): 615–632.

Sandler, Lucy Freeman. "Marginal Illustrations in the Rutland Psalter." *Marsyas* 8 (1959): 70–74.

The Psalter of Robert de Lisle. London: Harvey Miller, 1983.

Saxl, Fritz. "A Spiritual Encyclopedia of the Middle Ages." *Journal of the Warburg and Courtauld Institutes* 5 (1942): 82–139.

Schapiro, Meyer. *Romanesque Art: Selected Papers* I New York: Braziller, 1977.

Schmitt, Jean-Claude. "Ecriture et image: les avatars médiévaux du modèle grégorien." In E. Baumgartner and C. Marchello-Nizia, eds. *Théories et pratiques de l'écriture au Moyen Age*, pp. 119–151. Littérales, Paris X-Nanterre: Centre des Recherches du Département de Français, 1988.

"Les images classificatrices." *Bibliothèque de l'Ecole des Chartes* 147 (1989): 311–341.

La raison des gestes dans l'occident médiéval. Paris: Gallimard, 1990.

Scholem, Gershom. *Major Trends in Jewish Mysticism.* New York: Schocken Books, 1954.

Searle, John R. *The Rediscovery of the Mind.* Cambridge, MA: MIT Press, 1992.

Segal, Alan F. *Paul the Convert: The Apostolate and Apostasy of Saul the Pharisee.* New Haven: Yale University Press, 1990.

Seidel, Linda. *Songs of Glory: The Romanesque Façades of Aquitaine.* Chicago: University of Chicago Press, 1981.

"Installation as Inspiration: The Passion Cycle from La Daurade." *Gesta* 25 (1986): 83–92.

"Medieval Cloister Carving and Monastic Mentalité." In A. MacLeish, ed. *The Medieval Monastery*, pp. 1–16. Medieval Studies at Minnesota 2. St. Cloud, MN: North Star Press, 1988.

Jan van Eyck's Arnolfini Portrait: Stories of an Icon. Cambridge University Press, 1993.

"Legends in Limestone: Structure, Sculpture, and Site at St.-Lazare of Autun," forthcoming.

Settis, Salvatore. "Des ruines au musée: la destinée de la sculpture classique." *Annales ESC* 48 (1993): 1347–1380.

Sherman, Claire Richter. *Imaging Aristotle: Verbal and Visual Representation in Fourteenth-Century France.* Berkeley: University of California Press, 1995.

Sicard, Patrice. *Hugues de Saint-Victor et son école.* Turnhout: Brepols, 1991.

Diagrammes médiévaux et exégèse visuelle: le Libellus de formatione arche *de Hugues de Saint-Victor.* Turnhout: Brepols, 1993.

Sloane, Thomas O. "Schoolbooks and Rhetoric: Erasmus's Copia." *Rhetorica* 9 (1991): 113–129.

Bibliography

Smalley, Beryl. *English Friars and Antiquity in the Fourteenth Century*. Oxford: Blackwell, 1960.

The Study of the Bible in the Middle Ages. Third edition. Oxford: Blackwell, 1983.

Smith, Jonathan Z. *To Take Place: Toward Theory in Ritual*. Chicago: University of Chicago Press, 1987.

Smith, Macklin. *Prudentius' Psychomachia : A Reexamination*. Princeton University Press, 1976.

Snyder, Jane. *Puns and Poetry in Lucretius' "De Rerum Naturae"*. Amsterdam: Gruner, 1980.

Spence, Jonathan D. *The Memory Palace of Matteo Ricci*. New York: Viking Penguin, 1984.

Spiegel, Gabrielle M. "History, Historicism, and the Social Logic of the Text in the Middle Ages." *Speculum* (1990): 59–86.

Stern, David. "The Rabbinic Parable and the Narrative of Interpretation." In M. Fishbane, ed. *The Midrashic Imagination* (q.v.), pp. 78–95.

Stock, Brian. *Augustine the Reader: Meditation, Self-Knowledge, and the Ethics of Interpretation*. Cambridge, MA: Harvard University Press, 1996.

Sudnow, David. *Ways of the Hand: The Organization of Improvised Conduct*. Cambridge, MA: MIT Press, 1993.

Sumption, Jonathan. *Pilgrimage: An Image of Medieval Religion*. Totowa, NJ: Rowman and Littlefield, 1975.

Swartz, Michael D. *Mystical Prayer in Ancient Judaism*. Tübingen: Mohr, 1992.

Scholastic Magic: Ritual and Revelation in Early Jewish Mysticism. Princeton University Press, 1996.

Talmage, Frank. "Apples of Gold: The Inner Meaning of Sacred Texts in Medieval Judaism." In A. Green, ed. *Jewish Spirituality I* (q.v.), pp. 313–355.

Testard, Maurice. *Saint Augustin et Cicéron*. Paris: Etudes augustiniennes, 1958.

Troncarelli, Fabio. "Alpha e acciuga: Immagini simboliche nei codici di Cassiodoro." *Quaderni medievali* 41 (1996): 6–26.

Tronzo, William. "The Prestige of St. Peter's: Observations on the Function of Monumental Narrative Cycles in Italy." In H. L. Kessler and M. S. Simpson, eds. *Pictorial Narrative in Antiquity and in the Middle Ages* (q.v.), pp. 93–112.

Tufte, Edward R. *Envisioning Information*. Cheshire, CT: Graphics Press, 1990.

Underhill, Evelyn. *Mysticism*. 1911; rpt. New York: Dutton, 1961.

Van Deusen, Nancy. *Theology and Music at the Early University*. Leiden: E. J. Brill, 1995.

Vance, Eugene. "Roland and the Poetics of Memory." In J. Harari, ed. *Textual Strategies: Perspectives in Post-Structural Criticism*, pp. 374–403. Ithaca: Cornell University Press, 1979.

Mervelous Signals: Poetics and Sign Theory in the Middle Ages. Lincoln: University of Nebraska Press, 1986.

Varela, Francisco J., Evan Thompson, and Eleanor Rosch. *The Embodied Mind: Cognitive Science and Human Experience*. Cambridge: MA: MIT Press, 1991.

Vauchez, André. *The Spirituality of the Medieval West from the Eighth to the Twelfth Century*. Translated by C. Friedlander from *La spiritualité de moyen-âge occidental VIII-XII siècles* (Paris, 1975). Kalamazoo: Cistercian Publications, 1993.

Vogade, F. *Vézelay: histoire, iconographie, symbolisme*. Bellegarde: 1987.

Waddell, Chrysogonus. "The Early Cistercian Experience of the Liturgy." In M. B. Pennington, ed. *Rule and Life: An Interdisciplinary Symposium*, pp. 77–116. Kalamazoo: Cistercian Publications, 1971.

Waddell, Helen. *The Wandering Scholars: The Life and Art of the Lyric Poets of the Latin Middle Ages*. 1932; rpt. New York: Doubleday, 1961.

Walker, Andrew D. "*Enargeia* and the Spectator in Greek Historiography." *Transactions of the American Philological Association* 123 (1993): 353–377.

Wallach, Luitpold. *Alcuin and Charlemagne: Studies in Carolingian History and Literature*. Cornell Studies in Classical Philology 32. Ithaca: Cornell University Press, 1959.

Wallis, Faith. "The Ambiguities of Medieval 'Memoria'." *Canadian Journal of History / Annales canadiennes d'histoire* 30 (1995): 77–83.

Ward, John O. "From Antiquity to the Renaissance: Glosses and Commentaries on Cicero's *Rhetorica*." In J. J. Murphy, ed. *Medieval Eloquence* (q.v.), pp. 25–67.

"Quintilian and the Rhetorical Revolution of the Middle Ages." *Rhetorica* 13 (1995): 231–284.

Ciceronian Rhetoric in Treatise, Scholion and Commentary. Turnhout: Brepols, 1995.

Warnock, Mary. *Memory*. London: Faber and Faber, 1987.

Wehrli, Fritz. *Die Schule des Aristoteles*. 10 vols. Basel: Schwabe, 1944.

Weitzmann, Kurt. *Illustrations in Roll and Codex: A Study of the Origin and Method of Text Illustration*. Princeton University Press, 1947.

Late Antique and Early Christian Book Illumination. New York: Braziller, 1977.

Weitzmann, Kurt and Herbert Kessler. *The Frescoes of the Dura Synagogue and Christian Art*. Dumbarton Oaks Studies 28. Washington: Dumbarton Oaks, 1990.

Werckmeister, O. K. "Pain and Death in the Beatus of Saint-Sever." *Studi Medievali*, serie terza, 14 (1973): 566–626, plates I-XXVII.

"The First Romanesque Beatus Manuscripts and the Liturgy of Death." In *Actas del Simposio ... de Beato de Liébana* (q.v.), vol. 2, pp. 167–200.

Williams, John. "Le Beatus de Saint-Sever: état des questions." In J. Cabanot, ed. *Saint-Sever: Millénaire de l'Abbaye* (q.v.), pp. 251–263.

"Purpose and Imagery in the Apocalypse Commentary of Beatus of Liébana." In R. Emmerson and B. McGinn, eds. *The Apocalypse in the Middle Ages* (q.v.), pp. 217–233.

The Illustrated Beatus: Introduction. The Illustrated Beatus: A Corpus of Illustrations of the Commentary on the Apocalypse, vol. I. London: Harvey Miller, 1994.

Wirth, Karl-August. "Von mittelalterlichen Bildern und Lehrfiguren im Dienste der Schule und des Unterrichts." In B. Moeller *et al.*, eds. *Studien zum städtischen Bildungswesen des späten Mittelalters und der frühen Neuzeit*, pp. 256–370. Abhandlungen der Akademie der Wissenschaften in Göttingen, Philologisch-Historiche Klasse, Dritte Folge Nr. 137. Göttingen: Vandenhoeck & Ruprecht, 1983.

Wolfson, Elliot R. "Beautiful Maiden Without Eyes: *Peshat* and *Sod* in Zoharic Hermeneutics." In M. Fishbane, ed. *The Midrashic Imagination* (q.v.), pp. 155–203.

Wolfson, Harry A. "The Internal Senses." *Harvard Theological Review* 28 (1935): 69–133.

Wolska-Conus, Wanda. "La 'Topographie chrétienne' de Cosmas Indicopleustès: hypothèses sur quelques thèmes de son illustration." *Revue des Etudes Byzantines* 48 (1990): 155–191.

Woods, Marjorie C., ed. and trans. *An Early Commentary on the 'Poetria nova' of Geoffrey of Vinsauf*. New York: Garland, 1985.

——— "The Teaching of Writing in Medieval Europe." In J. J. Murphy, ed. *A Short History of Writing Instruction* (q.v.), pp. 77–94.

——— " 'In a Nutshell': *Verba* and *Sententia* and Matter and Form in Medieval Composition Theory." In C. Morse, P. Doob, and M. Woods, eds. *The Uses of Manuscripts in Literary Studies: Essays in Memory of Judson Boyce Allen*, pp. 19–39. Studies in Medieval Culture 31. Kalamazoo: Medieval Institute Publications, 1992.

Wright, Craig. *Music and Ceremony at Notre Dame of Paris: 500–1550*. Cambridge University Press, 1989.

Yates, Frances A. *The Art of Memory*. London: Routledge and Kegan Paul, 1966.

——— "Architecture and the Art of Memory." *Architectural Association Quarterly* 12 (1980): 4–13.

Young, James E. *The Texture of Memory: Holocaust Memorials and Meaning*. New Haven: Yale University Press, 1993.

Zinn, Grover A., Jr. "Mandala Symbolism and Use in the Mysticism of Hugh of St. Victor." *History of Religions* 12 (1972): 317–341.

——— "Hugh of St. Victor and the Art of Memory." *Viator* 5 (1974): 211–234.

——— "*De Gradibus Ascensionum*: The Stages of Contemplative Ascent in Two Treatises on Noah's Ark by Hugh of St. Victor." *Studies in Medieval Culture* 5 (1975): 61–79.

——— "Suger, Theology, and the Pseudo-Dionysian Tradition." In P. Gerson, ed. *Abbot Suger and St-Denis: A Symposium*, pp. 33–40. New York: Metropolitan Museum, 1986.

Ziolkowski, Jan M. ed. *Obscure Styles in Medieval Literature. Mediaevalia* 19 (1996).

——— "Theories of Obscurity in the Latin Tradition." *Mediaevalia* 19 (1996): 101–170.

Index

Note: reference numbers in **bold** refer to Plates, in *italic* to figures. The notes are indexed by subject only.

Index

Capitoline Tablet, Rome 201
captive gentiles trope 127–128, 168
carmina figurata 228
    Carolingian 140, 331 n29
Cassian, John *see* John Cassian
Cassian of Imola, St. 198
Cassiodorus, M. Aurelius 11, 24, 138, 157,
    159, 234–235, 300 n62
catenae (chains) of recollection 31, 101, 115,
    146–147, 150, 164, 167, 342 n113
Catherine of Cleves, Hours of **14**, 162–163, 164
Cecilia, St. 158–159
cellae see rooms for memory work
Celles, monastery of (Egypt) 168, 233
cellula deliciarum of recollection 164–165
cento (playful poem as by Virgil) 57–59
Centula-St.-Riquier 224, 266–268, *267*, 273
chains of recollection *see catenae*
character molded through memory work
    105–107
Chartres 69, 107, 222
Chaucer, Geoffrey 149
chiasmus 117
chick and eagle metaphor 113–114, 130
Chrysologus, Peter *see* Peter Chrysologus
Chrysostom, John *see* John Chrysostom
churches, structure as engine of prayer
    263–264, 275–276
Cicero, Marcus Tullius 7, 9, 13, 78, 102, 106,
    130–131, 156
    use of *intentio* 15
circumstantiae of rhetoric 18
Cistercian monasteries, structure **25, 26**, 256,
    257–261
Cistercian monasticism 84–85, 225
Cîteaux, monastery of 5
city, image of 19, 106–107
City of God, The (Augustine) 67, 129–130
Clairvaux monastery 225
Clark, Elizabeth 72
Clash of Gods, The (Mathews) 56–57
class and collective memory 44, 105
classroom procedure of novice monks 74–77
cloister structure and meditation 87, 269,
    272–275
clothing
    of buildings 18–19, 204, 230
    of pagans as metaphor for style 126–127
Cluny, abbey of 87, 92, 193, 224, 226–227
Codex Amiatinus **23**, 234, 236–237, 249
Codex Grandior 234–235, 236
cogitation
    meditation as a variety of 64
    recollective 117
cognition, relationship of memory to 10–11
collatio/collocare (inventive gathering) 16, 154
colligere (re-collection) 33, 64, 193, 330 n20,
    356 n90

color (ornament, way-finding) 61, 79, 81, 100,
    109, 117, 200, 208–209
columns, role in prayer of architectural 262,
    275
common place
    and classical culture 136
    the Cross as 166
    and etymologies, moral 159
    making a 44–46
    organizational 182
    in *Psychomachia* 144–145
    and recollection 13–16, 34–37, 258–259
competens silentium 3
Complaint of Nature, The (Alan of Lille) 197
Composite order (architecture) 262
composition
    Anselm of Bec's method 181
    in bed 176–179
    inventional mnemonic *picturae* 243
    monastic concept of 60, 262, 351 n59
    murals used in 177–178
    process of 70, 73–74, 79
    progymnasmata 130
    as taught in the Bestiary 140
    three stages of constructing 230
    see also ductus, rhetorical
Compostela, Santiago de 92
compunction (*compunctio cordis*) 96, 101, 103,
    105, 169, 175, 181, 197, 198
    see also anxiety in meditation
compunctus see punctus
concentration, lapses of *see* wandering mind
    in meditation
Conferences (Cassian) 61
Confessions (Augustine) 12, 31–32, 175
conscience, nature of 206–207
Consolation of Philosophy (Boethius) 173,
    197
conspectus (short-term memory) 63, 259
Constantine, Emperor 41, 262
constellations 5, 6, 25–27, 214, 217–218
constructio (raising of building) 230
conventions, social 46
"conversion" and forgetting 94–99
conversion theme in church structure 261–266
copia (copiousness) 61, 63, 64, 117, 322 n86,
    345 n8
Corinthians
    (13) 87, 232
    (13:10) 17, 149
    (13:15) 19
    (18:1) 23
Cosmas Indicopleustes 236, 301 n72, 348 n39
craft rules 33, 66
Crassus *see* Lucius Crassus
creativity
    cognitive 14–16, 23, 100, 171
    nature of 11–12, 69

Index

Octateuch manuscripts, Greek 236, 237
Odbert, Abbot 24
Ode on a Grecian Urn (Keats) 222–223
"On Conscience" (Peter of Celle) 206
"On Rhetoric and the Virtues" (Alcuin)
    123–124
Onians, John 261, 262
Opicinius de Canistris 245
Optatianus Porfirius 136–137
oratio brevis, etymologies as 157, 159
oratories, Cistercian 258–261
oratorium or *ecclesia* 258
orators, and art of memory 8, 237
oratory, Roman 176–178
orderliness and pattern 117
Origen 71, 87, 125
Origines (Isidore of Seville) 157
Orion, stories of 25, 26–27
ornament 20–1, 87, 116, 125–130
    basic features of 117
    decus 125
    and invention 274–275
    and prayer 262, 339 n79
    in *Psychomachia* 143–144
    punning decoration in margins 161–165
    putting the mind in play 122–124, 326 n131,
        327 n135
    stylistic 84–87, 114, 128–129, 130–131
orthodoxy 1
orthopraxis 1–3
ortulum (little garden) 273
ostomachia (Greek bone puzzle) 58
otherworld visions 182–183, 331 n30
overlay in public forgetting 54–57, 344 n7
Ovid 211
oxymoron 107, 117

pagan subject matter
    continued study of 125–130
    "forgetting" 88–91
    method of reading 128–129
page of memory trope 101–103, 283 n36, 296
    n23, 353 n70
paideia (educated class) and common ground
    45–46, 105
painting
    Adam of Dryburgh's procedure 248–249
    in the heart 133–135
    in the mind 130–133, 245–246
    and word-pictures 151, 249, 351 n61
palimpsest metaphor 97
Panofsky, Erwin 165
Pantheon (Rome) 39, 56, 58, 59
Paradise, image of 272, 275
paradox 117
parchment
    mind as a 128
    writing as metaphor 96–97, 102–103

parody of Virgil 59
paronomasia (punning) 118, 150
path, spiritual 74–75
pathos in memory work 4, 21
Patrologia latina (Migne) 62
pattern-making, cognitive 34–35, 84, 137–138,
    376 n32
Paul, St.
    image and writings 121
    (quotation) 7
    as wise master-builder 17–18, 19
Paulinus of Nola 179
pearls in marginal punning 162
pedagogus and student simile 50
pedagogy
    by vision 191–196
    pictures used in 199, 201–203, 208, 337 n71
    and poetry 213, 286 n61
penitence in remembering 143, 242
Persepolis 42
persuasion 107–108, 133, 224
Peter, Gregory's pupil in *Life of St. Benedict*
    191–192, 194–196
Peter (1 5:8) 187
Peter of Celle 73, 99, 132, 206–209, 238–239
    meditational reforms 257
    "On affliction and reading" 107–112
Peter Chrysologus 45, 62–63, 64, 125,
    158–159
Peter, St. 180, 226
Phainomena (Aratus) 24–25
phantasiai (mental images) 14, 132–133, 172,
    239
Philippic orations (Cicero) 106
Philo 17
Photinus 70–71
pia memoria 66, 115
Pichery 72
pictura
    Adam of Dryburgh's Triple Tabernacle
        247–250
    architectural 229–230
    definition of term 200, 203–205
    distinct from *imagines* 204
    trope of monastic rhetoric 203–205
pictures
    and books working together 247–250, 313
        n13, 319 n66, 326 n126
    cognitive 3, 10, 85, 130–133, 198–203
    literary 122–124, 145–146
    as memory sites 153–154, 289 n87
    mnemotechnic of 196–198
    painting for meditation 205–209, 211, 316
        n34
    and pedagogy 201–203, 208
    picture verses 135–142, *141*, 228–229, 250
    picturing poem 213–214
    placement in arrangement of 199–200

Index